Programming with class

A C++ Introduction to Computer Science

McGraw-Hill Series in Computer Science

SENIOR CONSULTING EDITOR

C. L. Liu, *University of Illinois at Urbana-Champaign*

CONSULTING EDITOR

Allen B. Tucker, *Bowdoin College*

Fundamentals of Computing and Programming

Computer Organization and Architecture

Computers in Society/Ethics

Systems and Languages

Theoretical Foundations

Software Engineering and Database

Artificial Intelligence

Networks, Parallel and Distributed Computing

Graphics and Visualization

The MIT Electrical Engineering and Computer Science Series

Fundamentals of Computing and Programming

*Abelson and Sussman: *Structure and Interpretation of Computer Programs*

Bergin: Data Abstraction: *The Object-Oriented Approach Using C++*

Heileman: *Data Structures, Algorithms, and Object-Oriented Programming*

Kamin and Reingold: *Programming with* **class***: A C++ Introduction to Computer Science*

Kernighan and Plauger: *The Elements of Programming Style*

Smith and Frank: *Introduction to Programming Concepts and Methods with Ada*

*Springer and Friedman: *Scheme and the Art of Programming*

Tremblay and Bunt: *Introduction to Computer Science: An Algorithmic Approach*

Tucker, Bernat, Bradley, Cupper, and Scragg: *Fundamentals of Computing I: Logic, Problem Solving, Programs, and Computers*

Tucker, Cupper, Bradley, Epstein, and Kelemen: *Fundamentals of Computing II: Abstraction, Data Structures, and Large Software Systems*

---

*Co-published by the MIT Press and The McGraw-Hill Companies, Inc.

Programming with class

A C++ Introduction
to Computer Science

Samuel N. Kamin
University of Illinois at Urbana-Champaign

Edward M. Reingold
University of Illinois at Urbana-Champaign

The McGraw-Hill Companies, Inc.

New York St. Louis San Francisco Auckland Bogotá Caracas
Lisbon London Madrid Mexico City Milan Montreal New Delhi
San Juan Singapore Sydney Tokyo Toronto

McGraw-Hill

*A Division of The **McGraw·Hill** Companies*

Programming with `class`:
A C++ Introduction to Computer Science

This book is printed on acid-free paper.

1 2 3 4 5 6 7 8 9 0 AGM AGM 9 0 9 8 7 6 5

ISBN 0-07-051833-5

This book was set in Times Roman by Publication Services, Inc.
The editor was Eric M. Munson;
the cover designer was Joseph Gillians;
the production supervisor was Denise L. Puryear.
Project supervision was done by Publication Services, Inc.
Quebecor Printing/Martinsburg was printer and binder.

Library of Congress Catalog Card Number:

95-81368

International Edition

When ordering this title, use ISBN 0-07-114415-3.

About the Authors

Samuel N. Kamin is an Associate Professor of Computer Science at the University of Illinois at Urbana-Champaign, specializing in the study of computer languages. He is the author of the textbook *Programming Languages: An Interpreter-based Approach,* and co-author of *Introduction to Programming with Mathematica.*

Edward M. Reingold is a Professor of Computer Science at the University of Illinois at Urbana-Champaign, specializing in the analysis of algorithms and data structures. He is the author or co-author of numerous journal articles, as well as the books *Computer Approaches to Mathematical Problems, Combinational Algorithms: Theory and Practice, Data Structures, Data Structures in Pascal,* and *PascAlgorithms.* He is a Fellow of the A. C. M.

Dedicated, with love, to our fathers

Sherwin Kamin, father of S.N.K.
Bernard Klersfeld, stepfather of S.N.K.
Harold Simon, father-in-law of S.N.K.

and

Haim Reingold, father of E.M.R.
Gerhard A. Nothmann, father-in-law of E.M.R.

אבות עטרה לבנים ובנים עטרה לאבות

בראשית רבה סג, ב

Fathers are a crown to their sons and sons are a crown to their fathers.

Genesis Rabbah 63,2

Contents

1 WHAT IS PROGRAMMING?

5 ITERATION

6 USER-DEFINED DATA TYPES

7 POINTERS AND LISTS

8 RECURSION

9 ARRAYS

10 A MULTI-FILE APPLICATION

List of Figures

List of Tables

List of Bug Alerts

Preface

Yes, take it all around, there is quite a good deal of
information in the book. I regret this very much, but
really it could not be helped.

—Mark Twain
Roughing It

The process of designing, writing, and debugging a computer program is
an exciting activity. As exciting as it is, however, it is fraught with frustrations that come from needing to know an enormous number of details
immediately, before even simple tasks are possible. It is an exacting and complex
task, rich in subtleties that contribute both to the inherent excitement and to the
frustrations.

In addition to the usual difficulties of learning to program, programming in
C++ is especially challenging because it is not a toy language (like Pascal) or a
teaching tool (like Modula-2); C++ is the most widely used professional language
based on the important idea of *object-oriented programming*.

So we find we must cover all the essentials of programming, such as one
might find in a book on a simpler programming language like Fortran, C, or Pascal, while giving due emphasis to the paradigm of object-oriented programming.
This has been a challenge, and our approach will likely be controversial, because
it inverts certain traditions in the teaching of this material. Our main innovation is
to give priority to the use of classes, the construction of data structures using objects and pointers, and the manipulation of these data structures via recursion. We
postpone the treatment of arrays until quite late (Chapter 9), because we believe
that data structures are easier to understand than arrays and that this organization
reflects the reality of C++ programming. Aficionados will recognize in this organization the influence of functional languages, which are widely admired for
their elegance.

It was not our intention to write merely an introductory C++ text but to
write an introductory computer science text as well. Our choice of programming
examples reflects this viewpoint. We have attempted to motivate our examples
from the student's own experiences. We have scrupulously avoided the inclusion of "bad" computer science. (A clear case is the bubble sort, an old chestnut
that finds its way into many, if not most, introductory programming books, even
though it cannot be recommended on any rational basis; we mention it only in

a brief exercise.) We have included examples that give a foretaste of more advanced areas of computer science, in the hopes of whetting the student's appetite; our examples include issues from computer architecture (computer representation of numbers and arithmetic operations on such representations), programming languages and compilers (parsing of arithmetic expressions, implementation of a picture-drawing language), data structures (sorting, searching, hashing), and graphics (line and circle drawing). We have, in almost all cases, provided appropriate analytical material to justify claims of efficiency; we don't expect our readers to be able to generate this kind of analysis on their own, but we want them to be aware that efficiency questions can be approached mathematically.

Throughout the presentation, we have attempted to adhere to an exemplary programming style. We use mnemonically suggestive identifier names, indent neatly and consistently, and try to avoid side effects in function calls. Our programming style leans decidedly toward the "functional," a symptom of many years of programming in LISP and its relatives; yet, as just discussed, we believe that both pedagogical considerations and the fashion in real-life C++ programming justify this style. In any case, we claim only that our style is exemplary, not that it is the only exemplary style.

How to Use This Book

There are two paths through this book. The direct path, following the order of the text, places classes and object-oriented programming as early as practicable, goes directly to pointers and data structures (especially lists), and then covers recursion in detail, leaving arrays as the last major topic.

Those who prefer a more conventional order can follow this path:

Chapters 1–6: Basic data types, control structures, and classes
Sections 7.1–7.2: Pointers
Sections 9.1–9.4, 9.6–9.7 (except 9.7.5): Arrays using iteration
Sections 7.3–7.8: Lists
Chapter 8: Recursion
Sections 9.5, 9.7.5: Arrays using recursion
Chapter 10: Files

In other words, you can skip directly from pointers to arrays, bypassing recursion; most of the examples using arrays in Chapter 9 do not use recursion (though some of our favorite examples do!), and we have been careful to ensure that knowledge of lists and recursion is not required outside of those examples.

There are three specific topics important in "real-world" programming, but inessential for neophytes, that we cover later than many introductory books: formatting output, dividing programs into multiple files, and file I/O. We have taken care that the sections covering them can be read independently of their immediate surroundings. Specifically:

- Formatting output is covered lightly in Chapter 2 and in more detail in the first part of Appendix D, which can be read after reading Chapter 2.

- Multi-file programs are covered in Section 10.1, which can be read after reading Chapter 6.
- File I/O is covered in Section 10.2 and the second part of Appendix D, which can also be read after Chapter 6.

In general, we deemphasize language details in favor of broader concepts of algorithm development, object-oriented design, and program correctness. Some features of C++ not mentioned in the text are covered, or at least introduced, in Appendix E, which has a table showing the earliest point at which each of its sections can be read.

Exercises

> I hear, I forget; I see, I remember; I do, I understand.
>
> —Chinese proverb

There are over 300 exercises in the book. Many of them are tied closely to the examples in text, requiring the reader to pore over the text material in order to do the exercise. Others involve novel uses of the text material. It cannot be overstressed that *the exercises are an integral part of the text*. Reading the text without looking at the exercises is not likely to lead to a deep understanding of the material. The best way to understand a program is to try to modify it. The way to understand an algorithm is to implement it. Doing the exercises helps provide a working knowledge of the material.

Some of the exercises (about a quarter of them) are marked in color with a hand (☞). These exercises are viewed as especially helpful in mastering the material, so solutions are provided at the back of the book. Solutions to the remaining exercises can be found in a *Solutions Manual,* available to teachers from the publisher without cost.

About 10% of the exercises are unusually difficult or extensive. Such exercises are marked with a star (★).

Marginalia

Outside margins contain key words and phrases from the nearby text. The outside margins are visible on both left- and right-hand pages as one flips through the text, making it easy to locate a particular discussion.

Inside margins are used occasionally to display a "speed limit" sign. Such a sign warns the reader that the nearby material is more subtle or difficult than other material and deserves special attention. The lower the posted speed limit, the more care should be taken in reading the material. Naturally, we have tried our best to smooth and widen all the roads, but some curvy ones are unavoidable, where a 15-mile-per-hour limit or even a 5-mile-per-hour limit is only prudent.

The use of a warning device in the margin was originated by the Bourbaki group, who, in their encyclopedia of mathematics, included a curvy road symbol in the margin near particularly tricky proofs. More recently, this idea was revived by D. E. Knuth.

Of course, what is subtle to one reader may not be to another. The presence of warning signs should not intimidate. We've used them to mark parts of the text that, in our experience, students are more likely to find vexing. Forewarned is forearmed!

Errata

In the introduction to his *Guide to the Perplexed,* the great twelfth-century philosopher, physician, and rabbinic commentator Moses Maimonides outlines seven categories of contradiction or error to be found in books:

1. The author quotes various sources that disagree.
2. The author has changed his mind on a point but neglects to remove all the rejected material.
3. Something is not to be taken literally but has inner content.
4. An apparent (but not real) contradiction stems from the necessity to explain one thing before another.
5. A simplification is made for purposes of explanation but is later explained in full.
6. A contradiction escapes the author.
7. The author is intentionally concealing something.

Maimonides avers that all the errors in his *Guide to the Perplexed* are of the fifth and seventh types. Would that the present authors could make such a claim!

There are undoubtedly errors of substance, style, spelling, and grammar in this book, try mightily as we did to prevent and eliminate them. All the programs and segments of programs were compiled and thoroughly tested before inclusion in the text.

Should anyone be so unlucky as to be waylaid by an error, or if anyone just happens to notice one, please bring it to our attention. We can be reached at the email addresses

```
kamin@cs.uiuc.edu
reingold@cs.uiuc.edu
```

Of course, we can be contacted by snail-mail at

Department of Computer Science
University of Illinois at Urbana-Champaign
1304 West Springfield Avenue
Urbana, IL 61801-2987 USA

World Wide Web Home Page

To facilitate electronic communication with our readers, we have established a home page for this book on the World Wide Web:

```
http://emr.cs.uiuc.edu/home/reingold/C++/index.html
```

This home page gives easy access to the C++ programs included in the book. All of the major pieces of C++ code in our presentation are available there; erroneous or bad-example code is not available, nor are some of the one- or two-line examples.

The latest errata list for the book is also available via the home page.

Acknowledgments

This project was initiated and supported by our editor at McGraw-Hill, Eric Munson; we owe many thanks to Eric and to his assistant, Holly Stark. One of Eric's key contributions was securing the services of Marjorie Anderson as development editor; Marjorie's input was extremely useful.

The team at Publication Services, Inc., Champaign, Illinois, did a highly professional job with the manuscript, from copyediting to design to typesetting. Our thanks to all of them.

Ken Urban wrote the solutions manual and contributed the solutions section in the book. He and his wife Regina Cassidy carefully proofread the entire manuscript; we are grateful to Ken and Regina for their efforts.

We prepared the original manuscript using LaTeX, drawing many of the figures with the powerful **pstricks** macros written by Timothy Van Zandt of Princeton University. He was instrumental in solving many of our most perplexing TeX difficulties.

We were fortunate to get feedback from a number of highly qualified and perceptive outside reviewers. Though we may not always have agreed with—or even enjoyed seeing—their comments, we always found them thoughtful and thought-provoking. Many thanks to

Manuel Bermudez (University of Florida)
Betty Cheng (Michigan State University)
Karla Fant (Portland State University)
Stephen Leach (Florida State University)
Henry Leitner (Harvard University)
Clayton Lewis (University of Colorado)
Kathleen Neumann (University of California at Los Angeles)
Vincent Russo (Purdue University)
David Spooner (Rensselaer Polytechnic Institute)
Jean Sullivan (Bowling Green State University)

Finally, our wives and daughters bore the brunt of this effort as much as we did ourselves. Our thanks and love, now and always, to them.

S.N.K.
E.M.R.

CHAPTER

1

What Is Programming?

Chapter Preview

Before writing programs in the C++ language, we demonstrate the thought processes and problem-solving techniques necessary for programming. We present a problem—to lead a mechanical mouse through a maze—and work through its solution. We introduce and explain some new vocabulary, including *algorithm*, *file*, *editor*, *compiler*, *syntax*, *debugging*, and *operating system*.

The precision essential to a computer's way of manipulating symbols constitutes both a great advantage and a severe limitation. Since what the symbols in a computer represent must be absolutely precise, and the programmer must be absolutely clear in defining each symbol, the attempt to write a computer program inevitably exposes hand-waving, fuzzy thinking, and implicit appeals to what everyone takes for granted. Submitting to this rigor is an immensely valuable discipline.

—Herbert L. Dreyfus and Stuart E. Dreyfus
Mind Over Machine

The image of a computer is magical to most of the world. It is the unseen force that messes up phone bills, bounces checks, and sends overdue notices from the library. The popular perception of "the computer" is as an all-powerful entity which, with seemingly little human effort or input, is responsible for running business, government, science, and many more mundane aspects of our lives. "The computer" evokes awe in the uninitiated; human errors are easily disguised by such phrases as "the computer was down" or "it must have been a computer error." But a computer is no more than an inanimate collection of wires and silicon, organized so that it can quickly perform simple operations like adding numbers. So how does it come to have such power? What is the sleight of hand that transforms this box of electrical components into such a powerful tool?

It is programming. A *program* is a set of directions that tells the computer exactly what to do; programs are thus the medium used to communicate with the computer. Programs can be written in many different programming languages—a *programming language* is an artificial language for specifying sequences of directions for the computer. Each programming language is appropriate for different types of applications and different types of computers. In this book we use the language C++. Whichever language is used, the same process bridges the gap from the challenge, "There is a job to be done," to the reply, "Here is a program to handle it."

program

programming language

Our first job in programming is to clarify the problem. *Exactly* what is required? How can the job be broken down into manageable pieces? What *algorithm*—sequence of steps—is appropriate to solve the problem? How can this algorithm be turned into a program? Does the program work? Is it written as clearly as it can be? Is it fast? Can it be changed easily if needed? Does it demand too great a fraction of the computer's resources? These are the questions confronting the *computer programmer*, the person who designs and writes the program.

algorithm

computer programmer

Mechanical Mouse in a Maze

We'll start learning to program by analyzing a problem that contains, in miniature, the basic components of any programming problem. We want to give instructions to a mechanical mouse so it can get through a maze. For our purposes, a *maze* is a rectangular arrangement of square rooms; adjacent rooms may be separated by a wall, or the boundary between them may be open. We'll place the mouse facing the entrance to a maze in which solid lines represent walls between rooms and dotted lines represent open boundaries:

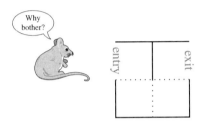

The mouse is like a computer in that it knows only how to follow certain very simple instructions: **step forward** into the next room, **turn right** in place, or **turn left** in place. We must *program* the mouse by writing the precise instructions it must follow to get through the maze. For the simple maze above, the instructions are

```
step forward;
turn right;
step forward;
turn left;
step forward;
turn left;
step forward;
turn right;
step forward;
```

This sequence of instructions is comparable to a computer program.

What happens if the maze has a different configuration? For example, what if we had the following?

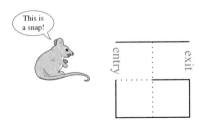

Then our preceding program would not work correctly, but the simpler program

```
step forward;
step forward;
step forward;
```

would work. It is easy to write out instructions to the mouse for any specific maze as long as we know the maze's internal configuration. But what if the inside of the maze is hidden from view, beneath an opaque cover? All we see is a mouse-eye view of things:

It is now a nontrivial problem for us to give the mouse proper instructions to get it through the maze. In fact, we have to approach the problem from a completely different perspective. In the language of computer programming, it is our task to figure out an *algorithm* to solve this task—a general method precise enough to be turned into a mouse program, and then to write the corresponding *program*, the exact sequence of mouse instructions.

algorithm

program

The first step in computer programming is always to make the problem precise. Where is the mouse initially placed with respect to the maze? What should happen if the maze has no exit? We'll assume the mouse is placed in front of the entrance to the maze so that a single **step forward** instruction takes it into the maze. Our instructions to the mouse must get it out the exit of the maze or back out the entrance if there is no path to the exit or no exit at all. This problem is, of course, impossible to solve unless the mouse is capable of examining the inside of the maze and making decisions based on what it finds as it goes along; the three instructions **step forward**, **turn left**, and **turn right** are not sufficient. The mouse, however, can also look forward myopically to see whether there is a wall immediately in front of it, and it can detect when it is outside the maze. These, then, are five instructions that the mouse can follow:

```
step forward
turn right
turn left
facing a wall?
outside the maze?
```

We are limited to these instructions to get the mouse through the maze.

The hardest part of any programming problem now faces us: how to extend a process that we understand well in any particular instance to more general situations. In other words, how do we describe precisely, and thus break down into its basic components, something that we do almost automatically? First, we must design an algorithm for getting through an unspecified maze, and then we need to express the algorithm in terms that the mouse can follow. The two parts of the problem are interdependent. The algorithm must be devised taking into consideration the types of instructions available to us, and the implementation of the algorithm requires a clear understanding of it.

For the mouse in the maze, the algorithm we will use is a familiar trick for going through a maze: Have the mouse walk with its right paw on the wall of the maze. This amounts to having the mouse walk hugging the wall to its right. In our first example above, the mouse would travel like this:

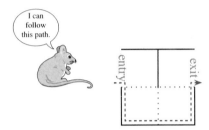

There is nothing in the five mouse instructions that says "walk hugging the wall to your right," so we need to express this "algorithm" with the set of five instructions that is available to our mouse. This is easier than it appears. We need to keep the wall to the mouse's right, but the only instruction the mouse understands about walls is **facing a wall?**. So to check whether it has a wall to its right, the mouse must **turn right** first and then ask whether it is facing a wall. Once the mouse is in the maze, the process of keeping its right paw on the wall then means

```
turn right;
if facing a wall? then
   turn left and if facing a wall? then
      turn left and if facing a wall? then
         . . .
```

continuing as long as necessary—that is, turn right and then keep turning left until no wall is in front. Assuming that the mouse isn't locked in a closed room, eventually the preceding instructions will have it facing an opening with a wall to its right.

It is awkward to write the instructions as we did above. Instead, we'll use some notation that is used in C++ for grouping instructions and write it as

```
turn right;
if (facing a wall?) {
   turn left and if (facing a wall?) {
      turn left and if (facing a wall?) {
         . . .
      }
   }
}
```

omitting the word "then" and using { and } to indicate the grouping of instructions and (and) to denote a question or condition. We still haven't said what the
"..." means. It means to continue with the same instructions while the mouse is
facing a wall, stopping only when the mouse is *not* facing a wall. So we'll write it
instead as

```
turn right;
while (facing a wall?) {
  turn left;
}
```

which means, "after turning right, repeat the process of checking whether you're
facing a wall, and if you are, turning left." The distinction between `while` and
`if` is that `while` means "continue checking as long as" and `if` means "check the
current state of things just one time."

After following these instructions, the mouse will be facing an opening. In
other words, it can now step forward (without crashing into a wall) and *repeat the
process again and again until it is out of the maze:*

```
turn right;
while (facing a wall?) {
  turn left;
}
step forward;
if (not outside the maze?) {
  turn right;
  while (facing a wall?) {
    turn left;
  }
  step forward;
  if (not outside the maze?) {
    turn right;
    while (facing a wall?) {
      turn left;
    }
    step forward;
    if (not outside the maze?) {
      ...
    }
  }
}
```

Again, we face the question of what the "..." means. Here it means continue with the same instructions while the mouse is *not* outside the maze. As
before, we rewrite it more precisely and concisely as

```
while (not outside the maze?) {
  turn right;
  while (facing a wall?) {
    turn left;
  }
  step forward;
}
```

This differs from what we had before, because we first ask whether the mouse is outside the maze *before* we do anything. Since the mouse is initially outside the maze, we must move it into the maze before we have it follow the preceding instructions:

```
step forward;  //  This takes the mouse into the entrance.
while (not outside the maze?) {
  turn right;
  while (facing a wall?) {
    turn left;
  }
  step forward;   //  How do we know that the
                  //  mouse is not facing a wall?

}
```

(We have used a double slash // to set off descriptive comments.)

How simple and elegant this program is! It reads almost like English, but it expresses exactly how the mouse (with its limited abilities) can be made to trace its way through a maze by keeping its right paw on the wall. Before reading further, lead the mouse through the following maze by executing the program and following its directions. The path the mouse follows is shown as a colored line—remember, the mouse is keeping its right paw on the wall:

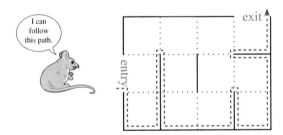

Notice that the mouse takes a circuitous route to the exit, going through every room once and through three of the rooms twice (which three rooms?)! (Of course, we could have taken a different approach to this problem, leading a different path through the maze.)

This program is the result of breaking down the problem at hand into a workable algorithm. The algorithm was then applied using the five simple instructions available to our specific mechanical mouse.

Exercises—First Set

1. What happens when the program is executed with the mouse placed in front of the entrance of a maze that has no exit?

2. Rework the maze-walking algorithm with the idea "walk hugging the wall to your left." Exactly what changes need to be made to the maze-traversal program to apply this new algorithm?

3. If the mouse could respond to the instruction `wall at right?`, could we use this instruction to simplify the maze-traversal program? If so, rewrite the maze-traversal program using `wall at right?`.

4. Could the additional instruction `turn around` be used to simplify the original algorithm? If so, rewrite the program using this instruction.

5. What happens when the program is executed with the mouse placed *inside* a maze having no entrance or exit?

☞ 6. Assuming the mouse starts at the entrance to a maze that has an exit, what is the maximum number of times that the mouse can go through any room of the maze?

☞ 7. Suppose the mouse can respond to the instruction `facing north?`. Write instructions to make the mouse face north.

8. Assume that every maze has at least the external walls, an entry, and an exit. Using the original set of five instructions, design an algorithm and write the corresponding program to force the mouse to enter the maze and crash into a wall. (Once you have exterminated the mouse, you can go on to the next section.)

1.2

Computers and Programming Languages

The computers you will learn to program are like the mechanical mouse. They "understand," in the sense that they can be made to respond in a predictable way to, a limited repertoire of simple instructions, called the *instruction set*. The task   *instruction set* of writing a program is that of expressing the solution to a problem algorithmically, in terms of the computer's instruction set. Of course, the computer's instruction set, while primitive from our point of view, is much more complex than the mouse's. The instruction sets vary from machine to machine, but all computer instruction sets include the following:

- They can perform the basic arithmetic operations for integers and fractions and have the ability to store intermediate results.
- They have some facility to deal with sequences of letters, symbols, and numbers, and they can compare items for equality or relative size.
- They are able to receive information (*input*) from such sources as keyboards,   *input* disks, telephones, tapes, or other computers, and they can send out information (*output*) to such devices as terminals, printers, disks, or tapes.   *output*

Just as the clever combination of simple instructions can get the mechanical mouse through a maze, so the clever combination of simple computer instructions can perform seemingly miraculous tasks. The great advantage of the computer is that it can execute its instructions at the rate of several million per second. Even though it responds only to simple commands, it can execute them so fast that the results can be astoundingly sophisticated.

The process of writing computer programs is exactly that illustrated for the mechanical mouse: We must understand the instructions available, we must understand the problem to be solved so that we can design an algorithm to solve it, and we must express that algorithm correctly in terms of the computer's instructions. These are difficult tasks, and over the years, computer scientists have developed many ways to make them more manageable. Most significantly, we are no longer compelled to limit ourselves to a computer's instruction set: We use considerably enhanced instruction sets ("high-level" programming languages) and *then have the computer itself translate the result into its own instructions* (to a "machine-level" language) so it can execute them.

There are many programming languages; C++ is just one. All share the essential property that, as in the mouse's language, the terms are used in precise ways following strict rules. The contrast with human language, with its ambiguities and subtleness, is stark; the precision required to communicate with computers is the hardest thing for beginning programmers to learn.

C++ was designed as a general-purpose language, a jack-of-all-trades. Programming languages go in and out of vogue, but don't let this deter you from learning C++ well. It is an extremely rich language, so the lessons you learn in mastering it will apply to programming in whatever language you end up using.

1.3

Programs and Algorithms

The mechanical mouse paradigm points out clearly that before you can begin writing a program (in C++ or any language), you have to have in mind a precise notion of what you want the program to do and how the program should do it. Unless you have carefully developed the algorithm, writing the program will be an impossibly difficult task, and the program that results will surely be a disaster! A good analogy is that knowledge of the English language will not suffice for an assignment to write a paper for a history class. You need to have thoroughly researched the topic and have organized the relevant material *before* you begin to write your paper. *After* carefully designing an algorithm, you must write the program in a good, readable style.

In this book we teach you how to design algorithms and how to express them well in C++. There are three separate tasks here: learning the "grammar" of C++, learning good taste in questions of style, and learning how to design and implement algorithms. Initially, writing syntactically correct programs seems the hardest part. Writing syntactically correct programs is a matter of mastering a set of grammatical rules; and being able to apply them in a practical way. Mastering C++ syntax is harder than it may appear only because the computer is completely unforgiving of errors. You may not have noticed the erroneous semicolon in the second to last sentence; if you did notice, it probably did not interfere with your comprehension. In C++, though, such an error would be fatal to your program! In the long run, however, this is only a matter of learning to abide by the rules of the language.

Writing programs in a good style is a more difficult task because there are few absolute rules, only general principles. Still, there is little creativity in writing a program in good style—just organization, attention to detail, and a feeling for it that comes with experience. Finally, as you master the intricacies of the language and are able to apply them in a practical way, it becomes clear that it is the last of the three tasks—the design and implementation of the algorithm—that is the most difficult, the most interesting, and the most important. It requires ingenuity and problem-solving skills: You learn as many techniques as possible to keep in your mental "tool box," and usually you'll be able to find some combination of variants of them to do the job. Occasionally, though, you'll be stumped and will have to develop something new. It is these problems that are the most frustrating. Initially, when your tool box is fairly empty, most problems fall into this class. As your collection of tools grows, your frustration level declines. Don't worry—it'll happen.

The design and implementation of algorithms requires attention to issues beyond C++. Not only must an algorithm correctly solve the problem, but it also needs to be efficient, comprehensible, and reliable in the presence of unexpected conditions. We address these issues (and others) in this book, as well as teaching you C++.

1.4

Practicalities

After you have designed the algorithm and written the program on paper, you begin the process of entering it into a *file* on the computer and *debugging* it— eliminating its errors—so it reaches a working, polished state. A file is the electronic equivalent of a container in which information such as text, data, or programs can be stored. Entering and modifying your program in a file is done using an *editor,* a program provided to you that understands instructions to insert or delete lines or characters, move them around, or look for particular patterns of characters. Editors permit the storage and retrieval of what you have written on a *disk,* the major memory component of a computer. Learning how to use an editor well can make the job of entering and debugging a program much easier. *file* *debugging* *editor* *disk*

Remember that the program you have written and entered is in C++, a *high-level language,* meaning that it allows the programmer to express himself or herself in terms of fairly complicated building blocks; other examples of high-level languages include BASIC, Fortran, and Pascal. High-level languages like C++ need to be translated into a more basic *machine-level language* that is directly executable by the hardware of the computer. So, once you have a file containing the C++ program, you use another program provided for you, a *compiler,* to take that file and translate it into a program in machine-level language that can actually be executed on the computer. If your program has *syntactic errors* (grammatical errors) in that it fails to adhere to the rules of C++, this translation cannot *high-level language* *machine-level language* *compiler* *syntactic errors* be completed and the computer will tell you, usually in a terse, unfriendly way. You must then figure out what needs to be changed in the program and use the editor to change it. Then you try again, and after a few iterations of this process, the program compiles properly into an executable form.

Just because the program compiles without errors does *not* guarantee or even suggest that it will work correctly! In other words, you may have written something that is grammatically correct; however, it really doesn't do at all what you expected. Such errors, which occur during the execution of the program, are called *run-time errors* or *logic errors;* they need to be fixed too, just like the syntax errors. Run-time errors can result from simple typing mistakes or from flaws in the algorithm. In either case, it's back to the editor to revise your program and back to the compiler (these two steps may be repeated many times) until the algorithm is correct, your program compiles, and finally it executes to completion. Did it get the right answers? If so, try enough additional data to be sure it really works; if not, find the errors, correct them, and recompile and rerun the program. This whole process of removing bugs (errors) from a program is called *debugging*.

run-time errors
logic errors

debugging

The foregoing description of the edit-compile-run cycle is illustrated in Figure 1.1. Just below the (Editor) is a C++ program. The (Compiler) translates this C++ program into a gibberish of primitive instructions that the computer can understand, known as "machine language." In the early days of computers, programmers wrote directly in this language, but now almost all programs are written in a high-level language like C++ (small wonder!). The machine language produced by the compiler is then loaded and run on the computer, producing the output shown.

Both the editor and the compiler work in an environment called the *operating system*. This is a huge, complicated program that manages the whole computer, including all the hardware connected to the machine as well as all the programs running on it. On multiple-user machines it is the operating system that logs you in or out (allows you to begin using the system or prepares for you to leave); creates, moves, destroys, or prints out files; invokes the editor and compilers; and runs your programs. At various times you will be giving commands to the operating system (moving a file, running a program), and at other times you will be working in the editor (typing in a new program, modifying an existing program). The operating system commands are usually quite different from the editor commands; be certain you know where you are at all times. On personal computers, there is no logging in or out, and the tasks of creating, moving, destroying, and printing out files and running programs are often done by a hybrid editor/compiler.

operating system

We have not attempted to describe the computer's hardware—especially the relationship between the heart of the computer (the CPU or central processing unit), the memory available to it, and the range of other devices connected to it. An analogy with the automobile will put things in perspective. In the early days of the automobile it was necessary to know a great deal about the inner workings of a car in order to drive: The motor, transmission, fuel system, brakes, and

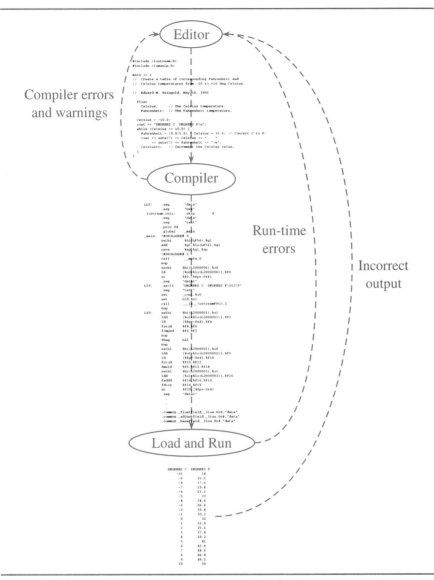

FIGURE 1.1   The cycle of editing, compiling, and debugging a program. The C++ program shown is the temperature table program on page 17; its output is from Figure 2.1 on page 18.

so on needed to be understood. As cars became better engineered and more "ergonomic," drivers needed to know less and less about the inner workings. Today, we learn to drive a car with no knowledge of what goes on internally. In the early days of computers one had to know a great deal about electronics and the internal workings of a computer to use it. Over the years, less and less such detailed knowledge was needed as the machines were made more "user friendly." Today, we can use a computer for many tasks with no idea of what goes on beneath the cover; furthermore, it is possible to write programs for computers with little understanding of the internal workings of the machine. Of course, to tackle problems that will push the computer to its limits, we'll need to know much, much more, but the brief description we give is sufficient for purposes of this text.

In the next chapter we will present the overall structure of a C++ program and introduce some of its basic features. Subsequent chapters will go deeper into C++ and the design and implementation of algorithms.

Exercises—Second Set

The following exercises refer to the specific computer system you are going to use as you study C++.

1. (a) If you are using a multiple-user system, the first thing you have to be able to do is "log on" and "log off." Find out what passwords or other information you will need for this and practice once or twice.
   (b) If you are using a personal computer, learn how to turn on and begin operating your machine.

2. Find out what editor you will be using. Using the manual for this editor (or some other available and reliable source), discover how to change characters or whole words and to move from line to line and character to character in both directions. Learn how to write a file, read a file, and change the name of a file.

3. Create a file **firstTry**, type in a few sentences, write the file, check to see that the file really exists, then remove the file.

4. Find out exactly what instructions and procedures are necessary on your system to compile and run a program.

Summary

The computer can do extraordinary things in the hands of a skillful programmer. By now you should have some idea of the steps involved in programming. The *problem* must first be clarified and an appropriate *algorithm* developed; the *program* can then be written, entered in a *file,* revised (as necessary) using an *editor,* *compiled,* and finally *run* and *debugged.*

Basic Elements of C++

Chapter Preview

To introduce C++, we look at a sample program and use it to illustrate the structure of a C++ program and some simple operations on numbers. A few basic tools for handling input and output and simple loops are presented—just enough for you to start writing your own programs. The final section introduces the debugging process as you will actually use it. This process results in well-written, working programs.

You must remember this, a kiss is still a kiss,
A sigh is just a sigh;
The fundamental things apply,
As time goes by.

—Herman Huupfeld
"As Time Goes By"

I n this chapter we discuss the fundamental parts of a C++ program. A program can be read, just as a story or poem can, and appreciated, even by someone who hasn't yet written a program. In fact, the first step in learning to *write* a program is learning how to *read* them. If a program is simple, well-written, and arranged neatly on the page, reading it can be a pleasure.

2.1

Two Simple Programs

We begin with two complete, but simple, working programs. In the following section we look at a more challenging one. Consider:

```
1   #include <iostream.h>
2   #include <iomanip.h>
3
4   main () {
5   //  Say hello.
6
7   //  Edward M. Reingold, November 12, 1993
8
9     cout << "Hello!";
10   }
```

When we compile and execute this program, it does nothing except to display the message

```
Hello!
```

on the terminal.

Let's look at each component of this program separately. First, the small line numbers in color are *not* part of the program (that is, they are not typed into the file containing the program); they are shown here so that we can refer to them in our discussions. Lines 1 and 2 are *compiler directives* that need to be included *compiler directives* at the beginning of every program; take them on faith now—we'll explain them in

heading

Chapter 10.[1] Line 3 is left blank for readability. It separates the compiler directives from the *heading*, lines 4 through 7, which introduces the program by using
the word **main** and some comment lines that identify the author and the date the
program was written and explain the purpose of the program. These comment
lines, which begin with a double slash **//**, are for human readers; the computer
ignores them.

It is line 9 that does the work:

```
9       cout << "Hello!";
```

This line sends the characters "H", "e", "l", "l", "o", and "!" to be displayed on
the terminal screen, one by one, forming the displayed message.

Now, let's look at a program that asks the user for the temperature in degrees
Fahrenheit and converts it to degrees Celsius. We want a dialog like

```
Please type the temperature (deg F): 68
68 deg F is 20 deg C
```

What the computer types is shown in black; the human response is in color. Here
is the program that produces just that dialog:

```
1       #include <iostream.h>
2       #include <iomanip.h>
3
4       main () {
5       //  Convert temperature from Fahrenheit to Celsius
6
7       //  Samuel N. Kamin, June 1, 1993
8
9         float temperature;   // The Fahrenheit temperature.
10
11        cout << "Please type the temperature (deg F): ";
12        cin >> temperature;
13        cout << temperature;
14        cout << " deg F is ";
15        cout << (5.0 * (temperature - 32)) / 9.0;
16        cout << " deg C";
17      }
```

The compiler directives and heading are similar to those in our first program, but the heart of the program, lines 9 through 16, is more complex. Five of
these lines send characters to the terminal screen (lines 11 and 13 through 16),
but lines 9 and 12 are different. Line 12 tells the computer that the human user is
expected to type something here. What should happen to the value typed? Line 12
says that the value is to be stored for later use under the symbolic name **temperature**; this symbolic name has been arranged for by the statement in line 9. Line 16
is also a bit different: It takes the value recorded for later use (**temperature**) and
does some arithmetic on it to produce the corresponding Celsius value—the ***** is

---

[1]These two lines say that the standard files **iostream.h** and **iomanip.h** should be included at this
point; these files contain the definitions needed to allow the program to read input and write output.
We discuss the subject in detail in Chapter 10.

used in C++ to indicate multiplication. We'll explain the storage of values such as **temperature** in Section 2.4.

A More Challenging Program

Here is a C++ program that, when executed, produces the table of equivalent Fahrenheit and Celsius temperatures shown in Figure 2.1:

```
 1   #include <iostream.h>
 2   #include <iomanip.h>
 3
 4   main () {
 5   //  Create a table of corresponding Fahrenheit and
 6   //  Celsius temperatures from -10 to +10 deg Celsius.
 7
 8   //  Ruth N. Reingold, October 22, 1993
 9
10     float
11       Celsius,     // The Celsius temperature.
12       Fahrenheit;  // The Fahrenheit temperature.
13
14     cout << "DEGREES C  DEGREES F\n";
15     Celsius = -10.0;
16     while (Celsius <= 10.0) {
17       Fahrenheit = (9.0/5.0) * Celsius + 32.0; // Convert C to F.
18       cout << setw(7) << Celsius << "     "
19             << setw(7) << Fahrenheit << "\n";
20       Celsius++;   // Increment the Celsius value.
21     }
22   }
```

As in the two previous examples, lines 1 and 2 are compiler directives that must be included. Also, as in the previous examples, the heading in lines 4 through 8 introduces the program by using the keyword **main**, identifies the author and the date, and explains the purpose of the program. The next three lines (10 through 12) describe the values to be manipulated by the program, just as in the previous temperature conversion program.

The heart of the program is the sequence of statements

```
14     cout << "DEGREES C  DEGREES F\n";
15     Celsius = -10.0;
16     while (Celsius <= 10.0) {
17       Fahrenheit = (9.0/5.0) * Celsius + 32.0; // Convert C to F.
18       cout << setw(7) << Celsius << "     "
19             << setw(7) << Fahrenheit << "\n";
20       Celsius++;   // Increment the Celsius value.
21     }
```

These statements describe exactly the actions that occur during the program's execution. The situation is much like that in the mouse-in-the-maze problem of

DEGREES C	DEGREES F
-10	14
-9	15.8
-8	17.6
-7	19.4
-6	21.2
-5	23
-4	24.8
-3	26.6
-2	28.4
-1	30.2
0	32
1	33.8
2	35.6
3	37.4
4	39.2
5	41
6	42.8
7	44.6
8	46.4
9	48.2
10	50

FIGURE 2.1   A table of corresponding Fahrenheit and Celsius temperatures from −10°C to +10°C, obtained as output from the sample program.

Chapter 1, only here the actions manipulate numbers instead of mice. The statement

```
15      Celsius = -10.0;
```

variables   for example, says that one of the symbolic names or *variables* being manipulated by the program is to have its value set to −10.0. Here, the variable called **Celsius** has its value set to −10.0. The variable names used in the program have to be declared (specified) at the beginning of the program, as they are in our example:

```
10      float
11          Celsius,      // The Celsius temperature.
12          Fahrenheit;   // The Fahrenheit temperature.
```

type   Not only do the variable names have to be given, but also the nature or *type* of each variable—here the two variables **Celsius** and **Fahrenheit** are declared to be **float**, that is, numerical values that may have a fractional part. Figure 2.2 shows how we might envision these variables as boxes whose contents are the

FIGURE 2.2   Memory locations for the variables **Celsius** and **Fahrenheit** from the temperature table program.

value of the variable. The box itself is the *location* in the computer's *memory*   *memory location*
where the value is stored.

The manipulation of these variables is the core of the program in which the
formula

$$°F = \tfrac{9}{5}°C + 32$$

is used repeatedly to convert $-10°C$, $-9°C, \ldots, 9°C, 10°C$ to the equivalent
Fahrenheit temperature. The repetition is done using the **while** statement introduced in Chapter 1, where the mouse continued turning left while it was facing a
wall. Here, the sequence of statements

```
17      Fahrenheit = (9.0/5.0) * Celsius + 32.0; // Convert C to F.
18      cout << setw(7) << Celsius << "     "
19           << setw(7) << Fahrenheit << "\n";
20      Celsius++;   // Increment the Celsius value.
```

is executed repeatedly as long as the value of **Celsius** is at most 10.0. Since the
value of **Celsius** is initially set to -10.0 in statement 15, and since the last statement in the sequence increases the value stored in **Celsius** by 1.0, eventually
the value of **Celsius** becomes bigger than 10.0, and program execution stops.
Each time these statements are executed, they calculate the value of Fahrenheit
temperature corresponding to the current value of **Celsius**, put that value in
Fahrenheit, and print both values on a new line of output. The **setw(7)** tells
C++ to have seven columns for each number, so that the numbers line up neatly.

Typical of the manipulations of variables in C++ is the statement on line 20,

```
20      Celsius++;   // Increment the Celsius value.
```

which says "increment the value of **Celsius** by 1"; this operation is illustrated
in Figure 2.3. We could also have written this as

```
Celsius = Celsius + 1.0;
```

The C++ language takes its name from this operation: C++ is the programming
language C "incremented" with many new features.

The repeated execution of statements, such as in the mouse problem in the
previous chapter and the temperature conversion above, is one of the computer's

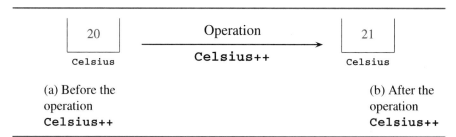

(a) Before the   (b) After the
operation   operation
Celsius++   **Celsius++**

FIGURE 2.3   The effect of the operation **Celsius++** when **Celsius** has the
value 20.

loops   great strengths. The design of such *loops*—instructions that iterate repeatedly un-til some condition is satisfied—is one of the most important skills in programming. We discuss loop design at length in Chapter 5, but in the meantime we use the **while** statement in instances where its meaning is clearly conveyed by its similarity to English. Furthermore, we do not expect you to be able to write programs using the **while** statement, except where the program required is a slight modification of one given in the text. In this way you will become comfortable with the idea of iteration without getting bogged down by the details.

Exercises—First Set

1. Enter, compile, and execute the sample program that writes the table of corresponding Fahrenheit and Celsius temperatures.

☞ 2. Explain why the table produced as output, shown in Figure 2.1, has 21 lines of temperature equivalences instead of 20.

☞ 3. Try the following experiments with the temperature table program on page 17. In each case, try to explain why you get the output that occurs.
   (a) Omit one of the semicolons.
   (b) Add an extra semicolon at the end of a line.
   (c) Change **main** to **mian**.
   (d) Change one of the { to [.
   (e) Change the constants 9.0 and 5.0 to 9 and 5, respectively.
   (f) Change the -10.0 to -5.0. Change it to 10.0. Change it to 20.0.
   (g) Change line 20 to **Celsius = Celsius + 0.5;**.
   (h) Change line 20 to **Celsius = Celsius + 2;**.
   (i) Change line 20 to **Celsius = Celsius - 1;**.

☞ 4. Try to modify the program so that it computes the table of equivalent temperatures for $-10°F, -9°F, \ldots, 10°F$ using the formula $°C = (°F - 32) \times \frac{5}{9}$.

5. Rewrite the temperature table program to convert from Fahrenheit temperature to kelvins (absolute temperature). The relationship between °F and K is

$$K = \tfrac{5}{9}(°F - 32) + 273.16$$

A kelvin is identical to one degree on the Celsius scale, but a temperature of zero kelvins is equal to $-273.16°C$.

2.3

Identifiers

identifiers   Examining the text of the temperature table program aside from the comments, the words we see are identifiers; *identifiers* are names that C++ recognizes. Some of those identifiers are provided to us by C++ identifiers like **float** and *keywords*   **while**, for example. Such identifiers are called *keywords*. Table 2.1 is a list of all

asm	auto	break	case	catch	char	class
const	continue	default	delete	do	double	else
enum	extern	float	for	friend	goto	if
inline	int	long	new	operator	private	protected
public	register	return	short	signed	sizeof	static
struct	switch	template	this	throw	try	typedef
union	unsigned	virtual	void	volatile	while	

TABLE 2.1 Keywords in C++.

keywords. Other than keywords, we can specify the meaning that other identifiers will have—such specification is part of the programming process.

Identifiers that you define yourself can consist of any sequence of letters and digits, but must begin with a letter. Punctuation and other symbols are not permitted. The following are all valid C++ identifiers:

    a   Sum   var1   finalTemp

whereas these are not:

    2for1   x+y   king kong

because they either begin with a nonletter, contain punctuation or symbols, or contain a blank. There is no limit to the length of an identifier. C++ considers upper- and lower-case letters distinct: the identifier **DATA** is not the same as **data** or **Data**; each of these is a separate identifier.

The underline character (_) *is* allowed as part of an identifier; it can be useful for making up descriptive identifier names such as **max_temperature** or **freezing_point**. We choose not to use it, however, instead following the convention of giving multiword descriptive names by using upper- and lower-case letters: **maxTemperature** or **freezingPoint**.

2.4

Variables

Take another look at these lines of the temperature table program:

```
10      float
11          Celsius,      // The Celsius temperature.
12          Fahrenheit;   // The Fahrenheit temperature.
```

The keyword **float** announces a *declaration* of variables used in the program. *Declaring a variable* announces its existence and makes it known within the program. Each variable in C++ has a name (an identifier) and a type (for example, **float**). The type of a variable describes the nature of values that can be stored in that variable's memory location. Each variable has only one type throughout the program, and that type determines what operations can be performed on it.

declaration

In our example of the temperature table program, both variables **Celsius** and **Fahrenheit** are of type **float**. There are other types in C++, but for now we discuss only the standard types **float** and **int**.

float

Values of type **float** are numbers having a fractional part:

        3.14159   7.12   9.0   0.5e+001   -16.3e+002

e-notation

The **e** is the way C++ uses scientific notation, *e-notation* in C++; the letter **e** separates the number from the exponent. For example, the speed of light is **2.997925e8** meters/second, and the radius of an electron is **2.817939e-15** meters.

Numbers of type **float** are stored by the computer as approximate values (unlike **int** numbers, which are stored exactly). Consequently, the same precision would result from using π = 3.141592653589793 as would result from using π = 3.14159265358979323846426433, since the precision available on most computers is less than 15 decimal places.

int

Variables of type **int** have values that must be whole numbers, for example:

        103   45   -632

The computer distinguishes between whole numbers of type **int** and whole numbers of type **float**. The variable **wholeNumber** defined by

        float wholeNumber;

allows **wholeNumber** to take on values such as 3.0, 2.0, and so on, as well as 3.12, 1.75, 16.2, and so on, while

        int wholeNumber;

confines **wholeNumber** to values such as −3, 2, 65.

2.5

Expressions

expression

Many programming tasks require computing the value of an *expression*. An expression can be a constant, a variable, or some arithmetic operation or function applied to constants or variables, resulting in a value, for example:

        x   cos(angle)   3+sizeOfBox   exp(maximum)

numeric operators

The symbols C++ uses for the operations addition, subtraction, multiplication, and division are **+**, **-**, *****, and **/**, respectively; these are called *numeric operators*. Numeric operators are used for values of type **float** and type **int** and have the expected meaning—that is, **+** adds two numbers, **-** subtracts one number from another, and ***** multiplies two numbers. However, the division operator **/** is idiosyncratic: Although it gives fractional values when used with values of type **float**, when used for values of type **int** it is similar to long division, giving

Type	Symbol	Operation	Example
float	+	Addition	4.50e01 + 5.30e00 = 5.03e01
	−	Subtraction	6.57e02 − 5.70e01 = 6.00e02
	*	Multiplication	7e03 * 3.0e00 = 2.1e04
	/	Division	9.6e01 / 2e01 = 4.8e00
int	+	Addition	45 + 5 = 50
	−	Subtraction	657 − 57 = 600
	*	Multiplication	7000 * 3 = 21000
	/	Division	10 / 3 = 3
	%	Remainder	10 % 3 = 1

TABLE 2.2   Arithmetic operations in C++. Division by zero results in an error; this includes both / and %.

only the "whole" portion of the quotient; the operator % gives the remainder.[2] Thus, for example,

8 / 4 is 2	7 / 4 is 1	63 / 8 is 7
8 % 4 is 0	7 % 4 is 3	63 % 8 is 7

Division by zero, with either the division operator / or the remainder operator %, causes an error message and terminates execution on some computers. On other computers, however, the operation just gives a nonsensical result.

division by zero

Table 2.2 shows all the arithmetic operations available in C++ for types **float** and **int**.

The value of an expression can be computed only if all of its constituent variables have been given values. For example,

```
(9.0 / 5.0) * Celsius + 32.0
```

can be evaluated only after **Celsius** has been assigned some value.

Division by Zero

BUG ALERT 2.1

Check your computer to see what effect division by zero has. On one computer, the statement

```
cout << 1/0;
```

printed the value zero with no warning; on another computer it caused the error message

```
Arithmetic Exception (core dumped)
```

and execution halted.

---

[2]The value of a % b takes its sign from a. Thus -10 % 3 is −1.

precedence rules

Just as in everyday arithmetic, expressions in C++ are evaluated according to a set of *precedence rules*. These rules tell us (and the computer) how to interpret an expression. What, for example, does the expression 2+4/2 mean? Is it to be treated as (2+4)/2 whose value is 3, or is it to be treated as 2+(4/2) whose value is 4? In C++ the rules are identical to those in everyday arithmetic: Subexpressions in parentheses are evaluated first; when there are no parentheses to make it otherwise, the multiplicative operations (*, /, and %) are done first, before the additive operations (+ and -). Sequences of +'s and -'s and sequences of *'s, /'s, and %'s are evaluated from left to right. Parentheses are evaluated from the inside out. For a summary of these precedence rules and some examples, see Table 2.3—since C++ has many operators aside from the arithmetic operators given here, the precedence rules in C++ are far more extensive than shown in Table 2.3; see Appendix A for a comprehensive description. It is generally better to use parentheses to avoid ambiguity for the human reader.

functions
argument

C++ has many predefined common mathematical *functions* that can be used in arithmetic expressions. The *argument* of a function is the expression to which the function is applied. For example, the trigonometric functions sine and cosine are available, and we can write sin(2 * theta) when we need that value in an expression; the argument here is 2 * theta. Some of the predefined numeric functions in C++ are shown in Table 2.4; a more complete list is given in Appendix B. To use any of these functions you must have the compiler directive

math.h

```
#include <math.h>
```

at the beginning of your program.

Rules	1. Evaluate all subexpressions in parentheses.
	2. Evaluate nested parentheses from the inside out.
	3. In the absence of parentheses, or within parentheses:
	(a) Evaluate *, /, or % before + or -.
	(b) Evaluate sequences of *, /, and % operators from left to right.
	(c) Evaluate sequences of + and - operators from left to right.
Examples	3.146 - 0.146 / 2.0 is the same as 3.146 - (0.146 / 2.0) or 3.146 - 0.073 = 3.073
	6 + 37 % 8 / 5 is the same as 6 + ((37 % 8) / 5) = 6 + (5 / 5) = 7
	However, 6 + 37 % (8 / 5) = 6 + 37 % 1 = 6 + 0 = 6

TABLE 2.3 Precedence rules with examples for evaluating arithmetic expressions in C++. Use parentheses to avoid ambiguity for human readers. See Appendix A for a comprehensive description.

Name	Description
acos	Arc cosine
asin	Arc sine
atan	Arc tangent
ceil	Ceiling (next larger integer)
cos	Cosine
cosh	Hyperbolic cosine
exp	Exponential (e^x)
floor	Floor (next smaller integer)
log	Natural logarithm (base e)
log10	Logarithm (base 10)
sin	Sine
sinh	Hyperbolic sine
sqrt	Square root
tan	Tangent
tanh	Hyperbolic tangent

TABLE 2.4   Some of the predefined numeric functions in C++; a more complete list is given in Appendix B. If you use any of these functions, you need to have `#include <math.h>` at the beginning of your program.

2.6

Assignment Statements

An *assignment statement* sets the value of a variable. Such a statement consists of a variable on the left side, an expression on the right side, and the symbol `=` (read "is assigned the value") between; the general form is thus

assignment statement

```
<variable> = <expression>;
```

We have used angle brackets "<" and ">" to denote *meta-symbols*; that is, `<variable>` stands for any C++ variable, and `<expression>` stands for any C++ expression.

meta-symbols

In the temperature table program, for example,

```
Celsius = -10.0;
```

is an assignment statement, as is

```
Fahrenheit = (9.0/5.0) * Celsius + 32.0; // Convert C to F.
```

Recall that variables have a type given in their declaration; in assignment statements, the variable on the left side always should be of the same type as the expression on the right. For example, in the statement

```
Celsius = -10.0;
```

the variable `Celsius` has type `float`, so the whole number `-10.0` is written with a decimal point, making it `float`. If the types differ, the value of the expression will be converted to the type needed. Thus an `int` value will be converted to a

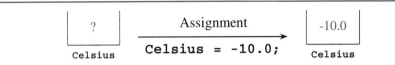

FIGURE 2.4   The effect of the assignment statement `Celsius = -10.0;` the previous value of `Celsius` is irrelevant.

`float`, without warning, when needed. A `float` value will be converted to an `int` by truncation, that is, cutting off the fractional part, so the value may be changed. For this reason, some C++ compilers warn you if a `float` value is converted to an `int` value. (The warning can be avoided by using a *cast*, but we will never need to do this; for the curious, the topic of casts is discussed in Appendix E; see page 603.)

An assignment statement has the effect of *replacing* the current value of the variable to which the assignment is made. In the case of

```
Celsius = -10.0;
```

the value of `Celsius` is replaced by the value `-10.0`. This is illustrated in Figure 2.4.

In the assignment statement

```
Celsius = Celsius + 1.0;    // Increment the Celsius value.
```

the variable on the left is assigned the value of the expression on the right, but the expression on the right contains the variable on the left. This means that 1.0 is added to the current value of the variable `Celsius`, and the result is stored in `Celsius`, giving a new value for the variable `Celsius`. This type of assignment statement demonstrates how an assignment statement acts: *First*, the expression on the right is evaluated, using whatever values were previously assigned to the variables. *Then*, the value of the expression on the right is assigned to the variable

---

BUG ALERT 2.2   **Finite Precision of Type `int`**

Integer values in the computer are limited in value by the internal structure of the computer. This limitation can have unexpected consequences, and no warning is given that you have overstepped the limit. Consider

```
int x = 100000 * 100000;
cout << x << "\n";
```

This produces the output

```
1410065408
```

instead of the correct value 10000000000, because the correct value is too large for our computer.

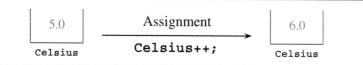

FIGURE 2.5 The effect of `Celsius++`.

on the left. Assignment statements that increment or decrement a variable by one are so common that C++ allows us to write them in an abbreviated form. As we saw in the temperature table example, the operator **++** increments a variable by 1:

```
Celsius++;   // Increment the Celsius value.
```

This is illustrated in Figure 2.5. Similarly, the operator **--** decrements a variable by 1:

```
Celsius--;   // Decrement the Celsius value.
```

2.7

Symbolic Constants

Suppose that instead of creating a table of corresponding Fahrenheit and Celsius temperatures from −10°C to 10°C, we want to create this table from some minimum temperature to some maximum temperature, with the minimum and maximum depending on where or when the table might be used. This change can be made by defining two symbolic constants. Assuming that the minimum and

Finite Precision of Type `float`   BUG ALERT 2.3

The computer's representation of type **float** with a finite number of decimal places means that computation with type **float** may not be exact in many cases. For example, if we write

```
float x = 1.0/5.0 + 1.0/5.0 + 1.0/5.0 - 0.6;
cout << x << "\n";
```

then instead of the accurate result 0, we get the output

```
8.88178e-17
```

because the values 1/5 and 0.6 are not represented precisely internally by the computer.

maximum are `-10.0` and `10.0`, respectively, we would write

```
const float
  lowTemp = -10.0,
  highTemp = 10.0;

float
  Celsius,      // The Celsius temperature.
  Fahrenheit;   // The Fahrenheit temperature.

Celsius = lowTemp;
cout << "DEGREES C  DEGREES F\n";
while (Celsius <= highTemp) {
  .
  . // Details on page 19.
  .
```

symbolic
constants
    The identifiers **lowTemp** and **highTemp** are called *symbolic constants*.

    Symbolic constants allow the use of names in place of numerals, making programs far more readable. A symbolic constant should be used when one needs the value of some fixed number throughout the program. For example, π or absolute zero or the number of kilometers per mile should be symbolic constants if used in a program. Unlike variables, the value of a symbolic constant never changes after it is set in the declaration.

2.8

Comments

comments
    We can make our programs more readable by describing, in English words, the actions of the C++ statements. Such descriptions are included as *comments*. Comments consist of any text following the symbol `//` to the end of the line. Although ignored by the computer, comments transform the formal, intricate format of a computer language into something that is more readily understood by humans.

BUG ALERT 2.4   **Erroneous Punctuation**

The most common mistakes for both new and experienced programmers are mismatching opening and closing braces and omitting a semicolon. The computer is unforgiving if you fail to follow its grammatical rules; unaware of your intent, it will try to run statements together in pursuit of a semicolon or closing brace. This results in peculiar and sometimes grotesque behavior. To help avoid this problem and to make your program more intelligible, the statements should be placed on the screen (or paper) with consistent, easily read indentations, as illustrated throughout this book.

At first you will want to spend your energy only on writing, debugging, and polishing a program; you will be tempted to avoid commenting or to add comments only *after* writing the entire program. Don't do it! The comments should be an integral part of the program, written, modified, and debugged, just as the program is. You'd be surprised how quickly you can forget the details of some section of code, and other people almost always need comments to understand your program. Reading a program should not be a detective game. Begin *every* program with a comment giving your name, the date, an explanation of the purpose of the program, and the method of solution used. Each section of a program should be commented by a description of its purpose.

2.9

Gluing Statements Together

Now that we have discussed most of the pieces of our sample program, it's time to examine the framework that holds these pieces together. The body of the program is enclosed within braces { } following the word **main ().** **main** is the identifier for the whole program. Within the program body, each atomic statement is terminated by a semicolon; *atomic statements* include assignment statements, declarations of constants and variables, input/output statements (discussed below), and some other types of statements discussed in later chapters. Braces { } group statements together into a single entity, called a *compound statement*, that can be used wherever a single C++ statement can be used; the closing brace is not followed by a semicolon. The entire body of the program is a compound statement enclosed within such braces.

atomic statements

compound statement

2.10

Layout of a C++ Program

The form in which a program is laid out on the page (or terminal screen) is not important to the C++ compiler; the compiler cares only about the keywords and punctuation (parentheses, commas, braces, and semicolons). The program can be compressed to have almost no blanks at all. Here is what the temperature table program looks like when compressed into dense lines of characters with no comments or identifiers meaningful to humans:

```
1    #include <iostream.h>
2    #include <iomanip.h>
3    main(){float C, F;C=-10.0;cout<<"DEGREES C  DEGREES F\n";while
4    (C<=10.0){F=(9.0/5.0)*C+32.0;cout<<setw(7)<<C<<"    "<<setw(7
5    )<<F<<"\n" ;C++;}}
```

This form of the program works just as well as the original version on page 17; the compiler does not object. In general, any division into lines is acceptable, as long as the compiler directives (lines 1 and 2) occupy separate lines, and characters within double quotes are kept on one line. There is no limit to the length of a line. However, the program in this last form is painfully difficult for a human to read and comprehend. It is next to impossible for a human to spot mismatched braces or parentheses, missing or extraneous semicolons, or misspelled identifiers. From the human point of view, this form of the program is a disaster!

Common sense dictates that a program should be laid out consistently in a way that clarifies, rather than obscures, its purpose and its method. Identifier names should be descriptive of their roles, statements should be properly aligned, blank spaces and lines should be included for readability, and matching pairs of braces and parentheses should be apparent at a glance. But there are no absolute rules of program layout. For some statements there is only one sensible choice; for others there may be several alternatives, each appropriate in some circumstances. As we present each C++ statement, we'll show reasonable layouts and arrangements of braces, as appropriate. The overall layout should look like

```
main () {



    }
```

with the statements of the program contained in the region shown here in light color.

2.11

Simple Input and Output

output
insertion operator
standard output stream
input
extraction operator
standard input stream

The purpose of the temperature table program is to print a table of Celsius and Fahrenheit temperatures. This process of printing data, usually on the computer screen, is called *output*. In C++ the operator << (the *insertion operator*) is the simplest way to produce output: it displays characters on the screen, referred to as cout in C++. cout is called the *standard output stream*. Similarly, *input* is obtained by the *extraction operator* >> as it is typed by the person sitting at the computer; this source of input is called cin in C++, the *standard input stream*. We will discuss streams at length later in the book; for now, we'll examine the bare bones needed for a program to read and write. The statement

```
cout << "DEGREES C  DEGREES F\n";
```

instructs the computer to print whatever is between the double quotes, that is

```
DEGREES C  DEGREES F
```

The "newline" character, \n, tells the computer to go to the start of the next output line. If we omit the newline character, we would write the same line but without skipping to the next line afterwards. Omitting the newline character allows us to compose output by writing one element of a line at a time. Should the need ever arise to write a double quotation mark itself, we use \", which will appear in the output *without* the preceding backslash. Strings like these that begin with the backslash \ are called *escape sequences* because the backslash allows us to "escape" from the ordinary meaning of the character that follows it. The most common ones are

escape sequences

\n	Newline—start printing on the next line
\"	Double quote mark
\\	Backslash

There are others, but they are rarely used and will be discussed as needed.

If we did not know in advance that the table of temperatures created by the temperature table program was to begin at $-10°C$ and go to $10°C$, but instead we were given the temperatures interactively ("on line"), we would need to use the extraction operator >> and the input stream **cin**. This stream can be used to assign the incoming data to program variables. The statement

```
cin >> lowTemp;
```

causes the program to stop and wait for you to type a number on the terminal, and then assigns the value you typed to the variable **lowTemp**. Of course, we had better warn the person sitting at the computer that input is expected by *prompting* for the input. Here is a program that asks a user to enter the minimum and maximum, which are then used in preparing the table:

prompting

```
1   #include <iostream.h>
2   #include <iomanip.h>
3
4   main () {
5   //  Create a table of corresponding Fahrenheit and
6   //  Celsius temperatures.
7
8   //  Haim Reingold, March 16, 1993
9
10    float
11      lowTemp,       // Starting Celsius temperature
12      highTemp,      // Ending Celsius temperature
13      Celsius,       // The Celsius temperature.
14      Fahrenheit;    // The Fahrenheit temperature.
15
16    cout << "Enter starting temperature (Celsius): ";
17    cin >> lowTemp;
18    cout << "Enter stopping temperature (Celsius): ";
19    cin >> highTemp;
20
21    Celsius = lowTemp;
22    cout << "DEGREES C  DEGREES F\n";
23    while (Celsius <= highTemp) {
24      Fahrenheit = (9.0/5.0) * Celsius + 32.0; // Convert C to F.
25      cout << setw(7) << Celsius << "      "
26          << setw(7) << Fahrenheit << "\n";
27      Celsius++;   // Increment the Celsius value.
28    }
29   }
```

This program asks the user to enter the starting and stopping temperatures by prompting

```
Enter starting temperature (Celsius): 0
```

After the user types a number for the starting value and then presses the "return" key, the program prompts

```
Enter stopping temperature (Celsius): 10
```

at which point the user enters the stopping value. (As before, we have shown what the computer types in black and the user's responses in color.)

Be warned that when you use **cout <<**, the characters to be output do not *buffer* go immediately to the screen but are kept in a holding area called a *buffer*; when the buffer is full, all the characters in it will be removed from it and displayed *output buffering* on the screen. This complicated arrangement, called *output buffering*, is used because there is an extremely lengthy startup time to output characters on the screen. Though output buffering saves computer time, it can cause strange behavior. Consider the following simple program:

```
1    #include <iostream.h>
2
3    main () {
4      cout << "Hello!";
5      cout << 1/0 << "\n";
6    }
```

When we run this program on one computer, we got the output

```
Arithmetic Exception (core dumped)
```

missing the characters **Hello!** that were sent to **cout** before the division by zero in line 5.

What happened to the missing output? It was waiting in the buffer, when the division-by-zero error happened and stopped the program. To prevent missing the last part of the output when the computer stops because of fatal error, you can *flush* send the command **flush** to **cout** to cause the buffer to be emptied immediately. Thus when we write

```
1    #include <iostream.h>
2
3    main () {
4      cout << "Hello!" << flush;
5      cout << 1/0 << "\n";
6    }
```

the output we get is

```
Hello!Arithmetic Exception (core dumped)
```

endl with nothing missing. The related command **endl**, when sent to **cout**, causes a newline (**\n**) to be sent to **cout**, followed by the flush command. That is,

```
cout << endl;
```

is equivalent to

```
cout << "\n" << flush;
```

Simple Loops

The `while` statement introduced in the mouse-in-the-maze problem in the previous chapter and used in the temperature table program is such a useful and common tool that it is worth going over one more example before we continue. It is used whenever a task is performed repeatedly, pending some end condition. Suppose we want the computer to print the following children's song:

```
10 in a bed and the little one said,
     "Roll over, roll over."
They all rolled over and one fell out,
9 in a bed and the little one said,
     "Roll over, roll over."
They all rolled over and one fell out,
8 in a bed and the little one said,
  .
  .
  .
1 in a bed and the little one said,
     "Alone at last."
```

The first thing to do is to decide which pieces of the song are to be printed just once and which pieces can be put inside the `while` loop. The song can be divided into the first line,

```
10 in a bed and the little one said,
```

the repeated lines,

```
     "Roll over, roll over."
They all rolled over and one fell out,
-- in a bed and the little one said,
```

each time including the current number, and the last line,

```
     "Alone at last."
```

We'll organize our program schematically as

```
<print first line of verse>
while (<more verses>) {
  <print rest of verse>
  <print first line of next verse>
}
<print rest of last verse>
```

We need one variable, which we'll call **numberInBed**, and a symbolic constant, **maxNumberInBed**, to specify how many verses of the song are to be written. The program is

```
1    #include <iostream.h>
2    #include <iomanip.h>
3
4    main () {
5    //  Print the nursery rhyme "Ten In a Bed."
6
7    //  Leah S. Gordon, December 29, 1993
8
9      const int maxNumberInBed = 10;
10     int numberInBed;
11
12     cout << maxNumberInBed
13         << " in a bed and the little one said,\n";
14     numberInBed = maxNumberInBed - 1;
15     while (numberInBed > 0) {
16       cout << "     \\"Roll over, roll over.\"\n"
17           << "They all rolled over and one fell out,\n"
18           << numberInBed
19           << " in a bed and the little one said,\n";
20       numberInBed = numberInBed - 1;
21     }
22     cout << "     \\"Alone at last.\"\n";
23   }
```

2.13

Debugging

The road to wisdom? Well, it's plain and simple to express:
Err and err and err again, but less and less and less.

—Piet Hein
Grooks

Now let's develop a program from the beginning. We do this over and over throughout the book. Each time we do it, we try to reproduce faithfully the thought processes that go into the development of the algorithm and its implementation as a program. In the early chapters we include errors ranging from simple syntactic mistakes to major design flaws in the algorithm. In later chapters, as your knowledge of C++ syntax grows more secure, we do not include syntactic errors but concentrate only on design flaws and implementation errors. It may be misleading to start out with a badly designed algorithm or a poor C++ implementation, but this is exactly the process you will be going through as you learn to write good programs, and we feel it is important to reproduce it in all its frustrating details. When we present erroneous versions of a program, you will be able to recognize them, because a warning such as "WRONG" will be printed over and over behind them in color.

Though the process—the spirit, so to say—of what we do in this section is just what you are likely to go through, the details will vary. You will make different mistakes, and we cannot possibly list all syntactic or logical errors that you may have to debug. Moreover, C++ compilers vary. The one you use may be more (or less!) helpful than ours and may give you different error messages.

The program we'll write computes the price of a coffee order from Peet's, a well-known chain of coffee shops in the San Francisco Bay area, that also sells coffee by mail. They compute the price for an order as

$$(\text{Price per pound}) \times \text{Weight} + \text{Shipping},$$

where

$$\text{Shipping} = (\text{Rate per pound}) \times \text{Weight} + \text{Fixed handling fee}.$$

The price per pound and the number of pounds ordered vary with each order, but the shipping cost per pound and the fixed handling fee do not. We want a program to calculate the total cost of a coffee order; corresponding to this problem description, we use the variables **pricePerPound** and **weight**, whose values are to be read, and the symbolic constants **fixedFee** and **ratePerPound**. We'll calculate and print the values of the variables **shippingPrice** and **totalPrice**.

Here is our first attempt:

```
 1  #include <iostream.h>
 2  #include <iomanip.h>
 3
 4  main () {
 5  //   Peet's Coffee
 6
 7  //   Eve M. Reingold, May 10, 1993
 8
 9    const int
10    ratePerPound = 1.25, // Shipping rate per pound
11    fixedFee,            // Shipping rate per shipment
12
13    int
14    pricPerPound,        // Coffee price per pound
15    weight,              // Amount ordered
16    shippingCost,
17    coffeeCost;
18
19    cout << "Peet's Coffee\n\nEnter price per pound: ;"
20    cin >> pricePerPound;
21
22    cout << "Enter number of pounds: ";
23    cin >> weight;
24
25    shipingCost = ratePerPound * weight + fixedFee;
26    totalPrice = pricPerPound * weight + shippingCost;
27
28    cout << "Coffee total is " << coffeeCost << "\N"
29         << "Shipping cost is " << shipingCost << "\N"
30         << "Total cost is " << totalPrice "\N";
31
32  }
33
```

debugging   We now have to correct the program by the process of *debugging*, the identification and correction of errors until a program works and is in good form (see Figure 1.1). The easiest errors to identify are those in syntax (like mismatched parentheses, missing or extraneous semicolons, and so on) because the program does not compile, the errors are pointed out by the compiler, and they are usually easy to fix.

Harder to identify, and far more serious, are logical errors. These go unnoticed by the compiler, but they cause fatal errors in the outcome of the program. Perhaps the most elusive errors are stylistic errors. A program may compile, run, and produce just the right results, and yet be a nightmare in form. We will repair the preceding program, fixing all three types of errors.

Before reading further, "desk check" (examine carefully without actually running) the program by scanning it carefully to find any errors. First look for errors in syntax, then in logic, and finally in style. Now being optimistic, we run the preceding program. On some computers, a sufficiently serious error may stop the compilation process and no further errors will be discovered; in other cases one may get a long list of errors. (Often, a simple error can cause the compiler to announce many errors; in effect, a single error may so confuse the compiler that it sees many errors where there is only one.) Compiling the program yields

```
Can't find include file iostream,h
```

because we asked for the wrong file. Correcting the name of the file to **iostream.h** (a period, not a comma) and then recompiling yields the error message

```
line 13: error: syntax error
```

which is unenlightening, to say the least! The problem is actually on an *earlier* line, line 11, where we used a comma instead of a semicolon to end the declaration. When we change line 11 to

```
11      fixedFee;            // Shipping rate per shipment
```

we get the error messages

```
line 20: error: ';' missing after statement
line 20: error: syntax error
```

Now the problem is not on line 20 as claimed, but on line 19: the semicolon and the closing quotation mark are transposed. Fixing this and recompiling we get

```
line 30: error: syntax error
```

This is quite puzzling, because we see nothing wrong with that output statement. (If you *do* see what's wrong with it, just pretend for the moment that you don't!) Not sure what to do, we "comment out" that statement by adding // at the start of each line,

```
28    //   cout << "Coffee total is " << coffeeCost << "\N"
29    //        << "Shipping cost is " << shipingCost << "\N"
30    //        << "Total cost is " << totalPrice "\N";
```

Wrong Line in Compiler Error Messages

You will often find that a syntax error reported by the compiler at a particular line actually reflects an error in some earlier line.

Capitalization Errors

One of the most common mistakes is inconsistency of capitalization in identifier names. The variables named `fixedFee`, `FixedFee`, and `fixedfee` are all different, because upper-case and lower-case letters are different characters to the computer.

and try the compiler again, only to find

```
line 10: warning:  const int  initialized with  double
line 11: error: uninitialized const fixedFee
line 20: error:  pricePerPound undefined
line 20: error:  pointer operand for  >>
line 25: error:  shipingCost undefined
line 26: error:  totalPrice undefined
line 11: warning:  fixedFee used but not set
line 14: warning:  pricPerPound used but not set
line 16: warning:  shippingCost not used
line 17: warning:  coffeeCost not used
```

so whatever is wrong with that final statement, we've got lots of other errors to attend to!

The error on line 10 says something is wrong with the initialization of `ratePerPound`—we've declared it an `int`, but assigned it a `float` value, so C++ warned us that this might be wrong. Indeed it *is* wrong, since the price of coffee per pound will be a dollar-and-cents value—that is, it must be declared as a `float`—so we change it. The next error is clear: We forgot to give the value for the `const fixedFee`, which should have been $1.95. The next error is also clear: We *tried* to declare the variable `pricePerPound`, but we misspelled it, leaving out the letter "e." So we look for all occurrences of this typo, finding another at line 26. The fourth error is absolutely unintelligible (what's a pointer?!), so we ignore it and go on to the fifth error, which points out another typo—`shipingCost` where we wanted `shippingCost`. We fix that typo and search for other instances, finding one at line 29, which we also fix. The sixth error tells us we forgot to declare `totalPrice`, though we used it in line 26.

Since the remaining four errors are only warnings, we ignore them and only make the changes above, giving us the program

```
 1    #include <iostream.h>
 2    #include <iomanip.h>
 3
 4    main () {
 5    //  Peet's Coffee
 6
 7    //  Eve M. Reingold, May 10, 1993
 8
 9      const float
10        ratePerPound = 1.25, // Shipping rate per pound
11        fixedFee = 1.95;     // Shipping rate per shipment
12
13      int
14        pricePerPound,       // Coffee price per pound
15        weight,              // Amount ordered
16        shippingCost,
17        coffeeCost,
18        totalPrice;
19
20      cout << "Peet's Coffee\n\nEnter price per pound: ";
21      cin >> pricePerPound;
22
23      cout << "Enter number of pounds: ";
24      cin >> weight;
25
26      shippingCost = ratePerPound * weight + fixedFee;
27      totalPrice = pricePerPound * weight + shippingCost;
28
29    //   cout << "Coffee total is " << coffeeCost << "\N"
30    //        << "Shipping cost is " << shippingCost << "\N"
31    //        << "Total cost is " << totalPrice "\N";
32
33    }
```

and compiling, we get only the warning messages

```
line 26: warning:  float   assigned to   int
line 17: warning:  coffeeCost not used
```

But the program compiles! So we run the program. Here's what happens:

```
Peet's Coffee

Enter price per pound: 8.95
Enter number of pounds:
```

The program doesn't give us a chance to enter the second number; it just stops! (Remember, we have shown the number 8.95 in color to indicate that it is entered at the terminal, whereas "Enter price per pound: " is program output.) This makes little sense, because the very next statement asks for the input. What do we do? As before, when we're not sure what happened, we try to go on to other errors, because often the other problems we've ignored will have unknown consequences; perhaps one of those consequences is just the problem we now face.

So we uncomment the output statements (lines 29 through 31) and try to compile the program, only to find:

```
line 31: error: syntax error
```

We're now completely lost, with no clue as to what to do, so we ask for outside help from someone who knows more than we do about C++ (the professor, teaching assistant, consultant). She asks whether we have searched for the error by selectively commenting out parts of the problematic output statement. She also points out that we've used \N and she's never seen that before. When we explain we wanted an end-of-line, she reminds us that it should be \n instead and she suggests we comment out the last two lines of the output statement and see what happens. We change these lines to read

```
29     cout << "Coffee total is " << coffeeCost << "\n";
30  //        << "Shipping cost is " << shippingCost << "\n"
31  //        << "Total cost is " << totalPrice "\n";
```

and compiling it we get the warnings

```
line 26: warning:  float  assigned to  int
line 17: warning:  coffeeCost used but not set
```

but since it compiled, we try again to run it:

```
Peet's Coffee

Enter price per pound: 8.95
Enter number of pounds: Coffee total is 32768
```

The strange value 32768 happened because we never assigned a value to the variable **coffeeCost**, which is just the price per pound times the number of pounds. We add a statement to compute it, using it in the calculation of **totalPrice**:

```
26     shippingCost = ratePerPound * weight + fixedFee;
27     coffeeCost = pricePerPound * weight;
28     totalPrice = coffeeCost + shippingCost;
```

The program compiles with the warning messages

```
line 26: warning:  float  assigned to  int
```

and when run gives

```
Peet's Coffee

Enter price per pound: 8.95
Enter number of pounds: Coffee total is 0
```

Uncommenting the next part of the final output statement (and moving the semicolon), compiling, and running the result gives

```
Peet's Coffee

Enter price per pound: 8.95
Enter number of pounds: Coffee total is 0
Shipping cost is 0
```

So the output statement is wrong on its last line. Looking at it closely, we see we've omitted a << before the end-of-line, so we fix this (again, we have to remember to remove the semicolon we added when we first commented out part of the statement) and try again:

```
Peet's Coffee

Enter price per pound: 8.95
Enter number of pounds: Coffee total is 0
Shipping cost is 1
Total cost is 1
```

Well, that's progress, because the program now runs to completion, albeit never allowing us to enter the weight. Also, the values we're printing out are nonsense. What's the source of this strange behavior? Let's try to execute the program again, but with a different value:

```
Peet's Coffee

Enter price per pound: 7
Enter number of pounds: 3
Coffee total is 21
Shipping cost is 5
Total cost is 26
```

Lo and behold, it worked! But why didn't it work when we entered **8.95** as the price per pound? Aha—we've declared all those variables to be **int**; *that* is what those warning messages must have meant! So, we fix the program by changing the declaration of the variables to **float** and the program works perfectly:

```
Peet's Coffee

Enter price per pound: 8.95
Enter number of pounds: 3
Coffee total is 26.85
Shipping cost is 5.7
Total cost is 32.55
```

That still doesn't explain why the computer wouldn't let us enter a weight in our earlier version. When we find the C++ expert and ask her, she explains that because **pricePerPound** was type **int**, the computer would take only an integer value for it. So when we typed **8.95**, the integer part "8" was taken as the value of **pricePerPound** and the ".95" was taken as the *next* value of input requested, namely the value of **weight**. Of course, **weight** was also declared as type **int**, so the value was truncated to zero, explaining the weird result.

Echoing Input

One way to detect errors in reading input is to echo the input value
read back to the user by writing it immediately after reading it. This
is useful during the development of the program.

Missing Output

When you think you may be missing output, use either **flush** or **endl**
to be sure that *all* the output has been sent to the screen.

No program is ever perfect, although at this point our Peet's Coffee program
is in excellent shape and we can leave it as it is:

```
1    #include <iostream.h>
2    #include <iomanip.h>
3
4    main () {
5    //  Peet's Coffee
6
7    //  Eve M. Reingold, May 10, 1993
8
9      const float
10       ratePerPound = 1.25, // Shipping rate per pound
11       fixedFee = 1.95;     // Shipping rate per shipment
12
13     float
14       pricePerPound,       // Coffee price per pound
15       weight,              // Amount ordered
16       shippingCost,
17       coffeeCost,
18       totalPrice;
19
20     cout << "Peet's Coffee\n\nEnter price per pound: ";
21     cin >> pricePerPound;
22
23     cout << "Enter number of pounds: ";
24     cin >> weight;
25
26     shippingCost = ratePerPound * weight + fixedFee;
27     coffeeCost = pricePerPound * weight;
28     totalPrice = coffeeCost + shippingCost;
29
30     cout << "Coffee total is " << coffeeCost << "\n"
31          << "Shipping cost is " << shippingCost << "\n"
32          << "Total cost is " << totalPrice << "\n";
33
34   }
```

Complicated programs released for public use require maintenance throughout their useful life, so debugging a large program is a task that never really ends while the program is in use. Such maintenance always involves many people over a period of many years. When is a program ready to be released for public use? Consider this news item from *The New York Times* of April 9, 1986:

HACKENSACK, N. J., April 8—For weeks, people have been traveling far and wide to reach the pay phones here. The attraction is free international telephone calls.

Technology in an electronic switching center here failed New Jersey Bell, and for nearly two months perhaps half the international calls placed from 400 pay phones around town went through without charge, according to a spokesman for the company, Ted Spencer.

"Apparently a problem developed in a computer program—in the software," Mr. Spencer said. "We don't have a record of the calls that got through. They bypassed the billing system."

Mr. Spencer said the problem has been resolved, adding that New Jersey Bell had no way of determining its financial loss.

Exercises—Second Set

1. Which of the following are valid C++ identifiers? In each case explain why or why not.

`first_entry`	`2nd`	`right-hand-side`	`dataType`
`FATHER`	`break`	`last one`	

2. Express these **float** values in e-notation:

   $$-6543210.0 \quad .897654321 \quad 3 \times 10^{45} \quad 0.000061 \quad 45.8 \times 10^{-3}$$

3. Give proper C++ expressions for the following:
   - (a) The Fahrenheit temperature as a function of the absolute temperature in kelvins (see Exercise 5, page 20, for the proper formula)
   - (b) The kelvin temperature as a function of the Celsius temperature
   - (c) The kelvin temperature as a function of the Fahrenheit temperature

4. Your European shoe size can be determined from the length of your foot in centimeters: Take the foot length, subtract 9, multiply by 3, divide by 2, round *up*, and add 15. Write a C++ program to read a person's foot length *in inches*, convert it to centimeters, and print the corresponding European shoe size. (There are 0.394 inches per centimeter.) Your output should look like:

   ```
   EUROPEAN SHOE SIZE

   Enter the length of your foot in inches: 9.5
   Your European shoe size is 38
   ```

5. A "target" heart rate is useful in establishing a suitable exercise level. To determine this rate, subtract your age from 220. The upper limit of your target heart rate is 85 percent of this value; the lower limit is 65 percent. For example, a 40 year-old person can achieve a healthy workout by reaching a heart rate between 117 and 153 beats per minute. Write a C++ program to read a person's age and print the range of that

person's target heart rate. Your output should look like:

```
TARGET HEART RATES

Enter your age: 40
Your target heart rate is 117 to 153 beats per minute.
```

6. The equation for ideal gases is

$$PV = nRT,$$

where P is the pressure of the gas, V is the volume, n is the number of moles of gas, T is the absolute temperature in kelvins, and R is the universal gas constant. Write a C++ expression for the pressure of an ideal gas using this equation. Choose meaningful identifiers for variables and constants.

7. A more precise equation for real gases (see the previous exercise) is the equation of state of van der Waals:

$$RT = \left(P - \frac{a}{v^2}\right)(v - b),$$

where $P, R,$ and T are as defined above; a and b are van der Waals' constants applicable to individual gases; and v is the molar volume (V/n). Write a C++ expression for the temperature of a gas using the van der Waals equation of state.

8. Snell's law in optics states that the relative index of refraction is

$$\frac{\sin \alpha}{\sin \beta},$$

where α is the angle of incidence and β is the angle of refraction. Write a C++ expression for the relative index of refraction using meaningful identifiers for variable names. (*Hint:* The function **sin** takes the angle in radians.)

9. The value at maturity of an initial investment P, invested over n periods, at an interest rate r, and compounded at the end of each period, is

$$P(1 + r)^n.$$

Write a C++ expression for this formula. (*Hint:* Use the functions **exp** and **log**.)

10. Coulomb's law states that the electrostatic force (in newtons) between two charges of q_1 and q_2 coulombs, separated by a distance of r meters in a vacuum, is

$$\frac{q_1 q_2}{4\pi\epsilon_0 r^2},$$

where $\epsilon_0 = 8.84 \times 10^{-9}$ farads per meter is the permittivity of free space. Write a C++ expression for the electrostatic force between two charges.

11. (a) The Tetens equation relates the saturation water vapor pressure to the air temperature. If the units of pressure are millimeters of mercury and the air temperature is Celsius, the formula for the saturation water vapor pressure is

$$4.579 \times 10^{7.49 \times \text{airtemp}/(\text{airtemp} + 236.87)}.$$

Write a C++ expression for the saturation water vapor pressure as a function of air temperature.

(b) Repeat part (a) for vapor over ice (instead of water); the constant 236.87 changes to 270.8, and 7.49 changes to 9.67.

12. Modify the program that prints "Ten in a Bed" to print the song "99 Bottles of Beer on the Wall":

```
99 bottles of beer on the wall,
99 bottles of beer,
If one of those bottles should happen to fall,
98 bottles of beer on the wall.

98 bottles of beer on the wall,
98 bottles of beer,
If one of those bottles should happen to fall,
97 bottles of beer on the wall.
    .
    .
    .
1 bottle of beer on the wall,
1 bottle of beer,
If that one bottle should happen to fall,
No more bottles of beer on the wall!
```

13. Modify the temperature table program to print a table of squares of the integers from 1 to 10.

14. Write and debug a program to calculate the selling price of items at a discount store where

$$\text{Selling price} = (\text{List price} - \text{Discount}) + \text{Tax}.$$

Use variables `listPrice`, `discount`, and `tax` whose values are to be read. Print the value of a variable `sellingPrice`.

15. The *Gregorian epact* of a year is the number of days since the new moon as of January 1 of that year, for the purpose of determining the date of Easter. The epact is given by the remainder when the expression

$$8 + (\text{Century}/4) - \text{Century} + ((8 * \text{Century} + 13)/25)$$

$$+ 11 * (\text{Golden number} - 1)$$

is divided by 30. In this expression, the century is the quotient when the year is divided by 100, and the golden number is one plus the remainder when the year is divided by 19. Write a program to print the Gregorian epact of a given year using the variables and expression defined above. Your output should look like this:

```
Gregorian epact

Enter the year: 1986
The Gregorian epact of 1986 is 19
```

16. The area of a triangle can be calculated from its side lengths by *Heron's formula*:

$$\text{Area} = \sqrt{s(s - a)(s - b)(s - c)},$$

where a, b, and c are the side lengths and s is the semiperimeter; that is, $s = (a + b + c)/2$. Write a program to read the three sides of a triangle and calculate its area by Heron's formula.

17. The (Euclidean) distance between two points (x_1, y_1) and (x_2, y_2) is

$$\text{Distance} = \sqrt{(x_2 - x_1)^2 + (y_2 - y_1)^2}.$$

Write a program to read the coordinates of two points and calculate the distance between them.

18. The *relative humidity* is the ratio of the amount of water vapor in the air to the amount of water vapor that the air could have if it were saturated (at that same temperature). The *dew point* is the temperature at which the actual water vapor pressure equals the saturation vapor pressure, that is, when the relative humidity is 1. The formula used by the United States National Weather Service to approximate the dew point in degrees Celsius from the actual temperature and the relative humidity (expressed as a percentage) is

Dew point = Temperature

$- (14.55 + 0.114 \times \text{Temperature}) \times (1 - 0.01 \times \text{Relative humidity})$

$- [(2.5 + 0.0007 \times \text{Temperature}) \times (1 - 0.01 \times \text{Relative humidity})]^3$

$- (15.9 + 0.117 \times \text{Temperature}) \times (1 - 0.01 \times \text{Relative humidity}).$[14]

Write a C++ program to read the temperature and relative humidity and then compute and print the dew point.

Summary

The essential parts of a C++ program are

```
#include <iostream.h>
#include <iomanip.h>

main () {
//  Author, date, explanation

  <declarations of variables>

  <program statements with relevant comments>
}
```

A *variable* is a named location in the computer's memory in which a value can be stored. A *symbolic constant* is also a named location in which a value can be stored, but unlike a variable, its value is never changed after it is set in the declaration. Variable and constant names are *identifiers*—strings of characters beginning with a letter and containing no punctuation or blanks; the name should reflect the role that the variable or constant plays in the program. Each variable or constant has a type associated with it; the simple types are `float` and `int`. A `float` value can be expressed either in ordinary decimal notation or in *e-notation*. Special identifiers, called *keywords*, are reserved for special purposes and therefore cannot be used as variable or constant names. The keywords used thus far are

```
const    float    int    while
```

A complete list is given in Table 2.1.

An *expression* is a constant, a variable, or some arithmetic operations or functions applied to constants and variables resulting in a value of one particular type. Some of the available predefined arithmetic functions in C++ are found in Table 2.4. Expressions are evaluated according to *precedence rules*. Subexpressions in parentheses are evaluated first. In the absence of parentheses, multiplicative operations (`*`, `/`, and `%`) take precedence over additive operations (`+` and `-`). A series of operations of equal precedence is evaluated left to right.

An *assignment statement* has the form

```
<variable> = <expression>;
```

such that the *<variable>* and *<expression>* are of the same type. This statement causes the expression to be evaluated and the resulting value assigned as the value of the specified variable. `int` variables or expressions are automatically converted to `float` when the right-hand side of the assignment is a `float` variable. Similarly, `float` values are truncated to `int` values when the right-hand side of the assignment is an `int` variable.

Comments, set off by `//`, are ignored by the computer but are essential to the human reader. Commenting is part of the development stage of a program; it should *never* be omitted or even delayed during program composition.

Statements within a program are either *atomic* or compound statements. Atomic statements, which include assignment statements, declarations of constants and variables, and input/output statements, are terminated by semicolons. Compound statements are enclosed in braces `{` and `}`. The entire body of the program is a compound statement enclosed within such braces.

Program layout is essential to the human reader, even though it is irrelevant to the C++ compiler. Careful layout makes a program easier to read, understand, and debug. Statements should be properly aligned, blank spaces and blank lines should be included to enhance readability, and pairs of braces should be apparent at a glance. Layout style should be consistent throughout a program.

Output is handled with the insertion operator `<<` and `cout`. *Input* is handled with the extraction operator `>>` and `cin`. The field width used for output and the number of digits can be controlled with the `setw` specification.

If a task in a program needs to be performed repeatedly, pending an end condition, the `while` statement is used:

```
while (<condition>)
  <statement>
```

The process called *debugging* is successive error identification and repair until a program works and is in good form.

3

Decision Making

Chapter Preview

Decisions are made in C++ with the **if** statement and the **switch** statement; we introduce these statements in this chapter. *Boolean expressions* determine the outcome of decisions using **if** statements; integers determine the outcome of decisions using **switch** statements.

<blockquote>
The prologues are over ... [i]t is time to choose.

—Wallace Stevens
Asides on the Oboe
</blockquote>

3.1

The `if` Statement

Programs often need to decide among one of several alternative actions. For example, the Social Security tax on wages (as of April of 1994) is computed as 12.4 percent of income, up to a maximum income of $57,600. To compute the tax, we must use the formula

$$\text{Tax} = \begin{cases} 0.124 \times \text{wages} & \text{if wages} \leq \$57600, \\ 0.124 \times \$57600 & \text{otherwise.} \end{cases}$$

Such a computation can be expressed neatly in C++ by the `if` statement used in Chapter 1 in the mouse-in-the-maze example:

```
if (wages <= maximumWage)
  tax = 0.124 * wages;
else
  tax = 0.124 * maximumWage;
```

When this is executed, the current value of **wages** is compared to the value of **maximumWage**. If the value of **wages** is less than or equal to the value of **maximumWage**, the statement **tax = 0.124 * wages** is executed. If the value of **wages** is greater than that of **maximumWage**, the statement **tax = 0.124 * maximumWage** is executed. Note that *just one* of the assignments is executed, *not* both.

This computation is embedded in the following complete C++ program, with the values 0.124 and 57600 replaced by suitably named symbolic constants.

```
 1   #include <iostream.h>
 2   #include <iomanip.h>
 3
 4   main () {
 5   //  Calculate and print the  Social Security
 6   //  Self-Employment Tax on wages (to be read in).
 7
 8   //  Deborah H. Reingold, November 6, 1994
 9
10     const float
11       maximumWage = 57600, // maximum wage subject to tax
12       taxRate = 0.124;     // tax rate on wages less than
13                            // the maximum
14     float
15       wages,               // amount of wages subject to tax
16       tax;                 // amount of tax
17
```

```
18      cout << "Your wages subject to Social Security Tax are: $";
19      cin >> wages;
20
21      if (wages <= maximumWage)
22        tax = taxRate * wages;
23      else
24        tax = taxRate * maximumWage;   // maximum allowable tax
25
26      cout << "Your Social Security Tax is: $" << tax << "\n";
27    }
```

When run, this program gives the following sample output for the case of **wages** less than **maximumWage**:

```
Your wages subject to Social Security Tax are: $20000
Your Social Security Tax is: $2480
```

and

```
Your wages subject to Social Security Tax are: $60000
Your Social Security Tax is: $7142.4
```

for **wages** greater than **maximumWage**.[1]

An **if** statement chooses one of two alternatives based on some true/false condition. The **if** statement is a single C++ statement divided into several parts—the keyword **if** followed by a parenthesized condition, followed by the "then" alternative (which will be executed if the condition is true); this is followed by the keyword **else** followed by the "else" alternative (which will be executed if the condition is false):

```
if (<condition>)
    <statement>    ←─ The "then" alternative
else
    <statement>    ←─ The "else" alternative
```

Each alternative can be a single statement or a compound statement enclosed by braces { ... }. Only the alternative chosen is executed; the other alternative is skipped entirely. If there is nothing to be done in the "else" alternative, it may be omitted:

```
if (<condition>)
    <statement>    ←─ The "then" alternative
```

For example, the result of

```
if (age >= 18)
    cout << "You are eligible to vote.\n"
```

is that the line of output

```
You are eligible to vote.
```

---

[1] We normally want dollars-and-cents amounts to be written with two digits following the decimal point, even if those digits are zeros. To see how to force the output into that format, see Appendix C, page 590.

will be printed if **age** is eighteen or larger; nothing will be printed if **age** is less than eighteen.

Each alternative in the **if** statement for the Social Security tax calculation was a simple statement. Here, by contrast, is an example of an **if** statement with a compound statement for each alternative. Given two positive integers, **firstNumber** and **secondNumber**, we want to calculate the **quotient** and the **remainder** of the larger integer divided by the smaller integer:

```
if (firstNumber <= secondNumber) {
  quotient  = secondNumber / firstNumber;
  remainder = firstNumber % secondNumber;
}
else {
  quotient  = firstNumber / secondNumber;
  remainder = secondNumber % firstNumber;
}
```

The *<statement>* in the "then" or "else" part of an **if** can be *any* statement, including another **if**. In the statement

```
if (<condition-1>)
  if (<condition-2>)
    <statement-1>
  else
    <statement-2>
else
  <statement-3>
```

<condition-1> is tested first. If it is true, the nested **if** (shown in color) is executed. That is, *<condition-2>* is tested; if it is true, *<statement-1>* is executed, otherwise *<statement-2>* is executed. If *<condition-1>* is false, *<statement-3>* is executed. The result is that exactly one of the three statements is executed:

- *<statement-1>* is executed if *<condition-1>* and *<condition-2>* are both true.
- *<statement-2>* is executed if *<condition-1>* is true and *<condition-2>* is false.
- *<statement-3>* is executed if *<condition-1>* is false, regardless of the truth of *<condition-2>*.

Notice how the indentation of the **if** statements displays the structure of the tests.

Another common example is when the else statement is an **if** statement:

```
if (<condition-1>)
  <statement-1>
else
  if (<condition-2>)
    <statement-2>
  else
    <statement-3>
```

Here, if `<condition-1>` is true, `<statement-1>` is executed. If not, `<condition-2>` is tested and if it is true, `<statement-2>` is executed; if it is false, `<statement-3>` is executed. Again, exactly one of the three statements is executed:

- `<statement-1>` is executed if `<condition-1>` is true.
- `<statement-2>` is executed if `<condition-1>` is false and `<condition-2>` is true.
- `<statement-3>` is executed if both `<condition-1>` and `<condition-2>` are false.

Again, the indentation of the `if` statements displays the structure of the tests—however in this case, it is customary to display the structure even more clearly as

```
if (<condition-1>)
  <statement-1>
else if (<condition-2>)
  <statement-2>
else
  <statement-3>
```

and this is the style we use.

An example of this last style calculates the wind-chill index for a given air temperature in °F and wind speed in miles per hour. The wind-chill index is computed from the empirically derived formula

$$\text{Wind-chill index} = \begin{cases} \text{temperature} & \text{wind} \le 4 \text{ mph,} \\ 91.4 - (10.45 + 6.69\sqrt{\text{wind}} & 4 \text{ mph} < \text{wind} \\ \quad - 0.447\text{wind}) \times \dfrac{91.4 - \text{temperature}}{22.0} & \le 45 \text{ mph,} \\ 1.6 \times \text{temperature} - 55.0 & \text{wind} > 45 \text{ mph.} \end{cases}$$

In C++ this formula becomes a "nested" `if` statement; that is, one `if` statement is inside another `if` statement:

```
if (windSpeed <= 4)        //  little or no wind
  windChillIndex = temperature;
else if (windSpeed <= 45)   //  moderate wind
  windChillIndex =
    91.4 - (10.45 + 6.69 * sqrt(windSpeed)
          - 0.447 * windSpeed) * (91.4 - temperature)/22.0;
else                       //  high wind
  windChillIndex = 1.6 * temperature - 55.0;
```

The complete C++ program to compute the wind-chill index is as follows. Notice that we need the compiler directive `#include <math.h>` because we are using the square root function **sqrt** (see Table 2.4 on p. 25):

```
1   #include <iostream.h>
2   #include <iomanip.h>
3   #include <math.h>
4
```

```
5   main () {
6   //  Calculate and print the wind chill index
7   //  for given air temperature and wind speed.
8
9   //  Rachel N. Reingold, January 31, 1993
10
11  //  The formula is taken from "Windchill" by William
12  //  Bosch and L.G. Cobb, UMAP Module 658, COMAP, Inc.,
13  //  Lexington, MA, 1984
14
15    float
16      temperature,       // air temperature (deg F)
17      windSpeed,         // wind speed (mph)
18      windChillIndex;    // wind chill index in deg F, the
19                         // equivalent temperature felt
20                         // by exposed skin
21
22    cout << "WIND-CHILL INDEX COMPUTATION\n\n";
23    cout << "The temperature (deg F) is: ";
24    cin >> temperature;
25    cout << "The wind speed (mph) is: ";
26    cin >> windSpeed;
27
28    // calculate the wind chill index according to
29    // formulas for different ranges of wind speed
30
31    if (windSpeed <= 4)      //  little or no wind
32      windChillIndex = temperature;
33    else if (windSpeed <= 45)   //  moderate wind
34      windChillIndex =
35        91.4 - (10.45 + 6.69 * sqrt(windSpeed)
36             - 0.447 * windSpeed) * (91.4 - temperature)/22.0;
37    else                     //  high wind
38      windChillIndex = 1.6 * temperature - 55.0;
39
40    cout << "The wind-chill index is " << windChillIndex << "\n";
41  }
```

Samples of the output for various temperatures and wind speeds are

```
WIND-CHILL INDEX COMPUTATION

The temperature (deg F) is: 72
The wind speed (mph) is: 3
The wind-chill index is 72
```

for almost no wind,

```
WIND-CHILL INDEX COMPUTATION

The temperature (deg F) is: 45
The wind speed (mph) is: 13
The wind-chill index is 30.7423
```

for moderate wind, and

```
WIND-CHILL INDEX COMPUTATION

The temperature (deg F) is: -12
The wind speed (mph) is: 52
The wind-chill index is -74.2
```

for high wind.

Nested **if** statements like this are useful and common, and you will often see them repeated several times, such as

```
if (<condition-1>)
   <statement-1>
else if (<condition-2>)
   <statement-2>
else if (<condition-3>)
   <statement-3>
...
else if (<condition-i>)
   <statement-i>
else
   <statement-(i+1)>
```

The action here is summarized as follows: *<condition-1>*, *<condition-2>*, *<condition-3>*, and so on, are tested in sequence until one of them is found to be true; the corresponding statement is then executed. If none of the conditions are true, *<statement-(i+1)>* is executed.

Nested **if** statements can become quite complicated; therefore, you should write them with clear indentations of corresponding conditions and alternatives. Indentation alone is not sufficient, though, because the compiler has no idea of the intent of a statement; it simply matches successive **if** and **else** statements. For example, consider the program fragment

```
if (<condition-1>)
   if (<condition-2>)
      <statement-1>
else
   <statement-2>
```

which consists of an **if**-then-**else** statement and an **if**-then statement (that is, an **if**-then-**else** statement with the **else** clause omitted—as we said, this is allowed in C++). The intent of the programmer is suggested by the indentation: *<statement-1>* should be executed if *<condition-1>* and *<condition-2>* are both true, *<statement-2>* should be executed if *<condition-1>* is false, and nothing at all should be done if *<condition-1>* is true and *<condition-2>* is false. However, the rule is that the **else** alternative is paired with the *nearest* unmatched **if** preceding it. This rule means that the fragment will be interpreted

SPEED
15

as

```
if (<condition-1>)
  if (<condition-2>)
    <statement-1>
  else
    <statement-2>
```

in spite of its appearance. In other words, if *<condition-1>* is false, this statement will do *nothing;* only if *<condition-1>* is true will *<condition-2>* be tested and a choice made between executing *<statement-1>* or *<statement-2>*.

To get the desired effect, the programmer can either insert a dummy **else**, as in

```
if (<condition-1>)
  if (<condition-2>)
    <statement-1>
  else;
else
  <statement-2>
```

or the "then" clause can be enclosed in a pair of braces:

```
if (<condition-1>) {
  if (<condition-2>)
    <statement-1>
}
else
  <statement-2>
```

The best solution, however, is to reorganize the code to

```
if (<not condition-1>)
  <statement-2>
else if (<condition-2>)
  <statement-1>
```

where *<not condition-1>* means the logical negation of *<condition-1>*. This way, the intent of these statements is clear and unambiguous to both the computer *and* the human reader. Getting this wrong results in a hard-to-locate error, called a *dangling* **else**.

dangling else

Dangling else

BUG ALERT 3.1

Remember to match each **else** with the correct **if**. The rule is that an **else** is paired with the nearest unmatched **if** preceding it.

3.2

Constructing Boolean Expressions

> I said the thing which was not. (For they have no word
> in their language to express lying or falsehood.)
>
> —Jonathan Swift
> *Gulliver's Travels*

boolean expressions

relational operators

logical (boolean) operators

The condition following the keyword **if** can be any expression; if its value is zero, it is taken as false, otherwise it is taken as true. This same interpretation holds for the condition of a **while** loop. "Conditions" are usually called *boolean expressions*. If a boolean expression is false, it has the value zero; if it is true, it has the value 1.

Boolean expressions are formed in C++ by comparing values with *relational operators* (Table 3.1) and by combining boolean values with the *logical (boolean) operators* || (or), && (and), and ! (not) (Table 3.2). For example, we can construct complicated conditions such as

```
(minimumWage <= wages) && (wages <= maximumWage)
```

to express, in C++, the condition `minimumWage` ≤ `wages` ≤ `maximumWage`.

Mathematics	C++	English
<	<	Less than
>	>	Greater than
≤	<=	Less than or equal to
≥	>=	Greater than or equal to
=	==	Equal to
≠	!=	Not equal to

Table 3.1   Relational operators in C++.

Expression	A	B	Result
A && B	True	True	True
	True	False	False
	False	True	False
	False	False	False
A || B	True	True	True
	True	False	True
	False	True	True
	False	False	False
!A	True		False
	False		True

Table 3.2   Boolean operators in C++.

Combining Relational Operations

The expression

```
(minimumWage <= wages <= maximumWage)
```

is syntactically correct in C++, but it does not have the meaning minimumWage $\leq$ wages $\leq$ maximumWage. As stated at the bottom of Table 3.3, operators of the same precedence are evaluated left to right, so the above expression is taken to mean

```
((minimumWage <= wages) <= maximumWage)
```

and since "false" is really 0 and "true" is really 1, the value of the condition (minimumWage <= wages) will be either 0 or 1; *that* value is the one compared to maximumWage. To combine relational operators to get the desired effect, you *must* use boolean operators:

```
(minimumWage <= wages) && (wages <= maximumWage)
```

Equal/Not Equal Comparisons with Type float

Recall from Bug Alert 2.3 (page 37) that numbers of type **float** are not always represented exactly in the computer. An important consequence of such inexact representation is that the relational operators == and != may give unexpected results. For example, the relational expression 1.0/5.0 + 1.0/5.0 + 1.0/5.0 - 0.6 == 0.0 has the value **false**.

In the absence of parentheses, operators are evaluated in the following order:

1. !   - (unary)
2. *   /   %
3. +   -
4. <   <=   >   >=
5. ==   !=
6. &&
7. ||

Operators within the same precedence level are evaluated left to right.

Table 3.3   Expanded precedence rules for arithmetic, relational, and boolean operators in C++. Notice that the minus sign occurs twice: first as a *unary* operator (as in -3) and then as a *binary* operator (as in $5 - 3$). See Appendix A for a more comprehensive description.

The relational operators have their usual mathematical meaning. The logical operators need some explanation. The operator ! before a boolean expression complements its value from true to false, and vice versa. The operator && combines two boolean expressions, giving an expression that is true if both of the constituent expressions are true and false if either of the constituent expressions is false. The operator || also combines two boolean values, but it gives an expression that is true if either or both of its constituent values are true.

We've just seen an example of &&. ! can be useful for rearranging **if**-then-**else** statements: The "dangling **else**" problem (see the code shaded ALERT on page 54) of Bug Alert 3.1 can be handled by reorganizing the code to read

```
if (!(<condition-1>))
  <statement-2>
else if (<condition-2>)
  <statement-1>
```

Note that the operator || gives the value true if *either* or *both* of the constituent parts are true. This is not always what we mean when we use the word "or" in English; we often use "or" to exclude the possibility of both being true. For example, in Patrick Henry's famous remark, "Give me liberty or give me death," it is unlikely that he wanted to include the possibility of *both* alternatives. The "or" available in C++ is thus called the *inclusive or* because it includes the possibility of both being true. We'll see below how to obtain the *exclusive or* from !, &&, and || in C++.

inclusive or

exclusive or

| BUG ALERT 3.4 | Equal Sign versus Double Equal Sign |

Remember, a single equal sign (=) is an *assignment statement* and a double equal sign (==) is a relational operator. The computer will happily accept

```
if (x=y)
  . . .
```

and will generate no error message, but the result is probably *not* what you want! Some C++ compilers generate a warning message for such usage.

| BUG ALERT 3.5 | Double Ampersands Mean "and"/Double Bars Mean "or" |

Remember to use *two* ampersands for "and" and two vertical bars for "or". A single ampersand (&) and a single vertical bar (|) are both legal operators in C++, with completely different meanings. So, if you write & or | when you mean && or ||, you will not get a syntax error, but the execution will not be what you wanted.

We discussed *precedence rules* of arithmetic operators in Chapter 2. These precedence rules need to be expanded to include boolean operators (see Table 3.3). The boolean operator ! has highest precedence, followed by &&, followed by ||. Notice that an expression without parentheses but having more than one operator of the same precedence is evaluated left to right. However, it's *always* best to use parentheses. That way your intentions are clear both to the computer and to humans.

expanded precedence rules

The evaluation of the boolean operators && and || has an additional complication. The expression A && B is evaluated as follows: First A is evaluated; if it is true, then B is evaluated and the result of the expression is is true if B is true and false if not. However, if A is false, there is no need to evaluate B, since A && B *must* be false regardless of the value of B, and so B *is not evaluated*. This sounds like a minor technical point, but it allows us to write, for instance,

```
if ((x != 0) && (1/x > 100)) {
   ...
}
else {
   ...
}
```

without fear that the evaluation of the condition will cause a division-by-zero error. The expression A || B is also evaluated only as far as necessary to determine its value: First A is evaluated; if it is false, then B is evaluated and the result of the expression is true if B is true and false if not. If A is true, there is no need to evaluate B, since A && B *must* be true regardless of the value of B, and so B *is not evaluated*.

Sometimes rather complicated boolean expressions are needed to express a condition. An example of an if statement that uses a complex boolean expression is the following program segment, which determines the **dayNumber** (number of days from the beginning of the year) given the **month** (1, 2, . . . , 12), the **day** of the month, and the **year**:

```
1   // Calculate dayNumber assuming all months have 31 days
2   dayNumber = (month - 1) * 31 + day;
3
4   //Correct for months beyond February
5   if (month > 2) {
6     // Assume non-leap year
7     dayNumber = dayNumber - ((4 * month + 23) / 10);
8     if ((((year % 4) == 0) && ((year % 100) != 0))
9          || ((year % 400) == 0))
10      // Correct for leap year
11      dayNumber = dayNumber + 1;
12   };
```

Line 2 calculates the day number under the simplifying assumption that every month has 31 days. This approximation is then corrected in two ways. First, it is corrected for months beyond February by the mysterious assignment statement

```
dayNumber = dayNumber - ((4 * month + 23) / 10);
```

This magic formula (of unknown origin) gives the following values for **month** $=$ $3, 4, \ldots, 12$:

month		3	4	5	6	7	8	9	10	11	12
$\dfrac{4 \times \text{month} + 23}{10}$		3.5	3.9	4.3	4.7	5.1	5.5	5.9	6.3	6.7	7.1
(4 * month + 23)/10	3	3	4	4	5	5	5	6	6	7	

Compare the sequence of values 3, 3, 4, 4, ... on the last line of the preceding table with the following corrections needed, in nonleap years for months beyond February, after assuming that each month has 31 days:

Date	1/1	2/1	3/1	4/1	5/1	6/1	7/1	8/1	9/1	10/1	11/1	12/1
Actual day of year	1	32	60	91	121	152	182	213	244	274	305	335
31(month − 1) + day	1	32	63	94	125	156	187	218	249	280	311	342
Correction needed	0	0	3	3	4	4	5	5	5	6	6	7

So we see that **(4 * month + 23)/10** gives the correction exactly for months beyond February.

The second correction in the program segment is for leap years, when February has 29 days instead of 28. In our (Gregorian) calendar, a year is a leap year if it is divisible by 4, except that century years also need to be divisible by 400 to be leap years. (For example, 2000 will be a leap year, but 1700, 1800, and 1900 were not leap years.) The boolean expression

```
(((year % 4) == 0) && ((year % 100) != 0))
|| ((year % 400) == 0)
```

is true if either (or both) of the subexpressions

```
((year % 4) == 0) && ((year % 100) != 0)
```

or

```
(year % 400) == 0
```

is true—the first of these is true if the year is divisible by 4 and is not a century year—a normal leap year. The second is true if the year is a century year divisible by 400. Thus the overall expression is true exactly when **year** is a leap year and false otherwise.

3.3

Analyzing Boolean Expressions

Now let's write a boolean expression that has the value true if either **A** or **B** is true, but not both (*exclusive or*). The description in the last sentence is virtually the boolean expression! We want to have

exclusive or

$$A \mid\mid B \text{ be true} \qquad (3.1)$$

to guarantee that at least one of **A** or **B** is true; we want in addition to have

$$A \text{ \&\& } B \text{ be false} \qquad (3.2)$$

to guarantee that **A** and **B** are not both true. This second condition is equivalent to insisting that

$$!(A \text{ \&\& } B) \text{ be true}$$

so we can insist that both (3.1) and (3.2) are simultaneously satisfied by writing

$$(A \mid\mid B) \text{ \&\& } !(A \text{ \&\& } B)$$

How can we be sure that this expression gives us what we want? The easiest way to show that a boolean expression is correct is to construct a *truth table*. Truth tables are an organized way to analyze boolean expressions by listing all the possible values of the boolean operands, the operators, the results of any subexpressions, and the final results. Table 3.2 contains three simple truth tables; the truth table for the more complex expression **(A || B) && !(A && B)** is shown in Table 3.4. Examining Table 3.4, we find that the value of the expression **(A || B) && !(A && B)** is true when either **A** or **B** is true, but not both—precisely the effect we desire.

truth table

The manipulation of boolean expressions uses rules similar to those of arithmetic; a synopsis of these rules appears in Table 3.5. Most of these rules are intuitive and easy to remember; DeMorgan's laws, however, are more complex and may require a truth table to convince you of their validity (see Table 3.6).

A	B	A || B	A && B	!(A && B)	(A || B) && !(A && B)
True	True	True	True	False	False
True	False	True	False	True	True
False	True	True	False	True	True
False	False	False	False	True	False

Table 3.4 Truth-table evaluation of the boolean expression (A || B) && !(A && B) to show that it is equivalent to the "exclusive or" of A and B.

Name	Rule
Absorption	p || (p && q) == p
	p && (p || q) == p
Associativity	((p && q) && r) == (p && (q && r))
	((p || q) || r) == (p || (q || r))
Commutativity	(p && q) == (q && p)
	(p || q) == (q || p)
DeMorgan's laws	!(p && q) == (!p || !q)
	!(p || q) == (!p && !q)
Distributivity	(p && (q || r)) == ((p && q) || (p && r))
	(p || (q && r)) == ((p || q) && (p || r))

Table 3.5   Some useful rules of boolean algebra. When applying these rules, the letters p, q, and r can be any constant, variable, or expression.

Input Values		Expression 1		Expression 2		
p	q	p || q	!(p || q)	!p	!q	!p && !q
True	True	True	False	False	False	False
True	False	True	False	False	True	False
False	True	True	False	True	False	False
False	False	False	True	True	True	True

Table 3.6   The two expressions shown to be equivalent here (shaded in gray) are the two sides of DeMorgan's second rule from Table 3.5.

Exercises—First Set

1. Suppose the final grade cutoffs for a computer science course are based on a computed score: 90 to 100 is an A, 80 to 89 is a B, 60 to 79 is a C, 50 to 59 is a D, below 50 fails. Write a nested **if** statement to write the final grade, given the variable **score**.

2. Write a boolean expression for the desired qualities in the following personal ad: "Wanted for companionship: 25–40, nonsmoking, under 66 inches, under 140 pounds, good-looking, able to relocate." Use the variables **smoking**, **goodLooking**, **ableToRelocate**, **age**, **height** (in inches), and **weight** (in pounds). Use **0** for **false** and **1** for **true**.

3. Rewrite your program in Exercise 4 on page 42 to check that the shoe size is within the range of available sizes, 17–46.

4. The entry fee for the local art museum is calculated as follows: children under 5 years, free; 65 years and older, $1.50; all others, $2.50. Write an **if** statement to print the **entryFee** (of type **float**) based on the input value **ageOfEntrant** (of type **int**).

☞ 5. Weather reports often mention "heating degree-days" and "cooling degree-days." For temperatures in Fahrenheit, the calculation of these is done by summing

$$65 - \frac{\text{High temperature of the day} + \text{low temperature of the day}}{2}$$

day by day. A positive value of the preceding expression contributes to the number of heating degree-days; a negative value contributes its absolute value to the number of cooling degree-days. Write an `if` statement to appropriately increment either the heating degree-days or the cooling degree-days by the contribution of any one day. Use the `int` variables `highTemp` and `lowTemp` and the `float` variables `degDays`, `heatingDegDays`, and `coolingDegDays`.

6. A more sensible definition of "heating degree-days" and "cooling degree-days" (see preceding exercise) might be to use the number of degrees (of the day's average temperature) above 85°F as the day's contribution to cooling degree-days and the number of degrees below 60°F as the day's contribution to heating degree-days. Write an `if` statement to increment appropriately either the heating degree-days or cooling degree-days by the contribution of any one day. Use the same variables as described in the previous exercise.

7. At wind-chill indices of −25 and below there is danger of freezing exposed flesh; at −75 and below there is *extreme* danger of freezing exposed flesh. Modify the wind-chill program (page 53) to print an appropriate warning.

8. A warm-weather counterpart to the wind-chill index is the discomfort index (also called the temperature-humidity index), defined by

$$\text{discomfortIndex} = 0.4(\text{dryTemp} + \text{wetTemp}) + 15,$$

where `dryTemp` is the "dry-bulb temperature," that is, the ordinary temperature in degrees Fahrenheit, and `wetTemp` is the "wet-bulb temperature," that is, the temperature in degrees Fahrenheit to which air can be cooled by evaporating water into it at constant pressure. A discomfort index of 85 is very uncomfortable. Write a C++ program to compute and print the discomfort index, given the dry- and wet-bulb temperatures. Also print a statement about whether or not the weather is comfortable. Your output should look something like this:

```
DISCOMFORT INDEX DETERMINATION

The dry-bulb temperature today is: 76
The wet-bulb temperature today is: 65


The discomfort index today is 71.4, a pleasant day.

DISCOMFORT INDEX DETERMINATION

The dry-bulb temperature today is: 106
The wet-bulb temperature today is: 90


The discomfort index today is 93.4, very uncomfortable.
```

9. An additional warm-weather index (see previous exercise) is the *humiture H,* which is defined as

$$H = T + h$$

where T is the current temperature in degrees Fahrenheit and h is the number of *humits*. A humit h is defined as

$$h = e - 10$$

where e is the vapor pressure in millibars (1013.25 millibars = standard atmospheric pressure at sea level = 760 millimeters of mercury). The discomfort zones of humiture are

     85   Mild discomfort
    100   Uncomfortable for everyone
    115   All activity should be restricted

Write a C++program to compute and print the humiture, given the temperature and vapor pressure. Also print a message to predict the discomfort level.

10. Wolfgang Amadeus Mozart's age at the time he composed a piece can be approximated from the Köchel number of that piece, under certain conditions: If the Köchel number is at least 100, then Mozart's age at the time of composition is approximately the Köchel divided by 25, plus 10. For example, Mozart's opera *The Marriage of Figaro* is K. 492, so we conclude that Mozart was about $(10 + 492/25) \approx 29$ years old when he wrote it. Write a program to read a Köchel number and print Mozart's age if it can be determined by this rule. Your output should look something like this:

```
MOZART'S AGE APPROXIMATION

Enter Kochel number: 492
Mozart was about 29 years old when he wrote that piece.

MOZART'S AGE APPROXIMATION

Enter Kochel number: 64
No information available about Mozart's age.
```

11. The following requirements for membership in the Congress of the United States are quoted from Article I of the Constitution of the United States:

> No Person shall be a Representative who shall not have attained to the Age of twenty five Years, and been seven Years a Citizen of the United States, and who shall not, when elected, be an Inhabitant of that State in which he shall be chosen.

> No Person shall be a Senator who shall not have attained to the Age of thirty Years, and been nine Years a Citizen of the United States, and who shall not, when elected, be an Inhabitant of that State for which he shall be chosen.

Using the `int` variables `age` and `lengthOfCitizenship`, write expressions to compute correct values for variables `eligibleForHouse` and `eligibleForSenate`, and use them to write a C++ program to print the eligibility of a candidate for Congress. (Disregard state residency.) The output should look something like this:

```
CONGRESS ELIGIBILITY


Enter age of candidate: 37
Enter years of U.S. citizenship: 3


The candidate is not eligible for election to either the
House of Representatives or the Senate.


CONGRESS ELIGIBILITY


Enter age of candidate: 47
Enter years of U.S. citizenship: 8


The candidate is eligible for election to the
House of Representatives
but not eligible for election to the Senate.


CONGRESS ELIGIBILITY


Enter age of candidate: 35
Enter years of U.S. citizenship: 25


The candidate is eligible for election to both the
House of Representatives and the Senate.
```

12. The following formulas are used to calculate the handicap used to compensate weight lifters for differing body weights. The handicap is expressed in terms of the weight in kilograms:

$$40 \le weight \le 125, \quad handicap = 6.31926 - 0.262349 \times weight$$
$$+ 0.511550 \times 10^{-2} \times weight^2$$
$$- 0.519738 \times 10^{-4} \times weight^3$$
$$+ 0.267626 \times 10^{-6} \times weight^4$$
$$- 0.540132 \times 10^{-9} \times weight^5$$
$$- 0.728875 \times 10^{-13} \times weight^6$$

$$125 < weight \le 135, \quad handicap = 0.5208 - 0.0012(weight - 125)$$
$$135 < weight \le 145, \quad handicap = 0.5088 - 0.0011(weight - 135)$$
$$145 < weight \le 155, \quad handicap = 0.4978 - 0.0010(weight - 145)$$
$$155 < weight \le 165, \quad handicap = 0.4878 - 0.0009(weight - 155)$$

(a) Write a program to read in a body weight and calculate the handicap.

(b) The handicap described in part (a) is multiplied by the lifter's score,

$$Score = squat + benchpress + deadlift$$

to calculate a handicapped score. Modify your program from part (a) to also read values for **squat**, **benchPress**, and **deadlift** (each in kilograms) and to calculate the lifter's handicapped score.

13. The United Parcel Service has the following limitations on the size and weight of packages accepted for shipment: A package cannot exceed 150 pounds or have a combined length plus girth (twice the width plus twice the depth) of over 130 inches. In addition, packages must not exceed 108 inches in length. The minimum charge for an "oversized" package (that is, package weighing less than 30 pounds but having a combined length plus girth of over 84 inches) is the same as for a package weighing 30 pounds. Write a program to read the **weight**, **length**, **width**, and **depth** of a package to be shipped by UPS and to print a message as to whether the package can be shipped under the above restrictions. Your output should look like this:

```
UPS PACKAGE ACCEPTABILITY

Enter the package weight in pounds: 42
Enter the package length in inches: 35
Enter the package width in inches: 10
Enter the package depth in inches: 5

This package is acceptable for shipment via UPS.

UPS PACKAGE ACCEPTABILITY

Enter the package weight in pounds: 18
Enter the package length in inches: 55
Enter the package width in inches: 10
Enter the package depth in inches: 5

This is an oversized package, but is acceptable for
shipment via UPS at the same rate as a 30 pound package.

UPS PACKAGE ACCEPTABILITY

Enter the package weight in pounds: 14
Enter the package length in inches: 45
Enter the package width in inches: 25
Enter the package depth in inches: 20

Sorry, this package is not acceptable for shipment via
UPS; it exceeds the maximum length plus girth.
```

14. (a) The Centers for Disease Control in Atlanta, Georgia, determine obesity by computing a person's "body mass index." The body mass index is a person's weight in kilograms divided by the square of his or her height in meters. For men, an index of 27.8 or more is considered obese; for nonpregnant women the cutoff is 27.3. Write a program to read a person's **sex**, **height**, and **weight**, determine the **bodyMassIndex**, and print a message as to obesity. Your program should convert height from inches to meters (one meter is 39.37 inches) and weight from pounds to kilograms (one kilogram is 2.20 pounds). Your output should look like this:

```
OBESITY CALCULATION

Enter your sex (0 for male, 1 for female): 1
Enter your height in inches: 69
Enter your weight in pounds: 141

Your body mass index is 20.90; you are not obese.

OBESITY CALCULATION

Enter your sex (0 for male, 1 for female): 1
Enter your height in inches: 61
Enter your weight in pounds: 145

Your body mass index is 27.47; you are obese.
```

(b) The body mass index correlates with one's overall risk of developing heart disease.

bodyMassIndex ≤ 25	Risk is very low to low
$25 <$ **bodyMassIndex** < 30	Risk is low to moderate
$30 \leq$ **bodyMassIndex**	Risk is moderate to very high.

Modify your program so that it also prints a message describing the risk of heart disease.

15. Use truth tables to verify the rules in Table 3.5.

16. Can the following boolean expressions ever be true? If so, give values of the variables that make them true; if not, explain why not, using the rules of Table 3.5.
    (a) `(x <= y) && (x >= z)`
    (b) `(x > y) && (y > z) && (x < z)`
    (c) `((x > 1) || (x < 4)) && (!(x < 4))`

☞ 17. Simplify the following boolean expressions using the rules of boolean algebra in Table 3.5.
    (a) `!((!!p) && (q || q))`
    (b) `(p || (p && q)) && !(!q && !r)`

18. Show the equivalence of the following boolean expressions in two ways, first using the rules of boolean algebra in Table 3.5 and second with a truth table.
    (a) `!(q || (p || p))` and `!(p || (p && q)) && !q`.
    (b) `(p || q) && (!(!p && !r))` and `p || !(!q || !r)`.

☞ 19. Using the variables **A** and **B**, write a C++ boolean expression that has the following values:

A	B	**Value**
True	True	False
True	False	True
False	True	True
False	False	True

The value of the expression is called the *nand* of **A** and **B**; together with the *nor* operation in the next exercise, the *nand* forms the basis of all computer circuitry.

20. Using the variables **A** and **B**, write a C++ boolean expression that has the following values:

A	B	Value
True	True	False
True	False	False
False	True	False
False	False	True

The value of the expression is called the *nor* of **A** and **B**.

21. Given the line $ax + by + c = 0$ and the point (u, v), the distance between them is given by

$$\left| \frac{au + bv + c}{\sqrt{a^2 + b^2}} \right|.$$

Write a program to read a, b, c, u, and v, and then calculate and print the distance between the line and point.

22. Given two lines with slopes s_1 and s_2, the angle between the lines is

$$\arctan\left(\frac{s_2 - s_1}{1 + s_1 s_2} \right).$$

If the lines are perpendicular, then $s_1 s_2 = -1$, and if they are parallel, then $s_1 = s_2$. Write a program to read the slopes of two lines, determine whether they are parallel, and if not, calculate and print the angle between them.

23. (a) Write a program to solve quadratic equations. The equation

$$ax^2 + bx + c = 0$$

has two roots, both real or both complex, given by

$$x_1, x_2 = \frac{-b \pm \sqrt{b^2 - 4ac}}{2a} = \frac{2c}{-b \mp \sqrt{b^2 - 4ac}}.$$

The quantity $b^2 - 4ac$ is the *discriminant*. If the discriminant is positive, the roots are real and unequal; if it is zero, the roots are real and equal; if it is negative, the roots are complex and unequal, and in this case you must calculate the real and imaginary parts of the root separately, because the C++ **sqrt** function works only for nonnegative values.

(b) When the discriminant is approximately $|b|$, the difference between it and $|b|$ is nearly zero and the limited precision of the internal computer representation causes a loss of precision in the calculation of the roots. In such cases, the formula that does *not* involve the difference gives the root more accurately. Modify your program from part (a) to use the more accurate formula in calculating each of the two roots.

3.4

Enumerated Types

Before proceeding with decision making using the **switch** statement, let's explore an additional variable type that is useful in the context of those statements. Until now we have used only the simple variable types **float** and **int**, predefined in C++. *Enumerated types* allow the programmer to define any ordered group of simple values (identifiers) as a type. Variables declared to be of an enumerated type may take on any value in the ordered group. For example:

enumerated types

```
enum weekday {Sunday, Monday, Tuesday, Wednesday,
              Thursday, Friday, Saturday};
enum month {January, February, March, April, May, June, July,
            August, September, October, November, December};

weekday d;
month m;
```

The variable **d** can take on any value within the ordered group **weekday**, that is, **Sunday**, **Monday**, and so on, while the variable **m** can take any value within the ordered group **month**, that is, **January**, **February**, and so on.

Enumerated types are really just integer constants in disguise: The first in the list is 0, the next is 1, the next 2, and so on. In the above, **Sunday** is 0, **Monday** is 1,..., **Saturday** is 6; similarly, **January** is 0,..., **December** is 11. This means that the values within the group have a relative order (**Sunday** precedes **Wednesday** as defined above). They can be used in any context where a value of that type can be used. We can write, for example,

```
d = Tuesday;
```

or

```
if (February < m)
    ...
```

The constants that make up the types can never be shared. We *cannot* use

```
enum color {blue, green, yellow, orange, white};
enum fruit {apple, orange, banana};
```

because **orange** is in both **color** and **fruit**.

Because enumerated types are just integers in disguise, their only real use is to make our programs more readable (as we'll see in the next section). For example, it is common to define a boolean type

```
enum boolean {false, true};
```

to be used wherever we want a true/false value. *We will use this definition throughout the book.* The use of **boolean** as an enumerated type to improve the readability of programs works properly because C++ allows *any* **int** value in the condition of an **if** or a **while** statement, considering a value zero to be false and any nonzero value to be true; the enum type **boolean** above means **false** is 0

Some C++ compilers consider

```
enum boolean {false, true};
```

to be an anachronism and issue a warning message. Newer compilers have a predefined type **bool**.

and **true** is **1**. Newer C++ compilers have a predefined type **bool**, making our type **boolean** unnecessary.

Writing enumerated types produces reasonable results. Consider

```
1    #include <iostream.h>
2    #include <iomanip.h>
3
4    enum boolean {false, true};
5
6    main () {
7
8      boolean a = false, b = true;
9      cout << "a = " << a << ", b = " << b << "\n";
10
11   }
```

which gives the output

```
a = 0, b = 1
```

as expected. However, reading enumerated types is problematic:

```
1    #include <iostream.h>
2    #include <iomanip.h>
3
4    enum boolean {false, true};
5
6    main () {
7
8      boolean a;
9      cout << "Enter boolean value (0 for false, 1 for true): ";
10     cin >> a;
11     cout << "a = " << a << "\n";
12
13   }
```

which gives the compiler warnings

```
line 10: warning: conversion of lvalue needed:
                  temporary used to initialize reference
line 8: warning:  a used but not set
```

and when executed causes

```
Enter boolean value (0 for false, 1 for true): 1
a = 0
```

To read in an **enum** value, we must read the value as an **int** and assign that value to the **enum** variable. That is, the following code

```
1    #include <iostream.h>
2    #include <iomanip.h>
3
4    enum boolean {false, true};
5
6    main () {
7
8      boolean a;
9      cout << "Enter boolean value (0 for false, 1 for true): ";
10     int temp;
11     cin >> temp;
12     a = temp;
13     cout << "a = " << a << "\n";
14
15   }
```

does what we want:

```
Enter boolean value (0 for false, 1 for true): 1
a = 1
```

switch **Statements**

Multitudes, multitudes in the valley of decision!

—Bible
Joel 3:14

C++ uses the **switch** *statement* to make a decision based on the value of an integer-valued expression or variable. The general form is

switch *statement*

```
switch (<expression>) {
  <statement with case label>
  <statement with case label>
  . . .
  <statement with case label>
}
```

The value of **<expression>** determines at which **<statement with case label>** execution starts; each of these statements is labeled by either the keyword **case** (together with an integer constant) or the keyword **default**. Once started, the execution continues, statement by statement, until either the end of the **switch** is reached or a **break** is encountered. This is not as complicated as it may sound—a few examples will demonstrate the range of possibilities. Consider

```
switch (age) {
  case 1:
  case 2:
  case 3:  cout << "Get a babysitter!\n"; break;
  case 4:
  case 5:
  case 6:
  case 7:
  case 8:
  case 9:  cout << "Movies rated G would be okay.\n"; break;
  case 10:
  case 11:
  case 12:
  case 13:
  case 14:
  case 15: cout << "Movies rated G or PG would be okay.\n"; break;
  case 16:
  case 17: cout << "Movies rated R might be okay.\n"; break;
  default: cout << "Movies rated R would be okay.\n"
}
```

This **switch** statement will print one of the five messages, depending on the value of **age**: for **age** $\leq$ 3 the babysitter message, for $4 \leq$ **age** ≤ 9 the "G" message, for $10 \leq$ **age** ≤ 15 the "G or PG" message, and for $16 \leq$ **age** ≤ 17 the "R might be okay" message; any other value of **age** will print the "R would be okay" message.

The controlling value for the **switch** needs to be an integer, but because enumerated types are really integers, we can use them in this context to make the intent of the code obvious. For example,

```
enum weekday {Sunday, Monday, Tuesday, Wednesday, Thursday,
              Friday, Saturday};
weekday d;
...
switch (d) {
  case Sunday:    cout << "Sunday";    break;
  case Monday:    cout << "Monday";    break;
  case Tuesday:   cout << "Tuesday";   break;
  case Wednesday: cout << "Wednesday"; break;
  case Thursday:  cout << "Thursday";  break;
  case Friday:    cout << "Friday";    break;
  case Saturday:  cout << "Saturday";  break;
}
```

This **switch** statement will write the name of the day of the week specified by d. Similarly,

```
switch (d) {
  case Monday:
  case Wednesday:
  case Friday:    cout << "C.S. meets at 9:00 today.\n";
                  cout << "History meets at 10:00 today.\n";
                  cout << "Math meets at 2:00 today.\n";
                  break;
```

```
    case Tuesday:
    case Thursday:   cout << "English meets at 9:00 today.\n";
                     cout << "Chemistry meets at 10:00 today.\n";
                     break;
    case Sunday:
    case Saturday:   cout << "Enjoy the weekend!\n";
    }
```

writes the class schedule of the day.

Or, for instance, we can set correctly the value of **numberOfDays** for a combination of **month** and **year**:

```
enum month {January, February, March, April, May, June, July,
            August, September, October, November, December};
month m;
...
switch (m) {
  case February:
    if ((((year % 4) == 0) && ((year % 100) != 0))
        || ((year % 400) == 0))
      numberOfDays = 29;
    else
      numberOfDays = 28;
    break;
  case April:
  case June:
  case September:
  case November: numberOfDays = 30; break;
  case January:
  case March:
  case May:
  case July:
  case August:
  case October:
  case December: numberOfDays = 31; break;
}
```

This example can be rewritten to use the keyword **default** to specify where to begin execution if the value of the expression is *not* one of the listed cases:

```
switch (m) {
  case February:
    if ((((year % 4) == 0) && ((year % 100) != 0))
        || ((year % 400) == 0))
      numberOfDays = 29;
    else
      numberOfDays = 28;
    break;
  case April:
  case June:
  case September:
  case November: numberOfDays = 30; break;
  default: numberOfDays = 31;
}
```

For values of **m** in the range 0 through 11 (that is, **January**...**December**) these two versions are equivalent; if **m** is not in this range, however, the former statement does not set the value of **numberOfDays**, while the latter sets the value of **numberOfDays** to 31.

What if there is no **case** for the value of the controlling expression and there is no **default** either? Then nothing is done in the **switch** statement.

If every statement in a **switch** ends with a **break**, then the statement is equivalent to a nested sequence of **if** statements. That is, the **switch**

```
switch (<expression>) {
  case <value-1>: <statements-1>; break;
  case <value-2>: <statements-2>; break;
  ...
  case <value-i>: <statements-i>; break;
  default: <statements-(i+1)>
}
```

is just a convenient way of writing

```
switchValue = <expression>;
if (switchValue == <value-1>)
  <statements-1>
else if (switchValue == <value-2>)
  <statements-2>
...
else if (switchValue == <value-i>)
  <statements-i>
else
  <statements-(i+1)>
```

The purpose of the **break** statement is to terminate the execution of the **switch** statement in which it is embedded. In general, every **case** and the **default** should have **break** as their last statement. If you omit a **break** at the end of one of them, program execution just continues with the statements of the following **case**, which may not be what you want. For example, the code

```
int i = 1;
switch (i) {
  case 0: cout << "0";
  case 1: cout << "1";
  case 2: cout << "2";
  case 3: cout << "3";
}
cout << "\n";
```

causes the output

```
123
```

since the code in cases 1, 2, and 3 is executed.

Omitting a **break** statement in a **switch** can cause extra statements
to be executed in the **case** with the missing **break**. Check **switch**
statements carefully.

Now let's try something a bit harder. Suppose we want to write a **switch**
statement to describe the actions to be taken in the game of Monopoly®. Monopoly
players move pieces around a board from square to square and, depending on
where the pieces land, take some action. The possible squares on which pieces
land are divided into the categories Chance, Community Chest, Free Parking,
Go to Jail, Jail (and Just Visiting), Go, four Railroads, two Utilities, Luxury Tax,
Income Tax, and the various real estate properties (Boardwalk, Park Place, and
so on). The actions to be taken on each square are as follows:

Chance:	Choose and follow the next card in the Chance pile.
Community Chest:	Choose and follow the next card in the Community Chest pile.
Free Parking:	Do nothing.
Go to Jail:	Move piece to jail.
Jail (and **Just Visiting**):	Do nothing.
Go:	Collect $200.
Railroad:	If unowned, may purchase; otherwise, pay owner rent of $25 per railroad owned.
Utility:	If unowned, may purchase; otherwise, pay owner rent of 4 × (dice roll) if one utility is owned, or 10 × (dice roll) if two utilities are owned.
Luxury Tax:	Pay $75.
Income Tax:	Pay 10% of total worth or $200.
Real Estate Property:	If unowned, may purchase; otherwise, pay owner appropriate rent.

Suppose we have

```
enum boolean {false, true};
enum monopolySquare {chance, communityChest, freeParking, goToJail,
                     jail, go, railroad, utility, luxuryTax,
                     incomeTax, realEstateProperty};
monopolySquare currentSquare;
boolean owned;  // true if currentSquare is owned
int totalWorth; // sum of values of all property owned
int numberRailroadsOwned, numberUtilitiesOwned;
```

We can use the following **switch** statement to print the appropriate directions to
the players:

```
switch (currentSquare) {
  case chance:
    cout << "Take a Chance card and follow instructions.\n";
    break;
  case communityChest:
    cout << "Take a Community Chest card and follow"
         << " instructions.\n";
    break;
  case freeParking:
  case jail: //  and Just Visiting
    break;    //  do nothing
  case goToJail:
    cout << "Move token to jail, do not pass Go,"
         << " do not collect $200.\n"
    break;
  case go:
    cout << "Collect $200.\n"
    break;
  case railroad:
    if (owned)
      cout << "Pay $" << 25 * numberRailroadsOwned << ".\n";
    else
      cout << "You may purchase this railroad.\n";
    break;
  case utility:
    if (!owned)
      cout << "You may purchase this utility.\n";
    else if (numberUtilitiesOwned == 1)
      cout << "Pay $" << 4 * diceRoll << ".\n";
    else
      cout << "Pay $" << 10 * diceRoll << ".\n";
    break;
  case luxuryTax:
    cout << "Pay $75.\n";
    break;
  case incomeTax:
    cout << "Pay 10% of total worth"
         << " (" << totalWorth/10 << ") "
         << "or $200.\n";
    break;
  case property:
    if (owned)
      cout << "Pay appropriate rent to owner.\n";
    else
      cout << "You may purchase this property.\n";
}
```

In addition, **switch** statements can be nested within **switch** statements to describe really complicated actions. An example is the operation of a digital alarm watch, which can be expressed neatly as a **switch** statement in which each case is itself a **switch** statement. We have taken part of the watch's operations and broken it down into seven states, or modes, each of which results in one of three possible actions, depending on which of three buttons labeled *A*, *B*, and *C* is pushed. Figure 3.1 shows the interrelationship between the states of the watch and the actions taken when buttons are pushed. In the C++ implementation of

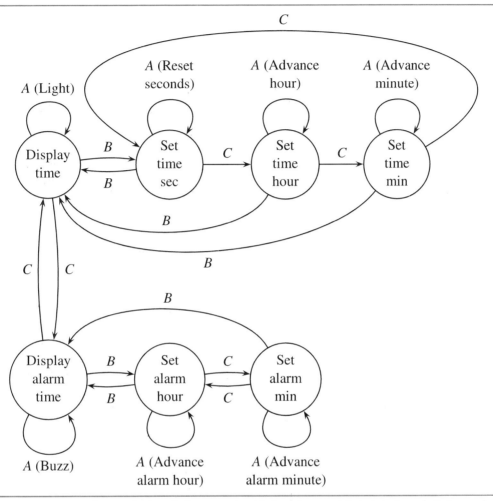

FIGURE 3.1 Operation of a simple digital alarm watch with three buttons labeled A, B, and C. For each state (mode) that the watch can be in, the arrows show what happens when one of the buttons is pressed. For example, in the "display alarm time" state, pushing button A causes the alarm to sound momentarily; if button C is pushed instead, the watch returns to the (normal) "display time" state.

the diagram in Figure 3.1, we use the declarations

```
enum state {displayTime, setTimeSec, setTimeHour, setTimeMin,
            displayAlarmTime, setAlarmHour, setAlarmMin};
enum button {A, B, C};

state s;      // current mode of watch
button btn;   // button being pushed
int
   clockHr,   // clock hour
   clockMin,  // clock minute
   clockSec,  // clock second
   alarmHr,   // alarm hour
   alarmMin;  // alarm minute
```

The enumerated type **state** refers to the seven different operative modes considered; the enumerated type **button** refers to the three different buttons that can be pushed. The following nested **switch** statement implements the diagram of Figure 3.1:

```
switch (s) {
  case displayTime:        // time display mode
    switch (btn) {
      case A:  // light
        cout << "turn light on momentarily\n"; break;
      case B:  // change state to setTimeSec
        s = setTimeSec; break;
      case C:  // change state to displayAlarmTime
        s = displayAlarmTime; break;
    }; break;
  case setTimeSec:         // set seconds for clock
    switch (btn) {
      case A:  // zero seconds
        clockSec = 0; break;
      case B:  // change state to displayTime
        s = displayTime; break;
      case C:  // change state to setTimeHour
        s = setTimeHour; break;
    }; break;
  case setTimeHour:        // set hours for clock
    switch (btn) {
      case A:  // increment hours
        clockHr = (clockHr + 1) % 24; break;
      case B:  // change state to displayTime
        s = displayTime; break;
      case C:  // change state to setTimeMin
        s = setTimeMin; break;
    }; break;
  case setTimeMin:         // set minutes for clock
    switch (btn) {
      case A:  // increment hours
        clockMin = (clockMin + 1) % 60; break;
      case B:  // change state to displayTime
        s = displayTime; break;
      case C:  // change state to setTimeSec
        s = setTimeSec; break;
    }; break;
  case displayAlarmTime:  // alarm display mode
    switch (btn) {
      case A:  // buzzer
        cout << "momentarily sound buzzer\n"; break;
      case B:  // change state to setAlarmHour
        s = setAlarmHour; break;
      case C:  // change state to displayTime
        s = displayTime; break;
    }; break;
  case setAlarmHour:        // set hours for alarm
    switch (btn) {
      case A:  // increment alarm hours
        alarmHr = (alarmHr + 1) % 24; break;
```

```
    case B:  // change state to displayAlarmTime
      s = displayAlarmTime; break;
    case C:  // change state to setAlarmMin
      s = setAlarmMin; break;
  }; break;
case setAlarmMin:        // set minutes for alarm
  switch (btn) {
    case A:  // increment alarm minutes
      alarmMin = (alarmMin + 1) % 60; break;
    case B:  // change state to displayAlarmTime
      s = displayAlarmTime; break;
    case C:  // change state to setAlarmHr
      s = setAlarmHr; break;
  }; break;
}
```

Imagine how messy it would be to express these decisions with only the **if** statement!

<hr>

3.6

Debugging Decision Making

A problem worthy of attack
Proves its worth by hitting back.

—Piet Hein
Grooks

To illustrate the process of debugging when a complicated case structure is involved, let's write a program to calculate a woman's panty hose size. Manufacturers of women's panty hose use a method similar to the following for determining a woman's size from her height and weight. First, compute

$$x = \texttt{floor}\left(\frac{1}{10}\text{height} - \frac{1}{50}\text{weight} - 2.4\right)$$

$$y = \texttt{floor}\left(\frac{1}{4}\text{height} - \frac{1}{20}\text{weight} - 20.5\right),$$

where **floor(x)** is the built-in function that gives the largest integer less than or equal to **x** (see Table 2.4 on page 25). The required size of panty hose is then

	$y = 0$	$y = 1$	$y = 2$	$y = 3$
$x = 1$	A	B	C	D
$x = 0$			E	F

Combinations of *x* and *y* other than those given in the table do not correspond to any of the sizes manufactured. So, we need a program to read a woman's height and weight and tell her what size panty hose to buy. Our output should look like this:

```
PANTY HOSE SIZE

Enter your height in inches: 69
Enter your weight in pounds: 142
Your size is D.


PANTY HOSE SIZE

Enter your height in inches: 72
Enter your weight in pounds: 160
Your size is not available.
```

Here is our first attempt:

```
1   #include <iostream.h>
2   #include <iomanip.h>
3   #include <math.h>
4
5   // Judith Kamin, March 29, 1995
6   // Determine panty hose size.
7
8   int height, // The woman's height...
9       weight; // ...and weight
10
11  main () {
12    cout << "PANTY HOSE SIZE\n\n"
13         << "Enter your height in inches: ";
14    cin >> height;
15    cout << "Enter your weight in pounds: ";
16    cin >> weight;
17
18    int x = floor(height/10.0 - weight/50.0 - 2.4);
19    int y = floor(height/4.0 + weight/20.0 - 20.5);
20
21    cout << "Your size is ";
22    switch (y) {
23      case 0: if (x == 0)
24                cout << "unavailable";
25              else
26                cout << "A";
27      case 1: if (x == 0)
28                cout << "unavailable";
29              else
30                cout << "B";
31      case 2: if (x == 0)
32                cout << "E";
33              else
34                cout << "C";
35      case 3: if (x == 0)
```

```
36          cout << "F";
37        else
38          cout << "D";
39    default: cout << "unavailable";
40    };
41    cout << ".\n";
42
43 }
```

This compiles with the warning messages

```
line 18: warning:  int  initialized with  double
line 19: warning:  int  initialized with  double
```

which we can ignore—the compiler is telling us that the values computed for **x** and **y** are computed as "double precision" (extended precision–type **float**) even though those two variables are type **int**—because the extra precision cannot hurt the calculation.

When we execute the program, we get

```
PANTY HOSE SIZE

Enter your height in inches: 68
Enter your weight in pounds: 140
Your size is Dunavailable.
```

Because we've forgotten to end the various cases in the **switch** with **break** statements, lines of code from extraneous cases are being executed. Fixing this, we have

```
1  #include <iostream.h>
2  #include <iomanip.h>
3  #include <math.h>
4
5  // Judith Kamin, March 29, 1995
6  // Determine panty hose size.
7
8  int height, // The woman's height...
9      weight; // ...and weight
10
11 main () {
12   cout << "PANTY HOSE SIZE\n\n"
13        << "Enter your height in inches: ";
14   cin >> height;
15   cout << "Enter your weight in pounds: ";
16   cin >> weight;
17
18   int x = floor(height/10.0 - weight/50.0 - 2.4);
19   int y = floor(height/4.0 + weight/20.0 - 20.5);
20
21   cout << "Your size is ";
22   switch (y) {
23     case 0: if (x == 0)
```

```
24          cout << "unavailable";
25        else
26          cout << "A";
27        break;
28    case 1: if (x == 0)
29          cout << "unavailable";
30        else
31          cout << "B";
32        break;
33    case 2: if (x == 0)
34          cout << "E";
35        else
36          cout << "C";
37        break;
38    case 3: if (x == 0)
39          cout << "F";
40        else
41          cout << "D";
42        break;
43    default: cout << "unavailable";
44    };
45    cout << ".\n";
46
47  }
```

which compiles. Execution gives

```
PANTY HOSE SIZE

Enter your height in inches: 68
Enter your weight in pounds: 140
Your size is D.
```

which is correct. So we try another case

```
PANTY HOSE SIZE

Enter your height in inches: 60
Enter your weight in pounds: 130
Your size is B.
```

which also looks reasonable. However, when we try

```
PANTY HOSE SIZE

Enter your height in inches: 50
Enter your weight in pounds: 200
Your size is C.
```

the result is suspicious, because C is a small size but 200 pounds is a large woman. To see what's going on, we add a debugging statement to tell us the values of **x** and **y**:

```
21      cout << "x = " << x << ", y = " << y << "\n";
```

and we find

```
PANTY HOSE SIZE

Enter your height in inches: 50
Enter your weight in pounds: 200
x = -2, y = 2
Your size is C.
```

revealing that the values of **x** (and maybe **y**) can be negative. This possibility complicates the problem enormously, because it means there are many cases that we didn't take into account.

Having discovered the inadequacy of our approach, we decide to start over. First, we decide to separate the computation of the size from the output. Since the size will be A, B, C, D, E, F, or none at all, we define an enumerated type

```
enum size {none, A, B, C, D, E, F};
```

and use a variable of type **size** to store the calculated size:

```
size s = none;
switch (y) {
  case 0: if (x == 1) s = A; break;
  case 1: if (x == 1) s = B; break;
  case 2: switch (x) {
              case 0:  s = E; break;
              case 1:  s = C; break;
          }
          break;
  case 3: switch (x) {
              case 0:  s = F; break;
              case 1:  s = D; break;
          }
}
```

being careful to initialize the value of **s** to **none** and to change its value *only* when both **x** and **y** have values that are acceptable. The desired output is now done with another **switch**, and the entire program is

```
 1   #include <iostream.h>
 2   #include <iomanip.h>
 3   #include <math.h>
 4
 5   // Judith Kamin, January 23, 1995
 6   // Determine panty hose size.
 7
 8   enum size {none, A, B, C, D, E, F};
 9
10   int height, // The woman's height...
11       weight; // ...and weight
```

```
12
13    main () {
14      cout << "PANTY HOSE SIZE\n\n"
15          << "Enter your height in inches: ";
16      cin >> height;
17      cout << "Enter your weight in pounds: ";
18      cin >> weight;
19
20      int x = floor(height/10.0 - weight/50.0 - 2.4);
21      int y = floor(height/4.0 + weight/20.0 - 20.5);
22
23      size s = none;
24      switch (y) {
25        case 0: if (x == 1) s = A; break;
26        case 1: if (x == 1) s = B; break;
27        case 2: switch (x) {
28                  case 0:  s = E; break;
29                  case 1:  s = C; break;
30                }
31                break;
32        case 3: switch (x) {
33                  case 0:  s = F; break;
34                  case 1:  s = D; break;
35                }
36      }
37
38      cout << "Your size is ";
39      switch (s) {
40        case A:    cout << "A"; break;
41        case B:    cout << "B"; break;
42        case C:    cout << "C"; break;
43        case D:    cout << "D"; break;
44        case E:    cout << "E"; break;
45        case F:    cout << "F"; break;
46        case none: cout << "not available";
47      }
48      cout << ".\n";
49
50    }
```

It is easy to verify that the first **switch**, and hence the whole program, gives correct values in all cases.

3.7

A Comment on the Future of Computers

The two fundamental boolean operations used to build computer circuitry are called the *nand* and the *nor;* these operations are not available directly in C++, but they can be expressed in terms of **&&**, **||**, and **!** (see Exercises 19 and 20 on page 67). These operations are implemented electronically in modern computers, but any technology could be used. Here is a description of a possible future implementation (excerpted from the British magazine *The Economist,* May 24, 1986):

> The electronic switches and wires inside computers have been getting steadily smaller. For that, thank the ingenuity of chipmakers and the properties of silicon. But switches made out of single molecules would bring a massive increase in the speed of computation. Dr. Robert Birge and his colleagues at Pittsburgh's Carnegie Mellon University think they know how it can be done.
>
> Dr. Birge's team plans to build molecular equivalents of the semiconductor "NAND" gate, the switch that forms the basis of computer logic. The NAND gate enables a computer to perform logical operations, such as: if A and B, then C. The fiendish cunning of the cleverest computer amounts to nothing more than hooking such gates together in the right sequence. But existing gates are made on semiconductor wafers and respond to electronic currents; Carnegie Mellon's gate would be opened and closed by the transfer of individual electrons within a custom-designed molecule.
>
> As in a semiconductor gate, the molecular gate might be constructed. As in a semiconductor gate, the molecular gate has two inputs (A and B) and an output. In this particular version, the two input arms of the molecule consist of cyanine dyes, each bonded to a group of quinones. The joint of the gate is a porphyrin; the output arm of the molecule is another dye. Architecturally, this gate is identical to a typical semiconductor gate. The big difference is size: some 10,000 molecular gates could sit upon the tip of a human hair.
>
> In a semiconductor gate, the input comes in the form of an electric current. In the molecular gate, the input is provided by a laser beam.
>
> It works like this: when the cyanine part of the molecule absorbs a photon from the laser, an electron is transferred to the quinone and thence to the porphyrin. If the porphyrin receives only one extra electron, nothing spectacular occurs. If it receives two—one from each of the input arms—the increase in electron density "fires" the gate, by changing the wavelength at which the output dye absorbs photons. This, in turn, enables the output of the gate to be read by interrogation with another laser beam. In a real computer, the molecular gates would be linked in chains like the circuits of a conventional computer.
>
> Turning the gate from a good idea into even a bad computer is a massive task. In addition to theoretical progress, the centre will have to find solutions to daunting practical problems—such as designing and synthesising the right molecules. Carnegie Mellon has built a machine to carry out the synthesis automatically—one reason that the project has already received a significant vote of confidence. IBM has given the centre nearly $2m—the only outside research award the computer giant has yet made in the field of molecular electronics.

Exercises—Second Set

☞   1. Write a program to read an integer $n \geq 0$ and write n followed by the appropriate ordinal suffix (that is, "th," "st," "rd," or "nd"). Your output should look something like this:

```
Enter an integer >= 0: 3
The ordinal form is 3rd.
```

☞   2. The following **switch** statement was found in a piece of code written by a rather poor programmer. Rewrite it as a single assignment statement to the variable **result**.

```
switch (x > 1.0) {
   case 1: if ((x-1.0) > 1.0e-5)
              result = 0;
           else
              result = 1;
           break;
   case 0: result = 1;
}
```

☞   3. Postage rates are calculated (as of January, 1995) according to the following rules:

First class, domestic:	$0.32 for the first ounce, $0.23 for each additional ounce
Foreign airmail:	$0.50 per half-ounce
Postcards, domestic:	$0.20
Book rate:	$1.24 for the first pound, 2–7 pounds $0.50 per additional pound, $0.31 for each additional pound beyond 7 pounds

Write a **switch** statement to determine the postage rate for sending an item given the **weight** in ounces (16 ounces = 1 pound) and the kind of mail **class** of enumerated type **postalClass**.

☞   4. The following **switch** statement was intended to set **s** to the sign of **x**, that is, to **-1** if **x** is negative, to **0** if **x** is 0, and to **1** if **x** is positive. What's wrong with it?

```
switch (x) {
   case 0:   s = 0;
   default: if (x<0)
               s = -1;
            else
               s = 1;
}
```

5. As part of a medical diagnosis system for a poison control center you have to prepare the **switch** statement to identify proper treatment for ingestion of various substances. The types of poison being considered are aspirin, alcohol, tobacco, chloroform, rat poison, strong acid, strong alkali, strychnine, and kerosene. Except for strong acids, strong alkalis, strychnine, and kerosene, the proper treatment is to administer fluid in large quantities, induce vomiting, and administer the universal antidote. For poisoning with strong acids, administer water and then milk of magnesia or baking soda solution; do not induce vomiting. For poisoning with strong alkalis, administer water and then vinegar or lemon juice; do not induce vomiting. For strychnine or kerosene ingestion, do not induce vomiting; get medical help immediately! Write the **switch** statement using the enumerated type **PoisonType**; the statement should print the proper treatment.

6. The famous nineteenth-century mathematician Carl Friedrich Gauss proposed the following method of calculating the date of Easter on the Gregorian calendar in the year

N, for years through 1999. Define

$$M = 15 + C - \mathtt{floor}(C/4) - \mathtt{floor}((8C + 13)/25)$$

and

$$L = 4 + C - \mathtt{floor}(C/4),$$

where C is the number of centuries prior to that the year, that is,

$$C = \mathtt{floor}(N/100).$$

Divide N by 4, 7, and 19, and call the resulting remainders a, b, and c, respectively. Divide $19c + M$ by 30, and call the remainder d. Divide $2a + 4b + 6d + L$ by 7, and call the remainder e. Then the date of Easter is either March $(22 + d + e)$ if $d + e \le 9$ or April $(d + e - 9)$ otherwise, with the following two exceptions:

1. If $d = 29$ and $e = 6$, Easter must be celebrated one week earlier, on April 19.

2. If $d = 28$, $e = 6$, and $M = 2, 5, 10, 13, 16, 21, 24,$ or 29, Easter must be celebrated one week earlier, on April 18.
   (a) Write a program to calculate the date of Easter. Your output should look something like this:

   CALCULATION OF THE DATE OF EASTER

   Enter the year: 1986
   The date of Easter is March 30.

   CALCULATION OF THE DATE OF EASTER

   Enter the year: 1985
   The date of Easter is April 7.

   (b) Similar rules apply for the Greek Orthodox calendar, except that $M = 15$, $L = 6$, and no exceptions occur. Write a program to calculate the date of Easter for the Greek Orthodox calendar.

7. Write a program to calculate the date following a given date. You will have to take into account leap years (see the **dayNumber** calculation on page 59). Your output should look something like this:

   TOMORROW'S DATE

   Enter the month for today's date: 10
   Enter the day for today's date: 22
   Enter the year for today's date: 1986
   Tomorrow's date is 10/23/1986

   TOMORROW'S DATE

   Enter the month for today's date: 12
   Enter the day for today's date: 31
   Enter the year for today's date: 1886
   Tomorrow's date is 1/1/1887

8. Modify your program in the previous exercise so that it first checks whether the date entered is legal. Your output should look like this:

```
TOMORROW'S DATE

Enter the month for today's date: 2
Enter the day for today's date: 29
Enter the year for today's date: 1987
That is not a legal date.


TOMORROW'S DATE

Enter the month for today's date: 14
Enter the day for today's date: 31
Enter the year for today's date: 1994
That is not a legal date.


TOMORROW'S DATE

Enter the month for today's date: 2
Enter the day for today's date: 28
Enter the year for today's date: 1997
Tomorrow's date is 3/1/1997
```

9. A certain medication for children is available in drops containing 1.23 grains of active ingredient per dropper-full, in syrup containing 2.46 grains per teaspoon, and in chewable tablets containing 1.23 grains per tablet. The recommended dosage is 0.0931 grains of active ingredient per pound of body weight for children weighing from 7 to 110 pounds. Drops can be given in multiples of half droppers-full, not exceeding three droppers-full. Syrup can be given in multiples of quarter teaspoons up to one teaspoon and in multiples of half teaspoons for more than one teaspoon. Tablets cannot be broken and are not to be given to a child weighing less than 27 pounds. Partial dosages are rounded to the nearest permissible dose (for example, 0.65 teaspoons of syrup would become 0.75 teaspoons). Write a program to read a child's weight in pounds and print the correct dosage of the medication in terms of droppers-full of drops, teaspoons of syrup, and tablets for that body weight. If more than one form of the medication is appropriate, give all possibilities. For example, your output might look like this:

```
DOSAGE CALCULATOR

Enter the child's weight in pounds: 38
Recommended dosage is 3.0 droppers of drops
or 1.5 teaspoons of syrup or 3 tablets.
```

10. A quadratic equation of the form

$$Ax^2 + Bxy + Cy^2 + Dx + Ey + F = 0$$

with the product $ABC \neq 0$ corresponds to a conic section (parabola, ellipse, circle, or hyperbola). The type of conic section is determined by the values of the *characteristic* and the *discriminant*. The characteristic is the value $B^2 - 4AC$, and the discriminant is

$$\begin{vmatrix} A & B/2 & D/2 \\ B/2 & C & E/2 \\ D/2 & E/2 & F \end{vmatrix} = A \begin{vmatrix} C & E/2 \\ E/2 & F \end{vmatrix} - \frac{B}{2} \begin{vmatrix} B/2 & E/2 \\ D/2 & F \end{vmatrix} + \frac{D}{2} \begin{vmatrix} B/2 & C \\ D/2 & E/2 \end{vmatrix},$$

where the expression

$$\begin{vmatrix} a & b \\ c & d \end{vmatrix},$$

called a *determinant*, has the value $ad - bc$. The resulting conic sections are classified as follows:

Discriminant	Characteristic	Type of Conic Section
0	$\neq 0$	Nondegenerate parabola
0	0	Degenerate parabola: two real or imaginary parallel lines
< 0	$\neq 0$	Nondegenerate ellipse or circle, real or imaginary
< 0	0	Degenerate ellipse: point ellipse or circle
>0	$\neq 0$	Nondegenerate hyperbola
>0	0	Degenerate hyperbola: two distinct intersecting lines

Write a program to read the coefficients A, B, C, D, E, and F, calculate the characteristic and discriminant, and print a message telling the type of conic section.

11. The musical scale in common use today is the equal-tempered chromatic scale with standard concert pitch of the fourth-octave A being 440 hertz. The twelve notes of each octave are logarithmically spaced. If we number the notes

1	2	3	4	5	6	7	8	9	10	11	12
C	C-sharp	D	E-flat	E	F	F-sharp	G	G-sharp	A	B-flat	B

the following formula relates the note numbers and frequencies in hertz:

$$\log_2 \frac{\text{Frequency}}{55} = \text{Octave number} + \frac{\text{Note number} - 22}{12}$$

where the octave number is according to the standard scheme in which middle C begins at octave number 4. Write a program to read a frequency and print the closest note and octave number.

12. An electrical supply company manufactures electrical extension cords rated at 3.0, 6.0, 7.0, 10.0, 13.0, and 15.0 amperes. If an extension cord of length at most 50 feet is to be used with an appliance, a cord with the same amperage rating as the appliance (or higher) can be safely used; if the length is more than 50 but less than 100 feet, a cord of at least the next higher amperage rating is needed. Write a program to determine and print the proper extension cord set selection, given the amperage of the appliance and the cord length. Your output should look something like this:

EXTENSION CORD AMPERAGE RATING

Enter appliance amperage: 5.8
Enter cord length in feet: 60
Use a cord rated at 7 amperes or more.

13. The children's game of Cootie is played with pencil, paper, and a die. The goal is to draw a complete picture of a "cootie" with a body, a head, two eyes, two antennae, six legs, and a tail:

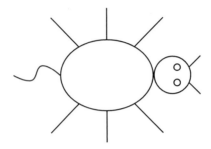

When the die is rolled, a 1 means the body may be drawn, 2 means the head may be drawn, 3 means a leg may be drawn, 4 means an antenna may be drawn, 5 means an eye may be drawn, and 6 means a tail may be drawn. The body must be drawn first; the head must be drawn before eyes or antennae.

(a) Assume boolean variables **body**, **head**, and **tail**, and **int** variables **eyes**, **antennae**, and **legs**. Write a boolean expression that is true when the cootie is complete and false otherwise.

(b) Write a **switch** statement that changes the values of the variables appropriately, depending on the value of an **int** variable **toss**. For example, if **toss** = 3, you can increment **legs**, but only if **body** is *true* and **legs** < 6.

Summary

The decision to take one of two alternative actions based on a true/false condition is implemented with an **if** statement:

```
if (<condition>)
    <statement>        ← The "then" alternative
else
    <statement>        ← The "else" alternative
```

The condition following the keyword **if** can be any expression; if the value of the expression is nonzero, it is considered true, while if the value is zero the expression is considered false. The statements may be any C++ statement, including another **if** statement. If a compound statement is used, it is framed by braces { and }. Care should be taken to indent these statements logically. If the **else** alternative is not needed, it may be omitted.

Boolean expressions are formed by comparing values with *relational operators* <, >, <=, >=, ==, and != or by combining values with *boolean operators* (&&, ||, !). Boolean expressions containing arithmetic, relational, and boolean operators are evaluated using the precedence rules, summarized in Table 3.3. Complicated boolean expressions can sometimes be simplified using the rules in Table 3.5. An organized way to examine the possible results of a boolean expression is to make a *truth table* (see Table 3.4).

Enumerated types allow the user to define any ordered group of simple values as a type. We use enumerated types to make our programs more readable. For example, we define a boolean type

```
enum boolean {false, true};
```

for use when we want a true/false value.

The **switch** statement is a way to decide on alternative actions based on **int**- or **enum**-type expressions:

```
switch (<expression>) {
  case <value>: <statements>
  case <value>: <statements>
  . . .
  case <value>: <statements>
  default: <statements>
}
```

The statements of the possible cases can be simple statements, compound statements within braces, or the empty statement (that is, no statement need be given). Statements are usually ended by a **break** statement, which causes execution of the **switch** to terminate. If a **break** is not present, the execution continues with the set of statements in the next case. If every **case** in a **switch** ends with a **break**, then the statement is equivalent to

```
  switchValue = <expression>;
if (switchValue == <value>)
  <statement>
else if(switchValue == <value>)
  <statement>
. . .
else if(switchValue == <value>)
  <statement>
else
  <statement>
```

The keywords introduced in this chapter are

```
break   case   if   else   enum   switch   default
```

CHAPTER

4

Functions

Chapter Preview

Large programs are written by subdividing them into *functions* to compartmentalize or *modularize* programming tasks. This chapter introduces user-defined functions and their components: parameters, local variables, and return types. Using functions, we will write a program to manipulate calendar dates.

Good things come in small packages.

—folk saying

B y now you are probably convinced that writing and debugging even a relatively small program is fraught with pitfalls and frustrations. Imagine how much more challenging it is to write large programs that do complicated things! Don't despair; the task of writing large programs can be made manageable by breaking the large problem into bite-size pieces, writing and debugging programs for these bite-size pieces, and then assembling the programs thus written into a single program. Encapsulating sections of C++ code is an *extremely* powerful technique.

The encapsulations of code are called *functions*. We have used functions all along, but in a highly restricted way. Whenever we used **floor**, **sqrt**, and so on, we were using functions provided as part of standard C++ (when we give the compiler directive **#include <math.h>**). The statement

```
windChillIndex =
    91.4 - (10.45 + 6.69 * sqrt(windSpeed) - 0.447 * windSpeed)
        * (91.4 - temperature)/22.0;
```

functions

calls (invokes) a standard function **sqrt**. The function **sqrt** expects to be told what to take the square root of; it is told by the *argument* (given in parentheses; also called the *parameter*) passed to it. In this case the numerical value named **windSpeed** is the argument. The function **sqrt** does its job of computing the square root and returning the value, and the program then continues from where it left off.

function call
argument
parameter

When a function **f** calls a function **g**, C++ begins executing the statements of **g** but *remembers that it was in the middle of executing* **f**. When **g** is done, it *returns* to executing **f**, continuing from where it had left off. This mechanism allows us to encapsulate computations (or actions) by putting those computations or actions into a C++ function.

function returns

To write your own function in C++, you need to specify the name of the function, its parameters, the type of value returned (its *return type*), and the C++ statements that do the computation (the *body of the function*). In general, it looks like this:

return type
body of the function

```
<type-returned> <name> (<parameterlist>) {

    <statements>  ← body of the function

}
```

For a specific example, suppose we want to write a program to print the words for the song "The Ants Came Marching":

The ants came marching 1 by 1, Hurrah! Hurrah!
The ants came marching 1 by 1, Hurrah! Hurrah!
The ants came marching 1 by 1,
The little one stopped to suck his thumb.
They all go marching down around the maze.
(Boom, boom, boom.)

The ants came marching 2 by 2, Hurrah! Hurrah!
The ants came marching 2 by 2, Hurrah! Hurrah!
The ants came marching 2 by 2,
The little one stopped to tie his shoe.
They all go marching down around the maze.
(Boom, boom, boom.)

$$\vdots$$

Each verse is similar, following a general pattern, but the number and the last phrase in the fourth line change each time. The similarity of the verses means we can encapsulate the writing of a verse by defining a function in which the body contains the statement

```
cout << "The ants came marching " << n << " by " << n
     << ", Hurrah! Hurrah!\n"
     << "The ants came marching " << n << " by " << n
     << ", Hurrah! Hurrah!\n"
     << "The ants came marching " << n << " by " << n
     << ",\n"
     << "The little one stopped to ";
```

This writes the verse except for the last phrase like "suck his thumb" or "tie his shoe." To encapsulate the statement as the body of a function, we write

```
void verse (int n) {
// Print the verse of "The Ants Came Marching"
  cout << "The ants came marching " << n << " by " << n
       << ", Hurrah! Hurrah!\n"
       << "The ants came marching " << n << " by " << n
       << ", Hurrah! Hurrah!\n"
       << "The ants came marching " << n << " by " << n
       << ",\n"
       << "The little one stopped to ";
}
```

We then can use this function to write the beginning of the first verse with

```
verse(1);
cout << "suck his thumb.\n";
```

and the beginning of the second verse with

```
verse(2);
cout << "tie his shoe.\n";
```

and so on.

How do these statements serve to write out the first and second verses? When we call the function **verse** by the statement

```
verse(1);
```

we begin executing the statements of the function **verse**. This function has the heading

```
void verse (int n)
```

saying that it expects to have an **int** value supplied to it; the keyword **void** says that the function will return no value (unlike **sqrt**, which returns the value of the square root of its argument). In the function **verse**, the **int** value is referred to by the identifier **n**. So when the function is executed by the call **verse(1)**, the identifier **n** in the function takes the value 1—the effect is that the output statements of the function produce the lines

```
The ants came marching 1 by 1, Hurrah! Hurrah!
The ants came marching 1 by 1, Hurrah! Hurrah!
The ants came marching 1 by 1,
The little one stopped to
```

Having reached the final line of **verse**, we return to where we were when we called **verse** and continue execution at that point. Since the last line written in the function **verse** does *not* end with a newline (**\n**), further output will be on the same line, and the statement

```
cout << "suck his thumb.\n";
```

completes the fourth line of the song. Similarly, the statements

```
verse(2);
cout << "tie his shoe.\n";
```

cause the first four lines of the second verse to be written.

To write the last two lines of each verse (the chorus), we use the statement

```
cout << "They all go marching down around the maze.\n"
     << "(Boom, boom, boom.)\n\n";
```

which we encapsulate into a C++ function like this:

```
void chorus () {
// Print the chorus of "The Ants Came Marching"
  cout << "They all go marching down around the maze.\n"
       << "(Boom, boom, boom.)\n\n";
}
```

This function has no parameters, so none appear in the heading, and we can use **chorus** to print the chorus by saying

```
chorus();
```

wherever needed. Whenever this function call is encountered, we begin executing the statements of **chorus**, returning to where we were after finishing the execution of the statements in **chorus**. With the functions **verse** and **chorus** we can write the first two verses and choruses of the song with the statements

```
verse(1);
cout << "suck his thumb.\n";
chorus();
verse(2);
cout << "tie his shoe.\n";
chorus();
```

Thus we can combine these pieces into the following program to write all the words of the song:

```
1    #include <iostream.h>
2    #include <iomanip.h>
3
4    //  Print the song "The Ants Came Marching"
5    //  Rebecca Kamin, September 12, 1995.
6
7    void verse (int n) {
8    // Print the verse of "The Ants Came Marching"
9      cout << "The ants came marching " << n << " by " << n
10          << ", Hurrah! Hurrah!\n"
11          << "The ants came marching " << n << " by " << n
12          << ", Hurrah! Hurrah!\n"
13          << "The ants came marching " << n << " by " << n
14          << ",\n"
15          << "The little one stopped to ";
16   }
17
18   void chorus () {
19   // Print the chorus of "The Ants Came Marching"
20     cout << "They all go marching down around the maze.\n"
21          << "(Boom, boom, boom.)\n\n";
22   }
23
24   main () {
25     verse(1);  cout << "suck his thumb.\n";     chorus();
26     verse(2);  cout << "tie his shoe.\n";       chorus();
27     verse(3);  cout << "climb a tree.\n";       chorus();
28     verse(4);  cout << "shut the door.\n";      chorus();
29     verse(5);  cout << "take a dive.\n";        chorus();
30     verse(6);  cout << "pick up sticks.\n";     chorus();
31     verse(7);  cout << "go to heaven.\n";       chorus();
32     verse(8);  cout << "shut the gate.\n";      chorus();
33     verse(9);  cout << "scratch his spine.\n"; chorus();
34     verse(10); cout << "say THE END.\n\n";
35   }
```

Notice that in this program we have arranged the statements on lines 25 through 34 three to a line, so that each group on a line writes a single stanza of the song. This arrangement makes the program more readable than a list of 39 statements, one per line. Note also the overall arrangement of the program. The two new functions follow the compiler directives and precede the `main` function. The order in which we define `verse` and `chorus` is immaterial. The rule is simply that functions must be defined before they are used.

As we have said, the general form of a function is

```
<type-returned> <name> (<parameterlist>) {
  <statements>   ←| body of the function |
}
```

The parameter list can consist of no parameters (as in `chorus`) and such a function definition looks like

```
<type-returned> <name> () {
  <statements>   ←| body of the function |
}
```

If there is a single parameter, the function definition looks like

```
<type-returned> <name> (<type> <identifier>) {
  <statements>   ←| body of the function |
}
```

(as in `verse`). There can also be two, three, or more parameters; in such cases the elements of the parameter list are separated by commas, and the function definition has the form

```
<type-returned> <name> (<type> <identifier>,
                        ...,
                        <type> <identifier>) {
  <statements>   ←| body of the function |
}
```

A function that returns no value, like `verse` or `chorus`, is defined with a *`<type-returned>`* of `void`.

Using an additional parameter, we can slightly simplify the program to print "The Ants Came Marching." We'll rewrite `verse` with a second parameter that says what the little ant stopped to do. The difficulty is that a number will not suffice for this purpose—we need a *character string*. Although we won't go into details of character strings until Chapter 9, we'll introduce them here so that we can use such values in simple instances. Strings of characters are defined in C++ as being of type `char` with a `*` preceding the variable name (the exact meaning of this declaration will be explained in Chapter 9); this type can be used just as we've used the types `int` and `float` to specify the types of variables. Using `char *`, we can rewrite `verse` as

character string

```
void verse (int n,      // How many ants came marching
            char *what) // What the little ant did
{
// Print the verse of "The Ants Came Marching"
```

```
        cout << "The ants came marching " << n << " by " << n
             << ", Hurrah! Hurrah!\n"
             << "The ants came marching " << n << " by " << n
             << ", Hurrah! Hurrah!\n"
             << "The ants came marching " << n << " by " << n
             << ",\n"
             << "The little one stopped to " << what << ".\n";
    }
```

Notice that we gave the parameter list *vertically*, with a comment next to each parameter explaining its role. We also gave a comment at the beginning of the function body explaining what the function does. This is a good practice to follow in all but the most trivial functions. The additional spaces and indentations are an aid to the human reader and are ignored completely by C++.

The new version of **verse** requires two parameters, an integer and a string. For example, the first verse of the song will be printed by the statement

```
    verse(1, "suck his thumb");
```

which consists solely of the function call. The remaining verses are similarly done. Thus, the entire song is printed by the sequence of statements

```
    verse(1, "suck his thumb");     chorus();
    verse(2, "tie his shoe");       chorus();
    verse(3, "climb a tree");       chorus();
    verse(4, "shut the door");      chorus();
    verse(5, "take a dive");        chorus();
    verse(6, "pick up sticks");     chorus();
    verse(7, "go to heaven");       chorus();
    verse(8, "shut the gate");      chorus();
    verse(9, "scratch his spine");  chorus();
    verse(10, "say THE END");
```

4.1

Scope of Variables

As a more elaborate example of the use of functions, we'll design a function to write an integer n in words, assuming that n is in the range $-999 \le n \le 999$. For instance, we want 313 to be written as the phrase "three hundred thirteen". We'll extend this to arbitrarily large integers in Chapter 8. Such a function would be needed in a program that prints salary checks, for example.

The way we write numbers in English words is idiosyncratic for small numbers, so we'll need to use a **switch** statement to write the names of the numbers $1, 2, \ldots, 19$. We'll make the **switch** statement into a function:

```
    void printSmallNumber (int n) {
    // Write the name of a number < 20.

      switch (n) {
        case  1: printString("one");        break;
        case  2: printString("two");        break;
        case  3: printString("three");      break;
```

```
         case  3: printString("three");      break;
         case  4: printString("four");       break;
         case  5: printString("five");       break;
         case  6: printString("six");        break;
         case  7: printString("seven");      break;
         case  8: printString("eight");      break;
         case  9: printString("nine");       break;
         case 10: printString("ten");        break;
         case 11: printString("eleven");     break;
         case 12: printString("twelve");     break;
         case 13: printString("thirteen");   break;
         case 14: printString("fourteen");   break;
         case 15: printString("fifteen");    break;
         case 16: printString("sixteen");    break;
         case 17: printString("seventeen");  break;
         case 18: printString("eighteen");   break;
         case 19: printString("nineteen");   break;
      }
   }
```

where we have a function **printString** to do the actual printing:

```
void printString (char *s) {
// Write a string.

   cout << s;
}
```

Similarly, we need a **switch** statement for the names of the decade numbers 20, 30, 40, . . . , 90; this is also made into a function:

```
void printDecade (int n) {
// Write the name of a multiple of 10.

   switch (n) {
     case 2: printString("twenty");  break;
     case 3: printString("thirty");  break;
     case 4: printString("forty");   break;
     case 5: printString("fifty");   break;
     case 6: printString("sixty");   break;
     case 7: printString("seventy"); break;
     case 8: printString("eighty");  break;
     case 9: printString("ninety");  break;
   }
}
```

In Chapter 8 we'll see a better way to write the functions **printSmallNumber** and **printDecade**.

We write the name of a number, n, between 1 and 999 by the following actions:

1. If $n > 99$, write the hundreds and then write n % 100.
2. If $99 \geq n > 19$, write the decade using the **printDecade** function above and then write n % 10.
3. If $19 \geq n$, write the number using **printSmallNumber**.

These actions can be expressed in C++ as

```
void printMediumNumber(int n) {
// Write the name of a number < 1000.

  if (n > 99) {
    printSmallNumber(n/100);
    printString("hundred");
    n = n % 100;
  }
  if (n > 19) {
    printDecade(n/10);
    n = n % 10;
  }
  if (n > 0)
    printSmallNumber(n);
}
```

Note that the three **if** statements are separate and are executed sequentially—they are *not* nested **if-else** statements.

There is a difficulty, however. Consider what happens when we make the call **printMediumNumber(432)**. The output is

```
fourhundredthirtytwo
```

How do we separate words by blank spaces? Notice that we don't want to write a blank automatically before each word, since we don't want a blank before the first word. Similarly, we can't automatically follow each word with a blank, because we don't want a blank after the last word. Moreover, a word such as "thirty" might be the only word, the first word, the last word, or in the middle. How should we handle the writing of a blank between words?

lazy approach   We'll solve the problem by taking what might be called a *lazy approach*: Write a blank only at the last possible moment. We'll do this by keeping a boolean variable **needBlank** that is **true** whenever a blank will be needed before the *next* word; before writing each word, we check the value of **needBlank** and act accordingly. Since words are always written by the function **printString**, we'll encapsulate the necessary manipulations in that function and declare **needBlank** outside all of these functions (as we explain below):

```
boolean needBlank; // keep track of whether a blank
                   // is needed before the next word

void printString (char *s) {
// Write a string, preceded by a blank if needed.

  if (needBlank)
    cout << " ";
  cout << s;
  needBlank = true;
}
```

The first thing we'll do in writing a number in words is to set **needBlank** to **false**; we'll do this before any call to **printString**. Then, when we write the first word, **s**, it will *not* be preceded by a blank. At the end of **printString**, however, after the string has been printed, we set the value of `needBlank` to `true`; `needBlank` then remains `true` while we write the rest of the words, so they will be preceded by blanks. Thus, the use of the variable `needBlank` forces `printMediumNumber(20)` to print "twenty," `printMediumNumber(120)` to print "one hundred twenty," and `printMediumNumber(128)` to print "one hundred twenty eight."

Finally, to complete our program to write numbers in words, we can extend the range of numbers to $-999 \leq n \leq 999$ in a straightforward way:

```
void printNumber(int n) {
// Write a number in English words.

  needBlank = false;
  if (n > 0)
    printMediumNumber(n);
  else if (n < 0) {
    printString("minus");
    printMediumNumber(-n);
  }
  else { // (n == 0)
    printString("zero");
  }
}
```

It is in this function that the `needBlank` is initialized before a number is printed. In Chapter 8 we extend this function to work for arbitrarily large integers.

Because the variable `needBlank` is declared outside any function, it is a *global variable*, available everywhere throughout the program following its definition. Conversely, a variable declared inside a function is called a *local variable*. A function's local variables are created when the function is called and disappear when the call ends. *Only that function can refer to the local variables within it*; neither the function that called it nor any function that it calls can refer to them. We had to make `needBlank` a global variable because its value must be preserved in between calls to `printString`. If it were a local variable in `printString`, its value would be lost as it was destroyed upon returning and recreated on a subsequent call to `printString`.

The following outline of C++ code illustrates the general situation with a locally declared variable **x**:

global variable
local variable

```
void g () {
  ...
}
```
} references to x not allowed here

```
int f () {
  float x = 1.4;
  ... g() ...
}
```
} references to x allowed here

```
void main () {
  ... f() ...
}
```
} references to x not allowed here

scope   We say that "the scope of **x** is the body of **f**." The *scope* of a variable is the part of the program in which it is legal to refer to that variable.

If you violate this scope rule, the C++ compiler will detect the error. For example, this program seems reasonable:

```
void incrxBy (int n) {
  x = x+n;
}

void main () {
  int x = 10;
  incrxBy(5);
  cout << x;   // prints 15, doesn't it?
}
```

but it is wrong. Since the body of **incrxBy** is not in the scope of **x**, **incrxBy** cannot refer to it. The result is a compiler error message something like

```
line 2: error:  x undefined
```

Note that **incrxBy** can declare a *different* variable called **x**. Then,

```
void incrxBy (int n) {
  int x;
  x = x+n;
}

void main () {
  int x = 10;
  incrxBy(5);
  cout << x;   // prints 10
}
```

is legal, but it doesn't do anything, because **incrxBy**'s variable **x** and **main**'s variable **x** are unrelated: **incrxBy**'s variable **x** comes into existence when **incrxBy** is called, gets incremented (without ever getting initialized), and then disappears when **incrxBy** returns. Variable **x** in **main** is unaffected, and calling **incrxBy** does nothing at all, so the value **10** is printed.

The variable **needBlank** was global, declared outside any function. It comes into existence when the program starts and remains in existence until the program stops; it can be seen and changed by any function. As we have seen, and will see further in later chapters, this feature provides a useful alternative method of communicating among functions.

Why not make all variables global—that is, allow every variable to be accessed anywhere? This would remove modularity from the program. The most *modular* flexible programs are those that can be taken apart, repaired, or expanded with *programming* modular parts. *Modular programming* means encapsulating separate tasks into separate functions that communicate with each other through parameters. A modular program avoids interference between variables; each function defines and controls its own variables. In modular programs, each function can be debugged individually, used in other programs, and modified as new conditions arise without worrying about the effect on other parts of the program.

When a function changes the value of a variable that it did not declare, the change is called a *side effect*. Avoid side effects wherever possible—the bugs *side effect* produced by side effects are very difficult to locate, because they make the pieces of a program interdependent in ways not immediately evident to the reader. For this reason, global variables should be used only where absolutely necessary, and communication between parts of a program should generally be through the parameters.

What if a local and global variable have the same name?

```
float x = 1.1419;

void f() {
  int x;

  ...          } What about references to x here?

}
```

The rule is that any reference to **x** in the body of **f** refers to the *local* variable. Thus, the global variable is effectively hidden by the local one. (Notice, by the way, that the local and global variables called **x** have different types. This is okay, because they are distinct, unrelated variables; *but it is very bad programming practice to use the identical name for both a global and a local variable!*)

Finally, there is an important rule that holds for both local and global variables (as well as functions): A name must be declared before it is used. This means that, in the following example, **x** cannot be used in **g**:

```
void g () {
  ...          } not in the scope of x
}

int x = 1;

void f () {
  ...          } in the scope of x
}
```

The scope of a global variable is not really the entire program or function, just the part of the program or function that follows the variable's declaration. Thus:

```
void f () {
  ...              } cannot refer to i here

  int i = 10;

  ...              } this is the scope of i
}
```

A variable can be declared anywhere within a function, but its scope is limited to the part that follows the declaration.

Finally, the scope of a variable declared in a compound statement (that is, within braces { }) is limited to that statement. For example, the function

```
void max (int i, int j, int k) {
    if (i > j) {
        int a;
        a = i;
    }
    else {
        a = j;
    }
    if (k > a)
        cout << k;
    else
        cout << a;
}
```

causes the error message

```
line 7: error:  a undefined
```

because the local variable **a** is not known outside of the *then* clause in which it is declared.

Returning a Value

The user-defined functions presented so far do not return a value, so the type returned is **void**. Many functions return a value as their result, however, such as **sqrt**. The distinction between these two cases is simple, but important: A call to a function that returns no value (that is, **void**) constitutes a C++ *statement* and can be used in any context that C++ statements can be used. A function call to a function that returns a value constitutes a value of the type returned by the function (that is, **int**, **float**, and so on) and can be used in any context that a C++ value of that type can be used, such as in expressions.

As an example of a function that returns a value, recall that in Chapter 3 we needed to determine whether a year was a leap year. This simple calculation can be encapsulated as a function that returns a boolean value:

```
int leapYear (int y) {

// Returns true if y is a leap year on the Gregorian
// calendar, that is, if y is a multiple of 4 and NOT
// a century year or is a century year divisible by 400

    return (((y % 4) == 0) && ((y % 100) != 0))
           || ((y % 400) == 0);
}
```

This function illustrates the mechanism used to specify what value is returned by a function—it is the value given after the **return**:

return *statement*

```
return <value>
```

In the case of **leapYear**, the value is the value of the boolean expression that does the leap year calculation.

Once the function **leapYear** has been declared, it can be used anywhere a boolean variable or expression can be used. For example, the **dayNumber** calculation from Chapter 3 computes the number of days from the beginning of the year given the month, day, and year:

```
dayNumber = (month - 1) * 31 + day;

//Correct for months beyond February
if (month > 2) {
  // Assume non-leap year
  dayNumber = dayNumber - ((4 * month + 23) / 10);
  if ((((year % 4) == 0) && ((year % 100) != 0))
      || ((year % 400) == 0))
    // Correct for leap year
    dayNumber = dayNumber + 1;
```

To encapsulate this as a function, we use the function **leapYear**, and we need a local variable in which to do the calculation:

```
1    int dayNumber (int month,
2                   int day,
3                   int year) {
4
5    // Calculate the day number in the year of month/day/year
6
7      // Calculate day number assuming all months have 31 days
8      int number = (month - 1) * 31 + day;
9
10     //Correct for months beyond February
11     if (month > 2) {
12       number = number - ((4 * month + 23) / 10);
13       if (leapYear(year))
14         number = number++;
15     };
16
17     return number;
18   }
```

Note the use of the variable **number** declared to be type **int** on line 8. This variable is local to the function **dayNumber**; this variable exists *only* during the computation in that function and not otherwise.

The function **leapYear** is also useful in writing a function to tell us the last day of a month:

```
int lastDayOfMonth(int m, int y) {

// Returns the number of days in a given month and year

  switch (m) {
    case 2: if (leapYear(y))
               return 29;
            else
               return 28;
    case 4:
    case 6:
    case 9:
    case 11: return 30;
    default: return 31;
  }
}
```

Then we can use **lastDayOfMonth** in writing a function to check a date for legality (Exercise 8 on page 88):

```
boolean dateIsLegal(int m, int d, int y) {

// Determine whether a given month, day, year is a legal date

  return
    (1 <= y) &&                            // year is okay
    (1 <= m) && (m <= 12) &&               // month is okay
    (1 <= d) && (d <= lastDayOfMonth(m,y));// day is okay
}
```

As these small examples indicate, proper naming and use of functions make the program more readable, and allow us to compartmentalize the program into logical units that are easy to write, debug, and modify.

As another example of a function that returns a value, let's convert the wind-chill index calculation from Chapter 3 (page 52) to a function with two parameters, the air temperature and the wind speed. The function looks similar to the program we wrote in Chapter 3:

```
float windChillIndex (
      float temp,   // air temperature (deg F)
      float speed   // wind speed (mph)
      )
{
// Calculate and print the wind-chill index
// for given air temperature and wind speed.
// The formula is taken from "Windchill" by William
// Bosch and L.G. Cobb, UMAP Module 658, COMAP, Inc.,
// Lexington, MA, 1984

  if (speed <= 4)       // little or no wind
    return temp;
  else if (speed <= 45) // moderate wind
    return (91.4 - (10.45 + 6.69 * sqrt(speed)
         - 0.447 * speed) * (91.4 - temp)/22.0);
```

```
                 else                     //  high wind
                   return (1.6 * temp - 55.0);
               }
```

We can use this function by embedding it in a program and achieve exactly
the same effect we had before:

```
 1    #include <iostream.h>
 2    #include <iomanip.h>
 3    #include <math.h>
 4
 5    //  Calculate and print the wind-chill index
 6    //  for given air temperature and wind speed.
 7
 8    //  D. Benjamin Gordon, August 25, 1994
 9
10    float windChillIndex (
11         float temp,    // air temperature (deg F)
12         float speed    // wind speed (mph)
13         )
14    {
15    //  Calculate and print the wind-chill index
16    //  for given air temperature and wind speed.
17    //  The formula is taken from "Windchill" by William
18    //  Bosch and L.G. Cobb, UMAP Module 658, COMAP, Inc.,
19    //  Lexington, MA, 1984
20
21      if (speed <= 4)         //  little or no wind
22        return temp;
23      else if (speed <= 45) //  moderate wind
24        return (91.4 - (10.45 + 6.69 * sqrt(speed)
25             - 0.447 * speed) * (91.4 - temp)/22.0);
26      else                     //  high wind
27        return (1.6 * temp - 55.0);
28    }
29
30    main () {
31      float
32        airTemp,      // air temperature (deg F)
33        windSpeed;    // wind speed (mph)
34
35      cout << "WIND-CHILL INDEX COMPUTATION\n\n"
36           << "The temperature (deg F) is: ";
37      cin >> airTemp;
38      cout << "The wind speed (mph) is: ";
39      cin >> windSpeed;
40      cout << "The wind-chill index is "
41           << windChillIndex(airTemp, windSpeed)
42           << "\n";
43    }
```

Now, however, the wind-chill calculation has been encapsulated so that we can
take it out and use it elsewhere, as needed. Moreover, if the definition of the wind-

chill index changes or becomes more refined, we can rewrite the function without disturbing the other code.

4.3

Parameters

formal parameters
actual parameters
arguments

The heading of a function specifies the identifier and the type of each of the parameters; these identifiers are called the *formal parameters* of the function. The *actual parameters*, or *arguments*, are supplied to the function when it is used. For example, in the wind-chill index program, the function `windChillIndex` has two formal parameters, `temp` and `speed`, both of type `float`. The body of the function `windChillIndex` uses the identifiers `temp` and `speed` when it needs to refer to its parameters. On the other hand, when `windChillIndex` is used in the program (line 41), the actual parameters (arguments) supplied are `airTemp` and `windSpeed`.

There must be an exact match in number, order, and types between the parameter list in the function heading (the formal parameters) and the arguments supplied when the function is called. However, there are exceptions to this rule. An `int` value will automatically be converted to a `float` value, if necessary. This exception is consistent with the way C++ treats `int` values in `float` expressions.

passing
parameters

An actual parameter can be any expression of the type required to match the corresponding formal parameter. To understand how parameters are *passed* to a function, let's examine what happens in the wind-chill index program when the function `windChillIndex` is called in the final output statement:

```
40      cout << "The wind-chill index is "
41              << windChillIndex(airTemp, windSpeed)
42              << "\n";
```

When the call occurs, the value of each formal parameter in the function is set to the value of the corresponding actual parameter. Thus the value of the formal parameter `temp` in `windChillIndex` is set to the value of the actual parameter, the value of the variable `airTemp` from the main program; similarly, the value of the parameter `speed` in `windChillIndex` is set to the value of the variable `windSpeed` from the main program. Once these values have been set, the function `windChillIndex` is executed—the computations use the values passed to the function.

value parameters

C++ provides two slightly different mechanisms for parameter passing. For the moment we will be concerned only with *value parameters*, which behave as described so far. Later in this chapter we will introduce the other type of parameter, *reference parameters*, which behave somewhat differently.

reference
parameters

Exercises—First Set

☞   1. Write a program to print the song "This Old Man":

> This old man, he played 1,
> He played nick nack on my drum;
> Nick nack paddy whack, give a dog a bone,
> This old man came rolling home.
>
> ⋮

The remaining verses are

2—on my shoe	5—on my hive	8—on my gate
3—on my tree	6—on my sticks	9—on my line
4—on my door	7—all round heaven	10—on my hen

Use the techniques shown so far in this chapter to encapsulate the chorus and repeated verse lines.

2. Encapsulate the central calculation of the Social Security tax program (on page 49) with a function that returns a value of type **float**, and modify the program to use this function.

3. Weather forecasters disagree about which hot weather index (discomfort index or humiture, see Exercises 8 and 9 on page 63) is more useful. Encapsulate your programs for these indices into two functions, **discomfortIndex** and **humitureIndex**, each of which returns **int** values. Incorporate these functions as well as the function **windChillIndex** in a program to print a weather message. At 50°F or less, print the wind-chill index; for temperatures greater than 50°F, print either the humiture or the discomfort index depending on the value of the variable **heatIndex**, of the user-defined type

   ```
   enum indexType {discomfort, humiture};
   ```

4. Encapsulate the calculation of the Gregorian epact (see Exercise 16, page 44) into a function, given the year.

5. The "exclusive or" is not available directly in C++ (see Table 3.4 on page 61). Write a function that computes the exclusive or.

6. Given the time of day in terms of the variables **hour, minute, second**, and **dayHalf** (that is, **AM** or **PM**), write a function called **fractionOfDay** to calculate and return the fraction of the day (type **float**) that has elapsed. For example,

   ```
   fractionOfDay(12, 0, 0, AM)
   ```

   would return 0.0,

   ```
   fractionOfDay(12, 0, 0, PM)
   ```

   would return 0.5, and

   ```
   fractionOfDay(11, 59, 59, PM)
   ```

   would return 0.999988426.

7. Write a function **triangle** that takes three **float** values and returns true if the three values are the sides of a triangle and false if not. For three lengths to form a triangle, the sum of any two lengths must exceed the third length.

8. Write a function called **majority** having three boolean parameters. The value returned should be true if any two of the arguments are true and false otherwise.

4.4

Reference Parameters

We stated above (page 103) that all communication between functions should be done via the parameters. There is a problem here; the communication is not really two-way. While the calling function can communicate to the function being called through the values of the parameters, the function being called can return only a single value.

Suppose we want to write a function that computes the next day from a date given as **month, day, year**. Returning a single value is not sufficient—we must return all three parts of the new date (the month, day, and year). How do we do it?

value parameters

The parameters we have described so far are called *value parameters*. A value parameter is a local variable. Its initial value within the function is given as the argument to the function; nothing that happens to the variable within the function is seen by the outside. All the parameters used in the functions so far have been value parameters.

reference parameters

C++ also allows for *reference parameters*, which facilitate communication from the function being called to whatever function called it. These parameters are indicated by appending an ampersand (**&**) to the type name in the parameter list. Any parameter so designated will have its initial value within the function taken from the argument list when it is called, just like a value parameter, but in addition, any changes made in the value of this parameter will be apparent to the calling program or function upon return.

Suppose, for example, we want to write a function that will increment a variable by 1. We would write

```
1    #include <iostream.h>
2    #include <iomanip.h>
3
4    void increment (int &n) {
5    // Increment the argument by 1.
6       n++;
7    }
8
9    main () {
10      int x = 0;
11      cout << "At first x = " << x << "\n";
12      increment(x);
13      cout << "But now x = " << x << "\n";
14   }
```

which, when executed, would produce the output

```
At first x = 0
But now x = 1
```

The **&** in line 4 is critical! If we omit the **&**, the output produced will be

```
At first x = 0
But now x = 0
```

since the change made in `increment` will be to the local variable (the parameter **n**), *not* to the actual parameter supplied, **x**.

Specifically, the distinction between value parameters and reference parameters is that when a function manipulates a value parameter, it is manipulating its own local variable—a local object whose initial value is that of the actual parameter. When a function manipulates a reference parameter, however, it is manipulating the actual parameter provided to it, not a local object. As a consequence, if the function makes a change, the change is made to the actual parameter; this means that the actual parameter corresponding to a formal parameter cannot be anything but a variable of the corresponding type. In particular, constants or, more generally, expressions cannot be used as the actual parameter when the formal parameter is a reference parameter.

Using reference parameters, we can write the function to compute the next day:

```
void nextDay(int& m, int& d, int& y) {

// Increment date m, d, y to next day

if (d != lastDayOfMonth(m,y))
  d++;
else { // last day of month
  d = 1;               // reset day
  m = (m % 12) + 1; // next month
  if (m == 1)          // next year
    y++;
  }
}
```

The statements

```
int year, month, day;
cout << "Enter year: ";  cin >> year;
cout << "Enter month: "; cin >> month;
cout << "Enter day: ";   cin >> day;
cout << "Date is " << month << "/" << day << "/" << year << "\n";
nextDay(month, day, year);
cout << "Next day is " << month << "/" << day << "/" << year << "\n";
```

cause the output

```
Enter year: 1994
Enter month: 12
Enter day: 31
Date is 12/31/1994
Next day is 1/1/1995
```

It is good programming practice to use reference parameters only in functions that do not return values (that is, that return **void**). Changing the value of a parameter is a form of side effect, and functions that return values should avoid side effects. Other side effects to be avoided in functions that return a value include the changing of a global variable, writing output, and reading input. The reason is simple: A "function" (in mathematical terms) computes a value; if, in the computation of that value, the state of the world is changed (say by changing a global value or reading input), then we cannot be sure that the *identical* function call will produce the same results the next time. Such a possibility makes debugging an even harder task!

Of course, functions of type **void** have no choice but to cause some side effects—they must be doing something! It is desirable, however, to limit their side effects to writing output, reading input, and changing the values of their parameters. Proper handling of errors may also necessitate the use of side effects. There are exceptions to every rule. Our use of **needBlank** in writing numbers in words (page 100) was a reasonable (and minimal) use of side effects for communication among various functions.

Exercises—Second Set

1. Write a function using the reference parameters **hour**, **minute**, **second**, and **dayHalf** (that is, **AM** or **PM**) to calculate the time of day, given a fraction of the day as a value parameter to the function (see Exercise 6 on page 109 for examples).

2. (a) Write a function to convert polar to rectangular coordinates. The parameters **r** and **theta** giving the polar coordinates should be value parameters, and the reference parameters **x** and **y** will be calculated. The formulas are $x = r \cos \theta$ and $y = r \sin \theta$.

   (b) Write a function to convert from rectangular coordinates (x, y) to polar coordinates (r, θ). The formulas are $r = \sqrt{x^2 + y^2}$ and $\theta = \arctan(y/x)$.

3. Write a function to perform the multiplication of two complex numbers. The value parameters to the function should be **real1**, **imag1**, **real2**, and **imag2**, and the reference parameters should be **realPart** and **imagPart**. The formula is

$$(a + bi) \times (c + di) = (ac - bd) + (bc + ad)i.$$

4. Write a function to perform the addition of two complex numbers. The value parameters to the function should be **real1**, **imag1**, **real2**, and **imag2**, and the reference parameters should be **realPart** and **imagPart**. The formula is

$$(a + bi) + (c + di) = (a + c) + (b + d)i.$$

5. A common task is to "swap" (interchange) the values of two variables. Write a function **swap** to perform this task; both parameters in **swap** (say, **firstVariable** and **secondVariable**) should be reference parameters.

6. Write a function **previousDay** to transform a given month, day, and year into the day before.

7. Take your program from Exercise 10, page 88, for quadratic equations and make it into a function.

★ 8. Write a function to solve cubic equations. The equation

$$ax^3 + 3bx^2 + 3cx + d = 0$$

has three roots: all real, or one real and two complex. Let

$$q = ac - b^2$$

$$r = \frac{3abc - a^2d}{2} - b^3$$

and

$$s_1 = (r + \sqrt{q^3 + r^2})^{1/3}$$

$$s_2 = (r - \sqrt{q^3 + r^2})^{1/3}.$$

Then the roots are

$$x_1 = \frac{s_1 + s_2 - b}{a}$$

$$x_2 = \frac{1}{a}\left[-\frac{s_1 + s_2}{2} + i\frac{\sqrt{3}}{2}(s_1 - s_2) - b \right]$$

$$x_3 = \frac{1}{a}\left[-\frac{s_1 + s_2}{2} - i\frac{\sqrt{3}}{2}(s_1 - s_2) - b \right]$$

If $q^3 + r^2 > 0$, there are one real and two complex roots; if $q^3 + r^2 = 0$, there are three real roots, of which at least two are equal; if $q^3 + r^2 < 0$, there are three real roots, but be careful, because the preceding solution requires finding the cube roots of complex quantities (see the formula given in Exercise 24 on page 149).

★ 9. Write a function to solve quartic equations. After dividing by the coefficient of x^4, the equation becomes

$$x^4 + ax^3 + bx^2 + cx + d = 0$$

which has four roots, all real, all complex, or two real and two complex. Find any real root y_1 of the cubic equation

$$8y^3 - 4by^2 + 2(ac - 4d)y - [c^2 + d(a^2 - 4b)] = 0$$

(see the previous exercise), and the four roots of the quartic are given by the roots of the two quadratic equations

$$x^2 + \left[\frac{a}{2} + \left(\frac{a^2}{4} + 2y_1 - b \right)^{1/2} \right]x + (y_1 + \sqrt{y_1^2 - d}) = 0$$

$$x^2 + \left[\frac{a}{2} - \left(\frac{a^2}{4} + 2y_1 - b \right)^{1/2} \right]x + (y_1 - \sqrt{y_1^2 - d}) = 0$$

(see Exercise 7 above).

★ 10. Investigate the way the times of sunrise and sunset are calculated from the latitude, longitude, and day of the year, and write a program to do the calculations. (See, for example, *Explanatory Supplement to the Astronomical Ephemeris and the American Ephemeris and Nautical Almanac*, prepared jointly by the Nautical Almanac Offices of the United Kingdom and the United States of America, Her Majesty's Stationery Office, London, 1961; or *Almanac for Computers 1984*, prepared by the Nautical Almanac Office, United States Naval Observatory, Washington, 1984.)

Modular Development and Debugging

Teach us to number our days,
that we may attain a wise heart.

—Bible:
Psalms 90:12

In this section we use functions to develop a program for a nontrivial application. You will see how a modular approach, in which you encapsulate program fragments, allows you to build a complicated, interrelated collection of functions with relative ease.

The problem we want to solve is this: Given two dates, compute the number of days elapsed from one date to the other. For example, from June 1, 1986 to June 20, 1986 there were 19 days. From December 25, 1983 to March 1, 1984 there were 67 days. John F. Kennedy was inaugurated on January 20, 1961 and assassinated on November 22, 1963, having been President of the United States for 1036 days. Though most people are aware of the basic rules by which the calendar works, the exact calculations are not obvious, and there are real applications for such a program, including the calculation of interest compounded daily and the prediction of such phenomena as eclipses.

Before we can start developing the program, we must ensure that we understand all the conditions to be satisfied. We will insist that the program work for any two dates from at least 1000 A.D. until 2200 A.D., and therein lies a subtle difficulty. There were two different calendars in operation during this time period: the *old style*, or *Julian*, calendar and the *new style*, or *Gregorian*, calendar. Our program will have to work properly with both. Therefore, we summarize the history and structure of these calendars before designing the algorithm and writing the program. Such background information is almost always needed to write a program.

The calendar in use today in most countries is the new style, or Gregorian, calendar, designed by a commission assembled by Pope Gregory XIII. The calendar is based on a 365-day year, divided into twelve months of lengths 31, 28, 31, 30, 31, 30, 31, 31, 30, 31, 30, and 31 days, in normal years and 366 days in leap years, the extra day added to make the second month 29 days long. A year is a leap year if it is divisible by 4 and is not a century year (multiple of 100) or if it is divisible by 400. The Gregorian calendar differs from its predecessor, the old style, or Julian, calendar only in that the Julian calendar did not include the century rule for leap years—all century years were leap years. (See Table 4.1 for a summary of these facts.)

Julius Caesar instituted the Julian calendar in 45 B.C. on the first of January, 709 years after the founding of Rome; it was a modification of the ancient Egyptian calendar. Since every fourth year was a leap year, a cycle of 4 years contained $4 \times 365 + 1 = 1461$ days, giving an average length of year of $1461/4 = 365.25$

Calendar	Leap Year Rule	Average Year Length
Julian (old calendar)	Every year divisible by 4	$\dfrac{4 \times 365 + 1}{4} = 365.25$
Gregorian (current calendar)	Years divisible by 4 *except* century years, which must be divisible by 400	$\dfrac{400 \times 365 + 97}{400} = 365.2425$
Month lengths (same on both calendars)	January = 31 days February = 28 days (29 in a leap year) March = 31 days April = 30 days May = 31 days June = 30 days	July = 31 days August = 31 days September = 30 days October = 31 days November = 30 days December = 31 days

Table 4.1   Summary of the rules governing the Julian (old style) and the Gregorian (current) calendars.

days. This is somewhat more than the actual length of the solar year, and over the centuries the calendar started to slip with respect to the solar year. By the sixteenth century, the date of the true vernal equinox had shifted from around March 21 to around March 11. If this error were not corrected, eventually Easter, whose date depends on the vernal equinox, would be in the summer. Pope Gregory instituted only a minor change in the calendar: Century years not divisible by 400 would no longer be leap years, giving an average length of year of $(400 \times 365 + 97)/400 = 365.2425$ days. However, he also corrected the accumulated 10-day error in the calendar by proclaiming that Thursday, October 4, 1582, the last date in the (old style) Julian calendar, would be followed by Friday, October 15, the first day of the new style (Gregorian) calendar. Catholic countries followed his rule, but Protestant and Orthodox countries resisted. Spain, Portugal, and Italy adopted it immediately, as did the Catholic states in Germany. The Protestant parts of Germany waited until 1700, Great Britain and its American colonies waited until 1752, Russia adopted the new calendar only after the revolution in 1918, and Bulgaria adopted it in 1920.

With this summary of the development of the calendar, we now face the heart of the problem: How are we to compute, say, the number of days George Washington lived—he was born February 11, 1732 on the Julian calendar and died on December 14, 1799 on the Gregorian calendar. Should we convert dates from one calendar to the other? If so, how do we do it? Before reading further, close the book and ponder the solution to this problem for an hour or so.

Here is our solution: We convert dates (on either calendar) to an *absolute date,* which we define as the number of days elapsed from some arbitrary starting point, absolute date 0. In this way, every day after that starting point is represented by a unique positive integer, and computing the number of days between two given dates will require only subtracting one absolute date from the other. Figure 4.1 shows the relationship between the Gregorian and Julian calendars, as they relate to the absolute date.

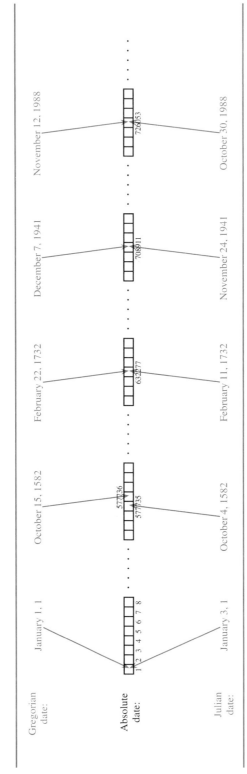

FIGURE 4.1 Time line displaying the relationship among the absolute date, the Julian calendar date, and the Gregorian calendar date. Each day is represented by a box; some boxes are labeled with the absolute date, corresponding Julian date, or Gregorian date.

What date should we choose as absolute date 0? We want a choice that makes the calculations easy, if possible, and will allow us to represent all dates from at least 1000 A.D. to 2200 A.D. We cannot easily use any date before the common era, since around 10 B.C. it was discovered that those in charge of the (Julian) calendar had added a leap day every third year instead of every fourth year, so to correct the error no further leap days were added until 4 A.D. A natural choice for absolute date 0, then, would be the day before January 1, 1 A.D. (Julian). However, that day was a Friday, and day-of-the-week calculations are more easily made if absolute date 0 is a Sunday (how? see page 125); such calculations are not mentioned in the specifications of the problem, but it costs us nothing to make the program robust enough to include them. Thus we choose to have Sunday, January 2, 1 A.D. (Julian) be absolute date 0. Another way to express this fact is to say that the *epoch* (that is, the start) of the Julian calendar is absolute date -2.

Before we face the problem of writing the program, we must figure out how to convert from Julian and Gregorian dates to absolute dates. The calculations are similar in each case. For a Julian date, say, Washington's birthday, February 11, 1732, we would calculate as follows: The years $1, 2, 3, \ldots, 1731$ contain $1731 \times 365 = 631{,}815$ days, ignoring leap years. Since every fourth year is a (Julian) leap year, the years $1, 2, 3, \ldots, 1731$ contain $1731/4 = 432$ leap days. Thus, the years $1, 2, 3, \ldots, 1731$ contain $631{,}815 + 432 = 632{,}247$ days. We must not include days of the Julian calendar that were before absolute date 0, so we must subtract 2 (that is, *add* the Julian epoch) giving 632,245 days from January 2, 1 A.D. (Julian) through December 31, 1731 (Julian). Now, since February 11 is the forty-second day of 1731, the absolute date of Washington's birthday is $632{,}245 + 42 = 632{,}287$.

The calculation for a Gregorian date is similar. If we extrapolate backward from the date of its inception, we find that the Gregorian date January 1, 1 A.D. corresponds to the Julian date January 3, 1 A.D., that is, to absolute date 1, so the epoch (that is, the start) of the Gregorian calendar is absolute date 0.[1] We can calculate just as we did for Julian dates, taking into account the century rule for Gregorian leap years. Thus the calculation goes as follows for February 22, 1732 (Gregorian): The years $1, 2, 3, \ldots, 1731$ contain $1731 \times 365 = 631{,}815$ days, ignoring leap years. As in the Julian case, we add $1731/4 = 432$ days to this for leap years, but we must subtract the century leap days wrongly included; for year n, we must subtract $(n/100)$, since $n/100$ is the number of century years that have passed. However, we've just subtracted away *all* the century years, including those that are multiples of 400; these *are* leap years, so we add them back. Thus we have found that there are

```
1731*365 + 1731/4 - 1731/100 + 1731/400
```

---

[1]Here is the explanation. The Julian and Gregorian calendars differed by 10 days in 1582. Since the years 100, 200, 300, 500, 600, 700, 900, 1000, 1100, 1300, 1400, and 1500 were Julian leap years but would not have been according to the Gregorian rule, going back to the year 1 means a Gregorian date would have been $12 - 10 = 2$ days before its Julian counterpart.

or 632,234 days from January 1, 1 A.D. (Gregorian) (which is absolute date 1) through December 31, 1731 A.D. (Gregorian). Since February 22 is the fifty-third day of 1732, the absolute date is $632,234 + 53 = 632,287$ (that is, February 22, 1732 is Washington's birthday according to the Gregorian calendar).

Notice that in the preceding calculations the integer values get fairly large. This can be a problem if the largest possible value on the computer is relatively small. For example, on so-called "16-bit" computers the largest integer value is $2^{15} - 1 = 32,767$ (the largest integer value that can be represented in 16 bits when one of those bits is used as the sign), then we would not be able to represent any date after absolute date 32,767, which is in 89 A.D. However, we continue here to assume what we have assumed all along: that we can represent integers at least as large as $2^{31} - 1 = 2,147,483,647$ (the largest integer value that can be represented in 32 bits when one of those bits is used as the sign), so that dates more than 5.8 million years hence can be represented.

Now that we've figured out what to calculate (the absolute date equivalent of the two dates) and how to calculate it, it's time to write the program. Although we cannot be clairvoyant and know in advance all the pieces that need to be written, we do know that we'll need to compute absolute dates and, for debugging purposes, read dates and check them for legitimacy. So we know we will need at least four functions, **getDate**, **dateIsLegal**, **absoluteFromGregorian**, and **absoluteFromJulian**, each of which performs a self-explanatory task. These are the only four functions that are apparent so far in the problem. As we think about how to write them, we will discover other functions needed as part of the task. Those functions, in turn, will lead to others, and so on. This is called a *top-down approach*, because we see the problem from the top in outline form and successively refine the outline by looking at each section in more detail, at each subsection in more detail, at each sub-subsection in more detail, and so on until we reach the bottom of the pyramid, where further refinement is unneeded; this process is called *stepwise refinement*. Following this approach suggests a logical order in which to begin writing the necessary parts. Eventually all (or most) of the constituent parts will become apparent. At that point we can begin writing them—the needs of debugging the individual parts dictates the order in which we write them.

top-down approach

stepwise refinement

We have already written a function to check that a date is legitimate, and it requires the functions **leapYear** and **lastDayOfMonth**, which we have also already written. Both of these functions need to be written for both the Gregorian and Julian calendars, however. It is easiest to start writing the program by concentrating on the Gregorian calendar, renaming the functions to indicate explicitly that they deal with this calendar:

```
boolean GregorianLeapYear (int y) {

// Returns true if y is a leap year according to the
// Gregorian calendar

// year must be a multiple of 4 and NOT a century
// year or must be a century year divisible by 400
```

```
      return (((y % 4) == 0) && ((y % 100) != 0))
             || ((y % 400) == 0);
   }

int lastDayOfGregorianMonth (int m, int y) {

// Returns the number of days in a given month and year
// on the Gregorian calendar

   switch (m) {
     case 2: if (GregorianLeapYear(y))
                 return 29;
             else
                 return 28;
     case 4:
     case 6:
     case 9:
     case 11: return 30;
     default: return 31;
   }
}

boolean GregorianDateIsLegal (int m, int d, int y) {

// Determine whether a given month, day, year is a legal date
// on the Gregorian calendar; date must be on or after
// Jan 1, 1 AD.

   return
     (1 <= y) &&                          // year is okay
     (1 <= m) && (m <= 12) &&             // month is okay
     (1 <= d) &&                          // day is...
     (d <= lastDayOfGregorianMonth(m,y)); //       ...okay
}
```

Now we take these three functions and use them as the basis of the three
similar functions for the Julian calendar:

```
boolean JulianLeapYear (int y) {

// Returns true if y is a leap year according to the
// Julian calendar

   // year must be a multiple of 4
   return ((y % 4) == 0);

}

int lastDayOfJulianMonth (int m, int y) {

// Returns the number of days in a given month and year
```

```
// on the Julian calendar

  switch (m) {
    case 2: if (JulianLeapYear(y))
                return 29;
            else
                return 28;
    case 4:
    case 6:
    case 9:
    case 11: return 30;
    default: return 31;
  }
}


boolean JulianDateIsLegal (int m, int d, int y) {

// Determine whether a given month, day, year is a legal date
// on the Julian calendar; date must be on or after Jan 3, 1 AD.

  return
    (1 <= y) &&                             // year is okay
    (1 <= m) && (m <= 12) &&                // month is okay
    (1 <= d) &&                             // day is...
    (d <= lastDayOfJulianMonth(m,y)) &&     //      ...okay
    (!((y == 1) && (m == 1) && (d < 3)));   // after Jan 2, 1 AD
}
```

We'd like to start debugging the six functions we've just written before we start writing something new. However, debugging what we have and checking our functions to compute absolute dates will require the ability to read the dates to be converted. Thus, it is reasonable to write the function **getDate** first. We must get a month, day, year, and calendar type:

```
void getDate (int& m, int& d, int& y, calendar& c) {

// Prompt the user for a date, accepting anything

  cout << "Enter month: ";    cin >> m;
  cout << "Enter day: ";      cin >> d;
  cout << "Enter year: ";     cin >> y;
  cout << "Enter 0 for Gregorian or 1 for Julian: ";
  int temp;
  cin >> temp;
  c = temp;

}
```

where we have defined

```
enum calendar {Gregorian, Julian};
```

This gives us the flexibility to allow other calendars (Jewish, Islamic, and so on, should we add them later).

Now we can debug the program pieces we have so far. The ability to debug sections of code separately is an advantage of modular programming. So we take the pieces that we have so far and put them into a program that does nothing but read a date with **getDate** and echo it back. In the following code we have put three dots in place of the details of the functions already given:

```
#include <iostream.h>
#include <iomanip.h>

enum boolean {false, true};

// GREGORIAN CALENDAR

int GregorianLeapYear (int y) {...}
int lastDayOfGregorianMonth (int m, int y) {...}
int GregorianDateIsLegal (int m, int d, int y) {...}


// JULIAN CALENDAR

int JulianLeapYear (int y) {...}
int lastDayOfJulianMonth (int m, int y) {...}
int JulianDateIsLegal (int m, int d, int y) {...}


// GENERAL CODE

enum calendar {Gregorian, Julian};

boolean dateIsLegal (int m, int d, int y, calendar c) {

// Determine whether a given month, day, year is a legal date
// on calendar c

  switch (c) {
    case Gregorian: return GregorianDateIsLegal(m,d,y);
    case Julian: return JulianDateIsLegal(m,d,y);
  }
}

void getDate (int& m, int& d, int& y, calendar& c) {...}

void printDate (int m, int d, int y, calendar c ) {

// Print a date

  cout << m << "/" << d << "/" << y;
  switch (c) {
    case Julian: cout << " (Julian)"; break;
    case Gregorian: cout << " (Gregorian)";
  }
}

main () {
  int year, month, day;
  calendar c;

  getDate(month,day,year,c);
```

```
      if (!dateIsLegal(m,d,y,c))
        cout << "\nThe date entered was not legal.\n";
      else {
        cout << "\nThe date entered was ";
        printDate(month,day,year,c);
        cout << "\n";
      }
    }
```

This debugging technique may seem like a waste of time—why not just continue to develop the program? The few minutes used for such a test can save hours of trouble later. It is far easier to pin down a problem with a handful of functions.

Once we are satisfied that all of the foregoing functions are correct, we are ready to write the **absoluteFromGregorian** and **absoluteFromJulian** functions, but first we need functions for the day number calculation (see page 59), modified for both the Gregorian and Julian calendars. For the Gregorian calendar:

```
int GregorianDayNumber (int month, int day, int year) {

// Calculate the day number in the year of Gregorian
// month/day/year

  // Calculate day number assuming all months have 31 days
  int number = (month - 1) * 31 + day;

  //Correct for months beyond February
  if (month > 2) {
    number = number - ((4 * month + 23) / 10);
    if (GregorianLeapYear(year))
      number = number + 1;
  };

  return number;
}
```

For the Julian calendar:

```
int JulianDayNumber (int month, int day, int year) {

// Calculate the day number in the year of Julian
// month/day/year

  // Calculate day number assuming all months have 31 days
  int number = (month - 1) * 31 + day;

  //Correct for months beyond February
  if (month > 2) {
    number = number - ((4 * month + 23) / 10);
    if (JulianLeapYear(year))
      number = number + 1;
  };

  return number;
}
```

It is good programming practice to define global symbolic constants for the absolute dates of the starting dates (epochs) of the two calendars. By defining such constants, all references to them can be centralized, and if we ever need to change the program (say, by choosing a different absolute date 0), it will be easy to do so:

```
const int GregorianEpoch = 0; // Absolute date of start
                              // of Gregorian calendar

const int JulianEpoch = -2;   // Absolute date of start
                              // of Julian calendar
```

The calculation of the absolute date from the Gregorian date is a matter of adding together the number of days in that year prior to that date, the number of days in years prior to that year, and the number of days before the epoch of the Gregorian calendar:

```
int absoluteFromGregorian (int month, int day, int year) {

// Calculate the absolute date of Gregorian date month/day/year

  return
    GregorianDayNumber(month,day,year) // days this year
      + 365*(year-1)                   // days in prior years
      + (year-1)/4                     // Julian leap years
      - (year-1)/100                   // century leap years
      + (year-1)/400                   // Gregorian leap years
      + GregorianEpoch;                // days before epoch
}
```

Similarly, for the Julian calendar, but with the Julian calendar's leap year rule:

```
int absoluteFromJulian (int month, int day, int year) {

// Calculate the absolute date of Julian date month/day/year

  return
    JulianDayNumber(month,day,year) // days this year
      + 365*(year-1)                // days in prior years
      + (year-1)/4                  // leap years
      + JulianEpoch;                // days before epoch
}
```

To test these functions, we add them to our program, changing the main program to

```
main () {
  int year, month, day;
  calendar c;

  getDate(month,day,year,c);
  if (!dateIsLegal(m,d,y,c))
    cout << "\nThe date entered was not legal.\n";
```

```
        else {
          cout << "\nThe date entered was ";
          printDate(month,day,year,c);
          cout << " = absolute date ";
          switch (calendar) {
            case Julian:
                  cout << absoluteFromJulian(month,day,year); break;
              case Gregorian:
                  cout << absoluteFromGregorian(month,day,year);
          }
          cout << "\n";
        }
    }
```

Satisfied that all this machinery works, we can finally write the main program we wanted all along—one that reads in two dates and computes the number of days elapsed between them:

```
main () {

    int y1, m1, d1, a1, y2, m2, d2, a2;
    calendar c1, c2;

    getDate(m1,d1,y1,c1);
    switch (c1) {
      case Julian: a1 = absoluteFromJulian(m1,d1,y1); break;
      case Gregorian: a1 = absoluteFromGregorian(m1,d1,y1);
    }

    getDate(m2,d2,y2,c2);
    switch (c2) {
      case Julian: a2 = absoluteFromJulian(m2,d2,y2); break;
      case Gregorian: a2 = absoluteFromGregorian(m2,d2,y2);
    }

    cout << a2-a1 <<" days from ";
    printDate(m1,d1,y1,c1);
    cout << " to ";
    printDate(m2,d2,y2,c2);
    cout << "\n";

}
```

4.6

Bells and Whistles

It often happens that after a program has been developed, either fully or partially, new applications come to light. In fact, it is usually the development and use of the program that stimulates suggestions for improvements or embellishments. So it is with the program for manipulating dates presented in the previous section;

among the possible additions to the date manipulations are determination of the day of the week from the date, conversion between equivalent Julian and Gregorian dates, determination of the season of the year, determination of the phase of the moon, inclusion of other calendars such as the Jewish, Islamic, and so on. We will examine one of these embellishments in this section, include others in the exercises, and use another in the next chapter to introduce additional programming techniques.

The day-of-the-week determination is simple to do because we were careful to start with absolute date 0 being a Sunday. Since the days of the week repeat in a cycle of 7, absolute dates 0, 7, 14, 21, ... will all be Sundays, absolute dates 1, 8, 15, 22, ... will all be Mondays, and so on. In other words, the remainder when the absolute date is divided by 7 determines the day of the week. We can write

```
int dayOfWeek(int m, int d, int y, calendar c ) {
switch (c) {
  case Julian: return (absoluteFromJulian(m,d,y) % 7);
  case Gregorian: return (absoluteFromGregorian(m,d,y) % 7);
  }
}
```

A more interesting question is how to convert between equivalent Julian and Gregorian dates. Since we already have C++ code to convert from these types of dates to absolute dates, writing a function that reverses the process (converts from an absolute date to a Julian or Gregorian date) will permit us to convert from a Julian date to the equivalent Gregorian date by using the absolute date as an intermediate. Thus, if we could write a function

```
int GregorianFromAbsolute(int date, int& m, int& d, int& y) {...}
```

that would set the values of **m**, **d**, and **y** to the date on the Gregorian calendar equivalent to the absolute date **date**, and a similar function

```
int JulianFromAbsolute(int date, int& m, int& d, int& y) {...}
```

that would set the values of **m**, **d**, and **y** to the date on the Julian calendar equivalent to the absolute date **date**, we would be able to write a function to convert, say, Julian to Gregorian dates as follows:

```
int GregorianFromJulian(int& m, int& d, int& y) {
  GregorianFromAbsolute(absoluteFromJulian(m,d,y),m,d,y);
}
```

Gregorian-to-Julian conversion is almost identical.

The question of how to write the function `GregorianFromAbsolute` remains. There is, unfortunately, no easy way to do this with the tools we have presented so far. The difficulty is that we know only the *theoretical average* number of days per year on the Julian or Gregorian calendars (365.25 and 365.2425, respectively). In practice, the *observed average* of the number of days per year will fluctuate around the theoretical value; these fluctuations make the conversion from absolute to Gregorian or Julian dates too messy to attempt without the techniques of Chapter 5. Think about the problem before seeing how we finally solve it in the next chapter.

4.7

Disastrous Results from Erroneous Input Data

In developing the program to compute the number of days elapsed between two given dates, we were careful to check the dates given for validity. How much trouble should a program go to in order to safeguard against improper input? Consider this excerpt from *The New York Times* of June 21, 1986:

> TYLER, Tex., June 20 (AP)—A computer malfunction apparently caused excessive radiation doses for two cancer patients at a treatment center, causing the death of one man, a Texas official said today. An identical machine at a Georgia treatment center unleashed a large radiation dose in June 1985 on a patient undergoing treatment for breast cancer, causing nerve damage.
>
> Bob Free, an investigator with the Texas Bureau of Radiation Control in Austin, said the two incidents at the East Texas Cancer Center appear to have been caused by a malfunction that occurred after the operator of the machine entered an erroneous command into the Canadian-made Therac 25 linear accelerator and then corrected it.
>
> The manufacturer, Atomic Energy of Canada, a Government-owned company, is taking corrective actions, which include a modification of the software, Mr. Higginbotham said.
>
> Dr. Kenneth Haile, director of the Kennestone Regional Oncology Center in Marietta, Ga., said an investigation into an accident there, begun as a result of the Texas cases, blamed a "software glitch" involving "an unforeseen sequence of computer commands." When a certain group of commands in the program were typed into the machine at a rapid rate of speed, it produced higher radiation than was called for, he said.
>
> Officials at the Texas center said a 66-year-old man, confined to a wheelchair and suffering from emphysema, died in April after receiving an excessive dose of radiation earlier in the month. Another patient, a 33-year-old man, received an excessive dose from the same machine March 25 and is being treated at a Dallas hospital, center officials said.
>
> In the case of the 33-year-old man, the operator began radiation treatment with the equipment after correcting an operator-entry command. The machine shut down immediately and flashed a malfunction message, Mr. Free said. The operator believed the patient had not received the treatment and reset the machine, he said. But the patient had experienced something like an electrical shock and was rolling off the table when the second dosage caught him in the shoulder and neck, Mr. Free said.
>
> Mr. Free said representatives of the clinic and manufacturer examined the machine and determined there was no electrical or other hazard. As a result, the ma-

chine was put back into use. Three weeks later, the same error was made on the 66-year old man. This time, Free said, the operator immediately shut down the machine.

Exercises—Third Set

Use any of the functions for date manipulations given in this chapter to complete the following exercises.

☞ 1. (a) Write a function to return the number of days left in a Gregorian year. The arguments to the function should be the month, day, and year.
   (b) Write a similar function for the Julian calendar.

2. Modify the function **printDate** so that it produces output like

   ```
   Sunday, August 31, 1986 (Gregorian)
   ```

   (Note the inclusion of the day of the week.)

3. According to some authorities the Julian year 4 A.D. was *not*, in fact, a leap year. Modify the functions developed in this chapter to do their computations in accordance with this opinion.

4. (a) To facilitate chronological reckoning, astronomers number days consecutively from January 1, 4713 B.C. (Julian), which is defined as *Julian day number* 0; days begin at Greenwich noon.[2] Under this numbering system, the year 1 A.D. is preceded by the year 0 (1 B.C.), which is preceded by the year −1 (2 B.C.), and so on. All years divisible by 4 are leap years, including years 0, −4, ... For example, the Julian day number for July 21, 1978 A.D. (Gregorian) is 2,443,711. Write a function **TotalJulianDayNumber** to compute the Julian day number from a date on either the Julian or Gregorian calendars.
   (b) Modify your function in part (a) so that it includes the fraction giving the time of day. For example, 0.125 corresponds to 3:00 P.M. Greenwich time and 7:30 A.M. Greenwich time corresponds to 0.8125 on the previous day, since 0.0 corresponds to noon.
   (c) The *modified Julian day number* is sometimes used to specify current dates; it is defined as the Julian day number minus 2,400,000.5. Modify your function in part (b) so that it computes the modified Julian day number. (*Warning*: Simply subtracting the value 2,400,000.5 may cause severe loss of precision.)

☞ 5. The seasons of the year are defined as

   Fall: September 21–December 20
   Winter: December 21–March 20
   Spring: March 21–June 20
   Summer: June 21–September 20

   Write a function that returns the season, given the month and day. Use the data type

   ```
   enum season {Fall, Winter, Spring, Summer};
   ```

---

[2] In *this* usage "Julian" does not refer to Julius Caesar but to the Renaissance physician Julius Scaliger (1484–1558), whose son Joseph (1540–1609) invented this reckoning system in order to be able to give a nonnegative day number to any event in recorded history.

6. (a) In a complete Gregorian cycle of 400 years there are $400 \times 12 = 4800$ thirteenths of the month. Since 7 does not divide 4800 evenly, it follows that the thirteenth of the month is more likely to fall on some days of the week than others. Write a program to compute the relative frequencies with which the thirteenth of the month falls on each weekday. (*Note*: Triskaidekaphobics will not be comforted by the results.)

   (b) In the United States, January 20 is inauguration day. Write a program to determine the relative frequencies with which this date falls on the various weekdays over a 400-year Gregorian cycle.

7. Daylight savings time moves the clock ahead one hour in the spring and back one hour in the fall. As of 1987 (and thus this applies only to the Gregorian calendar), daylight savings time begins on the first Sunday in April and ends on the last Sunday in October. Write a function **daysOfDaylightSavings** that computes the number of days of daylight savings time in a given year, which is a parameter of the function.

8. The signs of the zodiac are the 12 equal parts of the celestial sphere, each 30 degrees wide, bearing the name of a constellation for which they were originally named:

   Aries: March 21–April 19
   Taurus: April 20–May 20
   Gemini: May 21–June 21
   Cancer: June 22–July 22
   Leo: July 23–August 22
   Virgo: August 23–September 22
   Libra: September 23–October 23
   Scorpio: October 24–November 21
   Sagittarius: November 22–December 21
   Capricorn: December 22–January 19
   Aquarius: January 20–February 18
   Pisces: February 19–March 20

   Write a function that returns the sign of the zodiac, given the month and the day. Use the data type

   ```
   enum zodiacSign {Aries, Taurus, Gemini, Cancer, Leo, Virgo,
                    Libra, Scorpio, Sagittarius, Capricorn,
                    Aquarius, Pisces};
   ```

9. On average, the moon goes through its four phases (new, first quarter, full, third quarter) every 29.530588 days. Assuming that each of the phases is equally long and that the cycle repeats exactly after 29.530588 days, write a function that computes the number of days past the beginning of the current phase for any given absolute date. Use the data type

   ```
   enum moonPhase {newMoon, firstQuarter, fullMoon, thirdQuarter};
   ```

   and the function heading

   ```
   void phaseOfMoon (int absoluteDate,
                     moonPhase& phase,
                     int& daysPast)
   ```

The key piece of data you need is the exact phase of the moon at absolute date 0. Extrapolate from the new moon at 12:26 P.M. on December 4, 1983 (absolute date 724,248.5181, if we interpolate between December 4 and December 5 for the time of day). In comparing your results to the phases of the moon as specified on the calendar, you may be off by a day in either direction, because the assumptions made here are *not* very accurate.

10. Use the function **phaseOfMoon** in the previous exercise to calculate the date of Easter, defined as the Sunday following the full moon occurring after the vernal equinox (March 21 on the Gregorian calendar). (*Warning:* Since the moon phase calculation can be off by a day, your date for Easter can be off by as much as 4 weeks. There is no way to avoid this except by calculating the date of Easter as done in Exercise 6 on page 86.)

11. The Chinese New Year falls on the new moon nearest to the 15 degrees of Aquarius; on the Gregorian calendar this is about February 4. Use the function **phaseOfMoon** from Exercise 9 to calculate the date of the Chinese New Year for a given Gregorian year. (See the warning in the previous exercise.)

12. The Tibetan New Year, unlike the Chinese New Year (see previous exercise), falls on the full moon, as opposed to the new moon, nearest the 15 degrees of Aquarius. Use the function **phaseOfMoon** from Exercise 9 to calculate the date of the Tibetan New Year for a given Gregorian year. (See the warning in the two previous exercises.)

13. In the following parts, assume the enumerated type

    ```
    enum weekday {Sunday, Monday, Tuesday, Wednesday,
                  Thursday, Friday, Saturday};
    ```

    (a) Write a function

    ```
    int xdayOnOrBefore (int date, weekday x)
    ```

    to return the absolute date of the **x**-day of the week (Sunday, and so on) that falls in the seven-day period ending on absolute date **date**.

    (b) Explain how to use your function in part (a) to compute the absolute date of the **x**-day prior to a given absolute date, following a given absolute date, nearest to a given absolute date, and on or after a given absolute date.

    (c) Use your function in part (a) to write a function

    ```
    int nthXday (int n, weekday x, int month, int year)
    ```

    that determines the absolute date of the **nth x**-day in a given month in a given Gregorian year. Your function should count backward from the end of the month when **n** < 0.

14. Sadie Hawkins' day is the first Saturday in November. On this date, according to the *Li'l Abner* comic strip drawn by Al Capp, women and girls are encouraged to chase men. Write a function that returns the day in November on which Sadie Hawkins' day falls, given the year.

15. (a) Show how to compute the Julian year of occurrence of a given absolute date. (We will do this in the next chapter with loops, but a clever sequence of arithmetic operations suffices.)

    (b) Do the same for the Gregorian year.

16. The "ISO year" of the International Standardization Organization corresponds approximately to the Gregorian year, but weeks start on Monday and end on Sunday. The first week of the ISO year is the first such week that year in which there are at least 4 days. The ISO commercial date has the form *week day year*, in which *week* is in the range 1–52 and day is in the range 0–6 (1 = Monday, 2 = Tuesday, ..., 0 = Sunday). Write a function `absoluteFromISO` to compute the absolute date (with January 1, 1 A.D. Gregorian as absolute date 1) from an ISO date. Use the constant

```
const int ISO = 2;
```

and integrate your code with that given in this chapter for the Gregorian and Julian calendars.

17. (a) The Islamic calendar is computed, by the majority of the Moslem world, starting at sunset of July 16, 622 A.D. (Julian). In essence, Moslems count absolute date 227,016 = July 17, 622 A.D. (Julian) as the beginning of the Islamic year 1, with the understanding that a "day" begins the evening before. There are 12 Islamic months which contain, alternately, 29 or 30 days:

(1) Muharram	30 days	(7) Rajab	30 days
(2) Safar	29 days	(8) Sha'ban	29 days
(3) Rabi I	30 days	(9) Ramadan	30 days
(4) Rabi II	29 days	(10) Shawwal	29 days
(5) Jumada I	30 days	(11) Dhu al-Qada	30 days
(6) Jumada II	29 days	(12) Dhu al-Hijjah	29 or 30 days

The last month, Dhu al-Hijjah, contains 30 days in the 2nd, 5th, 7th, 10th, 13th, 16th, 18th, 21st, 24th, 26th, and 29th years of a 30-year cycle. Write a function `absoluteFromIslamic` to compute the absolute date (with January 1, 1 A.D. Gregorian as absolute date 1) from an Islamic date. Use the constants

```
const int IslamicEpoch = 227016; // Absolute date of start
                                 // of Islamic calendar
const int Islamic = 3;
```

and integrate your code with that given in the chapter for the Gregorian and Julian calendars and the ISO calendar of Exercise 16.

(b) A minority of Moslems begin their calendar at sunset of July 15, 622 A.D. (Julian). Everything else is as described in part (a) *except* that the 15th year in the 30-year cycle is a leap year, not the 16th. Modify your function `absoluteFromIslamic` to include a parameter to specify the majority or minority version of the Islamic calendar.

18. With the French Revolution, a new (but short-lived) calendar was adopted in France. The first day of the calendar was September 22, 1792 (absolute date 654,415). The year was divided into twelve months of thirty days each, followed by a five (six, in leap years)-day period called the "*sansculottides*." The months were named

(1) Vendémiaire (vintage)	(7) Germinal (seed)
(2) Brumaire (fog)	(8) Floréal (blossom)
(3) Frimaire (sleet)	(9) Prairial (pasture)
(4) Nivôse (snow)	(10) Messidor (harvest)
(5) Pluviôse (rain)	(11) Thermidor (heat)
(6) Ventôse (wind)	(12) Fructidor (fruit)

Each month was divided into *décades* of ten days each, with these days called Primidi, Doudi, Tridi, Quartidi, Quintidi, Sextidi, Septidi, Oxtidi, Nonidi, and Decadi. For example, November 1, 1792 would be referred to as "Décade II, Primidi de Brumaire de l'Année 1 de la Révolution." The days of the *sanscullottides* were given names: Vertu, Génie, Labour, Raison, and Récompense; the sixth day, Révolution, was added in leap years. For example, September 20, 1793 was called "Jour de la Raison de l'Année 1 de la Révolution." The leap year rule was originally based on the equinoxes and resulted in years 3, 7, and 11 being leap years; years 15 and 20 would have been leap years, had the calendar continued. The rule was then changed to make a year divisible by 4 a leap year, except that years divisible by 100 would be leap years only if they were divisible by 400, *except* that years divisible by 4000 were not leap years. (This rule was never implemented, however, because the calendar became defunct beforehand.)

(a) Write a function `absoluteFromFrench` to compute the absolute date (with January 1, 1 A.D. Gregorian as absolute date 1) from a French revolutionary date. (Treat the *sanscullottides* as a five- or six-day month.) Use the constants

```
const int FrenchEpoch = 654415; // Absolute date of start
                                // of French calendar
const int French = 4;
```

and integrate your code with that given in the chapter for the Gregorian and Julian calendars, the ISO calendar of Exercise 16, and the Islamic calendar of Exercise 17.

(b) Write a function `FrenchFromAbsolute` that converts an absolute date to its French revolutionary equivalent.

19. (a) The Copts, modern descendants of the Pharaonic Egyptians, use a calendar based on the ancient Egyptian solar calendar. Their calendar consists of twelve 30-day months (called by their Arabic names, Tot, Babe, Hatur, Kyak, Tobe, Amshir, Buramat, Baramude, Bashnas, Baune, Abib, and Meshri) followed by an extra five-day period (called Nisi). Once every fourth year a leap day is added to this extra period to make it six days (in which case it is called Kebus). The Copts count their years from August 29, 284 A.D. Julian (absolute date 103,605), the beginning of their year 1. Leap years occur when the Coptic year number leaves a remainder of 3 when divided by 4. Write a function `absoluteFromCoptic` to compute the absolute date (with January 1, 1 A.D. Gregorian as absolute date 1) from a Coptic date. (Treat Nisi as a five- or six-day month.)

(b) Write a function `CopticFromAbsolute` that converts an absolute date to its Coptic equivalent.

(c) The Ethiopian calendar is identical to the Coptic calendar except that the starting date is August 29, 7 A.D. Julian (absolute date 2430) and the month names are different (Maskarram, Tekemt, Hadar, Tahsas, Tarr, Yekatit, Magawit, Miaziah, Genbot, Sanni, Hamle, and Nas'hi; the five-day period is called Pagnem and the six-day period is called Quaggimi). Write a function `absoluteFromEthiopian` to compute the absolute date (with January 1, 1 A.D. Gregorian as absolute date 1) from an Ethiopian date. Also, write a function `EthiopianFromAbsolute` that converts an absolute date to its Ethiopian equivalent.

★ 20. Investigate the way the Hebrew calendar calculations are done [see, for example, "Calendrical Calculations" by N. Dershowitz and E. M. Reingold, *Software—Practice and Experience* **20** (1990), pages 899–928] and write a function `absoluteFrom-`

Hebrew to compute the absolute date (with January 1, 1 A.D. Gregorian as absolute day 1) from a given Jewish date. Since the Jewish calendar depends both on the lunar and solar cycles, this is much more complicated than either the purely solar Julian and Gregorian calendars or the purely lunar Islamic calendar.

★ 21. Investigate the way the Mayan calendar calculations are done [see, for example, "Calendrical Calculations, Part II: Three Historical Calendars" by E. M. Reingold, S. M. Clamen, and N. Dershowitz, *Software—Practice and Experience* **23** (1993), pages 383–404] and write a function **absoluteFromMayan** to compute the absolute date (with January 1, 1 A.D. Gregorian as absolute day 1) from a given Mayan date.

Summary

The task of writing large programs can be made manageable by breaking the (large) problem into bite-size pieces, writing and debugging programs for these bite-size pieces, and then assembling the programs thus written into a single program. C++ provides us with a way to encapsulate these bite-size pieces to make them independent of one another and easy to assemble. The encapsulations of code are called *functions*.

The program statements that constitute a function, called the *function definition*, look much like a whole program:

```
<type-returned> <name> (<parameterlist>)
<constant, type, and variable declarations>
<statements>
```

A function is used within a program by a *call* statement consisting of the function name, a parenthesized list of *actual parameters*, and a semicolon. There must be an exact match of the number, order, and types of the formal parameters and the actual parameters.

The mechanism used to specify the value to be returned by a function is the **return** statement:

```
return <value>
```

Except for functions that return **void**, a function returns a specific value as its result. A call to a function that returns **void** constitutes a C++ *statement* and can be used in any context in which C++ statements can be used; a call to a function that returns a *value* can be used in any context that a value of that type can be used.

The region of the program in which an identifier (variable, constant, or type) can be used is called its *scope*. A variable (or constant or type) to be used and understood everywhere in a program is declared at the beginning of the program and is called a *global variable* (or constant or type). In contrast, functions often include their own declarations of variables, constants, and types; these constants or variables are *local* and exist only during a call to that function. When a variable (or constant or type) is declared in a group of statements enclosed in braces { and }, then it is known only in that group of statements.

The most flexible programs are those that can be taken apart, reassembled, or expanded in modular parts. If the individual parts are well written, they can be individually debugged, used in other programs, and modified as new conditions arise without worrying about hidden interactions between parts of the program. For this reason, global variables should be avoided, but global constants and types are acceptable. Similarly, *side effects* should be avoided whenever possible. Side effects include a function changing the value of a variable that it did not declare.

Two types of parameters are used by functions. A *value parameter* is a local variable. Its initial value within the function is given as the argument to the function; nothing that happens to the variable within the function is seen by the outside. A *reference parameter* (indicated by an ampersand &) facilitates communication from the function being called back to whoever called it. Reference parameters allow the function to manipulate the actual parameter. Any changes made in the value of a reference parameter will be apparent in the calling function upon return.

The keywords introduced in this chapter are

```
void    char    return
```

5

Iteration

Chapter Preview

The `while` loop was introduced in Chapter 2 and was used in simple ways to cause the repetition of a group of statements. In this chapter we explore various mechanisms for the repetition of statements (iteration) and examine their use in detail. Special emphasis is placed on how to write a loop, how to ensure its correctness, and how to nest one loop within another.

"You are old, Father William," the young man said
"And your hair has become very white;
And yet you incessantly stand on your head—
Do you think, at your age, it is right?"

"In my youth," Father William replied to his son,
"I feared it might injure the brain;
But, now that I'm perfectly sure I have none,
Why, I do it again and again."

—Lewis Carroll
Alice's Adventures in Wonderland

W e introduced the concept of iteration in Chapter 1 by using a simple **while** loop to move the mouse through a maze. We used loops again in Chapter 2 to produce a table of equivalent temperatures in degrees Celsius and Fahrenheit. Our uses so far have been simple enough that the **while** loop was self-explanatory from its English-language meaning. Furthermore, we never asked you to write any loops—just to understand the loops we presented. In this chapter that will change. We'll discuss the construction of loops from simple instances to complex instances, and you'll learn how to design your own loops.

5.1

for **Loops**

Let's look again at the loop used in Chapter 2 to produce the Celsius/Fahrenheit table:

```
Celsius = -10.0;
while (Celsius <= 10.0) {
  Fahrenheit = (9.0/5.0) * Celsius + 32.0; // Convert C to F.
  cout << setw(7) << Celsius << "     "
       << setw(7) << Fahrenheit << "\n";
  Celsius++;   // Increment the Celsius value.
}
```

This kind of iteration, in which we increment a variable each time through the loop, is so common that C++ has a special form of looping mechanism that makes it easy to do exactly what is required—the **for** *statement*.

for statement

The **for** statement is written in the form

```
for (<statement1>; <condition>; <statement2>)
  <statement3>
```

and it causes **<statement3>**, called the *body of the loop*, to be executed repeatedly, as if we had written

```
<statement1>;
while (<condition>) {
  <statement3>;
  <statement2>;
}
```

Using a **for** statement, our temperature table loop can be rewritten as

```
cout << "DEGREES C  DEGREES F\n";
for (Celsius = -10.0; Celsius <= 10.0; Celsius++) {
  Fahrenheit = (9.0/5.0) * Celsius + 32.0;
  cout << setw(7) << Celsius << "     "
       << setw(7) << Fahrenheit << "\n";
}
```

The advantages of doing it this way are its compactness and simplicity. If we wanted to produce the table in reverse order, we could rewrite this as the **for** loop

```
for (Celsius = 10.0; Celsius >= -10.0; Celsius--)
```

so that all of the changes needed occur in the **for** statement, not spread throughout the loop.

We can use the **for** loop to write a function that computes k^n for integer values k and n, with $n \geq 0$. The heart of such a function, which we'll call **power**, is a **for** loop that multiplies by k a total of n times. We want to execute the instructions

```
int product = 1;
product = product * k;
       .
       .
       .
product = product * k;
```
$\left.\vphantom{\begin{array}{c} \\ \\ \\ \\ \\ \end{array}}\right\} n$ times.

We write

```
int product = 1;
for (int i = 1; i <= n; i++)
  // at this point power is k*k*k*...*k (i times)
  product = product * k;
```

This is equivalent to having written

```
int product = 1;
int i = 1;
while (i <= n) {
  // at this point power is k*k*k*...*k (i times)
  product = product * k;
  i++;
}
```

Scope of a Loop Index Variable

One consequence of the equivalence of the **for** loop and the **while** loop is that the **for** loop causes the variable i to be declared, initialized, and repeatedly incremented. After this **for** loop completes execution, the variable i has the value n+1. The scope of the variable i is the remainder of the program, so it must not be *declared* again in subsequent **for** loops. It can be used in those loops by writing i=1 rather than int i=1 as *<statement 1>*.

In the **while** loop above, if **n** is 0, the statement

```
product = product * k;
```

will never execute. The same is true in the **for** loop version—if the initial value of *<condition>* is false, then the body of the loop does not execute.

The complete function **power** would be

```
int power (int k,   // number to be raised to a power
           int n)   // power to which it's to be raised
{
   int product = 1;
   for (int i = 1; i <= n; i++)
      // at this point power is k*k*k*...*k (i times)
      product = product * k;
   return product;
}
```

Encapsulating it thus makes i into a local variable of the function **power**.

The function **power** is somewhat atypical, because the value of the loop variable i is never used in the body of the loop. In contrast, in the loop that produces the Celsius/Fahrenheit table the loop variable **Celsius** is used for computation within the body of the loop.

Let's look at an example that combines aspects of both the Celsius/Fahrenheit table calculation and **power**. We want to compute the mathematical function $n!$, read "n factorial," defined for nonnegative integers n by the formula

$$n! = \begin{cases} 1 & \text{if } n = 0, \\ 1 \times 2 \times \cdots \times n & \text{if } n \geq 1. \end{cases}$$

The function $n!$ appears often in mathematics and computer science because it has important combinatorial significance: It counts the number of ways to arrange n distinct objects in a row.

The calculation of $n!$ is done by executing the instructions

```
int product = 1;
product = product * 1;
```

```
product = product * 2;
      .
      .
      .
product = product * n;
```

We write

```
int product = 1;
for (int i = 1; i <= n; i++)
  // at this point product = 1 * 2 * ... * (i-1) = (i-1)!
  product = product * i;
```

However, we notice that the first multiplication (when i is 1) does nothing, so we change the initial value of i to 2. Encapsulating gives

```
int factorial (int n) {
  int product = 1;
  for (int i = 2; i <= n; i++)
    // at this point product = 1 * 2 * ... * (i-1) = (i-1)!
    product = product * i;
  return product;
}
```

As a final example of simple **for** loops, consider the problem of printing a calendar for a specified month, year, and calendar type. We want the output to look like this:

```
October, 1948
Sun  Mon  Tue  Wed  Thu  Fri  Sat
                              1    2
  3    4    5    6    7    8    9
 10   11   12   13   14   15   16
 17   18   19   20   21   22   23
 24   25   26   27   28   29   30
 31
```

In outline form, the function should

Print the title
Print the column headings
Print the numbers 1, 2, ..., lastDay in the correct columns

The last task is the hard one! We must skip some number of days on the first line so that 1 is printed in the correct column; then we write the dates one after another, writing a newline after writing a date corresponding to Saturday. Computing the **lastDay** is no problem, because we wrote **lastDayOfGregorianMonth** in Chapter 4 (page 118).

If the first day of the month is a Sunday, we skip 0 days on the first line; if it is a Monday, we skip 1 day, and so on. Since the absolute date is a multiple of 7 for Sunday, it is easy to calculate

```
int firstOfMonth = absoluteFromGregorian(month,1,year) % 7;
```

(see page 123 for details of **absoluteFromGregorian**) to tell us what day of the week the first of the month is and hence how many days to skip. In order to know when to end the current line by writing a newline, we also have to know which days are Saturdays. The first Saturday occurs on the $7 - $ **firstOfMonth** day of the month (why?), so if we write

```
int firstSaturday = 7 - firstOfMonth;
```

the Saturdays of the month will be on

```
firstSaturday
firstSaturday+7
firstSaturday+14
...
```

Thus, we know that the **ith** of the month is Saturday if

```
(i % 7) == (firstSaturday % 7)
```

(We might be tempted to write the test as

```
(i % 7) == firstSaturday
```

instead. Why is this wrong? What other statement could be changed to make this correct?)

Using symbolic constants **width** and **separation** to specify the width of a column in the calendar and the number of spaces between successive columns, respectively, the code needed to skip the days at the beginning and then print the dates properly is

```
// Leave firstOfMonth blank days on the first line
cout << setw(firstOfMonth*(width+separation)) << "";

// Write the days of the month, going to a new line
// after Saturday
for (int i = 1;
     i <= lastDayOfGregorianMonth(month,year);
     i++) {
  cout << setw(width) << i;
  if ((i % 7) == (firstSaturday % 7))
    // begin new week after Saturday
    cout << "\n";
  else
    // otherwise just add column separation
    cout << setw(separation) << "";
}
```

The statement

```
// Leave firstOfMonth blank days on the first line
cout << setw(firstOfMonth*(width+separation)) << "";
```

is a bit tricky. We are printing a string with *no* characters, but we are printing them in a field of width **firstOfMonth*(width+separation)**; this leaves **firstOfMonth** blank days at the beginning of the month.

The use of symbolic constants centralizes all references to the column width and separation in one place. Encapsulating the above lines of code as a function gives

```
void printGregorianCalendar (int month, int year) {

// Print a calendar for the specified month, year, (Gregorian)

    const int width = 3; //width of a column in the calendar
    const int separation = 2; //spaces between columns

    int firstOfMonth = absoluteFromGregorian(month,1,year) % 7;
                    // day of the week of the first of the month
                    // 0 means Sunday, 1 means Monday, etc.
    int firstSaturday = 7 - firstOfMonth;
                    // date of first Saturday in the month

    // Write the heading
    switch (month) {
      case 1:  cout << "January";   break;
      case 2:  cout << "February";  break;
      case 3:  cout << "March";     break;
      case 4:  cout << "April";     break;
      case 5:  cout << "May";       break;
      case 6:  cout << "June";      break;
      case 7:  cout << "July";      break;
      case 8:  cout << "August";    break;
      case 9:  cout << "September"; break;
      case 10: cout << "October";   break;
      case 11: cout << "November";  break;
      case 12: cout << "December";  break;
    }
    cout << ", " << year << "\n"
          << setw(width)            << "Sun"
          << setw(width+separation) << "Mon"
          << setw(width+separation) << "Tue"
          << setw(width+separation) << "Wed"
          << setw(width+separation) << "Thu"
          << setw(width+separation) << "Fri"
          << setw(width+separation) << "Sat"
          << "\n";

    // Leave firstOfMonth blank days on the first line
    cout << setw(firstOfMonth*(width+separation)) << "";

    // Write the days of the month, going to a new line
    // after Saturday
    for (int i = 1;
         i <= lastDayOfGregorianMonth(month,year);
         i++) {
      cout << setw(width) << i;
      if ((i % 7) == (firstSaturday % 7))
        // begin new week after Saturday
        cout << "\n";
```

```
        else
            // otherwise just add column separation
            cout << setw(separation) << "";
    }

    cout << "\n";
}
```

It would be better to encapsulate the writing of the month names in a separate function, but we'll leave that for you to do. Also, the above program is not quite perfect; see Exercise 1 on page 143.

5.2

Nested for Loops

Now that we've seen simple **for** loops, let's look at a harder example in which we must have one **for** loop nested inside another. We want a program to produce a wind-chill table that gives the equivalent wind-chill index for temperatures ranging from 50°F down to −60°F and wind speeds ranging from 0 mph up to 50 mph. Since the wind-chill index does not change much with small changes in either temperature or wind speed, we want the temperatures to descend from 50°F to −60°F by steps of 10°F and the wind speeds to increase from 0 mph to 50 mph in steps of 5 mph. Output of the program should look like that shown in Figure 5.1. Since we have already written the function **windChillIndex** (page 106), we can concentrate entirely on the necessary loop structure.

Here is the way to approach this type of loop construction. Write a list giving the sequence of actions that are to be done. For this example it is apparent from

```
TABLE OF WIND-CHILL INDICES
degrees F:    50    40    30    20    10     0   -10   -20   -30   -40   -50   -60

  0 mph:      50    40    30    20    10     0   -10   -20   -30   -40   -50   -60
  5 mph:      48    37    27    16     6    -5   -15   -26   -36   -47   -58   -68
 10 mph:      40    28    16     3    -9   -21   -34   -46   -58   -71   -83   -95
 15 mph:      36    22     9    -5   -18   -32   -45   -59   -72   -86   -99  -113
 20 mph:      32    18     4   -11   -25   -39   -53   -68   -82   -96  -111  -125
 25 mph:      30    15     0   -15   -30   -45   -59   -74   -89  -104  -119  -134
 30 mph:      28    13    -3   -18   -33   -49   -64   -79   -94  -110  -125  -140
 35 mph:      27    11    -5   -20   -36   -51   -67   -83   -98  -114  -130  -145
 40 mph:      26    10    -6   -22   -38   -54   -69   -85  -101  -117  -133  -149
 45 mph:      25     9    -7   -23   -39   -55   -71   -87  -103  -119  -135  -151
 50 mph:      25     9    -7   -23   -39   -55   -71   -87  -103  -119  -135  -151
```

FIGURE 5.1 The desired output from the program to produce a wind-chill table.

Figure 5.1 that we want to do the following:

Print the title
Print the heading line of the table
Print the first line of the table (0 mph wind-chill indices)
Print the second line of the table (5 mph wind-chill indices)
. . .
Print the ninth line of the table (50 mph wind-chill indices)

The pattern here is that after the title and heading line, we want to

Print the ith line of the table ($5 \times i$ mph wind-chill indices)

for $i = 0, 1, 2, \ldots, 10$. Thus we can outline the program to be written as

```
<print the title>
<print the heading line of the table>
for (int i = 0; i < = 10; i++) {
    <print the wind-chill indices for 5*i mph>
    <move to next output line>
}
```

Now we need to apply a similar analysis to the process of printing a line of wind-chill indices for `5*i` mph, one for each temperature $50°F, 40°F, \ldots, -60°F$. This amounts to

Print the label "`5*i mph:`" at the beginning of the line
Print the rounded wind-chill factor for `5*i` mph, $50°F$
Print the rounded wind-chill factor for `5*i` mph, $40°F$
. . .
Print the rounded wind-chill factor for `5*i` mph, $-60°F$

The pattern here is that after printing the label at the left of the row, we print the jth wind-chill index for $5 \times i$ mph and $10 \times j°F$ for $j = 5, 4, \ldots, -6$. After the last one is printed, we'll want to move to the next output line by writing a newline. Thus, the ith line of wind-chill indices is printed by

```
<print label 5*i mph>
for (int j = 5; j >= -6; j--) {
    <print the rounded wind-chill index of 5*i mph, 10*j degrees Fahrenheit>
}
```

Nesting this inside the other loop gives us the outline

```
<print the title>
<print the heading line of the table>
for (int i = 0; i <= 10; i++) {
    <print label 5*i mph>
    for (int j = 5; j >= -6; j--) {
        <print the rounded wind-chill index of 5*i mph, 10*j degrees Fahrenhei*
    }
    <move to next output line>
}
```

To print the heading line, we need to write the sequence of temperatures, 50°F, 40°F, ..., −60°F, across a line. This is done with a **for** loop almost identical to the inner **for** loop above:

```
for (int j = 5; j >= -6; j--) {
   <print the column heading 10*j degrees Fahrenheit>
}
<move to next output line>
```

Filling in the details of the printing of the various elements gives us the final program, in which we round a value by adding 0.5 to it and truncating (using the **floor** function):

```
#include <iostream.h>
#include <iomanip.h>
#include <math.h>

// Haim Reingold, March 16, 1994
// Produce a table of wind-chill indices

const int columnWidth = 5; //width of a column in the table

int round (float x) { return floor(x+0.5); }

float windChillIndex {...}  // details in Chapter 3

main () {
  cout << "TABLE OF WIND-CHILL INDICES\n";

  // write the column headings
  cout << "degrees F:";
  for (int j = 5; j >= -6; j--)
    cout << setw(columnWidth) << 10*j;  // column heading
  cout << "\n\n";

  for (int i = 0; i <= 10; i++) {
    cout << setw(columnWidth) << 5*i << " mph:"; // row label
    for (j = 5; j >= -6; j--)
      cout << setw(columnWidth)
           << round(windChillIndex(10*j,5*i));
    cout << "\n";
  }
}
```

Exercises—First Set

1. Fix the calendar printing program (page 140) to correct its minor flaws:
   (a) Encapsulate the printing of the month name into a function.
   (b) As written, the program prints an extra blank line when the last day of the month is Saturday; if the last day of the month is not a Saturday, the program prints **separation** extra blanks *after* the last day of the month. Fix these problems by appropriately testing whether **i** is the last day of the month.

2. Write a function **float sumOfRoots (int n)** to evaluate $\sum_{i=1}^{n} \sqrt{i}$.

3. (a) Evaluate the expression

$$\sum_{i=1}^{10,000} \frac{1}{i}$$

with two different **for** loops: First, use

```
for (int i = 1; i <= 10000; i++)
```

and then use

```
for (int i = 10000; i >= 1; i--)
```

★ (b) Explain why the values computed are not equal. Which is the more accurate value?

4. (a) Formulas for the sum of the first four powers of *n* integers are

$$\sum_{k=1}^{n} k = \frac{n(n+1)}{2}$$

$$\sum_{k=1}^{n} k^2 = \frac{n(n+1)(2n+1)}{6}$$

$$\sum_{k=1}^{n} k^3 = \frac{n^2(n+1)^2}{4}$$

$$\sum_{k=1}^{n} k^4 = \frac{n(n+1)(2n+1)(3n^2+3n-1)}{30}$$

Use these formulas in a program to produce a table of sums of powers of integers for the integers $1 \le n \le 40$. Your output should look like this:

```
SUMS OF POWERS OF INTEGERS
```

n	sum k	sum k*k	sum k*k*k	sum k*k*k*k
1	1	1	1	1
2	3	5	9	17
3	6	14	36	98
4	10	30	100	354
.				
.				
.				
40	820	22140	672400	21781332

(b) Write another program to produce the same table, but this time instead of using the formulas in part (a), accumulate the sums using the function **power** as you go along.

★ (c) Which program is more efficient? Why?

5. Modify your programs in the previous exercise so that a blank line is inserted after every fifth row of table entries; this makes the resulting table far more readable.

6. A certain famous state university issues paychecks to its faculty monthly on the twenty-first of the month. If the twenty-first is Saturday or Sunday, the checks are issued the previous Friday. Write a program to print a month-by-month list for the current year of the days and dates that paychecks will be issued.

7. (a) The sequence 0, 1, 1, 2, 3, 5, 8, ... of *Fibonacci numbers* is defined by the rule that each number is the sum of the previous two numbers. Write a program to print the first 20 Fibonacci numbers (using a symbolic constant `maxNumber = 20`).
   (b) Modify your program so that it prints the Fibonacci numbers four to a line.

8. Write a program to read a (Gregorian) year and determine which months have a Friday the 13th. Your output should look like this:

   ```
   OCCURRENCES OF FRIDAY THE 13TH


   Enter a year: 1903
   Friday the 13th occurs in February March November



   OCCURRENCES OF FRIDAY THE 13TH


   Enter a year: 1975
   Friday the 13th occurs in June



   OCCURRENCES OF FRIDAY THE 13TH


   Enter a year: 1945
   Friday the 13th occurs in April July
   ```

   (*Hint:* Every year contains at least one Friday the 13th.)

9. Write a program to determine how many Friday the 13ths occur in each year from 1900 to 1999 (Gregorian).

10. How often does your birthday fall on each day of the week during the years 1900 to 1999 (Gregorian)? Using symbolic constants for the years 1900 and 1999 and for the day and month of your birth, write a program to print the days of the week with the corresponding frequencies.

11. Write a program to compute and print the sum of the digits for the integers 150 to 180 (use symbolic constants!). The output should look like this:

    ```
    SUM OF DIGITS

    number    sum
      150      6
      151      7
        .
        .
        .
      180      9
    ```

12. Write a program to find and print a list of all numbers less than 3000 having the property that the number is equal to the sum of each digit in the number raised to the number of digits in the number. For example, $153 = 1^3 + 5^3 + 3^3$.

13. (a) Write a program to determine all integers less than 3,000,000 with the property that they equal the sum of factorials of their digits; $145 = 1!+4!+5!$ for example.
★ (b) Explain why no number above 3,000,000 can have this property.

14. Write a program to print an $n \times m$ array of asterisks; the variables n and m are positive integers to be read.

15. (a) There are 14 different year calendars possible—seven for January 1 falling on each day of the week in a nonleap year and seven more for a leap year. Print the 14 different calendars. (*Hint:* Use the function **printCalendar** inside a triple-nested loop.)
    (b) Write a program to print a table indicating which of the 14 different calendars to use for each year from 1900 to 1999 (Gregorian).

16. To assist a young friend learning to multiply, write a program to print the following multiplication table:

MULTIPLICATION TABLE

```
   1    2    3    4  ...  12

   2    4    6    8  ...  24

   3    6    9   12  ...  36

   .    .    .    .        .
   .    .    .    .        .
   .    .    .    .        .

  12   24   36   48  ... 144
```

17. Pascal's triangle consists of rows of coefficients of $(a + b)^n$ for $n = 0, 1, 2, \ldots$. The triangle looks like this:

```
                    1
                 1     1
              1     2     1
           1     3     3     1
        1     4     6     4     1
     1     5    10    10     5     1
                    .
                    .
                    .
```

where the values from left to right in the nth row are

$$\binom{n}{i} = \frac{n!}{i!(n-i)!}, i = 0, 1, 2, \ldots, n.$$

Write a program to print Pascal's triangle; the number of rows to be printed should be a symbolic constant. This is *not* an efficient method to produce Pascal's triangle—the point of the exercise is to construct the loops involved. (*Hint:* Use the **for** loop indices in **setw** to get the proper alignment of the values.)

18. Write a program to print the following table:

```
THE NUMBER OF EACH DAY OF THE YEAR

Day of                              Day of
Month   Jan   Feb   Mar   ...   Nov   Dec    Month

  1      1     32    60    ...   305   335      1
  2      2     33    61    ...   306   336      2
  3      3     34    62    ...   307   337      3
  .      .      .     .           .     .       .
  .      .      .     .           .     .       .
  .      .      .     .           .     .       .
 28     28     59    87    ...   332   362     28
 29     29      *    88    ...   333   363     29
 30     30            89   ...   334   364     30
 31     31            90   ...         365     31


*In leap years, after February 28,
add 1 to the tabulated number.
```

19. Using the formulas given on page 79, write a program to print a size chart of women's panty hose. Your output should look approximately like this:

```
PANTY HOSE SIZE CHART

weight (lbs):   100   105   110   ...   180   185   190

        58 in:         A     A     ...   F     F     F
        59 in:   A     A     A     ...   F     F     F
        60 in:   A     A     A     ...   F     F
        61 in:   A     A     A     ...   F
           .
           .
           .
        72 in:
```

20. Write a program to print a table for the years 1988 to 2008 of when the U.S. Supreme Court begins its session—it is always on the first Monday in October.

21. Write a function (similar to **printCalendar**) to print a "wall calendar" in the style shown in Figure 5.2. The function should have parameters to specify the month and year (assume the Gregorian calendar), as well as the dimensions of the box for each day.

```
+------------------------------------------------------------------------+
|OCTOBER, 1948                                                           |
+------------------------------------------------------------------------+
|Sunday   |Monday   |Tuesday  |Wednesday|Thursday |Friday   |Saturday |
+------------------------------------------------------------------------+
|         |         |         |         |         | 1       | 2       |
|         |         |         |         |         |         |         |
|         |         |         |         |         |         |         |
|         |         |         |         |         |         |         |
+------------------------------------------------------------------------+
| 3       | 4       | 5       | 6       | 7       | 8       | 9       |
|         |         |         |         |         |         |         |
|         |         |         |         |         |         |         |
|         |         |         |         |         |         |         |
+------------------------------------------------------------------------+
|10       |11       |12       |13       |14       |15       |16       |
|         |         |         |         |         |         |         |
|         |         |         |         |         |         |         |
|         |         |         |         |         |         |         |
+------------------------------------------------------------------------+
|17       |18       |19       |20       |21       |22       |23       |
|         |         |         |         |         |         |         |
|         |         |         |         |         |         |         |
|         |         |         |         |         |         |         |
+------------------------------------------------------------------------+
|24       |25       |26       |27       |28       |29       |30       |
|         |         |         |         |         |         |         |
|         |         |         |         |         |         |         |
|         |         |         |         |         |         |         |
+------------------------------------------------------------------------+
|31       |         |         |         |         |         |         |
|         |         |         |         |         |         |         |
|         |         |         |         |         |         |         |
|         |         |         |         |         |         |         |
+------------------------------------------------------------------------+
```

FIGURE 5.2   A sample of the desired output from the program of Exercise 21 to produce a wall calendar.

22. Parts of Europe use the calendar printed as follows with Monday as the first day of the week and Sunday as the last:

```
October, 1948 (Gregorian)

Mon   Tue   Wed   Thu   Fri   Sat   Sun

                          1     2     3
  4     5     6     7     8     9    10
 11    12    13    14    15    16    17
 18    19    20    21    22    23    24
 25    26    27    28    29    30    31
```

Rewrite the function **printCalendar** to produce this form of calendar.

23. Write a program to read a year (Gregorian) and print a calendar for that year in the following style:

```
CALENDAR PRINTING PROGRAM

Enter a Gregorian year: 1948
```

	M	T	W	T	F	S	S	M	. . .	T	W	T	F	S	S	M	T
Jan				1	2	3	4	5	. . .	27	28	29	30	31			
Feb						1	2	. . .	24	25	26	27	28	29			
Mar	1	2	3	4	5	6	7	8	. . .	30	31						
Apr				1	2	3	4	5	. . .	27	28	29	30				
May					1	2	3	. . .	25	26	27	28	29	30	31		
Jun		1	2	3	4	5	6	7	. . .	29	30						
Jul				1	2	3	4	5	. . .	27	28	29	30	31			
Aug						1	2	. . .	24	25	26	27	28	29	30	31	
Sep			1	2	3	4	5	6	. . .	28	29	30					
Oct					1	2	3	4	. . .	26	27	28	29	30	31		
Nov	1	2	3	4	5	6	7	8	. . .	30							
Dec			1	2	3	4	5	6	. . .	28	29	30	31				

(*Warning:* The output will require paper that is at least 120 characters wide.)

24. The nth roots of the complex number $x + iy$ are

$$r^{1/n}\left[\cos\left(\frac{\theta + 2k\pi}{n}\right) + i\sin\left(\frac{\theta + 2k\pi}{n}\right)\right]$$

for $k = 0, 1, 2, 3, \ldots, n - 1$ where $r = \sqrt{x^2 + y^2}$ and $\theta = \arctan(y/x)$. Write a program to read the real and imaginary parts of a complex number and a value for n, and then calculate and print the nth roots of a complex number. Be careful to avoid division by zero.

5.3

while **Loops**

Because you have been using simple **while** loops all along, you don't need much of an introduction. The C++ statement

```
while (<condition>)
    <statement>
```

repeatedly executes **<statement>** (which, of course, can be a compound statement surrounded by braces **{ }**) as long as **<condition>** is true. If we're careless in writing the loop and the condition never becomes false, the loop will continue to execute forever—an *infinite loop*.

infinite loop

while Conditions and Type float

Recall from Bug Alert 3.3 (page 57) that equal/not equal comparisons with type **float** may be unreliable because of inexact representation. This means that you must be careful *not* to have the end condition of a **while** loop rely solely on an expression such as **(x != 0)** where **x** is type **float**. In the unlucky event that **x** is inexactly represented, it may never be zero, and the loop will be an infinite loop.

Missing Output and Infinite Loops

Missing output (see page 32) can occur if a program gets into an infinite loop when characters are waiting in the output buffer. To be sure you've got all the output, use **flush** or **endl** when debugging loops.

Let's begin our study of **while** loops by writing a function that gets a date from the user and checks it for legitimacy, rejecting illegal dates and asking the user to try again. Most interactive programs need functions like this to ensure that the user's input is correct and can be processed. A standard way to write such code is as a **while** loop with the structure

```
<get data>
while (<data are unacceptable>) {
  <issue warning>
  try to get data again>
}
```

The step *get data* in this outline means get a month, day, year, and calendar type; such a step is done by our function **getDate** (page 120). Putting this function into the outline, we get

```
void getLegalDate (int& m, int& d, int& y, calendar& c ) {

// Prompt the user for a date, accepting only if it is proper

  cout << "\n";
  getDate(m,d,y,c);
  while (!dateIsLegal(m,d,y,c)) {
    cout << "\nNot a valid date, try again.\n\n";
    getDate(m,d,y,c);
  }
}
```

As our second example of **while** loops, let's solve the problem mentioned at the end of Chapter 4: We want to convert between Julian and Gregorian dates by using the absolute date as our intermediate stage. For the purposes of this section, all you need to recall is that the absolute date is the number of days elapsed since January 1, 1 A.D. (Gregorian), and is computed by the function

```
int absoluteFromGregorian (int month, int day, int year)
```

which we wrote in Chapter 4 (page 123). Now we need to write a function that goes in the other direction, converting an absolute date to its Gregorian or Julian equivalent.

Solving this problem requires determining the year, month, and day from the absolute date. First, we'll find the year. It would be nice if we could reason as follows: The average Gregorian (Julian) year has 365.2425 (365.25) days, so the year corresponding to an absolute date can be found by dividing the absolute date by 365.2425 (365.25). This simple reasoning is flawed, however, because the "average" is only theoretical—any given year will have either 365 or 366 days. Using the Gregorian calendar, for example, we find that January 1, 5 A.D., is absolute date 1462, but we find

$$\frac{1462}{365.2425} = 4.002820044,$$

suggesting that we need to round up to get the year. However, for December 31, 4 A.D., we would get

$$\frac{1461}{365.2425} = 4.000082137,$$

so rounding up is not correct. Similarly, rounding down is not correct either. There is no fixed, simple relationship between the absolute date and the year.

Instead of a fixed relationship, we turn to "brute force." That is, we exploit one of the computer's strengths to do the determination in a way that we would never dream of using by hand. We try, in turn, each year 1, 2, 3, . . . until we find the correct one. This method is inefficient, but it works! (We'll make it efficient later.) For an absolute date **date**, we want to ask, in turn,

Is **date** beyond year 1?
Is **date** beyond year 2?
Is **date** beyond year 3?
.
.
.

and we keep asking the question until we get "no" as the answer. Rewriting the sequence of questions in a parameterized form, that is,

```
year = 1;
Is date beyond year year?
year++;
```

Is `date` beyond year `year`?
`year++;`
Is `date` beyond year `year`?

.

.

.

makes the loop structure clear:

```
year = 1;
while (<date is beyond year>)
   year++;
```

How do we phrase the question "Is `date` beyond year `year`?" The last day of the year `year` is December 31, and its absolute date is given by

```
absoluteFromGregorian(12, 31, year)
```

where `absoluteFromGregorian` is the function we wrote in Chapter 4 (page 123). If

```
absoluteFromGregorian(12, 31, year) < date
```

then `date` is beyond the year `year`. We thus compute the year in which a given absolute date occurs with the program fragment

```
year = 1;
while (absoluteFromGregorian(12, 31, year) < date)
   year++;
```

We can improve the efficiency of this calculation by reflecting on how we would do this calculation by hand. Although we might have to go year-by-year at some point, we would not likely begin at year 1, especially if the absolute date were very large. We would be guided by common sense telling us that absolute date 706,828 occurs near the Gregorian year 1935, because $706{,}828/365.2425 \approx 1935$. To use this approach with the preceding `while` loop, we must always be certain to find an approximate year no later than the actual year. Since there are never more than 366 days in a year, the absolute date `date` cannot occur before the year, given by

$$\text{year} = \text{smallest integer past } \texttt{date/366}$$

Using the function `ceil`, which gives the next higher integer of a number (page 25), we can rewrite the loop to determine the year as follows:

```
year = ceil(date/366.0);
while (absoluteFromGregorian(12, 31, year) < date)
   year++;
```

The above is not quite correct, however, because `ceil(date/366)` does not give the result we expect: `date/366` gives an `int` result, just the quotient of the integer division. This causes problems when `date` < 366, because the result of the division will be truncated to 0, so the ceiling will be 0, and hence **year** will be 0; then we'll be calling **absoluteFromGregorian(12, 31, 0)**, which causes an error (why?). We want to compute **date/366** *exactly* and only then apply the ceiling function, so we must change the expression to **ceil(float(date)/366)**, giving

```
// find the year
year = ceil(float(date)/366);
while (absoluteFromGregorian(12, 31, year) < date)
  // date falls in a year after year
  year++;
```

Having found the correct year, we find the correct month, using the same logic that we applied to finding the year. We ask the series of questions

Is **date** beyond the end of January in year **year**?
Is **date** beyond the end of February in year **year**?
.
.
.

and rephrase them as the loop

```
// find the month
month = 1;
while (absoluteFromGregorian(
              month,
              lastDayOfGregorianMonth(month,year),
              year)
         < date)
    // date falls in a month after month in year year
    month++;
```

We could compute a higher starting value than 1 for **month**, just as we did for **year**, but it is not worth it, because the loop will be executed at most 11 times.

Now that we know the year **year** and the month **month**, we can find the day by computing the absolute date of the beginning of the month **month** in the year **year**:

```
day = date - absoluteFromGregorian(month,1,year) + 1;
```

Casting all the preceding into a function gives

```
void gregorianFromAbsolute (int date,    // absolute date
                            int& month,  // equivalent month,
                            int& day,    //          ... day,
                            int& year)   //          ... year
{

// Calculate the Gregorian month/day/year of absolute date

  // find the year
  year = ceil(float(date)/366);
  while (absoluteFromGregorian(12, 31, year) < date)
    // date falls in a year after year
    year++;
```

```
// find the month
month = 1;
while (absoluteFromGregorian(
               month,
               lastDayOfGregorianMonth(month,year),
               year)
         < date)
  // date falls in a month after month in year year
  month++;

// find day
day = date - absoluteFromGregorian(month,1,year) + 1;
}
```

5.3.1 Verifying Loops

Before we look at further examples of **while** loops and their construction, let's pause a moment and examine the preceding **while** loops. In particular, there are three issues that we need to discuss:

1. Do the loops always terminate?
2. Do they always compute the correct value when they terminate?
3. After how many iterations do they terminate?

Perhaps in the cases of the two loops in **GregorianFromAbsolute** the answers to these questions are obvious, but even so, we need to develop the tools to analyze and verify the correctness of more subtle loops that come later. Verifying that a loop terminates with the correct result is an essential part of loop construction! Knowing how many iterations it takes is essential to understanding its efficiency.

Verifying that a **while** loop terminates involves showing that no matter what happens in the body of the loop, eventually the condition will be false. In the case of

```
// find the year
year = ceil(float(date)/366);
while (absoluteFromGregorian(12, 31, year) < date)
  // date falls in a year after year
  year++;
```

we have only to observe that each time through the loop, **year** is increased by one, and that **absoluteFromGregorian(12, 31, year)** gets bigger and bigger as **year** gets bigger and bigger. Eventually then, the loop condition must fail, since **date** does not have its value changed during the loop.

The correctness of this loop follows from the parenthetical comment, "**date** falls in a year after **year**." More formally, the value **year** satisfies

$$1 \le \text{year} \le \text{actual year}$$

loop invariant   This property is called a *loop invariant*; that is, it is a description of the state of all variables that must be true at that point in the loop every time the loop is executed. Whenever we are at the beginning of the loop, the loop invariant tells us the relationships among all relevant variables. We have been careful to state such loop invariants in all but the most trivial loops in this book. You should be similarly careful in writing programs. Take it as a rule of thumb that if you cannot adequately give the loop invariant for a loop, you do not understand what the loop is doing!

We use the loop invariant to infer the correctness of the loop for determining the year **year** by the following reasoning:

1. The value **year** as assigned initially satisfies $1 \leq$ **year** $\leq$ actual year.
2. Once in the loop, we know that **date** falls after year **year**, so **year** < actual year; hence, **year** $+ 1 \leq$ actual year.
3. We do not go on to the next iteration of (or enter into) the loop if **date** falls within year **year**; that is, if **year** $=$ actual year.

These three statements mean, respectively, that

1. The loop invariant is true the first time through the loop.
2. The loop invariant remains true through an iteration of the loop.
3. The loop terminates at the value we want.

A similar analysis applies to the **while** loop for finding the month, based on the invariant "**date** falls in year **year** after month **month**."

5.3.2 Analyzing the Number of Iterations of a Loop

Finally, we're left with the question of how many iterations it will take before the loop terminates. The answer depends, of course, on how close our first approximation, `ceil(float(date)/366.0)`, is to the actual year. We won't be very precise here, but we'll give an analysis that supports a claim to efficiency.

In the Gregorian calendar the absolute date will be approximately 365.2425 $\times$ **year**, because 365.2425 is the theoretical average number of days per year. The starting value for the loop is then

$$\texttt{ceil(float(date)/366.0)} \approx \frac{365.2425 \times \textbf{year}}{366.0} = \textbf{year} - \frac{0.7575}{366.0}\textbf{year}$$

The error here is about $(0.7575/366.0) \times$ **year** $\approx 0.002 \times$ **year**—this tells us how many times the loop will advance **year**. For dates in the latter half of the twentieth century, $0.002 \times$**year** is approximately 4, meaning the loop will be executed 4 times. For earlier dates the loop will be executed fewer times, while for later dates it will be executed more times; for example, dates near 1000 A.D. will require about 2 iterations, whereas dates near 4000 A.D. will require about 9 iterations. In any case, the number of times the loop will be executed is small.

We will not go through such a detailed analysis for every loop we write in this book, but we will give the loop invariant, from which the correctness of the loop easily follows. We will also usually make some comments on the number of iterations. Again, we emphasize that you also should give loop invariants for your loops, as well as give some consideration to the number of iterations.

For our second example of **while** loop construction, we present one of the oldest numerical algorithms known—the greatest common divisor algorithm of

Euclid of Alexandria (circa 300 B.C.), which is found in Euclid's *Elements* (Book VII, propositions 1 and 2). Because this algorithm has great historical and mathematical importance, we'll use it to introduce a more intricate analysis of loops.

Given two positive integers u and v, we want to determine the largest integer that divides evenly into both u and v. For example, the greatest common divisor of 24 and 52 is 4, the greatest common divisor of 30 and 75 is 15, and the greatest common divisor of 13 and 42 is 1. Try to read the algorithm as described in Euclid's *Elements* (translated by Sir Thomas L. Heath, Dover Publications, New York, 1956):

> Thus it is required to find the greatest common measure of AB, CD. If now CD measures AB—and it also measures itself—CD is a common measure of CD, AB. And it is manifest that it is also the greatest; for no greater number than CD will measure CD. But, if CD does not measure AB, then, the less of the numbers AB, CD being continually subtracted from the greater, some number will be left which will measure the one before it . . .
>
> Now let CD, measuring BE, leave EA less than itself, let EA, measuring DF, leave FC less than itself, and let CF measure AE. Since then, CF measures AE, and AE measures DF, therefore CF will also measure DF. But it also measures itself; therefore it will also measure the whole CD. But CD measures BE; therefore CD also measures BE. But it also measures EA; therefore it will also measure the whole BA. But it also measures CD; therefore CF measures AB, CD. Therefore CF is a common measure of AB, CD.
>
> I say next that it is also the greatest. For, if CF is not the greatest common measure of AB, CD, some number which is greater than CF will measure the numbers AB, CD. Let such a number measure them, and let it be G. Now, since G measures CD, while CD measures BE, G also measures BE. But it also measures the whole BA; therefore it will also measure the remainder AE. But AE measures DF; therefore G will also measure DF. But it also measures the whole DC; therefore it will also measure the remainder CF, that is, the greater will measure the less: which is impossible. Therefore no number which is greater than CF will measure the numbers AB, CD; therefore CF is the greatest common measure of AB, CD.

Did you slog through all of that archaic description? Don't worry if you didn't—we included it here for its historical interest and to illustrate the necessity of a clear and concise description of an algorithm. Although, as we'll see, the algorithm here is simple, the language in which it is couched obscures its simplicity and structure. To understand what the archaic language means, we must be aware that Euclid wrote in terms of line segments AB, CD, and so on, instead of integers; he uses "measures" as we would use "divides evenly into."

Here is a more intelligible description of Euclid's algorithm: Given two positive integers u and v, we compute the greatest common divisor by taking the larger of these two integers, say, u, and subtracting the smaller of them, say, v, repeatedly as long as the difference is positive. Applying this to 13 and 42, we get

$$42 - 13 = 29$$
$$29 - 13 = 16$$
$$16 - 13 = 3$$

Now, Euclid's algorithm continues, we apply the *same process* to v, the smaller of the two original integers (in this case, 13), and the final difference (in this case, 3):

$$13 - 3 = 10$$
$$10 - 3 = 7$$
$$7 - 3 = 4$$
$$4 - 3 = 1$$

Again, we apply the same process, but this time to the last two final differences (3 and 1):

$$3 - 1 = 2$$
$$2 - 1 = 1$$
$$1 - 1 = 0$$

Arriving at a final difference of 0, we stop, having found that 1 (the last nonzero integer) is the greatest common divisor of 13 and 42.

The successive subtractions that Euclid used are just computing the remainder of an integer division: 42 divided by 13 leaves a remainder of 3, 13 divided by 3 leaves a remainder of 1, and 3 divided by 1 leaves a remainder of 0. In C++ we can compute the remainder directly with the % function, so we would shorten the preceding computation to

$$42 \ \% \ 13 = 3$$
$$13 \ \% \ 3 = 1$$
$$3 \ \% \ 1 = 0$$

concluding that since 1 is the last nonzero remainder, it is the greatest common divisor.

In general, we would formulate Euclid's algorithm as: Given two numbers u and v, compute

$$
\begin{aligned}
r_0 &= \text{larger of } u \text{ and } v \\
r_1 &= \text{smaller of } u \text{ and } v \\
r_2 &= r_0 \ \% \ r_1 \\
r_3 &= r_1 \ \% \ r_2 \\
&\vdots
\end{aligned}
$$

with the process stopping when r_i divides r_{i-1} evenly, that is, when $r_{i+1} = 0$. The greatest common divisor must be r_i. Why? Euclid's language may be archaic, but his logic is sound: Because $r_{i+1} = 0$, r_i divides r_{i-1}. But

$$r_i = r_{i-2} \ \% \ r_{i-1}$$

and hence

$$r_{i-2} = q \times r_{i-1} + r_i,$$

for some quotient q, and so r_i also must divide r_{i-2} (why?). Similarly, because r_i divides both r_{i-1} and r_{i-2}, it must divide r_{i-3}, since

$$r_{i-2} = r_{i-3} \% r_{i-1}.$$

Continuing upward in this way, we find that r_i must divide both r_0 and r_1; that is, it must divide our original numbers u and v. This convinces us that r_i is a common divisor of u and v.

Why must it be the largest? If there is a larger common divisor, say d, then we can follow the chain of equations downward: Because d divides both u and v (that is, r_0 and r_1), it follows that d must divide

$$r_2 = r_0 \% r_1$$

because $r_0 = q \times r_1 + r_2$. Similarly, because d divides r_1 and r_2, it must divide

$$r_3 = r_1 \% r_2$$

Continuing downward, we find that d must divide r_i, so $d \le r_i$. This convinces us that no common divisor is larger than r_i.

Observe that the properties of the % operator guarantee that the preceding process works just as well even if we do not worry about which is the larger of u and v. If we write

$$
\begin{aligned}
r_0 &= u \\
r_1 &= v \\
r_2 &= r_0 \% r_1 \\
r_3 &= r_1 \% r_2 \\
&\vdots
\end{aligned}
$$

then when $u \ge v$, this is what we had before. But if instead $u < v$, then $u \% v = u$, so the assignment

$$r_2 = r_0 \% r_1$$

assigns r_2 the value u, so we have

$$
\begin{aligned}
r_0 &= u \\
r_1 &= v \\
r_2 &= u \\
r_3 &= r_1 \% r_2 \\
r_4 &= r_2 \% r_3 \\
&\vdots
\end{aligned}
$$

In other words, the process continues as if we *had* worried about which of u or v was larger.

To implement Euclid's algorithm in C++, we need only to keep track of the last two values, not the entire history. We can write

```
int lastRemainder = u;
int remainder = v;
int nextRemainder;
```

```
if (remainder == 0) then lastRemainder is the gcd
nextRemainder = lastRemainder % remainder;
lastRemainder = remainder;
remainder = nextRemainder;
if (remainder == 0) then lastRemainder is the gcd
nextRemainder = lastRemainder % remainder;
lastRemainder = remainder;
remainder = nextRemainder;
if (remainder == 0) then lastRemainder is the gcd
nextRemainder = lastRemainder % remainder;
lastRemainder = remainder;
remainder = nextRemainder;
    .
    .
    .
```

Casting this into a **while** loop gives

```
int lastRemainder = u;
int remainder = v;
int nextRemainder;
while (remainder != 0) {
    // gcd of u and v is also gcd of remainder and lastRemainder
    nextRemainder = lastRemainder % remainder;
    lastRemainder = remainder;
    remainder = nextRemainder;
    // lastRemainder > remainder >= 0
}
```

This loop always terminates, because the value of **remainder** grows smaller at each step but is always nonnegative; eventually, it must reach 0, and the loop will end.

The loop invariant here comes directly from Euclid's logical argument that the last nonzero remainder must be the greatest common divisor. When we enter the loop for the first time, the loop invariant is true, because **lastRemainder = u** and **remainder = v**. If the loop invariant is true at one iteration of the loop, it follows that it must be true at the next iteration if the loop continues to another iteration. Let r_{i-1} and r_i be the values of **lastRemainder** and **remainder** at the beginning of the ith iteration (so that $r_0 = u$, $r_1 = v$); then on the $(i + 1)$st iteration we have

$$r_{i+1} = r_{i-1} \% r_i$$

The truth of the invariant on the ith iteration means that the greatest common divisor of u and v equals the greatest common divisor of r_i and r_{i-1}. But we can write $r_{i+1} = r_{i-1} -$ (a multiple of r_i), by the definition of %, it follows that the greatest common divisor of r_i and r_{i-1} is also the greatest common divisor of r_{i+1} and r_i, so the invariant will be true on the next iteration. If there is no $(i + 1)$st iteration, it must be because $r_{i+1} = 0$, meaning r_{i-1} is a multiple of r_i, so r_i is the greatest common divisor of r_{i-1} and r_i, and hence, by the invariant, $r_i =$ **lastRemainder** is the greatest common divisor of u and v. Thus, we know that the loop correctly determines the greatest common divisor.

Encapsulating the loop we have just written, we get a function for the greatest common divisor:

```
int greatestCommonDivisor(int u, int v) {
// finds greatest common divisor of nonnegative integers u and v
  int lastRemainder = u;
  int remainder = v;
  int nextRemainder;
  while (remainder != 0) {
    // gcd of u and v is also gcd of remainder and lastRemainder
    nextRemainder = lastRemainder % remainder;
    lastRemainder = remainder;
    remainder = nextRemainder;
    // lastRemainder > remainder >= 0
  }
  return lastRemainder;
}
```

How many iterations are necessary before the loop in the function ends? The answer to this question is simply stated, but its derivation involves a bit of mathematical thought. It can be proved that if both u and v have at most n digits, then the number of iterations is at most approximately $4.785n$.

To derive this limit on the number of iterations, we reason as follows (the non–mathematically inclined reader should skip the remainder of this section). We observed that the remainders decrease in value each time through the loop; we make this observation more precise by noting that in general

$$r_{i-1} \geq r_i + r_{i+1}$$

Why is this so? Assume that $u \geq v$, so that $r_0 \geq r_1$ because $r_0 = u$ and $r_1 = v$ (if $u < v$, there will be one extra iteration, as already discussed). We know that the definition of r_{i+1} is the remainder when r_{i-1} is divided by r_i:

$$r_{i+1} = r_{i-1} \% r_i$$

or, in other words,

$$r_{i-1} = (\text{some multiple of } r_i) + r_{i+1}.$$

Since $r_{i-1} > r_i$, the "multiple of r_i" cannot be zero, so

$$r_{i-1} \geq r_i + r_{i+1}$$

for $i = 1, 2, \ldots$ This means we have a chain of inequalities:

$$
\begin{aligned}
r_0 &\geq r_1 + r_2 \\
r_1 &\geq r_2 + r_3 \\
r_2 &\geq r_3 + r_4 \\
&\vdots
\end{aligned}
$$

Suppose that the algorithm ends after k iterations with $r_{k+1} = 0$, so r_k is the greatest common divisor sought. Then successive substitution in the chain of inequalities leads to

$$r_0 \geq r_1 + r_2$$
$$\geq (r_2 + r_3) + r_2 = 2r_2 + r_3$$
$$\geq 2(r_3 + r_4) + r_3 = 3r_3 + 2r_4$$
$$\geq 3(r_4 + r_5) + 2r_4 = 5r_4 + 3r_5$$
$$\geq 5(r_5 + r_6) + 3r_5 = 8r_5 + 5r_6$$
$$\vdots$$
$$\geq F_k r_k + F_{k-1} r_{k+1} = F_k r_k$$

where $F_0, F_1, F_2, \ldots$ are the so-called Fibonacci sequence $F_0 = 0$, $F_1 = 1$, $F_{i+1} = F_i + F_{i-1}$. (This sequence is discussed further in Chapter 8.) Since r_k is the greatest common divisor, $r_k \geq 1$ gives

$$r_0 \geq F_k.$$

If both u and v have at most n digits, then because $u = r_0 \geq v = r_1$, we know

$$10^n > F_k.$$

Mathematicians have proved that the value of F_k is

$$F_k = \text{round}\left[\frac{1}{\sqrt{5}} \left(\frac{1 + \sqrt{5}}{2} \right)^k \right] \approx \frac{1}{\sqrt{5}} \left(\frac{1 + \sqrt{5}}{2} \right)^k.$$

(How they proved this result needn't concern us now.) Thus,

$$10^n > \frac{1}{\sqrt{5}} \left(\frac{1 + \sqrt{5}}{2} \right)^k$$

and taking logarithms and solving for k gives

$$\frac{n}{\log_{10}\left(\frac{1+\sqrt{5}}{2}\right)} + \frac{\log_{10}\sqrt{5}}{\log_{10}\left(\frac{1+\sqrt{5}}{2}\right)} > k.$$

$1/\log_{10}\left(\frac{1+\sqrt{5}}{2}\right) \approx 4.785$, so k, the number of iterations, is at most approximately $4.785n$ on n-digit numbers.

Exercises—Second Set

1. There is a medieval puzzle about an old woman and a basket of eggs. On her way to market a horseman knocks her down and the eggs are all broken. The horseman will pay for the eggs, but the woman does not remember the exact number she had, only that when she took the eggs in pairs, there was one left over; similarly, there was one left over when she took them three, four, five, or six at a time. When she took them seven at a time, however, she came out even. Write a program to determine the smallest number of eggs the woman could have had.

2. Suppose we change the initialization in **GregorianFromAbsolute** to

   ```
   year = ceil(float(date)/365.2425);
   ```

   Explain why the loop no longer works correctly.

3. (a) Write a program `reverseDigits` that reads an integer and prints the number with its digits reversed. Your output should look like this:

```
DIGIT REVERSAL

Enter a positive integer: 12345

The integer with digits reversed is: 54321
```

Your program should ignore leading zeros, so that the reversal of `12000` is `21`.

(b) Rewrite your program from part (a) so that `reverseDigit` is a function with the heading:

```
int reverseDigits ( int n )
```

(c) A number **n** that satisfies

```
n = reverseDigits(n)
```

is called a palindrome. Thus, for example, 121 is a palindrome, but 41 is not. Use your function in part (b) to write a function with the heading

```
boolean palindrome ( int n )
```

to determine whether **n** is a palindrome.

(d) Consider the following process. Start with any positive integer that is not a palindrome, say, 48. Add 48 to its reversal, 84; we get $48 + 84 = 132$. Since 132 is not a palindrome, we add it to its reversal to get $132 + 231 = 363$ and we stop, having reached a palindrome. Write a program that reads an integer and applies the preceding process zero or more times until a palindrome results. Your program should count the number of times a number must be added to its reversal to reach a palindrome. Be sure your loop stops before an integer occurs that is too large for type **int** on your computer; for example, starting with 89 will require integers larger than $2^{31} - 1$ and so will be impossible on a 32-bit computer.

(e) Modify your program from part (d) to find the smallest integer that requires integers larger than can be represented on your computer with type **int**.

4. Find appropriate loop invariants for the two **while** loops in the algorithm for getting the mechanical mouse through the maze in Chapter 1. (*Hint:* It will be helpful to imagine that the mouse has a piece of chalk in its right paw and that it marks the wall as it walks along. Your invariant should include a statement to the effect that no wall in the maze can be marked twice.)

5. Write a date conversion function **IslamicFromAbsoluteDate** similar to the function **GregorianFromAbsoluteDate** given in this section. (See Exercise 17 on page 130.)

★   6. Write a date conversion function **HebrewFromAbsoluteDate** similar to the function **GregorianFromAbsoluteDate** given in this section. (See Exercise 20 on page 131.)

7. Consider the following process, which can be applied to any positive integer: If the integer is odd, multiply it by 3 and add 1; if the integer is even, divide it by 2. This process is repeated until the integer remaining is 1. As an example, consider 34; the process terminates in 13 steps, producing the following sequence: 34, 17, 52, 26, 13, 40, 20, 10, 5, 16, 8, 4, 2, 1. We stop the process when 1 occurs.

(a) Write a program to apply this process to each integer from 1 to 1000 and keep track of the largest number of steps required by the process to terminate and the largest intermediate number generated (52 in the example above).
(b) Modify your program in part (a) to continue as far past 1000 as you can without getting values too large for your computer.

5.4

do-while **Loops**

C++ has an alternative to **while** loops for indefinite repetition. The **do-while** loop looks like this:

```
do
    <statement>
while (<condition>);
```

and behaves just as its appearance suggests: *<statement>* is executed again and again until *<condition>* is false. The difference between this and a **while** loop is that in a **do-while** loop the boolean condition is checked *after* the body of the loop is executed, and as a consequence the body of the loop is *always* executed at least once.

Anything we can do with a **while** loop we can do with a **do-while** loop, and vice versa:

```
while (<condition>)
    <statement>;
```

is exactly the same as

```
if (<condition>)
    do
        <statement>
    while (<condition>);
```

In similar fashion,

```
do
    <statement>
while (<condition>);
```

is exactly the same as

```
<statement>
while (<condition>)
    <statement>;
```

where the same statement in the **do-while** loop body is copied before the **while** loop in addition to forming its body.

Although **do-while** loops offer us no new power, they can make the programs we write clearer for humans to read. The advantage of a **do-while** loop occurs when the body of the loop must always be executed at least once, no matter what. For example, we can use the loop

```
do
  <try to get input data>
while (<data are unacceptable>);
```

as a cleaner, more compact version of

```
<try to get input data>
while (<data are unacceptable>)
  <try to get input data>
```

Consider the following loop to count the number of digits in an **int number**:

```
numberOfDigits = 0;
rest = number;
while (rest > 0) {
  // The number of digits in number is numberOfDigits
  // plus the number of digits in rest
  rest = rest / 10;
  numberOfDigits++;
};
```

This loop provides correct output only for positive integers; it fails to work when **number** ≤ 0. We can correct this by changing the **while** condition to **rest != 0**, but this still fails for **number** $= 0$, which has, by convention, one digit. Instead of checking this case separately, it is easiest to make the loop work for *all* integer values by rewriting it as

```
numberOfDigits = 0;
rest = number;
do {
  // The number of digits in number is numberOfDigits
  // plus the number of digits in rest
  rest = rest / 10;
  numberOfDigits++;
} while (rest != 0);
```

In this way the body of the loop is always executed at least once, even for **number** $= 0$. Notice that the loop invariant was not affected by our reorganization of the loop.

5.5

Choosing an Appropriate Loop Structure

In this section we'll examine two problems involving loop construction and show how to derive the appropriate loop structure. For our first problem we want to read test scores and compute the minimum, maximum, and average scores. Imagine someone sitting at the computer and entering a sequence of scores; after entering the last score, the person signals the end of the data by entering a special character that indicates the *end of file* (eof). This character, which varies from computer to computer, is commonly a control-d (that is, the "control" key held while typing the "d" key); we will show it as ^D. The dialog should look like this:

end of file

```
Enter score (eof ends the data): 85
Enter score (eof ends the data): 62
Enter score (eof ends the data): 93
Enter score (eof ends the data): 87
Enter score (eof ends the data): 51
Enter score (eof ends the data): ^D

5 scores were entered.
The average score was 75.6
The maximum score was 93
The minimum score was 51
```

There are many questions to answer in writing this program. How do we calculate the average? The maximum? The minimum? What should the loop look like? Although these questions are interrelated, we can't answer all of them at once. The natural place to start is with the loop structure, so we will conceal the problems of how to compute the average, maximum, and minimum scores by lumping all this under the description "process the test score." The sequence of actions we want the program to take is

Read a test score
If end of file, stop the loop
Process the test score
Read a test score
If end of file, stop the loop
Process the test score
Read a test score
If end of file, stop the loop
⋮
Process the test score
Read a test score
If end of file, stop the loop

These actions can be grouped either with the test as the first statement of a loop (that is, use a **while** loop) or with the test as the last statement of a loop (that is, use a **do-while** loop), as shown in Figure 5.3. The organization as a **while** loop is preferable here, because to use the **do-while** loop we need

```
<read score>
if (<not end of file>)
  do {
    <process score>
    <read score>
  } while (<not end of file>);
```

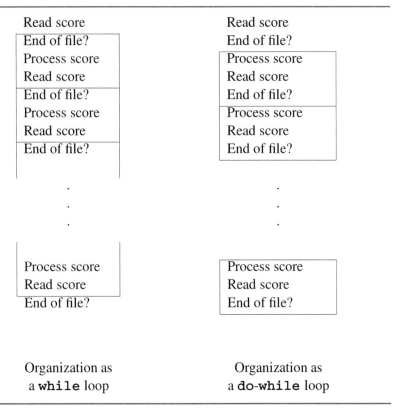

Read score	Read score
End of file?	End of file?
Process score	Process score
Read score	Read score
End of file?	End of file?
Process score	Process score
Read score	Read score
End of file?	End of file?

Organization as
a **while** loop

Organization as
a **do-while** loop

FIGURE 5.3   The two possible organizations of the loop for reading and processing
scores.

whereas using a **while** loop we can write

```
<read score>
while (<not end of file>) {
  <process score>
  <read score>
}
```

which is more desirable because it is shorter, clearer, and more natural.

With the loop structure set, we can examine what the processing entails. First, and most important, how do we test for the end-of-file condition? We just use **!cin.eof()** as a true/false value: **cin.eof()** is true when the last use of **cin** encountered the end of file; it is false if the last use of **cin** did *not* encounter the end of file. Thus, the loop we need looks like

```
<read score>
while (!cin.eof()) {
  <process score>
  <read score>
}
```

To compute the average value, we will need to keep track of the number of scores entered and their sum. Therefore, the processing must include statements such as

```
numberOfScores++;                        // new score
sumOfScores = sumOfScores + score;   // update sum
```

and the loop invariant must include the facts that the value of **numberOfScores** is the number of scores that have been read and that their sum is the value of **sumOfScores**. For such an invariant to be true the first time through the loop, the initialization of the loop must include

```
int sumOfScores = 0;
int numberOfScores = 0;
```

The program so far looks like this:

```
int sumOfScores = 0;
int numberOfScores = 0;

cout << "Enter score (eof ends the data): "; cin >> score;

while (!cin.eof()) {
  numberOfScores++;                        // new score
  sumOfScores = sumOfScores + score;   // update sum

  // The numberOfScores is the number of scores read so far and
  // sumOfScores is their sum

  cout << "Enter score (eof ends the data): "; cin >> score;
}
```

Once the loop has ended, the average score is easily computed as

```
float(sumOfScores) / numberOfScores
```

We need the **float** so that the division used will not be integer division, since we want some precision in the average value.

Notice that in the preceding loop we have the loop invariant in the middle of the loop; this allows a slightly simpler loop invariant. If we had put the loop invariant at the beginning of the loop, it would have to say that **numberOfScores** and **sumOfScores** do not include the last score read.

To add the computation of the maximum and minimum scores, we first decide what needs to be added to the loop invariant. Once written, the invariant will guide us in writing the C++ statements. In parallel with our invariant relationship between **numberOfScores** and **sumOfScores**, we want to have **maxOfScores** and **minOfScores**, with the property that they are, respectively, the largest and the smallest of the scores that have been read. The complete invariant can be stated as

```
// The numberOfScores is the number of scores read so far
// and sumOfScores is their sum; maxOfScores is the largest
// score and minOfScores is the smallest score read so far
```

To maintain the truth of this augmented invariant, we augment the loop to include the statements

```
if (maxOfScores < score)           // new largest score
  maxOfScores = score;
if (minOfScores > score)           // new smallest score
  minOfScores = score;
```

We also must initialize **maxOfScores** and **minOfScores** so that the loop invariant will be true the first time. This is done by making both **maxOfScores** and **minOfScores** equal to the first score read. Finally, we must be careful to check that at least one score was entered; otherwise the computation will result in an error, trying to divide by zero. The resulting program is

```
#include <iostream.h>
#include <iomanip.h>

// Arthur L. Reingold, October 31, 1994.

// Read scores and compute the minimum, maximum, and average
// scores.  Scores are read until the user types an
// end-of-file character.

void main() {
  int score;
  int sumOfScores = 0;
  int numberOfScores = 0;

  cout << "Enter score (eof ends the data): "; cin >> score;
  int maxOfScores = score;
  int minOfScores = score;

  while (!cin.eof()) {
    numberOfScores++;                          // new score
    sumOfScores = sumOfScores + score;  // update sum
    if (maxOfScores < score)                   // new largest score
      maxOfScores = score;
    if (minOfScores > score)                   // new smallest score
      minOfScores = score;

    // The numberOfScores is the number of scores read so far
    // and sumOfScores is their sum; maxOfScores is the largest
    // score and minOfScores is the smallest score read so far

    cout << "Enter score (eof ends the data): "; cin >> score;
  }

  if (numberOfScores == 0)
    cout << "\nNo scores were entered.\n";
  else if (numberOfScores == 1)
    cout << "\nOnly one score was entered.  It was "
         << sumOfScores << "\n";
  else
    cout << "\n\n" << numberOfScores
         << " scores were entered.\n"
         << "The average score was "
```

```
              << float(sumOfScores)/numberOfScores << "\n"
              << "The maximum score was " << maxOfScores << "\n"
              << "The minimum score was " << minOfScores << "\n";
    }
```

The break **Statement in Loops**

The **break** statement, which we introduced and used in the context of **switch** statements in Chapter 3, can also be used to terminate the execution of the iteration statements **for**, **while**, and **do-while**. When a **break** is encountered during the execution of one of these loops, the loop ends immediately, and execution continues with the statement following the loop.

The use of a **break** in loops can simplify writing code in what is sometimes called the *loop-and-a-half problem*. Let's reconsider the loop we used to read scores repeatedly in the example of the previous section. We needed the loop

```
<read score>
while (!cin.eof()) {
  <process score>
  <read score>
}
```

but what we really wanted was to execute the statements

```
<read score>
<process score>
```

as long as there are scores to process. The difficulty is that we had to do *<read score>* to find out that there are no more scores. In other words, we really want to execute the loop

```
while (true) {
  <read score>
  <process score>
}
```

an extra "half time," quitting in the middle when the *<read score>* fails. The **break** statement allows us to do just that:

```
while (true) {
  <read score>
  if (cin.eof()) break;
  <process score>
}
```

This style of read-process loop is advantageous when the "read" part is complex, because the code does not get reproduced in two places—both before and in the middle of the loop.

5.7

A Last Example

As the final example in this chapter, let's consider a problem for which we need all the ideas introduced on iteration. We want to read a number and determine its *prime factorization*. A number is *prime* if it is not divisible by any positive integer other than 1 and itself; 1 is not considered to be a prime. For example, 2, 5, 17, and 4,598,731 are primes, whereas 6 and 35 are not prime. Every integer $2, 3, 4, \ldots$ can be written as a product of powers of primes; for example,

$$
\begin{array}{llll}
& 10 = 2^1 5^1 & 20 = 2^2 5^1 & 30 = 2^1 3^1 5^1 \\
& 11 = 11^1 & 21 = 3^1 7^1 & 31 = 31^1 \\
2 = 2^1 & 12 = 2^2 3^1 & 22 = 2^1 11^1 & 32 = 2^5 \\
3 = 3^1 & 13 = 13^1 & 23 = 23^1 & 33 = 3^1 11^1 \\
4 = 2^2 & 14 = 2^1 7^1 & 24 = 2^3 3^1 & 34 = 2^1 17^1 \\
5 = 5^1 & 15 = 3^1 5^1 & 25 = 5^2 & 35 = 5^1 7^1 \\
6 = 2^1 3^1 & 16 = 2^4 & 26 = 2^1 13^1 & 36 = 2^2 3^2 \\
7 = 7^1 & 17 = 17^1 & 27 = 3^3 & 37 = 37^1 \\
8 = 2^3 & 18 = 2^1 3^2 & 28 = 2^2 7^1 & 38 = 2^1 19^1 \\
9 = 3^2 & 19 = 19^1 & 29 = 29^1 & 39 = 3^1 13^1 \\
\end{array}
$$

The product of the prime powers equal to *n* is called the *prime factorization* of *n*. Although it's beyond the scope of this book, the development of algorithms to factor a number into prime factors has a long, interesting history and many important applications. The most remarkable application today is in the design of secure encryption schemes for the transmission and storage of confidential data. We want to write a program with output like this:

```
Enter an integer (> 1) to be factored: 98888
    Prime  Exponent
       2       3
      47       1
     263       1
```

We'll want the program to continue prompting for input forever until the user types an end-of-file character. This means we want the overall structure of the program to be

```
while (true) {
  <read number to be factored>
  if (cin.eof()) break;
  <print heading>
  <find and print prime factors>
}
```

solving the loop-and-a-half problem with a **break** statement, as we saw in the previous section. The **<read number to be factored>** must ignore numbers less than 2 and end execution when the user types an end-of-file character:

```
      n = 0;
      while ((n < 2) && !cin.eof()) {
        cout << "\nEnter an integer (> 1) to be factored: ";
        cin >> n;
      }
```

Thus, we write

```
      const int w = 10;    // field width for list of primes

      void main() {
        int n;      // number to be factored
        while (true) {
          n = 0;
          while ((n < 2) && !cin.eof()) {
            cout << "\nEnter an integer (> 1) to be factored: ";
            cin >> n;
          }
          if (cin.eof()) break;
          cout << setw(w) << "Prime" << setw(w) << "Exponent" << "\n";
          factorize(n);
        }
        cout << "\n";
      }
```

Now we can concentrate on **factorize**, which finds and prints the prime factorization.

The algorithm is to find the smallest proper (larger than 1) divisor of the **n**; this divisor must be prime, for if it had a proper divisor, then *that* divisor would be a smaller proper divisor of **n**. Having found a prime divisor, we divide it out of **n** as many times as possible (keeping count of how many times we divide it out), and print a row for that prime divisor. Then we repeat the process with the reduced value of **n**. Thus the sequence of actions to be taken is

Find the smallest divisor (the prime)
Divide it out (the exponent)
Print the prime and exponent
Number remaining = 1?
Find the smallest divisor (the prime)
Divide it out (the exponent)
Print the prime and exponent
Number remaining = 1?

$\vdots$

This is exactly the right structure for a **do-while** loop:

```
      void factorize(int number) {
        do {
          <find the smallest divisor (the prime)>
          <divide it out to find the exponent>
          <print the prime and exponent>
        } while (number > 1);
      }
```

The middle line of the **do-while** loop—computing the exponent by dividing out the divisor as many times as possible—requires the actions

Exponent = 0
number a multiple of **divisor**?
Divide it out
Increment **exponent**
number a multiple of **divisor**?
Divide it out
Increment **exponent**
number a multiple of **divisor**?

$\vdots$

Since we know that **divisor** divides **number** evenly, the preceding actions will increment **exponent** at least once. These actions can be performed by either a **while** loop or a **do-while** loop:

```
exponent = 0;
while ((number % divisor) == 0) {
   // we've removed divisor exponent times
   number = number / divisor;
   exponent++;
}
```

works just as well as

```
exponent = 0;
do {
   // we've removed divisor exponent times
   number = number / divisor;
   exponent++;
} while ((number % divisor) == 0);
```

We decide to use the **while** form of the loop, preferring it in general when both forms are equally simple to apply, because the **<condition>** occurs at the start, making the code easier to read.

It remains to find the smallest (prime) divisor of **number**. We want to try 2, 3, 5, 7, 9, ... as possible divisors of **number**, continuing until we reach a value that is too large to be the smallest divisor of **number**.

We want to answer the sequence of questions

Does 2 divide **number**?
Does 3 divide **number**?
Does 5 divide **number**?
Does 7 divide **number**?
Does 9 divide **number**?

$\vdots$

But continuing how far? A moment's reflection tells us that if $p^2 > n$, then p cannot possibly be the smallest prime factor of n. Suppose an integer p divides n, and $p^2 > n$. Then we can write

$$n = p \times q$$

for some integer q (in fact, $q = n/p$). Because $p^2 > n$, $q < p$. For example,

$$60,887,083 = 96,493 \times 631$$

But that means that p is not the *smallest* prime divisor of n.

The loop can be written to stop when `divisor*divisor <= n`:

```
while (((number % divisor) != 0) &&
       (divisor*divisor <= number))
  // no value <= divisor remains as a factor of number
  if (divisor == 2)
    divisor = 3;
  else
    divisor = divisor + 2;
```

When this loop ends, we need to know whether it ended because it found a divisor or because **number** is prime; we do this by adding the statement

```
if ((number % divisor) != 0)  // number is prime...
  divisor = number;           // ...so it's a factor
```

after the end of the loop. In this way, `divisor` will be the smallest divisor of **number** (aside from 1), just as we need.

Now we make an important observation about the way this loop is to be used inside the outer loop. Because we will be finding the divisors in increasing order and eliminating them from **number**, when the preceding `while` loop begins, we know already that **number** has no divisor less than or equal to the divisor just found. There is no point, therefore, in reexamining all the values $2, 3, 5, \ldots,$ `divisor` as possible divisors of **number**; we should continue from where we left off.

Putting all these pieces together, including the loop invariants implicit in the foregoing discussion, yields the definition of `factorize`:

```
void factorize(int number) {
  int divisor = 2;     // trial divisor/prime factor
  int exponent;        // exponent of the prime factor
  do {// we've found all prime factors smaller than divisor,
    // printed them, and removed them from number

    // look for next prime factor
    while (((number % divisor) != 0) &&
           (divisor*divisor <= number))
      // no value <= divisor remains as a factor of number
      if (divisor == 2)
        divisor = 3;
      else
        divisor = divisor + 2;
    if ((number % divisor) != 0)  // number is prime...
      divisor = number;           // ...so it's a factor
```

```
        // find exponent of prime factor, removing that factor
        exponent = 0;
        while ((number % divisor) == 0) {
          // we've removed divisor exponent times
          number = number / divisor;
          exponent++;
        }
        cout << setw(w) << divisor << setw(w) << exponent << "\n";
    } while (number > 1);
}
```

Examining the loops of this program with regard to termination, correctness, and efficiency, we find that we need only consider the do-while (number > 1) loop and the while loops nested within it. Because the loops are interrelated, we must not look at them individually but as a unit. The loop to find the next divisor of **number** must eventually end, since **divisor** increases with each iteration and cannot grow beyond $\sqrt{\text{number}}$ without stopping the loop. When this loop ends, **divisor** divides **number**, so the loop to calculate the exponent must eventually result in **number** and **divisor** being relatively prime, which will cause that loop to end. Since each iteration of the do-while (number > 1) eliminates a prime factor from **number**, eventually we will have **number** = 1, causing the loop to end. The correctness of the result when each loop ends follows from the invariants.

As to the number of iterations, the do-while (number > 1) loop will go through one iteration per prime factor. On a computer in which the largest integer value is $2^{31} - 1$, the most prime factors occur when **number** $= 2 \times 3 \times 5 \times 7 \times 11 \times 13 \times 17 \times 19 \times 23 = 223,092,870$; thus, the loop can go through at most 9 iterations. The while loop that finds the next divisor can be iterated at most $\sqrt{\text{number}}/2$ times, or at most 23,171 times. The while loop that computes the exponent can be iterated at most 30 times, assuming 2^{31} is greater than the largest integer value.

5.8

You Bet Your Life

Writing well-designed, correct loops is not easy, and neither is writing the loop invariants that should accompany the loops. But there is no way to achieve mathematical certainty that the loops are correct without the loop invariants, so, difficult as it may be to formulate them, loop invariants should be an integral part of the program. *They should be written as the loops are written, not appended as an afterthought.* Read what C.A.R. Hoare, one of the pioneers of computer science, had to say on the subject in the British magazine *New Scientist* of September 18, 1986:

Digital computers must be the most reliable mechanisms built by the human race. Millions of computers throughout the world, and thousands in space, execute billions of instructions per second for billions of seconds without a single error in any of the millions of bits that comprise each computer. Yet few of us would trust our lives to a computer.

The fault lies not in the computer's hardware but in the programs which control it. Programs faithfully reproduce the errors, oversights, inadequacies and misunderstandings of the programmers who compose them. There are some large and widely used programs, operating systems and compilers in which hundreds of new errors are discovered each year. Even when programmers correct errors, the rate at which users continue to discover new ones remains constant over several decades. Indeed, some suspect that each correction introduces more than one new error. And only a few of the errors in these programs will ever be discovered before the programs are superseded by new products. These new products are, of course, equally unreliable.

Most of the errors that are found in general computer programs are extremely subtle: their effects are not serious, and it is easy to avoid them until the software's supplier gets round to correcting them. But computers are beginning to play an increasing role in "life-critical applications," situations where the correction of errors on discovery is not an acceptable option—for example, in control of industrial processes, nuclear reactors, weapons systems, oil rigs, aeroengines and railway signaling. . . .

When Brunel's ship the SS *Great Britain* was launched into the River Thames, it made such a splash that several spectators on the opposite bank were drowned. Nowadays, engineers reduce the force of entry into the water by rope tethers which are designed to break at carefully calculated intervals.

When the first computer came into operation in the Mathematisch Centrum in Amsterdam, one of the first tasks was to calculate the appropriate intervals and breaking strains of these tethers. In order to ensure the correctness of the program which did the calculations, the programmers were invited to watch the launching from the first row of the ceremonial viewing stand set up on the opposite bank. They accepted and they survived.

A similar solution has been proposed for programs that control the propeller and steering of a ship which has to keep stationary in rough seas close to the leg of an oil drilling rig. The action of the wind and waves is so sudden that no human helmsman could avoid collision, and the task must be delegated to a computer program. But if we require the programmer to demonstrate the reliability of his program by joining the crew of the ship, a question arises when he resigns his highly paid post. Is this because of boredom, seasickness or fear of something worse? . . .

I therefore suggest . . . the use of mathematics to calculate the parameters and check the soundness of a design before passing it for construction and installation. . . . A mathematical proof is, technically, a completely reliable method of ensuring the correctness of programs, but this method could never be effective in practice unless it is accompanied by the appropriate attitudes and managerial techniques. These techniques are in fact based on the same ideas that have been used effectively in the past.

It is not practical or desirable to punish errors in programming by instant death. Nevertheless, programmers must stop regarding error as an inevitable feature of their daily lives. Like surgeons or airline pilots, they must feel a personal commitment to adopt techniques that eliminate error and to feel the appropriate shame and resolution to improve when they fail.

Exercises—Third Set

☞　1. Suppose we rewrite the `if` statement in the scores program (page 168) as

```
if (maxOfScores < score)          // new largest score
   maxOfScores = score;
else if (minOfScores > score)     // new smallest score
   minOfScores = score;
```

Verify that the code still works properly and explain why this change is desirable.

☞　2. Think about how to augment the scores program to print the median of the scores. Can you do it with what you have learned so far in C++?

3. (a) Using your function `daysOfDaylightSavings` from Exercise 7 on page 128, write a program to determine the year with the maximum number of days of daylight savings from 1990 to 2100. Use symbolic constants `firstYear` = 1990 and `finalYear` = 2100.
   (b) Repeat part (a) for the year with the minimum number of days of daylight savings time.
   (c) Write a program to determine the average number of days of daylight savings per year time from 1990 to 2100.

4. Chicago beaches are open for swimming from July 4 to Labor Day each summer. (Labor Day is the first Monday in September.) Write a program to calculate and print the average number of days per year the Chicago beaches were open from 1950 to 2000 (use symbolic constants!).

5. Modify the prime factorization program so that it rejects an input value that is not greater than one.

6. Modify the prime factorization program so that it also computes the functions $\phi(n)$, $\sigma(n)$, $\tau(n)$, and $\mu(n)$, defined by

$$\phi(n) = \frac{n(p_1 - 1)(p_2 - 1) \cdots (p_k - 1)}{p_1 p_2 \cdots p_k}$$

$$\sigma(n) = (1 + p_1 + \cdots + p_1^{\alpha_1})(1 + p_2 + \cdots + p_2^{\alpha_2}) \cdots$$
$$(1 + p_k + \cdots + p_k^{\alpha_k})$$

$$\tau(n) = (\alpha_1 + 1)(\alpha_2 + 1) \cdots (\alpha_k + 1)$$

$$\mu(n) = \begin{cases} 0 & \text{if any } \alpha_i > 1 \\ (-1)^k & \text{otherwise} \end{cases}$$

where $n = p_1^{\alpha_1} p_2^{\alpha_2} \cdots p_k^{\alpha_k}$ is the prime factorization of n. The function $\phi(n)$ is called the *Euler totient function;* it is the number of numbers less than n and relatively prime to n. The function $\sigma(n)$ is the sum of all the positive divisors of n. The function $\tau(n)$ is the number of positive divisors of n. The function $\mu(n)$ is called the *Möbius function.*

7. A pair of numbers n and m is called *amicable* if $\sigma(m) - m = n$ and $\sigma(n) - n = m$, where σ is as defined in the previous exercise. Write a program to find all pairs n, m of amicable numbers such that $n > 1$, $m > 1$, and $n + m \leq 1000$.

8. Given an approximation to the cube root of x, we get a better approximation by computing

$$\text{Approximation} + \frac{1}{3}\left(\frac{x}{\text{Approximation}^2} - \text{Approximation}\right)$$

Use this idea to write a function to calculate the cube root of x. Use 1.0 as the first approximation and continue applying the given formula until the difference between successive approximations is less than a symbolic constant **error = 1.0e-6**.

9. Given two functions **action1** and **action2**, a program must be written that invokes these functions for several values of **i** and **j**. The order in which the actions are to be performed and the associated values (**i, j**) for each action are as follows:

```
action1(5, 6);
action2(5, 5);
action1(4, 6);
action2(4, 4);
action1(3, 6);
action2(3, 3);
action1(2, 6);
action2(2, 2);
action1(1, 6);
```

(a) Write a program that implements this using a **for** statement.
(b) Suppose that the pattern of actions is

```
action1(k,1);
action2(k,1);
action1(k,1);
action2(k,1);
action1(k,1);
    .
    .
    .
action2(k,1);
action1(k,1);
```

where the pattern starts and ends with **action1** and continues as long as **k** is greater than zero; neither action should be executed once **k** becomes zero. Assume that only **action1** can change the value of **k**. Write a program that implements this sequence of actions.
(c) Now assume that only **action2** can change the value of **k**. The pattern should still start and end with **action1**, so after **k** becomes zero, **action1** must be executed one final time. Write a program that implements this sequence of actions.

10. Write a program to help do payroll calculations. Your program should read wages and compute and print the State of Illinois tax due (3 percent of wages); your program should continue reading wages until an end of file is encountered. At the end of file, the program should print the total of all wages paid and the total of all Illinois state taxes due. The output of the program should look like this:

```
WAGE AND STATE OF ILLINOIS TAX CALCULATION

Enter wages (a negative value ends the program): $ 20450.00
State of Illinois tax due is $613.50
```

```
Enter wages (a negative value ends the program): $ 103575.00
State of Illinois tax due is $3107.25

Enter wages (a negative value ends the program): $ ^D

Total wages paid were $124025.00
Total State of Illinois tax due is $3720.75
```

11. It is known that for any integer $r \geq 1$, there is a power of 2 whose decimal representation has only 1's and 2's as its rightmost r digits. Write a program to find the smallest such power of 2 for each r, $1 \leq r \leq 9$. The output of the program should look like this:

```
TERMINAL DIGITS OF POWERS OF 2

  r          Power          Terminal Digits

  1            0                   1
  2            9                  512
  3           89                562112
  4           89                562112
  .
  .
  .
```

(*Hint:* Only retain the rightmost 9 digits during the calculations.)

12. (a) An amortization table shows the monthly payment schedule as a loan is repaid. Write a program to produce an amortization table. The formula for the interest portion of a month's payment is

$$\text{Interest} = \text{Balance} \times \frac{\text{Interest rate}}{12}$$

and the portion that is applied to the principal is

$$\text{Principal} = \text{Payment} - \text{Interest}$$

so the remaining balance is given by

$$\text{Remaining balance} = \text{Balance} - \text{Principal}$$

For example, at 5.5 percent interest on a loan of $20178.45 with $187.35 paid monthly, your program should produce the following output:

```
Enter amount of loan: $ 20178.45
Enter interest rate: 0.055
Enter monthly payment: $ 187.35

SCHEDULE OF DIRECT REDUCTION LOAN

Loan: $20178.45
Rate:  5.5%
Monthly Payment:  $187.35
```

Payment	Interest	Principal	Balance
			20178.45
1	92.48	94.87	20083.58
2	92.05	95.30	19988.28
3	91.61	95.74	19892.54
.			
.			
.			
146	3.24	184.11	523.20
147	2.40	184.95	338.25
148	1.55	185.80	152.45
149	0.70	152.45	153.15*

```
*The final payment is usually somewhat different from the regular
payment, and is shown starred on the last line.
```

(b) Repeat part (a) but with the annual interest paid printed after each 12 payments and also after the final payment.

13. The *gamma function* is defined for $x > 0$ as

$$\Gamma(x) = \int_0^\infty t^{x-1} e^{-t} dt$$

We have that $\Gamma(1) = 1$, and for $x > 1$,

$$\Gamma(x) = (x - 1)\Gamma(x - 1) \qquad (5.1)$$

Notice that when x is a positive integer,

$$\Gamma(x) = (x - 1)!$$

To compute $\Gamma(x)$ for $x > 1$, apply relation (5.1), above, r times until $0 < x - r \le 1$. For values of x in the range $0 \le x \le 1$ the gamma function is approximated by the formula

$$\Gamma(x + 1) \approx 1 - 0.57710166x + 0.98585399x^2 - 0.87642182x^3$$
$$+ 0.83282120x^4 - 0.56847290x^5 + 0.25482049x^6$$
$$- 0.05149930x^7$$

Write a function to calculate $\Gamma(x)$ for $x > 0$.

★ 14. The *stock market problem*: Read in the values of a stock for a sequence of consecutive days and find the best pair of days to have bought and sold the stock to maximize your profit. Your output should look like

```
STOCK MARKET PROBLEM

Enter value of stock on day 1: $ 17
Enter value of stock on day 2: $ 18
Enter value of stock on day 3: $ 16
Enter value of stock on day 4: $ 17
Enter value of stock on day 5: $ 21
```

```
Enter value of stock on day 6: $ 19
Enter value of stock on day 7: $ 20
Enter value of stock on day 8: $ ^D

Maximum profit from buying on day 3 and selling on day 5.
```

Of course, the buy date must be before the sell date (no short selling). (*Hint:* Keep track of the current best buy-sell pair and the current minimum value.)

Summary

Iteration, the repetition of an action, is accomplished through several different types of loop structures in C++. The **for** statement is written

```
for (<statement1>; <condition>; <statement2>)
    <statement3>
```

and it causes **<statement1>** to be executed once and then **<statement3>**, the body of the loop, and **<statement2>** to be executed repeatedly as long as **<condition>** is true (nonzero).

The **while** loop

```
while (<condition>)
    <statement>
```

repeatedly executes **<statement>** (which can be a compound statement surrounded by braces { and }) as long as **<condition>** is true (nonzero). If we're careless in writing the loop and **<condition>** never becomes false (zero), the loop will continue to execute forever—an infinite loop.

An alternative to **while** loops for indefinite repetition is available. The **do-while** loop is written:

```
do
    <statement>
while (<condition>);
```

and it behaves just as its appearance suggests: **<statement>** is executed again and again until **<condition>** is true; the major difference between this and a **while** loop is that in a **do-while** loop the condition is checked *after* the body of the loop is executed, and as a consequence the body of the loop is always executed at least once.

Anything we can do with a **while** loop we can do with a **do-while** loop, and vice versa. To decide which loop mechanism to use, write the sequence of actions to be taken, including the test for the end of the loop. It should then be apparent whether it is more convenient to test the end condition at the start of the loop (**while**) or at the end of the loop (**do-while**). Use a **for** loop in cases in which the number of iterations is known at the time the loop begins.

Every **while** or **do-while** loop should be examined to make certain that it cannot become an infinite loop. This is ordinarily done by demonstrating that each iteration of the loop changes the values of the variables in such a way that termination of the loop is inevitable. Some attempt should be made to estimate or establish a bound for the number of iterations of the loop in the worst case.

Verifying that a loop terminates with the correct results is done by writing a *loop invariant*. The loop invariant is the set of relationships between the program variables at a particular point of the loop, where it should be stated in program comments. The correctness of the loop can be inferred from the loop invariant by verifying that the loop invariant is true the first time through the loop, that the loop invariant remains true from one iteration to the next, and hence, that the loop terminates at the value we want.

The keywords introduced in this chapter are

```
for     do
```

CHAPTER

6

User-Defined Data Types

Chapter Preview

C++ programmers can define their own data types and use them as if they were built-in. With the `class` construct provided for this purpose, you can specify the representation of a new type of data and the operations applied to those data. The `class` construct allows you to make user-defined types as simple and natural as built-in types, including the ability to define operators like `+` and `<<` on user-defined types. We introduce two important concepts related to classes: *Representation independence* is the property of user-defined types that allows internal details of a class to be changed without affecting the class's users. *Mutability* is the ability to alter a value of a user-defined type simply by applying an operation.

I shall be accused of sowing class-hatred.

—T. G. Massey
Friend of People

All our programs up to this point manipulate simple, familiar kinds of data—integers and floating-point numbers. Those data are operated upon with the familiar arithmetic operations, printed using the left-shift operator, stored in variables, passed into functions, and returned as the results of function calls.

But the world is full of different types of data, so many that C++ can't possibly supply them all. So a major task in programming is *defining new data types*. The **enum** types are examples of data types defined by the programmer, but these really just provide convenient names for some small integers—you can't do anything with those types that you couldn't already do with **int**.

A more interesting example of a new data type, which we have already been working with implicitly, is the type *date*. Like the built-in data types, this one consists of a set of *values* with an appropriate set of *operations*—such as finding the month in which a given date falls or computing the number of days between two dates. This is the essence of a data type:

> **A data type is a set of values plus operations on those values.**

In C++, the **class** construct defines new data types. In this chapter, we introduce the basic form of a class and its principal components: *constructors*, *data members*, and *member functions*. We also discuss *operator overloading*, a way to achieve a considerable aesthetic improvement in many programs that use classes, and the notions of *mutability* and *immutability* of data.

6.1

A New Data Type: time

As the starting example in this chapter, we've chosen a data type similar to, but simpler than, dates. It is **time**, whose values represent a time (hour and minute) within a single day. You can think of a value of type **time** as two integers: an **hour** between 0 and 23, and a **minute** between 0 and 59. Picture **time** values

hour	14
minute	41

hour	0
minute	30

hour	23
minute	59

(a) 2:41 P.M.   (b) 12:30 A.M.   (c) 11:59 P.M.

FIGURE 6.1 Some examples of times.

graphically as

hour	7
minute	18

which represents the time 7:18 A.M. Some other examples and the times they represent are shown in Figure 6.1.

We'll provide this data type with two operations:

- Add a number of minutes to a given time to get a new time. We'll use the addition symbol for this operation. Here are some examples:

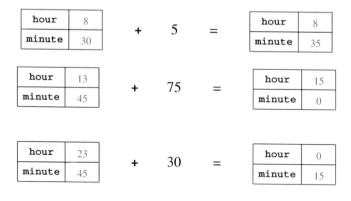

- Print a time in standard form:

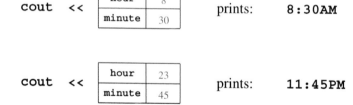

```
            hour    12
cout  <<                       prints:    noon
            minute   0
```

```
            hour    0
cout  <<                       prints:    midnight
            minute   0
```

The **class** construct permits you to program these operations, and it allows you to declare variables of type **time**, to write constants representing specific times, and apply these operations to **time** values. In other words, you will be able to use **time** in the same ways that you use the built-in types **int** and **float**.

6.2

Classes and Their Clients

User-defined data types are implemented using the C++ **class** construct. Functions that use the data type defined by a class are called *clients* of that class. The definition of a class must appear before its clients. We discuss class definitions first, and then clients.

class
client

6.2.1 Class Definitions

A class definition has the form

```
class  <name> {
private:
   <data members>

public:
   <constructor definitions>

   <member function definitions>
};
```

Such definitions are usually placed at the beginning of a program, just after the **#include**s, though they may appear anywhere, as long as they precede their clients.

Once the `<name>`, `<data members>`, `<constructor definitions>`, and `<member function definitions>` are filled in, this class will define a full-fledged data type, with values and operations on those values. Values of a user-defined data type are also called *objects*, or *instances*, of the type. (For example, the values shown in Figure 6.1 are examples of **time** objects.) The class can then be used like any other data type, by declaring variables of that type and applying operations to them. This will all be discussed in Section 6.2.2.

object
instance

The `<data members>` of the class specify the representation of data of this type, in the form of variable declarations. So a class to implement **time** might

A Semicolon *Must* Follow Each Class Definition

Note carefully the semicolon following the closing brace of a class definition. This semicolon is required, and omitting it causes many C++ compilers to produce cryptic error messages.

begin:

```
class time {
private:
  int hour, minute;

public:
  <constructor definitions>

  <member function definitions>
};
```

By giving these data members, we are telling C++ that **time** values are represented by two integers, giving the hour and minute, respectively. In other words, each object of this data type consists of two integers, as illustrated in Figure 6.1.

constructor   *Constructors* tell C++ how to initialize new objects of the class. A constructor is actually a function, but a special one: It has the *same name as the class* and has *no return type* (not even **void**). It can have any number of arguments, of any type.

An appropriate constructor for **time** has two integer arguments and uses them to initialize the two data members:

```
time (int h, int m) { hour = h; minute = m; }
```

With this constructor, our class looks like this:

```
class time {
private:
  int hour, minute;

public:
  time (int h, int m) { hour = h; minute = m; }

  <member function definitions>
};
```

To complete the class definition, we need to define the member functions. These are the functions we called **+** and **<<** in the examples in Section 6.1. Here, we'll call them **addMinutes** and **printTime**, respectively.

Member functions are different from regular functions in an important way: A member function of a class **C** *always* has one argument of type **C**. Because it *always* has this argument, the argument is not named explicitly in the member function's argument list but is instead left *implicit*. This means that the definition of **addMinutes** looks like this:

```
time addMinutes (int m) { ... }
```

There is no argument of type **time** mentioned, even though we know that the **addMinutes** function has to have an argument of type **time** in addition to its integer argument. It does have such an argument, but it is implicit. Similarly, the definition of **printTime** is

```
void printTime () { ... }
```

Since its only argument is of type **time**, and that is an implicit argument, it is declared with no arguments at all.

So far, the **time** class looks like this:

```
class time {
private:
  int hour, minute;

public:
  time (int h, int m) { hour = h; minute = m; }

  time addMinutes (int m) {  ... given below ... }

  void printTime () { ... given below ... }
};
```

It is helpful at this point to introduce a bit of terminology. When a client applies a member function to an object, it is called *sending a message* to that object; the object is called the *receiver* of the message. With respect to member functions, the term *arguments* refers to all the arguments *other than* the receiver. This view of member functions keeps the focus, properly, on the *receiver of the message*. You may find it useful to place yourself in the position of the receiver of a message and to think of yourself as responding to that message.

sending a message

receiver

arguments

For example, in writing **printTime**, you might think this way:

> I need to look at my **hour** and **minute** data members and decide whether I represent midnight (**hour** = 0, **minute** = 0), noon (**hour** = 12, **minute** = 0), or some other time. If the latter, then I'll print the hour as follows: 12 if **hour** is either 0 or 12; 1 if it is either 1 or 13; and so on. (In other words, I'll print **hour** itself if it is between 1 and 12, **hour** − 12 if it is between 13 and 23, and 12 if it is 0.) After I have printed the number, if **hour** is less than 12, I'll print **AM**; otherwise I'll print **PM**.

Now all you need to know is that to refer to the **minute** or **hour** data member of the receiver, you can use the name **minute** or **hour** as if it were a variable. Here, then, is the definition of **printTime**:

```
void printTime () {
  if ((hour == 0) && (minute == 0))
    cout << "midnight";
  else if ((hour == 12) && (minute == 0))
    cout << "noon";
  else {
    if (hour == 0)
      cout << 12;
    else if (hour > 12)
      cout << hour-12;
```

```
      else
        cout << hour;
      cout << ':' << setfill('0') << setw(2) << minute;
      if (hour < 12)
        cout << "AM";
      else
        cout << "PM";
    }
  }
```

The one item in this function that you haven't seen before is `setfill('0')`. When placed in the list of items to be output, as it is here, it tells the insertion operator (`<<`) that the next item printed (and only the next) is to have any blank columns filled with the character `0`. Here it is used to ensure that a time like 4:05 will be printed as `4:05` rather than `4: 5`. Appendix D covers `setw`, `setfill`, and a number of other facilities for formatting output. (`'0'` is a *character*—a type of data we'll be covering in Chapter 7.)

We now turn to the definition of **addMinutes**. The `time` object that receives the message `addMinutes(m)` has to return a new `time` object representing a time `m` minutes in the future. However, `m` may be a negative number, so that the resulting time may be *before* the time of the receiver; it may also be a very large number, representing several days. These possibilities make this function more complex than you might expect.

The simplest way to calculate the new time is to turn the existing time into a time based solely on minutes; specifically, `hour*60 + minute` represents the total number of minutes that have elapsed since midnight. Adding `m` to this number and converting it back to hours and minutes gives us the solution, almost:

```
time addMinutes (int m) {
  int totalMinutes = 60*hour + minute + m;
  return time(totalMinutes/60, totalMinutes % 60);
}
```

There are two problems with this function. First, if `m` is very large, then the value of `totalMinutes/60` can be larger than 23, and therefore not a valid hour. Second, if `m` is negative, `totalMinutes` may be negative, in which case both `totalMinutes/60` and `totalMinutes%60` will be negative. The first problem can be solved by making sure that `totalMinutes` is between $-(24 \times 60)$ and 24×60 (that is, it represents a valid number of minutes either today or yesterday). The second problem is solved by adding 24×60 to `totalMinutes`, if it is negative. This gives the correct version of **addMinutes**:

```
time addMinutes (int m) {
  int totalMinutes = (60*hour + minute + m) % (24*60);
  if (totalMinutes < 0)
    totalMinutes = totalMinutes + 24*60;
  return time(totalMinutes/60, totalMinutes % 60);
}
```

The complete definition of the class `time` is shown in Figure 6.2.

```
class time {
private:
  int hour, minute;
public:
  time (int h, int m) { hour = h; minute = m; }

  time addMinutes (int m) {
    int totalMinutes = (60*hour + minute + m) % (24*60);
    if (totalMinutes < 0)
      totalMinutes = totalMinutes + 24*60;
    return time(totalMinutes/60, totalMinutes % 60);
  }

  void printTime () {
    if ((hour == 0) && (minute == 0))
      cout << "midnight";
    else if ((hour == 12) && (minute == 0))
      cout << "noon";
    else {
      if (hour == 0)
        cout << 12;
      else if (hour > 12)
        cout << hour-12;
      else
        cout << hour;
      cout << ':' << setfill('0') << setw(2) << minute;
      if (hour < 12)
        cout << "AM";
      else
        cout << "PM";
    }
  }
};
```

FIGURE 6.2 The time class.

6.2.2 Clients

Following the definition of a class C, functions can create C objects, declare variables of type C, and send messages (that is, call member functions) defined in the class.

Declarations of variables of a user-defined type have the same syntax as for built-in types, except that the declaration must include arguments to the type's constructor. Given **time** defined as above, with a two-argument constructor, the variable **dawn** can be declared like this:

```
time dawn(5, 35);
```

This declaration creates a box for a **time** object and fills it with the value 5:35 A.M., as shown in Figure 6.3. Thus, by using constructors, a declaration of a variable can create the variable and at the same time create an instance of the class.

FIGURE 6.3 dawn, after initialization.

Constructors can be used in another way: to create an object without declaring a variable. A call to a constructor, such as

```
time(8, 30)
```

produces an instance of the **time** class, representing the time 8:30 A.M. It can be used anywhere an expression of type **time** can be used, such as the right-hand side of an assignment statement to a **time** variable:

```
dawn = time(5, 41);
```

The assignment evaluates the expression on the right, producing the object

and then replaces the previous value of **dawn** with this new value, as shown in Figure 6.4. This value stays in the **dawn** container until another assignment is made. Assignment to **time** variables (or variables of any other user-defined type) works exactly the same as assignment to **int** or **float** variables, with expressions like **time(8, 55)** and **time(19, 12)** acting as constants.

It is often useful to have more than one constructor, differing in the number or types of their arguments, and this is allowed in C++. We might have added two additional constructors, making our class look like this:

```
1   class time {
2   private:
3       int hour, minute;
4
5   public:
6       time (int h, int m) { hour = h; minute = m; }
7
8       time () { hour = 0; minute = 0; }
9
10      time (int m) { hour = m / 60; minute = m % 60; }
11
12      time addMinutes (int m) { ... }
13
14      void printTime () { ... }
15  };
```

The constructor in line 8 sets the new instance's time to midnight, and the one in line 10 interprets its argument as the number of minutes elapsed since midnight

FIGURE 6.4 dawn, after assignment.

(a number between 0 and 24 × 60) and sets the new instance's data members appropriately. With these constructors, the declarations

```
time t1, t2(720), t3(525);
```

are equivalent to

```
time t1(0, 0), t2(12, 0), t3(8, 45);
```

Since each of the three constructors we've defined has a different number of arguments, they could all be included in the **time** class—C++ can tell which one you intend to use in any declaration by looking at the number of arguments you've given. (Note that when using the zero-argument constructor, the parentheses you might expect to find for the empty argument list are omitted.)

Having created objects or variables of a class, the client can "send messages." Although message sending is really just a form of function calling, it has a special syntax in C++:

```
<receiver>.<message>(<arguments>)
```

The **<receiver>** is an object of the class, the **<message>** is a member function, and the **<arguments>** are the arguments named in the header of the member function. The **<receiver>** is an *implicit* argument of the member function, as we discussed above.

For example, here are two legal calls to the member functions of the **time** class:

```
dusk = dawn.addMinutes(60*12);
dusk.printTime();
```

Here, **dawn** is the receiver of the call to **addMinutes**, and **dusk** is the receiver of **printTime**.

To summarize, every member function has one special argument, called the receiver. In member function *definitions*, this argument is implicit—it is not

Remember to Initialize Objects!   BUG ALERT 6.2

Every **time** variable *must* be initialized by calling one of its constructors. The general rule is that whenever any variable of user-defined type is declared, it must be given with initializing arguments that match one of its constructors.

mentioned in the function header at all. In member function *calls*, this argument is given before the function name (instead of being in the argument list), followed by a period.

Writing a class definition and writing a client of that class are distinct activities, like writing a function definition and writing a program that calls that function. We now switch to writing a client of the **time** class. The program prints a schedule, a list of times, each followed by a sequence of underscore characters. Most of the work in this program will be done by the function **printSchedule**. Specifically, the call

```
printSchedule(time(8, 30), 30, 6);
```

prints six such lines, starting at **8:30AM** and incrementing by 30 minutes. The result is this output:

```
8:30AM  _____
9:00AM  _____
9:30AM  _____
10:00AM _____
10:30AM _____
11:00AM _____
```

The function **printSchedule** employs a simple **for** loop:

```
1   // Print a schedule for the period starting at time start,
2   // with numberOfAppts entries, apptLength minutes apart.
3   void printSchedule (time start,
4                       int apptLength,
5                       int numberOfAppts) {
6     for (int i=0; i<numberOfAppts; i++) {
7       start.printTime();
8       cout << "  _____ \n";
9       start = start.addMinutes(apptLength);
10    }
11  }
```

printSchedule is *not* a member function. If it were, its **time** argument would be implicit. It is just a client of **time**.

Make sure you understand the assignment in line 9 of **printSchedule**. It is natural to think that the expression

```
start.addMinutes(apptLength);
```

would change **start** by adding **apptLength** minutes to it, but that is not true. **addMinutes** does not change its receiver, but instead returns a new **time** object. **start** can only be changed by assigning a new **time** object to it, which is what we've done in line 9.

The rule about the placement of class definitions in a program is, as we stated earlier, the same as the rule about the placement of functions: The class must be defined before it is used. By the same token, the member functions of a class can use non-member functions defined earlier in the program.

Here is a complete program to print the schedule shown above. It has the usual **include** lines, then the definition of the **time** class and the function **printSchedule**, and finally a main program that calls **printSchedule** with the appropriate arguments.

```cpp
//
// Print lines of an appointment book, including
// times from 8.30 to 11.00.
//
// Author:  L. O. Kamin
// Last modified: 5/15/95

#include <iostream.h>
#include <iomanip.h>

//
// time objects represent times during a single day.
//
class time {
private:
  int hour, minute;

public:
  time (int h, int m) { hour = h; minute = m; }

  time addMinutes (int m) {
    // Return a time m minutes after the receiver's time
    // (or before it, if m is negative).
    int totalMinutes = (60*hour + minute + m) % (24*60);
    if (totalMinutes < 0)
      totalMinutes = totalMinutes + 24*60;
    return time(totalMinutes/60, totalMinutes%60);
  }

  void printTime () {
    // Print the receiver's time.
    if ((hour == 0) && (minute == 0))
      cout << "midnight";
    else if ((hour == 12) && (minute == 0))
      cout << "noon";
    else {
      if (hour == 0)
        cout << 12;
      else if (hour > 12)
        cout << hour-12;
      else
        cout << hour;
      cout << ':' << setfill('0') << setw(2) << minute;
      if (hour < 12)
        cout << "AM";
      else
        cout << "PM";
    }
  }
};
```

```
// Print a schedule for the period starting at time start,
// with numberOfAppts entries, apptLength minutes apart.
void printSchedule (time start,
                    int apptLength,
                    int numberOfAppts) {
  for (int i=0; i<numberOfAppts; i++) {
    start.printTime();
    cout << " _____\n";
    start = start.addMinutes(apptLength);
  }
}

int main () {
  printSchedule(time(8, 30), 30, 6);
}
```

Exercises—First Set

☞ 1. Add these member functions to the **time** class:
     (a) **void printMilitaryTime ()**. This function prints the time in 24–hour (military) format (for example, **1345 hours** instead of **1:45PM**).
     (b) **time addHours (int h)**. This function is analogous to **addMinutes**, but adds hours instead.
     (c) **boolean isPM ()**. This function tells whether the receiver is an afternoon time (noon or later) or a morning time.

☞ 2. Modify **printTime** so that it always prints the time right-justified in an eight-column field. As written above, the display of a time occupies either six or seven columns. With this change, the output of **printSchedule** will have twenty underline characters correctly aligned vertically. We've chosen eight columns so that the word **midnight** will fit.

☞ 3. Rewrite the class **time** to include seconds as well as minutes and hours. You need a third data member (**second**), an additional member function (**time addSeconds (int s)**), and revised constructor and **printTime** functions.

☞ 4. Review Section 4.2 and implement the class **date** with a constructor and two member functions. Use the Gregorian month-day-year representation, so that your class will have three data members (**month, day,** and **year**) of type **int**. Likewise, the constructor will have three arguments, giving the month, day, and year. The two member functions are **date incrementDay ()** and **void printDate ()**.

   • **date incrementDay ()** returns the **date** object representing the date following that given by the receiver. The calculation is shown in the function **nextDay** on page 111, although there is an important difference here: you will not be *changing* the receiver, but instead creating a new **date** object. Thus, this function will have the form

```
date incrementDay () {
  int newMonth, newDay, newYear;
  <calculate newMonth, newDay, newYear from month, day,
   and year of receiver>
  return date(newMonth, newDay, newYear);
}
```

   • **void printDate ()** prints the date in month/day/year format.

To test this class, write the function void printMonthlyCalendar (int m, int y), which will have output similar to printSchedule, but with each line labeled by a date in month/day/year format:

```
1/1/94   --------------------
1/2/94   --------------------
   .
   .
   .
1/31/94  --------------------
```

You will need to use the function lastDayOfMonth (page 106) to decide how many lines to print.

5. Given a complex number $x + iy$, we can define the following operations:

- $|x + iy| = \sqrt{x^2 + y^2}$ is the *absolute value* operation.
- $s(x + iy) = sx + isy$, where s is a real number, is *scaling*.

Define a **complex** class:

```
class complex {
private:
   float x, y;  // represents number x + iy
public:
   complex (float r, float i) {...}
   float absoluteValue () {...}
   complex scale (float a) {...}
   void printComplex () {...} // print as "x + i y"
};
```

Fill in the definitions of the constructor and the three member functions of this class. Then write a main program to exercise this class as follows: Repeatedly read three floating-point numbers, say x, y, and s, create and print the complex number $x + iy$, print its absolute value, then create and print $s(x + iy)$. Continue until the user terminates the program by entering the end-of-file character (^D).

6.3

More on Member Functions

Our set of operations in the time class is meager, so let's augment it. Along the way, we'll show how a member function can send another message to its receiver, we'll introduce *dot notation*, and we'll explain how to move the definitions of member functions outside of their classes.

6.3.1 Sending a Message to the Member Function's Receiver

Consider the operation that subtracts some number of minutes from a time:

$$t - i \text{ gives the same result as } t + (-i)$$

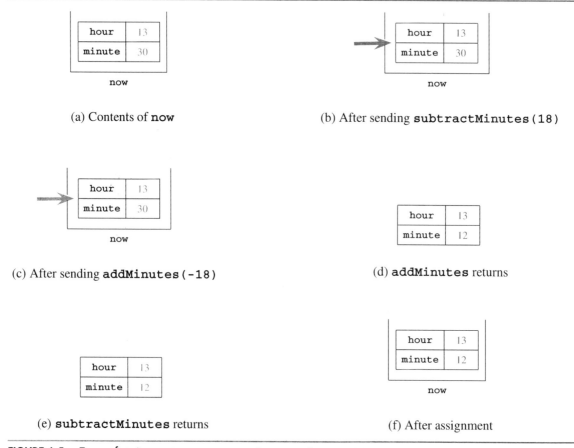

(a) Contents of **now**

(b) After sending **subtractMinutes(18)**

(c) After sending **addMinutes(-18)**

(d) **addMinutes** returns

(e) **subtractMinutes** returns

(f) After assignment

FIGURE 6.5   Trace of assignment now = now.subtractMinutes(18).

We'll include a member function **subtractMinutes** to perform this operation. A client could call **addMinutes(-i)** instead of **subtractMinutes(i)**,
but we'd like to offer the latter as a slight convenience.

The idea is to code **subtractMinutes** as a call to **addMinutes**:

```
time subtractMinutes (int m) {
    return <receiver-of-subtractMinutes>.addMinutes(-m);
}
```

where **<receiver-of-subtractMinutes>** is the **time** object that received
this call of **subtractMinutes**. However, we have no way to *name* the receiver
of a member function within the body of that function. So how can we finish this
code?

One possibility is to create a new **time** object that looks just like the receiver:

```
time subtractMinutes (int m) {
    return time(hour, minute).addMinutes(-m);
}
```

in which case the receiver of **addMinutes** is a new **time** value that is exactly like the receiver of **subtractMinutes** but isn't actually that object. But it's silly and inefficient to reconstruct a **time** object we already have.

A better solution is to use this C++ feature: Within the body of a member function like **subtractMinutes**, another member function of the same class (like **addMinutes**) can be called with the same receiver by calling that function *with no explicit receiver* at all. The function becomes

```
time subtractMinutes (int m) { return addMinutes(-m); }
```

If **t** is a variable of type **time**, and a client sends the **subtractMinutes** message to **t** with argument **n** (that is, makes the call **t.subtractMinutes(n)**), then **subtractMinutes** will send the **addMinutes** message to **t** with argument **-n**.

For example, consider the execution of the assignment

```
now = now.subtractMinutes(18);
```

in a client of **time**, assuming that **now** is a variable containing the time 1:30 P.M., as shown in Figure 6.5(a). After the call, we see in Figure 6.5(b) that the object stored in **now** is the receiver of the message (indicated by the double arrow). The body of **subtractMinutes** contains the call **addMinutes(-m)**. As noted, C++ interprets this to mean that the **addMinutes** message is to be sent to the current receiver. The situation is pictured in Figure 6.5(c). The **addMinutes** function behaves as described earlier, returning the time 1:12 P.M. (Figure 6.5(d)); **subtractMinutes** passes this result back to its sender. The assignment is made to **now**, with the result shown in Figure 6.5(f).

6.3.2 Referencing Data Members of a Different Instance

Another useful operation is to compare two times to see whether the first is "prior to" the second (assuming both represent times within the same day):

hour	h1
minute	m1

$<$

hour	h2
minute	m2

The comparison is true if either **h1** < **h2** or both **h1** = **h2** and **m1** < **m2**.

However, the coding is not obvious. Consider what the definition of this member function will look like:

```
boolean priorTo (time t) {
    return ((hour < <t's hour>) ||
            ((hour == <t's hour>) && (minute < <t's minute>)));
}
```

Coding this requires that we be able to look at the data members of **t**. But—and this is crucially important—we know how to see the data members only of the *receiver* of the message, and **t** is *not* the receiver. Rather, it is an argument that has type **time**; the receiver is, as always, implicit.

C++ provides a way for member functions of a class **C** (not clients, just member functions) to see the data members of arguments of type **C**, using *dot notation*: Give the name of the argument, followed by a period and then the name of the data member. Thus, the definition of **priorTo** is

dot notation

```
boolean priorTo (time t) {
  return ((hour < t.hour) ||
          ((hour == t.hour) && (minute < t.minute)));
}
```

(The resemblance to the notation for sending messages is not accidental; both correspond to selecting a member—whether data or function—of an object.)

With **priorTo** we can write another version of the **printSchedule** function in which we give the starting and ending times and the appointment length; all the appointment times between those two times are listed. (This program does not work if the starting and ending times are intended to be on different days.)

```
void printSchedule2 (time start,
                     time end,
                     int apptLength) {
  while (start.priorTo(end)) {
    writeLine(start);
    start = start.addMinutes(apptLength);
  }
}
```

A complete listing of the **time** class, with all its new member functions, is given in Figure 6.6. We label it "version 1" in anticipation of further work in Section 6.4.

6.3.3   Member Function Prototypes vs. Definitions

It is possible to split the definitions of classes into two parts: the *declaration*, in which everything except the *bodies* of the member functions is given, and the *definitions* of those member functions. The declaration of version 1 of the **time** class would be

```
class time {
private:
  int hour, minute;

public:
  time (int h, int m) ;

  time addMinutes (int m) ;

  void printTime () ;

  time subtractMinutes (int m) ;

  boolean priorTo (time t) ;
};
```

```
class time {
private:
  int hour, minute;

public:
  time (int h, int m) { hour = h; minute = m; }

  time addMinutes (int m) {
    int totalMinutes = (60*hour + minute + m) % (24*60);
    if (totalMinutes < 0)
      totalMinutes = totalMinutes + 24*60;
    return time(totalMinutes/60, totalMinutes%60);
  }

  void printTime () {
    if ((hour == 0) && (minute == 0))
      cout << "midnight";
    else if ((hour == 12) && (minute == 0))
      cout << "noon";
    else {
      if (hour == 0)
        cout << 12;
      else if (hour > 12)
        cout << hour-12;
      else
        cout << hour;
      cout << ":" << setfill('0') << setw(2) << minute;
      if (hour < 12)
        cout << "AM";
      else
        cout << "PM";
    }
  }

  time subtractMinutes (int m) { return addMinutes(-m); }

  boolean priorTo (time t) {
    return ((hour < t.hour) ||
            ((hour == t.hour) && (minute < t.minute)));
  }
};
```

FIGURE 6.6   Version 1 of `time` class, with added operations.

This is, as we said, just like the **time** class in Figure 6.6 in terms of data members and member function types, but only the *first lines* of member functions are given. The full definitions of the member functions can be supplied later in the program (not earlier!), and they look exactly like their definitions in Figure 6.6, with one difference: The characters **time::** need to be placed before each member function's name. Thus, the definitions of the constructor and the functions **addMinutes** and **subtractMinutes** are

```
time::time (int h, int m) { hour = h; minute = m; }

time time::addMinutes (int m) {
  int totalMinutes = (60*hour + minute + m) % (24*60);
  if (totalMinutes < 0)
    totalMinutes = totalMinutes + 24*60;
  return time(totalMinutes/60, totalMinutes%60);

time time::subtractMinutes (int m) { return addMinutes(-m); }
}
```

We'll leave it to you to supply the definitions of **printTime** and **priorTo**.

function prototype

These first lines of functions—giving the return type, function name, and argument types, and ending with a semicolon—are called *function prototypes*. The prototype of a function need not give the names of the function's argument, as long as it gives their types. Thus, this declaration of **time** is equivalent to the one we just gave:

```
class time {
private:
  int hour, minute;

public:
  time (int, int) ;

  time addMinutes (int) ;

  void printTime () ;

  time subtractMinutes (int) ;

  boolean priorTo (time) ;
};
```

It is also possible to mix definitions and declarations of member functions in a class declaration. Thus, we could give this mixed declaration of **time**:

```
class time {
private:
  int hour, minute;

public:
  time (int h, int m) { hour = h; minute = m; }

  time addMinutes (int m) ;

  void printTime () ;

  time time::subtractMinutes (int m) { return addMinutes(-m); }

  boolean priorTo (time t) {
    return ((hour < t.hour) ||
            ((hour == t.hour) && (minute < t.minute)));
  }
};
```

followed by the separate function definitions of `time::addMinutes` and `time::printTime`.

Why do we mention this? Some C++ compilers will print an error message when presented with the version of `time` in Figure 6.6, but not with the versions just given. As a rule, the fewer member function definitions appearing within the class declaration, the better the chance that the compiler will be able to handle it. The rather technical reason for this is discussed in Section E.4 of Appendix E. (Prototypes of ordinary, non-member functions are also used very often; we will see them in Chapters 8 and 10 and in Appendices B and C.)

This causes a dilemma for us: We prefer the form we've used in Figure 6.6 because it is a little neater looking, but it can cause compilers to complain. So we have adopted this rule: We will give member function definitions within the declaration of the class—as in Figure 6.6—when we do not believe it will cause an error. If we know it will cause an error in any compiler, we will give the definition of the offending member function separately. A common cause of this problem, by the way, is member functions that contain **while** loops, so throughout this book you will see such member functions defined outside of their classes.

Exercises—Second Set

1. Add these new member functions to `time`:
   (a) `boolean equals (time t)`. This function returns true if two times are the same, false otherwise.
   (b) `boolean after (time t)`. `t1.after(t2)` is true if, and only if, `t2.priorTo(t1)` is true.
   (c) `int subtractTimes (time t)`. This function returns the difference, in minutes, between two times (presumed to occur on the same day).

2. Add the member function `int daysBetween (date d)`, which computes the number of days between the receiver and `d`, to the `date` class (Exercise 4 on page 194).

3. We did not define the following three operations in the `complex` class of Exercise 5 on page 195:

   - The *complex conjugate* of $x + iy$ is $x - iy$.
   - $(x + iy) + (x' + iy') = (x + x') + i(y + y')$ is *addition*.
   - $(x + iy)(x' + iy') = (xx' - yy') + i(xy' + x'y)$ is *multiplication*. (Notice that scaling is just a special case, where $y = 0$.)

   Add these new member functions to the `complex` class:
   (a) `complex add (complex c)`
   (b) `complex multiply (complex c)`
   (c) `complex conjugate ()`

   Modify the main program you wrote in Exercise 5 to include these new operations. Now, each input line should contain four numbers, x, y, x', and y'; the complex numbers $x + iy$ and $x' + iy'$ should be created, the three new operations should be performed on them, and the results printed.

4. The class **rational** contains rational numbers (that is, fractions) and has the usual arithmetic operations:

(a) $\dfrac{n}{d} + \dfrac{n'}{d'} = \dfrac{nd' + n'd}{dd'}$

(b) $-\dfrac{n}{d} = \dfrac{-n}{d}$

(c) $\dfrac{n}{d} \times \dfrac{n'}{d'} = \dfrac{nn'}{dd'}$

(d) $1\Big/\dfrac{n}{d} = \dfrac{d}{n}$

In addition, there should be a constructor, which takes two integers n and d to the rational number n/d, and an operator **floor**, which returns the integer part of a rational number (namely, n/d, using integer division).

Fill in this class definition:

```
class rational {
private:
   int n, d;
public:
   rational (int num, int den) {...}
   rational plus (rational r) {...}
   rational negate () {...}
   rational minus (rational r) {...}
   rational times (rational r) {...}
   rational reciprocal () {...}
   rational divide (rational r) {...}
   int floor () {...}
};
```

Write a main program similar to the one used in the previous exercise, where the inputs x, y, x', and y' represent the rational numbers x/y and x'/y'. (Be aware that the integers **n** and **d** tend to get very large, quickly exceeding the range of variables of type **int**. The result is that many examples will fail to work even when your code is correct. See Exercise 3 on page 207 for a partial solution.)

6.4

Changing Data Representations

The most important choice a programmer makes is how to represent data objects, as reflected in the data members of a class. Occasionally, the choice is obvious, but usually it isn't. We've represented time by two integers, an hour and a minute, because it seemed the most natural thing to do, but it is not the only possibility.

Another representation of time is as a single integer, the number of minutes since midnight. A class using this representation would have a single data member, **minutes**, and we might picture the object representing 8:30 A.M. like this:

| minutes | 510 |

```
class time {
private:
  int minutes;
  time (int m) { minutes = m; }

public:
  time (int h, int m) { minutes = 60*h + m; }

  time addMinutes (int m) {
    int newmin = (m + minutes) % (24*60);
    if (newmin < 0) newmin = newmin + 24*60;
    return time(newmin);
  }

  void printTime () {
    int hour = minutes / 60;
    int minute = minutes % 60;
    if ((hour == 0) && (minute == 0))
      cout << "midnight";
    else if ((hour == 12) && (minute == 0))
      cout << "noon";
    else {
      if (hour == 0)
        cout << 12;
      else if (hour > 12)
        cout << hour-12;
      else
        cout << hour;
      cout << ":" << setfill('0') << setw(2) << minute;
      if (hour < 12)
        cout << "AM";
      else
        cout << "PM";
    }
  }

  time subtractMinutes (int m) { return addMinutes(-m); }

  boolean priorTo (time t) { return (minutes < t.minutes); }
};
```

FIGURE 6.7   Version 2 of `time`.

An alternative definition of **time** using this representation is shown in Figure 6.7. A noteworthy aspect of this alternative version of **time** is the use of an additional one-argument constructor; it was added because it is more convenient for many of the operations than the two-argument constructor. The new constructor is placed *before* the **public** keyword—something we hadn't previously allowed. The reason for this will be discussed shortly.

From the point of view of a client, how does this version of the **time** class differ from our first one? Not at all! In fact, the client functions we've written, **printSchedule** and **printSchedule2**, produce identical results for these two classes. A third version of the **time** class, in which the time is represented on a 12–hour clock together with an A.M./P.M. indication, is shown in Figure 6.8. In this representation, 8:30 A.M. is represented by the object

hour	8
minute	30
AM	true

Again, no client sees any difference between this version and either of the previous ones.

The ability to *change the representation of data in a class without affecting its clients* is the most important feature of the C++ class construct. It is called *representation independence*, meaning that the clients can use the class without knowing or caring what data members its objects contain. For the same reason, user-defined data types are sometimes called *abstract data types*.

representation independence

abstract data type

That the data members of the various **time** classes are private (they appear after the **private** keyword) is essential to maintaining the representation independence of these classes. We now explain exactly what the **public** and **private** keywords do.

We have seen that if a member function of a class **C** wants to see a data member of a **C** object other than the receiver, it uses dot notation. The general rule is, roughly, that to access a member (data or function) of an object **x**, use dot notation. However, that statement is not entirely accurate, because it suggests that *any* client of **C** can access the data members of a **C** object by using dot notation, which is *not* true. This function, for example, is not a legal client of **time**:

```
void print24HourTime (time t) {
    cout << t.hour << t.minute << " hours";
}
```

and results in a compiler error message like

```
In function 'void  print24HourTime (class time)':
    member 'hour' is a private member of class 'time'
    member 'minute' is a private member of class 'time'
```

The reason for this error message is that *the data members of* **time** *are private*, because they appear after the **private** keyword in the definition of the class. Being private means precisely that clients cannot gain access to them. So the correct rule is:

private

> To access a *public* member of an object **x**, use dot notation. A member function—but not a client—can use dot notation to access a *private* member of an object other than its receiver. It can access any member of its receiver, whether public or private, simply by naming the member (without using dot notation).

We've referred here to "members" in general; indeed, it is possible to have both **public** data members (declared after the **public** keyword) and **private**

```
class time {
private:
  int hour, minute;
  boolean AM;

public:
  time (int h, int m) {
    AM = h < 12;
    minute = m;
    if (h == 0)
      hour = 12;
    else if (h <= 12)
      hour = h;
    else
      hour = h-12;
  }

  time addMinutes (int m) {
    int totalMinutes = 60*hour + minute + m;
    if (!AM)
      totalMinutes = totalMinutes + 12*60;
    totalMinutes = totalMinutes % (24*60);
    if (totalMinutes < 0)
      totalMinutes = totalMinutes + 24*60;
    return time(totalMinutes/60, totalMinutes%60);
  }

  void printTime () {
    if ((hour == 12) && (minute == 0))
      if (AM)
        cout << "midnight";
      else
        cout << "noon";
    else {
      cout << hour << ":"
           << setfill('0') << setw(2) << minute;
      if (AM)
        cout << "AM";
      else
        cout << "PM";
    }
  }

  time subtractMinutes (int m) { return addMinutes(-m); }

  boolean priorTo (time t) {
    int h = hour, ht = t.hour;
    if (h == 12) h = 0;
    if (ht == 12) ht = 0;
    return ((AM  && !t.AM) ||
            ((AM == t.AM) &&
             ((h < ht)
              || (hour == t.hour && minute < t.minute))));
  }
};
```

FIGURE 6.8 Version 3 of time.

member functions (declared after the `private` keyword). Public data members are accessible, via dot notation, to any client; private member functions are accessible *only* to other member functions.

We advise you *never* to use public data members, even though C++ allows them, because they severely compromise representation independence. For example, a client function that refers to the `hour` field of a `time` object—if `hour` were public, that is—might work fine with version 1 of the `time` class, but it would not compile at all if we changed to version 2, and it would compile but possibly give incorrect results with version 3. The data members are private, however, so a client cannot refer to the `hour` field, and none of these things can happen.

On the other hand, a class can allow clients to see the values of the private data members of its objects by defining member functions that return those values, such as

```
int getHour () { return hour; }
int getMinute () { return minute; }
```

accessor function   With these *accessor functions* included, a client can write `dawn.getHour()` even though writing `dawn.hour` is illegal.

This subtle distinction—between making data members public, on the one hand, and making them private and providing accessors, on the other—is important, because accessors do not compromise representation independence. All we need to do is to provide the same functions, with the same results, in the alternative representations. For example, we could add `getHour` and `getMinute` to version 2 so that they would give the same results as the previous definitions do in version 1, like this:

```
int getHour () { return minute / 60; }
int getMinute () { return minute % 60; }
```

Now, even a client that uses these accessor functions won't be able to tell version 1 from version 2. (In Exercise 1 on page 207, you are asked to add accessors to version 3.)

Constructors follow slightly different rules, because they are not invoked using dot notation. Still, the principle is the same: C++ will invoke a *public* constructor on behalf of a client, assuming the correct number of arguments of the correct type are provided. It will invoke a *private* constructor only on behalf of a member function. In version 2, the one-argument constructor is used by the member function `addMinutes`, but it cannot be used by any clients. We can now see that the one-argument constructor was declared `private` to maintain representation independence. Because the other classes do not have a one-argument constructor, no client should be able to see the one-argument constructor in version 2.

Why is representation independence so important? Large programs are developed over a period of months or even years, often by many programmers. Many different types of data are used, and their representations can change over time. If all the programmers were directly accessing the representations of those data—in effect, relying on those *specific* representations—each change might cause parts of the program to stop working. The ultimate result—as has been frequently observed in practice—is a program so fragile that it cannot be changed at all. In the real world, however, a program that does not change is soon obsolete. By keeping the representation private, the effective life of the program is increased.

Why would one ever want to change the representation of a data item? It is difficult to see how it could make much difference, in practice, which of the three versions of `time` were used, because `time` is so simple. Still, it can be used to illustrate the two main reasons why data representations are sometimes changed: to *improve efficiency* and to *increase functionality*.

Later in this book—in Section 9.6, for example—we will see examples of different representations for the same type of data that differ markedly in their efficiency. Even for `time` we can see how efficiency considerations might dictate a choice of representation. For example, version 2 executes `addMinutes` more efficiently than either of the others; a program that uses this operation heavily would benefit from using version 2. On the other hand, version 3 executes `printTime` the fastest.

A more common reason to change representations is to allow for increased functionality, by permitting the addition of a new member function that cannot be implemented using the old representation. Suppose we wanted to add the new member function `daysElapsed` to `time`, which returns the number of days that have passed since the receiving object was first initialized. For example, the following statements would output **2**:

```
time startwork(8, 0);
startwork = startwork.addMinutes(2*60*24);
cout << startwork.daysElapsed() << "\n";
```

The existing member functions should give exactly the same results, of course, as they do now, so that functions that use them won't be broken by the addition of this new function.

The difficulty we have is that none of our three versions of `time` can support the new operation, because they only represent clock time within a 24-hour period. It is not hard to change the representation to accommodate this addition. A modification of version 2 is given in Figure 6.9; only by enforcing representation independence can we ensure that no existing programs will need to be changed when this version of `time` is introduced.

Exercises—Third Set

1. Add the accessors `getHour` and `getMinute` to version 3 of `time`.

2. As shown in Chapter 4, there are many ways to represent dates. In Exercise 4 on page 194 you used the Gregorian form. Reimplement that class (along with the `daysBetween` operation from page 201) using the "absolute date" form. This way `incrementDay` and `daysBetween` will be easier to implement, `printDate` harder.

3. Choosing a representation for a user-defined type is a matter not only of deciding the names and types of the data members of the class, but also of deciding exactly how those data members are used. In Exercise 4 on page 202, you represented rational

```
class time {
private:

  int minutes;

  time (int m) {minutes = m;}

public:

  time (int h, int m) {minutes = 60*h + m;}

  time addMinutes (int m) { return time(m + minutes); }

  time subtractMinutes (int m) { return addMinutes(-m); }

  int priorTo (time t) {
    int m = minutes % (24*60);
    if (m < 0)
      m = 24*60 + m;
    int tm = t.minutes % (24*60);
    if (tm < 0)
      tm = 24*60 + tm;
    return (m < tm);
  }

  int daysElapsed () { return (minutes / (24*60)); }

  void printTime () {
    int positiveMinutes = minutes;
    if (minutes < 0)
      positiveMinutes = (minutes % (24*60)) + 24*60;
    int hour = positiveMinutes / 60;
    int minute = positiveMinutes % 60;
    if ((hour == 0) && (minute == 0))
      cout << "midnight";
    else if ((hour == 12) && (minute == 0))
      cout << "noon";
    else {
      if (hour == 0)
        cout << 12;
      else if (hour > 12)
        cout << hour-12;
      else
        cout << hour;
      cout << ":" << setfill('0') << setw(2) << minute;
      if (hour < 12)
        cout << "AM";
      else
        cout << "PM";
    }
  }
};
```

FIGURE 6.9   The time class with daysElapsed.

numbers as arbitrary pairs of integers. However, you can use the same data members in a more "economical" way, which would tend to keep the numbers somewhat smaller, by keeping rational numbers in *reduced form*. Specifically, you can ensure that the data members **n** and **d** are relatively prime (have no common factors) by dividing out their greatest common divisor. Make this change and test it to ensure that clients see no difference in the results. Add one new function, **equal**, and notice how this representation makes it simpler. (Even with this change, **n** and **d** may overflow the range of **int** values. The ultimate solution is to use infinite-precision integers; see Chapter 7.)

4. In Exercise 3 on page 201 you represented a complex number using two real numbers: the real and imaginary parts of the complex number. There is a one-to-one correspondence between complex numbers and points on the plane; number $x + iy$ corresponds to point (x, y). An alternative representation, *polar representation*, identifies points by giving numbers r and θ (the *magnitude* and *argument*, respectively); (r, θ) represents the point that is at distance r from the origin along a line at angle θ from the x-axis. The same operations as you defined in Exercise 3 can be defined using polar representation, with clients seeing no change in the observable behavior of the class.

The absolute value and scaling operations are very simple: The absolute value of (r, θ) is r, and $a(r, \theta)$ is (ar, θ). The other operations are

- $(r, \theta) \times (r', \theta') = (rr', \theta + \theta')$.
- $(r, \theta) + (r', \theta') =$

$$\left(\sqrt{r\cos\theta + r'\cos\theta' + r\sin\theta + r'\sin\theta'}, \right.$$

$$\left. \arctan(r\sin\theta + r'\sin\theta', r\cos\theta + r'\cos\theta') \right)$$

where $\arctan(y, x)$ gives the tangent of the angle from the positive x-axis to the point (x, y).

- Conjugate of $(r, \theta) = (r, -\theta)$.

Implement the class **polarComplex** with the same operations and types (including constructor) as **complex**. Use the same main program as in Exercise 3, only changing **complex** to **polarComplex**, and test that the results are exactly the same as for the class **complex**. (Don't forget to include **math.h**. It contains the two-argument function **atan2**, which computes the arctan function.)

6.5

Overloading Functions and Operators

The same function name can be used for several different functions in C++. This eases the burden of coining names for functions, especially when you have several functions that do essentially the same thing for different types of data. However, the various functions that share a name need to have different numbers or types of arguments; that way, C++ knows which function to use in any particular call.

A common example is a function to print a value followed by a newline character. Having such a function can save you some typing if you often want to print a single value on a line, such as when you're debugging a program. Rather than requiring us to use a variant of this name for each type of argument (`printLineInt`, `printLineFloat`, `printLineTime`, etc.), C++ allows us to call them all `printLine`:

```
void printLine (int i) {cout << i << endl;}
void printLine (float x) {cout << x << endl;}
void printLine (time t) {t.printTime(); cout << endl;}
```

Calls such as `printLine(pi)` or `printLine(dawn)` will invoke the correct version of the function. If `printLine` is to be used for debugging, you may want to label the values. You can pass a label as a parameter of type **char ***, as explained in Chapter 4.

```
void printLine (char *label, int i) {
  cout << label << " " << i << endl;}
void printLine (char *label, float x) {
  cout << label << " " << x << endl;}
void printLine (char *label, time t) {
  cout << label << " "; t.printTime(); cout << endl;}
```

Now, the call `printLine("dawn = ", dawn)` will invoke the last version, as it should.

overloading

We say that the name `printLine` is *overloaded*, and this feature of C++—the ability to give multiple function definitions for a single name—is called *overloading*. We have already seen an example of overloading: multiple constructors in a class. Though we presented it as a feature unique to constructors, it is really just an example of overloading.

The overloading of `printLine` is easy to understand, but that is not always the case. Consider this example:

```
void f(int i, float x) {...}
void f(float x, int i) {...}
  ...
f(10, 20);
```

The programmer doesn't know which version of **f** will be called: C++ can convert the **20** to a **float** and use the first definition of **f**, or convert the **10** to a **float** and use the second definition.

The rules that C++ uses to decide which function to call are extremely complicated and are beyond the scope of this book. They also vary among C++ compilers. We advise you to solve Exercise 1 at the end of this section, which will give you some experience and show you what to expect from your compiler.

6.5.1   Overloading Operators

operator overloading

A handy feature of C++ is that it allows the overloading of *operators*—the special symbols like + and <<. *Operator overloading* permits a more elegant presentation of code, in which we can write **dawn + 10** instead of **dawn.addMinutes(10)**, and **cout << dawn** instead of **dawn.printTime()**.

To do this, we use the "full name" of the operator symbol. This name is composed of the word **operator** followed by the operator symbol; for example, **operator+** is the full name of the plus operator. The full name can be used with ordinary function-calling syntax. Thus, you can write the expression `cout << x+4` as

```
operator<<(cout, operator+(x, 4))
```

Of course, you would never want to write it this way. Still, it is useful to know an operator's full name, because by using its full name an operator can be overloaded just like any other function, as in

```
time operator+ (time t, int m) { return t.addMinutes(m); }
```

Now, an expression **expr1 + expr2**, where **expr1** is of type **time** and **expr2** is of type **int**, will be interpreted by C++ as a call to this definition of **operator+**.

In addition to the requirement that the C++ compiler must be able to resolve the overloading, there are some additional constraints on the overloading of operators. One obvious rule is that any overloading of an operator must have the correct number of arguments, depending on the operator (for example, two for **+**, one or two for **-**). Another is that an operator cannot be overloaded unless at least one of the arguments in the overloaded version is of user-defined type (or the operator is overloaded as a member function, as discussed below); this prevents the chaos that would result from having basic operations like integer addition redefined.

The operator **<<** is frequently overloaded. You may not even think of this as an operator, because you probably don't think of **cout** as a value. Actually, it is a variable containing an object of the class **ostream** (for "output stream"), which is predefined for you by C++. **ostream** has a number of public member functions that can be applied to **cout** using ordinary dot notation, but most of the time all you'll need is **operator<<**, so that is all we've shown you.

Like any operator, **operator<<** can be overloaded to apply to values of a user-defined type. You should be careful to conform to the conventional argument and return types for this operator. Here is a proper overloading of **operator<<** to print **time** objects:

```
ostream& operator<< (ostream& os, time t) {
  t.printTime();
  return os;
}
```

As with all binary operators, the first argument in the argument list corresponds to the one that appears on the left when the operator is used, and the second corresponds to the one on the right. This overloading of **operator<<** is used as follows:

```
cout << dawn;
```

The argument on the left is an **ostream** reference, and the one on the right is a **time** object, just as they were declared to be in the definition above.

Note that **operator<<** returns an **ostream** reference. The reason for this is to allow cascading of outputs, as in

```
cout << dawn << "\n";
```

The expression `cout << dawn` is evaluated first. The overloading of `operator<<` above is invoked; it prints the value of `dawn` and then returns the stream `cout`. Thus, when the second `operator<<` is called, its arguments are `cout` and `"\n"`. This invokes the built-in definition of `operator<<` for printing characters. By respecting the convention that `operator<<` returns its `ostream &` argument, we ensure that values of any type on which it is overloaded can appear in such a cascade of outputs.

With the overloadings of `+` and `<<` given above, `printSchedule` can be written as

```
void printSchedule (time start,
                    int apptLength,
                    int numberOfAppts) {
  for (int i=0; i<numberOfAppts; i++) {
    cout << start << " _____ \n";
    start = start + apptLength;
  }
}
```

6.5.2   Overloaded Operators as Member Functions

If the first argument of an operator is of a user-defined type, the overloaded operator can be defined as a member function. Aside from its name, such a function is exactly like any other member function. Thus, the definition of `operator+` can be given as a member function, looking exactly like the definition of `addMinutes`:

```
// Overloading of operator+ as a member function of time
time operator+ (int m) {
    int totalMinutes = ...
    ...
}
```

An expression `expr1 + expr2`, where `expr1` is of type `time` and `expr2` is of type `int`, is interpreted as the expression

```
expr1.operator+(expr2)
```

and `printSchedule` would be written exactly as shown above. Note that this definition of `operator+` is given *in place of* the function `addMinutes`, whereas the previous overloading of `operator+` called the member function `addMinutes` and therefore was defined *in addition to* it.

Keep in mind that an operator can be overloaded as a member function only when its *first* argument is of user-defined type. Thus, `operator<<` *cannot* be overloaded as a member function of `time`, because its first argument is of type `ostream &`, not `time`.

A complete version of `time`, with operators overloaded as appropriate, is given in Figure 6.10. The definition of `operator+`, as explained above, looks just like the definition of `addMinutes`; only its name is different. Similarly, `operator<` has the same definition as `priorTo`. `operator<<` cannot be overloaded as a member function, so member function `printTime` remains as before, and `operator<<` is overloaded as a client.

```
class time {
private:

  int hour, minute;

public:

  time (int h, int m) { hour = h; minute = m; }

  time operator+ (int m) {   // + overloaded as member
    int totalMinutes = (60*hour + minute + m) % (24*60);
    if (totalMinutes < 0)
      totalMinutes = totalMinutes + 24*60;
    return time(totalMinutes/60, totalMinutes%60);
  }

  void printTime () {
    if ((hour == 0) && (minute == 0))
      cout << "midnight";
    else if ((hour == 12) && (minute == 0))
      cout << "noon";
    else {
      if (hour == 0)
        cout << 12;
      else if (hour > 12)
            cout << hour-12;
          else cout << hour;
      cout << ":" << setfill('0') << setw(2) << minute;
      if (hour < 12)
        cout << "AM";
      else
        cout << "PM";
    }
  }
  time operator- (int m) { // - overloaded as member
    return operator+(-m);
  }

  boolean operator< (time t) { // < overloaded as member
    return ((hour < t.hour) ||
            ((hour == t.hour) && (minute < t.minute)));
  }
};

// << overloaded as client
ostream& operator<< (ostream& os, time t) {
  t.printTime();
  return os;
}
```

FIGURE 6.10   time with operator overloading.

As a matter of good programming style, when we overload `operator<`, we should do the same for all the other comparison operators: `operator>`, `operator==`, `operator>=`, `operator<=`, and `operator!=`. Clients will expect it. We have left that as an exercise.

The definition of `operator-` looks strange. We would like to write its body as

```
return <receiver of message>+(-m)
```

using the infix form of `operator+`, but as before, we have no way to refer to the receiver. Using the full name of the operator allows us to write the function just as in the previous versions of the class.

Exercises—Fourth Set

1. You can see how your C++ compiler resolves overloading in specific cases by experiment. For example, consider this program, which tests what a compiler does for the difficult overloading case discussed on page 210:

```
int f(float x, int i) {return i;}

int f(int i, float x) {return i;}

main () {
  cout << f(10, 20) << endl;
}
```

Though one of our compilers gives an error message—the right thing to do!—the other prints **20**, indicating that the first definition of **f** was called. Furthermore, changing the order in which the two definitions are given,

```
int f(int i, float x) {return i;}

int f(float x, int i) {return i;}

main () {
  cout << f(10, 20) << endl;
}
```

produces the output **10**.

Run these two programs to see what your compiler does. Then write programs to determine how your compiler resolves the following overloading situations:
   (a) Function **f** has two definitions. In the first it has one argument, of type `float`; in the second it has two arguments, of types `int` and `float`, respectively. It is called with a single integer argument.
   (b) **g** is two definitions, both with two arguments. In one, both arguments are of type `int` and in the other they are of type `float`. **g** is called with one integer and one float argument.
   (c) **h** has two definitions. In one, its two arguments have types `int` and `boolean`, respectively, and in the other the argument types are reversed. What happens if **h** is called with two boolean arguments? With two integer arguments? Does the order in which the two definitions of **h** are given affect the answer in either case?

☞ 2. Rename both `subtractMinutes` and `subtractTimes` (page 201) as `difference`. Then overload `operator-` with both definitions.

☞ 3. In Figure 6.10 we showed how to overload `operator<` as a member function of `time`. Now add overloaded definitions of the other comparison operators: `operator>`, `operator==`, `operator>=`, `operator<=`, and `operator!=`. They can be added either as client functions (except `operator==`, which should be added as a member function), or as members. Do it both ways.

4. The extraction operator (`>>`) can be overloaded to provide a convenient syntax for input of values of user-defined type. To read a new value of type `T`, it should be declared as

```
istream& operator>> (istream&, T&)
```

Overload this operator to read `time` objects. These objects should be typed in as two numbers separated by one or more spaces, the first number between 0 and 23, the second between 0 and 59. Note that `operator>>`, like `operator<<`, can be overloaded only as a client of `time`, not as a member, since its first argument is not of type `time`. Bear in mind that within this overloaded definition the usual definition of `>>` for reading integers can be used, and be sure to return the first argument of `operator>>` as its result, as is done in `operator<<`.

5. In Exercise 5 on page 195 and Exercise 3 on page 201 you implemented the `complex` class. Overload the arithmetic operators as complex operators as follows: `add` as `operator+`, `printComplex` as `<<`, and both `scale` and `multiply` as `*`.

Mutable and Immutable Types

Of all the member functions in all our versions of `time`, only the constructors ever *assign* values to data members. A `time` instance has its data members filled in by a constructor, and they are never changed. Some of the member functions return *new* `time` objects with different data members, but none ever changes the data members of its receiver. `time` objects are therefore called *immutable*, and the `time` class is an *immutable class* or *immutable type*.

immutable class

    A class need not be immutable; member functions are allowed to change data members by assignment. Such member functions are called *mutating operations*, and a class that has mutating operations is called a *mutable class* or *mutable type*.

mutable class

    Consider as an example the following mutating operation on `time`, using the original (version 1) representation:

```
void advanceMinutes (int m) {
   int totalMinutes = (60*hour + minute + m) % (24*60);
   if (totalMinutes < 0)
     totalMinutes = totalMinutes + 24*60;
   hour = totalMinutes/60;
   minute = totalMinutes%60;
}
```

This is similar to **addMinutes**, but **advanceMinutes** changes the data members of the receiver and doesn't return anything, while **addMinutes** returns a new object giving the later time and leaves its receiver alone. The difference to clients is illustrated by this code:

```
1    time lunchtime(12, 0), dinnertime(0, 0);
2    lunchtime.printTime();                // prints:  noon
3    lunchtime.advanceMinutes(10);
4    lunchtime.printTime();                // prints:  12:10PM
5    dinnertime = lunchtime.addMinutes(6*60);
6    lunchtime.printTime();                // still prints:  12:10PM
7    dinnertime.printTime();               // prints:  6:10PM
```

A trace is shown in Figure 6.11. After line 1 **lunchtime** and **dinnertime** contain **time** objects as shown in part (a). In line 3 the **advanceMinutes** message is sent to **lunchtime**; this situation is shown in part (b). The result, shown in part (c), is that the **minute** member is changed to 10. In line 5 **addMinutes** is sent to **lunchtime** (Figure 6.11(d)); it does not change the data members of any objects but returns a new **time** object (Figure 6.11(e)). Finally, this new object is stored in **dinnertime**.

Note that it is illegal to write

```
lunchtime = lunchtime.advanceMinutes(10);
```

because **advanceMinutes** doesn't return anything. Similarly,

```
lunchtime.addMinutes(10);
```

is wrong, because the return type of **addMinutes** is not **void**.

The point is that line 3 *changed* the contents of **lunchtime** by *changing the data members of the object it contained,* whereas line 5 *changed* **dinnertime** by *replacing its contents with an entirely new object.* The difference between a class that has mutating operations and one that does not is

> For an *immutable* class **C** the value of a variable of type **C** can be changed *only* by an assignment statement. For a *mutable* class, the value of a variable can be changed either by assignment or by sending a message.

Our goal is to write programs that are clear and easy to understand. Mutating operations make programs harder to understand, because they make it difficult to know when a variable's value will change. It is unfortunate that in C++—as in most languages—there is no requirement that mutating operations be clearly identified as such wherever they are called. The best policy is to avoid them whenever the use of nonmutating operations is equally convenient.

There are, however, times when mutating operations are more sensible than nonmutating ones. A good example is a class that implements a *transition diagram.* As we saw in Section 3.5, a diagram describing the "states" of a device such as an alarm watch is a useful way of conceptualizing certain programs. There, the

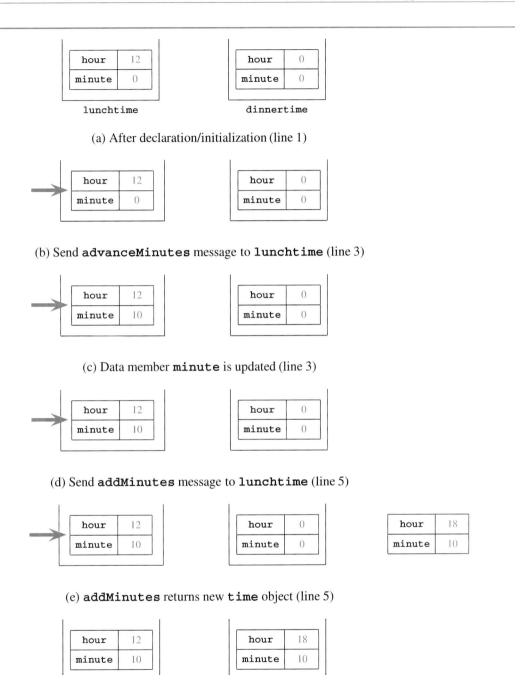

(a) After declaration/initialization (line 1)

(b) Send **advanceMinutes** message to **lunchtime** (line 3)

(c) Data member **minute** is updated (line 3)

(d) Send **addMinutes** message to **lunchtime** (line 5)

(e) **addMinutes** returns new **time** object (line 5)

(f) After assignment to **dinnertime** (line 5)

FIGURE 6.11   Trace of statements using **advanceMinutes**.

switch statement was used to implement the transitions, with **enum** types used to name the states. In this section, we will see how user-defined types can implement transition diagrams.

Review the diagram on page 77, which represents the control of an alarm watch with three buttons (*A*, *B*, and *C*). Pushing the buttons in the right sequence allows the setting of either clock time or alarm time. In this section, we'll use a slightly simplified diagram, shown in Figure 6.12.

The class **alarmClock** will represent a clock with a particular time, alarm setting, and state. It is natural to represent such a clock by these three values:

```
enum state {displayTime, setTimeHour, setTimeMin,
            displayAlarmTime, setAlarmHour, setAlarmMin};
state s;
time clockTime, alarmTime;
```

Note something in this class that we haven't seen before: Two of the data members of **alarmClock** are themselves objects of another user-defined type.

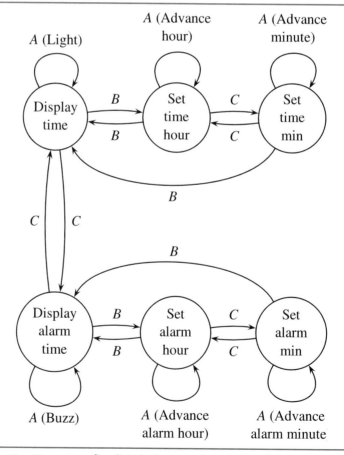

FIGURE 6.12   Operation of a digital alarm watch with three buttons (a simplified version of Figure 3.1 on page 77).

For example, a clock whose face reads 11:45 A.M., set to ring at 7:00 A.M., in the display-time state, would be represented by

state	displayTime	
clockTime	hour	11
	minute	45
alarmTime	hour	7
	minute	0

For this class we'll provide a zero-argument constructor that sets the clock to midnight, reflecting what happens in real life when a digital clock is first plugged in.

```
alarmClock () {
  s = displayTime;
  clockTime = time(0, 0);
  alarmTime = time(0, 0);
}
```

But this is wrong; the problem is very subtle, and before we discuss its solution we'd like to look at the member functions.

The main idea behind this class is that "pushing a button" is interpreted as "sending a message." Thus, the three buttons will be implemented as mutating member functions. There will be one clock, which will change its settings rather than producing a new **alarmClock**. Thus, the outline of the class is

```
class alarmClock {
private:
  enum state {displayTime, setTimeHour, setTimeMin,
              displayAlarmTime, setAlarmHour, setAlarmMin};
  state s;
  time clockTime, alarmTime;

public:
  alarmClock () { ... }

  void readDisplay () { ... }

  void readAlarm () { ... }

  void A () ;

  void B () ;

  void C () ;
};
```

where we have chosen to give prototypes of **A**, **B**, and **C** and to give their definitions after the class, as explained on page 199. The complete definition of the **alarmClock** class is shown in Figure 6.13.

When the clock receives the **A** message, its response will depend upon its state, as shown in Figure 6.12. Usually, the response will involve changing the state, and it may also change the clock or alarm time or display one or the other. For example,

```
void alarmClock::A () {
  switch (s) {
    case displayTime:  cout << "turn light on\n"; break;
    case setTimeHour:  clockTime = clockTime+60; break;
    case setTimeMin:   clockTime = clockTime+1; break;
    case displayAlarmTime: cout << "sound buzzer\n"; break;
    case setAlarmHour: alarmTime = alarmTime+60; break;
    case setAlarmMin:  alarmTime = alarmTime+1; break;
  }
}
```

The **B** and **C** member functions are equally straightforward. Both are shown, along with a correct version of the zero-argument constructor, in Figure 6.13.

Now back to the error in our original zero-argument constructor. What we attempted to do in our first version, on page 219 (set the state to **displayTime** and set the clock and alarm times to midnight) was conceptually correct. However, C++ complained with this message:

```
In method 'alarmClock::alarmClock ()':
line 68: too few arguments for constructor 'time'
line 68: in base initialization for class 'time'
line 68: too few arguments for constructor 'time'
line 68: in base initialization for class 'time'
```

It says that **clockTime** and **alarmTime** haven't been initialized. We've already noted that C++ insists that all instances be initialized, by calling a constructor, when created; certainly, when a new **alarmClock** object is created, it will in turn create two **time** objects. So, it would be reasonable for C++ to complain, except that **clockTime** and **alarmTime** *are* initialized in lines 70 and 71. So what's the problem?

initialization list   Though C++ insists that the two **time** objects be initialized, it will not look *inside* the body of the **alarmClock** constructor to make sure there are assignments to them. Instead, it provides special syntax, called *initialization lists*. Here is the correct form of the constructor:

```
alarmClock ()  : clockTime(0, 0), alarmTime(0, 0) {
  s = displayTime;
}
```

where we have shown the initialization list in blue. It tells C++ to initialize the **clockTime** and **alarmTime** data members by calling the two-argument

```
class alarmClock {
private:
  enum state {displayTime, setTimeHour, setTimeMin,
              displayAlarmTime, setAlarmHour, setAlarmMin};
  state s;
  time clockTime, alarmTime;

public:
  alarmClock () : clockTime(0, 0), alarmTime(0, 0) {
    s = displayTime;
  }

  void readDisplay () { cout << clockTime << "\n"; }

  void readAlarm () { cout << alarmTime << "\n"; }

  void A () ;

  void B () ;

  void C () ;
};

void alarmClock::A () {
  switch (s) {
    case displayTime:      cout << "turn light on\n"; break;
    case setTimeHour:      clockTime = clockTime+60; break;
    case setTimeMin:       clockTime = clockTime+1; break;
    case displayAlarmTime: cout << "sound buzzer\n"; break;
    case setAlarmHour:     alarmTime = alarmTime+60; break;
    case setAlarmMin:      alarmTime = alarmTime+1; break;
  }
}

void alarmClock::B () {
  switch (s) {
    case displayTime:      s = setTimeHour; break;
    case setTimeHour:      s = displayTime; break;
    case setTimeMin:       s = displayTime; break;
    case displayAlarmTime: s = setAlarmHour; break;
    case setAlarmHour:     s = displayAlarmTime; break;
    case setAlarmMin:      s = displayAlarmTime; break;
  }
}

void alarmClock::C () {
  switch (s) {
    case displayTime:      s = displayAlarmTime; break;
    case setTimeHour:      s = setTimeMin; break;
    case setTimeMin:       s = setTimeHour; break;
    case displayAlarmTime: s = displayTime; break;
    case setAlarmHour:     s = setAlarmHour; break;
    case setAlarmMin:      s = setAlarmMin; break;
  }
}
```

FIGURE 6.13   The alarmClock class.

constructor of `time`, with both arguments 0. This way, C++ can guarantee that these two data members are initialized.

Initialization lists begin with a colon (`:`) following the function header. The order in which data members are named in an initialization list is immaterial. The arguments to constructors appearing in the initialization list (the `time` constructor in this example) need not always be constants. If the `alarmClock` constructor had arguments, they could be used as well, and so could global variables.

You must have an initialization list on any constructor for a class (such as `alarmClock`) that has data members of user-defined types (such as `clockTime` and `alarmTime`). The only exception is when the class of those data members has a zero-argument constructor, in which case that constructor will be called if the data member is not included in the initialization list.

Initialization lists can also be used for nonuser-defined types. Thus, the constructor can be written in this way:

```
alarmClock () : clockTime(0, 0), alarmTime(0, 0),
                state(displayTime)
   {}
```

This form of constructor—a long initialization list with an empty function body—is common. We'll use it often.

Finally, a warning about mutable data types and functions is necessary. When objects of user-defined type are passed as arguments to functions, remember that they are passed *by value* (just like `int`s, `float`s, and so on, as explained in Chapter 4). In other words, when an object is passed as an argument, it is *copied*. Consider this function, which uses the mutating member function `advanceMinutes` that we previously added to `time`, and its call from `main`:

```
void advanceHours (time t, int h) {
  t.advanceMinutes(60*h);
}

main () {
  time dawn(5, 0);
  advanceHours(dawn, 3);
  cout << dawn << "\n";
}
```

The output from this program is `5:00AM`! When `dawn` is passed from `main` to `advanceHours`, it is copied. The `advanceMinutes` message is sent *to the copy*, and it changes the data members *of the copy*, but `dawn` itself is unchanged.

Clearly, in this case the result is surprising and unintended. The solution is simple: Pass the `time` object by reference. With this change in `advanceHours`,

```
void advanceHours (time& t, int h) {
  t.advanceMinutes(60*h);
}
```

the main program above prints `8:00AM`.

6.7

Debugging Classes

To illustrate the process of debugging classes, let's write a program to evaluate polynomials. The user's input will be in two parts, the first describing a polynomial (in one variable), and the second giving various values of the variable at which the polynomial is to be evaluated. Here is an example:

```
Enter exponents and coefficients, then -1: 0 4 1 7.9 3 2.25 -1
Enter x value: 4
The value of the polynomial at 4 is 179.6
Enter x value: -1.3
The value of the polynomial at -1.3 is -11.2132
Enter x value: ^D
```

The first line of input describes the polynomial $4 + 7.9x + 2.25x^3$. Subsequent lines of input give values of x at which to evaluate this polynomial. The values of exponents can be given in any order, but they must not be repeated and are confined to the range 0 to 4.

We'll define a class **Polynomial** whose data members contain the coefficients. Since each coefficient is represented by a data member, it is rather tedious to deal with polynomials of very high order, which is why this class only allows for order-4 polynomials. The most important member function in **Polynomial** is

```
float Polynomial::evaluateAt (float x)
```

which evaluates the receiver at value **x**. Once the polynomial has been read and a **Polynomial** object has been created, we read values from the terminal and call **evaluateAt** to compute the values.

Here is our first attempt at the **Polynomial** class:

```
1   //
2   // Program to read and evaluate a polynomial
3   // of order less than or equal to 4.
4   //
5   // Author: D. Kamin
6   // Last modified: 7/10/95
7   //
8
9   #include <iostream.h>
10  #include <iomanip.h>
11
12  //
13  // Objects of class Polynomial represent polynomials
14  // of order less than or equal to 4.
15  //
16  class Polynomial {
17  private:
18    float coeff0, coeff1, coeff2, coeff3, coeff4;
19    // Coefficients of x^0 term, x^1 term, ..., x^4 term
20
21  public:
```

```
22      Polynomial () : coeff0(0.0), coeff1(0.0), coeff2(0.0),
23                      coeff3(0.0), coeff4(0.0),
24      {}
25
26      float evaluateAt (float x) {
27        return coeff0
28               + coeff1 * x
29               + coeff2 * x * x
30               + coeff3 * x * x * x
31               + coeff4 * x * x * x * x;
32      }
33
34      float setCoeff (int i, float c) {
35      // Set coefficient of x^i term to c
36        switch (i) {
37          case 0: coeff0 = c;
38          case 1: coeff1 = c;
39          case 2: coeff2 = c;
40          case 3: coeff3 = c;
41          case 4: coeff4 = c;
42        }
43      }
44    };
```

Since the coefficients will be entered in any order, and some may be missing, it seems easiest to set them individually as they are input, so we added the mutating operation **setCoeff**. To input the polynomial, overloading **operator>>** is easy, so that's what we'll do. Here are the definitions of **operator>>** and **main**:

```
46    istream& operator>> (istream& is, Polynomial p) {
47      int i;
48      float f;
49      cout << "Enter exponents and coefficients, then -1: ";
50      cin >> i;
51      while (i != -1) {
52        cin >> f;
53        p.setCoeff(i, f);
54        cin >> i;
55      }
56      return is;
57    }
58
59    void main () {
60      float x;
61
62      cin >> poly;
63      cout << "Enter x value: ";
64      cin >> x;
65      while (!cin.eof()) {
66        cout << "The value of the polynomial at "
67             << x << " is " << poly.evaluateAt(x) << endl;
68        cout << "Enter x value: ";
69        cin >> x;
70      }
71    }
```

This fails to compile:

```
line 24: error: syntax error
line 27: error:  coeff0 undefined
line 27: error:  coeff1 undefined
line 27: error:  + of void*
line 27: error:  coeff2 undefined
line 27: error:  coeff3 undefined
line 27: error:  coeff4 undefined
line 46: error:  Polynomial undefined, size not known
line 53: error:  member setCoeff undefined
line 62: error:  poly undefined
line 62: error:  pointer operand for  >>
line 67: error:  pointer operand for  <<
line 67: error:  pointer operand for  <<
line 67: error:  function operand for  <<
Sorry, too many errors
14 errors
```

Looking at line 24 above—which just contains {}—we don't see anything promising. As is often the case, the error is actually on the previous line: the comma at the end of line 23.

We have learned that in our compiler there is little point in looking past the first error, because one error like this can make the compiler very confused and cause many other errors. So we fix this line and run the compiler again. Unfortunately, there are more errors:

```
line 16: warning: "inline" ignored,
         Polynomial::setCoeff() contains switch
line 16: warning: no value returned from Polynomial::setCoeff()
line 62: error:  poly undefined
line 62: error:  pointer operand for  >>
line 67: error:  pointer operand for  <<
line 67: error:  pointer operand for  <<
line 67: error:  function operand for  <<
5 errors
```

The error on line 16—the first line of the class definition—is cryptic. It refers to a problem we mentioned earlier in this chapter: Sometimes member functions cannot be defined inside classes but must be defined outside them. Our compiler is telling us that it cannot compile a member function *inside* the class definition if that member function contains a **switch** statement. (See Section E.4 of Appendix E for an explanation.) So we move **setCoeff** out of the class:

```
//
// Objects of class Polynomial represent polynomials
// of order less than or equal to 4.
//
```

```
class Polynomial {
private:
  float coeff0, coeff1, coeff2, coeff3, coeff4;
  // Coefficients of x^0 term, x^1 term, ..., x^4 term

public:
  Polynomial () : coeff0(0.0), coeff1(0.0), coeff2(0.0),
                  coeff3(0.0), coeff4(0.0)
  {}

  float evaluateAt (float x) {
    return coeff0
        + coeff1 * x
        + coeff2 * x * x
        + coeff3 * x * x * x
        + coeff4 * x * x * x * x;
  }

  void setCoeff (int i, float c) ;
};

void setCoeff (int i, float c) {
// Set coefficient of x^i term to c
  switch (i) {
    case 0: coeff0 = c;
    case 1: coeff1 = c;
    case 2: coeff2 = c;
    case 3: coeff3 = c;
    case 4: coeff4 = c;
  }
}
```

Our attempt to compile is again met with stubborn resistance from our compiler:

```
line 40: error:  coeff0 undefined
line 41: error:  coeff1 undefined
line 42: error:  coeff2 undefined
line 43: error:  coeff3 undefined
line 44: error:  coeff4 undefined
line 64: error:  poly undefined
line 64: error:  pointer operand for  >>
line 69: error:  pointer operand for  <<
line 69: error:  pointer operand for  <<
line 69: error:  function operand for  <<
10 errors
```

It says that none of the data members are recognized as such in the definition of **setCoeff**. We see that there was no such problem in the constructor or in **evaluateAt**.

This is one case where there's no substitute for experience, because you could probably stare at this for an hour and not see the error. We've omitted the

`Polynomial::` in defining `setCoeff` outside of the class. As a result, C++ does
not realize that it is a member function, so the data members have no meaning.

This is easily fixed:

```
void Polynomial::setCoeff (int i, float c) {
  ...
}
```

and the result apparently eliminates all errors in the class definition, leaving errors
only in **main** (line numbers in **main** have increased by 2 due to the changes in
`Polynomial`):

```
line 64: error:  poly undefined
line 64: error:  pointer operand for  >>
line 69: error:  pointer operand for  <<
line 69: error:  pointer operand for  <<
line 69: error:  function operand for  <<
5 errors
```

The error on line 64 is pretty obvious: no declaration of the variable **poly**.

Adding the declaration

```
Polynomial poly;
```

in **main**, our program finally compiles without errors. So we run it:

```
Enter exponents and coefficients, then -1: 0 4 1 7 -1
Enter x value: 3
The value of the polynomial at 3 is 0
Enter x value: ^D
```

But this is wrong. Polynomial $4 + 7x$, evaluated at $x = 3$, is 25, not zero.

At this point we're lost. The first thing we should do is make sure that the
polynomial is being input correctly. In order to take a look at **poly** after it has
been read, we'll add a function **print** as a member function of **Polynomial**:

```
void print () {
  cout << coeff0
       << " + " << coeff1 << "x"
       << " + " << coeff2 << "x^2"
       << " + " << coeff3 << "x^3"
       << " + " << coeff4 << "x^4"
       << endl;
}
```

and call it from **main**:

```
void main () {
  float x;
  Polynomial poly;

  cin >> poly;
  cout << "Polynomial is ";  poly.print();
  cout << "Enter x value: ";
  cin >> x;
```

```
      while (!cin.eof()) {
        cout << "The value of the polynomial at "
             << x << " is " << poly.evaluateAt(x) << endl;
        cout << "Enter x value: ";
        cin >> x;
      }
    }
```

This program compiles, and when we run it, we see the problem immediately:

```
Enter exponents and coefficients, then -1: 0 4 1 7 -1
Polynomial is 0 + 0x + 0x^2 + 0x^3 + 0x^4
Enter x value: ^D
```

For some reason, **poly** has all zero coefficients!

It is hard to see how **setCoeff** could fail to set *any* coefficients to anything other than zero. And it is equally hard to see how **operator>>** could be failing to read in values correctly. Just to be sure, though, let's put the call to **print** inside **operator>>**:

```
istream& operator>> (istream& is, Polynomial p) {
  int i;
  float f;
  cout << "Enter exponents and coefficients, then -1: ";
  cin >> i;
  while (i != -1) {
    cin >> f;
    p.setCoeff(i, f);
    cin >> i;
  }
  cout << "Polynomial is ";  p.print();
  return is;
}
```

Compiling and running this program, we get something of a surprise:

```
Enter exponents and coefficients, then -1: 0 4 1 7 -1
Polynomial is 4 + 7x + 7x^2 + 7x^3 + 7x^4
Polynomial is 0 + 0x + 0x^2 + 0x^3 + 0x^4
Enter x value: ^D
```

It seems as if the polynomial is nonzero within **operator>>** but is zero after **operator>>** returns! Furthermore, the polynomial is wrong: *All* the coefficients but the first are 7, even though we only set the coefficient of x to 7 (the rest should be zero). The bugs are piling up!

The more disabling of the two problems is that the polynomial seems to be changing its value during the return from **operator>>**. After a little thinking, we see the problem: **poly** should have been passed into **operator>>** as a *reference* parameter. As it is, **poly** is passed as an ordinary value parameter, meaning it is copied in when the function is called, and it itself never changes. Just adding an ampersand to the argument list of **operator>>**,

```
istream& operator>> (istream& is, Polynomial& p) {
  ...
}
```

leads to much better results:

```
Enter exponents and coefficients, then -1: 0 4 1 7 -1
Polynomial is 4 + 7x + 7x^2 + 7x^3 + 7x^4
Polynomial is 4 + 7x + 7x^2 + 7x^3 + 7x^4
Enter x value: 3
The value of the polynomial at 3 is 844
Enter x value:
```

The polynomial is being passed back from **operator>>**, though it is still wrong. On the other hand, **evaluateAt** seems to be working. The polynomial $4 + 7x + 7x^2 + 7x^3 + 7x^4$, evaluated at $x = 3$, is indeed 844.

Placing the call to **print** *inside* the loop in **operator>>** would be the way to go next, but a quick look at **setCoeff** reveals that we made a classic error: omitting the **break** statements in a **switch** statement. The effect is that whenever any case within the **switch** statement is chosen, every statement *after* the chosen one is also executed. Fixing **setCoeff**,

```
void Polynomial::setCoeff (int i, float c) {
// Set coefficient of x^i term to c
  switch (i) {
    case 0: coeff0 = c; break;
    case 1: coeff1 = c; break;
    case 2: coeff2 = c; break;
    case 3: coeff3 = c; break;
    case 4: coeff4 = c; break;
  }
}
```

leads, at last, to a working version of the program:

```
Enter exponents and coefficients, then -1: 0 4 1 7 -1
Enter x value: 3
The value of the polynomial at 3 is 25
Enter x value: 4
The value of the polynomial at 4 is 32
Enter x value: 3.5
The value of the polynomial at 3.5 is 28.5
Enter x value: ^D
```

We need to test the program for other inputs to gain real confidence in it. We'll try one more example:

```
Enter exponents and coefficients, then -1: 3 1.2 5 0.11 -1
Enter x value: 2
The value of the polynomial at 2 is 9.6
Enter x value: ^D
```

Oops! $1.2x^3 + 0.11x^5$, evaluated at $x = 2$, is not equal to 9.6. In fact, this is the value of $1.2x^3$ evaluated at $x = 2$. It seems as if the x^5 term has been ignored.

Well, of course it has! We said at the outset that only exponents in the range 0 to 4 were to be considered. Still, we can't just leave the program like this. Changing **setCoeff** to catch the error,

```
void Polynomial::setCoeff (int i, float c) {
// Set coefficient of x^i term to c
  switch (i) {
    case 0: coeff0 = c; break;
    case 1: coeff1 = c; break;
    case 2: coeff2 = c; break;
    case 3: coeff3 = c; break;
    case 4: coeff4 = c; break;
    default:
      cout << "Coefficient of x^" << i <<" ignored;"
           << " exponents must be in range 0-4.\n";
  }
}
```

gives more desirable behavior in this case:

```
Enter exponents and coefficients, then -1: 3 1.2 5 0.11 -1
Coefficient of x^5 ignored;  exponents must be in range 0-4.
```

Further testing shows that the program works as expected. Here is our final version:

```
1    //
2    // Program to read and evaluate a polynomial
3    // of order less than or equal to 4.
4    //
5    // Author: D. Kamin
6    // Last modified: 7/10/95
7    //
8
9    #include <iostream.h>
10   #include <iomanip.h>
11
12   //
13   // Objects of class Polynomial represent polynomials
14   // of order less than or equal to 4.
15   //
16   class Polynomial {
17   private:
18     float coeff0, coeff1, coeff2, coeff3, coeff4;
19     // Coefficients of x^0 term, x^1 term, ..., x^4 term
20
21   public:
22     Polynomial () : coeff0(0.0), coeff1(0.0), coeff2(0.0),
23                     coeff3(0.0), coeff4(0.0)
24     {}
25
26     float evaluateAt (float x) {
27       return coeff0
28             + coeff1 * x
29             + coeff2 * x * x
30             + coeff3 * x * x * x
31             + coeff4 * x * x * x * x;
32     }
33
```

```
34      void setCoeff (int i, float c) ;
35    };
36
37    void Polynomial::setCoeff (int i, float c) {
38    // Set coefficient of x^i term to c
39      switch (i) {
40        case 0: coeff0 = c; break;
41        case 1: coeff1 = c; break;
42        case 2: coeff2 = c; break;
43        case 3: coeff3 = c; break;
44        case 4: coeff4 = c; break;
45        default:
46          cout << "Coefficient of x^" << i <<" ignored;"
47                << "  exponents must be in range 0-4.\n";
48      }
49    }
50
51    istream& operator>> (istream& is, Polynomial& p) {
52      int i;
53      float f;
54      cout << "Enter exponents and coefficients, then -1: ";
55      cin >> i;
56      while (i != -1) {
57        cin >> f;
58        p.setCoeff(i, f);
59        cin >> i;
60      }
61      return is;
62    }
63
64    void main () {
65      float x;
66      Polynomial poly;
67
68      cin >> poly;
69      cout << "Enter x value: ";
70      cin >> x;
71      while (!cin.eof()) {
72        cout << "The value of the polynomial at "
73              << x << " is " << poly.evaluateAt(x) << endl;
74        cout << "Enter x value: ";
75        cin >> x;
76      }
77    }
```

Exercises—Fifth Set

☞ 1. Change **alarmClock** to use a version of **time** that includes the mutating operation **advanceMinutes**, defined on page 215, instead of **addMinutes**.

2. Using the version of **time** from Exercise 3 on page 194, which includes seconds, modify the **alarmClock** class to mimic the transition diagram in Figure 3.1 on page 77 exactly.

3. Mutating operations can enhance the efficiency of a class without changing the meanings of any operations. For example, we know that for the **time** class the representation

in terms of total number of minutes (version 2) is most efficient for calculations (for example, **addMinutes**), while the representation using the A.M./P.M. indicator (version 3) is best for printing. It is possible to get the advantages of both representations by *choosing the representation as you go*.

To do this, define **time** to have five data members: **minutes** from version 2; **hour**, **minute**, and **AM** from version 3; and the **boolean** data member **allvalid**. **allvalid** has the following meaning: If it is true, then all four of the other data members are valid—that is, the **minutes** field gives the total number of minutes for the given hour and minute in the morning or afternoon. If **allvalid** is false, then **minutes** contains the correct value, but **hour**, **minute**, and **AM** should not be trusted. When the two-argument constructor is called, **allvalid** should be set to true and the other four data members set as shown in the constructors for versions 2 and 3. However, when **addMinutes**, or any other computational operation, is applied, the returned value should set only **minutes** correctly and should set **allvalid** to false. This avoids the complicated calculation needed to find the correct values of **hour**, **minute**, and **AM**. When the **printTime** message is sent, however, these should be calculated, and **allvalid** should be set to true. This way, the calculations you do before printing the date are inexpensive, but if you print a time more than once, the calculations needed to print it are done only once. (This is an application of a rule of computation called *lazy evaluation*: Avoid doing expensive calculations until the last possible moment—they may turn out not to be necessary after all; furthermore, having done them, remember the result and avoid recalculating them.)

Program **time** this way.

4. The children's game of Cootie was described in Exercise 13 on page 90. Create a class to represent the current state of the picture:

```
class cootie {
private:
  ...
public:
  cootie () {...} // blank sheet of paper

  void drawBody () {...}

  void drawHead () {...}

  void drawAntenna () {...}

  void drawLeg () {...}

  void drawTail () {...}

  void drawEye () {...}

  void status () {...} // what parts are missing?

  boolean complete () {...} // true if picture complete
};
```

The various **draw** functions should print an appropriate error message if the operation is illegal as explained on page 90. The **status** operation should print a summary of what parts are yet to be drawn.

Write a main program to exercise the `cootie` class. It should repeatedly read a number between 1 and 6, giving the value of the die throw, and print the status after each throw. When the picture is complete, it should start a new blank page and play again, until the user stops playing by entering the end-of-file character (^D).

★   5. In computerized drawing programs, one places a shape on the screen and can then perform various operations such as moving, resizing, and rotating. Define the `rectangle` class to represent rectangles and perform those operations:

```
class rectangle {
private:
  int x1, y1,     // one corner
      x2, y2;     // the opposing corner
public:
  rectangle (int X1, int Y1,    // (X1, Y1) is one corner
             int X2, int Y2)    // (X2, Y2) is opposite corner
  {...}

  void move (int deltax, int deltay) {
    // Move this rectangle deltax in the x direction,
    // deltay in the y direction
    ...
  }

  void reshape (int x, int y, int newx, int newy) {
    // (x, y) is one of the four corners.  It is to be moved
    // to (newx, newy), leaving the opposite corner stationary
    ...
  }

  void rotate () {
    // Rotate rectangle 90 degrees, leaving center fixed
    ...
  }

  rectangle duplicate (int delta) {
    // Create a new rectangle identical to this one, except
    // that it is moved by delta in both directions
    ...
  }

  void display () {
    // Print the four corners of the rectangle in clockwise order
    ...
  }
};
```

Integers are used here instead of floating-point numbers because the points represent positions on the screen, viewed as a grid (see Section 9.7 for a detailed explanation).

Write a main program to test these functions. It should repeatedly read a line of input, consisting of one or more numbers, until the user enters the end-of-file character. On each line, the first number represents the operation to be performed: 0 to create a new rectangle, 1 for move, 2 for reshape, 3 for rotate, 4 for duplicate, and 5 for display. Operations 1, 2, 3, and 5 operate on the most recently created (whether by operation

0 or 4) rectangle. For operations 0, 1, 2, and 4, the initial integer is followed by the appropriate number of integers, according to the number of arguments that member function has.

Summary

A *class* has a name and consists of a collection of *data member* declarations—which look exactly like variable declarations—followed by *constructors* and *member function* definitions. For example, a class named C with data members i and **x**, of types **int** and **float** respectively, two constructors, and member functions **f** and **g**, would have the form

```
class C {
private:
  int i;
  float x;
```
←| **Data members** |

```
public:
  C (int a) { i = a; x = 0.0; }

  C (int a, float y) { i = a; x = y; }
```
←| **Constructors** |

```
  int f (...) { ... }

  void g (...) { ... }
};
```
←| **Member functions** |

Every value of type C—also called an *object* or *instance* of C—contains its own copies of the data members of C. The constructors all have the name C and *no* return type; they are used to initialize the data members. The member functions are the operations provided by the class. Members are classified as *public* or *private*, depending on whether they follow the **public** or **private** keyword.

The name C is used as a type name in the rest of the program. *Clients* of C can declare variables of type C using ordinary variable declaration syntax, except that constructor arguments must be provided:

```
  C c1(10), c2(0, -.05);
```
←| **Declaration of variables of type C** |

Member functions are somewhat different from ordinary functions both in their definitions and their usage. Clients call member functions of C with the syntax

```
  int j = c1.f(<argument-list>);

  c2.g(<argument-list>);
```
←| **Sending messages** |

In the first example c1 is the *receiver* of the *message* **f**; in the second, c2 is the receiver of **g**.

An equivalent definition of class C is obtained by giving *prototypes* of the constructors and member functions inside the class definition and giving the definitions of those functions after the class:

```
class C {
private:
  int i;
  float x;

public:
  C (int) ;
                          }← Constructor prototypes
  C (int, float) ;

  int f (...) ;
                          }← Member function prototypes
  void g (...) ;
};

C::C (int a) { i = a; x = 0.0; }
                                        }← Constructor definitions
C::C (int a, float y) { i = a; x = y; }

int C::f (...) { ... }
                                }← Member function definitions
void C::g (...) { ... }
```

The only difference is that some C++ compilers will give error messages for the first form but not for the second (see Section E.4 of Appendix E).

In the definitions of member functions, the receiver is *not* listed as an argument, but its data members may be referred to by naming them:

```
int C::f (...) { ... i ... x ... }
```

They can access the members of other C objects using dot notation:

```
int C::f (..., C c, ...) {

    ... i ...          ← Member i of receiver

    ... c.i ...        ← Member i of argument

    ... x ...          ← Member x of receiver

    ... c.x ...        ← Member x of argument

}
```

However, data members can be accessed in this way *only* by member functions of C.

Clients of a class cannot directly observe how that class represents its objects if the class's data members are private, as they should always be. The programmer of the class can change the data members at will, just ensuring that member functions behave correctly. This is called *representation independence* and is an important property of classes.

Overloading allows you to give many different functions the same name, so long as each definition with that name has a different number and different types of arguments. Constructors are frequently overloaded, as in the foregoing example.

Operator overloading allows you to give new overloaded definitions to operators like **+** and **<<**. This is accomplished by using the *full names* of those operators: **operator+** for **+**, **operator<<** for **<<**, and so on. These functions can be overloaded using ordinary function definitions, so long as at least one of the arguments is of user-defined type. They may be overloaded as clients:

```
C operator+ (C x, C y) { ... }

ostream & operator<< (ostream & os, C x) {
  // print x
  return os;
}
```

If the argument on the left of a binary operator, or the sole argument of a unary operator, is of user-defined type, the operator may also be overloaded as a member function:

```
C C::operator+ (C y) { ... }
```

Bear in mind the distinction between *mutating* and *nonmutating* operations of a class. Mutating operations modify the data members of their receiver; non-mutating operations do not. Clients must be aware of which type of operation they are using. Often, nonmutating operations of class **C** return a value of type **C**, while the corresponding mutating operations return **void**.

The keywords introduced in this chapter are

```
class    operator    private    public
```

Pointers and Lists

Chapter Preview

Up to now, the amount of data we have been able to store in a program has been limited to the number of variables we declared; this is inadequate when the amount of data a program needs to store cannot be predicted in advance. In this chapter, we use classes together with two other new features—*pointers* and the **new** operator—to overcome this limitation. Our major examples in this chapter will be programs to construct and manipulate *lists* of data.

If somebody there chanced to be
Who loved me in a manner true,
My heart would point him out to me,
And I would point him out to you.

—Gilbert and Sullivan
Ruddigore

Most real-life computer programs store lots of information while they're running. Often, they can't even predict how much they'll have to store. Your text editor, for example, doesn't know how much you're going to type until you finish typing it.

That's the biggest shortcoming of what we've covered so far in this book: There has been no way to store huge amounts of data. Sure, we can declare as many variables as we want, but how many would it take before the program became unwieldy? A hundred? A thousand?

In this chapter we introduce techniques to solve this problem. These techniques allow us to store as much data as we want by dynamically creating objects to store them. First, we'll introduce a new data type, called a *pointer*, which is widely used in C++ programs and is especially useful with classes. Then we'll use classes to define a data object called a *list* to solve our storage problems.

7.1

Pointers

Pointers constitute a built-in data type. Pointer values point to other data items, *pointer*
as shown in Figure 7.1. As with any other data type, you can declare variables to

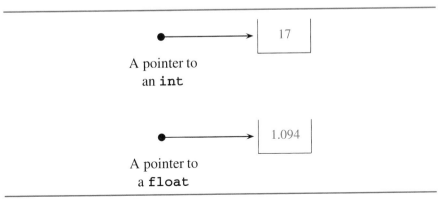

A pointer to
an `int`

A pointer to
a `float`

FIGURE 7.1 Examples of pointers.

be of pointer type. Pointers also have their own operations, which we introduce after explaining how pointer variables are declared and how pointers are created.

7.1.1   Declaring Pointer Variables

address

A pointer variable contains a pointer like the ones shown in Figure 7.1. Another way to think of this is that the pointer variable contains the *address*, or *location*, of another data item. A pointer variable is constrained to point to one type of data throughout its lifetime. A pointer-to-**int** variable, for example, can point to any integer, but *only* to an integer. To declare **gradePtr** to be a pointer-to-**int**, write

```
int *gradePtr;
```

C++ programmers call such a variable an "int pointer" or "int star." In general, for a built-in or user-defined type **T**, a pointer-to-**T** variable is declared using an asterisk (**T***) as above:

```
time *lunchtimePtr;
float *xPtr;
```

If a function returns a pointer, it is declared using the same notation:

```
time *getTimePtr (..) {...}
```

Multiple pointer variables can be declared in a single declaration, but carefully note the required syntax:

```
float *xp, *yp, *zp;
```

This declaration of three **float** pointers is quite different from this (perfectly legal) declaration of two **float** pointers and one **float**:

```
float *xp, y, *zp;
```

7.1.2   Creating Pointers

address-of operator

If **x** is a variable, then **&x** is a pointer to it, as shown in Figure 7.2. **&** is called the *address-of operator*, and its precedence is the same as that of *unary* minus (see Appendix A).

You can assign the pointers created using the address-of operator to variables. Thus, the declarations and initializations

```
1    float pi = 3.14159;  // assign value to pi
2    float *piPtr = &pi;   // assign pi's address to piPtr
```

&x   x

FIGURE 7.2   The address-of operator.

FIGURE 7.3 `piPtr` is a `float` pointer.

result in the situation shown in Figure 7.3. Line 1 allocates and initializes a `float` variable; line 2 allocates a `float` pointer and initializes it to point to the variable declared in line 1.

There is one pointer constant, called **NULL**, which points to nothing. In pictures, the *null pointer* is drawn as

null pointer

It is always legal to assign the null pointer to a pointer variable:

```
piPtr = NULL;
```

The importance of **NULL** will become clear later on in the chapter.

7.1.3 Dereferencing

To do anything useful with pointers, we need to see what a pointer points to; this operation, called *dereferencing*, is expressed with an asterisk. If `piPtr` is a pointer-to-`float`, then `*piPtr` is the number to which it points. Thus

dereferencing

```
float pi = 3.14159;
float *piPtr = &pi;
cout << "pi = " << *piPtr << "\n";
```

prints

```
pi = 3.14159
```

`*` has the same precedence as `&`.

A good way to read the declaration `T *x` is "the expression `*x` has type `T`." In pointer variable declarations, we always place the asterisk right next to the variable (even though any other placement of spaces, including their complete omission, would be legal) to emphasize this reading of the declaration. Note that this reading does not work at all for reference-type variables; declaring a parameter `int &x` does *not* mean that the expression `&x` is of type `int`; to discourage that reading, we always place the ampersand next to the type name, as in `int& x`.

7.1.4 Assignment and Pointers

The dereferencing operator can also be used on the left-hand side of an assignment, indicating an assignment into the location to which the pointer points. Thus

BUG ALERT 7.1   **Don't Dereference Null Pointers**

Among the most common bugs in C++ programs is dereferencing an uninitialized or **NULL** pointer. Usually, there is a characteristic error message you can expect—depending on which C++ compiler you're using—though it may not seem to relate to pointers at all. For example, the following program:

```
main () {
   int *p = NULL;
   cout << *p;
}
```

produces the run-time error message

```
Segmentation fault (core dumped)
```

in one computer, and

```
Bus error
```

on another. Worst of all, one system produces an output of **0** and no error message. Why is this so bad? Because dereferencing a null pointer is unquestionably a mistake—there is never a good reason to do it—and on this system, the program just continues to run as if everything were fine; the error will simply show up later, in a completely unexpected and puzzling way.

```
1    float pi = 3.1415926536;
2    float *piPtr = &pi;
3    *piPtr = 3.1416;
4    cout << "pi = " << *piPtr << "\n";
```

prints

```
pi = 3.1416
```

Let's follow this sequence of statements in pictures. Figure 7.4(a) depicts the situation after line 2, Figure 7.4(b) after line 3. There are two things to note

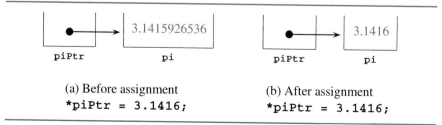

(a) Before assignment
*piPtr = 3.1416;

(b) After assignment
*piPtr = 3.1416;

FIGURE 7.4   Tracing the assignment ***piPtr = 3.1416;**.

about Figure 7.4(b):

- **piPtr** still points to **pi**, because *there was no assignment to* **piPtr**, so it hasn't changed.
- ***piPtr** and **pi** are the same. We could have changed ***piPtr = 3.1416** to **pi = 3.1416**; we could have changed **<< *piPtr** in line 4 to **<< pi**; or both. All three variants have the same output.

It is critical that you understand the difference between

```
piPtr = ...
```

and

```
*piPtr = ...
```

The first changes the pointer contained in **piPtr**, while the second changes the variable to which **piPtr** points. Pictures help a lot; we'll work through two examples, and then you can do the exercises to be sure you understand.

As our first example, consider the code in Figure 7.5. Figure 7.6 shows the values of all the variables after statements 1 through 7, after which we can see what statement 8 will print. After statement 2, the state is as shown in Figure 7.6(b). The pointer-to-**int** variables **p**, **q**, and **r** have been *created* but *not initialized*. They are empty, as shown. Assignments 3 and 4 lead to Figure 7.6(d), using the address-of operator to create pointers to **i** and **j** and assigning them to **p** and **q**, respectively. Statement 5 is a *pointer assignment* that says, "Let **r** contain the same pointer as **q** does." Accordingly, the pointer in **q**—the one that points to **j**—is copied to **r**. Now, both **q** and **r** point to **j**.

Statement 6, ***q = *p + 5;** is more complicated. In English it means, "Take the contents of the variable that **p** points to, add 5 to it, then assign that value to the cell to which **q** points." Let's break this down: ***p** means "the contents of the variable that **p** points to"; this variable is **i**, which contains 10. Adding 5 to it gives 15. ***q =** means, "Assign into the location pointed to by **q**." That location is the variable **j**, so 15 is assigned to it, as shown in Figure 7.6(f).

Lastly, in statement 7, we have another pointer assignment, with the pointer contained in **r** being copied to **p**, leading to the state shown in Figure 7.6(g). Thus, statement 8 prints **10, 15, 15**.

Our second example uses pointers to **time** objects, but we need to introduce *arrow notation*. The notation **p->x** is equivalent to **(*p).x**. In other words, *arrow notation*

```
1    int i = 10, j = 20;
2    int *p, *q, *r;
3    p = &i;
4    q = &j;
5    r = q;
6    *q = *p + 5;
7    p = r;
8    cout << i << ", " << j << ", " << *p << "\n";
```

FIGURE 7.5 Code illustrating pointer manipulations.

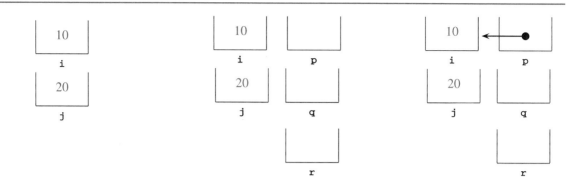

(a) `int i = 10, j = 20;` (b) `int *p, *q, *r;` (c) `p = &i;`

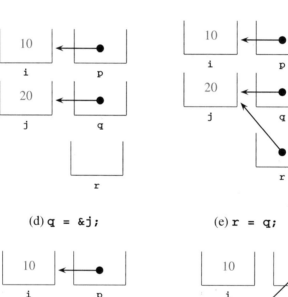

(d) `q = &j;` (e) `r = q;`

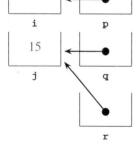

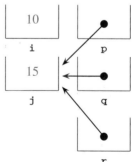

(f) `*q = *p + 5;` (g) `p = r;`

FIGURE 7.6   Trace of statements in Figure 7.5.

it is used when **p** is a pointer to a class instance and **x** is a member of that class. Thus, if **timePtr** is a pointer-to-time, then **timePtr->printTime()** is equivalent to **(*timePtr).printTime()** and **timePtr->hour** is equivalent to **(*timePtr).hour**. (Of course, the latter is illegal outside of the **time** class, because **hour** is private.)

Now consider these statements, which use the mutating **advanceMinutes** operation defined in Section 6.6:

```
1      time *morningnews = &time(7,0);
2      time *eveningnews = &time(17,30);
3      time *localnews = eveningnews;
4      eveningnews->advanceMinutes(30);
5      localnews = &time(17, 30);
6      *morningnews = morningnews->addMinutes(30);
```

The state of this program after each of these statements is shown in Figures 7.7 and 7.8. After statements 1 and 2, **morningnews** and **eveningnews** point to distinct **time** objects. The pointer assignment in statement 3 causes **localnews** to point to the same object as **eveningnews** (Figure 7.7(c)). In statement 4 the mutating operation **advanceMinutes** modifies the object to which **eveningnews** points; of course, **localnews** still points to that object (Figure 7.7(d)). In statement 5 a new **time** object is created, and its address is assigned to **localnews**, so that all three variables now point to distinct objects. Finally, the object created by the call to **addMinutes** in statement 6 is assigned to **morningnews**, resulting in Figure 7.8(b).

7.1.5 Pointers on Pointers

Before we consider fancier uses of pointers, you ought to know a few details about type checking, pointer comparison, and display of pointer values.

Since C++ knows what type of value a pointer points to, type checking is the same as for other operations: expression **&e** has type pointer-to-**T**, where

---

Initializing Pointers to Objects BUG ALERT 7.2

The initialization of pointers to class objects must not be confused with the initialization of the objects themselves. In fact, it is not necessary to initialize pointer variables at all (any more than it is for **int** variables), even though it is necessary to initialize class objects. So, the declaration

```
time *p;
```

is legal, but the declaration

```
time t;
```

is not, because **time** does not have a zero-argument constructor.

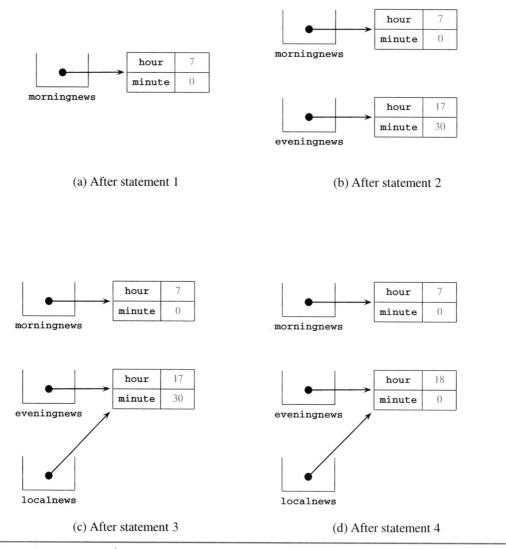

(a) After statement 1

(b) After statement 2

(c) After statement 3

(d) After statement 4

FIGURE 7.7   Pointers to **time** objects.

T is the type of e. An expression ***e** has type **T** if e has type pointer-to-**T**. An assignment **e1 = e2** is legal only if **e1** and **e2** have the same type. Here are some examples:

```
int x, *p, *q;
x = *p;      // legal: both sides have type int
*p = x;      // legal: both sides have type int
*p = *q;     // legal: both sides have type int
p = q;       // legal: both sides have type pointer-to-int
p = &x;      // legal: both sides have type pointer-to-int
p = x;       // illegal: p has type pointer-to-int, x type int
*p = q;      // illegal: *p has type int, q type pointer-to-int
```

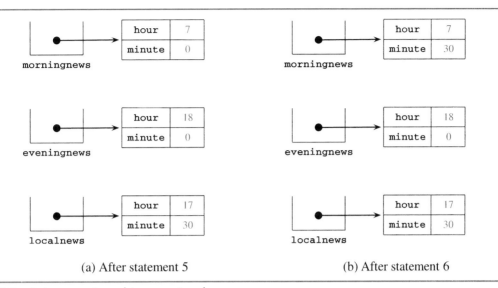

(a) After statement 5   (b) After statement 6

FIGURE 7.8   Pointers to `time` objects, continued.

Pointers can be compared for equality using the `==` and `!=` operators. Two pointers are equal if they point to the same variable. Note the difference between the comparisons `p == q` and `*p == *q`, if `p` and `q` are pointers-to-int. `*p == *q` is an *integer* comparison, `p == q` a pointer comparison. One indication of the difference is that if `p == q` is true, then certainly `*p == *q` must be true as well, as illustrated in Figure 7.9(a), but we may have `*p == *q` without `p == q` (Figure 7.9(b)). The most common use of pointer comparison is to test whether a pointer is null: `p == NULL`.

Debugging programs that use pointers can be difficult, in part because there is no obvious way to display a pointer. If you attempt to print a pointer, you will see a rather strange-looking number, possibly also containing some letters. On the authors' computer this program,

```
int main () {
  int i = 10;
  int *p = &i;
  cout << p << "\n";
}
```

(a) p == q (so *p == *q)   (b) *p == *q, but p != q

FIGURE 7.9   Pointer comparison.

produces this output:[1]

```
0xeffff9ec
```

This is a number written in hexadecimal (base 16) notation. (The opening `0x` indicates that it is hexadecimal; the digits used in hexadecimal numbers are $0, \ldots, 9$ and $a, \ldots, f$.) It is not important to understand what this number is—only to be able to compare it to other hexadecimal numbers. To see this, take our program in Figure 7.6(g) and add a statement at the end to display pointer values:

```
cout << "address of i = " << &i
     << ", address of j = " << &j
     << "\np = " << p << ", q = "
     << q << ", r = " << r << "\n";
```

The output from this statement is

```
address of i = 0xeffff9ec, address of j = 0xeffff9e8
p = 0xeffff9e8, q = 0xeffff9e8, r = 0xeffff9e8
```

The hexadecimal numbers on these lines may be unreadable, but what is clear is that all three on the last line are the same, and all are equal to the address of `j` shown on the first line. This confirms the picture in Figure 7.6(g), which shows all three pointers pointing to `j`.

7.1.6 `this`

Returning to the `time` class of Chapter 6, consider how we might add the member function `boolean after(time t)`. This function should tell us whether the receiver represents a time later than `t`, the opposite of `priorTo`. We might try to code this as

```
boolean after (time t) { return !priorTo(t); }
```

but this code will also return true if `t` is the *same time* as the receiver; that is, if we think of `priorTo` as `<`, then `after` should be `>`, but this definition gives `>=`.

The correct code would do something like this:

```
boolean after (time t) {
    return t.priorTo(<receiver of this message>);
}
```

The problem is that we again need to refer to the receiver of the message. The last time we were in this predicament (with `subtractMinutes` on page 196), we found that we could send a message *to the receiver of the current message* without explicitly naming the receiver. Here we have no such easy solution, because we are passing the receiver of the current message as an argument rather than sending a message to it.

However, C++ provides a way to refer directly to the receiver of a message. Within a member function, the variable `this` always contains a pointer to the

---

[1] Pointers are implemented differently by different compilers, so your output may be—probably will be—different from ours, but it will almost certainly be a strange-looking number.

receiver of the message. **this** is declared implicitly in every member function of every class, with type pointer-to-that-class.

So, the solution to our problem is

```
boolean after (time t2) { return t2.priorTo(*this); }
```

Note that we need to use ***this** because **this** is a *pointer*-to-**time**, whereas **priorTo** takes an argument of type **time**.

Exercises—First Set

1. Predict the output of line 8:

```
1    main () {
2      float x, y, *p, *q, *r;
3      x = 100.0;
4      q = &y;
5      p = &x;
6      r = q;
7      *r = x*2;
8      cout << x << " " << y << "\n";
9      cout << p << " " << q << " " << r << "\n";
10   }
```

Run it to check your answer. Draw pictures of all the variables, and explain the output produced by line 9.

2. The following program should exchange the contents of variables i and j, producing output:

```
20 10
```

However, it has a number of errors, both syntactic and logical. Fix it.

```
void swap (int *p1, int *p2) { *p1 = *p2; *p2 = *p1; }

main () {
  int i = 10, j = 20;
  int *ip, jp;
  ip = i;
  jp = j;
  swap(ip, jp);
  cout << i << " " << j << "\n";
}
```

3. It is legal to have pointers that point to other pointers. For example,

```
int **p;
```

declares a variable of type pointer-to-pointer-to-**int**. Then, the expression ***p** has type pointer-to-**int**, and ****p** has type **int**. Suppose a program begins with these declarations:

```
int i = 10;
int *pi = &i;
int **ppi = &pi;
int **pppi = &ppi;
```

Give four distinct assignment statements to increment the contents of **i**. The first should use only the variable **i** itself, the second only **pi**, and the third and fourth only **ppi** and **pppi**, respectively.

The new **Operator**

The address-of operator **&** is not the only way to create a pointer. Another way is to use the **new** operator.

If **T** is a type, then the expression

```
new T
```

creates a new value of type **T**, calls the zero-argument constructor if **T** is a user-defined type, and returns a pointer to that new value. (Of course, if **T** is a built-in type, no constructor is called; if it is a user-defined type with no zero-argument constructor, this expression will produce an error message.)

You can use any of **T**'s constructors by passing arguments to it when using the **new** operator:

```
new T (<constructor-arguments>)
```

All uses of **new** return a *pointer* to the new object. For example, after executing these statements,

```
int *ip, *jp;
time *now, *later;
ip = new int(10);
jp = ip;
now = new time(11,30);
later = new time(*now);
```

the various objects and pointers will be as shown in Figure 7.10. **later** is initialized to be an exact copy of *now*; note that passing **now** as the argument in the last line would be an error, since **now** is a pointer rather than a **time** instance. You can perform the usual operations on these pointers, particularly dereferencing, so that

```
cout << *ip << "\n";
*jp = 20;
cout << *ip << "\n";
cout << *now << "\n";
*later = *later + 60;
cout << *later << "\n";
```

will print

```
10
20
11:30AM
12:30PM
```

The necessity for **new** may not be immediately apparent. In fact, an argument could be made that it is not really needed. After all, whenever you write

```
... new T() ...
```

you could instead write

```
... &T() ...
```

which produces a **T** value and returns a pointer to it.

To explain the difference, we need to look more closely at the mechanism by which memory space is allocated for variables. Recall from Chapter 4 that the

SPEED
5

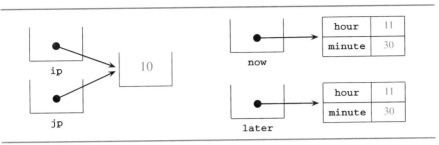

FIGURE 7.10 Results of **new** operators.

local variables of a function come into existence only when the function is called, and go out of existence when the function returns. You can think of it this way: Suppose that all the variables in a function and their contents were written on a piece of paper. When another function is called, a new piece of paper is placed on top of the first, and the variables of that function are written on it. If it in turn calls another function, another piece of paper is added to the pile. When a function returns, the piece of paper on top is taken away and thrown in the trash. This procedure wastes a lot of paper, but it mimics the computer's use of a *stack* to hold the parameters and local variables of functions. In the computer, each "piece of paper" is called a *stack frame*.

stack

stack frame

We can picture the situation when the program begins—when **main** is executing—as consisting of a single stack frame:

Function **main**
. . . space for local variables of **main** . . .

If **main** calls function **f**, **f**'s stack frame is placed on top of **main**'s stack frame. **main**'s stack frame is still in the computer, but it is not needed as long as **f** executes:

Function **main**
Call to function **f**
Where we came from: main . . . space for arguments and local variables of **f** . . .

If **f** calls **g**, the stack looks like

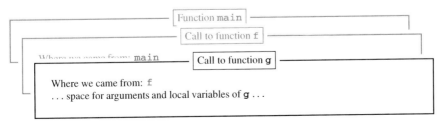

When **g** returns, the stack reverts to its previous state, and **g**'s stack frame is tossed in the trash.

Now consider this program, in which the function **maketime** creates a **time** object and returns its address:

```
time *maketime (int m) {
    time newtime(m / 60, m % 60);
    return &newtime;
}

main () {
    time now(0, 0), *timePtr;
    timePtr = maketime(60*4+15);
    now = now + 30;
    cout << *timePtr << "\n";
}
```

At first, the only stack frame is **main**'s, with local variables **now** and **timePtr**:

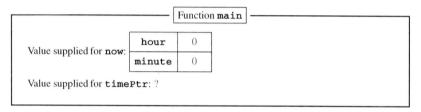

We've written ? for the value of **timePtr** to signify that it has not been initialized. **main** calls **maketime** with argument 255, so when **maketime** begins, the stack looks like

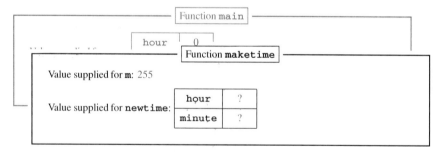

The **time** constructor is immediately called for **newtime**. We won't trace through this call, but after its return the data members of **newtime** are filled in:

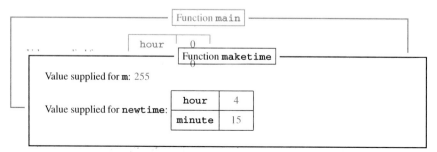

maketime is now ready to return. It returns the address of **newtime**, which is assigned to **timePtr**, and the stack now looks like this:

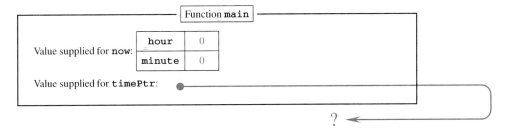

But here **timePtr** points to nothing, or rather to the place where **newtime** *used to be*. The piece of paper on which **newtime** was written has been thrown in the garbage! Next, **operator+**, defined in the **time** class, is called. It has one local variable, **totalMinutes**, plus the parameter **m**:

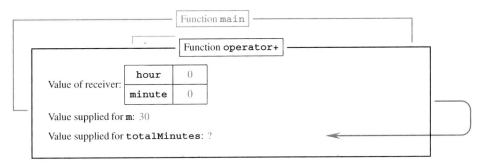

When we return from the call to **operator+**, the stack looks like

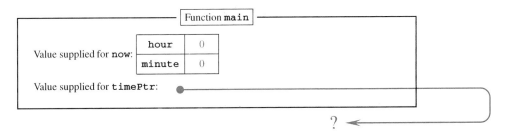

The value of **timePtr** is a pointer, but we have no idea what it points to anymore. Printing ***timePtr** produces the output[2]

    18:30PM

which is not a valid output. **timePtr** points to *something*, and the program attempts to print that thing as if it were a **time** object, but it only results in garbage being printed.

---

[2]This is one of those cases in which your output may differ from ours.

dangling pointer

A pointer like the one contained in `timePtr`, pointing to a data item inside a stack frame that has been removed from the stack, is called a *dangling pointer*. Dangling pointers are a major source of subtle bugs, because they can have extremely puzzling symptoms.

In summary, we created a `time` object in `maketime` that had to survive beyond the call to `maketime`, but, being contained in a local variable, it did not. How can we create an object that will survive longer than the function that created it?

heap

C++ provides an area of memory separate from the stack, called the *heap*, in which objects can be placed. Objects allocated in the heap never disappear unless the program explicitly requests it (see Section 7.8). All objects created using **new** are allocated in the heap.

Consider, then, the same program with a new definition of `maketime`:

```
time *maketime (int m) {
    time *newtimePtr = new time(m / 60, m % 60);
    return newtimePtr;
}
```

We'll trace it as before, but we'll also show the heap off to the side. Initially it is empty. Here are the stack and heap when `maketime` is called:

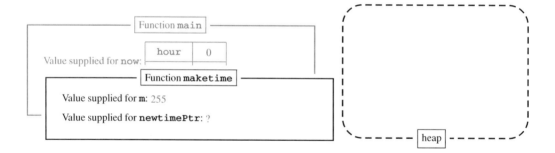

This version of `maketime` creates a new `time` object using **new**, so it goes into the heap:

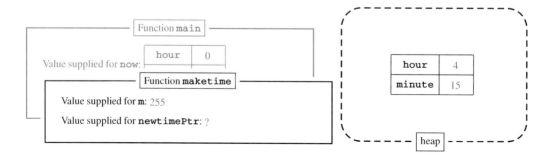

new returns the address of that new object, which is assigned to **newtimePtr**:

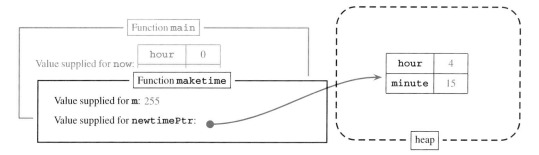

maketime returns this address and **main** assigns it to **timePtr**:

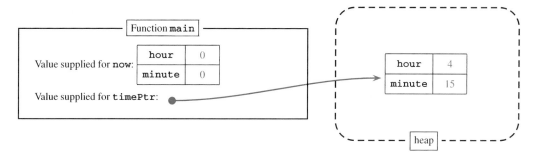

Even though **maketime**'s local variables are gone, the **time** object that it created in the heap lives on. **timePtr** does not contain a dangling pointer. The call to **operator+** proceeds without having any effect on the new object. Printing ***timePtr** produces the correct output:

    4:15AM

The lesson of this discussion is that objects created using **new** are stored in the heap and survive for the entire run of the program. Pointers to such objects will not become dangling pointers. On the other hand, pointers to objects allocated as local variables become dangling pointers as soon as the function that allocates the objects returns. So, use a pointer to a local variable only when you are certain that the pointer will not survive longer than the object to which it points.

7.3

Lists

The list could surely go on, and there is nothing more wonderful than a list, instrument of wondrous hypotyposis.

—Umberto Eco
The Name of the Rose

linked list

In this section we show how to store an unpredictably large number of data items by placing them in a structure called a *linked list*. This will give us, for the first time, the ability to deal with large quantities of data.

Our ability to construct lists—which we will do momentarily—is based on the fact that objects of class **T** can contain pointers to **T** objects. Note that **T** objects *cannot* contain other **T** *objects*. Thus, the declaration of member **m** here is illegal:

```
class T {
private:
   T m;
   ...
}
```

However, they *can* contain *pointers* to **T** objects. A linked list is constructed out of objects containing a value and a pointer to the next object in the list. A list of integers constructed in this way is shown in Figure 7.11.

cell

head

tail

Linked lists are used very frequently in computer programming. The individual objects in a linked list are called *cells*. The first cell in a list (the one containing 17 in Figure 7.11) is called the *head* of the list; the remainder of the list is its *tail*. In this section we show how to define classes whose objects are list cells, and we describe programs for operations such as inserting elements into a list.

The list of integers shown in Figure 7.11 is constructed using the pointer-within-an-instance idea from the previous section. Given the class

```
class intList {
private:
  int value;
  intList *nextEntry;

public:
  intList (int v, intList *next)
    : value(v), nextEntry(next)
  {}

  int getValue () { return value; }

  intList *getNextEntry () { return nextEntry; }
};
```

the list in Figure 7.11 can be constructed using the code

```
intList *cell4 = new intList(-14, NULL);
intList *cell3 = new intList(616, cell4);
intList *cell2 = new intList(10945, cell3);
intList *cell1 = new intList(17, cell2);
```

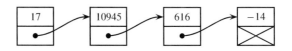

FIGURE 7.11   Representing the list 17, 10945, 616, −14.

Here, `cell1` points to the head of the list. Notice how we had to construct the cells in reverse order.

We also see clearly the importance of the `NULL` pointer. Without it, there would be no way to create the first cell—what arguments could we pass to the constructor?

We don't need to have a variable pointing to each cell in the list. These statements construct the same list using a single variable, `list`, which points to the head of the list:

```
1    intList *list = new intList(-14, NULL);
2    list = new intList(616, list);
3    list = new intList(10945, list);
4    list = new intList(17, list);
```

A trace of these statements is shown in Figure 7.12. Even better coding is

```
intList *list = new intList(17,
               new intList(616,
                 new intList(10945,
                   new intList(-14, NULL))));
```

We need the `intList` class not to construct four-element lists, but to construct unpredictably large lists. A simple example of this is a program that reads in a list of numbers from the user—as long as the user wants—then prints the list in reverse order. (This is simpler than reading them in and printing them in the order in which they were entered; that program will come later.)

We already have the `intList` class, which allows us to store the numbers as we read them. There are two parts to this problem:

1. Read the numbers and store them in a list, in reverse order.
2. Print the list.

Suppose the user's input is the list

```
Enter number: 2
Enter number: 3
Enter number: 5
Enter number: 7
Enter number: 11
Enter number: 13
Enter number: 17
Enter number: 19
Enter number: 23
Enter number: 29
Enter number: 31
Enter number: 37
Enter number: ^D
```

Our program will construct the list:

(a) After statement 1

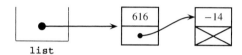

(b) After statement 2

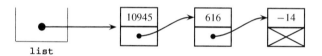

(c) After statement 3

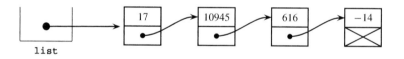

(d) After statement 4

FIGURE 7.12   Building the list 17, 10945, 616, −14.

and then print it, producing the output

```
37
31
29
23
19
17
13
11
7
5
3
2
```

The outline of our program, then, is

```
#include <iostream.h>
#include <iomanip.h>

class intList { ... };

intList *readReverseList () { ... }

ostream& operator<< (ostream& os, intList *list) { ... }

main () {
   intList *theList;
   theList = readReverseList();
   cout << theList;
}
```

and we need to write the two functions **readReverseList** and **operator<<**. **readReverseList** constructs the list shown above and returns a pointer to its head (the leftmost cell). **operator<<** prints the elements of a list in sequential order. (These are *not* member functions of **intList**; the accessor functions **getValue** and **getNextEntry** are **intList**'s only member functions, though we will add new ones later.)

Let's write **operator<<** first, because it's easier. The idea is to start at the beginning of a list and repeat the action

Print the value in the current cell and then go to the next cell.

until there is no "next cell"—that is, until the **nextEntry** field is **NULL**. This type of repetition is exactly suited to the **while** loop, covered in Chapter 5:

```
ostream& operator<< (ostream& os, intList *list) {
  while (list != NULL) {
    cout << list->getValue() << "\n";
    list = list->getNextEntry();
  }
  return os;
}
```

Let's follow this program for a couple of iterations. Suppose the function **readReverseList** has been called, and **theList** points to this list:

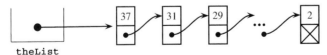

When **operator<<** is called, **list** will be copied from **theList**:

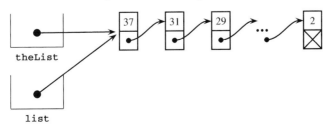

Since `list` is not **NULL**, the loop body is entered. It prints `list->getValue()` (that is, 37) and then assigns `list->getNextEntry()` (the pointer to the next cell) to `list`. Now the picture is

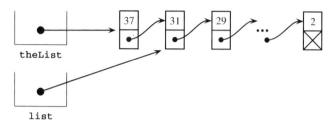

`list` is still not **NULL**, so the loop body is again entered. It prints **31** and assigns to `list` the pointer to the next cell:

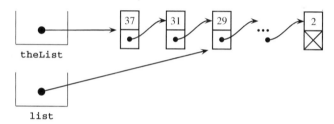

This continues until we get to the end of the list:

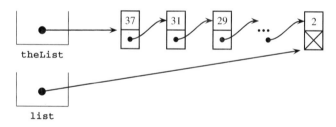

`list` is still not **NULL**, so we enter the loop body once again, printing **2** and assigning to `list` the value of `list->nextEntry`:

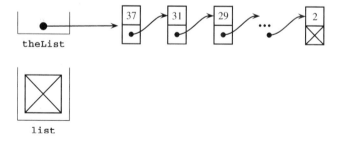

Now, `list != NULL` is false, the while loop ends, and we return from **printList**.

We now turn to **readReverseList**. It reads numbers from the user and keeps doing so until the user types an end-of-file character. For each number read, readReverseList creates a new intList object using **new** and puts that number into it. Then readReverseList must put the entry into the list it has been constructing:

```
intList *readReverseList () {
  int inputval;
  intList *front = NULL;

  cout << "Enter number: "; cin >> inputval;

  while (!cin.eof()) {
    front = new intList(inputval, front);
    cout << "Enter number: "; cin >> inputval;
  }
  cout << "\n";
  return front;
}
```

Again, let's follow this program for a few steps, assuming the user's input consists of the numbers 2, 3, ..., 37. Initially, front is **NULL**:

front

Since **cin** has input remaining, we read it and create a new intList object. That object contains the integer just read and the value of front:

and its address is assigned to front:

front

Since there is more input, we read the next number, 3, and again construct an intList object containing that number and the contents of front:

and assign to front the address of the object just created:

front

This continues until the last number, 37, has been read:

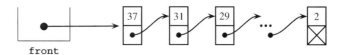

front

`readReverseList` is done, and it returns the address of the head of the list, which is contained in `front`.

As another example, let's write the function

```
intList *find (int key, intList *list)
```

which looks for **key** in **list** and returns the address of the cell that contains it if it is found, **NULL** otherwise.

find goes sequentially through the list, just as **printList** does, but instead of printing the value in each cell, it compares it to **key**:

```
intList *find (int key, intList *list) {
  while (list != NULL && list->getValue() != key)
    list = list->getNextEntry();
  return list;
}
```

If at any iteration of the loop we find **key**, we immediately end the loop and return the address of the cell that contains it. The other way the loop can terminate is if **list** is the null pointer, which occurs only if **key** has not been found anywhere in the list. In this case, we return the null pointer, which is the correct action.

A useful operation is the one that computes the length of a list. It involves a simple iteration over the list:

```
int length (intList *list) {
  int l = 0;
  while (list != NULL) {
    l++;
    list = list->getNextEntry();
  }
  return l;
}
```

Another useful operation returns the address of the nth cell in a list. Following C++ convention, we will assume the list cells are numbered from zero, so for a list of length l, the legal arguments to **nth** are $0 \ldots l - 1$. Arguments less than 0 are treated like 0, that is, **nth** returns the head of the list; for arguments greater than $l - 1$, **nth** returns **NULL**.

```
intList *nth (intList *list, int n) {
  while (list != NULL && n > 0) {
    list = list->getNextEntry();
    n--;
  }
  return list;
}
```

We can also read a list and print it in *forward* order, by first reading it in reverse order as above and then reversing it. The function **reverse** will take an **intList** pointer, construct a new list containing the same elements as its argument but in reverse order, and return the address of the head of the new list. The structure of this function is similar to **readReverseList**, even though it doesn't read any input. It uses a **while** loop to look at each element of the argument list, and creates a list cell on each iteration:

```
intList *reverse (intList *list) {
  intList *newList = NULL;
  while (list != NULL) {
    // list originally pointed to a list x0, x1, ..., xn.
    // Now, list points to list xi, x(i+1), ..., xn, for some i,
    // and newList points to the list x(i-1), x(i-2), ..., x0.
    newList = new intList(list->getValue(), newList);
    list = list->getNextEntry();
  }
  return newList;
}
```

For example, if the argument list is 37, 31, ..., 2, as above, then before entering the **while** loop the first time, the variables look like

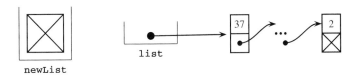

After one iteration, **newList** has one element:

After two iterations, it has two elements:

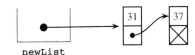

By the time **list** reaches the end of its list, **newList** will point to the list 2, 3, ..., 37.

With **reverse**, we can write a program to read a list of numbers and print it in forward order:

```
intList *readForwardList () {
  int inputval;
  intList *front = NULL;

  cout << "Enter number: "; cin >> inputval;

  while (!cin.eof()) {
    front = new intList(inputval, front);
    cout << "Enter number: "; cin >> inputval;
  }
  cout << "\n";
  return reverse(front);
}

main () {
  intList *list = readForwardList();
  cout << list;
}
```

Finally, we can add a new element to the end of an existing list using the function **addToEnd**. This doesn't really add the new element to the list; rather, it creates a new list looking just like its argument but with the new element at the end (just as **reverse** produces a new list):

```
intList *addToEnd (intList *list, int n)  {
  return reverse(new intList(n, reverse(list)));
}
```

This is almost too easy! Reverse the list, add the new element to the beginning—which we know how to do—and then reverse the result.

Exercises—Second Set

☞ 1. Define the following functions on lists:
   (a) **int sum (intList *list)** sums all the numbers in **list**.
   (b) **int frequency (intList *list, int p)** counts the number of times that **p** occurs in **list**.
   (c) **void minmax (intList *list, int& min, int& max)** computes the minimum and maximum values in **list** and returns them in the corresponding reference parameters.

☞ 2. Define the following functions that construct new lists. Use the same approach as we did for **addToEnd** above: Construct the list in reverse, then call **reverse** to put it in forward order.
   (a) **intList *copy (intList *list)** simply creates a fresh copy of a list identical to **list**.
   (b) **intList *extractPositive (intList *list)** returns a list consisting of just the positive integers occurring in **list** (in the same order as they occur there). If **list** contains no positive numbers, then return the **NULL** pointer.

(c) `intList *remove(int n, intList *list)` which returns a list identical to `list` except that all occurrences of `n`, if any, are removed. If `list` has no occurrences of `n`, then an exact copy is returned. If `list` has just one cell, and it contains `n`, then return the `NULL` pointer.

3. Write the function `intList *addInOrder(int n, intList *list)`. This function assumes its second argument is a list that contains integers in numerical order. It creates a new list the same as `list`, but with `n` inserted in the appropriate position. If the list already contains `n`, then `addInOrder` should not add it again, but should instead return an exact copy of `list`.

   By using `addInOrder` to build a list, you can ensure that it will be sorted numerically.

4. Lists of numbers might represent grades on an exam, as was suggested in Chapter 5 (page 168). Write a program that reads in a list of integers, then prints their mean and then, on separate lines, each score together with its difference from the mean. For example, if the input were 75 85 90, the output would be

   ```
   Average: 83.33
   Grades:
   75 -8.33
   85 1.67
   90 6.67
   ```

   (The output of fractions may not be exactly the same as ours.)

5. The *standard deviation* of a set of scores is a measure of how much the scores tend to clump near the mean. If everyone taking an exam gets nearly the same score, the standard deviation will be near zero, whereas if scores are spread evenly throughout a broad range, the standard deviation will be high. The standard deviation of a typical school exam graded on a 0-to-100 scale, with an average of 75, might be 10 to 15.

   The formula for computing the standard deviation of a set of scores $x_1, x_2, \ldots, x_n$, with a mean of $\bar{x} = \left(\sum_{i=1}^{n} x_i\right)/n$ is given by the formula

   $$s = \sqrt{\frac{\sum_{i=1}^{n}(x_i - \bar{x})^2}{n}}$$

   or, equivalently,

   $$s = \sqrt{\frac{\sum_{i=1}^{n} x_i^2}{n} - \bar{x}^2}$$

   Repeat the previous exercise, but augment the program by having it print the standard deviation of the set of scores as well as its mean.

6. The standard deviation is sometimes used in grading students in a class to factor out the differences among exams. Suppose there are two exams of equal weight, both with a mean score of 70. The first has a narrow range of scores, the highest being 84, while the second has scores ranging as high as 98. Consider a student who did average on the first test and got a score of 90—far from the best score in class—on the second; and consider another who did average on the second test but best in the class on the first. The second student should be regarded as having done better, but when their scores are totaled, the first student has 160, the second only 154. The second student is penalized

for having had an excellent performance on an exam in which excellence was rewarded by a mere 14-point advantage over mediocrity.

The difference between the two exams shows up as a difference in their standard deviations. The exam grades can be made more directly comparable by translating them to *z-scores*. A student's *z*-score is the difference between that student's score and the class average, measured in standard deviations; that is, if the mean is $\bar{x}$ and the standard deviation is *s*, then the *z*-score for a grade x_i is $(x_i - \bar{x})/s$. For example, a score exactly one standard deviation above the mean translates to a *z*-score of 1.

Modify the program from the previous exercise so that it prints out the average and standard deviation of the exam and then prints a list of all the scores *and* corresponding *z*-scores.

7.4

List Operations as Member Functions

Many functions are easier to write as member functions than as client functions. By exploiting our ability to send messages to any of the cells in a list, we can perform many operations on lists without using a **while** loop.

Let's consider how we might program the various list operations from the previous section as member functions. The basic change in point of view—from "applying a function" to "sending a message"—will result in a profound change in the way we write these functions.

We'll add, as member functions of the **intList** class, the six functions defined in the previous section, plus a function similar to **addInOrder**, which was assigned in Exercise 2 in the last exercise set. Because the first argument of **operator<<** is of type **ostream &**, we cannot overload it as a member of **intList**, so we will instead define a member function **print** that does the same thing.

```
class intList {
private:
  int value;
  intList *nextEntry;

public:
  intList (int v, intList *next)
    : value(v), nextEntry(next)
  {}

  int getValue () { return value; }

  intList *getNextEntry () { return nextEntry; }

  void print () ;

  intList *find (int key) ;

  int length () ;
```

```
intList *nth (int n) ;

void addToEndM (int n) ;

intList *reverseM () ;

intList *addInOrderM (int n) ;
};
```

The `intList *` argument that each of these operations previously had is now an implicit argument; thus, the three functions that had only one argument now have none, and the three that had two arguments now have one. A more significant change occurs in the last three functions, where we've changed the names and, in the case of `addToEnd`, changed the return type; this function used to return new lists, but now it returns nothing. We'll explain these changes when we get to those operations.

In writing code for member functions, a good policy, as we have said, is to place yourself in the position of an object. In writing `print`, your thinking might go like this:

> I have an integer called **value** and a list pointer called **nextEntry**. To print myself means printing **value** and then printing the rest of the list—that is, the list pointed to by **nextEntry**—which I can do by sending it the **print** message.

This leads directly to the following code, which is almost right:

```
void intList::print () {
  cout << value << "\n";
  nextEntry->print();
}
```

The idea is right, but there is a problem: Sometimes `nextEntry` is `NULL`, and the penultimate line causes an error. (Recall that `nextEntry->print()` really means `(*nextEntry).print()`). If `nextEntry` is null, then `*nextEntry` is an attempt to dereference the null pointer.) What is the proper thing to do in this case? Just print the value and don't send the `print` message:

```
void intList::print () {
  cout << value << "\n";
  if (nextEntry != NULL) nextEntry->print();
}
```

We can now overload `operator<<` on list pointers, just having it send the `print` message to its argument:

```
ostream& operator<< (ostream& os, intList *list) {
  list->print();
  return os;
}
```

Taking the "object-oriented" view, in which we place ourselves in the position of an object receiving the `print` message, led us to a simple and correct version of the function. Let's try it out again with **find**. If you receive the message **find(k)**, you might reason like this:

> If I contain **k** as my value, I should return my own address (namely, **this**). If I don't contain **k** and my **nextEntry** field is NULL—so **k** isn't in the list at all—I should return **NULL**. Finally, if I don't contain **k** but my **nextEntry** field is non-NULL, I should send a message to my tail to look for **k**.

You are led to this code:

```
intList *intList::find (int key) {
  if (value == key)
    return this;
  else if (nextEntry == NULL)
    return NULL;
  else
    return nextEntry->find(key);
}
```

Programming **length()** is another straightforward application of the object-oriented method. You again have to consider the possibility that your **nextEntry** field is null, meaning you are the last cell in the list:

> To compute my length, I need to find the length of the list that my **nextEntry** points to—which I can do by sending it the **length** message—and add 1 to the result. If my **nextEntry** field is null, then I am the only item in the list, so I should just return 1.

This leads to

```
int intList::length () {
  if (nextEntry == NULL)
    return 1;
  else
    return 1 + nextEntry->length();
}
```

The definition of **nth** as a member function is another example of this type of reasoning. Recall that **nth** finds the cell occurring at a particular position in the list; the first cell is defined to be at position zero, the second is at position 1, and so on. Here is how you might think this through:

> I have received the message **nth(n)**, asking me to return the nth cell in this list. If $n = 0$, I should return the head of the list, namely myself, or **this**. If $n > 0$, I need to get a cell out of the tail of this list, but instead of cell **n**, I should request cell **n - 1**. For example, suppose $n = 1$, that is, the message requested the second cell in the list; that is exactly the cell my tail will return if I send it the message **nth(0)**. In other words, the second cell in the list is the same as the first cell in the tail of the list. Similarly, the third cell in the list is the same as the second cell in the tail, so if $n = 2$, I should send the message **nth(1)** to my tail. In general, if cell **n** was requested, I should request cell **n - 1** from my tail.

This reasoning leads directly to this solution:

```
intList *intList::nth (int n) {
  if (n == 0)
    return this;
  else if (nextEntry == NULL)
    return NULL;
  else
    return nextEntry->nth(n-1);
}
```

In Chapter 6 we introduced the notion of mutable and immutable classes. As an example, all our `time` classes were immutable, until we added the mutating operation `advanceMinutes` in Section 6.6. If a variable contains an immutable object, its value can be changed only by explicit assignment; if it contains a mutable object, its value may be changed by sending it a message.

This distinction is important when programming member functions in `intList`. Mutating and nonmutating versions of the same operation can differ significantly in their complexity and efficiency. We do, however, need to update the notions of mutating and nonmutating to apply them to lists. Consider the `addToEnd` operation, which adds a new item to the end of an existing list. Suppose its receiver is the list pointed to by `chapterPages`:

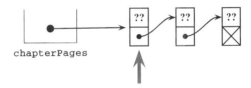

We want to "add 000 to the end of this list," but there are two different ways of interpreting that:

- The *nonmutating* interpretation: Create a new list just like this one, but with one additional element.

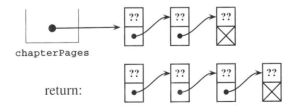

This is just what `addToEnd`, defined in the previous section, does.
- The *mutating* interpretation: Change this list so that it has one more element.

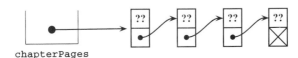

The difference between these interpretations is that the nonmutating version leaves `chapterPages` unchanged. In the mutating version, `chapterPages` is different and will produce different results if we send it messages like `print` or `find` than it would have before. So, for list operations, we will call them *mutating* if *any* cell in the list is changed.

We can write either mutating or nonmutating functions as member functions. In this section, we've chosen to write mutating versions of `addToEnd`, `reverse`, and `addInOrder` because they're a bit easier to understand, and we have indicated this by adding the letter `M` to their names. The nonmutating versions of these functions will be presented in the next section.

First, we will take a look at `addToEndM`, the mutating version of `addToEnd`. Since it is going to change its receiver rather than construct and return a new list, there is no need for it to return a pointer to its result. So its return type is `void`.

As usual in writing any member function, you need to place yourself in the position of an object (that is, the list cell) receiving an `addToEndM` message, with argument `n`. There are two possibilities. The first is that you are a cell *not* at the end of the list:

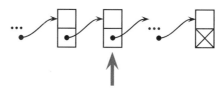

You can tell that you're not at the end, because your `nextEntry` data member is non-`NULL`. In this case, there is nothing to do but send the `addToEndM` message along to the next entry.

Eventually, the message will reach the last cell, which is the only one that can do anything about it. This brings us to the second possibility—that you are yourself the last cell in the list:

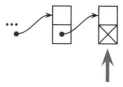

You know you're the last cell, because your `nextEntry` field is `NULL`. There are two things you need to do now: Create a new cell containing `n`, and set your `nextEntry` field to point to it:

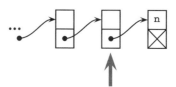

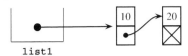

(a) Initial value of `list1`

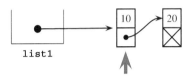

(b) After `list->addToEndM(30)`

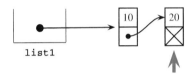

(c) After `nextEntry->addToEndM(30)`

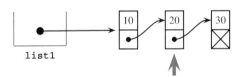

(d) After `nextEntry = new intList(30, NULL)`

FIGURE 7.13   Tracing the `addToEndM` function.

The code for **addToEndM** is thus

```
void intList::addToEndM (int n) { // mutating version
  if (nextEntry != NULL)
    // we're a cell in the middle of the list
    nextEntry->addToEndM(n);
  else // we're the last cell
    nextEntry = new intList(n, NULL);
}
```

Let's examine this in detail. Suppose **list1** is an **intList *** variable initialized by

```
intList *list1 = new intList(10, new intList(20, NULL));
```

as shown in Figure 7.13(a). Figure 7.13 traces the call **list1->addToEndM(30)**.

1. When it is sent to ***list1**, the **addToEndM** message recognizes that the pointer **list1->nextEntry** is not **NULL**, so it sends the **addToEndM** message to ***nextEntry**, leading to Figure 7.13(d).

2. `list1->nextEntry`, receiving the **addToEndM** message, sees that its **nextEntry** field *is* NULL, so it executes the **new** operator. It then creates a new **intList** object, containing 30 and NULL, and modifies its own **nextEntry** field to point to that object.

Now let's look at the mutating version of **reverse**. If its argument is a list,

it will reverse the list by changing all the pointers in its **nextEntry** fields to point backwards:

Like **addToEndM**, this function modifies the list "in place"; that is, it changes what is in the cells rather than creating new cells with different member values. The head of the reversed list, however, is now the cell containing 2. When a client sends the **reverse** message to a list, the client must be told where the head of the reversed list is, which is why **reverseM** has the type

```
intList *reverseM () ;
```

This is the trickiest function we've seen so far:

```
1    intList *intList::reverseM () { return reverseM(NULL); }
2
3    intList *intList::reverseM (intList *prev) {
4      if (nextEntry == NULL) {
5        nextEntry = prev;
6        return this;
7        }
8      else {
9        intList *front = nextEntry->reverseM(this);
10       nextEntry = prev;
11       return front;
12       }
13   }
```

Most of the code is in the one-argument version of **reverseM**, which is the one we'll concentrate on. We've used overloading to provide a zero-argument version as a convenience to our clients. This member function passes to its receiver the address that should be placed into the **nextEntry** field, and returns the new front of the list. As usual, we place ourselves in the position of a cell receiving a **reverseM** message. If our **nextEntry** field is NULL, we do two things:

1. Recalling that the **prev** argument is supposed to be our new **nextEntry** field, we assign it (line 5).
2. Also, we should return the new beginning of the list. But that's us! Hence, line 6.

If our **nextEntry** field is non-**NULL**, we are in this situation:

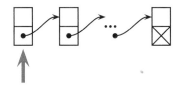

and we want to end up in this one:

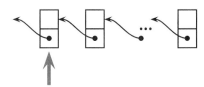

Thus, the next cell in the list should change *its* **nextEntry** field to point to us (line 9). That call will return the new front of the list, which is the cell shown all the way out on the right. So after changing our **nextEntry** field (line 10), we should return the address of the new front of the list to our caller (line 11).

Incidentally, since the one-argument version of **reverseM** is really just an auxiliary operation, not intended for use by clients, it should be placed in the **private** part of the class.

As our last example in this section, **addInOrderM** is the mutating version of the function **addInOrder** described in Exercise 3 (page 265). This **intList *addInOrderM (int n)** adds the integer **n** to its receiver in a position that keeps the list in numerical order, assuming it was so to begin with. If you consistently use **addInOrderM** to build your list, the list is always in numerical order. This function also returns the new address of the head of the list; this is necessary because the new cell containing *n* may go at the front of the list (if *n* is less than the element at the head of the list). However, most of the time, the receiver of the message will continue to be the head of the list.

Here is the definition of **addInOrderM**; its explanation follows.

```
1    intList *intList::addInOrderM (int n) {
2      if (n < value)
3        return new intList (n, this);
4      else if (n == value)
5        return this;
6      else if (nextEntry == NULL) {
7        nextEntry = new intList(n, NULL);
8        return this;
9      }
10     else {
11       nextEntry = nextEntry->addInOrderM(n);
12       return this;
13     }
14   }
```

Consider a cell in the middle of a numerically ordered list, which receives the **addInOrderM**(*n*) message. Its actions will depend not only on whether it is in the middle or at the end of the list, but also on how its value—call it p—compares with n. There are, in total, four cases to consider:

1. p is greater than n:

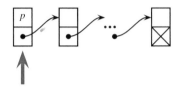

Line 3 allocates a new cell to hold n and places it on the front of the list:

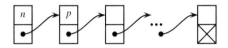

and returns its address.

2. p equals n. Here we need to make a choice about what the function is supposed to do. There are two alternatives: insert a new cell with value n, or simply ignore the request. We've chosen the latter course; line 5 reflects this decision.

3. p is less than n, but the receiver's **nextEntry** field is **NULL**:

Here, we should end up with the list

and should return the address of the cell containing p; this is accomplished by statements 7 and 8.

4. p is less than n, and **nextEntry** is non-**NULL**:

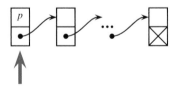

For this case, the receiver passes the message on to its **nextEntry**, and then sets **nextEntry** to whatever is returned by that call (line 11). It returns its own address (line 12) as the result.

As shown in Exercise 2 on page 265, `addInOrderM` can be used to "sort" a list of numbers as they are read in. However, this is not the only way to do so and, in fact, is not efficient. Another method is to read in the entire list as is, then call a function that *sorts* lists—arranges them in increasing order. The problem of sorting efficiently has been extensively studied. Efficient methods for sorting are discussed in Chapters 8 and 9.

Exercises—Third Set

1. Program `readForwardList` using `addToEndM`. It should have exactly the same effect as the version given on page 264 but without using `reverse`. Then program it again, this time the same way as on page 264 using `reverseM` instead of `reverse`.

2. Program these operations from Exercise 1 on page 264 as member functions:
   (a) `int sum ()`
   (b) `int frequency (int n)`

3. Program a mutating version of `remove`, previously given (as a nonmutating, non–member function) in Exercise 2c on page 265:

   ```
   intList *removeM (int n)
   ```

   Make sure that you can handle the case in which the item being removed is the *first* one in the list. As before, if the receiver is a one-element list containing `n`, return the null pointer.

4. Program the mutating operation `intList *removeNthM (int i)`, which removes the `i`th cell from its receiver and returns the new head of the list. The latter will normally be the same as the current head, but when `removeNthM` is called with argument `1`, the new head will be the second cell in the list. If `i` is greater than the length of the receiver, do nothing.

5. Use `removeNthM` to solve the "Josephus problem," named for the Jewish historian of the Roman–Jewish War of the first century. The story goes that ten Jews were trapped in a cave by Roman soldiers, and that they determined to commit suicide rather than surrender. They decided to do so in an unusual way: They all stood in a circle, and, with one man chosen to begin, every other man committed suicide. The question is, which man was the last to die?

   We want you to solve this problem in a more general setting. For given positive integers m and n, construct a list of the numbers from 1 to n. Then, starting from 1, remove every mth item; if this takes you past the end of the list, then consider the list to be a circle and continue from the beginning. For example, if n is 10 and m is 6, you would start with the list:

   ```
   1 2 3 4 5 6 7 8 9 10
   ```

   Eliminate element 1, leaving

   ```
   2 3 4 5 6 7 8 9 10
   ```

   Then count off 6 and eliminate element 7:

   ```
   2 3 4 5 6 8 9 10
   ```

Then count off 6 from there, looping around to the front, and eliminate element 4:

```
2 3 5 6 8 9 10
```

Continue in this way, eliminating 2, then 10, and so on. Continue in this way until only one man is left, and print his number.

6. Define a new class, `pairList`, which is like `intList` except that each cell contains two integers instead of just one. Its operations are the same as those of `intList`, except that `getValue` is replaced by `getFirstValue` and `getSecondValue`, and its constructor is also changed appropriately. Define the operation `pairList *search (int val)`, which looks for a cell that has `val` as its first value and returns a pointer to that cell.

Using `pairList`, define the class `grades` that keeps a grade list, consisting of student ID numbers (integers) and grades on one exam, and reports grades in terms of z-scores.

```
class grades {
private:
  pairList *allGrades;
  float mean, stdDev;
  boolean meanValid;
public:
  grades ()  // start with empty lists
  {...}

  void addGrade (int studentID, int grade) ;

  float average () ;

  float standardDeviation () ;

  int getScore (int studentID) ;

  float getZScore (int studentID) ;
};
```

`mean` and `stdDev` hold the mean and standard deviation of the scores but should not be computed each time a new grade is added. Instead, compute them only when one of the functions `average`, `standardDeviation`, or `getZScore` is called. Set `meanValid` to true when `mean` and `stdDev` are valid, and to false when they may not be.

7. Augment the `grades` class in the previous exercise to allow for changing an individual student's grade and for adjusting the grades for the entire class. Do this as follows:

1. Add to `pairList` the member functions `void changeFirst (int v)` and `void changeSecond (int v)`, which change the first or second value in the cell of their receiver to `v`, and `void adjustFirst (int f)` and `void adjustSecond (int f)`, which add `f` to the first or second values in their receiver.
2. Use these operations to add these member functions to the `grade` class: `void changeGrade (int studentID, int grade)` replaces the grade of the given student with `grade`; `void adjust (int f)` adds `f` to every grade.

Make sure that subsequent calls to `average`, `standardDeviation`, and `getZScore` deliver the correct answers.

★   8. Recall the **rectangle** class in Exercise 5 on page 233. It allowed the creation of rectangles for a computerized drawing program, with operations **move**, **reshape**, **rotate**,
duplicate, and **display**. You can use the **pairList** class to define a class **polygon**
that offers similar features.

In a drawing program, polygons are created by clicking the mouse at each of
the vertices (then usually double-clicking on the final vertex). The system will automatically close the polygon, joining the last vertex to the first. Define the **polygon**
class with the same operations as the **rectangle** class, except that you will not include
rotate and you will add one new operation, **nextVertex**; also, the constructor will
have different arguments.

```
class polygon {
private:
  pairList *vertices;   // all the points in the polygon

public:
  polygon (int x, int y) ; // polygon starts with one vertex

  void nextVertex (int x, int y) ; // add new vertex

  void move (int deltax, int deltay) ;
    // Move this polygon deltax in the x direction,
    // deltay in the y direction

  void reshape (int x, int y, int newx, int newy) ;
    // (x, y) is one of the vertices.  It is to be moved
    // to (newx, newy), leaving the other vertices stationary

  polygon duplicate (int delta) ;
    // Create a new polygon identical to this one, except
    // that it is moved by delta in both directions

  void display () ;
    // Print the vertices of the polygon in the order
    // in which they were created.
};
```

Modify the main program you used to exercise the **rectangle** class to do likewise for
polygon.

7.5

Debugging Programs with Lists

Let's return to the polynomial evaluation program of Section 6.7 and extend its
capabilities. That program used the class **Polynomial**, which represented polynomials in a single variable x. We wrote a program in which the user entered the
coefficients of a polynomial and then evaluated it for various values of x:

```
Enter exponents and coefficients, then -1: 0 4 1 7.9 3 2.25 -1
Enter x value: 4
The value of the polynomial at 4 is 179.6
```

```
Enter x value: -1.3
The value of the polynomial at -1.3 is -11.2132
Enter x value: ^D
```

The program was based on the class **Polynomial**, which had a zero-argument constructor (which initialized all coefficients to zero) and two member functions:

```
float evaluateAt (float x)
void setCoeff (int i, float c)
```

However, due to our limited ability to store coefficients—we simply stored each one in a separate data member—we restricted the class to polynomials of order 4. It was obvious how we could extend it to higher orders, but equally obvious how tedious that would be.

In this section we extend the **Polynomial** class to handle polynomials of any order. For polynomials of order 4 or less, the new **Polynomial** class should work exactly like the old one, and any program using it should see no difference (that is the beauty of representation independence!), but it should work correctly for polynomials of high order:

```
Enter exponents and coefficients, then -1: 20 1 19 -1 -1
Enter x value: 1.5
The value of the polynomial at 1.5 is 1108.42
```

That is, $x^{20} - x^{19}$, evaluated at $x = 1.5$, is 1108.42.

The main program and definition of **operator>>** are the same as in Section 6.7:

```
istream& operator>> (istream& is, Polynomial& p) {
  int i;
  float f;
  cout << "Enter exponents and coefficients, then -1: ";
  cin >> i;
  while (i != -1) {
    cin >> f;
    p.setCoeff(i, f);
    cin >> i;
  }
  return is;
}

void main () {
  float x;
  Polynomial poly;

  cin >> poly;
  cout << "Enter x value: ";
  cin >> x;
  while (!cin.eof()) {
    cout << "The value of the polynomial at "
         << x << " is " << poly.evaluateAt(x) << endl;
    cout << "Enter x value: ";
    cin >> x;
  }
}
```

In the `Polynomial` class, we will use a list of `float`s, called `coeffs`, to represent the coefficients—using the first cell to represent the coefficient of x^0, the second for the coefficient of x^1, and so on. In other words, for any i, `coeffs->nth(`i`)` will be the coefficient of x^i. This list will be initialized to contain one cell and will grow as necessary; if, for example, it contains coefficients for powers of x up to 3, and the polynomial receives the message `setCoeff(6, 1.05)`, then three cells will be added to `coeffs`, containing 0.0, 0.0, and 1.05. We will store in data member `order` the highest exponent of x for which a coefficient has been given (which is one less than the length of `coeffs`). Thus, the declaration of `Polynomial` is

```
//
// Objects of class Polynomial represent polynomials
//
class Polynomial {
private:
  floatList *coeffs;   // list of coefficients
  int order;           // order of highest non-zero
     // coefficient;  equal to length of coeffs minus one

public:
  Polynomial () : coeffs(new floatList(0.0, NULL)),
                  order(0)
  {}

  float evaluateAt (float x) ;

  void setCoeff (int i, float c) ;
};
```

The class `floatList` is identical to `intList`, except that `float` is used in place of `int` everywhere:

```
class floatList {
private:
  float value;
  floatList *nextEntry;

public:
  floatList (float v, floatList *next)
    : value(v), nextEntry(next)
  {}

  float getValue () { return value; }

  floatList *getNextEntry () { return nextEntry; }

  void setValue (float x) { value = x; }

  void addToEndM (float x) ;

  floatList *nth (int n) ;
};
```

We won't give the definitions of **addToEndM** and **nth**, which have been given for **intList**. Note the one new member function, **setValue**, which changes the value in a cell; we will see shortly how this is used in **setCoeff**.

evaluateAt iterates over **coeffs**, multiplying the coefficients by larger powers of **x** and adding the products. **setCoeff** uses **nth** to find the appropriate cell and **setValue** to set its value; the only complication is when **setCoeff** is called to supply a coefficient of a power larger than **order**, in which case the list must be extended. Here are these member function definitions along with the auxiliary function **extendList**:

```
70    float Polynomial::evaluateAt (float x) {
71      float xtoi = 1.0;  // x raised to the i(th) power
72      floatList *fl = coeffs;
73      float value = 0;   // accumulated sum of terms
74
75      for (int i = 0; i <= order; i++) {
76        // xtoi = x raised to the i(th) power, and
77        // value - sum of terms up to x^(i-1) term
78        value = value + fl->getValue() * xtoi;
79        xtoi = x * xtoi;
80      }
81    }
82
83    void extendList (floatList *fl,   // Extend this list
84                     int size,        // by this many elements
85                     float init) {    // initialized to this
86      for (int i=0; i<size; i++)
87        fl->addToEndM(init);
88    }
89
90    void setCoeff (int i, float c) {
91      // Set coefficient of x^i term to c
92      if (i > order)
93        extendList(coeffs, i-order, 0.0);
94      floatList fl = coeffs.nth(i);
95      fl->setValue(c);
96    }
```

We have now presented the entire program. Note that the order of these parts of the program is not the same as the order in which we have presented them (as you can see by the line numbers). The definitions of **floatList** and of its member functions come first; the declaration of **Polynomial** and the definitions of **evaluateAt** and **setCoeff** come next; and the definitions of **operator>>** and **main** are last.

Our first attempt to compile this program is unsuccessful:

```
line 81: warning: no value returned from Polynomial::evaluateAt()
line 92: error:  order undefined
line 93: error:  coeffs undefined
line 93: error:  - of void*
line 94: error: cannot make a floatList from a any
line 95: error: non pointer -> setValue
5 errors
```

These errors are fairly obvious. The first one is unusually clear—we have indeed failed to return anything from `evaluateAt`. We need to add the statement `return value;` at the end. The errors starting on line 92 come from the same omission as in Section 6.7: In the definition of `setCoeff`, we forgot to write the `Polynomial::` part.

After correcting these omissions, the compiler gives us a shorter list of errors:

```
line 95: error: non object . nth
line 95: error: cannot make a floatList from a any
line 96: error: non pointer -> setValue
3 errors
```

The first error here is also clear, if you know how to read it. It says that we have used dot notation to get a member of something that is not an object. The offending expression is `coeffs.nth(i)`, and the problem is that `coeffs` is a pointer, not an object. Assuming the other two errors are related to this one, we fix this line:

```
95      floatList fl = coeffs->nth(i);
```

and recompile:

```
line 95: error: cannot make floatList from floatList *
line 96: error: non pointer -> setValue
2 errors
```

We were wrong: the same two errors are still present. We had two separate errors on the same line! The error message says the compiler is trying to convert a `floatList` pointer to a `floatList`. Indeed, we have declared `fl` to be a `floatList`, when we had intended to make it a pointer. Change this line to

```
95      floatList *fl = coeffs->nth(i);
```

At last, the program compiles. However, it does not run correctly:

```
Enter exponents and coefficients, then -1: 0 10 1 20 -1
Enter x value: 1
The value of the polynomial at 1 is 10
Enter x value: ^D
```

Polynomial $10 + 20x$, evaluated at $x = 1$, should be 30, not 10.

We have no way of knowing whether the problem is in reading the polynomial or in evaluating it. But notice that 10 is the answer we would have gotten if only the x^0 coefficient were considered. This suggests that `setCoeff` may be failing to set the coefficient for higher powers of x, so let's take a look at it. When `setCoeff(1, 20)` is called, it should extend `coeffs` by one cell and then set that cell's value to 20. All of this looks okay, but there is one omission: We have failed to change the data member `order`, which is supposed to contain the highest exponent for which a coefficient has been given. `setCoeff` should be changed to

```
void Polynomial::setCoeff (int i, float c) {
  // Set coefficient of x^i term to c
  if (i > order) {
    extendList(coeffs, i-order, 0.0);
    order = i;
  }
  floatList *fl = coeffs->nth(i);
  fl->setValue(c);
}
```

This new version still fails to produce correct output:

```
Enter exponents and coefficients, then -1: 0 10 1 20 -1
Enter x value: 1
The value of the polynomial at 1 is 20
Enter x value: ^D
```

It seems to have ignored the x^0 coefficient and considered only the x^1 coefficient.

This time, we can't find the error by inspection, so we use the same strategy as in Section 6.7: Print the polynomial after reading it, so we can tell whether the problem is in inputting the polynomial or in evaluating it. Printing the polynomial requires that we add a **print** member function to **floatList** (this is identical to the function shown on page 259, except that instead of skipping a line after each number we will just skip a space). Then we can add a **print** member function in **Polynomial**:

```
void print () {
  cout << "Polynomial of order " << order
       << " with coefficients ";
       coeffs->print();
       cout << endl;
}
```

and the call **poly.print()** in **main**. Now we get this output:

```
Enter exponents and coefficients, then -1: 0 10 1 20 -1
Polynomial of order 1 with coefficients 10 20
Enter x value: 1
The value of the polynomial at 1 is 20
Enter x value: ^D
```

The polynomial was read correctly, so let's concentrate on **evaluateAt**. Again, inspection doesn't reveal any obvious errors, so we place an output statement inside the loop to trace the evaluation process:

```
85   float Polynomial::evaluateAt (float x) {
86     float xtoi = 1.0;   // x raised to the i(th) power
87     floatList *fl = coeffs;
88     float value = 0;   // accumulated sum of terms
89
90     for (int i = 0; i <= order; i++) {
91       // xtoi = x raised to the i(th) power, and
```

```
92        // value - sum of terms up to x^(i-1) term
93        value = value + fl->getValue() * xtoi;
94        cout << "value, coeff, xtoi = " << value << " "
95             << fl->getValue << " " << xtoi << endl;
96        xtoi = x * xtoi;
97      }
98      return value;
99    }
```

We have made an error, unfortunately, in entering this output statement:

```
line 95: error:  pointer operand for  <<
line 95: error:  function operand for  <<
line 95: error:  pointer operand for  <<
line 95: error:  pointer operand for  <<
line 95: error:  pointer operand for  <<
line 95: error:  float operand for  <<
line 95: error:  pointer << float
line 95: error:  function operand for  <<
8 errors
```

Can you see what's wrong? As usual, the error messages don't tell us much. The error is that we have treated **getValue** as a data member rather than a member function. Line 95 should be

```
95              << fl->getValue() << " " << xtoi << endl;
```

Now, the program compiles and gives this output:

```
Enter exponents and coefficients, then -1: 0 10 1 20 -1
Polynomial of order 1 with coefficients 10 20
Enter x value: 1
The value of the polynomial at 1 is value, coeff, xtoi = 10 10 1
value, coeff, xtoi = 20 10 1
20
Enter x value: ^D
```

(We didn't think to print a newline before the output statement in the loop, so the first line of output from that statement appears at the end of the fourth line.) The first time through the loop, **value** and **coeff** are 10, and **xtoi** is 1; these are all fine. The second time through, however, something is wrong: **value** is 20, when it should be 30, and **coeff** is 10, when it should be 20. It is surprising that **coeff** has the same value on both iterations of the loop, as if the call **fl->getValue()** is returning the same value on each iteration. Of course! We are looking at the same cell, since we haven't changed **fl**!

Fixing this—we're so confident, we also remove the output statement— gives this definition of **evaluateAt**:

```
float Polynomial::evaluateAt (float x) {
  float xtoi = 1.0;  // x raised to the i(th) power
```

```
    floatList *fl = coeffs;
    float value = 0;    // accumulated sum of terms

    for (int i = 0; i <= order; i++) {
      // xtoi = x raised to the i(th) power, and
      // value - sum of terms up to x^(i-1) term
      value = value + fl->getValue() * xtoi;
      xtoi = x * xtoi;
      fl = fl->getNextEntry();
    }
    return value;
}
```

Finally, the output is correct:

```
Enter exponents and coefficients, then -1: 0 10 1 20 -1
Polynomial of order 1 with coefficients 10 20
Enter x value: 1
The value of the polynomial at 1 is 30
Enter x value: 2
The value of the polynomial at 2 is 50
Enter x value: 1.5
The value of the polynomial at 1.5 is 40
Enter x value: -1
The value of the polynomial at -1 is -10
Enter x value: ^D
```

After removing the code to output the polynomial, we arrive at the final version of the program.

```
1   //
2   // Program to read and evaluate a polynomial
3   // of arbitrary order
4   //
5   // Author: J.M. Kamin
6   // Last modified: 7/10/95
7   //
8
9   #include <iostream.h>
10  #include <iomanip.h>
11
12  enum boolean {false, true};
13
14  class floatList {
15  private:
16    float value;
17    floatList *nextEntry;
18
```

```
19  public:
20    floatList (float v, floatList *next)
21      : value(v), nextEntry(next)
22    {}
23
24    float getValue () { return value; }
25
26    floatList *getNextEntry () { return nextEntry; }
27
28    void setValue (float x) { value = x; }
29
30    void addToEndM (float x) ;
31
32    floatList *nth (int n) ;
33  };
34
35  floatList *floatList::nth (int n) {
36    if (n <= 0)
37      return this;
38    else if (nextEntry == NULL)
39      return NULL;
40    else
41      return nextEntry->nth(n-1);
42  }
43
44  void floatList::addToEndM (float x) { // mutating version
45    if (nextEntry != NULL)
46      nextEntry->addToEndM(x);
47    else
48      nextEntry = new floatList(x, NULL);
49  }
50
51  //
52  // Objects of class Polynomial represent polynomials
53  //
54  class Polynomial {
55  private:
56    floatList *coeffs;  // list of coefficients
57    int order;          // order of highest non-zero
58      // coefficient;  equal to length of coeffs minus one
59
60  public:
61    Polynomial () : coeffs(new floatList(0.0, NULL)),
62                    order(0)
63    {}
64
65    float evaluateAt (float x) ;
66
67    void setCoeff (int i, float c) ;
68  };
69
70  float Polynomial::evaluateAt (float x) {
71    float xtoi = 1.0;  // x raised to the i(th) power
72    floatList *fl = coeffs;
```

```
73      float value = 0;    // accumulated sum of terms
74
75      for (int i = 0; i <= order; i++) {
76        // xtoi = x raised to the i(th) power, and
77        // value - sum of terms up to x^(i-1) term
78        value = value + fl->getValue() * xtoi;
79        xtoi = x * xtoi;
80      }
81      return value;
82    }
83
84    void extendList (floatList *fl,   // Extend this list
85                      int size,       // by this many elements
86                      float init) {   // initialized to this
87      for (int i=0; i<size; i++)
88        fl->addToEndM(init);
89    }
90
91    void Polynomial::setCoeff (int i, float c) {
92      // Set coefficient of x^i term to c
93      if (i > order) {
94        extendList(coeffs, i-order, 0.0);
95        order = i;
96      }
97      floatList *fl = coeffs->nth(i);
98      fl->setValue(c);
99    }
100
101   istream& operator>> (istream& is, Polynomial& p) {
102     int i;
103     float f;
104     cout << "Enter exponents and coefficients, then -1: ";
105     cin >> i;
106     while (i != -1) {
107       cin >> f;
108       p.setCoeff(i, f);
109       cin >> i;
110     }
111     return is;
112   }
113
114   void main () {
115     float x;
116     Polynomial poly;
117
118     cin >> poly;
119     cout << "Enter x value: ";
120     cin >> x;
121     while (!cin.eof()) {
122       cout << "The value of the polynomial at "
123            << x << " is " << poly.evaluateAt(x) << endl;
124       cout << "Enter x value: ";
125       cin >> x;
126     }
127   }
```

7.6

Nonmutating Operations on Lists

We have written both nonmutating (**print**, **find**, **length**, **nth**) and mutating (**addToEndM**, **reverseM**, **addInOrderM**) operations on lists. The principle is the same: Place yourself in the position of an object receiving a message. However, the three mutating functions are somewhat more difficult to write in nonmutating form. In this section we will do just that, as well as define one more nonmutating operation, **remove**, that removes an element from a list.

The nonmutating version of **addToEnd**—which we'll call just **addToEnd**—returns a new list, just as the nonmember function of the same name did, so its type is

```
intList *addToEnd (int n) ;
```

Sending the **addToEnd** message to a list directs that list to make an exact copy of itself, but with a new cell at the end containing *n*. It should return the address of the head of the new list.

As in the mutating version, once you've placed yourself in the position of a list receiving this message, the basic question you have to ask yourself is, Am I the cell at the end of the list, or not? Again, the question is answered by looking at **nextEntry**. If it's null, you're the last cell in the list; otherwise you're at the beginning or somewhere in the middle. So the function will look like

```
intList *intList::addToEnd (int n) {
  if (nextEntry == NULL) {
    ...
  }
  else {
    ...
  }
}
```

When **nextEntry** is null, you need only consider this simple question: How do you add *n* to the end of a one-element list? Just consider the situation. The receiver looks like

and you need to construct a new list that looks like

Thus, you will need to create two cells using **new**, and return the address of the one containing *m*:

```
ncell = new intList(n, NULL);
mcell = new intList(value, ncell);
return mcell;
```

Consider now the other case, where **nextEntry** is not null. The receiver can just pass the message along to its tail, knowing that it will eventually get back a copy of it (with the new cell appended). In other words, if the receiver is a cell like this one,

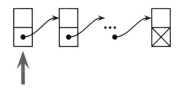

then the call **nextEntry->addToEnd(n)** will produce a new list and return its address:

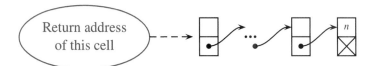

Now we must figure out how to return a new copy of the entire list, including a copy of ourselves. We already have a copy of the tail of the list, though, so we can return a copy of the entire list by allocating a single new cell and copying our own value into it:

```
ncell = nextEntry->addToEnd(n);
```

We end up with this definition:

```
intList *intList::addToEnd (int n) { // non-mutating version
  intList *ncell, *mcell;
  if (nextEntry == NULL) {
    ncell = new intList(n, NULL);
    mcell = new intList(value, ncell);
    return mcell;
    }
  else {
    ncell = nextEntry->addToEnd(n);
    mcell = new intList(value, ncell);
    return mcell;
    }
}
```

or, more concisely,

```
intList *intList::addToEnd (int n) { // mutating version
  if (nextEntry == NULL)
    return new intList(value, new intList(n, NULL));
  else
    return new intList(value, nextEntry->addToEnd(n));
}
```

To emphasize further the difference between **addToEnd** and **addToEndM**, compare these statements to those on page 216:

```
1    intList *list1, *list2, *list3;
2    list1 = new intList(2, NULL);
3    list2 = new intList(2, NULL);
4    list1->addToEndM(3);
5    list3 = list2->addToEnd(3);
6    cout << list1;  // prints:  2 3
7    cout << list2;  // prints:  2
8    cout << list3;  // prints:  2 3
```

In lines 2 and 3, two copies of the list containing just the number 2 are constructed, and **list1** and **list2** are assigned their addresses. In line 4, the list that **list1** points to is mutated using **addToEndM**; the output of line 6 reflects this. In line 5, a new list is constructed using **addToEnd**, which makes a copy of **list2** and adds a 3 at the end; this list's address is assigned to **list3**, and the output of line 8 reflects that. Most importantly, **list2** has not changed during any of the assignments or function calls, and this is shown in the output of line 7.

The nonmutating version of reverse—**reverse**—constructs a new list, with all new cells that contain the same numbers as are in its receiver, but in reverse order, and returns the address of the new list. For a one-element list (**nextEntry == NULL**), the receiver just needs to make a copy of itself, because a one-element list is the same forwards and backwards. So the function will look like this:

```
intList *intList::reverse () {
  if (nextEntry == NULL)
    return new intList(value, NULL);
  else
    ...
}
```

For the case when **nextEntry** is non-**NULL**, the receiver can send it the **reverse** message and expect a new, reversed, copy to be returned. That is, if the receiver is in this position,

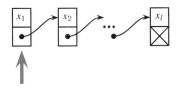

then **nextEntry->reverse()** should return

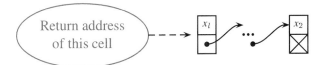

Now, the receiver can just place its value (x_1) onto the end of the list and return the address of the resulting list, giving this code:

```
intList *intList::reverse () {
  if (nextEntry == NULL)
    return new intList(value, NULL);
  else
    return (nextEntry->reverse())->addToEnd(value);
}
```

Now, these statements,

```
intList *numbers =
  new intList(2, new intList(3, new intList(4, NULL)));
cout << numbers->reverse();
```

print

4

3

2

This code works fine and is adequately efficient for short lists, but it is extremely inefficient when the lists get long. Here's why: Suppose the length of **list** is l, and we send it the **reverse** message. Let's trace the execution of this message and, as a measure of its cost, count the number of times **new** is executed:

- **list** sends the message to its **nextEntry**, which sends it to its **nextEntry**, and so on, until the final cell receives it:

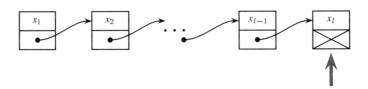

No executions of **new** have occurred up to this point.
- The x_l cell copies itself, calling **new** once, and returns to the x_{l-1} cell.
- The x_{l-1} cell sends the **addToEnd** message to the list returned by the x_l cell. Inspection of **addToEnd** shows that, when sent to a list of length m, it calls **new** $m + 1$ times. Thus, in this case, **new** is called twice, and the x_{l-1} cell returns a two-element list to the x_{l-2} cell.
- The x_{l-2} cell calls **addToEnd**, which calls **new** 3 times.
- Continuing in this way, the x_2 cell eventually returns a list of length l to the x_1 cell, which calls **addToEnd**, which calls **new** $l + 1$ times.

In total, **new** was executed

$$1 + 2 + \cdots + l + (l + 1) \; = \; \frac{l^2}{2} + \frac{3l}{2} + 1$$

times. Because the l^2 term dominates here (that is, for large n, $l^2/2$ is much larger than $3l/2$), we say the cost of **reverse** is a *quadratic function* of the length of the list being reversed. This is inefficient.

quadratic function

How inefficient? Well, here is a table of some values of $l^2/2 + 3l/2 + 1$:

l	10	100	500	1000	1500	2000
Calls to **new** made by **reverse** on list of length l	116	10,151	250,751	1,001,501	2,252,251	4,003,001

and here are some timings taken from our computer for reversing lists of those lengths, given in seconds:[3]

l	10	100	500	1000	1500	2000
Time to run **reverse** on list of length l	0	0.2	10.1	57.3	149.5	302.8

The point to observe in both these tables is that the cost of reversing a list grows much faster than the length of the list. That is, when we double the length of the list, we *quadruple* the time it takes to reverse it. If we only doubled it, we would say the time grew *linearly*.

linear function

Notice that **reverseM** does not exhibit this quadratic growth in time. In fact, it is impossible to get usable timing results for reversing lists of up to length 2000 using **reverseM**, because they all run in "zero" seconds. This suggests that reversing a list *can* be accomplished in linear time. The question is how to program a *nonmutating* reverse function with linear growth in time.

The concept of an *accumulator* argument is helpful here. An accumulator is an argument that gets passed from one invocation of a function to its next invocation, always containing the current value of the final result. In this case, whenever a cell sends the **reverse** message to its **nextEntry**, it will pass an argument that contains the reverse of all the cells up to, and including, itself. In other words, when the ith cell in a list gets the **reverse** message,

accumulator

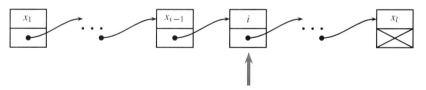

---

[3] Two points need to be made about this table. First, we obtained the timings using a system command that reports the time in tenths of a second. The time of zero for reversing a 10–element list is, of course, not literally true, but it is far enough below one-tenth of a second that it rounds to zero. Second, you will find, if you attempt to reverse a list of 2000 elements, that you cannot do it; the program will crash. This phenomenon will be explained in Section 7.8, where we will also show how we were able to run the function on long lists despite this problem.

its argument will be the list containing the the first $i - 1$ values in the list, in reverse order; when it then sends the **reverse** message to the $(i + 1)$st cell, it will pass it a list containing the first i values in reverse.

As usual, we need to consider two cases:

1. When the receiver's **nextEntry** is null (the receiver is the last cell in the list), the accumulator argument contains the first $l - 1$ elements in reverse order. To obtain the *entire* list in reverse order, just allocate a new cell for x_l and put it at the beginning of the list being constructed.
2. When **nextEntry** is non-**NULL**, the only thing to do is to send the reverse message to it, making sure to pass the correct accumulator argument.

Adding a zero-argument form (as we did for **reverseM**; again, the one-argument form should be private), we get the functions

```
intList *intList::reverseAcc () { return reverseAcc(NULL); }

intList *intList::reverseAcc (intList *acc) {
  if (nextEntry == NULL)
    return new intList(value, acc);
  else
    return nextEntry->reverseAcc(new intList(value, acc));
}
```

The function **reverseAcc** reverses a list immutably in linear time. To see this, just observe that it sends only the **reverseAcc** message (never **addToEnd** or anything else), and it calls **new** exactly once for each time it sends that message to **nextEntry**. The resulting timings are indistinguishable from those of **reverseM**; our system reports that **reverseAcc** takes no time to reverse a list of length 2000. (For longer lists, **reverseAcc** is somewhat slower than **reverseM**, because **reverseM** never calls **new**, which is a fairly time-consuming operation.)

In conclusion, we'll add one more nonmutating member function, **remove**, previously given as Exercise 1 on page 265 (as a nonmutating, non-member function), and then as Exercise 3 on page 275 (as a mutating member function).

For example, given the list

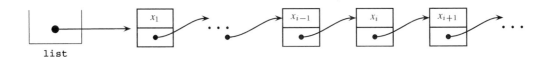

the call **list->remove** (x_i) returns

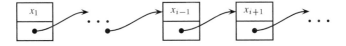

Here is the **remove** function:

```
1   intList *intList::remove (int n) {
2     if (value == n)
3       return nextEntry;
4     else if (nextEntry == NULL)
5       return this;
6     else
7       return new intList(value, nextEntry->remove(n));
8   }
```

To be precise, the call **list->remove**(n) removes the cell containing the *first* occurrence of n. This is consistent with **addInOrder**, which, if used consistently, produces lists that have at most one occurrence of any integer.

The function has three cases to consider:

1. If the receiver itself contains n,

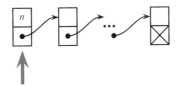

   then it returns its **nextEntry**:

   as seen in line 3. This is correct, since this is the same as the original list, without the cell containing n.
2. If not, then the receiver needs to consider, as usual, whether it is at the end of the list or in the middle. If it is at the end (**nextEntry == NULL**), then there are no occurrences of n, so it should just return itself (line 5).
3. If the value of the receiver is not n and it is not the last cell in the list, then the resulting list should contain a cell that contains the same value as the receiver but points to a list from which n has been removed. To accomplish this, the receiver needs to send the **remove** message to **nextEntry** and then create a cell that contains the same value as itself but points to the list returned from that call. This is done in line 7.

Unlike our previous nonmutating operations, **remove** does *not* construct a completely new list with all new cells. Instead, if it is sent to a list that looks like this:

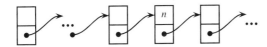

it will return a list like this:

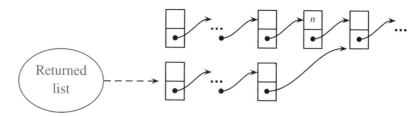

It is still correct to say that it is a nonmutating operation, by the criterion we gave earlier: After the **remove** message is sent to a list **list**, that list still looks exactly the same as before. That is, **cout << list** will produce the same result.

However, the situation is now decidedly more complex. If we subsequently apply a *mutating* operation, such as **addToEndM**, to **list**, it will not only change **list**—it will also change the list that was returned by **remove**! Thus:

```
intList *lista =
    new intList(1,
        new intList(2,
            new intList(3, NULL)));   // lista is 1,2,3
intList *listb = lista->remove(2);    // listb is 1,3
lista->addToEndM(4);                  // lista is 1,2,3,4
cout << listb;                        // listb is ?!
```

has output

```
1
3
4
```

This is just an example of how confusing mutating operations can be.

Exercises—Fourth Set

1. Program **readForwardList** (page 264) yet again, using **intList::addToEnd**.

2. Program **addInOrder** (page 265) as a nonmutating member function. (The mutating version was given on page 273.)

3. If we use a mutating operation to remove the only item in the list, we will end up with an *empty list*, and we have no way of representing empty lists. If the list is

list

and we make the call **list->removeM**(*x*), it is impossible for the receiver to *change itself* into an empty list.

If all the variables in clients are of type **intList ***, rather than **intList**, then we can represent the empty list by the null pointer, as is very commonly done. However, we then have to check whether the variable is **NULL** whenever we want to send it a message. In other words, if a variable **list** points to an **intList** object but may be **NULL**, it is wrong to write simply **list->print()**; if **list** is null, that call will cause the program to crash. Instead, we have to say

```
if (list != NULL) list->print();
```

and the same holds for all the member functions. It would be neater if we had a variable representing a list to which we could *always* safely send any message.

One way to achieve this is to define a new class, **intListHeader**, whose only data member is a pointer-to-**intList**. It has the same member functions as **intList**; when we send it a message like **print**, it just "delegates" the duty to its data member. However, this class first checks whether its data member is **NULL**. A client using **intListHeader**, can always send messages without having to check for null pointers. Program **intListHeader**.

4. *Histograms,* also called *bar charts,* are a popular method of presenting quantitative data graphically. The histogram in Figure 7.14 shows the number of students in a class receiving grades on an exam in various categories.

Define a class **histogram**, having two member functions: **incrCategory (int category)** and **categoryFreq (int category)**. The **category** argument in each function is a number in the range 0 to 9. 0 is for grades 0 through 9, 1 for grades 10 through 19, and so on until category 9 for grades 90 through 100 (we've enlarged this last category rather than give 100 its own category). In brief, category i, when $i < 9$, represents grades $10i$ through $10i + 9$. **incrCategory** adds 1 to the frequency count for that category, and **categoryFreq** reports the count for that category. You should represent a histogram by a list of integers. The most natural implementation uses **nth** and **setValue**, much as we did in Section 7.5.

Then write a main program to read in a list of grades and construct and print a histogram.

```
            Distribution of
            student grades

            Range   Count

             0- 9   ******************
            10-19
            20-29   ****
            30-39   ****
            40-49   *********
            50-59   ***********************
            60-69   *************************
            70-79   ********
            80-89   ******
            90-100  ****
```

FIGURE 7.14   A histogram.

```
                    Distribution of
                    student grades
                    (* = exam 1, + = exam 2)

                    Range    Count

                     0- 9    ******************

                             ++++++++++++

                    10-19

                    20-29    ****

                             ++

                    30-39    ****

                             +++

                    40-49    *********

                             +++++++++

                    50-59    ***********************

                             +++++++++++++++++++++

                    60-69    *************************

                             ++++++++++++++++++++++++++

                    70-79    ********

                             +++++++++++++++

                    80-89    ******

                             +++++++++

                    90-100   ****

                             +++++++
```

FIGURE 7.15 A grouped histogram (see Exercise 5).

5. Grouped histograms are used to show outcomes of related events, such as grade distributions on several exams of the same class, or the results of the same survey sent to differing groups of people. Figure 7.15 shows a histogram for grades on two exams (we've reduced the number of categories to ten so that the histogram would fit on a page). It shows that the students did somewhat better on the second exam than the first.
   Write a histogram class with operations

   - `void incrCategory (int cat, int which)`, where `which` is either 1 or 2 (the exam number); category `cat` in that exam is to be incremented.
   - `int categoryFreq (int cat, int which)`

   Use it to produce a histogram like the one in Figure 7.15. The main program should read two numbers from each line, giving scores on each of the exams.

6. In the `Polynomial` class in Section 7.5 it is possible to create a list of coefficients that is very "sparse," in the sense that it contains mostly zeros. For example, the polynomial $0.001x^{100} + 1.011x^{150} + 0.025x^{200}$ would be represented by a list of 201 elements, all but three containing zero.

An alternative implementation method uses *parallel lists*, in which one list— call it `terms`—holds the powers of *x* that have nonzero coefficients, and the other— `coeffs`—holds the corresponding coefficients. For example, the polynomial we just described would be represented by these two lists:

parallel lists

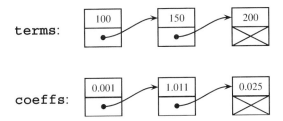

It is not necessary for `terms` to be in increasing order, so setting the value of a new coefficient is just a matter of adding a new cell to each of the lists. To evaluate the polynomial at *x*, follow both lists "in parallel," raising *x* to the power given in `terms` and multiplying by the number given in the corresponding cell of `coeffs`. Implement the `Polynomial` class using parallel lists. (When testing your solution, bear in mind that, due to the limitations of computer arithmetic, it may not be possible to compute very large powers of *x* accurately. Testing it for relatively small powers of *x*—say, below 20—is safer.)

7. The class `grades` from Exercise 6 (page 276) could have been implemented using parallel lists instead of the `pairList` class. The advantage would be that a new class is not needed; by the same token, grades on more than one exam could be easily accommodated without having to define a new class.

Alter the `grades` class to include scores on two exams.

```
class grades {
private:
  intList *studentIDs, *exam1, *exam2;
  float mean1, stdDev1;
  float mean2, stdDev2;
  boolean meansValid;
public:
  grades ()  // start with empty lists
  {...}

  void addGrade (int studentID, int grade1, int grade2) {...}

  float average (int i) {...}

  float standardDeviation (int i) {...}

  int getScore (int studentID, int i) {...}

  float getZScore (int studentID, int i) {...}
};
```

The new integer arguments are always 1 or 2, indicating the exam for which the information is being requested. The means and standard deviations are computed for both exams at once, so that `meansValid` holds when all of those numbers are up to date.

Character Lists

Until now, every program we've written has operated on numbers. You might conclude that numbers are the only kinds of data computers *can* operate on. Indeed, in the very early years of computing that was the case.

nonnumerical computation

But it isn't any more. Most programs written nowadays perform primarily *nonnumerical computations*. Inputs to these programs might be letters or other characters, or perhaps signals from a mouse or other device, and the outputs are words or pictures.

In this section we give an example of one type of nonnumerical program, a *string-processing* program, whose inputs and outputs are sequences of characters. Our example is a simple version of a "mail-merge" program. These programs, commonly found as parts of text-processing programs such as WordPerfect® and Microsoft Word®, are used to produce customized form letters. Given a letter with some "blanks" and a list of addresses (and perhaps other information), a mail-merge program will print a customized copy of the letter for each address. We will program a simple version of this idea.

Several new features of C++ will be introduced along the way to doing this example. We need to explain what characters are and how to read and write them. Our main tool, though, will be the class **charList**, similar to **intList**. Indeed, once we know how to do the input and output, the actual processing in the mail-merge example is within the list-processing capabilities covered in the previous sections.

7.7.1 Characters

character

A *character* is any key you can strike on the keyboard or that can show up on the computer screen. This includes upper- and lower-case letters, punctuation marks, and even digits. Each time you type a key on the keyboard, the computer receives a character as input; each time a letter or digit shows up on the screen, it is because the computer printed a character.

You can store characters in your program by declaring variables of type **char**:

```
char firstLetter, middleInitial;
char MorF;
```

There are *character constants*, written using single quotes:[4]

```
char vitamin = 'A',
     chromosome = 'y',
     middleInitial = 'N';
```

---

[4]Not to be confused with the *double* quotes used for strings. Although we've given strings the type **char ***—pointer-to-**char**—we cannot explain this until Chapter 9. In the meantime, think of characters and strings as unrelated types.

Just as integer constants can be assigned to `int` variables, so character constants can be assigned to `char` variables.

Some operations you might expect would be defined for characters do indeed work correctly. For example, the program

```
1   main () {
2     char vitamin = 'A',
3         chromosome = 'y',
4         middleInitial = 'N';
5     cout << vitamin;
6     if (chromosome == middleInitial)
7       cout << chromosome;
8     else
9       cout << middleInitial;
10  }
```

prints

   AN

However, before going into more detail about character operations, we need to say more about characters themselves. Characters seem simple enough when you think solely in terms of letters and punctuation marks, but the concept can get confusing when some other cases are considered.

One source of trouble is the *space character*, `' '`. It is sometimes difficult to *space character* think of a space as a real character, but it is. A space appears between two words on the screen because the computer sent a space character to the terminal. (Notice that in the last program there was no space printed between the `'A'` and the `'N'`; to get one, you need to add `cout << ' '` after line 5.)

A worse source of confusion involves the digit characters, `'0'`, `'1'`,..., `'9'`. These are completely different from the *integers* 0, 1,..., 9. It is a serious, but common, mistake to assign an integer to a character variable, as in

```
char level = 3;
```

For reasons we will explain in Chapter 9, C++ does not consider this a mistake at all and will not print any error message. However, the statement `cout << level` after this declaration will not print 3; try it. The correct way to assign the *character* `'3'` to a variable is

```
char level = '3';
```

After this assignment, the statement `cout << level` will print 3.

Finally, there are the so-called *nonprinting characters*, which don't really *nonprinting* show up on the screen at all but are still useful. The most important of these is the *characters* *newline* character. This is the character you send to the computer when you strike *newline* the enter or return key. When the computer prints it, it causes the terminal to skip to the beginning of the next line for subsequent output. To print it in a program, you use the character constant `'\n'`. \n is called an *escape sequence*, and \ is the *escape character*, as was discussed on page 31. Without the escape character, *escape character* you would just have a lower-case n; with it you have the newline character.

null character   There are several other nonprinting characters, but the only one you'll need to know, which we'll explain later on in this section, is the *null character*, written '\0' (backslash-zero). Not all escape sequences are nonprinting, though. Because the backslash is *always* assumed to be used as an escape character, the question arises: How can you write a backslash as a character constant? The answer is to embed it in an escape sequence by introducing it with another backslash: '\\' represents a (single) backslash character. As another useful example, '\'' represents a single quote constant.

To review, here are the character constants you need to know:

'A',..., 'Z'	Upper-case letters
'a',..., 'z'	Lower-case letters
'0',..., '9'	Digits
'.', ',', '!', '"', etc.	Punctuation marks
'\n'	Newline
'\\'	Backslash
'\''	Single right quote
'\0'	Null character

7.7.2 Character Operations

Some character operations are obvious. << operates exactly as you'd expect on characters: It prints the character and nothing else (no extra spaces or newlines). == compares characters for exact equality; case is significant ('e' == 'E' is false).

Input is more subtle. The extraction operator >> works, but not exactly as you might want:

```
cin >> ch
```

reads a character from the standard input stream (the keyboard) into the character variable **ch**, *but only after skipping spaces and newlines.* (This is what >> does when reading numbers as well, if you hadn't noticed.) An alternative is to write[5]

```
ch = cin.get()
```

which reads the next character typed on the keyboard, even if it is a space or newline. (If there is no input left, then we don't care what it returns; we'll test for this, as always, by testing whether **cin.eof()** is zero.)

---

[5]We mentioned on page 211 that **cout** is an object of class **ostream**. Similarly, **cin** is an object of class **istream** (for "input stream"), which is predefined by C++. **eof()** and **get()** are member functions of **istream**.

Here is a simple program illustrating these two ways of reading characters. It reads the first three characters you type:

```
main () {
  char c1, c2, c3;
  cin >> c1 >> c2 >> c3;
  cout << c1 << c2 << c3 << "\n";
}
```

Note that input doesn't "happen" until you type an entire line—that is, until you hit the return or enter key. So the program will read the first three characters you type and print them after you've pressed the return key (even if you may have typed some other characters first):

```
abcdef
abc
```

To be more precise, it reads the first three *nonblank* characters, because, as we mentioned, the `>>` operator skips spaces:

```
a b   cdef
abc
```

Similarly, it skips newline characters:

```
a
b
cdef
abc
```

To read every single character, including blanks and newlines, we need to use `cin.get()` instead of `>>`:

```
main () {
  char c1, c2, c3;
  c1 = cin.get();
  c2 = cin.get();
  c3 = cin.get();
  cout << c1 << c2 << c3 << "\n";
}
```

With this version, input without spaces gets the same result as before:

```
abcdef
abc
```

However, blanks are not ignored:

```
a b cdef
a b
```

Newlines count as well:

```
a
b
a
b
```

```
class charList {
private:
  char value;
  charList *nextEntry;

public:
  charList (char v, charList *next)
    : value(v), nextEntry(next)
  {}

  char getValue () { return value; }

  charList *getNextEntry () { return nextEntry; }

  charList *reverseM () ;

  charList *reverseM (charList *prev) ;
};

charList *charList::reverseM () { return reverseM(NULL); }

charList *charList::reverseM (charList *prev) {
  if (nextEntry == NULL) {
    nextEntry = prev;
    return this;
  }
  else {
    charList *newfront = nextEntry->reverseM(this);
    nextEntry = prev;
    return newfront;
  }
}
```

FIGURE 7.16   The charList class.

Note in the last case that the program only lets you type two lines. Once it had read three characters (`'a'`, `'\n'`, `'b'`), it waited for the next newline character and then printed its result and stopped.

Of course, there is no reason to confine ourselves to reading three characters. Using **charList**, we can read *and store* all the characters we want, just as we did with lists of integers using **intList**. Our first version of **charList**—we'll add some enhancements later—is given in Figure 7.16; it is barely different from **intList**, except that **int** is changed to **char**. Here, for example, is a program to read input from the terminal, store it, and repeat it when the user types ^D:

```
ostream& operator<< (ostream& os, charList *list) {
  while (list != NULL) {
    os << list->getValue();
    list = list->getNextEntry();
  }
  return os;
}
```

```
istream& operator>> (istream& is, charList *&cl) {
  cl = NULL;

  char ch = is.get();
  while (!cin.eof()) {
    cl = new charList(ch, cl);
    ch = is.get();
  }
  cl = cl->reverseM();
  return is;
}

main () {
  charList *input;
  cin >> input;
  cout << input;
}
```

(In `operator>>` we have passed a `charList` pointer by reference. Like any other argument passed by reference, this allows the function to assign to that argument and thereby return a result from the function indirectly. When **main** calls `operator>>` and passes `input`, the assignments to `cl` inside `operator>>` will actually assign to `input`, which is, of course, what is desired.)

7.7.3   A Mail-Merge Program

In a mail-merge program the user provides a template of a letter, with blanks at specific places, and a list of items to be used to fill in the blanks, such as the recipient's name. The program generates personalized copies of the letter. Our program uses a simple input format. The letter template is given first, with the percent sign (%) used to indicate the blanks. The template and all date items are terminated by pound signs (#). Thus, in the following sample input, everything up to the the blank line following **Edna McWoman** is the letter.

```
%

Dear %,

You may have already won TEN MILLION DOLLARS.

%, I know you would just love to have all this wonderful
money, so SEND IN THE ENTRY FORM, now!

Your pal,

Edna McWoman

#
Joseph Shmoe
10 Wasta Way
Makesme, IL#
```

```
Joseph#
Joe#
Joan Simone
1001 Outta Place
Okeydo, KY#
Joanie#
Joan#
```

Suppose there were n blanks in the letter. The letter will be followed by p sequences of characters (possibly including newlines), each terminated by a pound sign; we'll refer to all of these as *field*s. The fields are used in order to replace the blanks in the letter, yielding p/n customized letters. The fields probably include an address, but they may also include other information, such as a name to use in the salutation. (The letter may not contain any %'s or #'s, and the fields cannot contain #'s; but see Exercise 2 at the end of this section.) In the foregoing example, there are three blanks, and the letter is followed by six fields, yielding these two letters as its output:

field

```
Joseph Shmoe
10 Wasta Way
Makesme, IL

Dear Joseph,

You may have already won TEN MILLION DOLLARS.

Joe, I know you would just love to have all this wonderful
money, so SEND IN THE ENTRY FORM, now!

Your pal,

Edna McWoman

Joan Simone
1001 Outta Place
Okeydo, KY

Dear Joanie,

You may have already won TEN MILLION DOLLARS.

Joan, I know you would just love to have all this wonderful
money, so SEND IN THE ENTRY FORM, now!

Your pal,

Edna McWoman
```

One point should be noted carefully here. Within a field, all characters up to the ending **#** are counted, including newlines. However, the **#** *and the newline following it* are not included in the field.

We'll start our program by reading all the input into two lists. `letter` will point to the letter template itself (that is, everything up to the first **#**), and `fields` will contain all the fields and other information (everything after the first **#**). To do the input, we define a function that reads characters up to a certain character called the *delimiter*:

```
charList *readUpto (char delim) {
  charList *input = NULL;
  char inputchar;

  inputchar = cin.get();
  while (!cin.eof() && inputchar != delim) {
    input = new charList(inputchar, input);
    inputchar = cin.get();
  }
  return input->reverseM();
}
```

Note that the call `readUpto('\0')` reads all the remaining input. This depends on the one significant property of the null character: It can *never* be input from the keyboard. So `readUpto` will read all the characters in the input looking for a null character; the null character will never show up, and `readUpto` will stop only when it reaches end of file.

Our program, then, begins like this:

```
main () {
  charList *letter, *letterPtr, *fields;
  char c;

  letter = readUpto('#');    // read template
  c = cin.get();  // skip newline
  fields = readUpto('\0');  // read fields
```

The basic idea is to process all the characters in `letter` one at a time, using the pointer variable `letterPtr`, printing each character from `letter` except **%** and substituting the next item from the list pointed to by `fields` each time the character **%** appears in the letter. When the end of the letter is reached, reset `letterPtr` to the beginning of the letter (but do *not* reset `fields`) and do it again. The entire process ends when the end of `fields` is reached.

A useful auxiliary function prints the characters in a list starting from the current cell and continuing through some delimiter character:

```
void printUpto (charList *&cl, char delim) {
  while (cl != NULL && cl->getValue() != delim) {
    cout << cl->getValue();
    cl = cl->getNextEntry();
  }
}
```

`printUpto` uses one combination of features that we haven't seen before, namely a *reference to a pointer* (`charList *&cl`). `printUpto` is called to print the various parts of `letter` and the `fields`. (In `letter` these parts are separated by %, and in `fields` they are separated by #.) After printing one part, we want to make sure that the next time `printUpto` is called, it will print from where it left off. The easiest way to do this is to have `printUpto` change its pointer argument to point to the list cell following the last one it printed. Thus, `cl` is an argument that needs to be changed by `printUpto`, so `printUpto` declares it as a reference type.

Here is the entire main program:

```
main () {
  charList *letter, *letterPtr, *fields;
  char c;

  letter = readUpto('#');   // read template
  c = cin.get();  // skip newline
  fields = readUpto('\0');  // read fields

  while (fields != NULL) {
    letterPtr = letter;
    while (letterPtr != NULL) {
      printUpto(letterPtr, '%');
      if (letterPtr != NULL) {
        letterPtr = letterPtr->getNextEntry();   // skip '%'
        printUpto(fields, '#');
        fields = fields->getNextEntry();   // skip '#'
        fields = fields->getNextEntry();   // skip '\n'
      }
    }
  }
}
```

The outer loop iterates over `fields`. Within this loop, an inner loop iterates over the letter, repeatedly looking for a % (if it is not found, it means the last part of the letter has been printed), then printing the next segment in `fields`.

Exercises—Fifth Set

1. Overload == and != on `charList` objects. (Note: It is not possible to overload these operators on pointers-to-`charList`, but only on `charList`s themselves.)

     Use these new operations to write a program to test whether a line of input constitutes a *palindrome*: a sentence that reads the same forward and backward. Input a line of characters, store them in a `charList`, and compare the list to its reversal, reporting the outcome. Then read the next line, and continue until the user inputs the end-of-file character.

2. The format of the input to our mail-merge program is flawed in two ways:

    1. The characters # and % cannot appear in the letter, and # cannot appear in any of the fields.
    2. Since there is no special character separating one set of fields from the next, the accidental omission of one field would throw off the entire set of letters.

    Rectify the first problem by allowing # and % to be "escaped" in the input; that is, if the characters \# appear in the input, # appears in the output, and similarly for \%. \

itself must be escaped in the same way. Rectify the second problem by using % instead of # to separate fields within a single group (that is, to separate the fields for a single customization of the letter) and # to separate groups. Be sure to test your program on an input that has missing fields.

3. The **grades** class in Exercise 6 (page 276) can be implemented in a more realistic way if names can be associated with grades, instead of merely having ID numbers. Define a new list class, **charIntPairList**, just like **pairList**, except that instead of two integer values, the cells contain one integer and one pointer-to-**charList**. Modify the **grades** class so that student IDs are replaced by student names, of type **charList** *, but the operations otherwise remain the same.

Write a main program that reads input lines containing a name and a number and stores them in a **grades** object. When the end of file is reached, print a listing giving the class average and standard deviation, and then each student's name, raw score, and z-score.

4. In the game of Hangman, one player chooses a word and writes down a number of blanks equal to the length of the word. The other player guesses a letter. If that letter appears in the word, the first player fills in all its occurrences; if it doesn't, the first player fills in part of a hanging man's body. This process is repeated until either all the blanks are filled in (and the second player wins), or the hanging man is complete (and the first player wins). Write a program to play Hangman. Its first input should be a word; its subsequent inputs should be characters. After each character that occurs in the word, print out the current status—that is, the word with all the letters that have been guessed filled in and the remainder left as dashes; after each character that does not occur, print the number of wrong guesses remaining. Give the second player a total of eight wrong guesses (gallows; head; neck; two arms; trunk; two legs). When the game ends—the word is complete or the challenger has made eight wrong guesses—print an appropriate message and read another word.

The delete Operator

new creates objects in the heap. These objects take up space, and because two objects cannot occupy the same space, you eventually run out of heap. This would happen if, for example, you tried to create too long a list:

```
intList *L = NULL;
for (int i=0; i<1000000; i++)
  L = new intList(i, L);
L->print();
```

The heap on our computer is not big enough to hold a million list cells, so when this loop executes, it crashes with the message

```
Segmentation fault (core dumped)
```

Your computer may be bigger than ours, so this program might run, but if you increase the size enough, it *will* crash. (Your error message may also differ from ours.)

Computers have finite size, and no matter how large the computer, there will be some list too long for it to hold. But consider this program:

```
intList *makeBigList () {
  intList *L = NULL;
  for (int i=0; i<100; i++)
    L = new intList(i, L);
  return L;
}

main () {
  intList *L;
  for (int i=0; i<10000; i++)
    L = makeBigList();
  L->print();
}
```

This is an odd program, to be sure, because it creates 10,000 lists and ignores all but the last. Nonetheless, it creates only 100-element lists, well within the size of any heap, so you might expect it to work, but it crashes just like the last one.

Although it doesn't need more than 100 cells at one time, it does try to *allocate* a million cells, just like the first program. A cell is allocated in the heap each time **new** is executed, even if some of the cells it allocated earlier are no longer in use.

We can do something about that, however, using the following C++ statement,

```
delete <pointer>;
```

where **<pointer>** is a pointer to an object in the heap. This statement returns the object to the pool of available cells. In other words, if we write

```
delete L;
... new intList(...,...) ...
```

the cell allocated in the second line may be the same one deleted in the first line.

This feature gives us a way to make our last program work. By deleting each list after it is created, the program will be able to run to completion without crashing:

```
void deleteList (intList *L) {
  intList *M;
  while (L != NULL) {
    M = L->getNextEntry();
    delete L;
    L = M;
  }
}

main () {
  intList *L = NULL;
  for (int i=0; i<10000; i++) {
    deleteList(L);
    L = makeBigList();
  }
  L->print();
}
```

(Notice that the following main program would not work:

```
main () {
  for (int i=0; i<100; i++) {
    delete L;
    L = makeBigList();
  }
}
```

because it deletes only the single cell at the head of the list L. **deleteList** deletes all 100 cells in the list.)

Unfortunately, deleting cells in real applications is extremely tricky, and we do not intend much more than the simple introduction we've already given.

However, in one place we've already had to use **delete**, without saying so, and that is in measuring the run time of **reverse** on page 291. The first table on that page shows how many times **new** is called to allocate **intList** cells. You can see that it is impossible to reverse a 1000-element list using **reverse**, because it allocates over a million cells, and we have just seen that our computer cannot allocate that many cells. We were able to make the timings by adding calls to **delete** within **reverse**, allowing cells to be returned to the heap.

Look again at the definition of **reverse**:

```
intList *intList::reverse () {
  if (nextEntry == NULL)
    return new intList(value, NULL);
  else
    return (nextEntry->reverse())->addToEnd(value);
}
```

A small modification makes it easier to see what to do:

```
1    intList *intList::reverse () {
2      if (nextEntry == NULL)
3        return new intList(value, NULL);
4      else {
5        intList *L = nextEntry->reverse();
6        intList *M = L->addToEnd(value);
7        return M;
8      }
9    }
```

Recall that **addToEnd** makes a copy of its receiver before adding the new element at the end. Thus, after statement 6, L and M point to completely separate lists that share no cells. Of these, only M is useful; L can be deleted. Adding a call to **deleteList**,[6]

---

[6]Since deleteList is a client of intList, it must follow the declaration of intList; but intList:: reverse calls deleteList, so it must follow the prototype of deleteList. The definition of deleteList can be placed between the declaration of intList and the definition of reverse.

```
intList *intList::reverse () {
  if (nextEntry == NULL)
    return new intList(value, NULL);
  else {
    intList *L = nextEntry->reverse();
    intList *M = L->addToEnd(value);
    deleteList(L);
    return M;
  }
}
```

yields a version of **reverse** that can reverse very long lists. This is the version we used to get the timings on page 291. Of course, this version is somewhat slower than it was before adding the call to **deleteList**, but for long lists it is the best we can do.

Summary

Pointers are data items that point to other data items. A pointer variable **Tptr**, restricted to point to data of type **T**, is declared like this:

```
T *Tptr;
```

Pointers are subject to various operations. Unary ***** is the *dereferencing* operator: ***Tptr** gives the contents of the variable that **Tptr** points to, and when used on the left of the = sign, it permits assignment into that variable. Unary **&** is the *address-of* operator: If **aT** is a variable of type **T**, **&aT** is a pointer to it, so that **Tptr = &aT** is a legal assignment. The comparison operator == can be used to test *pointer equality* between two pointers of the same type. A useful abbreviation when using pointers to class instances is **->**; if **p** is such a pointer, and **m** is a member of the class, **p->m** is equivalent to **(*p).m**.

Every member function of a class **C** has an implicit argument of type **C**. This implicit argument has type pointer-to-**C**. It is called **this**, and it can be used in member functions when it is necessary to refer to the receiver of a message as a whole.

The operator **new** is used to create an object in the heap. If **T** is a type, the expressions

```
new T                 ←  T is built-in, or has zero-argument constructor

new T(<arguments>)    ←  Constructor arguments are supplied
```

allocate **T** objects in the heap and return pointers to those objects. In contrast to ordinary variables, which come into existence when the function that declares them is called and go out of existence when it returns, heap-allocated objects remain in the heap for the entire execution of the program (unless explicitly deallocated by calling the **delete** operator).

A class **C** may not contain a data member of type **C**, but it may contain a data member of type **C*** (pointer-to-**C**). Together with the **new** operator, this allows the construction of *lists*, which can store an unlimited amount of data. It allows the

```
class intList {
private:
  int value;
  intList *nextEntry;

  intList *reverseM (intList *) ;

  intList *reverseAcc (intList *) ;

public:
  intList (int, intList *) ;

  int getValue () ;

  intList *getNextEntry () ;

  void print () ;

  int length () ;

  void addToEndM (int) ;

  intList *addToEnd (int) ;

  intList *reverseM () ;

  intList *reverse () ;

  intList *reverseAcc () ;

  intList *addInOrderM (int) ;

  intList *find (int) ;

  void setValue (int) ;

  intList *nth (int) ;

  intList *remove (int) ;
};
```

FIGURE 7.17   intList declaration, with all functions.

construction of many other *data structures* as well, some of which will be covered in future chapters.

We gave many examples using the class **intList** (as well as the nearly identical class **charList**). Figure 7.17 gives the declaration of **intList** with prototypes of all the functions we've defined in this chapter.

The keywords introduced in this chapter are

```
char    delete    new    this
```

Recursion

Chapter Preview

In this chapter we explore *recursion.* A function is *recursive* if it calls itself during its execution. First, we rework some examples from earlier chapters into simpler, more elegant recursive forms; then we move on to new examples. Of primary importance in algorithm design is the recursive *divide-and-conquer principle,* which we apply to the problem of sorting a list; `mergeSort`, an efficient all-around sorting algorithm, is the result. We also apply divide-and-conquer to multiplication of very large numbers to obtain an extremely efficient algorithm. The analysis of the rate of growth of the time required for a recursive computation is usually done with *recurrence relations,* which closely parallel the recursive computation—we discuss some simple examples. Optional sections on mutual recursion and curve drawing are included to enhance your insight into the intricacies of recursion.

My New Zoo, McGrew Zoo, will make people talk.
My New Zoo, McGrew Zoo, will make people gawk
At the strangest odd creatures that ever did walk.
I'll get, for my zoo, a new sort-of-a-hen
Who roosts in another hen's topknot, and *then*
Another one roosts in the topknot of his,
And another in *his,* and another in HIS,
And so forth and upward and onward, gee whiz!

—Dr. Seuss
If I Ran the Zoo

L et's return to the problem of counting the digits in a number and view it a little differently. Here is the way we wrote a loop to count the digits in **number** on page 164:

```
numberOfDigits = 0;
rest = number;
do {
    // The number of digits in number is numberOfDigits
    // plus the number of digits in rest
    rest = rest / 10;
    numberOfDigits++;
}
while (rest != 0);
```

The number of digits in an integer n can be defined as

$$\text{Number of digits in } n = \begin{cases} 1 & \text{if } -9 \le n \le 9, \\ 1 + \text{number of digits in } n/10 & \text{otherwise.} \end{cases}$$

So, for example, we can compute the number of digits in 321 as

$$1 + [\text{number of digits in } 321/10 = 32]$$
$$= 1 + [1 + (\text{number of digits in } 32/10 = 3)]$$
$$= 1 + [1 + (1)]$$
$$= 3.$$

This definition of the number of digits is an example of a *recursive definition,* *recursive definition* because it is self-referential—defined in terms of simpler instances of itself.

Writing self-referential definitions is the heart of writing recursive functions in C++, because we can turn them into elegant C++ functions such as

```
int numberOfDigits (int n) {
   if (( -10 < n) && (n < 10))
      return 1;
   else
      return 1+numberOfDigits(n/10);
}
```

The recursive definition of the number of digits has a circularity about it. *Circular* definitions are certainly unacceptable, because they lead nowhere, but the "circularity" here is not really a circle; rather it is a *spiral* that eventually terminates. The number of digits is defined by reference to the number of digits in a smaller value, which is defined in terms of the number of digits in a still smaller value, which eventually is defined in terms of the number of digits in a one-digit number. Since a one-digit number obviously has one digit, we can retrace our way outward on the spiral to compute the number of digits; that is what we did above.

As another example, recall that in Chapter 5 (page 138) we wrote a function to compute $n! = 1 \times 2 \times \cdots \times n$ (remember, $0! = 1$). This function can be defined recursively by noticing that multiplying $(n - 1)!$ by n gives the value of $n!$. That is, $n!$ can be defined in terms of $(n - 1)!$ as long as $n > 0$; the inward spiral of defining $n!$ in terms of $(n - 1)!$, which is then defined in terms of $(n - 2)!$, which is then defined in terms of $(n - 3)!$, and so on, stops, because we define $0!$ to be 1:

$$n! = \begin{cases} 1 & \text{if } n = 0, \\ n \times (n - 1)! & \text{if } n \geq 1, \end{cases}$$

so in C++ we write

```
int factorial (int n) {
  if (n == 0)
    return 1;
  else
    return n*factorial(n-1);
}
```

We have a conceptually simpler program.

The functions **numberOfDigits** and **factorial** differ from other functions we've seen because they are *recursive*—as part of their computation, they call themselves. We used this idea in simple ways in Chapter 7; for example, to print an **intList L** (page 267) we wrote

```
void intList::print () {
  cout << value << "\n";
  if (nextEntry != NULL) nextEntry->print();
}
```

which says that to print an **intList** we print its first value and then print the remainder of the list, if it isn't empty.

In this chapter we explore the consequences of translating a recursive definition directly into C++. Such implementations of a recursive definition usually yield programs that are easier to write and understand than the corresponding iterative versions are.

8.1

How to Write a Recursive Function

In general, the way to think about recursion is this: If you want to compute $f(x)$, *assume* you can compute $f(y)$ for any value y smaller than x, then see whether you can use $f(y)$ to express the computation of $f(x)$. It may not always be obvious which smaller value y to use, or even what "smaller" means, but the idea will become clear through examples.

As an example of expressing a computation of $f(x)$ in terms of $f(y)$ for values of y less than x, suppose we want a function that prints positive integers digit by digit, with each digit expressed as a word; that is, we want to produce the output

```
six five two zero one
```

for the integer 65201. Such a function might be used by the telephone company for an automated information service in which the requested phone number is read digit by digit to the customer.

For single-digit numbers, the task is easy:

```
void printDigit (int n) {
// Write the name of a number n, 0 <= n < 10.

  switch (n) {
    case  0: cout << "zero";   break;
    case  1: cout << "one";    break;
    case  2: cout << "two";    break;
    case  3: cout << "three";  break;
    case  4: cout << "four";   break;
    case  5: cout << "five";   break;
    case  6: cout << "six";    break;
    case  7: cout << "seven";  break;
    case  8: cout << "eight";  break;
    case  9: cout << "nine";   break;
  }
}
```

(In Chapter 9 we'll see that `printDigit` can be simplified.) But what do we do for multidigit numbers?

Suppose we call our function `printDigits`; then, assuming we can call `printDigits` for some value smaller than 65201, how can we use that call to print the answer above? We call `printDigits(6520)`, then print a space, and then print the units digit **one**. More generally, we can print a number **n** in this way by calling `printDigits(n/10)`, printing a space, and then `printDigit(n%10)`:

```
void printDigits (int n) {
// Write n digit by digit in words.

  printDigits(n/10);
  cout << " ";
  printDigit(n%10);
}
```

The point is, don't worry about how `printDigits` will print n/10—just assume it works and go from there.

However, this function does not quite work—it goes into an infinite loop for any argument (do you see why?). We are missing the *base cases* where the   *base cases* inward spiral terminates. These are the arguments small enough that there is no use passing smaller values to the function—that is, values so small that no recursive call is needed. In **printDigits** the base cases are the one-digit numbers:

```
 1    void printDigits (int n) {
 2    // Write n digit by digit in words.
 3
 4      if (n < 10)
 5        printDigit(n);
 6      else {
 7        printDigits(n/10);
 8        cout << " ";
 9        printDigit(n%10);
10      }
11    }
```

recursion
bottoming out

We say that the recursion *bottoms out* for the base cases, here **n** < 10.

How does the computer execute the instructions in our recursive function **printDigits**? The computer executes a recursive computation in a manner similar to the way a human would, and to explain it, we'll describe what's going on as though we were doing the computation with pencil and paper. You should be following this description with pencil and paper yourself, performing the actions indicated.

Suppose we call **printDigits** with the value 321 from somewhere in **main**:

```
main () {
  .
  .
  .
  printDigits(321);
  .
  .
  .
}
```

On a piece of paper, write the lines

┌──────────────────── Call to function **printDigits** ────────────────────┐
│ Where we came from: main   │
│ Value supplied for **n**: 321   │
│   │
└──┘

and put this piece of paper down in front of you. In general, there will be a stack of such papers in front of you—keep them carefully in order! (Naturally, the computer doesn't use pieces of paper but *stack frames,* as discussed in Chapter 7 on page 251.)

The first thing we do now is execute **printDigits** with the value of the parameter **n** as given on the piece of paper on top of the stack, in this case 321. **printDigits** compares **n** with 10; because 321 > 10, the **else** clause is executed and a recursive call to **printDigits** is about to occur. The value of the parameter is **n/10**, where the present value of **n** is what's on the top piece of paper on the stack. The value written there is 321, so **n/10** is 32; this is the value of the actual parameter in the recursive call. So we fill out another piece of paper and add it to the top of the stack in front of us. The top piece of paper on the stack now reads

Remember that there is one piece of paper below this one, as shown.

printDigits compares the value of its parameter **n** (written on the top piece of paper) with 10. Since $32 > 10$, the **else** clause is executed and a recursive call to **printDigits** occurs. The value of the parameter is **n/10**; the value of **n** on the top piece of paper is 32, so **n/10** is 3. We fill out another piece of paper and add it to the top of the stack above the two pieces of paper already there:

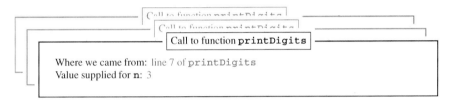

printDigits compares the value of its parameter **n** (written on the top piece of paper) with 10. Since $3 < 10$, the true clause of the **if** is executed (line 5), and we call **printDigit(3)** to write the word **three** and this call to **printDigits** has finished—the recursion has bottomed out. The computer looks at the top piece of paper on the stack and sees that the call was from the first line of the **else** clause in **printDigits**. Removing and destroying the top piece of paper, the computer continues at the next (second) line of the **else** clause, right past the point at which it left off. The removal of the top piece of paper leaves the following stack:

| Call to function **printDigits** |
| Where we came from: line 7 of **printDigits** |
| Value supplied for **n**: 32 |

The second line of the **else** clause (line 8) says **cout << " ";** so a blank is printed. The next line of the **else** clause (line 9) calls **printDigit(n%10)** with the value of **n** as given on the top piece of paper, 32, so the word for **32 % 10**, **two**, is written, and this call to **printDigits** has finished.

Again, the computer consults the top of the stack, and we see that this call was from the first line of the **else** clause (line 7) in **printDigits**. Removing and destroying the top piece of paper, the computation continues at the next (second) line of the **else** clause (line 8) with the stack of papers now looking like this:

```
┌──────────────────── Call to function printDigits ────────────────────┐
│ ┌──────────────────────────────────────────────────────────────────┐ │
│ │ Where we came from: main                                          │ │
│ │ Value supplied for n: 321                                         │ │
│ │                                                                    │ │
│ └──────────────────────────────────────────────────────────────────┘ │
└──────────────────────────────────────────────────────────────────────┘
```

Again, the second line of the **else** clause says to print a blank. The next line of the **else** clause says **printDigit(n%10)**, and the value of n given on the top piece of paper is 321, so the word **one** is written, and this call to **printDigits** has finished.

Consulting the top of the stack, we see that this call was from the main program. Removing and destroying the top (only) piece of paper on the stack, we return, triumphant, to the main program!

Before we go on, notice that in the **if** statement of **printDigits**, both clauses write a single digit as their last action. When **n** is 10 or larger, we write the units digit **n%10**, whereas when **n** is less than 10, we write **n**, which is equal to **n%10**. Hence the recursive structure can be simplified to

```
1    void printDigits (int n) {
2    // Write n digit by digit in words.
3
4      if (n > 9) {
5        printDigits(n/10);
6        cout << " ";
7      };
8      printDigit(n%10);
9    }
```

In this simplified version, the recursive call is made when **n** is 10 or more and afterwards, regardless of the value of **n**, the digit **n%10** is written.

Let's return to the general question of how the value of $f(y)$ can help us compute $f(x)$. In some cases it may not be obvious how such a value can help us no matter how we choose y. Consider another number-printing problem. A function **printDecimal** is to print an integer in a form sometimes used in elementary-school arithmetic books, giving each digit along with its power of 10. For example, **printDecimal(294)** should print

```
2*10^2 + 9*10^1 + 4*10^0
```

where the symbol ^ denotes exponentiation.

We found that the recursive call **printDigits(n/10)** was useful for **printDigits(n)**, but here **printDecimal(n/10)** or **printDecimal(29)** would print

```
2*10^1 + 9*10^0
```

which is of no use, because the powers of 10 are wrong. Instead, we could print the first digit, then print the power of 10, and then call `printDecimal(94)`; this would lead to

```
void printDecimal (int n) {
  int i = largestPowerOfTenIn(n);
  cout << n/i << "*" << i << " + ";
  printDecimals(n%i);
}
```

We'll leave it to you to give the definition of `largestPowerOfTenIn` and fill in the base cases. In any case this is an inelegant solution, because we now need to write a separate function `largestPowerOfTenIn`, when that calculation could instead be incorporated into the recursive structure of `printDecimal` itself. The best approach here is to define a two-argument version of `printDecimal`, with header

```
void printDecimal (int n, int p)
```

which prints the number $n \times 10^p$, omitting the last p digits (which, of course, are all zeros). (Recall that we're allowed to have two versions of `printDecimal`, using the overloading feature of C++.) For example, `printDecimal(29, 10)` would print

```
2*10^11 + 9*10^10
```

The one-argument version of `printDecimal` calls the two-argument version:

```
void printDecimal(int n) {
// Write a number in decimal.
  printDecimal(n, 0);
}
```

Now that we've changed the problem, it becomes easier. We can *assume* that `printDecimal` works correctly as long as we pass it a first argument less than n, and again ask, How can we use such a call to get the correct answer for the original call? Consider the call `printDecimal(n/10, p+1)`. This prints all but the final digit of n, pairing each digit with the appropriate power of 10. The only work left is to print the last digit:

```
void printDecimal (int n, int p) {
// Write a number n * 10^p in decimal.
  printDecimal(n/10, p+1);
  cout << " + ";
}
```

Now we need to consider the base cases. The obvious case is when $n < 10$. This occurs for the leftmost digit, so we ought not to print the leading +:

```
1    void printDecimal (int n, int p) {
2    // Write a number n * 10^p in decimal.
3
4      if (n > 9) {
5        printDecimal(n/10, p+1);
6        cout << " + ";
7      }
8      cout << n%10 << "*10^" << p;
9    }
```

and that's it!

auxiliary parameter
The use of an *auxiliary parameter,* such as **p** in **printDecimal**, is a common technique in a recursive process. It was not part of the original problem statement, but for the recursion to dovetail properly an auxiliary value must be supplied at each call. The value supplied for the initial call is a constant, and must be given to get the whole thing started. It is customary to envelop such recursive functions in a "protective layer" that supplies the proper initial value of all such auxiliary parameters; this allows the user of such a function to supply *only* the values needed as seen from the outside. We generally use overloading to play that role.

8.2

More Examples of Recursion

For practice in writing recursive code, let's rewrite the function **power** from Chapter 5 (page 137) recursively, based on the clever observation that

$$k^n = \begin{cases} 1 & \text{if } n = 0, \\ (k^{n/2})^2 & \text{if } n \text{ is even,} \\ k \times (k^{n/2})^2 & \text{if } n \text{ is odd,} \end{cases}$$

where $n/2$ means integer division, as in C++. If we translate this directly into C++, we obtain

```
int power (int k,   // number to be raised to a power
           int n)   // power to which it's to be raised
{
    if (n == 0)
        return 1;
    else {
        if ((n % 2) == 0)
            return power(k, n/2)*power(k, n/2);
        else
            return k*power(k, n/2)*power(k, n/2);
    }
}
```

which is correct, but inefficient (we'll see to what extent later in this chapter) because **power(k, n/2)** is called *twice* for the same values of the parameters when **n** is nonzero. Instead, we can use a temporary variable to store **power(k,** n/2) after computing it—that way we won't need to recompute it:

```
1    int power (int k,    // number to be raised to a power
2               int n)    // power to which it's to be raised
3    {
4      if (n == 0)
5        return 1;
6      else {
7        int t = power(k, n/2);
8        if ((n % 2) == 0)
9          return t*t;
10       else
11         return k*t*t;
12     }
13   }
```

The variable **t** is a *local variable*. We've used local variables in functions before (in Chapter 4), but here we have a local variable in a recursive function, and that's a new wrinkle. Let's trace through **power** to see why it's something new.

Suppose we call **power(7, 5)** from somewhere in **main**:

```
main () {
   .
   .
   .
   int x = power(7, 5);
   .
   .
   .
}
```

On a piece of paper, write the lines

n is compared to 0; since the value of **n** on the top piece of paper is 5, the **else** clause (lines 7 through 11) is executed. The first action in the **else** clause is to set **t** to **power(7,2)**, which causes a recursive call, so the stack of papers now looks like

Again, **n** is compared to 0; since the value of **n** on the top piece of paper is 2, the **else** clause is executed. The first action in the **else** clause is to set **t** to **power(7,1)**, which causes a recursive call, so the stack of papers now looks like

Call to function power

Call to function power

Call to function **power**

Where we came from: line 7 of power
Value supplied for **k**: 7
Value supplied for **n**: 1
Value of **t**: as yet uninitialized

Yet again, **n** is compared to 0; since the value of **n** on the top piece of paper is 1, the **else** clause is executed. The first action in the **else** clause is to set **t** to **power(7,0)**, which causes a recursive call, so the stack of papers now looks like

Call to function power

Call to function power

Call to function power

Call to function **power**

Where we came from: line 7 of power
Value supplied for **k**: 7
Value supplied for **n**: 0
Value of **t**: as yet uninitialized

Now the value of **n** on the top piece of paper *is* 0, so **power** returns the value 1 from line 5; this causes the top piece of paper to be removed from the stack and **t** to be set to the value returned, namely 1. The stack now is

Call to function power

Call to function power

Call to function **power**

Where we came from: line 7 of power
Value supplied for **k**: 7
Value supplied for **n**: 1
Value of **t**: 1

We continue with the execution of **power**, line 8. Since the value of **n** on the top piece of paper is 1, **n % 2** is 1, and we return the value **k*t*t** = 7 from the **else** clause (line 9), leaving the stack

Call to function power

Call to function **power**

Where we came from: line 7 of power
Value supplied for **k**: 7
Value supplied for **n**: 2
Value of **t**: 7

We continue with the execution of **power**, line 8. Since the value of **n** on the top piece of paper is 2, **n % 2** is 0, and we return the value **t*t** = 49 from the **else** clause (line 11), leaving the stack

```
┌──────────────────────────── Call to function power ────────────────────┐
│                                                                          │
│  ┌────────────────────────────────────────────────────────────────┐     │
│  │ Where we came from: main                                        │     │
│  │ Value supplied for k: 7                                         │     │
│  │ Value supplied for n: 5                                         │     │
│  │ Value of t: 49                                                  │     │
│  └────────────────────────────────────────────────────────────────┘     │
│                                                                          │
└──────────────────────────────────────────────────────────────────────────┘
```

Again, we continue with the execution of **power**, line 8. Since the value of **n** on the top piece of paper is 5, **n % 2** is 1, and we return the value **k*t*t** = 16,807 from the **else** clause (line 11), ending the call to **power** from **main**.

Whenever you are uncertain about what is happening in a recursive computation, simulate it with pieces of paper. This is the only sure-fire way to see the actions occurring. Try it for **power(2,14)**.

As an example illustrating all of the recursive techniques discussed so far, let's adapt our function **printNumber** (page 100), which can write numbers below 1000 in words, to write larger numbers in words.

Think about how you read a number like 12,345,679: "Twelve million, three hundred forty-five thousand, six hundred seventy-nine." The number is broken up into three-digit segments (called *millenary groups*), each of which is expressed in words with the appropriate power of 1000 appended (thousand, million, billion, and so on). To express 12,345,679 in words, we take the first (leftmost) millenary group, "12," and express it in words; add the word "million"; express the next millenary group, "345," in words; add the word "thousand"; and then express the last (rightmost) millenary group, "679," in words. In other words, we

Express 12,000,000 in words.
Then express 345,000 in words.
Finally, express 679 in words.

To do this recursively, it is easier (and, although strange at first, more natural) to restate this as

Express 12,345,000 in words.
Then express 679 in words.

To "express 12,345,000 in words," we

Express 12,000,000 in words.
Then express 345,000 in words.

In general, we can describe this process recursively by

Express all but the last (rightmost) millenary group in words.
Express the rightmost millenary group in words.

That is,

Express $(n/1000) \times 1000$ in words.
Express $n\%1000$ in words.

Think about this recursive strategy. We already know how to express $n\%1000$ in words, since it is a value in the range for which `printMediumNumber` (page 100) works; the value $n/1000$ can be expressed in words by a recursive call, but it must be followed by the name of the appropriate millenary.

These ideas are sound, but for the recursion to dovetail properly, so that a recursive call does the precise subtask we need done, we have to formulate the function a bit more generally to write in words a number *given its millenary group*. (This is the same idea we needed in `printDecimal`.) That is, we want to write a number of the form $n \times 1000^i$ in words, given n and i. For example, if you think of writing the number

$$ABC, DEF, GHI, JKL \times 10^9 = ABC, DEF, GHI, JKL, 000, 000, 000,$$

we would

Express $ABC, DEF, GHI, 000, 000, 000, 000$ in words.
Express JKL in words.
Write the name of $10^9 = 1000^3$ in words ("billion").

This amounts to thinking of $n \times 1000^i$ as being

$$n \times 1000^i = (n/1000) \times 1000^{i+1} + (n\%1000) \times 1000^i.$$

More generally, to express $n \times 1000^i$ in words, we

Express $(n/1000) \times 1000^{i+1}$ in words.
Express $n\%1000$ in words.
Write the name of the ith power of 1000 in words.

Starting the preceding recursion with $i = 0$ properly expresses $n \times 1000^0$ in words.

Thus, we'll make the heading of the function

```
void printBigNumber(int n, int i) {
// Write the name of a number n * 1000^i, n > 0, i >= 0.
```

To implement this, we'll need a function to print the names of the powers of 1000:

```
void printMillenary (int n) {
// Write the name of the power of a 1000.

  switch (n) {
    case 1: printString("thousand"); break;
    case 2: printString("million");  break;
    case 3: printString("billion");  break;
    case 4: printString("trillion"); break;
  }
}
```

where `printString` is as we wrote in Chapter 4 (page 100). All we need to do to write larger numbers is to extend this function to include "quintillion," "sextillion," and so on (see Exercise 2 on page 369).

We already have the C++ function to express numbers n less than 1000 in words: `printMediumNumber` on page 100. This function will handle the writing of n % 1000. We need to prepend to it the recursive call to express $(n/1000) \times 1000^{i+1}$ and to append the writing of the name of the *i*th power of 1000. The call sequence will look (roughly) like this:

```
printBigNumber(n/1000,i+1);
printMediumNumber(n % 1000);
printMillenary(i);
```

However, the writing of n % 1000 and the millenary must *not* be done when n % 1000 is zero, nor must *anything* be done when n is zero. Hence, we have

```
void printBigNumber(int n, int i) {
// Write the name of a number n * 1000^i, n > 0, i >= 0.

//  This would need to be completely rewritten for British
//  nomenclature; see Exercise 7 (page 330).

  if (n > 0) {
    printBigNumber(n/1000,i+1);
    if ((n % 1000) != 0) {
      printMediumNumber(n % 1000);
      printMillenary(i);
    }
  }
}
```

and the driver, **printNumber**, is just as before (page 101), except that it now calls **printBigNumber** instead of **printMediumNumber**:

```
void printNumber(int n) {
//  Write a number in English words according to the
//  American nomenclature. The number can be as large as
//  needed--it is only necessary to extend the switch
//  statement in printMillenary to include "quadrillion",
//  "quintillion", "sextillion", and so on.

  needBlank = false;
  if (n > 0)
    printBigNumber(n,0);
  else if (n < 0) {
    printString("minus");
    printBigNumber(-n,0);
  }
  else { // (n == 0)
    printString("zero");
  }
}
```

The power of the technique of using **needBlank** is now more apparent than it was in Chapter 4. This variable, which is global, is accessible at all recursive levels. If it is changed at any recursive level, that change is felt up and down the line.

The function **printNumber** displays the role that global (versus local) variables play in recursive functions. Keep in mind the following distinctions:

1. Parameters communicate information from one level to the next in the recursion.
2. Local variables are invisible from one level to the next—each level has its own copies of local variables. Local variables from other levels of recursion are not accessible.
3. Global variables establish communication among all levels of recursion simultaneously.

Points 1 and 3 are relatively clear just by the nature of parameters and global variables. Point 2 is quite subtle and often confusing for the newcomer to recursion. Remember that a *local* variable is just that: local. Outside the immediate invocation of the function it is completely unknown. This means that different levels of recursion do not have access to, or the ability to modify, the local variables of other levels of recursion. The variable **t** in **power** is an example of this property; setting its value at one level of recursion doesn't interfere with its value at higher (or lower) recursive levels.

8.3

Debugging Recursive Functions

As difficult as debugging can be with the C++ constructs introduced in previous chapters, debugging recursive functions can be even harder if not approached properly. In this section we'll show you an example of what you should do when faced with a recursive computation that goes awry.

Let's rewrite Euclid's algorithm for the greatest common divisor of two positive integers (page 160). Recall that the greatest common divisor of u and v was computed by

$$
\begin{aligned}
r_0 &= u \\
r_1 &= v \\
r_2 &= r_0 \% r_1 \\
r_3 &= r_1 \% r_2 \\
&\vdots
\end{aligned}
$$

which we expressed using a **while** loop. Notice, however, that the computation can also be expressed recursively, since the lines from "$r_3 =$" onwards are computing the greatest common divisor of $r_1 = v$ and $r_2 = u \% v$. Thus the recursive definition is

$$
\gcd(u, v) = \begin{cases} u & \text{if } v = 0, \\ \gcd(u \% v, v) & \text{otherwise.} \end{cases}
$$

Direct translation of this definition into C++ yields

```
int gcd (int u, int v) {
    if (v == 0)
        return u;
    else
        return gcd(u % v, v);
}
```

Then we execute it with the statements

```
int M, N;
cout << "Enter integer: "; cin >> M;
cout << "Enter another integer: "; cin >> N;
cout << gcd(M,N) << "\n";
```

Alas, when we actually try to execute the function call `gcd(3, 2)`, we get the message

```
Segmentation fault
```

What happened? To find out, we temporarily add a statement to print the values of the parameters u and v every time we enter the function gcd:

```
int gcd (int u, int v) {
   cout << "In gcd, u=" << u << ", v=" << v << "\n";
   if (v == 0)
      return u;
   else
      return gcd(u % v, v);
}
```

and find

```
Enter integer: 3
Enter another integer:2
In gcd, u=3, v=2
In gcd, u=1, v=2
In gcd, u=1, v=2
In gcd, u=1, v=2
In gcd, u=1, v=2
          .
          .
          .
```

and we see that we have the equivalent of an infinite loop! To see why, let's go through the pencil-and-paper exercise of executing the call by hand. The first piece of paper on the stack is

Call to function gcd
Where we came from: main Value supplied for **u**: 3 Value supplied for **v**: 2

Because **v** is nonzero, the **else** clause is executed, resulting in the recursive call `gcd(1, 2)`, since u % v = 3 % 2 = 1. Thus we add a piece of paper on top of the stack:

Where we came from: else clause of gcd
Value supplied for **u**: 1
Value supplied for **v**: 2

v is zero, so the **else** clause is executed, and the recursive call **gcd(1, 2)** occurs because **u % v = 1 % 2** = 1. So we add a piece of paper on top of the stack:

Where we came from: else clause of gcd
Value supplied for **u**: 1
Value supplied for **v**: 2

However, this piece of paper is identical to the one beneath it on the stack, and so it, in turn, causes another identical piece of paper to be added to the stack:

Where we came from: else clause of gcd
Value supplied for **u**: 1
Value supplied for **v**: 2

This then causes the same thing to happen again, and so the stack of papers keeps growing forever, without bound:

Where we came from: else clause of gcd
Value supplied for **u**: 1
Value supplied for **v**: 2

The computer does not have an inexhaustible supply of "paper" to use. Eventually it will run out of memory, causing the "segmentation fault."

The error we made in **gcd** is that we are trying to use a truly circular definition, which, of course, can lead nowhere. Algorithmically, our error was to provide a reduced value for the *first* parameter, **u**, while only checking the *second* parameter, **v**, for the end condition. We never change the value of the second parameter, and an infinite computation results. The lesson to be learned here is that we must be careful to have the recursive function or function test a condition that will ultimately cause the recursion to bottom out at the base case.

Here is the way we *should* have written the recursive definition of the greatest common divisor:

$$\gcd(u, v) = \begin{cases} u & \text{if } v = 0, \\ \gcd(v, u\%v) & \text{otherwise} \end{cases}$$

(with the parameters interchanged in the recursion), and here is how it looks in C++:

```
int gcd (int u, int v) {
  if (v == 0)
    return u;
  else
    return gcd(v, u % v);
}
```

Now it is the second parameter that gets reduced in a recursive call, and it is the second parameter that is tested to see whether it is zero.

Verifying that the recursion eventually bottoms out is similar to verifying that a **while** loop eventually terminates. For a loop, we demonstrate that each time through the loop brings us closer, in some sense, to satisfying the end condition. In the iterative version of the greatest common divisor, we noted (page 159) that the value tested in the **while** loop grows smaller at each step; however, it is always a nonnegative integer, so it must reach 0 eventually, ending the loop. For recursion, we usually show that each subsequent recursive call is a step closer to bottoming out. In our correct recursive version of **gcd**, we note that each recursive call has a reduced value for the second parameter; this value is always a nonnegative integer, so any nested sequence of recursive calls will eventually bottom out with the second parameter being 0. In the functions **printDigits** and **printNumber**, the first parameter, n, is reduced, so eventually the recursion bottoms out when it reaches 0.

Exercises—First Set

1. Modify **printDecimal** to print 1 instead of 10^0, 10 instead of 10^1, 100 instead of 10^2, and so on.

2. Rewrite **printDecimal** so that it prints the binary form instead of the decimal form. That is, write a function **printBinary** that prints

   ```
   1*2^5 + 0*2^4 + 0*2^3 + 0*2^2 + 1*2^1 + 1*2^0
   ```

   when **printBinary(35)** is called.

3. Rewrite **printDecimal** so that it prints the number in the opposite order. That is, it should print

   ```
   4*10^0 + 9*10^1 + 2*10^2
   ```

   when **printDecimal(294)** is called.

4. Modify **printDecimal** so that it does *not* print powers of 10 that are zero. In other words, it should print

   ```
   1*10^3 + 2*10^0
   ```

   when **printDecimal(1002)** is called.

☞ 5. Modify **printNumber** to add commas to its output. For example, it should write "one hundred ninety-four thousand, five hundred eleven" for 194511. Remember, it should *not* write a comma at the end of "twenty-four thousand" when it writes 24000.

6. Write a function with the heading

   ```
   int sumOfSquares (int n)
   ```

   to compute and return $\sum_{i=0}^{n} i^2$.

7. The British call very large numbers by different names than Americans do. In the British system, "billion" means 10^{12}, "trillion" means 10^{18}, "quadrillion" means 10^{24}, and "quintillion" means 10^{30}. The British would read the number 1,234,567,890 as "one thousand two hundred thirty-four million, five hundred sixty-seven thousand, eight hundred ninety," while they would read 12,034,000,000,000 as "twelve billion, thirty-four thousand million." Write a version of **printNumber** for British nomenclature.

8. Write a C++ function to calculate the *n*th number in the Newman-Conway sequence defined by $P(1) = P(2) = 1$, and, for $n \geq 3$, $P(n) = P(P(n-1)) + P(n - P(n-1))$.

8.4

Nonlinear Recursion: the Towers of Hanoi

Although we've now written a number of recursive functions, each of them could have been organized iteratively; it would be a little awkward, but not too difficult. Now let's examine a problem in which replacing the recursion with iteration *would* be difficult. First, notice that in all the problems solved recursively thus far, each call to the recursive function leads to *at most* one new recursive call; *linear recursion* such a use of recursion is called *linear*. Because the recursion has been linear, it is not difficult to replace with iteration.

Towers of Hanoi As our first example of nonlinear recursion, we'll solve a well-known puzzle, the *Towers of Hanoi*. This problem has become popular in computer science because it is such an excellent introductory example. We are given poles labeled *left, middle,* and *right,* along with *n* graduated disks. Initially, the disks are on the pole labeled *left,* and the poles labeled *middle* and *right* are empty (see Figure 8.1). The problem is to determine a sequence of moves so that the *n* disks end up on *right,* with the following restrictions on the moves that can be made:

- Only one disk can be moved at a time.
- A disk must be moved directly from one pole to another.
- No disk may be placed on top of a smaller disk. Thus the disks on *right* at the end must also be in order by size.

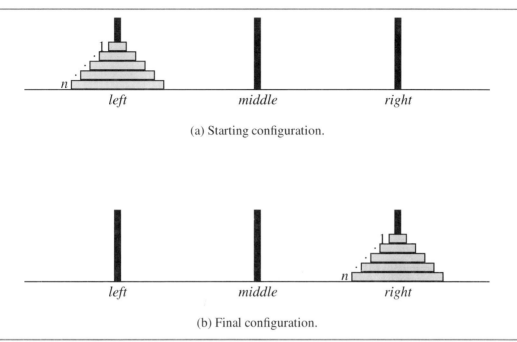

(a) Starting configuration.

(b) Final configuration.

FIGURE 8.1 The starting (a) and final (b) configurations in the Towers of Hanoi problem. Disks must be moved one at a time with no disk ever placed on top of a smaller disk.

In his book *Mathematical Recreations and Essays* (11th edition, The Macmillan Company, 1960), W. W. Rouse Ball quotes a whimsical "history" of the Towers of Hanoi problem, which is actually a puzzle introduced in 1883 by a man named "Claus" (an anagrammatic pseudonym for the well-known French mathematician Edouard Lucas):

> De Parville gave an account of the origin of the toy which is a sufficiently pretty conceit to deserve repetition. In the great temple at Benares, says he, beneath the dome which marks the centre of the world, rests a brass plate in which are fixed three diamond needles, each a cubit high and as thick as the body of a bee. On one of these needles, at the creation, God placed sixty-four discs of pure gold, the largest disc resting on the brass plate, and the others getting smaller and smaller up to the top one. This is the Tower of Bramah. Day and night unceasingly the priests transfer the discs from one diamond needle to another according to the fixed and immutable laws of Bramah, which require that the priest on duty must not move more than one disc at a time and that he must place this disc on a needle so that there is no smaller disc below it. When the sixty-four discs shall have been thus transferred from the needle on which at the creation God placed them to one of the other needles, tower, temple, and Brahmins alike will crumble into dust, and with a thunderclap the world will vanish.

Solving the Towers of Hanoi problem by hand gets confusing—try it for only five disks and see! That's because in doing it by hand we're thinking iteratively. However, if we think recursively, the solution is straightforward. The recursive algorithm is this:

1. Move the top $n - 1$ disks from *left* to *middle,* using *right* as needed as an intermediate pole.
2. Move the *n*th disk from *left* directly to *right* (the other $n - 1$ disks are on *middle,* in order).
3. Move the $n - 1$ disks from *middle* to *right,* using *left* as needed as an intermediate pole.

This recursive strategy is illustrated in Figure 8.2.

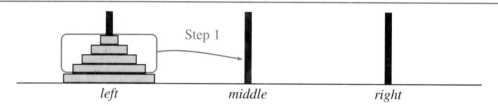

(*a*) Step 1: Recursively move the top $n - 1$ disks from *left* to *middle,* using *right* as needed as an intermediate pole

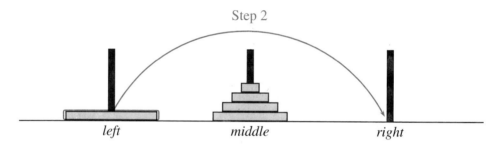

(*b*) Step 2: Move the *n*th disk from *left* directly to *right*

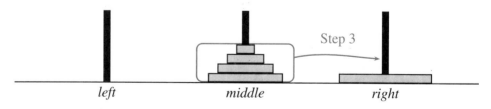

(*c*) Step 3: Recursively move the $n - 1$ disks from *middle* to *right,* using *left* as needed as an intermediate pole

FIGURE 8.2   The three steps in the recursive solution to the Towers of Hanoi problem.

Implementing the recursive strategy of Figure 8.2 in C++ is simple, once we see what information is needed in the communication from one level to the next. The information needed consists of the number of disks to be moved, the starting pole, the intermediate pole, and the destination pole. Consequently, we'll write the function with four parameters, one for each of these items. The heading is

```
void towersOfHanoi (
            int n,              // how many disks
            pole start,         // from which pole
            pole temporary,     // using which intermediate pole
            pole destination)   // to which pole
{
```

where we have defined

```
enum pole {left, middle, right};
```

The function **towersOfHanoi** should write the sequence of moves to be made, so we'll need to be able to write an object of type **pole**. Thus we need

```
ostream& operator<<(ostream& os, pole p) {
// Write the name of a pole

  switch (p) {
    case left:   os << "left";   break;
    case middle: os << "middle"; break;
    case right:  os << "right";  break;
  }
  return os;
}
```

Now we can write the function to print the solution to the Towers of Hanoi problem:

```
void towersOfHanoi (
            int n,              // how many disks
            pole start,         // from which pole
            pole temporary,     // using which intermediate pole
            pole destination)   // to which pole
{
  if (n > 0) {
    // Move the top n-1 disks from start to temporary
    towersOfHanoi(n-1, start, destination, temporary);

    // Move the bottom disk from start to destination
    cout << "Move the top disk from the " << start
         << " pole to the " << destination << " pole.\n";

    // Move those n-1 disks from temporary to destination
    towersOfHanoi(n-1, temporary, start, destination);
  }
}
```

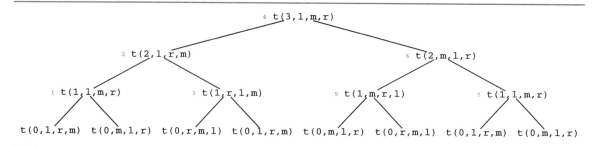

FIGURE 8.3 The recursive calls made during the execution of `towersOfHanoi(3, left, middle, right)`. The lines emanating downward from a call show, in order from left to right, the recursive calls made during that call. Obvious abbreviations have been used for the sake of compactness. The small colored labels 1 through 7 indicate which output line, if any, is written by the particular call.

For example, the call `towersOfHanoi(3, left, middle, right)` produces the seven lines of output

```
Move the top disk from the left pole to the right pole.
Move the top disk from the left pole to the middle pole.
Move the top disk from the right pole to the middle pole.
Move the top disk from the left pole to the right pole.
Move the top disk from the middle pole to the left pole.
Move the top disk from the middle pole to the right pole.
Move the top disk from the left pole to the right pole.
```

It is instructive to draw a diagram showing the calls made during the production of these seven output lines. Figure 8.3 shows the diagram; observe that the recursion bottoms out when $n = 0$. Each call that prints a line of output is labeled with the number of the line it prints.

To make the function `towersOfHanoi` number its output lines (to agree with the small colored labels shown in Figure 8.3), we use a global variable `lineNumber` in the following way: Before calling `towersOfHanoi`, we initialize `lineNumber` to 0. In `towersOfHanoi` we increment and print `lineNumber` just before printing the move; remember that because `lineNumber` is a global variable, all levels of recursion refer to the same variable `lineNumber`. As we did with `printDecimal`, we use overloading to encapsulate the whole business:

```
int lineNumber;

void towersOfHanoi (
            int n,              // how many disks
            pole start,         // from which pole
            pole temporary,     // using which intermediate pole
            pole destination)   // to which pole
    {
      if (n > 0) {
        // Move the top n-1 disks from start to temporary
        towersOfHanoi(n-1, start, destination, temporary);
```

```
        // Move the bottom disk from start to destination
        lineNumber++;
        cout << lineNumber << ". Move the top disk from the "
            << start << " pole to the " << destination
            << " pole.\n";

        // Move those n-1 disks from temporary to destination
        towersOfHanoi(n-1, temporary, start, destination);
    }
}


void towersOfHanoi (int d) {
// Print directions for moving d disks from left pole to
// right pole using middle pole as an intermediate.

    lineNumber = 0;
    towersOfHanoi(d, left, middle, right);
}
```

The call **towersOfHanoi(3)** produces the output lines

```
1. Move the top disk from the left pole to the right pole.
2. Move the top disk from the left pole to the middle pole.
3. Move the top disk from the right pole to the middle pole.
4. Move the top disk from the left pole to the right pole.
5. Move the top disk from the middle pole to the left pole.
6. Move the top disk from the middle pole to the right pole.
7. Move the top disk from the left pole to the right pole.
```

8.5

Recursive Algorithms and Recurrence Relations

One advantage of recursion over iteration is that, in many cases, some simple rules allow you to determine how much time a recursive algorithm requires; computer scientists have found it convenient to classify algorithms in a rough way by the amount of time they require. This classification is not based on the *absolute* amount of time required (which can vary enormously depending on the particular computer and language used), but rather on how fast the time required *grows* as the size of the problem increases. For example, in the case of lists, the "size of the problem" is ordinarily the number of elements in the list. If the size of the problem is measured by a variable n, we can express the time required as a function of n, $T(n)$. When this function $T(n)$ grows rapidly, the algorithm becomes unusable for large n; conversely, when $T(n)$ grows slowly, the algorithm remains useful even when n becomes large.

We say an algorithm is *quadratic,* or $\Theta(n^2)$ (read "theta of n squared"), if *Θ-notation* the time it takes quadruples when n doubles. Similarly, we say an algorithm is *linear,* or $\Theta(n)$ (read "theta of n"), if the time it takes doubles when n doubles.

We say an algorithm is *logarithmic*, or $\Theta(\log n)$ (read "theta of log n"), if the time it takes increases by a constant, independent of n, when n doubles.[1]

There are other classes of algorithms as well. An algorithm is *cubic*, or $\Theta(n^3)$, if it takes eight times as long when n doubles. An algorithm is $\Theta(n^4)$ if it takes 16 times as long when n doubles. An algorithm is *exponential*, or $\Theta(c^n)$, if it takes c times as long when n increases by one; that is, the time gets *squared* when n doubles. An algorithm is *constant time*, or $\Theta(1)$, if its time does not increase at all when n increases—that is, if it takes an amount of time independent of n. In general, an algorithm is $\Theta(T(n))$ if the time it requires on problems of size n grows like the function $T(n)$ as n increases. Table 8.1 summarizes the common growth rates encountered in computer science.

This classification is useful in determining whether an algorithm will prove usable as the size of the problem grows. Some of the algorithms that we've presented so far and will present in later chapters are given as examples in the right-hand column of Table 8.1. As a general rule, algorithms whose time requirements grow faster than $\Theta(n \log n)$ cannot be reasonably applied to "large" problems; if they grow faster than $\Theta(n^3)$, they cannot be reasonably applied to "intermediate" problems.

We have been careful to discuss, when appropriate, the analysis of the time required by the algorithms we present. The topic of analysis of algorithms is crucial in computer science, and you will probably study it in detail in later courses. We introduce you to it here to foster good programming habits—to help build a sense of appropriateness in designing algorithms and implementing them as programs.

Consider the simple recursive function to compute $n!$ given on page 314. The heart of it is the statement

```
if (n == 0)
   return 1;
else
   return n*factorial(n-1);
```

In determining the rate of growth of the time required for this function, let $T(n)$ be the time for computing $n!$. The recursive definition for $n!$,

$$0! = 1$$
$$n! = n \times (n - 1)!$$

yields an analogue in terms of $T(n)$, namely,

$$T(0) = a$$
$$T(n) = b + T(n - 1) \tag{8.1}$$

---

[1] *Warning:* This footnote is pedantic; read at your own risk! There is another, similar notation that you may see in other books for describing the time required by algorithms. We say an algorithm is $O(n)$ (read "big-oh of n") if the time it requires grows *no faster than* doubling when n doubles. Note the words "no faster than." Any algorithm whose time increases *no faster than* $f(n)$ is said to be $O(f(n))$, so algorithms that are $O(\log n)$ or $O(n)$ are also $O(n^2)$. It is a more precise statement, for example, to say that something is a $\Theta(n)$ algorithm than to say it is an $O(n)$ algorithm. Saying it is $\Theta(n)$ says it grows no faster than doubling when n doubles *and that it grows no slower*.

Rate of Growth	Comment	Examples
$\Theta(1)$	Time required is constant, independent of problem size	Hashing (Chapter 9)
$\Theta(\log \log n)$	Very slow growth of time required	
$\Theta(\log n)$	Logarithmic growth of time required—doubling the problem size increases the time by only a constant amount	Power of k (page 321); binary search of an array (Chapter 9)
$\Theta(n)$	Time grows linearly with problem size—doubling the problem size doubles the time required	Adding/subtracting/comparing `digitLists` (next section); linear search of lists (Chapter 7) and arrays (Chapter 9)
$\Theta(n \log n)$	Time grows faster than linearly, but not much faster—doubling the problem size more than doubles the time required	Merge sort (later in this chapter); average behavior of quicksort (Chapter 9)
$\Theta(n^2)$	Time grows quadratically—doubling the problem size quadruples the time required	Naïve list reversal (page 290); simple sorting (Chapter 9)
$\Theta(n^3)$	Time grows cubically—doubling the problem size results in an 8-fold increase in the time required	
$\Theta(n^4)$	Doubling the problem size results in a 16-fold increase in the time required	
$\Theta(c^n)$	Time grows exponentially—increasing the problem size by 1 results in a c-fold increase in the time required; doubling the problem size *squares* the time required	Direct translation of Fibonacci recurrence (page 341)

TABLE 8.1 Common growth rates of algorithms, with examples.

where a is the small constant amount of time to return the value 1 when $n = 0$, and b is another small constant amount of time: that to multiply the recursively found value by n and return the value of that product. The equation $T(n) = b + T(n-1)$ states that the time to compute $n!$ is the time to compute $(n-1)!$, $T(n-1)$, plus the time to multiply the value $(n-1)!$ by n.

The equation

$$T(n) = \begin{cases} a & \text{if } n = 0, \\ b + T(n-1) & \text{if } n \geq 1 \end{cases}$$

recurrence
relation is called a *recurrence relation;* it completely determines the rate of growth of
$T(n)$, because for $n > 0$ we have, by repeated substitution,

$$
\begin{aligned}
T(n) \quad &= \quad b + T(n - 1) \\
&= \quad b + [b + T(n - 2)] = 2b + T(n - 2) \\
&= \quad 2b + [b + T(n - 3)] = 3b + T(n - 3) \\
&\ \ \vdots \\
&= \quad (n - 2)b + [b + T(1)] = (n - 1)b + T(1) \\
&= \quad (n - 1)b + [b + T(0)] = nb + T(0) \\
&= \quad nb + a
\end{aligned}
$$

Therefore, **factorial** requires an amount of time $T(n)$ that increases propor-
tionally with n as n increases. We say, in other words, that **factorial** is a $\Theta(n)$
algorithm.

Applying a similar analysis to **numberOfDigits** (page 313), we find

$$
T(k) = \begin{cases} c & \text{if } k = 1, \\ d + T(k - 1) & \text{if } k > 1 \end{cases}
$$

where $k \approx \log_{10} n$ is the number of decimal digits in n, c is the small constant
amount of time to return 1, and d is the small constant amount of time to divide
by 10, add 1, and return that value. As above, we find

$$
\begin{aligned}
T(k) \quad &= \quad d + T(k - 1) \\
&= \quad 2d + T(k - 2) \\
&\ \ \vdots \\
&= \quad kd + c
\end{aligned}
$$

so $T(k)$ is $\Theta(k)$, and **numberOfDigits** is linear time in $k \approx \log_{10} n$, the length
of the number n; that is, $\Theta(\log n)$.

In the Towers of Hanoi problem the resulting recurrence relation is different.
Let's count the number of lines of output written; that will tell us the rate of growth
of the time required, since each line takes a small constant time to write. The
structure of **towersOfHanoi** is

```
if (n > 0) {
   towersOfHanoi(n-1, ...);
   write a line of output
   towersOfHanoi(n-1, ...);
}
```

so the number of lines to be written is given by

$$
L(n) = \begin{cases} 0 & \text{if } n = 0, \\ 1 + 2L(n - 1) & \text{if } k > 0. \end{cases}
$$

Here the factor of 2 occurs because there are *two* recursive calls when $n > 0$. We
find by repeated substitution that

$$
\begin{aligned}
L(0) \quad &= \quad 0 \\
L(1) \quad &= \quad 1 + 2L(0) = 1 + 0 = 1 \\
L(2) \quad &= \quad 1 + 2L(1) = 1 + 2 = 3
\end{aligned}
$$

$$L(3) = 1 + 2L(2) = 1 + 6 = 7$$

$$\vdots$$

$$L(n) = 1 + 2L(n-1) = 1 + 2(2^{n-1} - 1)$$
$$= 2^n - 1$$

Hence, with n disks `towersOfHanoi` will write $2^n - 1$ lines (moves). The number of moves that the Brahmins must make to transfer the golden disks is $2^{64} - 1 = 18{,}446{,}744{,}073{,}709{,}551{,}615$; assuming that they make one move each second, it will take them 584,942,417,355 years to finish the job if they never make a mistake. The world is safe for the time being!

Many of the recurrence relations that arise in the analysis of algorithms are easy to solve, as were those above. Unfortunately, there is no general method to determine the solution of a recurrence relation. There are various general classes of recurrence relations for which solutions are known, but the methods of solution are largely *ad hoc*. In this book, if a recurrence relation cannot be solved by the most elementary algebraic techniques, we just give its solution without any justification. The mathematically inclined reader may wish to try to verify that the solution we give is correct, but we will expect only that you be able to follow the logical steps and understand the conclusions of analyses we present; we do *not* expect you to be able to develop such analyses on your own.

There is one important and broad class of recurrence relations that arises from recursive computations of the form

```
<type> compute (int n) {
  <something requiring time g(n) in which the
  recursive call compute(n/B)is made A times>
}
```

where A and B are positive constants, independent of n, and $B > 1$. (We return to such algorithms in more detail later in this chapter.) If the time required is $T(n)$, then

$$T(n) = g(n) + AT(n/B),$$

because $g(n)$ time is used at the current recursive level and there are A recursive calls, each requiring time $T(n/B)$. These are called *divide-and-conquer recurrences,* and they occur frequently enough in computer science that we give in Table 8.2 a summary of the rate of growth of $T(n)$ for a few common cases of interest, some of which arise in the discussion of algorithms in this book. We'll need Table 8.2 to compare the efficiencies of various algorithms.

divide-and-conquer recurrences

Now let's analyze our two versions of **power** (page 320) and compare them to our iterative version (page 137). The iterative computation of k^n requires time $\Theta(n)$, since the statement **product = product * k** is executed n times.

The recursive version of **power** that we claimed was inefficient on page 320 uses *two* recursive calls when **n** is nonzero, so the time required is described by the recurrence relation

$$T(n) = \begin{cases} a & \text{if } n = 0, \\ b + 2T(n/2) & \text{if } n \geq 1, \end{cases}$$

$g(n)$	A, B	Growth rate of $T(n)$
$\Theta(1)$	$A = 1$	$\Theta(\log n)$
	$A \neq 1$	$\Theta(n^{\log_B A})$
$\Theta(\log n)$	$A = 1$	$\Theta[(\log n)^2]$
	$A \neq 1$	$\Theta(n^{\log_B A})$
$\Theta(n)$	$A < B$	$\Theta(n)$
	$A = B$	$\Theta(n \log n)$
	$A > B$	$\Theta(n^{\log_B A})$
$\Theta(n^2)$	$A < B^2$	$\Theta(n^2)$
	$A = B^2$	$\Theta(n^2 \log n)$
	$A > B^2$	$\Theta(n^{\log_B A})$

TABLE 8.2   Rate of growth of the solution to the recurrence $T(n) = g(n) + AT(n/B)$, the so-called divide-and-conquer recurrence relations. A and B are positive constants, independent of n, and $B > 1$.

where a is the small constant amount of time to determine that **n** is 0 and then to return 1, and b is the small constant amount of time to determine that **n** is greater than 0, if it is even or odd, and then to return the square of $k^{n/2}$, computed recursively. There is actually slightly more time required if n is odd, because in that case we have to multiply by k; however, this difference does not affect the growth rate of $T(n)$. Table 8.2 tells us that $T(n)$ is $\Theta(n)$ because $g(n) = b$; that is, $g(n)$ is $\Theta(1)$, $A = 2$, $B = 2$, and $\log_2 2 = 1$. This is the same, to within a constant factor, as the time for the iterative computation.

The recursive version of **power** that we claimed was efficient (page 321) uses only one recursive call when **n** is nonzero, so that the time required is described by the recurrence relation

$$\hat{T}(n) = \begin{cases} a & \text{if } n = 0, \\ b + \hat{T}(n/2) & \text{if } n \geq 1. \end{cases}$$

Table 8.2 tells us that $\hat{T}(n)$ is $\Theta(\log n)$ because $g(n)$ is $\Theta(1)$, $A = 1$, $B = 2$, and $\log_2 2 = 1$. This is a *great deal* less time than $\Theta(n)$; hence, our claim to efficiency is justified.

The inefficiency of a recursive computation need not be as obvious as the **power** example. Consider the Fibonacci numbers, defined by (page 145)

$$F_i = \begin{cases} 0 & \text{if } i = 0, \\ 1 & \text{if } i = 1, \\ F_{i-1} + F_{i-2} & \text{if } n \geq 2. \end{cases}$$

(We used these numbers in the analysis of Euclid's algorithm in Chapter 5 and in Exercise 7.) If we write a recursive function that mimics the definition, we obtain

```
int fibonacci (int n) {
  switch (n) {
    case 0:  return 0;
    case 1:  return 1;
    default: return fibonacci(n-1) + fibonacci(n-2);
  }
}
```

The time required by this algorithm to compute F_n is described by the recurrence

$$T(n) = \begin{cases} a & \text{if } n \leq 1, \\ b + T(n-1) + T(n-2) & \text{if } n \geq 2. \end{cases}$$

This does not have the form $T(n) = g(n) + AT(n/B)$, so we cannot use Table 8.2, but it turns out that $T(n)$ is $\Theta([(1 + \sqrt{5})/2]^n)$. This is outrageously inefficient; so inefficient, in fact, that computing even relatively small Fibonacci numbers becomes prohibitively time-consuming—computing $F_{40} = 102,334,155$ on a fast computer took almost 5 minutes, slower than we could do it by hand!

Why is this recursive Fibonacci computation so bad? We can understand why by drawing a picture of the calls made in a sample computation for Fibonacci numbers. What happens when we call **fibonacci** to compute F_7? The answer is found in Figure 8.4. Computing F_7 means recursive calls to compute both F_6 and F_5. Computing F_6 means recursive calls to compute both F_5 and F_4. Eventually, F_2 will be computed a total of 8 times, F_3 will be computed 5 times, and so on. Clearly, the computation should be arranged in an iterative fashion so that each F_i is computed just once, not many times.

To eliminate the needless repetition, we should express the recursive definition of the Fibonacci numbers in terms of pairs of adjacent values,

$$(F_n, F_{n+1}) = \begin{cases} (0, 1) & \text{if } n = 0, \\ (F_n, F_{n-1} + F_n) & \text{if } n \geq 1, \end{cases}$$

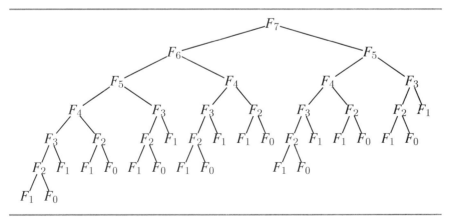

FIGURE 8.4   The sequence of recursive calls to compute F_7 by the inefficient function **fibonacci**. Note the amount of repetition.

so that the pair (F_n, F_{n+1}) is expressed in terms of the prior pair (F_{n-1}, F_n). To write this as a function, we need to be able to compute and return two values, and we saw how to do that in Chapter 4:

```
void fibonacci (int n, int& fn, int& fn1) {
   // Compute the nth and (n+1)st Fibonacci numbers,
   // returning the values as fn and fn1, respectively.
   if (n == 0) {
      fn = 0;
      fn1 = 1;
   }
   else {
      int u, v;
      fibonacci(n-1, u, v);
      fn = v;
      fn1 = u + v;
   }
}
```

which we invoke by

```
int fibonacci (int n) {
   // Compute the nth Fibonacci number.
   int a, b;
   fibonacci(n, a, b);
   return a;
}
```

The amount of time used to compute F_n by this method is described by a recurrence

$$T(n) = \begin{cases} a & \text{if } n = 0, \\ b + T(n-1) & \text{if } n \geq 1, \end{cases}$$

where a is the small constant amount of time to return the pair $(0, 1)$ when $n = 0$, and b is the small constant amount of time to take the recursively determined values u and v and use them to compute and return v and $u + v$. As we saw on page 337, $T(n)$ is $\Theta(n)$, so we have a computation of F_n that is linear in n instead of exponential in n.

However, now that we have the idea of using recursion on pairs of Fibonacci numbers, we can do even better! We can use the identities

$$F_{2k} = 2F_k F_{k+1} - F_{k+1}^2,$$
$$F_{2k+1} = F_k^2 + F_{k+1}^2,$$

and hence

$$F_{2k+2} = 2F_k F_{k+1} + F_{k+1}^2,$$

as the basis of a recursive computation:

```
void fibonacci (int n, int& fn, int& fn1) {
   // Compute the nth and (n+1)st Fibonacci numbers,
```

```
// returning the values as fn and fn1, respectively.
if (n == 0) {
  fn = 0;
  fn1 = 1;
}
else {
  int u, v;
  fibonacci(n/2, u, v);
  if ((n % 2) == 0) {
    fn = 2*u*v - u*u;
    fn1 = u*u + v*v;
  }
  else {
    fn = u*u + v*v;
    fn1 = 2*u*v + v*v;
  }
}
}
```

For this function the amount of time used to compute F_n is described by a recurrence $T(n) = a + T(n/2)$ and Table 8.2 tells that $T(n) = \Theta(\log n)$.

Finally, we observe that we can simplify the code a bit by defining a **class** `intPair`

```
class intPair {
private: int xValue, yValue;
public:
  intPair (int u, int v) {xValue = u; yValue = v;}
  int x () {return xValue;}
  int y () {return yValue;}
};
```

and using it to return the pair of values:

```
intPair fibonacciPair (int n) {
  // Compute the nth and (n+1)st Fibonacci numbers,
  // returning the pair of values.
  if (n == 0)
    return intPair(0,1);
  else {
    intPair p = fibonacciPair(n/2);
    if ((n % 2) == 0)
      return intPair(2*p.x()*p.y() - p.x()*p.x(),
                     p.x()*p.x() + p.y()*p.y());
    else
      return intPair(p.x()*p.x() + p.y()*p.y(),
                     2*p.x()*p.y() + p.y()*p.y());
  }
}

int fibonacci (int n) {
  // Compute the nth Fibonacci number.
  return fibonacciPair(n).x();
}
```

Exercises—Second Set

1. Write a recursive function to compute the *Jacobi symbol* $J(a, n)$, defined for relatively prime integers a and n, $a > 0$ and $n > 0$ by the formula

$$J(a, n) = \begin{cases} 1 & \text{if } a = 1, \\ J(a/2, n)(-1)^{(n^2-1)/8} & \text{if } a \text{ is even,} \\ J(n \% a, a)(-1)^{(a-1)(n-1)/4} & \text{otherwise.} \end{cases}$$

★ 2. (a) Develop a recursive definition for the number of ways to make change for n dollars, assuming that pennies, nickels, dimes, quarters, half dollars, dollar bills, and five-dollar bills are available.
   (b) Use your definition as the basis of a program to compute the number of ways to make change for a specified amount.
   (c) Modify your program in part (b) to list *all* the ways of making change, instead of just computing the number of ways.

3. *Ackermann's function* $A(m, n)$ is defined for nonnegative integers by the recurrence

$$A(m, n) = \begin{cases} n + 1 & \text{if } m = 0, \\ A(m - 1, 1) & \text{if } m > 0, n = 0, \\ A(m - 1, A(m, n - 1)) & \text{if } m > 0, n > 0. \end{cases}$$

Write a program to compute this function. Be warned that the value of $A(m, n)$ grows super-rapidly!

4. In the Towers of Hanoi problem, what must the state of affairs be when the largest disk is moved, for the last time, to the destination pole?

5. Which disk is moved on the billionth move in the Towers of Hanoi problem with 64 disks? (Find the answer by discovering the pattern of moves, not by running on the computer.)

6. Write an iterative solution to the Towers of Hanoi problem that alternates between two moves: (i) Move the smallest disk from its present pole to the next pole in clockwise order. (ii) Move any disk but the smallest.

7. Suppose that you are given the Towers of Hanoi with the n disks distributed arbitrarily on the three poles, subject to the restriction that no disk is on top of a smaller disk. Design an algorithm to move the n disks to a specified destination pole, subject to the usual restriction that no disk ever be placed on top of a smaller disk.

★ 8. Prove that the n-disk Towers of Hanoi problem *cannot* be done in fewer than $2^n - 1$ moves.

★ 9. Develop a recursive function for the *adjacent Towers of Hanoi problem:* Moves of disks can be made only between adjacent poles—that is, between **left** and **middle** and between **right** and **middle**, but not between **left** and **right**.

★ 10. Develop a recursive function for the *cyclic Towers of Hanoi problem:* Moves of disks can be made only from **left** to **middle**, from **middle** to **right**, and from **right** to **left**.

★ 11. Develop an algorithm for the Towers of Hanoi problem with four poles instead of three. Because the fourth pole is available, it is possible to move n disks in *many* fewer than the $2^n - 1$ required with only three poles. (*Hint:* Choose some function $f(n)$, say, $f(n) = \sqrt{n}$, and use the following strategy. Consider the problem as needing to move $n/f(n)$ "superdisks" in the three-pole problem, where a superdisk is really a pile of $f(n)$ disks. Moving a superdisk is done by a call to `towersOfHanoi` using the extra pole.)

8.6

Recursion on Lists

We have already seen, in Chapter 7, a number of important examples of the recursive manipulation of lists: printing, searching, inserting, and reversing lists, in both mutating and nonmutating forms. In this section we'll consider a few more examples. We will begin by using the class `intList` from Chapter 7:

```
class intList {
private:
  int value;
  intList *nextEntry;

public:
  intList (int v, intList *next)
    : value(v), nextEntry(next)
  {}

  int getValue () { return value; }

  intList *getNextEntry () { return nextEntry; }
};
```

8.6.1   Summing the Values in a List

As our first example, suppose we want a function **sum** that adds all the values in an `intList`. We apply the same kind of reasoning that we've been using and try to express **sum** in terms of itself. We'll write **sum** in two ways. First we'll write it as a client, with the header

```
int sum (intList *list)
```

and then as a member of `intList`.

Our method for writing recursive functions is to assume that the function works on smaller lists, such as the tail of `list`. So, how can we use the value of `sum(list->getNextEntry())` to compute the value of **sum(list)**? The answer is simple: If **sum(list->getNextEntry())** is the sum of all the integers in the tail of the list, then

```
list->getValue() + sum(list->getNextEntry())
```

is the sum of all the integers in `list`. This leads to

```
int sum (intList *list) {
  return list->getValue() + sum(list->getNextEntry());
}
```

This does not quite work, because sometimes a list doesn't have a tail. The best base case for this recursion to bottom out is when its argument is **NULL**:

```
int sum (intList *list) {
  if (list == NULL)
    return 0;
  else
    return list->getValue() + sum(list->getNextEntry());
}
```

When we write **sum** as a member function, the header is

```
int intList::sum ()
```

and the idea is the same: Assume that sending the **sum** message to the tail of the receiver correctly sums the integers in the tail, and then ask how to obtain the sum of all the integers in the receiver. The answer is to add the value in the receiver to the sum of the tail:

```
int intList::sum () {
  return (value + nextEntry->sum());
}
```

Here the receiver cannot be **NULL**, because, by definition, it points to the receiving object. However, it may not have a tail, in which case its **nextEntry** field is **NULL**, so we need

```
int intList::sum () {
  if (nextEntry == NULL)
    return value;
  else
    return (value + nextEntry->sum());
}
```

8.6.2 Constructing Index Entries

Now for something harder. Let's suppose that we're using `intList` to keep track of all the page numbers in a book on which a particular topic is mentioned. For example, if a term occurs on pages 1, 3, 4, 6, 7, 8, 9, 12, and 13, then the list would be

We want to write a function that prints this list of pages in the form that is conventionally seen in an index. Sequences of three or more consecutive pages are to be given by a *range of pages*. The preceding list would appear in an index as

```
1, 3, 4, 6-9, 12, 13
```

Such a function is most clearly written with recursion, but the recursion is a bit tricky.

To begin, notice that each index entry except the last is followed by a comma. We'll use the same technique we used to get blank spaces in the right places when writing numbers in words—a global variable `needComma` that is true when the previous index entry needs to be followed by a comma before we print the next entry:

```
boolean needComma;  // a global variable used to keep track
                    // of whether a comma is needed before
                    // the next index entry
```

Using this variable, the function to write a single index entry spanning pages `first` to `last` is

```
void printIndexEntry (int first, int last) {
// Print the range of pages first-last as an index entry,
// preceded by a comma if necessary.

  if (needComma)
    cout << ", ";
  if (first == last)        // one-page run
    cout << first;
  else if (first+1 == last) // two-page run
    cout << first << ", " << last;
  else                      // run of 3 or more pages
    cout << first << "-" << last;
  needComma = true;         // after printing any entry
}
```

This function is the basis for our scanning a list of pages and printing the index entries; we must call **printIndexEntry** for each run of pages that we find in the list. We will scan the list accumulating pages in a single run of pages until the run ends. When the run ends, we'll call **printIndexEntry**.

As we scan the list, we can represent the current run of pages by its starting and ending page. If the current run stretches from **first** to **last**, then the value of the next page in the list tells us whether to extend the current run or to end it. When the current run ends, we write it with a call to **printIndexEntry** and then, if it wasn't the final run, use the next page to begin a new run. Thus, there are three cases:

1. The last run has ended; this happens when there are no more pages in the list—that is, when the list is **NULL**.
2. The current run needs to be extended by one page; this happens when the next page in the list is one more than the last page.

3. The current run has ended, but there are more pages in the list; this happens when the next page is *not* one more than the last page and we are not at the end of the list.

Putting this into C++, we have

```
void printIndexList (int first,
                     int last,
                     intList *L) {
// Print a list L of index entries, preceded by the run
// first-last; runs of three or more pages are coalesced
// into one hyphenated entry.

// L must be in sorted order without duplicate entries,
// beginning with a page >= last; also, first <= last.

  if (L == NULL)                      // end of final run
    printIndexEntry(first, last);
  else if (last+1 == L->getValue())// extend the run
    printIndexList(first,
                   last+1,
                   L->getNextEntry());
  else {                             // end of current run
    printIndexEntry(first, last);
    printIndexList(L->getValue(),
                   L->getValue(),
                   L->getNextEntry());
  }
}
```

Notice that we start a new run (of one page) by making the starting and ending pages equal to the next page in the list.

As seen by the outside world, the function must initiate **printIndexList** properly, with the first index entry becoming the current run. It is here that we must initialize the value of **needComma**; the initial value must be **false** because no comma is needed before we print the first index entry. As in earlier examples, we use overloading:

```
void printIndexList (intList *L) {
// Print a list L of index entries with runs of three or
// more pages coalesced into one hyphenated entry.  The list
// L must be in sorted order with no duplicate entries.

  needComma = false;     // no comma before first entry
  printIndexList(L->getValue(),
                 L->getValue(),
                 L->getNextEntry());
}
```

8.6.3   Merging and Splitting Lists

As our next example, we consider the problem of merging two sorted lists into a single sorted result. Suppose we have the lists

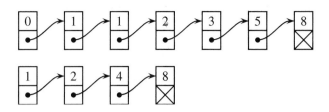

We want to transform these lists into the list

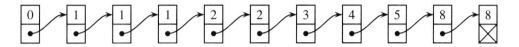

We'll write the function **merge** as a *mutating member function* that transforms the cells of the given lists into the merged result by changing the pointer fields, returning a pointer to the merged result; later in this section we'll rewrite it as a nonmutating, client function.

Since we are writing a member function, the lists to be merged will be **this** and a parameter **intList *L**; of course **this** cannot be empty, but **L** can be the empty list, **L = NULL**. We can think of the merge recursively with the following cases:

1. If **L = NULL**, the result of the merge will just be **this**.
2. If **L** is not **NULL**, and the value in **this** is greater than the value in **L**, then the value in **L** must precede the result of merging **this** with the remainder of **L**.
3. Otherwise, the value in **this** must precede the result of merging the remainder of **this** with **L**.

In C++ this is expressed as

```
intList *mergeM (intList *L) {
// Merge sorted lists THIS and L.

  if (L == NULL)
    return this;
  else if (value > (L->getValue())) {
    L->nextEntry = mergeM(L->nextEntry);
    return L;
  }
  else {
    nextEntry = L->mergeM(nextEntry);
    return this;
  }
}
```

This code is mutating, because the **next** fields in the cells are changed as the list items are processed. Since each element of each list is returned at most once by a **return** statement in this function, the total time required to merge two lists is proportional to the sum of their lengths.

Now let's consider the opposite of merging: splitting a list into two pieces—one piece consisting of the first, third, fifth, ... elements of the original list and the other piece consisting of the second, fourth, sixth, ... elements of the original list. Both of these lists must keep the items in their same relative order as in the original list. Thus, we want the list

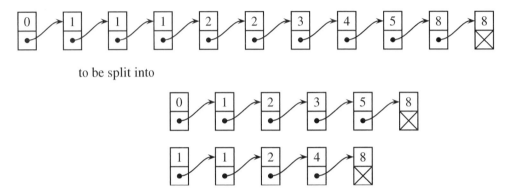

to be split into

Expressing such a split recursively depends on the following idea. The original list is to be split into the first, third, fifth, ... elements and the second, fourth, sixth, ... elements; when we remove the first item from the original list, what was the second element on the original list becomes the first element on the foreshortened list, what was the third element of the original list becomes the second element of the foreshortened list, and so on. That means that if we split the foreshortened list, the roles of even-indexed and odd-indexed positions become interchanged!

Since this is a member function, the list to be split is **this**. Let's assume it's split into the two lists **L1** and **L2**. Then **L1**, which is to be the odd-indexed items from **this**, should consist of the first item from **this**, followed by the *even-indexed* items from the foreshortened **this** (because those were the other odd-indexed elements of the original **this**). Similarly, **L2**, which is to be the even-indexed items from **this**, should contain the *odd-indexed* items from the foreshortened **this** (because those were the even-indexed elements of the original **this**). Hence, in C++ we have

```
void splitM (intList *&L1, intList *&L2) {
// Split list THIS into halves L1 and L2.
// L1 gets the 1st, 3rd, 5th, ... elements of L,
// L2 gets the 2nd, 4th, 6th, ... elements of L.

  L1 = this;
  if (nextEntry == NULL) // One item
    L2 = NULL;
  else                   // Two or more items
    nextEntry->splitM(L2, nextEntry);
}
```

Notice that **L2** becomes the *first* parameter in the recursive call to **split**; **L2** thus gets the first, third, ... items from the foreshortened **this**, which are, as we said, really the second, fourth, ... items from the original **this**.

Let's rewrite these two functions in a nonmutating form as client functions. Because these are to be client functions instead of member functions, the merge function will have two `intList` parameters, say `L1` and `L2`, which are the lists to be merged, and it will return an `intList` that is the result of the merge; `L1` and `L2` will be unchanged. There is one major difference between the function as a client and the function as a member. Both `L1` and `L2` can be `NULL`, so the recursion will bottom out differently than it did in the mutating version. If `L1` is `NULL`, we return `L2`, and if `L2` is `NULL`, we return `L1`. If neither is `NULL`, we take the one with the smaller first item and that becomes the first element on the merged list; the remainder of the merged list is simply the result of merging the remaining items on the two lists. However, we need to use **new** to create new cells for the merged list:

```
intList *merge (intList *L1, intList *L2) {
// Merge sorted lists L1 and L2.

  if (L1 == NULL)
    return L2;
  else if (L2 == NULL)
    return L1;
  else if ((L1->getValue()) < (L2->getValue()))
    return new intList(L1->getValue(),
                    merge(L1->getNextEntry(), L2));
  else
    return new intList(L2->getValue(),
                    merge(L1, L2->getNextEntry()));
}
```

The function to split a list in a nonmutating way as a client is nearly the same as the member function, but now we have three parameters instead of two: the list to be split and the two output lists into which it will be split. As in the case of merging, the recursion bottoms out slightly differently. If the list to be split is empty (not possible in the client case, because **this** cannot be **NULL**), both output lists are **NULL**. If it is not empty, we use a temporary variable for the recursive call, which splits all of the list *except* the first item, and then append the list pointed to by that temporary variable to a copy of the first element of the list to be split:

```
void split (intList *L, intList *&L1, intList *&L2) {
// Split list L into halves L1 and L2.
// L1 gets the 1st, 3rd, 5th, ... elements of L,
// L2 gets the 2nd, 4th, 6th, ... elements of L.

  if (L == NULL) {      // No items in L
    L1 = NULL;
    L2 = NULL;
  }
  else {                // One or more items in L
    intList *l;
    split(L->getNextEntry(), L2, l);
    L1 = new intList(L->getValue(), l);
  }
}
```

8.6.4   Simple Arithmetic on Very Long Integers

Now that we've had some practice manipulating lists recursively, we're ready for an example that demonstrates the full power that comes with lists and their ability to grow and shrink as needed during the execution of a program. We'll write functions that do arithmetic with *arbitrarily large* integers. In the rest of this section we describe how we use lists to represent numbers with many, many digits and to implement some simple operations on such numbers, such as adding, subtracting, and comparing them. In the next section, we implement multiplication.

Using lists to represent extremely large numbers is done naturally by storing a number as a list of digits. For example, we could represent the number $2^{2^7} = 340,282,366,920,938,463,463,374,607,431,768,211,456$ by the list

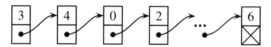

Even though this corresponds precisely to the way we would represent the number on paper, it is far more convenient for algorithmic purposes to keep the digits in the opposite order:

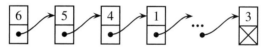

so that the *least significant* digit (the units digit) comes first and the *most significant* digit (the highest-power-of-ten digit) comes last. The convenience of this digit order for recursive computation follows from the natural recursive definition of a number represented by its digits in base 10:

$$n = (n\%10) + 10 \times (n/10), \tag{8.2}$$

because the first element of the list is $n\%10$ and the rest of the list is $n/10$.

The value 10 is not essential here. We could be representing numbers in any base, but 10 is most familiar, so we'll use that in our examples. However, all of our functions will be written to use a symbolic constant

```
const int radix = 10;
```

To represent a positive integer we use a `digitList`:

```
class digitList {
private:
  int digit;
  digitList *nextDigit;

public:
  digitList (int d, digitList *next)
    : digit(d), nextDigit(next)
  {}

  int getDigit () { return digit; }

  digitList *getNextDigit () { return nextDigit; };
```

```
digitList *copy() {
// Copy digitList.

  if (nextDigit == NULL)
    return new digitList(digit,NULL);
  else
    return new digitList(digit, nextDigit->copy());
}

int length() {
// Length of digitList.

  if (nextDigit == NULL)
    return 1;
  else
    return 1+nextDigit->length();
}

digitList *leftDigits(int n);  // To be discussed later.

digitList *rightDigits(int n); // To be discussed later.

};
```

This class is not sufficient to represent negative numbers, but we'll worry about that later, after we've developed some functions to manipulate positive numbers. To make things simple, we insist that our numbers have no leading zeros; because the digits are stored least-significant-first in digit lists, this rule means that digit lists have no trailing zeros. We make this restriction because leading zeros do not affect the value of a number but can slow down computation by making lists unnecessarily longer. A consequence of this decision is that we *must* represent the value 0 by the empty list **NULL**.

First, we'll need some auxiliary functions. We have provided member functions to determine the length of a **digitList** and to make a copy of one. Also, we will need member functions to get the leftmost and rightmost digits in a **digitList**, but we'll write those when we need them, in the next section.

We also need a number of client functions. For example, we need a client function that writes a **digitList**, such as

```
ostream& operator<<(ostream& os, digitList *L) {
// Print a digitList.

  if (L->getNextDigit() != NULL)
    // high-order digits
    os << L->getNextDigit();
  // lowest-order digit
  os << L->getDigit();
  return os;
}
```

We'll also need to convert an ordinary positive value of type **int** to a **digitList**:

```
digitList *digitize(int n) {
// Convert integer n into a digitList
```

```
        if (n == 0)
          return NULL;
        else
          return new digitList(n % radix, digitize(n / radix));
    }
```

These two client functions are straightforward—the recursive structure is nearly identical to functions we've seen earlier in this section.

For a first client function to manipulate digit lists as integers, let's write a function to compare two digit lists to determine their relative size. Given digit lists **L1** and **L2**, the function should return 0 if the two numbers are equal, should return 1 if **L1** > **L2**, and should return -1 if **L1** < **L2**. The idea is to use recursion to compare the tails of the two lists, **L1->getNextDigit()** and **L2->getNextDigit()**, and then use that information, together with the relative sizes of **L1->getDigit()** and **L2->getDigit()**, to determine the relative sizes of **L1** and **L2**. The recursion bottoms out if either (or both) of the lists are empty—that is, zero:

```
    int compareDigitLists(digitList *L1, digitList *L2) {
    // Compare digitLists L1 and L2.  Return 0 if equal,
    // return 1 if L1 > L2, and return -1 if L1 < L2.

      if ((L1 == NULL) && (L2 == NULL))
        return 0;   // Both numbers 0
      else if (L1 == NULL)
        return -1; // L1 is 0, L2 is not
      else if (L2 == NULL)
        return 1;   // L2 is 0, L1 is not
      else
        switch (compareDigitLists(L1->getNextDigit(),
                                  L2->getNextDigit())) {
          case 1: return 1;   // Units digit is irrelevant
          case -1: return -1; // Units digit is irrelevant
          case 0: // Tails are equal; units digits critical
            if (L1->getDigit() > L2->getDigit())
              return 1;
            else if (L1->getDigit() == L2->getDigit())
              return 0;
            else
              return -1;
        };
    }
```

Notice how the recursive structure of this function mimics the recursive structure in Equation (8.2). If one tail is strictly greater than the other, the units digit is irrelevant to their relative size; but if the two tails are equal, the units digit determines the relative size. If we had stored the digits most-significant-first, this function (and the others to follow) would have been much more difficult to write.

The addition of two digit lists is done recursively (of course!), with the structure of the recursion following Equation (8.2); however, we need to propagate a carry. To handle the propagation of the carry in general, we'll write the addition function to add two digit lists *and a carry*. To add two digit lists **L1** and **L2** and a carry c, we note that if neither list is empty, we just add the carry and the two units digits `L1->getDigit()` and `L2->getDigit()` and then make the units digit of that sum the units digit of the result. The rest of the result is found by recursively adding the tens digit of that sum with the tails of the two lists:

```
int t = c + L1->getDigit() + L2->getDigit();
return
  new digitList(t % radix,
                addDigitLists(t / radix,
                              L1->getNextDigit(),
                              L2->getNextDigit()));
```

In fact, if L2 is **NULL**, the identical recursion works, except L2 disappears:

```
int t = c + L1->getDigit();
return
  new digitList(t % radix,
                addDigitLists(t / radix,
                              L1->getNextDigit(),
                              NULL));
```

If L1 is **NULL**, we can simply call the function again with the lists switched:

```
return addDigitLists(c, L2, NULL);
```

Finally, if *both* lists are **NULL**, we are just adding the carry to two zero values, so the result is the carry itself, properly "digitized":

```
return digitize(c);
```

Putting all these pieces together yields

```
digitList* addDigitLists(int c, digitList *L1, digitList *L2) {
// Add digitLists L1 and L2 plus carry c.

  if ((L1 == NULL) && (L2 == NULL))
    return digitize(c);
  else if (L1 == NULL)
    return addDigitLists(c, L2, NULL);
  else if (L2 == NULL) {
    int t = c + L1->getDigit();
    return
      new digitList(t % radix,
                    addDigitLists(t / radix,
                                  L1->getNextDigit(),
                                  NULL));
  }
  else {
    int t = c + L1->getDigit() + L2->getDigit();
    return
      new digitList(t % radix,
                    addDigitLists(t / radix,
                                  L1->getNextDigit(),
                                  L2->getNextDigit()));
  }
}
```

Subtraction is nearly identical to addition in its structure, but there are three critical differences. First, instead of a carry, we have a borrow. Second, since we have no way at the moment to have negative numbers as digit lists, we cannot do subtraction unless the *subtrahend* (the number being subtracted) is less than or equal to the *minuend* (the number from which we are subtracting); otherwise it is a fatal error. Third, unlike addition, a subtraction can generate leading zeros, which we need to "trim" away. For example, subtracting 11,021,948,

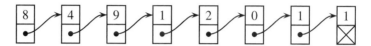

from 11,121,945,

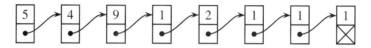

yields 99,997, but the list looks like

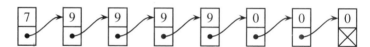

because the subtraction leaves the three zeros at the end of the list. Such extraneous zeros increase the time needed to manipulate the numbers in linked form, so we'll have to get rid of them.

The first difference, a borrow instead of a carry, is simple enough—it has to be subtracted just as the carry was added. The second difference, "improper" subtraction, will be guarded against by killing the program with an error message if "proper" subtraction is impossible. The program is killed by a call to the standard library function **exit**, which we get by having **#include <stdlib.h>** at the beginning of the file (see Appendix C). Finally, the third difference, trimming away any leading zeros, is handled by recursively removing all the zeros from the right end of the digit list:

```
digitList *trimDigitList(digitList *L) {
// Copy of digitList L with leading zeros deleted.

  if (L == NULL)
    return NULL;
  else {
    digitList *trimmed = NULL;
    trimmed = trimDigitList(L->getNextDigit());
    if ((L->getDigit() == 0) && (trimmed == NULL))
      return NULL;
    else
      return new digitList(L->getDigit(), trimmed);
  }
}
```

This function uses a slightly tricky recursion. If the list is not empty, its tail is trimmed; then, if the trimmed tail is empty and the units digit is zero, the trimmed result is just **NULL**. Otherwise, the units digit is appended to the front of the trimmed tail.

Now, with all these ideas, we can write

```
digitList* subDigitLists(int b, digitList *L1, digitList *L2) {
// Subtract digitList L2 from L1 minus borrow b.

    int t; // the units digit of the difference minus borrow b
    int B; // the borrow resulting from the difference of the
           // units digits and borrow b

    if (L1 == NULL) {
      if ((L2 == NULL) && (b == 0))
        return NULL;
      else {
        cout << "Improper subtraction; fatal error.\n";
        exit(0);
      }
    }
    else if (L2 == NULL) {
      t = L1->getDigit() - b;
      if (t < 0) {  // borrow a one
        B = 1;
        t = t + radix;
      }
      else          // no borrow
        B = 0;
      return trimDigitList(
        new digitList(t, subDigitLists(B,
                                       L1->getNextDigit(),
                                       NULL)));
    }
    else {
      t = L1->getDigit() - L2->getDigit() - b;
      if (t < 0) {  // borrow a one
        B = 1;
        t = t + radix;
      }
      else          // no borrow
        B = 0;
      return trimDigitList(
        new digitList(t, subDigitLists(B,
                                       L1->getNextDigit(),
                                       L2->getNextDigit())));
    }
}
```

We use the machinery just described to define a new class, **Integer**. An object of this class consists of a **digitList**, together with a sign, in the **private** portion of the class:

```
digitList *digits;
int sign;
```

The **private** portion also includes the auxiliary functions (see Section 6.4)

```
int length () {
  if (digits == NULL)
    return 0;
  else
    return digits->length();
}

Integer copy () {
  if (digits == NULL)
    return Integer(0);
  else
    return Integer(sign, digits->copy());
}
```

These functions are kept private, because we do not want general access to them, but the member functions will need them. The **public** portion consists of the constructors, an output function, and overloadings of arithmetic operators. The constructors are

```
1   Integer (): sign(1), digits(NULL) {}
2   Integer (digitList *L): sign(1), digits(L) {}
3   Integer (int i, digitList *L): sign(sgn(i)), digits(L) {}
4   Integer (int i): sign(sgn(i)), digits(digitize(abs(i))) {}
```

The constructor on line 1, which has no parameters, forms an **Integer** with the value zero. The constructor on line 2 makes a **digitList** into an **Integer** by setting the **sign** to be positive. The one on line 3 takes a sign value and a **digitList** and forms them into an **Integer**. Finally, the one on line 4 takes an **int** and converts it to an **Integer**. In these last two constructors, we need a handy way to get the sign of an **int**, so we write

```
int sgn (int i) {
// Sign of integer i.

  if (i < 0)
    return -1;
  else
    return 1;
}
```

The output function is simply

```
void print (ostream& os) {
// Print an Integer.

  if (sign == -1)
    os << "-";
  if (digits == NULL)
    os << 0;  // empty list is zero
  else
    os << digits;
}
```

which allows us to write the client function

```
ostream& operator<<(ostream& os, Integer L) {
  L.print(os);
  return os;
}
```

The overloadings of the normal **int** operators for the class **Integer** have no subtleties, but some examples are worth looking at just for practice. First, to do addition, we already have the basics, with the addition and subtraction of digit lists, but we now have to use the sign properly to determine whether to add or subtract the corresponding digit lists. Here is the member function to do just that:

```
Integer operator+ (Integer L) {
  if (sign == L.sign)
    return Integer(sign, addDigitLists(0, digits, L.digits));
  else if (compareDigitLists(digits, L.digits) > 0)
    return Integer(sign, subDigitLists(0, digits, L.digits));
  else
    return Integer(L.sign,
                   subDigitLists(0, L.digits, digits));
}
```

With this overloading, we can further overload the + operator to add an **Integer** to an **int** with the member function:

```
Integer operator+ (int i) { return *this + Integer(i); }
```

But the addition of an **int** to an **Integer** cannot be a member function (why?), so we'll get to that later when we describe some of the client functions.

The subtraction operators are similarly overloaded:

```
Integer operator- (Integer L) {
  if (sign != L.sign)
    return Integer(sign, addDigitLists(0, digits, L.digits));
  else if (Integer(digits) > Integer(L.digits))
    return Integer(sign, subDigitLists(0, digits, L.digits));
  else
    return Integer(-sign,
                   subDigitLists(0, L.digits, digits));
}
Integer operator- () { return Integer(-sign, digits); }
Integer operator- (int i) { return *this - Integer(i); }
```

We should also overload the various boolean operators:

```
boolean operator== (Integer L) {
  return ((sign == L.sign)
          && (compareDigitLists(digits,L.digits) == 0));
}
boolean operator>= (Integer L) {
  return ((sign > L.sign) ||
      ((sign == L.sign)
       && (compareDigitLists(digits,L.digits) != -1)));
}
```

```
boolean operator> (Integer L) {
  return ((sign > L.sign) ||
      ((sign == L.sign)
        && (compareDigitLists(digits,L.digits) == 1)));
}
boolean operator== (int i) { return (*this == Integer(i)); }
boolean operator!= (Integer L) { return !(*this == L); }
boolean operator!= (int i) { return !(*this == i); }
boolean operator> (int i) { return (*this > Integer(i)); }
boolean operator>= (int i) { return (*this >= Integer(i)); }
boolean operator< (Integer L) { return !(*this >= L); }
boolean operator< (int i) { return !(*this >= i); }
boolean operator<= (Integer L) { return !(*this > L); }
boolean operator<= (int i) { return !(*this > i); }
```

and we need to overload functions that add, subtract, and compare an **int** to an **Integer** (in that order). These are client functions:

```
Integer operator+ (int i, Integer L) { return Integer(i) + L; }
Integer operator- (int i, Integer L) { return Integer(i) - L; }
Integer operator== (int i, Integer L) {
  return Integer(i) == L;
}
Integer operator!= (int i, Integer L) {
  return Integer(i) != L;
}
Integer operator>= (int i, Integer L) {
  return Integer(i) >= L;
}
Integer operator> (int i, Integer L) { return Integer(i) > L; }
Integer operator<= (int i, Integer L) {
  return Integer(i) <= L;
}
Integer operator< (int i, Integer L) { return Integer(i) < L; }
Integer operator* (int i, Integer L) { return Integer(i) * L; }
```

As an example of the use of the class **Integer**, consider

```
int n;
cout << "Enter positive integer: "; cin >> n;
Integer l = 1;
for (int i = 1; i <= n; i++)
  l = l+l;
cout << "2^" << n << " = " << l << "\n";
```

which produces, for instance,

```
Enter positive integer: 64
2^64 = 18446744073709551616
```

We'll see how to implement multiplication for the class **Integer** in the next section.

Before concluding this section, we should discuss the time required by the various list manipulation functions that we've written in this section. Every one of those functions is *linear* in the length of the lists; this means that if the length of the lists doubles, the time required will double as well. Keep this in mind as you read the next section.

Divide-and-Conquer Algorithms

Divide et impera [Divide and rule]

—Ancient political maxim cited by Machiavelli

The single most important paradigm in the design of algorithms is the *divide-and-conquer principle*. The principle itself is simple: Break a problem into smaller subproblems of the same type, solve those subproblems recursively, and meld the solutions found for the individual subproblems into a solution for the entire problem.

The efficient recursive function **power** (page 321) is a good example of divide-and-conquer. The computation of k^n is reduced to performing a couple of elementary arithmetic operations once the value of $k^{n/2}$ has been obtained recursively. This example, however, is not complex enough to display the elegance and subtlety that usually accompanies divide-and-conquer algorithms.

Here's a typical example of the divide-and-conquer idea. We want to sort a box of n index cards in alphabetical order. We take the n index cards, split them arbitrarily into two piles of $n/2$ cards each, sort each of the piles separately, and then merge the two piles into a single sorted pile. This sorting technique, pictured in Figure 8.5, is called the *merge sort*.

merge sort

Schematically, merge sort is simple. Furthermore, we can use Table 8.2 (page 340) to get an idea of its behavior as the number of items n gets large: Let $T(n)$ be the time required by merge sort for sorting n index cards by hand. The time needed to do the merging is, as we saw on page 349, proportional to the number of cards being merged, so that

$$T(n) = cn + 2T(n/2),$$

because we must sort the two halves (time $T(n/2)$ each) and then merge (time proportional to n). This is a divide-and-conquer recurrence, and we see by Table 8.2 that the growth rate of $T(n)$ is $\Theta(n \log n)$, since $A = B = 2$ and $g(n)$ is $\Theta(n)$. This is excellent performance for a sorting algorithm; simpler approaches yield only $\Theta(n^2)$ algorithms (see Chapter 9). See Table 8.3 for a comparison of running times.

The hard work in writing merge sort is already done! We just need to use the splitting and merging functions that we wrote in the previous section. As there,

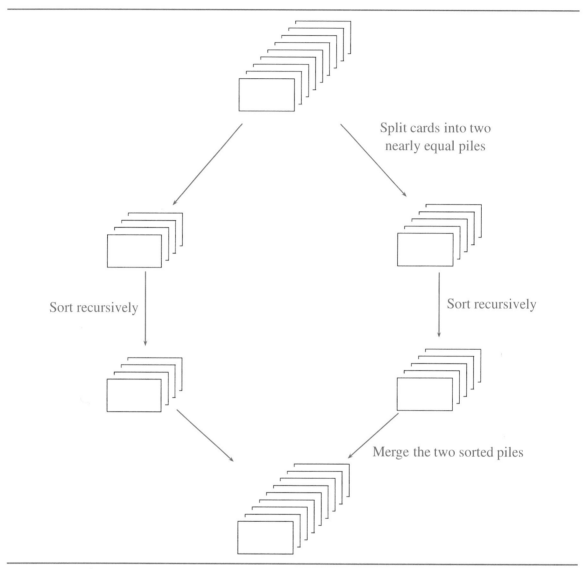

FIGURE 8.5   Schematic representation of merge sort.

we'll do this two ways, first as a mutating member function and then as a nonmutating client function.

The mutating member function has the recursion bottom out when the list consists of a single element (remember, **this** cannot be **NULL**) which is, trivially, already sorted. If there is more than one item in **this**, we use two temporary variables to call **splitM** and then merge the lists pointed to by those temporary

Number of elements n	Simpler sort $n^2 \times 10^{-6}$	Merge sort $100n \log_2 n$
10	10^{-4} seconds	3×10^{-3} seconds
100	10^{-2} seconds	10^{-1} seconds
1,000	1 second	1 second
10,000	1 minute, 40 seconds	13 seconds
100,000	2 hours, 46 minutes	2 minutes, 46 seconds
1,000,000	11 days, 13 hours	33 minutes, 16 seconds

We assume that the $\Theta(n^2)$ sort uses n^2 computer instructions, each taking 10^{-6} seconds, to sort n items, while merge sort uses $100n \log_2 n$ such computer instructions. We have added an extra factor of 100 for merge sort because it is a far more complicated algorithm, making it slower for small numbers of items.

TABLE 8.3   Approximate times for a simple $\Theta(n^2)$ sort versus merge sort.

variables to form the sorted result of the function:

```
intList *mergeSortM () {

// Sort list by recursively splitting and merging.

  if (nextEntry == NULL) // Just 1 item
    return this;
  else {              // At least 2 items
    // Split it in two parts...
    intList *L1, *L2;
    splitM(L1,L2);
    // ...then sort and merge the two parts
    return (L1->mergeSortM())->mergeM(L2->mergeSortM());
  }
}
```

To make this code work properly to sort the empty list, we create a client function

```
void sort (intList *&L) {
// Sort L in place.

  if (L != NULL)
    L = L->mergeSortM();
}
```

which applies the member function only when the list to be sorted is not empty.

For the nonmutating client version of merge sort, we only need to change the way the recursion bottoms out. When the list to be sorted contains zero or one item, we just return the original list. Otherwise, if the list has two or more items, we do as we did in the member function and use the split and merge functions (the nonmutating client versions this time, however):

```
intList *mergeSort (intList *L) {
// Sort L by recursively splitting and merging.

  if ((L == NULL) || (L->getNextEntry() == NULL))
     return L;              // Zero or one items
  else {                    // Two or more items
     // Split it in two parts...
     intList *L1, *L2;
     split(L, L1, L2);
     // ...then sort and merge the two parts
     return merge(mergeSort(L1), mergeSort(L2));
  }
}
```

Since this function works properly on the empty list, there is no need for an additional "wrapper" client function as we needed above.

Now that we've seen the idea of divide-and-conquer, let's apply it to develop an algorithm to multiply elements of the class **Integer** from the previous section. The algorithm is a bit counterintuitive, because we would never dream of using such a technique by hand. Plan to reread this discussion a second time before continuing to the implementation in C++. As in the previous section, for clarity we focus on the case **radix** = 10, but when we write the C++ code, we will use the identifier **radix**.

To multiply x and y, assume that x has exactly $l \geq 2$ digits and that y has at most l digits. Let $x_0, x_1, x_2, \ldots, x_{l-1}$ be the digits of x and $y_0, y_1, \ldots, y_{l-1}$ be the digits of y (some of the significant digits at the end of y may be zeros, if y is shorter than x), so that

$$x = x_0 + 10x_1 + 10^2 x_2 + \cdots + 10^{l-1} x_{l-1},$$

and

$$y = y_0 + 10y_1 + 10^2 y_2 + \cdots + 10^{l-1} y_{l-1},$$

Chop x into two pieces: the leftmost n digits and the remaining digits:

$$x = x_{\text{left}} + 10^n x_{\text{right}},$$

where $n = l/2$. Similarly, chop y into two corresponding pieces:

$$y = y_{\text{left}} + 10^n y_{\text{right}},$$

Because y has at most the number of digits that x does, y_{right} might be 0. The product $x \times y$ can be written

$$x \times y = (x_{\text{left}} + 10^n x_{\text{right}}) \times (y_{\text{left}} + 10^n y_{\text{right}}),$$
$$= x_{\text{left}} \times y_{\text{left}} + 10^n (x_{\text{right}} \times y_{\text{left}} + x_{\text{left}} \times y_{\text{right}}) + 10^{2n} x_{\text{right}} \times y_{\text{right}}.$$

This is an awkward way to write the product $x \times y$, but here's why it's worth it: We already know that we can add or subtract two members of the class **Integer**. Thus, by writing member functions **leftDigits**, **rightDigits**, and **shift** for the class **Integer**, we can implement multiplication by

```
Integer operator* (Integer Y) {
// Multiply Integers THIS and Y with a simple
// divide-and-conquer method.

  int lengthX = length();
  int lengthY = Y.length();
  if ((lengthX == 0) && (lengthY == 0))
    // Both numbers zero
    return Integer(0);
  else if ((lengthX == 1) && (lengthY == 1))
    // Both numbers single digit
    return Integer((digits->getDigit())
                 * (Y.digits->getDigit())
                 * sign * Y.sign);
  else {
    int n = max(lengthX, lengthY) / 2;
    Integer Xleft = leftDigits(n);
    Integer Xright = rightDigits(lengthX - n);
    Integer Yleft = Y.leftDigits(n);
    Integer Yright = Y.rightDigits(lengthY - n);
    return Xleft * Yleft
          + (Xright * Yleft + Xleft * Yright).shift(n)
          + (Xright * Yright).shift(2*n);
  }
}
```

We have already written the member function **length** for the class **Integer**; the member functions **leftDigits**, **rightDigits**, and **shift** are

```
Integer leftDigits (int n) {
// Copy of leftmost n digits of THIS.
  if (digits == NULL)
    return Integer(sign, NULL);
  else
    return
      Integer(sign, trimDigitList(digits->leftDigits(n)));
}

Integer rightDigits (int n) {
// Copy of rightmost n digits of THIS.
  if (digits == NULL)
    return Integer(sign, NULL);
  else
    return
      Integer(sign, trimDigitList(digits->rightDigits(n)));
}

Integer shift (int n) {
// Shift THIS n places (positive n shifts right, negative n
// shifts left).
  if (n == 0)
    return copy();
  else if (n > 0)
    return
      Integer(sign,
              new digitList(0, shift(n-1).digits));
```

```
        else if (digits != NULL)
          return Integer(sign, digits->getNextDigit()).shift(n+1);
        else
          return Integer(0);
    }
```

where we write the member functions for the class `digitList`:

```
digitList *digitList::leftDigits(int n) {
// Copy of the leftmost n digits of digitList.
// NULL if n <= 0.

  if (n <= 0)
    return NULL;
  else if (nextDigit == NULL)
    return new digitList(digit,NULL);
  else
    return new digitList(digit,nextDigit->leftDigits(n-1));
}

digitList *digitList::rightDigits(int n) {
// Copy of the rightmost n digits of digitList.
// NULL if n <= 0.

  if (n <= 0)
    return NULL;
  else if (length() <= n)
    return this->copy();
  else
    return nextDigit->rightDigits(n);
}
```

To analyze the time required by our divide-and-conquer multiplication function, we use Table 8.2 (page 340). If $T(n)$ is the time to multiply two n-digit numbers with this function, then

$$T(n) = kn + 4T(n/2).$$

Why? The kn part is the time to do the three additions that form $x \times y$ from the last statement in the function; each of these additions involves n-digit numbers. The $4T(n/2)$ part is the time to (recursively) form the four needed products $x_{\text{left}} \times y_{\text{left}}$, $x_{\text{right}} \times y_{\text{left}}$, $x_{\text{left}} \times y_{\text{right}}$, and $x_{\text{right}} \times y_{\text{right}}$, each of which is a product of about $n/2$ digits. What about the time to chop the numbers into two pieces and shift numbers by n and $2n$ positions? These operations are $\Theta(n)$.

Table 8.2 tells us that

$$T(n) = \Theta(n^{\log_2 4}) = \Theta(n^2).$$

So the divide-and-conquer algorithm is no more efficient than the elementary-school method, which will be implemented in Exercise 5 on page 369.

However, we can be more economical in our formation of subproducts if we are a little clever. We can write

$$x \times y = (x_{\text{left}} + 10^n x_{\text{right}}) \times (y_{\text{left}} + 10^n y_{\text{right}}),$$
$$= x_{\text{left}} \times y_{\text{left}}$$
$$+ 10^n (x_{\text{right}} \times y_{\text{left}} + x_{\text{left}} \times y_{\text{right}})$$
$$+ 10^{2n} x_{\text{right}} \times y_{\text{right}}$$
$$= B + 10^n C + 10^{2n} A,$$

where

$$A = x_{\text{right}} \times y_{\text{right}}$$
$$B = x_{\text{left}} \times y_{\text{left}}$$
$$C = (x_{\text{left}} + x_{\text{right}}) \times (y_{\text{left}} + y_{\text{right}}) - A - B.$$

This is an even more awkward way to write the product $x \times y$, but the recurrence for the time required changes to

$$T(n) = kn + 3T(n/2).$$

The kn part is the time to do the two additions that form $x \times y$ from A, B, and C and the two additions and the two subtractions in the formula for C; each of these six additions/subtractions involves n-digit numbers. The $3T(n/2)$ part is the time to (recursively) form the three needed products $x_{\text{right}} \times y_{\text{right}}$, $x_{\text{left}} \times y_{\text{left}}$ and $(x_{\text{left}} + x_{\text{right}}) \times (y_{\text{left}} + y_{\text{right}})$, each of which is a product of about $n/2$ digits.[2] As before, the time to chop and shift is $\Theta(n)$.

Table 8.2 now tells us that

$$T(n) = \Theta(n^{\log_2 3}).$$

Now

$$\log_2 3 = \frac{\log_{10} 3}{\log_{10} 2} \approx 1.5849625 \cdots$$

which means that this divide-and-conquer multiplication technique will be faster than the straightforward $\Theta(n^2)$ method for large numbers of digits.

The implementation is similar to our foregoing implementation:

```
Integer operator* (Integer Y) {
// Multiply Integers THIS and Y with a clever
// divide-and-conquer method.

  int lengthX = length();
  int lengthY = Y.length();
  if ((lengthX == 0) && (lengthY == 0))
    // Both numbers zero
    return Integer(0);
```

---

[2]This is not fully accurate, but it's close enough to the truth for the arguments to be made precise by a more complicated analysis that we forgo. In fact, $(x_{\text{left}} + x_{\text{right}}) \times (y_{\text{left}} + y_{\text{right}})$ might be the product of two $(n/2 + 1)$-digit numbers.

```
        else if ((lengthX == 1) && (lengthY == 1))
            // Both numbers single digit
            return Integer((digits->getDigit())
                            * (Y.digits->getDigit())
                            * sign * Y.sign);
        else {
          int n = max(lengthX, lengthY) / 2;
          Integer Xleft = leftDigits(n);
          Integer Xright = rightDigits(lengthX - n);
          Integer Yleft = Y.leftDigits(n);
          Integer Yright = Y.rightDigits(lengthY - n);
          Integer A = Xright * Yright;
          Integer B = Xleft * Yleft;
          Integer C = (Xleft + Xright) * (Yleft + Yright) - A - B;
          return B + C.shift(n) + A.shift(2*n);
        }
}
```

So now we can write, for example,

```
int n;
cout << "Enter positive integer: "; cin >> n;
Integer l = 2;
for (int i = 1; i <= n; i++)
  l = l*l;
cout << "2^(2^" << n << ") = " << l << "\n";
```

which will produce

```
Enter positive integer: 6
2^(2^6) = 18446744073709551616
```

Does the multiplication by this clever divide-and-conquer algorithm give us an improvement over the the more simple-minded divide-and-conquer algorithm or over the "standard" multiplication that we learned in elementary school? Yes and no. Yes, to the extent that our analysis tells us that for *large* numbers of digits the divide-and-conquer method is superior. No, in the sense that 25 digits are not "large" enough to show its superiority.

How large do the numbers have to be for the divide-and-conquer $\Theta(n^{\log_2 3})$ algorithm to surpass the $\Theta(n^2)$ simple algorithm? We reason as follows: When a $\Theta(n^{\log_2 3})$ algorithm is used, doubling n results in a threefold increase in time, since $(2n)^{\log_2 3} = 2^{\log_2 3} n^{\log_2 3} = 3n^{\log_2 3}$. When a $\Theta(n^2)$ algorithm is used, doubling n results in a fourfold increase in time, since $(2n)^2 = 4n^2$. So if we double the number of digits, say, from 50 to 100, we expect the elementary-school algorithm to take four times as long per multiplication, whereas our divide-and-conquer algorithm will take three times as long per multiplication. On one computer, testing revealed that the multiplication of two 50-digit numbers required an equal amount of time for the two algorithms; on that computer, then, multiplying two 100-digit numbers will be somewhat faster for the divide-and-conquer algorithm. Similarly, multiplying two 200-digit numbers, the divide-and-conquer algorithm will be almost twice as fast as the elementary-school algorithm; multiplying two 800-digit numbers will be more than three times as fast.

Finally, we wrote the code and did all of our thinking in decimal (base 10) notation. If we change the radix to a higher power of 10, we get a significant increase in speed, because each basic computer hardware operation (addition, multiplication, and so on) can handle decimal numbers with more than one digit *at no additional cost*. Thus, changing the radix to 10,000 (on a 32-bit computer—this consideration will be addressed in Exercise 4 below) by

```
const int radix = 10000;
```

we get a fourfold increase in speed. For example, computing $2^{2^{15}}$ with a radix of 10 took 15 seconds on our computer; when the radix was 10,000, it took less than 4 seconds.

Exercises—Third Set

1. Rewrite the nonmutating function **split** (see page 351) so that it splits the list into three parts.

2. Rewrite **printNumber** to write an **Integer** in words. In addition to other changes, you will have to extend **printMillenary** to higher powers of 1000:

Power of 1000	Name	Power of 1000	Name	Power of 1000	Name
1	thousand	8	septillion	15	quattuordecillion
2	million	9	octillion	16	quindecillion
3	billion	10	nonillion	17	sexdecillion
4	trillion	11	decillion	18	septendecillion
5	quadrillion	12	undecillion	19	octodecillion
6	quintillion	13	duodecillion	20	novemdecillion
7	sextillion	14	tredecillion	21	vigintillion

☞ 3. What is the time required by the divide-and-conquer multiplication algorithm for the class **Integer** if it is applied to a one-digit number and a number with n digits? Explain.

4. Explain how to change the function

```
ostream& operator<<(ostream& os, digitList *L)
```

so that it works properly with larger values of **radix**. What is the largest value of **radix** that can be used on a 16-bit computer? Explain. By how much will the speed of the algorithm be increased compared to using a **radix** of 10?

☞ 5. Implement the "ordinary" elementary-school multiplication algorithm for the class **Integer**. Begin by writing a recursive function to multiply an **Integer** by a single digit; then use that function, along with shifts, to multiply an **Integer** by an **Integer**.

6. Implement / and % for the class **Integer**. Then rewrite the recursive greatest common divisor function for the class **Integer**.

7. Write a function to overload the input operator >> for the class **Integer**.

8.8

Mutual Recursion (Optional)

The recursive functions presented so far are "directly" recursive in the sense that they call themselves. How about a scenario in which a function **A** calls a function **B**, **B** calls a function **C**, and finally, the dog bites its own tail when function **C** calls function **A**? Such a recursive structure is certainly more complex than anything described so far, but is it useful, and is it possible in C++? The answer is yes to both questions, and in this section you'll see an example of just such recursion; it is an important example, because it is the underlying basis for the way the computer takes C++ programs and translates them into a form that can be executed directly on the computer (see Chapter 10).

Let's imagine that you're making calculations with integers. You might want to write a program to imitate a pocket calculator to evaluate the expressions. We'd want a program that will perform as follows:

```
Enter expression: (10*(2+3)*(1+1))
Value of expression = 100
```

To simplify our task somewhat, we'll only worry about syntactically correct expressions composed of positive integers, **+**, *****. The ideas we're about to present can be extended to the full range of arithmetic operations and to numbers of type **float**, but we'll stick to the most basic possibilities.

The hardest part of this problem now confronts us. We all know the evaluation "rules" for arithmetic expressions, but how do we make them precise enough to write a program? For example, we know that the value of **2 + 3 * 4** is 14 because we wouldn't dream of doing the calculation as **(2 + 3) * 4**. Why not? The answer, of course, is that we view ***** as "stronger" than **+**, so that unless parentheses are inserted to make it otherwise, the ***** takes *precedence* over the **+**. This is the way C++ evaluates expressions too, as we discussed back in Chapter 2.

We can codify this precedence rule of ***** over **+** by saying that we view an arithmetic expression as a sum of terms

$$\text{term}_1 + \text{term}_2 + \cdots + \text{term}_n,$$

where these terms may themselves be products. For instance,

$$1 + 2 + 3 + 4 + 5$$

is such a sequence of terms. So is

$$1 * 2 + 3 * 4 + 5 + 6 * 7 * 8.$$

Because of our understanding of the relative roles of **+** and *****, we don't need parentheses to tell us what this expression means.

Good enough! An arithmetic expression may be a sum of terms, but what is a "term"? Well, **3*4** is okay as a term, but **3+4** isn't; **3+4** is the sum of two terms. **5** is okay as a term. **6*7*8** is too. It seems, then, that a term is just a product of one or more multiplicative factors:

$$\text{factor}_1 * \text{factor}_2 * \cdots * \text{factor}_m.$$

Now we have an arithmetic expression being the sum of terms and a term being the product of factors. What is a "factor"? Clearly, a number can be a factor. Can **3+4** be a factor? Only if we put parentheses around it; but if we put parentheses around *any* expression, it can be used multiplicatively. This gives us a beautiful recursive definition of arithmetic expressions:

> **expression = term + term + $\cdots$ + term**
> **term = factor * factor * $\cdots$ * factor**
> **factor = a number or a parenthesized expression**

These definitions are mutually recursive, because the definition of an expression relies on that of a term, which relies on that of a factor, which relies on that of an expression.

Here is how we could use this definition to understand the expression **1*2+(3*4+5)*6+7**:

1. **1** is a factor and **2** is a factor, so **1*2** is a term.
2. **3** is a factor and **4** is a factor, so **3*4** is a term; **5** is a factor and hence a (trivial) term. This means that **3*4+5** is the sum of two terms and is thus an expression; because it is parenthesized, it is therefore a factor. **6** is a factor, making **(3*4+5)*6** a product of factors and thus a term.
3. **7** is a (trivial) factor and hence a term.
4. Since **1*2**, $(3*4+5)*6$, and **7** are each terms, their sum is an expression.

This is a verbose way to view the expression **1*2+(3*4+5)*6+7**, but it has a precision that allows us to evaluate it automatically. Assuming that the three terms are properly evaluated, respectively, to 2, 92, and 7, we just add them. In a similar fashion, terms are evaluated by multiplying pairs of factors. Our problem now is to specify this as a program.

Recursive definitions lead to recursive programs, as we have seen many times in this chapter. There is considerable extra complication here, though, because we have three definitions (of an expression, of a term, and of a factor), *each* of which leads to a corresponding function (**expression**, **term**, **factor**, respectively). What do we do first? First, we write the function **expression**, whose job it is to scan the expression, evaluating it. In so doing we assume someone else has been given the part of the job to write the function **term**, which evaluates the "terms" of an expression; we just have to call **term** appropriately.

Even this limited task is not too easy to do. Let's assume that the expression we're to translate is stored (without blanks) in a **charList** pointed to by **e** (see page 302). Our function **expression** is supposed to look at **e** and evaluate that expression pointed to, *moving the pointer **e** as it goes* to indicate what part of the expression has already been processed.

Our definition,

$$\text{Expression} = \text{term}_1 + \text{term}_2 + \cdots + \text{term}_n,$$

is what guides us. Since we assume that the function **term** will be provided to us, let's insist that whoever writes **term** will have to make it work in a way consistent with the way **expression** is to work: changing the value of e along as it goes. To process the terms of the sum, we want to do the following:

Call **term** to evaluate the first term.
If e->getValue() ≠ '+', we're done;
    otherwise set e = e->getNextEntry() to skip the +.
Call **term** and add result to the value of preceding terms.
If e->getValue() ≠ '+', we're done;
    otherwise set e = e->getNextEntry() to skip the +.
Call **term** and add result to the value of preceding terms.
If e->getValue() ≠ '+', we're done.
    otherwise set e = e->getNextEntry() to skip the +.
Call **term** and add result to the value of preceding terms.
  .
  .
  .

This is readily expressed in loop form as

```
int value = term(e);
while (e->getValue() == '+') {
  e = e->getNextEntry(); // skip + sign
  value = value + term(e);
}
```

and is encapsulated as

```
int expression (charList *&e) {
  int value = term(e);
  while (e->getValue() == '+') {
    e = e->getNextEntry(); // skip + sign
    value = value + term(e);
  }
  return value;
}
```

The parameter e is declared as **charList *&e** so that it is a pointer reference parameter and we can change its value. If the function **term** is supplied as promised, this will work fine.

Of course, there really isn't someone else to write the function **term**; we have to do it ourselves. As we did before, let's assume that someone else will provide us with the function **factor** and all we need to do is call that function as appropriate. Fortunately, our experience at writing **expression** above makes writing **term** fairly easy. We have the definition

Factor = a number or a parenthesized expression

Here's what we want to do:

> Call `factor` to handle the first factor.
> If e->getValue() ≠ '*', we're done;
>   otherwise set e = e->getNextEntry() to skip the *.
> Call `factor` and multiply result by the value of preceding factors.
> If e->getValue() ≠ '*', we're done;
>   otherwise set e = e->getNextEntry() to skip the *.
> Call `factor` and multiply result by the value of preceding factors.
> If e->getValue() ≠ '*', we're done;
>   otherwise set e = e->getNextEntry() to skip the *.
> Call `factor` and multiply result by the value of preceding factors.
>
> .
> .
> .

As in the case of **expression**, this **while** loop is encapsulated into

```
int term (charList *&e) {
  int value = factor(e);
  while (e->getValue() == '*') {
    e = e->getNextEntry(); // skip times sign
    value = value * factor(e);
  }
  return value;
}
```

Again, the parameter e is declared as `charList *&e` so that it is a pointer reference parameter and we can change its value.

Now all we need is the function **factor**. The definition of a factor was the simplest of the three: A factor is either a number or a parenthesized expression. Therefore, **factor** will look like this:

```
if (isDigit(e->getValue()))
  <scan and evaluate digits until a nondigit is found>
else
  <evaluate the parenthesized expression>
```

Scanning (and evaluating) the digits in the true case is done with a **while** loop, and the **else** clause needs only to skip over the parentheses and call **expression**:

```
int factor (charList *&e) {
  int value = 0;
  if (isDigit(e->getValue())) { // number
    while ((e != NULL) && (isDigit(e->getValue()))) {
      value = 10*value + charToInt(e->getValue());
      e = e->getNextEntry();
    }
  }
```

```
        else { // parenthesized expression
          e = e->getNextEntry();   // skip opening parenthesis
          value = expression(e);
          e = e->getNextEntry();   // skip closing parenthesis
        }
        return value;
      }
```

where we have defined

```
      boolean isDigit (char ch) {
        return ((ch == '0') || (ch == '1')
               || (ch == '2') || (ch == '3')
               || (ch == '4') || (ch == '5')
               || (ch == '6') || (ch == '7')
               || (ch == '8') || (ch == '9'));
      }

      int charToInt (char ch) {
        switch (ch) {
          case '0': return 0;     case '1': return 1;
          case '2': return 2;     case '3': return 3;
          case '4': return 4;     case '5': return 5;
          case '6': return 6;     case '7': return 7;
          case '8': return 8;     case '9': return 9;
        }
      }
```

(We'll see in Chapter 9 how to write these last two functions in a better way.)

We've got all the pieces finished, but how can we assemble them? C++ insists that a function be placed physically before any function that calls it. This means that **expression** can't be placed before **term**, but **term** can't be placed before **factor**, and naturally, **factor** can't be placed before **expression**! According to C++'s rules, none of the functions can be the first one, physically, in the program.

The way out of this difficulty in C++ is to give advance warning of our intention to define a function when it is needed before its definition. Recall that we did something similar in Chapter 6 for member functions: giving prototypes for them inside the class and defining them after it. The prototype looks just like the definition, *but* the function's body is omitted and a semicolon is in place of the body. This is the mechanism that C++ uses to facilitate mutually recursive functions. It allows us to put the functions **expression**, **term**, and **factor** together. We write

```
      int term (charList *&e);      // prototype
      int factor (charList *&e);    // prototype

      int expression (charList *&e) { // definition
        .
        . // details above
        .
      }
```

```
int term (charList *&e) {          // definition
  .
  . // details above
  .
}

int factor (charList *&e) {        // definition
  .
  . // details above
  .
}
```

Now, we just define

```
int evaluate (charList *e) { return expression(e); }
```

and we can write

```
charList *L = readForwardCharList();
cout << "Value of expression = " << evaluate(L) << "\n";
```

to prompt for and evaluate an expression, where we have

```
charList *readForwardCharList () {
  charList *input = NULL;
  cout << "Enter expression: ";

  do { input = new charList(cin.get(), input); }
  while (input->getValue() != '\n');

  return input->reverseM();
}
```

and **reverseM** is as given in Chapter 7 (page 272).

Exercises—Fourth Set

☞ 1. (a) What happens (and why) when the expression evaluator is given the syntactically incorrect expression (1+1?
   (b) What happens (and why) when the expression evaluator is given the syntactically incorrect expression 1+1)?

☞ 2. Rewrite **expression** and **term** to use recursion instead of the **while** loop by using the recursive definitions

> expression = term + expression
> term = factor * term
> factor = a number or a parenthesized expression

☞ 3. Rewrite **factor** so that instead of using a **while** loop to get the digits of the number, a recursive procedure **number** is called to do the job. To what recursive definition of a number does your procedure correspond?

4. What happens in the expression evaluator if the user enters blank spaces in the midst of the expression to be evaluated? Modify the program so that blanks are ignored.

5. Augment the expression evaluator to include the operations − and /.

★ 6. Rewrite the expression evaluation code so that instead of evaluating an expression, it translates the expression into *postfix form,* or *reverse Polish notation* (RPN), in which both of the two operands precede the operator. For example, the expression (10*(2+3)*(1+1)) would be translated into 10 2 3 + * 1 1 + *. This is the order in which the expression would be entered on an RPN-style calculator.

8.9

Curve Drawing (Optional)

Interesting examples of recursion come from functions that draw certain intricate, recursively defined curves. These examples are not "useful" instances of recursion, but they'll help to sharpen your use and understanding of recursion. In this section we'll examine two such recursively defined curves.

8.9.1   Example: Sierpiński Curves

Figure 8.6 shows the first four curves in the sequence of *Sierpiński curves*; curves of orders 2 to 4 are formed by taking four copies of the previous curve and "pasting" them together, as shown in Figure 8.7. We want to write a function that draws such curves, but because we don't have any drawing ability in C++ (we'll see a form of drawing ability in Chapters 9 and 10), we have to be satisfied with writing (in English) the sequence of pen moves necessary to draw the curve. For example, for the curve in Figure 8.6(a), we start at the point indicated by the small colored arrowhead at the lower left and follow the directions

```
north 1 cm   east 1 cm
north 2 cm
north 1 cm   west 1 cm
north 1 cm   east 1 cm
 east 1 cm south 1 cm
 east 2 cm
 east 1 cm north 1 cm
 east 1 cm south 1 cm
south 1 cm   west 1 cm
south 2 cm
south 1 cm   east 1 cm
south 1 cm   west 1 cm
 west 1 cm north 1 cm
 west 2 cm
 west 1 cm south 1 cm
 west 1 cm north 1 cm
```

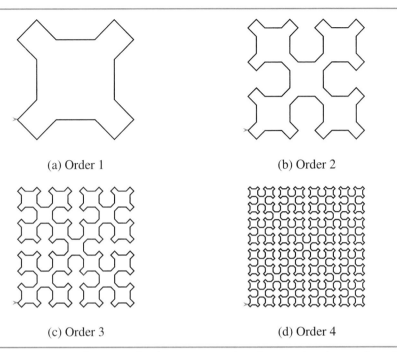

(a) Order 1   (b) Order 2

(c) Order 3   (d) Order 4

FIGURE 8.6   Sierpiński curves of orders 1, 2, 3, and 4, shown reduced in size from the description in the text. The small colored arrowhead at the lower left of each curve indicates the starting point when the curve is drawn.

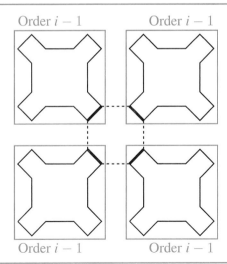

FIGURE 8.7   The recursive structure of the Sierpiński curve of order i. The dashed lines must be added and the adjacent bold lines deleted to form the order i curve from four order $i - 1$ curves.

The directions here need a bit of explanation. When we say "north 2 cm," the meaning is obvious—move the pen to 2 centimeters north of its present location. When we say "north 1 cm east 1 cm," we mean move the pen (directly) to the location 1 centimeter north and 1 centimeter east of its current location; thus, this direction results in a 45° diagonal line of length $\sqrt{2}$. Although slightly unnatural at first glance, this is convenient, and it's the way some drawing languages actually work. In any case, it is not difficult to modify the functions we are about to present so that they instead produce a list of the x and y coordinates of successive points on the curve (Exercise 2 on page 389).

For the curve in Figure 8.6(b), we start at the lower left corner and follow the directions

```
north 1 cm   east 1 cm
north 2 cm
north 1 cm   west 1 cm
north 1 cm   east 1 cm
 east 1 cm  south 1 cm
 east 2 cm
 east 1 cm  north 1 cm
north 2 cm
 west 1 cm  north 1 cm

    .

    .

    .

south 2 cm
south 1 cm   east 1 cm
 west 1 cm  south 1 cm
 west 1 cm  north 1 cm
 west 2 cm
 west 1 cm  south 1 cm
 west 1 cm  north 1 cm
```

The function **Sierpinski** we are to write should produce the preceding output lines when called with **Sierpinski(1)** and **Sierpinski(2)**, respectively.

The obvious recursive structure shown in Figure 8.7 does not help us in drawing the curve, because we want to describe a continuous sequence of pen motions—there is no way to "paste" the pieces together with the dotted lines in Figure 8.7 and eliminate the extraneous edges at the intersection of the four corners shown in bold in Figure 8.7. Instead, we'll use a different description of the Sierpiński curve, as four instances of the *Sierpiński edge* shown in Figure 8.8(a), put together to form Figure 8.8(b). Each instance of the Sierpiński edge is composed, recursively, of smaller Sierpiński edges, as shown in Figure 8.9.

To write a function to draw a Sierpiński curve, we need a function to draw a Sierpiński edge; that function will be recursive, using the decomposition in Figure 8.8(b). We'll need to be able to draw the edge in different orientations—pointing north, south, east, and west. So the function to draw a Sierpiński edge will need two parameters: one that specifies the "order" of the edge and one that

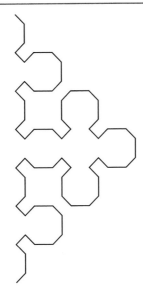

(a) The Sierpiński edge of order 3, pointing north

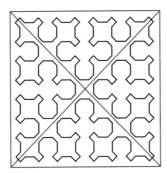

(b) Four Sierpiński edges of order 3 put together to form a Sierpiński curve of order 3

FIGURE 8.8   Sierpiński edge and its use to form the Sierpiński curve.

specifies its orientation. The heading will be

```
void edge (direction d, int i) {
// Draw the edge of an i-th order Sierpinski curve in the
// orientation specified by the direction d
```

assuming we've defined

```
enum direction {north, east, south, west};
```

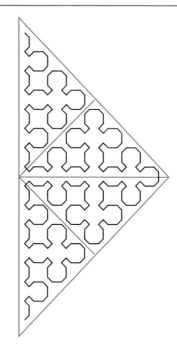

(a) In detail

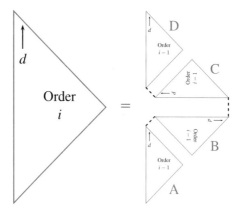

(b) Schematically (the dashed lines are the connections between the four edges of order $i - 1$ in forming the edge of order i; The arrows labeled d indicate the direction in which an edge is pointing)

FIGURE 8.9   The recursive structure of the Sierpiński edge.

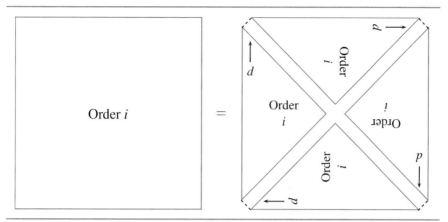

FIGURE 8.10 Schematic diagram of the *i*th-order Sierpiński curve formed from *i*th-order Sierpiński edges. The arrows labeled *d* indicate the direction in which an edge is pointing.

This function calls itself recursively to draw the Sierpiński edge, based on the arrangement shown in Figure 8.9(b).

Following the schematic diagram in Figure 8.10, the function **Sierpinski** must call the function **edge** four times to draw edges pointing first north, then east, then south, and finally west. After drawing an edge, the connecting line to the next edge must be drawn. If the edge is pointing north, the connecting line to the next edge goes north and east; if the edge is pointing east, the connecting line to the next edge goes east and south. In general, if the edge is pointing in direction **d**, the next edge will be pointing in the direction $-90°$ (that is, $90°$ clockwise) from **d**, that is, the direction to its right. Thus, the connecting line goes diagonally: 1 unit in direction **d** and 1 unit in direction **right(d)**, where **right** is a function that tells us what direction is to the right (clockwise) from a given direction:

```
direction right (direction d) {
// Return the direction to the right (clockwise)

  switch (d) {
    case north: return east;
    case east:  return south;
    case south: return west;
    case west:  return north;
  }
}
```

As in various examples so far, we need to be able to write an enumerated type, in this case **direction**. We use

```
ostream& operator<< (ostream& c, direction d) {
// Write a direction
```

```
      switch (d) {
        case north: c << "north"; break;
        case east:  c << " east"; break;
        case south: c << "south"; break;
        case west:  c << " west"; break;
      }
      return c;
    }
```

With these two functions we can specify `Sierpinski`:

```
void Sierpinski (int i) {
// Draw Sierpinski curve of order i

    direction d = north;
    do {
      edge(d, i);
      cout << d << " 1 cm " << right(d) << " 1 cm\n";
      d = right(d);
    } while (d != north);
}
```

We still have to do the hard part of writing the recursive function `edge`. Following the schematic diagram of Figure 8.9, we draw a Sierpiński edge of order **i** pointing in direction **d** as follows:

Draw edge A in Figure 8.9(b).
Connect to edge B.
Draw edge B in Figure 8.9(b).
Connect to edge C.
Draw edge C in Figure 8.9(b).
Connect to edge D.
Draw edge D in Figure 8.9(b).

where edges A, B, C, and D are each of order $i - 1$. Edges A and D point in direction **d**, edge B points to the right of **d** (90° clockwise), and edge C points to the left of **d** (90° counterclockwise). Writing the function

```
direction left (direction d) {
// Return the direction to the left (counterclockwise)

    switch (d) {
      case north: return west;
      case east:  return north;
      case south: return east;
      case west:  return south;
    }
}
```

in parallel to `right`, the edges A, B, C, and D of order $i - 1$ are now done by recursive calls:

```
edge(d, i-1);
```
Connect to edge B.

```
edge(right(d), i-1);
Connect to edge C.
edge(left(d), i-1);
Connect to edge D.
edge(d, i-1);
```

Connecting to the next edge is done in a way clear from Figure 8.9(b)—connecting edge A to edge B requires going (diagonally) 1 unit each in directions `d` and `right(d)`; connecting edge B to edge C requires going 2 units in direction `d`; connecting edge C to edge D requires going (diagonally) 1 unit each in directions `d` and `left(d)`.

When and how does this recursion bottom out? An edge of order 1 is formed by drawing only the connecting lines just described. For example, an edge of order 1 pointing north looks like this:

and this is exactly the dashed-line portion of Figure 8.9(b). Thus the preceding recursive description is correct for an edge of order 1, provided the recursive call to produce an edge of order 0 does nothing! This is a convenient situation, so the function **edge** is

```
void edge (direction d, int i) {
// Draw the edge of an i-th order Sierpinski curve in the
// orientation specified by the direction d

  if (i >= 1) {
    edge(d, i-1);
    cout << d << " 1 cm " << right(d) << " 1 cm\n";
    edge(right(d), i-1);
    cout << d << " 2 cm\n";
    edge(left(d), i-1);
    cout << d << " 1 cm " << left(d) << " 1 cm\n";
    edge(d, i-1);
  }
}
```

8.9.2 Example: Hilbert Curves

Our second curve drawing example is to draw the so-called *Hilbert curves,* the first four of which are shown in Figure 8.11. Each curve of order 2 and above is formed by four copies of the previous curve, just as with the Sierpiński curves, but here the constituent curves of order $i - 1$ are rotated and reflected as they combine to form the curve of order i. Figure 8.12 shows the basic pattern in the Hilbert curve, and Figure 8.13 shows how four copies of the basic pattern are combined to form the curve of next higher order.

This time we want to produce a list of the coordinates of successive points on the Hilbert curve, assuming we start at the origin (0,0). Thus, for example, for

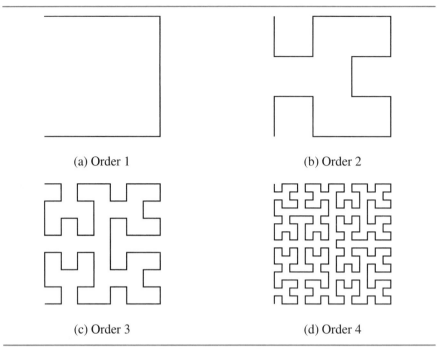

(a) Order 1   (b) Order 2

(c) Order 3   (d) Order 4

FIGURE 8.11   Hilbert curves of orders 1, 2, 3, and 4, shown reduced in size from the description in the text.

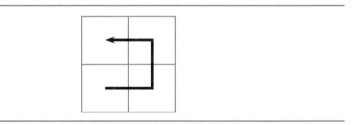

FIGURE 8.12   The basic pattern of the Hilbert curve.

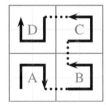

FIGURE 8.13   Recursive structure of the Hilbert curve of order i. Each of the four quadrants contains a Hilbert curve of order $i - 1$ in the orientation shown: Quadrant A contains the mirror image of a curve of order $i - 1$ rotated $-90°$; quadrants B and C contain a curve of order $i - 1$; quadrant D contains the mirror image of a curve of order $i - 1$ rotated $90°$. The dotted lines connect the four curves together.

the Hilbert curve of order 1 shown in Figure 8.11(a), we want the output

```
0 0
1 0
1 1
0 1
```

which lists the coordinates of the four vertices on the curve in Figure 8.11(a), assuming that the lower left end of the curve is at (0,0) and each edge is 1 unit long. Similarly, the output

```
0 0
0 1
1 1
1 0
2 0
3 0
3 1
2 1
2 2
3 2
3 3
2 3
1 3
1 2
0 2
0 3
```

describes the Hilbert curve of order 2 shown in Figure 8.11(b).

We'll write a function **Hilbert** to produce the list of coordinates desired, based on the recursive structure of Figure 8.13. Because the function needs to be able to draw (that is, list the coordinates of the vertices of) Hilbert curves in different orientations, we have to provide the function with three pieces of information: the order of the curve desired, which way the curve is to face, and whether it's to be reflected or not. However, it happens to be easier to supply the information about the orientation as a complete set of four compass directions in the following way: Assume that we are facing north, so that east is to our right, south is behind us, and west is to our left, and that, in this orientation, the curve we are to draw is schematically as shown in Figure 8.13. Assume further that we have a function to draw the curve in Figure 8.12. We can describe the drawing of Figure 8.13 by

> Draw the mirror image of Figure 8.12, rotated $-90°$.
> Connect to quadrant B by going east.
> Draw Figure 8.12.
> Connect to quadrant C by going north.
> Draw Figure 8.12.
> Connect to quadrant C by going west.
> Draw the mirror of image of Figure 8.12, rotated $90°$.

Now for the clever part: Instead of leaving this description in terms of the absolute compass directions north, east, south, and west, let's rewrite it in terms of our relative orientation based on which way we are facing:

Draw the mirror image of Figure 8.12, rotated $-90°$.
Connect to quadrant B by going `right`.
Draw Figure 8.12.
Connect to quadrant C by going `facing`.
Draw Figure 8.12.
Connect to quadrant C by going `left`.
Draw the mirror of image of Figure 8.12, rotated $90°$.

where `facing` is the direction we're facing (north, at the moment), `right` is the direction to our right (east, at the moment), and `left` is the direction to our left (west at the moment).

To describe how to draw the mirror image of Figure 8.12, rotated $-90°$, we change *our* orientation from

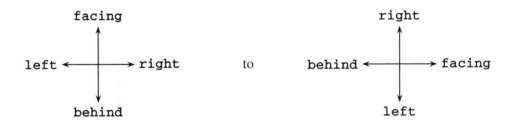

We can do this easily if we supply the orientation to `Hilbert` by specifying what direction we are facing, what direction is to our right, what direction is behind us, and what direction is to our left. Thus we'll make the heading of `Hilbert` be

```
void Hilbert (
    int i,          // the order of the Hilbert curve to be drawn
    direction facing, // the compass direction we are facing
    direction right,  // the compass direction to our right
    direction behind, // the compass direction at our back
    direction left,   // the compass direction to our left
    int& x, int& y)   // the starting coordinates
{
// Print the coordinates of successive points on the Hilbert
// curve of order i, starting at location (x,y), oriented as
// specifed by the "local" compass
```

With `Hilbert` having this structure, we specify that the drawing be the mirror image and rotated $-90°$ from our current orientation (that is, quadrant A of Figure 8.13) by switching around the directions: We'll be facing what is currently `left`, to our right will be what is currently `behind`, behind us will be what is currently `right`, and to our left will be what is currently `facing`. Thus, to draw a Hilbert curve of order $i - 1$ in such an orientation, we call

```
Hilbert(i-1, right, facing, left, behind, x, y);
```

Now we move to the `right` (to quadrant B of Figure 8.13) and draw a Hilbert curve of order $i - 1$ in our present orientation with

```
Hilbert(i-1, facing, right, behind, left, x, y);
```

and move in the direction `facing` (to quadrant C of Figure 8.13) and draw the same thing again. Finally, we move to our `left` (to quadrant D of Figure 8.13) and draw the mirror image of the Hilbert curve of order $i - 1$, rotated $-90°$:

```
Hilbert(i-1, left, behind, right, facing, x, y);
```

which corresponds to

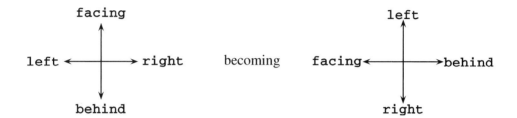

This is tricky, so study it carefully.

The function `Hilbert` is thus

```
void Hilbert (
    int i,          // the order of the Hilbert curve to be drawn
    direction facing, // the compass direction we are facing
    direction right,  // the compass direction to our right
    direction behind, // the compass direction at our back
    direction left,   // the compass direction to our left
    int& x, int& y)   // the starting coordinates
{
// Print the coordinates of successive points on the Hilbert
// curve of order i, starting at location (x,y), oriented as
// specifed by the "local" compass

    if (i == 0)
        cout << x << " " << y << "\n";  // print coordinates
    else {
        Hilbert(i-1, right, facing, left, behind, x, y);
        move(right, x, y);
        Hilbert(i-1, facing, right, behind, left, x, y);
        move(facing, x, y);
        Hilbert(i-1, facing, right, behind, left, x, y);
        move(left, x, y);
        Hilbert(i-1, left, behind, right, facing, x, y);
    }
}
```

where the function `move` properly adjusts the values of the variables **x** and **y** as we move in one direction or another:

```
void move (direction d, int& x, int& y) {
// Move one unit in direction d from point (x,y).

  switch (d) {
    case north: y++; break;
    case east:  x++; break;
    case south: y--; break;
    case west:  x--; break;
  }
}
```

Notice that the recursion in the function `Hilbert` bottoms out when we call for drawing a 0th-order curve. We can think of a 0th-order Hilbert curve as being simply a vertex of the curve whose coordinates are to be printed.

Finally, we define a function `Hilbert` to supply the initial call to `Hilbert` with the actual compass points for the various directions and to initialize the starting point to (0,0):

```
void Hilbert (int i) {
// Draw a Hilbert curve of order i.
  int x = 0;
  int y = 0;
  Hilbert(i, north, east, south, west, x, y);
}
```

The curves in Figure 8.11 would be produced by the call

```
Hilbert(order);
```

with **order** taking the values 1, 2, 3, and 4, respectively.

Square Limit (Incidental)

The later work of Dutch artist Maurits Cornelis Escher (1898–1972) is highly geometric and often recursive in character. In his woodcut *Square Limit* (1964), fish figures are arranged in an interesting recursive structure, which we'll explore here. Figure 8.14 shows a simplified, computer-generated version of *Square Limit*.

The drawing in Figure 8.14 can be viewed schematically as a combination of edge and corner pieces, as shown in Figure 8.15. In the schematic drawing of Figure 8.15, each component has a small arrow to indicate its orientation; its size, relative to the other components, is as shown.

Both the corner and edge pieces are composed entirely of two square figures, which we call A-pieces and B-pieces in Figure 8.16. These pieces form the edge and corner pieces, as shown in Figure 8.17, where the pattern continues indefinitely. The edge piece is expressed recursively as a combination of B-pieces and smaller edge pieces (see Figure 8.18). Similarly, the corner piece is expressed

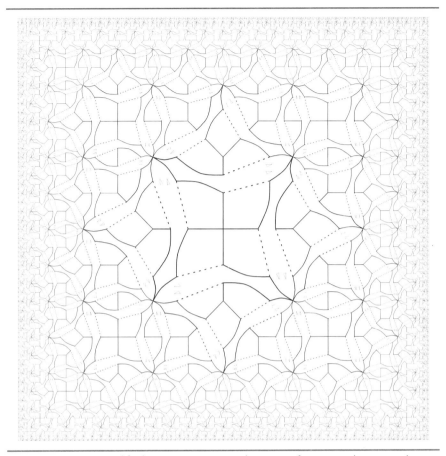

FIGURE 8.14   A simplified computer-generated version of M. C. Escher's woodcut
Square Limit.

recursively in terms of edge pieces and a smaller corner piece (see Figure 8.19). Finally, the A- and B-pieces can be described in terms of the two extremely simple 45°–45°–90° triangular pieces shown in Figure 8.20(a), by combining them as shown in Figure 8.20(b).

What a remarkable and lovely example of recursion!

Exercises—Fifth Set

1. (a) What should an order-0 Hilbert curve look like?
   (b) What should an order-0 Sierpiński curve look like?

2. Modify `Sierpinski` to produce the **x** and **y** coordinates of successive points on the curve.

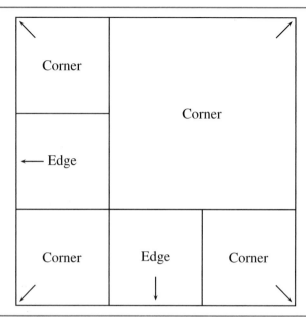

FIGURE 8.15 A schematic view of Escher's *Square Limit*. The arrows indicate the orientation of the pieces (see Figures 8.18 and 8.19), and the relative sizes of the pieces are as drawn.

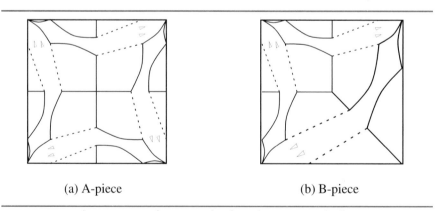

(a) A-piece   (b) B-piece

FIGURE 8.16 The two square figures used to form the corner and edge pieces.

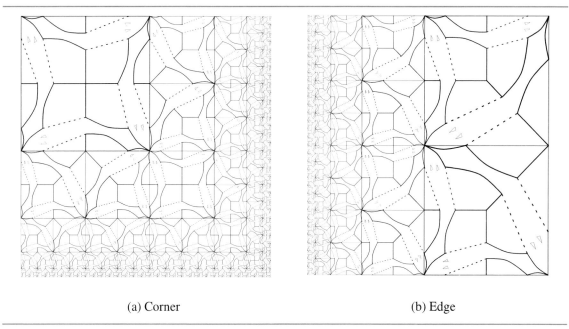

(a) Corner   (b) Edge

FIGURE 8.17   The corner and edge pieces, made from A-pieces and B-pieces.

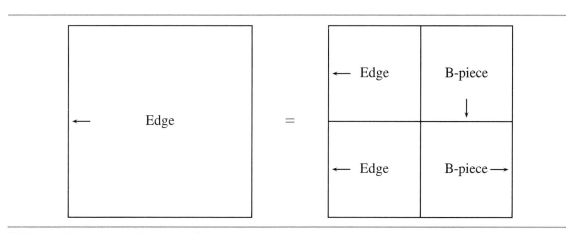

FIGURE 8.18   Recursive description of an edge piece.

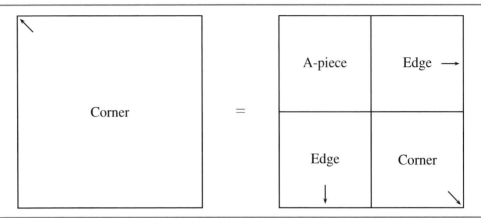

FIGURE 8.19 Recursive description of a corner piece.

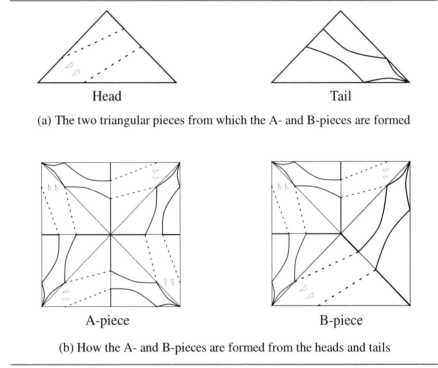

(a) The two triangular pieces from which the A- and B-pieces are formed

(b) How the A- and B-pieces are formed from the heads and tails

FIGURE 8.20 The decomposition of an A-piece and a B-piece in terms of the two triangular pieces.

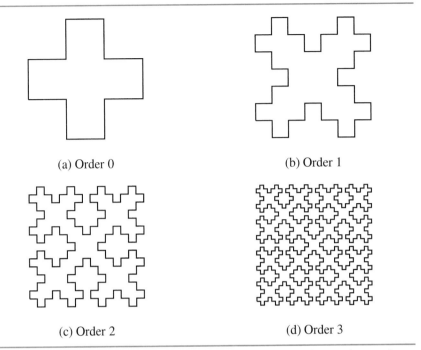

(a) Order 0   (b) Order 1

(c) Order 2   (d) Order 3

FIGURE 8.21   Rectilinear Sierpiński curves of orders 0, 1, 2, and 3, as discussed in Exercise 3.

3. There is a variant of the Sierpiński curve in which all lines are either vertical or horizontal. Figure 8.21 shows the first few examples of this curve. Modify the function **Sierpinski** so that it prints the directions for drawing these curves.

4. An interesting curve called the *dragon curve* is formed by the following recursive method. Start with a right angle:

Replace each line segment with a smaller right angle:

Now, again replace each line segment with a smaller right angle:

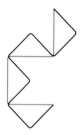

After several more iterations, the curve looks like this:

(The right angles in these drawings have been rounded slightly to show the structure of the curves more clearly.) These dragon curves are the result of taking a strip of paper, folding it in half, folding it in half again, and so on for some number of folds (the folds are parallel to each other) and then unfolding the paper so that each fold is at a 90° angle. Write a program to "draw" dragon curves—either as we "drew" the Sierpiński curves or as we "drew" the Hilbert curves.

5. If we unfold and flatten the folded paper obtained as described in the previous exercise, the pattern of folds will be $\vee$ after one fold, $\wedge\vee\vee$ after two folds, $\wedge\wedge\vee\vee\wedge\vee\vee$ after three folds, and so on (try it!). The pattern for $n + 1$ folds is obtained from the pattern for n folds as follows: Take the *reflected* pattern for n folds, add the fold $\vee$ at the end, and then add the original pattern for n folds. "Reflected" means upside down and in reverse order. (Again, try it!)
   (a) Using 1 for $\vee$ and 0 for $\wedge$, write a recursive function to produce the pattern for n.
   (b) Use your function from part (a) to get a function to draw the dragon curve.

6. In a variant of the dragon curves in the previous exercises, the right angle that replaces a line segment is always put on the same side of the line segment (in the dragon curves the right angles are alternately on one side and then the other). This sequence of curves begins

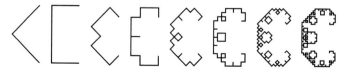

and starts to look more and more like an ornate "C". Write a program to "draw" members of this sequence of curves.

7. The following sequence of curves, called the *Sierpiński gasket,* is closely connected to the Towers of Hanoi problem; for details see either "The Towers and Triangles of Professor Claus (or, Pascal Knows Hanoi)," by D. G. Poole, *Mathematics Magazine* **67,** 5 (December, 1994), pp. 323–344, or "Four Encounters with Sierpiński's Gasket," by Ian Stewart, *The Mathematical Intelligencer* **17**, 1 (January, 1995), pp. 52–64.

Write a program to "draw" members of this sequence of curves.

Summary

A function is *recursive* if, as part of its action, it calls itself. The recursive version of a computation is often simpler and more elegant than the iterative form. Recursion is a powerful tool; it can make difficult programming jobs more manageable.

To simulate a recursive function to check its execution, use a stack of papers. Each time you encounter a call to the function, put down a sheet of paper on which all relevant information is written, consisting of the place the function was called from, the values of any parameters, and the values of any local variables.

Keep in mind the following distinctions concerning parameters, global variables, and local variables for recursive functions:

1. Parameters communicate information from one level to the next in the recursion.
2. Local variables are invisible from one level to the next. Each level has its own copies of local variables. Different levels of recursion do not have access to, or the ability to modify, the values of the local variables of other levels of recursion.
3. Global variables establish communication among all levels of recursion simultaneously.

One benefit of recursion over iteration is that the analysis of the rate of growth of the time required is often simpler. The analysis is carried out using *recurrence relations*.

The single most important paradigm in the design of algorithms is the *divide-and-conquer principle;* it is the backbone of many of the most efficient algorithms. This principle is: Break a problem into smaller subproblems of the same type, solve those subproblems recursively, and meld the solutions found for the individual subproblems into a solution for the entire problem.

In *mutual* recursion, a function calls itself indirectly through other functions. Mutually recursive functions require a prototype of the function, because C++ insists that a function physically precede any function calling it.

CHAPTER

9

Arrays

Chapter Preview

In this chapter we introduce *arrays*, a structure for storing large amounts of data. We discuss two of the most important operations performed on arrays: *sorting* and *searching*. Also, in C++, arrays are used to represent character strings, and we describe this representation. Most of the chapter is devoted to *one-dimensional arrays*. The final section treats *two-dimensional arrays*, which are used to represent grids of information, such as mathematical matrices, or characters on a computer screen. Arrays are an alternative to lists, and we discuss their comparative advantages. Unlike lists, arrays are of fixed size and can never grow once they are created; on the other hand, items in an array can be referenced much more quickly than can items in a list.

Little boxes on the hill side, little boxes made of ticky
tacky.
Little boxes, little boxes, little boxes all the same.
There's a green one and a pink one and a blue one and
a yellow one,
And they're all made out of ticky tacky, and they all
look just the same.

—Malvina Reynolds
"Little Boxes"

A n *array* is a sequence of variables of identical type. It can be used to *array*
store large amounts of data, without the need to declare many individual
variables.

We show how to declare arrays and use them. The simplest kind of array
processing uses a `for` loop to look at each element in the array. We give a number
of examples of these types of loops. We show how to pass arrays to functions,
which is slightly different from passing ordinary variables.

We then give many examples of the use of arrays. One important use is
to represent strings of characters; another is to sort lists of numbers; yet another
is to store large tables, allowing one to use a key (such as a person's name or
social security number) to obtain information associated with that key (such as an
address). These three uses of arrays are discussed in detail in Sections 9.4, 9.5,
and 9.6, respectively.

Two-dimensional arrays are used to represent mathematical matrices, characters on a computer screen, the kinds of tables that one often sees in books or
newspapers, and many other things. Section 9.7 introduces two-dimensional arrays and presents two important applications: one in graphics and the other in
mathematical programming.

Lists, introduced in Chapter 7, could also be used for all these purposes.
The comparative advantages of arrays and lists are discussed in the optional Section 9.1.6.

9.1

Array Basics

9.1.1 Creating Arrays

An array contains a fixed number, called its *length*, of variables of identical type. *length*
Like any other variable, an array is created by giving a declaration, which includes

397

the length of the array, as in

```
int counts[10];
char lastname[15];
time appointmentTimes[10];
```

The bracketed number is the length of each array. We can picture the array
counts like this:

Each box in this picture is an **int** variable. The numbers in color atop each box

subscript give that variable's *subscript*, or *index*; an array of length 10 has subscripts from
index 0 to 9.

Similarly, the declaration of **lastname** would create a sequence of fifteen
char variables, and the declaration of **appointmentTimes** would create a sequence of ten **time** objects.

Arrays can contain any type of value, built-in or user-defined. However, for
the moment, we will confine ourselves to arrays of numbers and characters. In
Section 9.6 we will see arrays of user-defined types.

9.1.2 Subscripting an Array

The essential feature of arrays is the ability to use subscripts to obtain a specific
array subscripting variable in an array. The notation for this *array subscripting* operation uses square
brackets, as in

```
counts[0]    // the first variable in counts
counts[1]    // the second variable in counts
counts[9]    // the last variable in counts
counts[10]   // error!!
```

Each of these subscripted arrays, except the last, is an **int** variable, and can be
used in all the same ways that any **int** variable is used: on the left-hand side of an
assignment statement, in an arithmetic expression, as the argument of a function,
and so on.

Here, for example, is a program to read in ten integers and print them in
reverse order:

```
void main () {
  int counts[10];

  cout << "Enter ten numbers: ";
  cin >> counts[0] >> counts[1] >> counts[2] >> counts[3]
      >> counts[4] >> counts[5] >> counts[6] >> counts[7]
      >> counts[8] >> counts[9];
```

```
    cout << counts[9] << " " << counts[8] << " "
         << counts[7] << " " << counts[6] << " "
         << counts[5] << " " << counts[4] << " "
         << counts[3] << " " << counts[2] << " "
         << counts[1] << " " << counts[0] << "\n";
}
```

9.1.3 Computing Subscripts

It is of paramount importance in using arrays that *array subscripts can be expressions*—they don't have to be constants.

For example, if i is an integer variable, `counts[i]` refers to one of the variables in `counts`. If $i = 0$, it refers to `counts[0]`; if $i = 1$, it refers to `counts[1]`; and so on. Of course, values of i that are not in the range 0 to 9 must be avoided.

More complex expressions can also be used as subscripts. `counts[2*i]` refers to `counts[0]` if i is zero, `counts[2]` if i is 1, and so on. In this case, any value of i greater than 4 would result in an error. `counts[i/2]`, on the other hand, is legal as long as i is between zero and 19; it refers to `counts[0]` if i is 0 or 1, `counts[1]` if i is 2 or 3, and so on.

Arrays Are Subscripted from Zero   BUG ALERT 9.1

A source of confusion in using arrays in C++ is subscripting from zero, which seems unnatural at first. Just remember that to create an array `A` of `n` variables of type `T`, use the declaration

```
T A[n];
```

Then keep in mind that the element `A[n]` does not exist—only `A[0]` through `A[n-1]` do.

Arrays Can Be Copied, but Not Assigned   BUG ALERT 9.2

Arrays contain variables, but they are not variables themselves. In particular, if `A` and `B` are arrays, you cannot write

```
    A = B;
```

The compiler will issue an error message.

You can, on the other hand, *copy* `B` to `A`; that is, you can copy the contents of each variable in `B` to the corresponding variable in `A`. The loop

```
    for (int i=0; i<n; i++)
      A[i] = B[i];
```

does this copying, assuming that `A` and `B` are arrays of size `n`.

9.1.4 Initializing Arrays

Arrays can be initialized by giving a list of all their elements, as in

```
int primes[10] = {2, 3, 5, 7, 11, 13, 17, 19, 23, 29};
```

Indeed, in this case you do not even have to declare the size of the array. The following declaration has the same effect as the one just given:

```
int primes[] = {2, 3, 5, 7, 11, 13, 17, 19, 23, 29};
```

This notation can be used only at the time an array is declared; it is illegal to write

```
int primes[10];
primes = {2, 3, 5, 7, 11, 13, 17, 19, 23, 29};
```

Note: Some C++ compilers allow initialization lists only for *global* arrays—those declared outside of any function—and will give an error message if you attempt to initialize a local array. Accordingly, we will use array initialization only for global arrays.

9.1.5 Simple Array-Processing Loops

The simplest kind of array processing uses a `for` loop to generate the subscripts of an array.

For example, this loop initializes the array `counts` to contain the numbers 0, 10, 20, and so on up to 90:

```
1    for (int i=0; i<10; i++)
2       counts[i] = i*10;
```

index variable   The variable `i`, which varies from 0 to 9, is called the *index variable* of the loop. The first time through the loop, `i` is zero, so the assignment in line 2 assigns zero to `counts[0]`; the second time through, `i` is 1 and 10 is assigned to `counts[1]`; the third time, 20 is assigned to `counts[2]`; and so on. The last time through the loop, `i` is 9, so 90 is assigned to `counts[9]`. In the end, `counts` looks like this:

	0	1	2	3	4	5	6	7	8	9
counts	0	10	20	30	40	50	60	70	80	90

As another example, here is a more concise version of the program we gave earlier to read ten numbers into `counts` and print them in reverse order:

```
1    void main () {
2      int counts[10];
3
4      cout << "Enter ten numbers: ";
5      for (int i=0; i<10; i++)
6        cin >> counts[i];
7
```

```
8      for (i=0; i<10; i++)
9        cout << counts[9-i] << " ";
10     cout << "\n";
11   }
```

The loop in line 5 executes `cin >> counts[i]` ten times, with `i` varying from 0 to 9. Similarly, the loop in lines 8 and 9 executes the output statement 10 times, with `i` varying from 0 to 9. However, at each iteration of the loop, the value of `counts[9-i]` is printed. Thus, in the first iteration, with `i` equal to zero, `counts[9]` is printed; in the second, with `i` equal to one, `counts[8]` is printed; and so on. Another way to write this output loop is

```
       for (i=9; i>=0; i--)
         cout << counts[i] << " ";
```

where the index variable `i` varies from 9 down to 0.

Although an array cannot grow once it has been declared, you can accommodate a varying amount of data by making the array very large and only filling as much of it as you need. The following program reads and echoes a sequence of numbers; the sequence is terminated by an end-of-file character and is of unknown length. However, if we assume that there will never be more than 1000 numbers in the input, we can make an array large enough to hold them all:

```
const int inputMax = 1000;

main () {
  int inputs[inputMax];
  int size = 0;
  int n;

  // Input up to inputMax numbers
  cout << "Enter first number: ";
  cin >> n;
  while (!cin.eof()) {
    // The first size inputs are stored in
    // inputs[0] .. inputs[size-1]
    inputs[size] = n;
    size++;
    cout << "Enter next number: ";
    cin >> n;
  }

  // Print numbers, one per line
  for (int i=0; i<size; i++)
    cout << inputs[i] << "\n";
}
```

Here we use a `while` loop to read the input, as we have always done. The variable `size` varies from 0 up to the number of items read; in other words, `size` is the index variable of this loop. After reading the inputs, `inputs[0],...,` `inputs[size-1]` contain those items. It is a simple matter to print them in order.

As another example of array processing, this program reads a sequence of student ID numbers and scores on two exams and prints a listing giving the average score for each student. The input is in the form of three numbers for each

Remember to Increment Index Variable in `while` **Loop**

When an array is processed by a **while** loop, you must initialize the index variable before the loop and increment it inside the loop. A common error in programming is to forget to increment the index variable.

This advice does not apply when a **for** loop is used, since the form of the **for** loop makes it difficult to make this mistake.

line, the ID number followed by two scores:

```
405567 57 69
998923 94 86
770904 90 77
   . . .
```

and the output is in two columns:

```
ID Number    Average

   405567       63
   998923       90
   770904       83
    . . .
```

Here is the program:

```
const int inputMax = 100;

main () {
  int IDNumbers[inputMax],
      exam1[inputMax],
      exam2[inputMax];
  int size;
  int i;

  // Read ID numbers and exam grades; size counts inputs
  size = 0;
  cout << "Enter ID number, and two exam grades: ";
  cin >> IDNumbers[size] >> exam1[size] >> exam2[size];
  while (!cin.eof()) {
    size++;
    cout << "Enter ID number, and two exam grades: ";
    cin >> IDNumbers[size] >> exam1[size] >> exam2[size];
  }

  cout << "\n\n" << setw(12) << "ID Number" << "    "
       << "Average" << "\n\n";
  for (i=0; i<size; i++)
    cout << setw(10) << IDNumbers[i] << "      "
         << setw(3) << (exam1[i] + exam2[i])/2 << "\n";
}
```

| **Check Array Indices for Out-of-Bounds Errors** | **BUG ALERT 9.4** |

When C++ subscripts an array, it does not check that the index is within the bounds of the array. It is *your* responsibility to make sure you use only legal subscripts. In some cases, an out-of-bounds index causes an immediate run-time error, which is bad enough, but in some cases it simply causes the answers you get to be wrong, and gives no warning. (Some C++ compilers are capable of producing programs that check every array subscripting operation, causing a run-time error for an out-of-bounds subscript; check your compiler manual.)

9.1.6 (Optional) Arrays vs. Lists

There is nothing we can do with arrays that we can't already do with lists. If `L` is an `intList`, and `A` is an integer array, we have these correspondences, using the `nth` and `setValue` functions defined in Chapter 7:

Operation	On lists	On arrays
Get `i`th value	`L.nth(i)->getValue()`	`A[i]`
Assign `x` to `i`th location	`L.nth(i)->setValue(x)`	`A[i] = x`

However, arrays lack a key capability of lists: Arrays cannot grow or shrink. Once an array is declared with a certain size, it always has exactly that size.

Why, then, do we bother with arrays? They have one property that can crucially affect the efficiency of programs: In arrays, access to individual elements is done in a constant amount of time, independent of the subscript. Getting the one-thousandth variable in an array of a thousand items takes exactly the same amount of time as getting the first item in that array. This is called *random access*. It is in stark contrast to the `nth` operation in lists, in which getting the `i`th element takes time proportional to `i`. This is *sequential access*.

random access

sequential access

Especially in the later sections of this chapter—Sections 9.6 and 9.7, for example—we will write programs that are considerably more efficient using array subscripting than if we had used lists and the `nth` function.

Exercises—First Set

☞ 1. Read a sequence of numbers terminated by the end-of-file character into an array `A` (just as was done in the program on page 401), and perform the following operations (where `n` is the number of inputs):
   (a) Compute and print running sums in both forward and backward directions. Specifically, compute and print arrays `B` and `C`, where $B[i] = B[0]+B[1]+\cdots+B[i]$, and $C[i] = C[n-1]+C[n-2]+\cdots+C[i]$.

(b) Compute pairwise differences: `D[i] = D[i+1]-D[i]`.

(c) Compute three-way averages: `E[i] = (E[i]+E[i+1]+E[i+2])/3`.

(d) Compute the increasing values within the array. That is, start with `F[0] = A[0]`. Then compute `F[1]` to be the value `A[i]`, where `i` is the smallest index such that `A[i]>A[0]`. Then compute `F[2]` to be the value `A[j]`, where `j` is the smallest index greater than `i` such that `A[j]>A[i]`, and so on. For example, if the inputs are 5, −5, 10, 13, 4, 40, 25, 6, then `F` should contain the values 5, 10, 13, and 40.

2. Exercise 7 on page 265 asked you to read a sequence of grades and report their average and standard deviation and then list each student's raw score and z-score. Repeat that exercise using arrays instead of lists. You may set an upper limit of 100 on the number of students, printing an error message and stopping the program if that number of inputs is exceeded.

3. The function

```
void dayNumber (int  month, int day, int year)
```

defined on page 105, computes the number of days from the first of the given year to the given date (using the Gregorian calendar). If all months had 31 days, this calculation would be simple, but because they don't, we had to use the "magic formula" `(4 * month + 23) / 10` as a correction factor. That this formula works is fortuitous, but it is hardly good style to depend on this kind of thing. A simple solution is to store the lengths of all the months in an array and then calculate the first day of the given month by adding up the lengths of the months that precede it. All that is needed after that is to correct for leap years.

(a) Program **dayNumber** using a global array **monthLengths**, initialized to hold the lengths of the months.

(b) The array **monthLengths** can be used to compute the inverse of **dayNumber**. Program the function

```
void computeNormalDate (int dayNumber,
                        int year,
                        int& month,
                        int& day)
```

to find the month and day for the given day number in the given year.

9.2

Passing Arrays to Functions

The programs shown earlier in this chapter were not organized into functions, as we have done with all our programs since Chapter 4. The use of arrays does not diminish the need for functions in any way, but passing arrays to functions is a subtle topic that needs some explanation. The purpose of this section is to provide that explanation and to show some examples of functions that operate on arrays.

9.2.1 Arrays as Arguments

Consider this rewriting of the program given on page 401, which reads and echoes a sequence of numbers:

```
1   const int inputMax = 1000;
2
3   void readArray (int A[], int& size) {
4     size = 0;
5     int n;
6     cout << "Enter first number: "; cin >> n;
7     while (!cin.eof()) {
8       A[size] = n;
9       size++;
10      cout << "Enter next number: "; cin >> n;
11    }
12  }
13
14  void writeArray (int A[], int s) {
15    for (int i=0; i<s; i++)
16      cout << A[i] << "\n";
17  }
18
19  main () {
20    int inputs[inputMax];
21    int s;
22
23    readArray(inputs, s);
24    writeArray(inputs, s);
25  }
```

This is a better version of the program, because it is structured in terms of its two logical parts: Function **readArray** does the input, and function **writeArray** does the output.

Two important points about these functions need to be noted. First, notice how the argument **A** to **readArray** and **writeArray** is declared. It appears as an array declaration, but without the length. By giving no length in this declaration, you are telling C++ that its argument will be an array of integers, without telling it how long the array will be. This allows the function to work for arrays of any size. Second, assignments into the array that occur in **readArray** are "seen" by the main program and, subsequently, by **writeArray**. This is odd, because to ensure that the assignment to **size** within **readArray** would be seen in the main program, we gave that argument a reference type. For the array, we didn't need to.

These two points are really one and the same. When an array is passed to a function, C++ actually passes a *pointer* to the beginning of the array. There is just one array, the one created in line 25 (called the array's *definition*). The functions' argument lists contain *declarations* of an array, but the functions don't have to make room for the array, so there is no need to give its length; hence the special notation for parameter declarations. Also, because the functions receive a pointer to the array **inputs**, rather than a copy of it, assignments made to **A** in **readArray** are actually made to **inputs**. Thus, after return from **readArray**, **inputs** contains the new values.

Here is the stack when **readArray** is called:

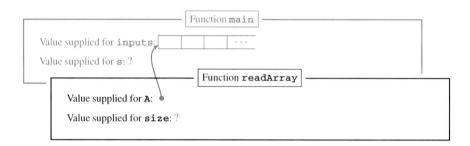

For C++ it makes little difference whether **A** is regarded as an *array* of integers or as a *pointer* to an integer. Indeed, C++ treats arrays and pointers as interchangeable, so that this definition of **readArray** works exactly the same as the last:

```
void readArray (int *A, int& size) {
  size = 0;
  int n;
  cout << "Enter first number: "; cin >> n;
  while (!cin.eof()) {
    A[size] = n;
    size++;
    cout << "Enter next number: "; cin >> n;
  }
}
```

What about changing the definition of **inputs** in **main** the same way?

```
main () {
  int *inputs;
  int s;

  readArray(inputs, s);
  writeArray(inputs, s);
}
```

This almost makes sense, but it doesn't work, because the array is never created. At some point, memory for the array needs to be allocated. This is where the difference between a *definition* and a *declaration* comes in. A definition declares an array *and* allocates space for it; a declaration doesn't allocate space.

9.2.2   Array Functions Using Existing Space

We now give three functions to illustrate the passing of arrays to functions. All do basically the same thing—reverse the elements of an array—but they vary in how they give their results. **reverseCopy** has two array arguments and copies

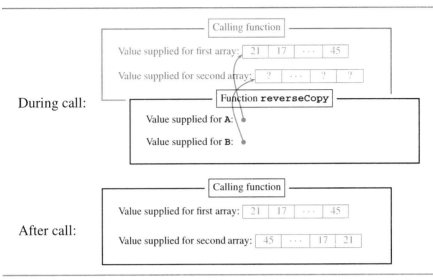

During call:

After call:

FIGURE 9.1   void reverseCopy (int A[], int B[], int size)

the contents of the first into the second in reverse order. **reverseInPlace** is a *mutating* operation: It has one array argument, and it reverses the contents of that array. **reverse** copies the contents of its array argument, in reverse order, into a fresh array allocated in the heap; it is a nonmutating operation.

   reverseCopy, illustrated in Figure 9.1, takes two arrays, **A** and **B**, and places the reversed contents of **A** into **B**. This function looks at each item in **A** ("iterates over" **A**) and copies it into a variable at the opposite end of **B**. The correspondence is as follows:

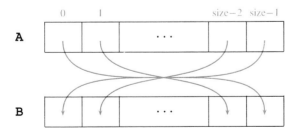

The formula is simple. The contents of **A[i]** are copied into **B[(size-1)-i]**.

```
void reverseCopy (int A[], int B[], int size) {
   for (int i=0; i<size; i++)
      // A[0]..A[i-1] have been moved to
      //   B[size-1]..B[size-i]
      B[size-1-i] = A[i];
}
```

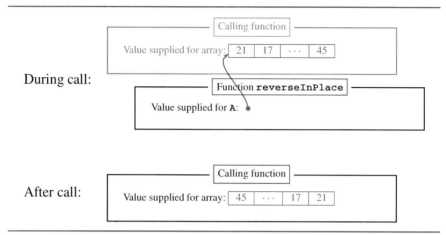

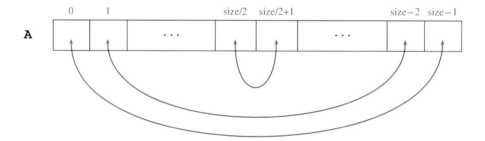

FIGURE 9.2   `void reverseInPlace (int A[], int size)`

The second function, **reverseInPlace**, takes just one array, **A**, and reverses its contents; it is illustrated in Figure 9.2. Here the contents of **A** are swapped:

There is a question about what to do in the middle, but we'll get to that. The function is

```
void swap (int& x, int& y) {
  int temp = x;
  x = y;
  y = temp;
}

void reverseInPlace (int A[], int size) {
  for (int i=0; i<size/2; i++)
    // A[0]..A[i-1] have been swapped with
    //   A[size-1]..A[size-i]
    swap(A[i], A[size-1-i]);
}
```

The subtle part of **reverseInPlace** is the termination of the loop. There are two cases:

- `size` is even. For example, suppose `size` is 6:

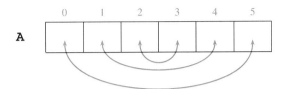

We need to execute the **swap** function three times, with **i** ranging from 0 to 2. Since $2 = (6/2) - 1$, the loop terminates correctly in this case.
- `size` is odd, say 5:

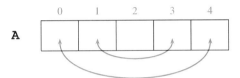

swap should be executed twice, with **i** ranging from 0 to 1; the middle element can just be left alone. Since $1 = (5/2) - 1$, the loop again terminates correctly.

We'll leave it up to you to prove that the loop works correctly for all values of `size`.

9.2.3   Allocating Arrays on the Heap

The third function that we will consider, **reverse**, illustrated in Figure 9.3, takes one array, **A**, and places the reversed contents of **A** in a newly allocated array in the heap. It cannot be written without introducing a new feature, or rather a variation on a feature we've used before: **new**. We know, of course, how to allocate an object of user-defined type in the heap using **new**. Allocating integers, **floats**, pointers, or any other primitive type is just as easy, though rarely useful:

```
int *ip = new int;
time *fp = new float;
```

Arrays, however, are different, because they require a notation to tell **new** how many variables to allocate. That notation is

```
new <type>[<size>]
```

This expression allocates an array of length **<size>** with variables of type **<type>** and returns a pointer to the first item in the array.

reverse allocates an array in the heap and copies its argument into that array in reverse. It returns the array by returning a pointer to it.

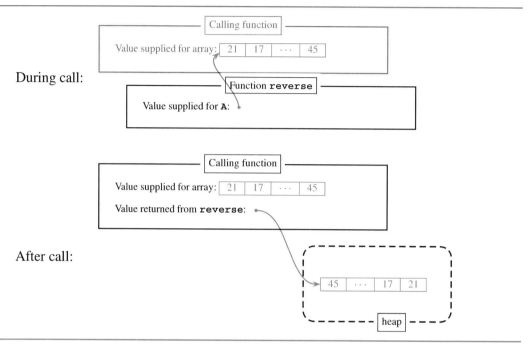

During call:

After call:

FIGURE 9.3   `int *reverse (int A[], int size)`

```
int *reverse(int A[], int size) {
  int *B = new int[size];
  reverseCopy(A, B, size);
  return B;
}
```

B is an array just like any other, except that it happens to be in the heap. Notice that the length of the new array is a variable. C++ will allocate an array of length exactly **size** in the heap. This does not contradict our earlier statement that arrays are of fixed size. *Once defined*, an array cannot change its size. However, its definition—whether as a stack-allocated or heap-allocated data item—can contain variables used to compute its length dynamically.

reverse cannot be used exactly as **reverseCopy** can. If **S** and **T** are integer arrays, you call **reverseCopy** this way,

```
reverseCopy(S, T, n);
```

to copy **S** into **T** in reverse (assuming **S** has length **n**). However, you cannot call **reverse** like this,

```
T = reverse(S, n);
```

because, as noted in Bug Alert 9.2 on page 399, it is not legal to assign to an array. However, you can pass the result of calling **reverse** into a function that takes an array or pointer argument.

You might think there is a fourth approach to writing an array-reversal function: Take one array argument, copy it in reverse into a local array, then return the local array:

```
int *reverseIntoLocal (int *A, int size) {
  int B[inputMax];
  ... // reverse A into B
  return B;
}
```

However, this is erroneous. As illustrated in Figure 9.4, it leads to a dangling pointer (as described on page 252). The array **B** exists only during the call of **reverseIntoLocal**. Returning a pointer to it is a mistake, because it ceases to exist after return from the function, and the pointer points to nothing.

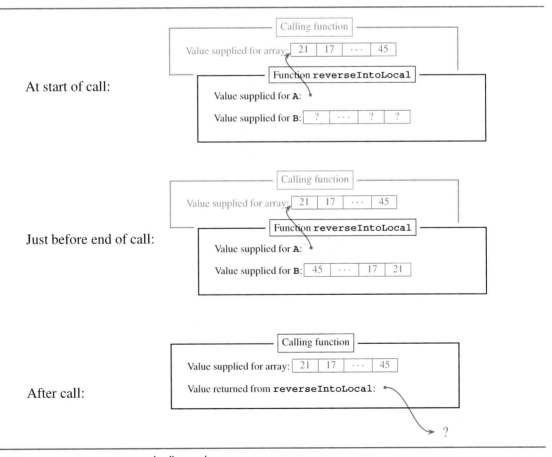

FIGURE 9.4   Attempt to return stack-allocated array.

Objects Are Passed by Value

Objects can contain arrays as data members. However, when such an object is passed as an argument to a function, the entire object is passed by value. That is, the object—*including the array it contains*—is copied. As explained on page 222, this means that any alterations done to the array by the calling function will not be seen by the caller. Again, one solution is to pass the object by reference.

Exercises—Second Set

1. Write the following functions (which are analogous to those assigned in Chapter 7 on page 265):

    (a) `int sum (int A[], int size)` sums the elements `A[0]...A[size-1]`.

    (b) `int frequency (int A[], int size, int p)` counts the number of occurrences of `p` among the values `A[0]...A[size-1]`.

    (c) `int max (int A[], int size)` returns the maximum among the values `A[0]...A[size-1]`.

    (d) `void insert (int A[], int size, int p)` inserts `p` into `A` as the first element. The existing elements of `A` (`A[0]...A[size-1]`) are shifted over one position to the right; you can assume that `A` is large enough to hold this new element.

    (e) `void insertInOrder (int A[], int size, int p)` inserts `p` into `A` so as to leave `A` in numerical order, if it was in order originally. The elements of `A` greater than `p` are shifted one position to the right.

    (f) `int find (int A[], int size, int p)` returns the location at which `p` first occurs in `A`, or -1 if it does not occur at all.

2. Given a polynomial $a_n x^n + a_{n-1} x^{n-1} + \cdots + a_0$, we evaluate it by *Horner's method*, rewriting it as

$$(\cdots(((a_n x) + a_{n-1})x + a_{n-2})x + \cdots + a_1)x + a_0$$

Assuming the coefficients a_i are stored in an array `float a[n+1]`, write a program to read a value for x and evaluate the polynomial using Horner's rule.

3. The *sieve of Eratosthenes* is a method of finding prime numbers by sifting out composite numbers. Start with

    2   3   4   5   6   7   8   9   10   11   12   13   14   15   16 $\cdots$ n

    Starting with 2, the first prime number, cross off every second number (except 2), leaving

    2   3   4   5   6   7   8   9   10   11   12   13   14   15   16 $\cdots$ n

    Then, starting from 3 (the next prime number), cross off every third number except 3, leaving

    2   3   4   5   6   7   8   9   10   11   12   13   14   15   16 $\cdots$ n

    The numbers in color are those that have already been found to be prime, and the ones in gray are the multiples of the numbers in color. At each step, find the smallest number p still in black—it is the next prime number—and color p, and make every pth number after p gray. Continue this process until the smallest number in black exceeds $\sqrt{n}$; at that point all the black numbers are primes (see page 173). Write a program to compute the prime numbers less than n (a symbolic constant) by the sieve of Eratosthenes, using a boolean array `crossedOff[n+1]` to represent the sequence. If `crossedOff[i]` is `true`, then `i` has been crossed off; if it is `false`, `i` has not yet been crossed off. (Elements `crossedOff[0]` and `crossedOff[1]` will just be ignored.)

★ 4. The most important feature of spreadsheet programs like Lotus 1–2–3® and Microsoft Excel® is that the value contained in one cell can be computed as a function of the values in other cells. If cell A1 contains the wholesale cost of a product, and A2 its retail cost, then you can enter the formula `A2-A1`, representing the profit on that item, into cell A3. It will be computed automatically when you enter the formula, and recalculated automatically whenever the contents of A1 or A2 change.

One issue that arises in writing a spreadsheet program is what to do if there is a *circular* dependency among the items in the spreadsheet. Suppose the user inadvertently enters the formula `A4+1` into cell A3 and `A3+1` into cell A4. Such a mistake must be detected, so that the user can be warned, but how?

We'll simplify the problem by having only a single row of cells instead of the usual grid of cells and, more importantly, by allowing each cell to depend on at most one other cell. Abstractly, we have a structure like this, where an arrow from cell i to cell j represents the fact that cell i is a function of cell j. For example, cell 3 contains a formula that refers to cell 6:

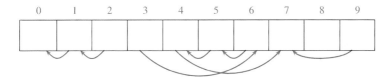

Your program should have as its input a sequence of n numbers (terminated by end of file) in the range $-1, \ldots, n - 1$, giving the contents of the array `cells`. If `cells[i]` contains $j \geq 0$, it means that cell `i` is a function of cell `j`; if `cells[i]` contains -1, it means that cell `i` does not depend on any other cell. The dependencies illustrated above would be given as the ten numbers

```
-1 0 1 6 7 4 5 -1 -1 7
```

To determine whether there is a circularity in the set of dependences, define an array of booleans called `visited` and initialize it to all `false`. For each cell `i`, set `visited[i]` to `true` and then follow the arrows from `i`, setting `visited[j]` to `true` when an arrow leads to cell `j`. If it ever occurs that an arrow leads to a cell `k` such that `visited[k]` is already `true`, there is a cycle. In that case, print a message indicating that cell `k` is in a cycle; otherwise, print a message indicating that there are no cycles.

9.3

Debugging Arrays

A *histogram* or *bar chart* is a graphical presentation of quantitative data in discrete categories. In Exercise 4 (page 295), you were asked to write a class `histogram` with operations

```
void incrCategory (int cat) ;
int categoryFreq (int cat) ;
```

Then you were to read a sequence of numbers representing grades on an exam and increment the frequency count for the corresponding category: category 0 for grades 0 through 9, category 1 for grades 10 through 19, and so on, with category 10 for grades 90 through 100. Finally, when the input was exhausted, you were to print the histogram, as shown on page 295.

In this section, we will write a similar program, using a class `histogram` with the same member functions but different categories. Here is the problem:

A survey sent to a collection of historians asked them to indicate their choice for "most important year in American history." They were permitted to choose from the following set of years:

Year	Event
1776	Declaration of Independence
1805	Lewis and Clark reach the Pacific Ocean
1865	Lee surrenders, ending the Civil War
1908	Ford introduces the Model T
1917	America enters World War I
1929	Stock market crash; beginning of the Great Depression
1945	End of World War II

We have their responses, in the form of a sequence of years, and our job is to read them and print a histogram showing the number of votes for each year, as shown in Figure 9.5.

So we want a `histogram` class with the same operations as in the earlier exercise, but with categories corresponding to the seven candidate years. In other words, if `h` is a `histogram` object, sending the message `h.incrCategory(1776)` should add 1 to the 1776 category, and similarly for the other six years.

Our approach is to use two integer arrays of length 7: `categories` will contain the numbers 1776, 1805, and so on, and `frequencies` will contain the num-

```
               Historian survey

               Year    Count

               1776    **************
               1805    *******
               1865    *************
               1908    *****
               1917    ***
               1929    ******
               1945    ********
```

FIGURE 9.5   A histogram.

	0	1	2	3	4	5	6
categories	1776	1805	1865	1908	1917	1929	1945

frequencies	14	7	13	5	3	6	8

FIGURE 9.6 Parallel arrays used in `histogram` class.

ber of votes for each year. This technique is known as *parallel arrays*, since we   *parallel arrays*
can think of the two arrays as being lined up in parallel, as shown in Figure 9.6; for
every i, `frequencies[i]` gives the number of votes for year `categories[i]`.

Here is our first cut at the `histogram` class and its clients, functions
`readYears` and `printHistogram`, which are called by `main`. The function
`printHistogram` uses an auxiliary function `printYear` to print a single line of
the histogram:

```
13    const int size = 7;
14
15    class histogram {
16    private:
17      int categories[size];  // Contains 1776, ..., 1945
18      int frequencies[size]; // Contains frequencies for
19                             // 1776, ..., 1945
20
21    public:
22      histogram () ;
23
24      void incrCategory (int cat) ;
25
26      int categoryFreq (int cat) ;
27    };
28
29    histogram::histogram () {
30      categories[0] = 1776;
31      categories[1] = 1805;
32      categories[2] = 1865;
33      categories[3] = 1908;
34      categories[4] = 1917;
35      categories[5] = 1929;
36      categories[6] = 1945;
37      for (int i=0; i<size; i++)
38        frequencies[i] = 0;
39    }
40
41    void histogram::incrCategory (int cat) {
42      // cat is one of the years 1776, ..., 1945;
43      // increment the associated frequency.
44      int i = 0;
```

```
45        while (categories[i] != cat) i++;
46        frequencies[i]++;
47    }
48
49    int histogram::categoryFreq (int cat) {
50        // cat is one of the years 1776, ..., 1945;
51        // return the associated frequency.
52        int i = 0;
53        while (categories[i] != cat) i++;
54        return frequencies[i];
55    }
56
57    void printYear (int year, histogram h) {
58        // Print year and then print a number of asterisks
59        // corresponding to the frequency of year in h.
60        freq = h.categoryFreq(year);
61        cout << setw(4) << year << "   ";
62        for (int j=1; j<=freq; j++)
63            cout << '*';
64        cout << "\n";
65    }
66
67    void printHistogram (histogram h) {
68        cout << "Historian survey\n\n"
69             << "Year    Count\n\n";
70        printYear(1776, h);
71        printYear(1805, h);
72        printYear(1865, h);
73        printYear(1908, h);
74        printYear(1917, h);
75        printYear(1929, h);
76        printYear(1945, h);
77    }
78
79    void readYears (histogram h) {
80        // Read years up to end-of-file and
81        // increment their frequencies in h.
82        int year;
83
84        cin >> year;
85        while (!cin.eof()) {
86            h.incrCategory(year);
87            cin >> year;
88        }
89    }
90
91    void main () {
92        histogram yearHisto;
93
94        readYears(yearHisto);
95        printHistogram(yearHisto);
96    }
```

As usual, we get syntax errors:

```
line 60: error:  freq undefined
1 error
```

This refers to the line in which we have initialized the local variable `freq` in `printYear`. This is a simple error—we haven't declared `freq`. After fixing it,

```
60      int freq = h.categoryFreq(year);
```

the program compiles without syntax errors.

It is always a good idea to start testing a program using simple input data. We will first test it by inputting each of the allowable years exactly once. The output should show exactly one asterisk for each year, but instead it shows none:

```
Historian survey

Year    Count

1776
1805
1865
1908
1917
1929
1945
```

The problem may be in `readYears`, `printHistogram`, or the `histogram` class. To see whether the histogram is being read correctly, we place this output statement in `main` after the call to `readYears`:

```
95      cout << yearHisto.categoryFreq(1776) << endl;
```

Presumably, the problem is the same for every year, so looking at just one year should tell us as much as if we looked at every year. In any case, the output from this version is

```
0
1776
1805
1865
1908
1917
1929
1945
```

So the frequency for this category is zero, which casts suspicion on `readYears` (as opposed to `printHistogram`).

To see what is happening in `readYears`, we place the same output statement inside it, just before the return:

```
79    void readYears (histogram h) {
80       // Read years up to end-of-file and
81       // increment their frequencies in h.
82       int year;
83
```

```
84      cin >> year;
85      while (!cin.eof()) {
86        h.incrCategory(year);
87        cin >> year;
88      }
89      cout << h.categoryFreq(1776) << endl;
90    }
```

This time, the output is

```
1
0
1776
1805
1865
1908
1917
1929
1945
```

So **readYears** is incrementing the categories in **h**, but it is failing to do so in its argument, **yearHisto**. This is a familiar problem: **yearHisto** should have been passed by reference. We fix this:

```
79    void readYears (histogram& h) {
```

(We will also change **printHistogram** to make **h** a reference parameter, for the slight gain in efficiency.)

The output is much more satisfactory now:

```
1
1
1776    *
1805    *
1865    *
1908    *
1917    *
1929    *
1945    *
```

We remove the two output statement that we added for debugging, and when we test the program on the original input, everything is okay:

```
Historian survey

Year    Count

1776    **************
1805    *******
1865    *************
1908    *****
```

```
1917   ***
1929   ******
1945   ********
```

Perhaps we should be happy now, but this code is ugly in spots. For one thing, the definitions of **incrCategory** and **categoryFreq** are too similar, suggesting that a separate function should be defined to do the shared work. Add member function **int findCat (int)** to return the index (between 0 and 6) of a year.

```
13   const int size = 7;
14
15   class histogram {
16   private:
17     int categories[size];  // Contains 1776, ..., 1945
18     int frequencies[size]; // Contains frequencies for
19                            // 1776, ..., 1945
20
21     int findCat (int cat) {
22
23   public:
24     histogram () ;
25
26     void incrCategory (int cat) ;
27
28     int categoryFreq (int cat) ;
29   };
30
31   histogram::histogram () {
32     categories[0] = 1776;
33     categories[1] = 1805;
34     categories[2] = 1865;
35     categories[3] = 1908;
36     categories[4] = 1917;
37     categories[5] = 1929;
38     categories[6] = 1945;
39     for (int i=0; i<size; i++)
40       frequencies[i] = 0;
41   }
42
43   int histogram::findCat (int cat) {
44     // Find location of cat, if any
45     int i = 0;
46     while (i<size && categories[i] != cat) i++;
47     return i;
48   }
49
50   void histogram::incrCategory (int cat) {
51     // cat is one of the years 1776, ..., 1945;
52     // increment the associated frequency.
53     frequencies[findCat(cat)]++;
54   }
55
```

```
56   int histogram::categoryFreq (int cat) {
57     // cat is one of the years 1776, ..., 1945;
58     // return the associated frequency.
59     return frequencies[findCat(cat)];
60   }
```

This has syntax errors:

```
line 23: error: syntax error
line 102: error: '}' missing at end of input
line 102: error: syntax error
line 102: error: '}' missing at end of input
4 errors
```

The syntax error on line 23—the prototype of **findCat**—is easy to see: a brace instead of a semicolon (which obviously caused the other errors as well). After we fix that, the code compiles without incident and gives identical output.

A more serious problem is in the basic design of the program. It is unfortunate when a long list of constants—such as the list of years in this example—has to be repeated. Here, the same list of years appears in the **histogram** constructor and in the client function **printHistogram**. This can lead to errors, because we always need to make sure the two sets of years are identical. Since the **histogram** class "knows" the years, there should be a way of getting them from it.

For this purpose, we add three new member functions:

```
int numberOfCategories ()
void reset ()
void nextCategory ()
```

that work like this: **numberOfCategories** simply returns 7 (we make it a function to allow for future changes). **reset** has no apparent effect, but it sets a counter to zero. After **reset** is called, **nextCategory** is called repeatedly, and each time it is called, it gives the next year in the histogram. Thus, when first called after the call to **reset**, it returns 1776; when next called (unless **reset** is called again), it returns 1805, and so on.

These functions were designed so that **printHistogram** could be written like this:

```
82   void printHistogram (histogram& h) {
83     cout << "Historian survey\n\n"
84          << "Year   Count\n\n";
85     h.reset();
86     int lines = h.numberOfCategories();
87     for (int i=0; i<lines; i++)
88       printYear(h.nextCategory(), h);
89   }
```

The loop iterates exactly seven times. Each time, there is a call to **nextCategory** to get the next year, and **printYear** is called (as before) with that year. The beauty of this change is that all the clients of **histogram** are independent of the precise years that were studied in the survey, or even the number of years. We can use those clients again for the next survey, with different years.

To implement the new member functions, we need a new data member to keep track of the next category that **nextCategory** should return.

```
15   class histogram {
16   private:
17     int categories[size];  // Contains 1776, ..., 1945
18     int frequencies[size]; // Contains frequencies for
19                            // 1776, ..., 1945
20     int current;           // Next category to return
21
22     int findCat (int cat) ;
23
24   public:
25     histogram () ;
26
27     void incrCategory (int cat) ;
28
29     int categoryFreq (int cat) ;
30
31     int numberofCategories () { return size; }
32
33     void reset () { current = 0; }
34
35     void nextCategory () {
36       current++;
37       return categories[current];
38     }
39   };
```

This code has a few syntax errors:

```
line 37: error: unexpected return value
line 15: sorry, not implemented: cannot expand inline
    function histogram::nextCategory() with return statement
line 86: error:  member numberOfCategories undefined
line 88: error: bad argument  1 type for
    printYear(): void  (int  expected)
4 errors
```

Line 37 is the last line in the definition of **nextCategory**. The return value in this function is "unexpected" because the function was wrongly declared to have return type **void**; it should be **int**. The error in line 15 (the first line of the class definition) says that the function **nextCategory** cannot be defined in the class (you may not get this error from your compiler), so we have to move it out. Line 86 is the first call of the member function **numberOfCategories**, and the compiler claims to know nothing about it. Stupid mistake: in the class, we misspelled this function, using a lower-case o. Finally, the error in line 88 is the same as the one in line 37. We fix all these errors:

```
15   class histogram {
16   private:
17     int categories[size];  // Contains 1776, ..., 1945
18     int frequencies[size]; // Contains frequencies for
```

```
19                            // 1776, ..., 1945
20      int current;          // Next category to return
21
22      int findCat (int cat) ;
23
24  public:
25      histogram () ;
26
27      void incrCategory (int cat) ;
28
29      int categoryFreq (int cat) ;
30
31      int numberOfCategories () { return size; }
32
33      void reset () { current = 0; }
34
35      int nextCategory () ;
36  };


69  int histogram::nextCategory () {
70      // Return next year, and update current to
71      // return following year next time.
72      current++;
73      return categories[current];
74  }
```

The program compiles and almost produces the right output:

```
1805    *******
1865    *************
1908    *****
1917    ***
1929    ******
1945    *******
  14    *******
```

However, it has omitted the first year (1776) and has added a bogus year (14) at the end.

numberOfCategories and **reset** seem too simple to be wrong, so the likely culprit is either **nextCategory** or **printHistogram**. Let's trace these two functions by hand: **printHistogram** calls **reset**, which sets **current** to zero. **lines** is set to 7, and **nextCategory** is called. It increments **current** to 1 and returns **categories[1]**. We have found the error! The first year—1776—is contained in **categories[0]**, not **categories[1]**. How can we fix this? We want to *return* **categories[current]** and *then* increment **current**, but that is impossible. We'll have to increment **current** first and then return **categories[current-1]**:

```
69  int histogram::nextCategory () {
70      // Return next year, and update current to
71      // return following year next time.
72      current++;
73      return categories[current-1];
74  }
```

There is an important point to make about the previous version. We only traced it far enough to see why 1776 was skipped. But where did the 14 come from? If we had traced further, we would have found that 14 was returned from `nextCategory` after it incremented `current` to 7. In other words, it was returned as the contents of `categories[7]`. But 7 is an erroneous subscript for `categories`; as an array of seven elements, it should only allow subscripts between 0 and 6! We have here an illustration of what we said in Bug Alert 9.4 on page 403: C++ went ahead and got the eighth element of `categories` and then of `frequencies`, even though these arrays have no eighth element, without ever flagging an error. Luckily, the mistake was immediately obvious in the output.

We have arrived at our final version of the program:

```
//
// Histogram - read years and print histogram giving
// frequency of occurrence of each year.  Allowable years
// are 1776, 1805, 1865, 1908, 1917, 1929, and 1945.
//
// Author: Max Kamin
// Last modified: 7/17/95
//

#include <iostream.h>
#include <iomanip.h>

const int size = 7;

class histogram {
private:
  int categories[size];  // Contains 1776, ..., 1945
  int frequencies[size]; // Contains frequencies for
                         // 1776, ..., 1945
  int current;           // Next category to return

  int findCat (int cat) ;

public:
  histogram () ;

  void incrCategory (int cat) ;

  int categoryFreq (int cat) ;

  int numberOfCategories () { return size; }

  void reset () { current = 0; }

  int nextCategory () ;
};

histogram::histogram () {
  categories[0] = 1776;
  categories[1] = 1805;
  categories[2] = 1865;
  categories[3] = 1908;
```

```
      categories[4] = 1917;
      categories[5] = 1929;
      categories[6] = 1945;
      for (int i=0; i<size; i++)
        frequencies[i] = 0;
    }

    int histogram::findCat (int cat) {
      // Find location of cat, if any
      int i = 0;
      while (i<size && categories[i] != cat) i++;
      return i;
    }

    void histogram::incrCategory (int cat) {
      // cat is one of the years 1776, ..., 1945;
      // increment the associated frequency.
      frequencies[findCat(cat)]++;
    }

    int histogram::categoryFreq (int cat) {
      // cat is one of the years 1776, ..., 1945;
      // return the associated frequency.
      return frequencies[findCat(cat)];
    }

    int histogram::nextCategory () {
      // Return next year, and update current to
      // return following year next time.
      current++;
      return categories[current-1];
    }

    void printYear (int year, histogram& h) {
      // Print year and then print a number of asterisks
      // corresponding to the frequency of year in h.
      int freq = h.categoryFreq(year);
      cout << setw(4) << year << "   ";
      for (int j=1; j<=freq; j++)
        cout << '*';
      cout << "\n";
    }

    void printHistogram (histogram& h) {
      cout << "Historian survey\n\n"
           << "Year   Count\n\n";

      h.reset();
      int lines = h.numberOfCategories();
      for (int i=0; i<lines; i++)
        printYear(h.nextCategory(), h);
    }

    void readYears (histogram& h) {
      // Read years up to end-of-file and
      // increment their frequencies in h.
```

```
      int year;

      cin >> year;
      while (!cin.eof()) {
        h.incrCategory(year);
        cin >> year;
      }
    }

    void main () {
      histogram yearHisto;

      readYears(yearHisto);
      printHistogram(yearHisto);
    }
```

9.4

Strings

Sequences of characters—or *strings*—are usually represented in C++ using *string* arrays. The C++ compiler provides a number of functions for performing operations on arrays of characters. In this section, we will learn about some of these "library functions," as well as programming many functions on strings ourselves.

Recall from Section 7.7 of Chapter 7[1] that **char** is a built-in data type with constants written in single quotes (`'k'`, `'4'`, `'\n'`, and so on), which can be compared using `==` and `!=`. **operator>>** can be used to read a single character after skipping white space; **cin.get()** is used to read the next character in the input stream, white space or otherwise.

We can do a lot more with characters, and it can all be described easily after we emphasize a single fact: When an integer operation is applied to a character, the character is automatically converted to a number. Thus, expressions like

```
      'a'+1      '0' <= ch   'A'-'a'
```

are legal, and useful.

The number to which any character is converted follows an international convention called *ASCII* (for *American Standard Code for Information Inter-* *ASCII code* *change*). You can obtain the code for any particular character by converting it to an integer and printing it; the easiest way to do this is to assign it to an integer variable. Thus,

```
      main () {
        int i;
        i = 'a';
        cout << "The ASCII code for 'a'" << " is " << i << "\n";
      }
```

---

[1]The first part of that section, which introduces the **char** data type, can be read independently of the rest of Chapter 7.

Upper-case letters		Lower-case letters		Digits		Special Characters	
A	65	a	97	0	48	bell	7
B	66	b	98	1	49	tab	9
C	67	c	99	2	50	newline	10
D	68	d	100	3	51	space	32
E	69	e	101	4	52	!	33
F	70	f	102	5	53	"	34
G	71	g	103	6	54	#	35
H	72	h	104	7	55	$	36
I	73	i	105	8	56	%	37
J	74	j	106	9	57	&	38
K	75	k	107			'	39
L	76	l	108			(	40
M	77	m	109			)	41
N	78	n	110			*	42
O	79	o	111			+	43
P	80	p	112			,	44
Q	81	q	113			-	45
R	82	r	114			.	46
S	83	s	115			:	58
T	84	t	116			;	59
U	85	u	117			<	60
V	86	v	118			=	61
W	87	w	119			>	62
X	88	x	120			?	63
Y	89	y	121			@	64
Z	90	z	122			[	91
						\	92
						]	93
						^	94
						_	95
						{	123
						|	124
						}	125
						~	126

FIGURE 9.7   ASCII codes for some characters.

has output

```
The ASCII code for 'a' is 97
```

Similarly, you can convert an integer back to a character. The statements

```
main () {
  char ch = 85;
  cout << "85 is the ASCII code for " << ch << "\n";
}
```

print

```
85 is the ASCII code for U
```

Tables giving the ASCII code of every character are widely available. Instead of simply presenting such a table, we'll write a program to generate it. For this program we rely on the fact that in the ASCII coding scheme the groups of lower-case letters, upper-case letters, and digits all have codes that are consecutive integers. For example, `'a'+1` is the code for `'b'`, `'S'+1` is the code for `'T'`, `'2'+1` is the code for `'3'`, and so on. Thus, the program

```
main () {
  int i;
  char c;
  for (i = 'a'; i <= 'e'; i++) {
    c = i;
    cout << "Character: " << c << ", ASCII code: " << i << "\n";
  }
}
```

prints

```
Character: a, ASCII code: 97
Character: b, ASCII code: 98
Character: c, ASCII code: 99
Character: d, ASCII code: 100
Character: e, ASCII code: 101
```

For our program, we'd like the output to be arranged neatly in four columns. In addition to the letters and digits, our table includes some of the special characters, like arithmetic operators and the newline character. The output we want is shown in Figure 9.7.

```
#include <iostream.h>
#include <iomanip.h>

enum boolean {false, true};

void printCharOrSpaces (
          int seqnum,    // which character in its sequence
          int firstChar, // first character in this sequence
          int seqmax     // number of characters in sequence
          )
{
  // Print character whose ASCII code is seqnum+firstChar,
  // unless seqnum > seqmax;  in that case, print spaces
  int code = seqnum+firstChar;
  char ch = code;
  if (seqnum > seqmax)
    cout << setw(6) << " ";
  else
    cout << ch << "   " << setw(3) << code;
}

int specialCodes[34];

void printSpecial (int i) {
  // print i-th special character; i <= 33.
  int code = specialCodes[i];
```

```
    char specialChar = code;
    switch (code) {
      case 7:    cout << "  bell "; break;
      case '\t': cout << "  tab  "; break;
      case '\n': cout << "newline"; break;
      case ' ':  cout << " space "; break;
      default:   cout << "    " << setw(5) << specialChar;
    }
    cout << "  " << setw(3) << code;
  }

  main () {
    int i;

    specialCodes[0] = 7;
    specialCodes[1] = 9;
    specialCodes[2] = 10;
    for (i=3; i<=17; i++) specialCodes[i] = 32+(i-3);
    for (i=18; i<=24; i++) specialCodes[i] = 58+(i-18);
    for (i=25; i<=29; i++) specialCodes[i] = 91+(i-25);
    for (i=30; i<=33; i++) specialCodes[i] = 123+(i-30);

    cout << "  Upper-case    Lower-case"
         << "                  Special\n";
    cout << "   letters      letters"
         << "        Digits       Characters\n\n";

    for (i=0; i<34; i++) {
      cout << "    ";
      printCharOrSpaces(i, 'A', 25);
      cout << "      ";
      printCharOrSpaces(i, 'a', 25);
      cout << "        ";
      printCharOrSpaces(i, '0', 9);
      cout << "        ";
      printSpecial(i);
      cout << "\n";
    }
  }
```

Notice how characters are converted to integers and back; indeed, aside from the way they are printed by operator<<, it is hard to detect any difference between them. Many manipulations involving characters depend on viewing them as integers. A simple example is a function to convert upper-case letters to lower-case:

```
    char upperToLower (char ch) {
      if ('A' <= ch && ch <= 'Z')
        // ch is an upper-case letter
        return ch + ('a'-'A');
      else
        return ch;
    }
```

'A', 'Z', and ch are converted to integers for the comparisons: 'A' to 65, 'Z' to 90, and ch to its ASCII code. If the ASCII code is between 65 and 90, ch is indeed an upper-case letter. Now, 'a' and 'A' are converted to their ASCII codes (97 and 65) for the calculation ch + ('a'-'A'), so the effect is to add $97 - 65 = 32$

to the code of **ch**. If **ch** is **'A'**, this gives $65 + 32 = 97$, the code for **'a'**; if **ch** is **'B'**, this gives $66 + 32 = 98$, the code for **'b'**; and so on. This code is returned from the function and is converted back to a character in the process, because **char** is the return type of the function. For example,

```
cout << upperToLower('G');
```

prints **g**.

The functions **isDigit** and **charToInt**, used in Chapter 8 (page 374), can be coded more concisely using character codes. **isDigit** takes an input character and returns a boolean value indicating whether that character is one of the digits **'0'**, ..., **'9'**. **charToInt** takes such a digit character and returns the corresponding integer value, 0 for **'0'**, 1 for **'1'**, and so on, up to 9 for **'9'**. Using the automatic conversion from **char** to **int**, these become easy to code:

```
boolean isDigit (char ch) { return (ch >= '0' && ch <= '9'); }

int charToInt (char ch) { return ch - '0'; }
```

Note carefully the difference between the number that **charToInt** returns (the numeric value corresponding to decimal digit **ch**) and the ASCII value of **ch**.

With this understanding of characters, we can return to the discussion of *strings*. Strings are just arrays of characters, with one additional property: The useful part of the array is terminated by a special character, called the *null character*, which is written **'\0'** (backslash-zero) and has ASCII code 0. Thus, a string is a character array containing a null character. When a string is used, the characters after the null character are ignored. The length of the array determines the largest string that it can hold. An array of length n can hold a string consisting of $n - 1$ characters and the null character, so the smallest is of length zero. Some examples of strings are

string

null character

| t | o | p | \0 | | | | | | |
(maximum useful length 9; 3 used)

| b | o | t | t | o | m | \0 | | | |
(maximum useful length 9; 6 used)

| \0 | | | | | | | | | |
(empty string; no useful characters)

The use of **\0** as a terminator, or *sentinel*, character, gives strings a limited ability to grow and shrink. The length of the array containing the string limits the maximum length of the string, but the string—that is, the characters up to the null character—can grow and shrink within it.

sentinel

This representation of character strings is standard in C++, and many library functions are written for it. Furthermore, whenever you write a string in double quotes—**"This is a string"**—C++ creates a null-terminated array just big enough to hold it, namely one more than the number of characters in the string:

| T | h | i | s | | i | s | | a | | s | t | r | i | n | g | \0 |

The "empty" locations in this array contain the space character (ASCII code 32).

Character arrays can be initialized using string notation, and, as with integer arrays, you may omit the size of the array and let C++ compute it:

```
char date[20] = "February 2, 1980";
char time[] = "eight o'clock";
```

date is a 20-element array containing characters F, e, b, and so on up to character 0, followed by the null character; the last four locations are not initialized. time is a 14-element array, just large enough to hold the characters e, i, and so on, plus the terminating null character.

We present some simple examples to get the basic idea of working with strings. Finding the length of the useful part of a string is a matter of iterating over the array looking for the null character:

```
int strlen (char str[]) {
  // Compute length of str
  int i = 0;
  while (str[i] != 0)
    i++;
  return i;
}
```

Note that comparing a character to the null character '\0' is equivalent to comparing it to the integer 0, because the null character is converted to its ASCII code (which is zero) for the comparison.

Another example of a string-processing function is the function **strcpy**, which copies one string into another. It is essentially the same as the array-copying loop shown on page 399, except that it terminates when it reaches the null character.

```
void strcpy (char target[], char source[]) {
  // Copy source to target
  int i = 0;
  while (source[i] != 0) {
    target[i] = source[i];
    i++;
  }
  target[i] = 0;
}
```

Note the purpose of the last line: The loop terminates after detecting the null character in **source**, before it is has been copied into **target**.

strcpy allows us to fill character arrays with specific strings, like this:

```
char str[10];
strcpy(str, "Patty");
```

BUG ALERT 9.6   **Leave an Extra Position in Character Arrays**

When deciding how large a character array you need, don't forget to take into account the one extra location you need for the null character.

Note that

```
char str[10];
str = "Patty";
```

is illegal. You may not assign an entire array to another, but you may copy the individual elements from one into another.

An example that combines strings and integer arrays is the following function to check whether two strings are anagrams of one another—words made from rearranging the same set of letters (ignoring case). We maintain two arrays of 26 integers each and use these arrays to count the frequency of each letter in each string. Then we compare the two arrays. If they have the same count for each character, the two strings are anagrams:

```
 1   const int sizeOfAlphabet = 26;
 2
 3   int *charCount (char str[]) {
 4     int *counts = new int[sizeOfAlphabet];
 5     int i;
 6     for (i=0; i<sizeOfAlphabet; i++)
 7       counts[i] = 0;
 8     i = 0;
 9     while (str[i] != 0) {
10       counts[upperToLower(str[i])-'a']++;
11       i++;
12     }
13     return counts;
14   }
15
16   boolean equalArrays (int A[], int B[], int size) {
17     for (int i=0; i<size; i++)
18       if (A[i] != B[i]) return false;
19     return true;
20   }
21
22   boolean anagram (char str1[], char str2[]) {
23     return equalArrays(charCount(str1),
24                        charCount(str2),
25                        sizeOfAlphabet);
26   }
```

The heart of the anagram program consists of the two functions **charCount** and **equalArrays**.

charCount is given a string **str** containing upper- and lower-case letters. To count the number of occurrences of each letter in **str**, **charCount** allocates a 26-element integer array in the heap (line 4) and initializes it to zeros. Then it iterates over the elements of **str** (the loop starting at line 9), and, for each letter, it calculates its position in the alphabet and increments the corresponding location in **counts**. The key line is line 10:

```
counts[upperToLower(str[i])-'a']++;
```

Suppose **str[i]** is the letter **d**. It is lower-case, so the call to **upperToLower** just returns it; subtracting **a** returns the integer 3, and **counts[3]** is incremented. If `str[i]` is an upper-case letter, `upperToLower` returns its lower-case counterpart, so subtracting **a** results in an integer between 0 and 25. Thus, after going through the entire string, `counts` contains the frequency count of each character in `str`. It is returned as the result of `charCount`.

`equalArrays` compares two integer arrays, returning `true` if the corresponding variables in each array contain the same value. The `anagram` function is simple: It calls `charCount` twice and then calls `equalArrays` to compare the results of the two calls to `charCount`.

An important operation on strings is comparing them to see which comes *lexicographic order* first in alphabetic, or *lexicographic*, order. This is the natural order for printing strings in many applications.

In lexicographic ordering, two strings,

s =	s[0]	s[1]	s[2]	$\cdots$	s[m-1]	\0	$\cdots$

t =	t[0]	t[1]	t[2]	$\cdots$	t[n-1]	\0	$\cdots$

are compared as follows: First compare `s[0]` to `t[0]`. If `s[0]` precedes `t[0]` in the alphabet (which can be determined by comparing them using `operator<`, which will compare their ASCII codes), then **s** alphabetically precedes **t** (**s < t**); if `t[0]` precedes `s[0]`, **t < s**; if `s[0] = t[0]`, we don't have an answer yet and need to repeat the process with `s[1]` and `t[1]`, and so on. If we run out of characters in **s** before coming to a decision—that is, `s[i] = t[i]` for all $i < m$— then either **s** is a prefix of **t** ($m < n$), in which case **s < t**, or the strings are equal ($m = n$). Similarly, if we run out of characters in **t** first, and $n < m$, then **t < s**.

The function `boolean less (char a[], char b[])` returns `true` if a precedes b lexicographically:

```
boolean less (char a[], char b[]) {
  int i = 0;
  while (b[i] != 0) {
    if (a[i] == 0) return true;
    else if (a[i] < b[i]) return true;
    else if (a[i] > b[i]) return false;
    i++;
  }
  return false;
}
```

This function can be written more neatly using recursion; see Section 9.5.1.

Note that the ordering given by `less` depends directly on the ASCII codes of the characters and can sometimes be surprising. For example, `Zorro` precedes `abracadabra`, because the ASCII code of **z** is less than that of **a**. To ignore case when doing comparisons—which you normally want to do—`less` has to be repaired:

```
boolean less (char a[], char b[]) {
  int i = 0;
  char ai = upperToLower(a[i]),
       bi = upperToLower(b[i]);
```

```
    while (bi != 0) {
      if (ai == 0) return true;
      else if (ai < bi) return true;
      else if (ai > bi) return false;
      i++;
      ai = upperToLower(a[i]);
      bi = upperToLower(b[i]);
    }
    return false;
  }
```

A number of the operations we've written on strings—or operations very similar to them—are already available in the "string library." If you put

```
    #include <string.h>
```

at the start of your program, you automatically obtain definitions of **strlen**, **strcpy**, and many other useful functions. Another function defined there is

```
    int strcmp (char *s1, char *s2)
```

which is a more general version of **less**; it compares **s1** and **s2** lexicographically, returning a negative number if **s1** is less than **s2**, a positive number if **s2** is less than **s1**, and zero if they are equal. We have listed the functions available in **string.h** in Appendix C.

Exercises—Third Set

☞　1. Write the following functions on strings:
　　(a) **void upcase (char *)** changes all lower-case letters in its argument to upper-case.
　　(b) **char *join (char *, char *)** creates a new string (in the heap) and copies into its first argument followed by its second argument. For example, **join("The rockets' ", "red glare")** returns a pointer to a string in the heap containing **The rockets' red glare**.
　　(c) **char *joinInOrder (char *, char *)** is similar to **join**, but it appends the strings in lexicographic order, so that the calls **joinInOrder("ab", "cd")** and **joinInOrder("cd", "ab")** both return a pointer to the string **abcd**.
　　(d) **void squeezeSpaces (char *)** removes all space characters in its argument by moving following nonspace characters over the spaces. Thus, if **str** contains the string **Four score and seven years** before it is passed to **squeezeSpaces**, it will contain **Fourscoreandsevenyears** afterwards.

☞　2. Write a program to read characters from the keyboard and echo them with one change: Any lower-case letter that follows a period (possibly with intervening space or newline characters) is capitalized.

　　3. Write a function to compute the value of a string as a Scrabble® word: All letters are worth 1 point, except D and G are worth 2 points; B, C, M, and P are worth 3 points; F, H, V, W, and Y are worth 4 points; K is worth 5 points; J and X are worth 8 points; and Q and Z are worth 10 points. Use an array of 26 integers to store the values of the letters.

　　4. Write a program to read characters from the keyboard (up to end of file) and calculate the number of characters, the number of lines (that is, the number of newline

characters), and the number of words (sequences of nonblank characters, where a blank character is a space, newline, or tab).

5. Word-processing programs ignore multiple spaces and line breaks in the user's input and simply place as many words on each line as possible, with one space between each pair of words. Write a program to do this line-filling, with lines of length `lineLength` (a symbolic constant). If a word is too big to fit on one line, break it into as many lines as necessary.

6. Extend your program from Exercise 5 to fill out lines to the width of the column. Spaces should be added between words as evenly as possible.

7. The *rail-fence cipher* provides a simple way to encrypt a message. The message is written with alternate letters on each of two rows (ignoring spaces), and the encrypted form is read row by row and put into groups of five letters. For example, the message

       BEWARE THE IDES OF MARCH

   is written

       B W R T E D S F A C
       E A E H I E O M R H

   and thus enciphered as

       BWRTE DSFAC EAEHI EOMRH

   Write a program that reads a string from the keyboard and writes the rail-fence encrypted version.

★ 8. Write a *self-reproducing* C++ program. That is, the program should print an exact copy of itself.

9.5

Sorting Arrays

sorting   *Sorting* is the operation of placing an array of data into a given order. The problem has already been described in Section 8.7, where `mergeSort` was presented. Sorting is a very common operation in computers, and one for which many algorithms are known.

In this section we present two simple sorting algorithms and one complicated one. The simple algorithms, *selection sort* and *insertion sort,* run rather slowly for large arrays, but for small ones they do well. The complicated algorithm, *quicksort,* is a beautiful example of recursion and one of the crown jewels among computer algorithms.

We will look closely at the efficiency of the three algorithms we present. Because sorting is a common and time-consuming operation, computer scientists have continually sought more efficient methods. As we will see, the difference in efficiency between two algorithms can be tremendous.

9.5.1 Processing Arrays Recursively

The basic idea of writing a recursive function, as expounded in Chapter 8, is to *assume* the function works for smaller values. For arrays a "smaller" value means a shorter array. In many cases, it is not necessary actually to construct a smaller array. Instead, you can use a subarray. A *subarray* of an array **A** is a contiguous set of elements of **A**. It can be represented by two subscripts: the lower and upper bounds of the subarray.

subarray

For example, the following function sums the elements of the subarray of **A** given by **lo** and **hi**, that is, the elements **A[lo], A[lo+1], ..., A[hi]**:

```
float sum (float A[], int lo, int hi) {
  float theSum = 0.0;
  for (int i=lo; i<=hi; i++)
    theSum = theSum + A[i];
  return theSum;
}
```

The entire array can be summed by calling **sum(A, 0, size-1)**, where **size** is the length of **A**.

Subarrays are especially useful for writing functions recursively, which often results in cleaner code. *Assume* that the function works on smaller subarrays and use that ability to compute the answer for *this* subarray. Then, of course, handle the base cases.

Consider **sum** again. We need to compute the sum of the subarray **A[lo]** ... **A[hi]**. Assume that **sum** will correctly compute the sum of any smaller subarray, such as **A[lo+1]** ... **A[hi]**. How can we use that value to find the sum of **A[lo]** ... **A[hi]**? Easy: Add **A[lo]** to it.

```
float sum (float A[], int lo, int hi) {
  return A[lo] + sum(A, lo+1, hi);
}
```

What is an appropriate base case? In other words, what is the smallest subarray **sum** can be given as an argument? If **lo** = **hi**, the subarray has one element, which is small, but we may as well allow **hi** to be less than **lo**, indicating a subarray of zero elements:

```
float sum (float A[], int lo, int hi) {
  if (hi < lo)
    return 0.0;
  else
    return A[lo] + sum(A, lo+1, hi);
}
```

Another example of subarrays is the array-reversal problem we studied in Section 9.2. Consider how you might use subarrays to write **reverse-InPlace** (page 408). In defining **reverseInPlace(float A[], int lo, int hi)**, we assume that we can reverse any subarray smaller than **A[lo]** ... **A[hi]**. How does this help? Suppose we reverse the elements in **A[lo+1]** ... **A[hi-1]**. Then all we need to do is swap **A[lo]** and **A[hi]** to reverse the entire subarray.

```
void reverseInPlace (float A[], int lo, int hi) {
   reverseInPlace(A, lo+1, hi-1);
   swap(A[lo], A[hi]);
}
```

What are appropriate base cases? Again, as long as the subarray `A[lo]...A[hi]` has at least one element, the recursive solution works. However, in the case of a one-element subarray—that is, when `lo=hi`—`swap` does nothing. So we will use one-element subarrays as the base cases:

```
void reverseInPlace (float A[], int lo, int hi) {
   if (hi > lo) { // subarray has more than one element
      reverseInPlace(A, lo+1, hi-1);
      swap(A[lo], A[hi]);
   }
}
```

The idea of using subarrays is illustrated by each of the sorting algorithms in this section. Before we go on to those, here is one more example: the lexicographic ordering function on strings, **less**, from page 432. The recursive structure of this function is very simple: If the lexicographic comparison of two strings is not settled by their first characters, then lexicographically compare the substrings obtained by removing the first characters. Thus, the substrings are those starting at some point within the strings and including the rest of the array. Since the upper bound on the subarrays is always the same, we don't bother to pass it as an argument.

```
boolean less (char a[], char b[], int lo) {
   if (b[lo] == '\0')
      return false;
   else if (a[lo] == '\0')
      return true;
   else if (a[lo] != b[lo])
      return (a[lo] < b[lo]);
   else
      return less(a, b, lo+1);
}

boolean less (char a[], char b[]) {
   return less(a, b, 0);
}
```

The following are base cases:

- When **b** is empty, in which case **a** is certainly not less
- When **a** is empty but **b** is not, in which case **a** is less
- When both are nonempty and the first characters are different, in which case the comparison of the strings depends upon the comparison of those characters

9.5.2 Selection Sort

selection sort   *Selection sort* is perhaps the simplest of all sorting methods. It follows a natural scheme for sorting items by hand:

Starting with an array **A**, find the smallest item and place it at the front:

27	12	3	18	11	7

Find the next smallest item and place it in the second position:

3	12	27	18	11	7

Do the same for the third item:

3	7	27	18	11	12

And the fourth item:

3	7	11	18	27	12

Finally, the fifth item:

3	7	11	12	27	18

A is now sorted:

3	7	11	12	18	27

Selection sort can be written using subarrays. In the diagram of selection sort we first looked at the entire array (or, to put it differently, the subarray A[0] ... A[5]). After placing the smallest element in A[0], we ignored that position and proceeded to sort the subarray A[1] ... A[5]. We proceeded with smaller and smaller subarrays, finally sorting A[4] ... A[5]. In short, to sort A[lo] ... A[hi], place the minimum element in A[lo] and then sort A[lo+1] ... A[hi].

This discussion suggests that if we have a function findMinimum that locates the smallest element in a subarray, selection sort can be written with a simple use of recursion:

```
void selectionSort (float A[], int lo, int hi) {
  // A[0]..A[lo-1] contain the smallest values in A,
  // in ascending order.
  if (lo < hi) { // subarray has more than one element
    swap(A[lo], A[findMinimum(A, lo, hi)]);
    selectionSort(A, lo+1, hi);
  }
}
```

The function int findMinimum (float A[], int lo, int hi) returns the location of the smallest value in the subarray A[lo] ... A[hi]. It is itself recursive: The smallest element in the subarray A[lo] ... A[hi] is either A[lo] or the smallest element in the subarray A[lo+1] ... A[hi], depending on which is smaller.

```
int findMinimum (float A[], int lo, int hi) {
  if (lo == hi)
    return lo;
  else {
    int locationOfMin = findMinimum(A, lo+1, hi);
    if (A[lo] < A[locationOfMin])
      return lo;
    else
      return locationOfMin;
  }
}
```

The sequence of arrays displayed on page 437 gives an exact trace of the call selectionSort(A, 0, 5), when A is the array pictured there.

Let's analyze the cost—that is, the running time—of this algorithm. Consider first the cost of findMinimum. Letting n = hi - lo, we see that the recurrence relation describing the time for a call to findMinimum is exactly the same as the one given on page 336:

$$T(n) = \begin{cases} a & \text{if } n = 0, \\ b + T(n-1) & \text{if } n \geq 1. \end{cases}$$

Here a is the cost of the comparison lo == hi, $T(n-1)$ is the cost of the recursive call to findMinimum, and b is the cost of the comparison A[lo] < A[locationOfMin]. Thus, we can reach the same conclusion as we did on page 336: findMinimum runs in time linear in the size of the subarray; in other words, it is a $\Theta(n)$ algorithm.

The selectionSort function itself satisfies a different recurrence relation. Letting $n = $ hi - lo again, the time $T(n)$ to run selection sort satisfies the equation

$$T(n) = \begin{cases} a & \text{if } n = 0, \\ bn + T(n-1) & \text{if } n \geq 1. \end{cases}$$

Now we have the term bn on the second line: On a subarray of length n, selectionSort not only recursively sorts a subarray of length $n - 1$ (giving the $T(n - 1)$ term) but also performs an operation that takes time $\Theta(n)$—namely, the call to findMinimum. A solution to this recurrence can be obtained by repeated substitution:

$$\begin{aligned}
T(n) &= nb + T(n-1) \\
&= nb + [(n-1)b + T(n-2)] = 2nb - b + T(n-2) \\
&= 2nb - b + [(n-2)b + T(n-3)] = 3nb - 3b + T(n-3) \\
&= 3nb - 3b + [(n-3)b + T(n-4)] = 4nb - 6b + T(n-4) \\
&\vdots \\
&= n^2 b - \sum_{i=1}^{n-1} ib + T(0) \\
&= n^2 b - (n^2/2 - n/2)b + T(0) \\
&= n^2 b/2 - nb/2 + a
\end{aligned}$$

Thus, selection sort is $\Theta(n^2)$. To see just how efficient or inefficient this might be, we ran the program

```
const int size = 1000;

main () {
  float A[size];
  for (int i=0; i<size; i++) A[i] = i;
  selectionSort(A, 0, size-1);
}
```

with **size** = 1000, 2000, 4000, 8000, and 16,000. This table shows the characteristic quadratic behavior, in which *doubling* the size of the array *quadruples* the running time:

Array size	1000	2000	4000	8000	16,000
Running time for selection sort, in seconds	4.3	17.6	69.1	278.3	1120.8

By contrast, the running time of an $n \log n$ algorithm like **mergeSort** only slightly more than doubles when the length of the list doubles. Thus, selection sort is comparatively slow for long arrays. However, it is quite fast for short ones.

9.5.3 Insertion Sort

Insertion sort is nearly as simple as selection sort, and also nearly as slow, but it has a property that is often useful: The closer an array is to being sorted, the faster insertion sort works.   *insertion sort*

Insertion sort is based on another natural method of sorting by hand:

Starting with array **A**, sort the first two elements:

27	12	3	18	11	7

Move the third element so that the first three are sorted:

12	27	3	18	11	7

Move the fourth element so that the first four are sorted:

3	12	27	18	11	7

Move the fifth element so that the first five are sorted:

3	12	18	27	11	7

Move the sixth element so that all six are sorted:

3	11	12	18	27	7

A is now sorted:

3	7	11	12	18	27

The recursive structure of insertion sort is perhaps even simpler than that of selection sort. As usual, we ask how solving a smaller problem can help us solve the problem at hand; specifically, how can the (assumed) ability to sort arrays of length $n - 1$ be used to sort an array of length n? The answer is really simple, as shown above: Sort the array of length $n - 1$ and then insert the nth element in the proper place in that sorted array. In terms of subarrays, this says: To sort subarray `A[0]...A[hi]` (here, we only need subarrays whose lower bound is zero), sort `A[0]...A[hi-1]` and then insert `A[hi]` into that subarray. `insertInOrder(A, hi, x)` inserts `x` into subarray `A[0]...A[hi-1]` (using location `A[hi]` to allow for the extra element). Insertion sort looks like this:

```
void insertionSort (float A[], int hi) {
  // Sort  A[0] ... A[hi]
  if (hi > 0) {
    insertionSort(A, hi-1);
    insertInOrder(A, hi, A[hi]);
  }
}
```

The function `insertInOrder` moves an element into a subarray. Its recursive structure is also simple: To insert `x` into subarray `A[0]...A[hi-1]`, do one of two things: If $x \geq$ `A[hi-1]`, just place `x` into `A[hi]`; if $x \leq$ `A[hi-1]`, move `A[hi-1]` into `A[hi]` and insert `x` into subarray `A[0]...A[hi-2]`:

```
void insertInOrder (float A[], int hi, float x) {
  // Insert x into A[0] ... A[hi-1], filling in
  // A[hi] in the process.  A[0] ... A[hi-1] are sorted.
  if (hi == 0 || A[hi-1] <= x)
    A[hi] = x;
  else {
    A[hi] = A[hi-1];
    insertInOrder(A, hi-1, x);
  }
}
```

worst-case

Insertion sort is harder to analyze than selection sort, because its running time depends upon exactly what is in `A`. However, if we make *worst-case* assumptions, it appears to be $\Theta(n^2)$: Because a call to `insertInOrder` can take time proportional to `hi` (that is, linear in the size of the subarray), the analysis will exactly mirror that of selection sort. In fact, this worst-case running time is achieved when `A` is initially sorted in descending order.

We will run insertion sort, again on arrays of sizes 1000, 2000, 4000, 8000, and 16,000, using this main program, which calls `insertionSort` on an array that is sorted in descending order:

```
const int size = 1000;

main () {
  float A[size];
  for (int i=0; i<size; i++) A[i] = size-i;
  insertionSort(A, size-1);
}
```

The results are given in the following table:

Array size	1000	2000	4000	8000	16,000
Running time for insertion sort, in seconds	4.2	16.7	67.6	273.9	1080.1

The times are almost identical to those for selection sort. However, there is a big difference. Selection sort will have this running time regardless of the contents of **A**, even if **A** is already sorted, but consider the efficiency of insertion sort in that case: Whenever **insertInOrder** is called, **x** will be larger than any element in the subarray **A[0]...A[hi-1]**, so that **insertInOrder** will do nothing but place **x** in **A[hi]**. In other words, **insertInOrder** will run in constant, rather than linear, time. This completely changes the recurrence relation governing **insertionSort**, and we find that in this case **insertionSort** runs in linear time. We can attempt to confirm this analysis by running this main program:

```
main () {
  float A[size];
  for (int i=0; i<size; i++) A[i] = i;
  insertionSort(A, size-1);
}
```

Indeed, this runs so fast we can barely measure it:

Array size	1000	2000	4000	8000	16,000
Running time for insertion sort, in seconds	0.0	0.0	0.0	0.1	0.1

Partially sorted arrays give times that are between these extremes. Here are tests of several different arrays:

- Every odd-even pair of elements is inverted, but the array is otherwise sorted. That is, it looks like

1	0	3	2	5	4	7	6	$\cdots$	999	998

We can test **insertionSort** on this array by running the main program above, but with the following loop to initialize **A**:

```
for (int i=0; i<size; i+=2) {
  A[i] = i+1;
  A[i+1] = i;
}
```

The program again runs extremely fast:

Array size	1000	2000	4000	8000	16,000
Running time for insertion sort, in seconds	0.0	0.0	0.0	0.1	0.2

- The array is split into two halves, each of which is sorted, but the elements in the first half are all larger than those in the second half:

500	501	502	$\cdots$	998	999	0	1	$\cdots$	499

The initializing loop for this array is

```
for (int i=0; i<size/2; i++) {
  A[i] = size/2 + i;
  A[size/2 + i] = i;
}
```

The timing results are

Array size	1000	2000	4000	8000	16,000
Running time for insertion sort, in seconds	2.1	8.6	34.1	137.1	541.6

This is considerably faster than sorting an array in descending order—about twice the speed.
- The sequences $0, 1, \ldots, \texttt{size}/2 - 1$ and $\texttt{size}/2, \texttt{size}/2 + 1, \ldots, \texttt{size} - 1$ are interleaved:

0	500	1	501	$\cdots$	499	999

obtained from the loop

```
for (int i=0; i<size/2; i++) {
  A[2*i] = i;
  A[2*i+1] = size/2 + i;
}
```

The timing results are

Array size	1000	2000	4000	8000	16,000
Running time for insertion sort, in seconds	1.0	4.2	16.7	67.6	272.3

We see that in the worst case, insertion sort, like selection sort, takes time quadratic in the size of the array. It is possible to show—though the mathematics is beyond the scope of this book—that the "average" cost of insertion sort, taken over all possible arrangements of an n-element array, is quadratic in n. However, unlike selection sort, it can be much more efficient for arrays that are partially sorted.

9.5.4 Quicksort

Quicksort[2] is an elegant and ingenious divide-and-conquer sorting method, perhaps the best all-around method known. It can, in principle, run as slowly as selection sort, but in practice it almost always runs as fast as merge sort.

quicksort

Quicksort makes clever use of the subarray concept. To sort **A**, first move all the smaller elements of **A** into the bottom half and all the larger elements into the top half, and then sort the two halves recursively. If every element in the bottom half is less than every element in the top half, then after we sort the two halves, the entire array will be sorted. More specifically, given that **A** is of size **size**, do the following steps:

1. *Partition* **A** into its smaller elements and its larger ones, placing the smaller ones in positions **A[0]** ... **A[m-1]** for some **m** (not necessarily in order), the larger ones in positions **A[m+1]** ... **A[size-1]** (not necessarily in order), and the "middle" element in **A[m]**. Thus, the array **A**,

5	27	12	3	18	11	7	19

might be partitioned as

5	7	3	11	12	27	18	19

with **m** = 4.

2. *Recursively sort* **A[0]** ... **A[m-1]**. In our example, **A** becomes

3	5	7	11	12	27	18	19

3. *Recursively sort* **A[m+1]** ... **A[size-1]**. In our example, **A** becomes

3	5	7	11	12	18	19	27

[2]It is traditional in computer science to write "quicksort" as a single word.

The overall structure of the `quickSort` function, then, is

```
int partition (float A[], int lo, int hi) {
    <Choose middle element among A[lo] ... A[hi]>
    <move other elements so that A[lo] ... A[m-1] are all less
    than A[m] and A[m+1] ... A[hi] are all greater than A[m]>
    <m is returned to the caller>

    ...

}

void quickSort (float A[], int lo, int hi) {
    int m;

    if (hi > lo+1) { // there are at least 3 elements,
                     // so sort recursively
        m = partition(A, lo, hi);
        quickSort(A, lo, m-1);
        quickSort(A, m+1, hi);
    }
    else // 0, 1, or 2 elements, so sort directly
        if (hi == lo+1 && A[lo] > A[hi])
            swap(A[lo], A[hi]);
}
```

The base case in this recursion occurs when the subarray `A[lo]`...`A[hi]` contains either zero elements ($lo = hi+1$), one element ($lo = hi$), or two elements ($lo = hi-1$). If the subarray contains no elements, we ignore it. If it contains one element, it is already sorted, and there is nothing to do. If it contains two elements, then if they are out of order, they need to be swapped.

Clients sort an array `A` of length `size` by calling

```
quickSort(A, 0, size-1)
```

pivot The `quickSort` function itself is done, but the hard part remains: writing **partition**. There are really two problems here: choosing the "middle" element in the subarray and doing the partitioning. For the middle, or *pivot,* element, we want to find the *median* of the subarray `A[lo]`...`A[hi]`—the element `A[j]` such that exactly half the elements in the subarray are less than it and half are greater. Then the recursive calls in `quickSort` will sort subarrays half as long as the original array, which gives the greatest efficiency.

Unfortunately, we can't do this. There is no simple way to find the median element among `A[lo]`...`A[hi]` except to sort it and choose the element in the middle, which is what we're trying to do in the first place. Instead, we'll have to *guess* at the median element and hope for the best. In practice, a good way of choosing the pivot—that is, of guessing the median of the subarray—is to take the median of three of its elements, specifically `A[lo+1]`, `A[(lo+hi)/2]`, and `A[hi]`. This is the method we use. (See Exercise 7 at the end of this section for a further discussion of this issue.)

Having made our choice, for better or worse, we begin the partitioning process. We hope we have chosen the median of the subarray, so that the partitioning process will divide the subarray exactly in half, but there is no way to be sure.

Only when the partitioning process is done can we know how many elements are less than the pivot and how many are greater. The dividing line between these is the index we've called **m**.

Suppose our subarray looks like this at the start:

From the three highlighted elements we select the median, **A[hi]**, to be our pivot element. Swapping it with **A[lo]**, we can begin the partitioning process.

Again, we have no way of knowing how many elements are less than the pivot and how many are greater. We will shuffle the elements in **A[lo+1]...A[hi]** around so that all the elements less than the pivot (**A[lo]**) appear to the left of all the elements greater than the pivot:

Only when the partitioning is done do we see where the dividing line between the small elements and the large ones is. The integer we call **m** is the largest subscript that contains a value less than the pivot. In this example, we got a decent split, but not a perfect one: The pivot element was a bit larger than the median, so the left partition is larger than the right partition. Since we know **A[lo]** is greater than the small elements and less than the large ones, we can swap it with **A[m]**:

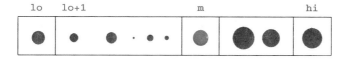

partition has now done its job. Sorting **A[lo]...A[m-1]** and **A[m+1]...A[hi]** will leave us with a sorted array.

We now describe how the partition process itself works. The **quickSort** function calls a three-argument version of **partition**, passing it the array and the low and high bounds of the subarray; **partition** returns the location **m**, where the array was split. There is a four-argument version of **partition**,

```
int partition (float A[], int lo, int hi, float pivot)
```

that does the real work. The three-argument version,

```
int partition (float A[], int lo, int hi) {
  swap(A[lo], A[medianLocation(A, lo+1, hi, (lo+hi)/2)]);
  int m = partition(A, lo+1, hi, A[lo]);
  swap(A[lo], A[m]);
  return m;
}
```

moves the pivot element into `A[lo]`, calls the four-argument `partition` to shuffle the elements in the subarray `A[lo+1]...A[hi]`, and then swaps `A[lo]` and `A[m]`. (`medianLocation` finds the middle elements among `A[lo+1]`, `A[(lo+hi)/2]`, and `A[hi]`; it will be shown on page 448.)

The four-argument version of `partition` is given a subarray and the pivot element, and does the main partitioning work: shuffling the elements in the subarray so that the elements less than the pivot precede the elements greater than the pivot. The method is based on a clever use of subarrays. As usual, we *assume* that `partition` will work on any smaller subarray, and we ask ourselves how we can use that capability to partition the subarray `A[lo]...A[hi]`.

For example, *assume* that we can partition `A[lo+1]...A[hi]`. Does that help? Indeed it does: If `A[lo] < pivot`, it is all we need! Therefore, part of the `partition` function is

```
int partition (float A[], int lo, int hi, float pivot) {
  if (A[lo] <= pivot) // A[lo] in correct half
    return partition(A, lo+1, hi, pivot);
  ...
}
```

What if `A[lo] > pivot`? In that case we know that `A[lo]` belongs in the upper half of the subarray, so we swap it with `A[hi]`. We don't have any idea where the new value of `A[lo]` belongs, since we haven't looked at it, but we do know that the new value of `A[hi]` belongs where it is, so we don't need to look at it any more. In other words, we can finish the job by partitioning the subarray `A[lo]...A[hi-1]`. This is a smaller subarray, so we *assume* that `partition` can handle it. So `partition` now looks like

```
int partition (float A[], int lo, int hi, float pivot) {
  if (A[lo] <= pivot) // A[lo] in correct half
    return partition(A, lo+1, hi, pivot);
  else {               // A[lo] in wrong half
    swap(A[lo], A[hi]);
    return partition(A, lo, hi-1, pivot);
  }
}
```

The appropriate base case here is the one-element subarray (`lo=hi`). When we see a one-element subarray, however, we have to decide whether it is a small element or a large element. If it is small (less than `pivot`), then it is at the middle point (the point referred to as `m` above); otherwise, it is just above the middle point. This observation gives us the final version of this function:

```
int partition (float A[], int lo, int hi, float pivot) {
  if (hi == lo)
    if (A[lo] < pivot)
      return lo;
    else
      return lo-1;
  else if (A[lo] <= pivot) // A[lo] in correct half
    return partition(A, lo+1, hi, pivot);
  else {                    // A[lo] in wrong half
    swap(A[lo], A[hi]);
    return partition(A, lo, hi-1, pivot);
  }
}
```

Let us illustrate this process. We'll use a six-element subarray:

The three-argument version of **partition** is called. It chooses the third element in the subarray (that is, **A[(lo+hi)/2]**) as the pivot, swaps it into **A[lo]**, and calls the four-argument version. The situation as we are about to begin the partitioning process is as follows:

At each step of the process, we place a box around the subarray being partitioned in that call; the circles outside of that box, aside from the pivot element shown in color, are already in the correct half of the subarray. Because **A[lo]** is greater than the pivot, we swap it with **A[hi]**,

and call **partition** recursively with a smaller subarray:

Because **A[lo]** is smaller than **pivot**, it is already in the correct half, so we simply call **partition** recursively, with a smaller subarray:

With `A[lo]` greater than `pivot`, we again swap,

and call **partition** recursively:

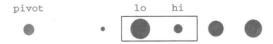

Again, `A[lo]` is greater than `pivot`, so we swap

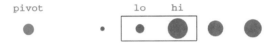

and call **partition** recursively:

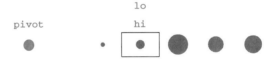

With `lo` and `hi` equal, the partitioning process is finished. Since `A[lo]` is less than the pivot, `lo` is returned as the dividing line between the two halves.

The quicksort algorithm is now complete. The function `medianLocation` finds the subscript of the median of three values in an array, given their subscripts:

```
int medianLocation (float A[], int i, int j, int k) {
  if (A[i] <= A[j])
    if (A[j] <= A[k])
      return j;
    else if (A[i] <= A[k])
      return k;
    else
      return i;
  else // A[j] < A[i]
    if (A[i] <= A[k])
      return i;
    else if (A[j] <= A[k])
      return k;
    else
      return j;
}
```

```
int partition (float A[], int lo, int hi, float pivot) {
  if (hi == lo)
    if (A[lo] < pivot)
      return lo;
    else
      return lo-1;
  else if (A[lo] <= pivot) // A[lo] in correct half
    return partition(A, lo+1, hi, pivot);
  else {                   // A[lo] in wrong half
    swap(A[lo], A[hi]);
    return partition(A, lo, hi-1, pivot);
  }
}

int partition (float A[], int lo, int hi) {
  swap(A[lo], A[medianLocation(A, lo+1, hi, (lo+hi)/2)]);
  int m = partition(A, lo+1, hi, A[lo]);
  swap(A[lo], A[m]);
  return m;
}

void quickSort (float A[], int lo, int hi) {
  int m;

  if (hi > lo+1) { // there are at least 3 elements,
                   // so sort recursively
    m = partition(A, lo, hi);
    quickSort(A, lo, m-1);
    quickSort(A, m+1, hi);
  }
  else // 0, 1, or 2 elements, so sort directly
    if (hi == lo+1 && A[lo] > A[hi])
      swap(A[lo], A[hi]);
}
```

Let's now look at the running time of **quickSort**. Superficially, it is a straightforward divide-and-conquer algorithm, like merge sort: Divide the data in half, sort each half, then combine the results. However, for quicksort, the division of the array may or may not be "in half," depending upon the choice of the pivot element in **partition**. If the array is partitioned exactly in half—that is, our guess for the median turns out to be exactly right every time—then the recursive calls sort arrays of size $n/2$. This leads to an analysis identical to the one for merge sort (page 361), with time complexity proportional to $n \log n$. On the other hand, if we are unlucky and the partitioning elements turn out very poorly—in the worst case, the second smallest or second largest element in the subarray—then the division of the subarrays is not "in half" at all. Instead, **A[lo]** and **A[lo+1]** contain the smallest values in the subarray, and subarray **A[lo+2]** ... **A[hi]** has to be sorted recursively (or **A[hi-1]** and **A[hi]** contain the largest values, and **A[lo]** ... **A[hi-2]** has to be sorted recursively). Far from dividing the array in half, the partitioning process has produced a subarray two items shorter than the one it was handed. An analysis similar to the analysis of selection sort tells us the cost of quicksort in this case will be $\Theta(n^2)$.

In fact, it is not easy to contrive examples on which quicksort will show its worst-case performance. Running it on the same cases as we used for insertion sort, the times for **quickSort** are given in the following table:

Array size, n	1000	2000	4000	8000	16000
$\boxed{0\mid 1\mid 2\mid 3\mid\cdots\mid n-1}$	0.2	0.5	1.6	4.4	13.0
$\boxed{n-1\mid n-2\mid n-3\mid\cdots\mid 1\mid 0}$	0.1	0.3	0.7	1.9	5.3
$\boxed{1\mid 0\mid 3\mid 2\mid\cdots\mid n-1\mid n-2}$	0.2	0.6	1.6	4.7	13.5
$\boxed{n/2\mid\cdots\mid n-1\mid 0\mid\cdots\mid n/2-1}$	0.1	0.3	0.9	2.3	6.5
$\boxed{0\mid n/2\mid 1\mid n/2+1\mid 2\mid\cdots}$	0.1	0.2	0.4	1.0	2.3

quickSort does far better than insertion sort and selection sort do in their worst cases, though not as well as insertion sort's best cases. Most important, if we consider the *average* performance over all possible arrangements of n values in an array, **quickSort** runs in time $\Theta(n \log n)$, whereas insertion sort is $\Theta(n^2)$—a dramatic difference.

Exercises—Fourth Set

☞ 1. Collections of objects are usually sorted by comparing only parts of those objects. For example, suppose we define the class **appointment**:

```
class appointment {
private;
   time appointmentTime;
   char description[100];
public:
   ...
};
```

where **time** is the class defined in Figure 6.10 on page 213. Two **appointment** objects will be compared by comparing the **time** objects they contain. Now suppose

```
appointment *Schedule[30];
```

contains a sequence of appointments, but it is given in the order in which the appointments were made, not in their chronological order. Rewrite **selectionSort** with prototype

```
void selectionSort (appointment *sched[], int lo, int hi)
```

and then do likewise for **insertionSort** and **quickSort**. In each case, the only movement of data should be the swapping of pointers.

2. All the sample arrays used in this section contained distinct elements, but all the algorithms can sort arrays that contain duplicate elements. The duplicates are simply bunched together, as you would expect, so that

10	3	1	3	5	10

when sorted, becomes

1	3	3	5	10	10

The question arises of whether the relative positions of duplicate elements are preserved in the sorted array. That is, if we mark the duplicate elements,

$$10_1 \quad 3_1 \quad 1 \quad 3_2 \quad 5 \quad 10_2$$

does the sorting process retain the order,

$$1 \quad 3_1 \quad 3_2 \quad 5 \quad 10_1 \quad 10_2$$

or reverse it,

$$1 \quad 3_2 \quad 3_1 \quad 5 \quad 10_2 \quad 10_1$$

or sometimes one and sometimes the other? This may not be significant when sorting arrays of numbers, but when we are sorting appointments, as in Exercise 1, the original order tells us which appointment was made first. In case of a scheduling conflict, this information can be useful.

A sorting algorithm that retains the original order of duplicate elements is called *stable*. Determine whether each of the three sorting algorithms studied in this section is stable and either explain why it is or give an example showing that it is not.

3. Rewrite **selectionSort** and **insertionSort** using only iteration (both for the functions themselves and their auxiliary functions, **findMinimum** and **insertInOrder**). Then write the **partition** function of **quickSort** in iterative form (**quickSort** itself is very difficult to write iteratively; don't try it). You may find that these versions, though not as neat, run much faster than the recursive versions we've given. This is because, with some C++ compilers, the simple act of calling a function is rather time-consuming.

4. The *bubble sort* algorithm repeatedly scans the array from left to right interchanging adjacent elements that are out of order; the scan is repeated until no out-of-order pairs are found on a scan. The name of this sorting algorithm comes from the way larger elements "bubble up" toward the right end of the array. Implement the bubble sort and compare its execution speed to the other sorting algorithms we have shown. *Note:* The bubble sort makes a good exercise, but it is inferior to insertion sort in every regard.

5. Quicksort is not especially fast in sorting small arrays. It might be improved if it were modified as follows:

```
if (hi-lo < size)
  insertionSort( ...);
else {
  ... // as above
}
```

where **size** needs to be determined by experimentation. Make this modification, comparing the times with the original version of **quickSort** on several sets of test data and different values of **size**. Is there any value of **size** on which this version consistently beats the original?

To go a little further, we can leave the individual subarrays of length **size** unsorted until the end. The array will be filled with these subarrays, which are internally unsorted but are correctly ordered among themselves. In such a case, insertion sort runs very well. So change **quickSort** to

```
if (hi-lo < size)
  ;       // do nothing
else {
  ... // as above
}
```

and call **insertionSort** after calling **quickSort**. Compare the running times of this version to those of the previous versions.

★ 6. The merge sort method described in Chapter 8 can be used with arrays. Its general structure is

```
void mergeSort (float A[], int lo, int hi) {
  if ((hi-lo) < 2)
    <sort the array directly>
  else {
    mergeSort(A, lo, (lo+hi)/2);
    mergeSort(A, (lo+hi)/2+1, hi);
    <merge the two sorted halves of A>
  }
}
```

However, the difficulty is in that last line: There is no easy way to merge two halves of **A** into a sorted whole. It is fairly simple, on the other hand, to merge the two halves into a separate array, which can then be copied back into **A**. Write the function

```
void merge (float A[], int lo, int middle, int hi, float B[])
```

which merges sorted subarrays **A[lo]...A[middle]** and **A[middle+1]...A[hi]** into **B[0]...B[hi-lo]**. Use this to finish **mergeSort** and check the timings on our sample arrays.

7. Comparisons of sorting methods based on contrived examples, such as the ones we used to test insertion sort and quicksort (see the table on page 450), cannot be relied on to predict the efficiency of these algorithms in practice. A more realistic example is an array that is completely random.

   In this exercise we will construct such an array and use it to explore the efficiency of our sorting methods, especially **quickSort**. If you place the line

   ```
   #include <stdlib.h>
   ```

   at the beginning of your program, you can call the function **float drand48()**. It returns a different floating-point number x, in the range $0 \le x < 1$, each time it is called. Furthermore, the sequence of numbers it returns is *pseudorandom*, meaning there is no apparent pattern to them. Thus, an array of **n** random numbers can be produced by a loop like this:

   ```
   float A[n];
   for (int i=0; i<n; i++) A[i] = rand();
   ```

   (a) Use such a randomly generated array to compare the three sorting methods. Letting **n** be 1000 will be enough to show the differences. Although we cannot predict exactly what sequence of random numbers you will get, you are almost sure to see these results: selection sort will be the slowest, insertion sort somewhat faster, and quicksort by far the fastest of the three.

   (b) We can use such random arrays to explore an important aspect of quicksort: the choice of the pivot element in **partition**. Recall that in choosing a pivot element, the goal is to approximate the median element of the subarray **A[lo] ... A[hi]**. We chose the median of **A[lo+1]**, **A[(lo+hi)/2]**, and **A[hi]**. We will use the random array to explore other possibilities.

      Set **n** large enough so that sorting the array with **quickSort** takes about 20 seconds (probably somewhere between 30,000 and 50,000 elements), and try the following methods of choosing the pivot element:

      - **A[lo]**. This would have been a very poor choice for our contrived examples (why?), but it should work fairly well for random data.

      - The middle element among **A[lo]**, **A[hi]**, and **A[(lo+hi)/2]**. This is almost identical to the guess we used, but you will be surprised at how poorly it performs on an array that is in strictly decreasing order. Look at the partitions obtained for this array to see why it runs so slowly.

      - A randomly-chosen element. You can generate a random integer in the range **lo ... hi** using this assignment:[3]

      ```
      int randomInt = lo + drand48()*(hi-lo+1)
      ```

      drand48() generates a number x such that $0 \le x < 1$. If, for example, **lo** = 0 and **hi** = 10, the number on the right-hand side will be $0 + 11x$, which is a number in the range $0 \le 11x < 11$. When it is assigned to **randomInt**, it will be truncated to an integer between 0 and 10, as required.

---

[3] Your compiler may produce a warning message, because you are assigning a **float** to an **int** variable. You can ignore the warning, or see Section E3.3 of Appendix E to see how to suppress it.

9.6

Tables

A common use of computers is to store large amounts of data and retrieve them quickly. Of course, "quickly" is relative, but, as we've seen in our discussion of sorting, the choice of algorithm can make the difference between a program that finishes almost instantly and one that takes so long that it is nearly useless. When data must be retrieved quickly, the way they are stored turns out to be the most crucial decision. In this section, we'll explore several ways of storing the data and compare their efficiency.

This section presents our first use of arrays of objects. In principle, there is nothing special about that, but a question arises about initialization of the objects in the array, which we will need to discuss. You will also see the first use of arrays of pointers.

Our application in this section is the construction of *concordances*—sets of all the words occurring in a piece of text. Scholars use concordances to study important books. Concordances of the Bible, for example, available in both printed and electronic form, list each word and the locations (book, chapter, and verse) of all its occurrences. The concordance that we will develop in this section is a sequence of all the words occurring in a piece of text, together with their frequency of occurrence, but not their locations. In Exercise 2 at the end of the section, you will be asked to add the location.

The overall structure of the program is shown in Figure 9.8. It consists of a class called `table`, with operations `addOccurrence` and `listEntries`. The main program repeatedly calls a function `readWord` to read the next word from the input, then calls `addOccurrence` to add that word to the concordance. When the input is exhausted, the main program calls `listEntries` to print the concordance.

The crucial part of this code, from an efficiency standpoint, is the function `addOccurrence`, which must first seek the word being added among the set of words previously seen, so that its count can be incremented. The `listEntries` function is not trivial either, because it sorts the words in order to print them; but we have `mergeSort` and `quickSort`, so we can do that job quickly.

How should we represent the table and retrieve items from it? We explore three alternatives:

- *Unsorted array.* The strings are stored in an array in the order in which they are read.
- *Sorted array.* The strings are stored in alphabetical order. This representation permits a remarkably efficient method of search, though it does not perform well overall.
- *Hash table.* The strings are stored in an array, but the position of each string is calculated from the characters in the string. This turns out to be, by far, the best representation.

After programming the `table` class using each of these representations, we'll try it on various input texts: a set of 10,000 distinct words; a set of 100

```
class word {
  // word objects are character strings plus integers
};

class table {
  // data members used to represent table

public:
  void addOccurrence (char *str) {
    // increment count for str, if it is in table
    // add it with a count of 1, otherwise
  }

  void listEntries () {
    // print concordance, in alphabetical order
  }
};

char *readWord () {
    // read the next sequence of alphabetic characters
    // from input, place in array in heap, return address
}

main () {
  char *word;
  table concordance;

  word = readWord();
  while (word != NULL) {
    concordance.addOccurrence(word);
    word = readWord();
  }

  concordance.listEntries();
}
```

FIGURE 9.8   Top-level view of concordance program.

words repeated 100 times; and the first 10,000 words of this chapter. For example, the output on the last of these inputs begins like this (due to the ASCII ordering scheme, words beginning with capitals come first):

```
A  124
ASCII  20
According  1
Accordingly  1
Actual  2
After  7
Again  1
All  1
Allocating  1
Although  2
American  1
```

We will compare the running time of each representation on each input. We will see how their performance varies according to the characteristics of the input.

Before we get to these versions of the **table** class, let's look at the book-keeping details. We can see in Figure 9.8 that there is a class **word**, containing strings (**char ***) and integers. The various table representations store **word** objects or pointers to **word** objects. The definition of this class, as well as overloadings of **operator<<** and **operator==** on **word** objects, follows. **operator==** compares only the strings contained in two **word** objects (it uses the library function **strcmp**, mentioned on page 433). We will use definitions of **<** (lexicographic ordering), **<=**, **>**, **>=**, and **!=** at various places in this section; their definitions are simple variations on the definition of **operator==** (just as for the **Integer** class in Chapter 8). Note also the one-argument constructor, which converts a string to a **word** object, and the zero-argument constructor; we will soon see why both are needed.

```
class word {
private:
  char *theString;
  int theFrequency;

public:
  word () : theString(NULL), theFrequency(0) {}

  word (char *w) : theString(w), theFrequency(1) {}

  char *getString () {return theString;}

  int getFrequency () {return theFrequency;}

  void incrFrequency () {theFrequency++;}
};

ostream& operator<< (ostream& os, word w) {
  os << w.getString() << "  " << w.getFrequency();
  return os;
}

boolean operator== (word s1, word s2) {
  return (strcmp(s1.getString(), s2.getString()) == 0);
}
```

readWord extracts the next sequence of alphabetic characters from the input stream (the boolean function **isAlphabetic** is similar to **isDigit** on page 429), allocates a character array in the heap to hold it, and returns the address of that array. It simplifies matters if we place an absolute limit on the length of the largest word; this allows us to store the characters in an array as we read them and then copy the array into the heap. We've chosen 100, arbitrarily, as the limit.

```
boolean isAlphabetic (char ch) {
  return (('a' <= ch && ch <= 'z')
      || ('A' <= ch && ch <= 'Z'));
}
```

```
char *readWord () {
  // Get next word (sequence of letters) from cin
  // Non-alphabetic character terminates word
  // Return NULL when at end-of-file
  const int maxWordSize = 100;
  char wordbuffer[maxWordSize]; // store word before
                                // copying to heap
  char *word;       // address in heap
  char ch;
  int i=0;

  ch = cin.get();
  // skip over non-alphabetic characters
  while (!cin.eof() && !isAlphabetic(ch))
    ch = cin.get();
  // ch is a letter, or at eof
  if (cin.eof()) return NULL;
  // read alphabetic characters and place in buffer
  while (isAlphabetic(ch)) {
    wordbuffer[i] = ch;
    i++;
    ch = cin.get();
  }
  wordbuffer[i] = '\0';
  // allocate array in heap, copy buffer into it
  word = new char[strlen(wordbuffer)+1];
  strcpy(word, wordbuffer);
  return word;
}
```

Notice that we have returned the string by allocating it in the heap. As we discussed on page 411, it would be a mistake to simply return the local array **word**.

We now return to the nub of the matter: the **table** class. The simplest approach is to place each word in an array without ordering the words in any way. Each time **addOccurrence** is called, the array is searched from the beginning for the word. If it is not there, it is put in an available location at the end of the array. When the **listEntries** message is sent, the array is sorted and printed.

This version of the **table** class is shown in Figure 9.9. The table is represented by an array of **word** objects, together with an integer **size** indicating how many items are currently in the array. As always when using arrays, we need to give a maximum size; we've chosen 20,000, to allow for inputs larger than our sample inputs.

Defining arrays of objects uses the same syntax as any other array declaration, as you can see in Figure 9.9:

```
word words[maxTableSize];
```

but there is a subtle problem here: C++ always insists on initializing objects, and here it will want to initialize each of the objects in this array. Where will it find the arguments to its constructors?

This is not a problem if the class has a zero-argument constructor. In that case C++ uses the zero-argument constructor on every object in the array. This is the reason for our having the zero-argument constructor in **word**.

```
const int maxTableSize = 20000;

class table {
private:
  word words[maxTableSize];
  int size;

public:
  table () : size(0) {}

  void addOccurrence (char *str) {
    word w(str);
    int i = 0;
    while (i < size && words[i] != w) i++;
    if (i == size) { // add w as new entry
      words[size] = w;
      size++;
    }
    else  // word already in table; increment count
      words[i].incrFrequency();
  }

  void listEntries () ;
};

void table::listEntries () {
  quickSort(words, 0, size-1);
  for (int i = 0; i < size; i++)
    cout << words[i] << "\n";
}
```

FIGURE 9.9   Version 1 of the `table` class: unsorted array.

An alternative to the zero-argument constructor is to use an initialization list. Just as with arrays of built-in types, an initialization list is a list of objects of the class, enclosed in braces, as in

```
time words[6] = {
  word(""), word(""), word(""), word(""), word(""), word("")};
```

You can also give a sequence of arguments to a one-argument constructor, if the class has one, as in

```
time words[6] = {
  "", "", "", "", "", "", ...
};
```

C++ will look for a constructor with the right type of argument, and apply it to each of the values in the initialization list. However, this approach won't work for us. Since `words` is an array of length `maxTableSize`, which is 20,000, the initialization list would have to be 20,000 items long! That is why we've defined a zero-argument constructor instead.

Turning to Figure 9.9, we see that **addOccurrences** first creates a **word** object (this is where the one-argument constructor **word::word (char *)** is used).

It then iterates over the array **words** until it either finds the word or reaches the end of the array (this innocent-looking loop consumes almost all the execution time of the program). If it reaches the end of the array (i = **size**), it adds **word** to the end of the array; otherwise, it increments the frequency count of **word**. **listEntries** sorts the elements of **words** from **words[0]** to **words[size-1]** and then prints them all.

How would we expect this program to perform? There are two costly steps: First, **addOccurrence** is called for each word read. It looks at the words in **words** until it either finds the word it's looking for or reaches the end. The other costly part of the computation is the sorting when **listEntries** is called.

As our first sample input, we'll use a set of 10,000 distinct words; the maximum length of any word is 20 letters. Since this input contains no repeated words, **addOccurrence** will look at every word previously read each time it is called. This will give our familiar quadratic behavior: 0 comparisons for the first word, 1 for the second, 2 for the third, ..., $n - 1$ for the nth, the total being $1 + 2 + \cdots + (n - 1) = n^2/2 - 3n/2 + 1$. So this part is likely to be quite costly. (By contrast, **listEntries** should be much more efficient, because we can use **quickSort**, which takes time proportional to $n \log n$ and so should not contribute significantly to the cost.) In fact, the program takes 136.5 seconds on our computer.

An easy case (for all the representations) is a text file containing few distinct words but many repetitions of each. Files like this occur rarely in practice, so we've concocted one by taking the first 100 words in the first input file and repeating them 100 times. The program indeed does much better on this file, running in 2 seconds.

Finally, we've taken a piece of ordinary text—the first 10,000 words of this chapter—as our last input. This sample contains 1513 distinct words. On this input, the program runs in 10.2 seconds. These results are summarized in the first line of Table 9.1 below, along with the timings for all our other versions of this program.

Our second version of **table** (Figure 9.10) is distinguished from the first only in that the words are maintained in increasing order in the array. However, this one change turns out to be very interesting. The basic idea is simple: **addOccurrence** looks for its argument in the array **words** and either finds it and increments its count or doesn't find it and has to insert it. In that case, the program

Version of `table`	Distinct words	100 words repeated	Book chapter
Version 1—unordered array	136.5	2	10.2
Version 2—ordered array	22.5	1.4	2.3
Version 3—hash table (20,000 items)	6.8	1.0	1.4
Version 4—hash table (19,991 items)	6.1	0.9	1.3

TABLE 9.1 Timings for four versions of `table`, in seconds. All inputs contain 10,000 words. The last line reflects the code shown in Figure 9.11.

```
class table {
private:
   word words[maxTableSize];
   int size;

public:
   table () : size(0) {}

   void addOccurrence (char *str) {
     word w(str);
     int i = 0;
     i = binarySearch(w, words, 0, size-1);
     if (i < size && words[i] == w) // word already in table
       words[i].incrFrequency();
     else { // words[i] > w (and words[i-1] < w, if i>0)
            // place w in position i and shift rest of words
       for (int j = size-1; j >= i; j--)
         words[j+1] = words[j];
       words[i] = w;
       size++;
     }
   }

   void listEntries () ;
};

void table::listEntries () {
   for (int i = 0; i < size; i++)
     cout << words[i] << "\n";
}
```

FIGURE 9.10   Version 2 of the `table` class: sorted array.

shifts all the words above the argument word's location in the array to the right and inserts the new element, just as was done in insertion sort.

The interesting part is *how* **addOccurrence** looks for its argument in **words**. Using arrays, **addOccurrence** has at its disposal a method of search, *binary search* called *binary search*, that is far more efficient than simply looking at each element. We now explain how binary search works and why it is so efficient.

The idea of binary search is the same as what you use when looking up a word in a dictionary. Rather than go through each page one at a time, you start by flipping to the middle. If the page you open to has words that come before the word you're looking up, you confine your interest to the pages after it; otherwise, to the pages before it. In either case, you have completely eliminated about half the dictionary from consideration. In the half that's left, you repeat the process, again eliminating about half of those pages. In short, you start in the middle and successively narrow down the search until you find your page.

search key When searching for an item—what we'll call the *search key*—in a sorted array, the approach works brilliantly. Suppose we are searching in subarray **wl[0]** ...**wl[size-1]** are occupied. Look first at **wl[(size-1)/2]**, the word right in the middle. If it equals the word you're looking for, you're done. If it is greater, you can immediately narrow your search to the subarray `wl[0]...wl[(size-1)/2-1]`; if it's less, you can narrow the search to `wl[(size-1)/2+1]...wl[size-1]`. The code reflects the recursive nature of this process:

```
int binarySearch (word w, word wl[], int lo, int hi) {
  // Search for w among wl[lo], ..., wl[hi], assuming
  // wl is sorted.  The integer returned is either the
  // location of w in wl, or the location where w
  // would be if it were in wl.
  if (lo > hi) // empty region
    return lo;
  else {
    int middle = (lo+hi)/2;
    if (wl[middle] < w)
      return binarySearch(w, wl, middle+1, hi);
    else if (wl[middle] == w)
      return middle;
    else
      return binarySearch(w, wl, lo, middle-1);
  }
}
```

The terminating condition for the search, if the key is not found, is when `lo > hi` (that is, the empty subarray).

We illustrate this process with an example, searching in an eight-element array of numbers, **A**:

4	15	19	30	36	40	51	57

We are searching for 36. We'll trace the calls to **binarySearch**, showing the value of **lo** and **hi** at each call.

First call:

lo							hi
4	15	19	30	36	40	51	57

36 is compared to `A[(0+7)/2]`—`A[3]`—which is 30. Since 36 is greater, the first four elements of the array are eliminated.

Second call:

				lo			hi
4	15	19	30	36	40	51	57

The middle element is `A[(4+7)/2]`—`A[5]`—which is 40. Since it is greater than 36, **hi** is decreased.

Third call:

		lo	hi		
4	15	19	30	36	40	51	57

Now, the middle element is `A[(4+5)/2]`—`A[4]`—which is equal to 36, so the binary search is complete and returns 4.

An important property of `binarySearch` is that when the key is not found, the index returned by the binary search process is always the index of the position into which the new element should be placed. That is, it returns the index of the smallest element greater than the key, or the index of the position at the end of the array, if the key is greater than any element in it. For example, suppose in the illustration we just gave, we had been searching for 33 instead of 36; the search would have proceeded exactly as it did, and in the next call, `lo` would have been 4, `hi` would have been 3, and we would have returned 4. This is precisely the location into which 33 should be placed. You should do some examples on your own to see how binary search works and to convince yourself that it does indeed have this property.

The performance of this function can be determined by a simple analysis using Table 8.2 on page 340. At most one recursive call is made in `binarySearch`, and either call halves the size of the subarray. Thus, the time $T(n)$ to search in a subarray of size n is subject to the equation

$$T(n) = g(n) + T(n/2)$$

where g is the cost of comparing `lo` and `hi`, computing `(lo+hi)/2`, referencing `wl[middle]`, and so on. Each of the computations that contribute to g is independent of n, so $g(n)$ is a constant; that is, $\Theta(1)$. Reading Table 8.2, with $A = 1$ and $B = 2$, we find that `binarySearch` has growth rate $\Theta(\log n)$, where n is the size of the subarray. For a 1000-element array, this means a key can be found in 10 comparisons, as compared to an average of 500 comparisons for a sequential search.

The second version of `table` does indeed have better performance than the first, as shown on the second line of Table 9.1. This is not surprising for the sample inputs that contain repetitions, since this version of the class is much more efficient than the previous one at finding words that are in the table. It is surprising, though, that it should be so much faster on the first input, which has no repetitions; there, the cost it will pay for inserting elements should be at least as high as the cost of searching for elements in the unordered case. We explore this mystery in Exercise 6 at the end of this section.

Our fundamental problem remains unresolved. We still don't have a table representation in which both search *and* insertion are fast. The quadratic factor continues to show up.

However, there is an excellent solution, that decisively beats everything else *hash table*   we've tried. It is the *hash table*,[4] and its central premise is that instead of search-

---

[4]This discussion assumes knowledge of lists, since they are used in hash tables.

ing through the table for each key starting at `words[0]`, we make mathematical "hash" of the contents of the key itself to compute a value—call it `hash(key)`, or the *hash value* of `key`—that is also a valid position in the table, and we store the key at `words[hash(key)]`. The effect is to spread the keys out in the array, so that when searching for a key, we ideally don't have to look at more than one entry in the table. The only problem is what to do if two keys have the same hash value; the answer is to store them all in a list and put the address of that list in `words[hash(key)]`.

Let us illustrate. The array starts with all its elements containing **NULL**. Now suppose we enter the word **The** and it happens that `hash("The")` is 792. We allocate a list cell containing **The** (that is, it contains a pointer to **The**), and place it in `words[792]`:

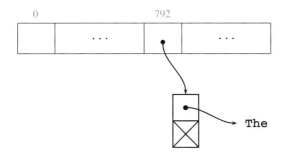

Here, the word **The** actually represents a **word** object containing a pointer to the string **The** in the heap, but for our current purposes there is no point in including all that detail.

Suppose the next three words added are **Republic** (hash value = 114), **of** (645), and **Plato** (299):

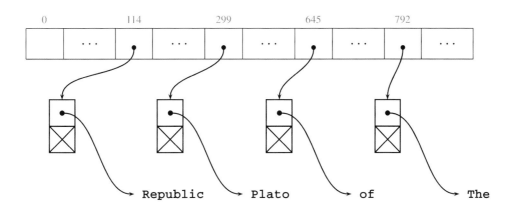

Suppose the next word is **Socrates** and its hash value is 299, the same as that of **Plato**. We look in **words[299]** and find that it is occupied, but not by **Socrates**. So we add **Socrates** to the list:

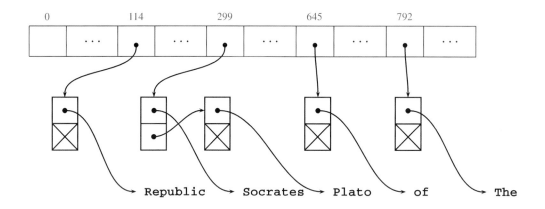

bucket   The major factor determining the efficiency of hash tables is the length of the individual lists, or *buckets*. If the array of pointers is too small, the buckets will inevitably be long, and **addOccurrence** will have to pay the cost of linear searching in each bucket. Even if the array is big enough, however, a poorly chosen hash function may place a lot of keys into just a few buckets, violating the basic principle of hash tables: spreading out the keys in the array. It has been observed that in many applications a poor hash function is the principal cause of inefficiency.

What do hash functions look like? Here's a simple one:

```
const int maxTableSize = 20000;

int hash (char w[]) {
    int i = 0, sum = 0;
    while (w[i] != 0) {
        sum = sum + w[i];
        i++;
    }
    return sum % maxTableSize;
}
```

That is, sum the ASCII codes of all the characters in the string. (We take the sum modulo **maxTableSize** in the last line, just in case we get a string so long that **sum** exceeds the size of the array, though this possibility is very remote.) However, with **maxTableSize** equal to 20,000, this hash function has an obvious weakness. Since ASCII codes for letters are all in the range 65 to 122, and since words rarely exceed ten letters, the effective range of hash values is only about 65 to 1220—barely more than 5 percent of the array. The goal of a hash function is to *spread out* the keys in the array; this function does a pretty poor job of it.

We make two improvements to this hash function to get a better spread: multiplying the running sums by 256 (the maximum integer value of a character) and changing the size of the array to a prime number, 19,991. (For reasons that go beyond what we can explain here, it is generally a good idea to choose a prime number for the size of a hash table.)

```
const int maxTableSize = 19991;

int hash(char w[]) {
  // compute hash value between 0 and maxTableSize-1
  int i = 0, sum = 0;
  while (w[i] != 0) {
    sum = (sum * 256 + w[i]) % maxTableSize;
    i++;
  }
  return sum;
}
```

The final version of the **table** class, using this hash function, is shown in Figure 9.11. Aside from the changes we've already outlined, **listEntries** changes a lot: It first has to gather up all the words into the beginning of an array and then sort them.

The class **wordList** is analogous to our other list classes. Its entries contain pointers to **word** objects. We'll use only the **find** and **print** operations, identical (except for the types) to their definitions in Section 7.4.

```
class wordList {
private:
  word *value;
  wordList *nextEntry;

public:
  wordList (word *v, wordList *next)
    : value(v), nextEntry(next)
  {}

  word *getValue () { return value; }

  wordList *getNextEntry () { return nextEntry; }

  wordList *find (word *w) ;

  void  print () {
    cout << *value << "\n";
    if (nextEntry != NULL)
      nextEntry->print();
  }
};

wordList *wordList::find (word *w) {
  if (*value == *w) return this;
  else if (nextEntry == NULL) return NULL;
  else return nextEntry->find(w);
}
```

```
const int maxTableSize = 19991;

int hash(char w[]) {
  // compute hash value between 0 and maxTableSize-1
  int i = 0, sum = 0;
  while (w[i] != 0) {
    sum = (sum * 256 + w[i]) % maxTableSize;
    i++;
  }
  return sum;
}

class table {
private:
  wordList *words[maxTableSize];

public:
  table () ;  // initialize words to all NULL

  void addOccurrence (char *str) {
    word *w = new word(str);
    // Calculate preferred location of w
    int h = hash(str);
    if (words[h] == NULL)
      words[h] = new wordList(w, NULL);
    else {
      wordList *findw = words[h]->find(w);
      if (findw == NULL)
        words[h] = new wordList(w, words[h]);
      else
        findw->getValue()->incrFrequency();
    }
  }

  void listEntries () ;
};

table::table () {
  for (int i=0; i<maxTableSize; i++)
    words[i] = NULL;
}

void table::listEntries () {
  wordList *allwords = NULL, *bucket;

  for (int j=0; j<maxTableSize; j++) {
    bucket = words[j];
    while (bucket != NULL) {
      allwords = new wordList(bucket->getValue(), allwords);
      bucket = bucket->getNextEntry();
    }
  }

  mergeSort(allwords)->print();
}
```

FIGURE 9.11 Version 3 of the `table` class: hash table.

Note that in this version of table, listEntries calls mergeSort to sort the list of words. The definition of mergeSort is identical to that given in Section 8.7 (with intList replaced by wordList), with one exception: The comparison

```
L1->getValue() < L2->getValue()
```

in merge (page 349) is changed to

```
*(L1->getValue()) < *(L2->getValue())
```

because getValue in wordList returns a word pointer and we want to compare words.

Table 9.1 on page 459 shows the timings for this version of table, as well as the timings when the first, "bogus," hash function is used. The good hash function clearly gives better performance (the gap would would increase dramatically if we increased the number of distinct words). By *instrumenting the code*—adding statements to calculate and output the sizes of the buckets—we can see why. Consider the sample input derived from this chapter (the most realistic of the three sample inputs). It contains 1319 distinct words out of a total of 10,000, so that 8681 of the calls to addOccurrence result in successful searches.

instrumenting the code

The first ("bogus") hash function produces a hash table with the following characteristics:

Number of nonempty buckets:	678
Average length of nonempty buckets:	1.9
Maximum bucket length:	8
Buckets of length 1:	359
Buckets of length 2:	156
Buckets of length 3:	82
Buckets of length 4:	37
Buckets of length 5:	19
Buckets of length 6:	18
Buckets of length 7:	5
Buckets of length 8:	2

As a simple kind of analysis, consider how many comparisons were needed to make the 8681 successful searches. We can't know exactly without further instrumenting the code, but the structure of the hash table gives us a good estimate: 8681 times the average cost of searching for any of the 1319 words in the table. The cost of searching for any of the 359 words contained in a bucket of length 1 is 1; the cost of searching for any of the 156 words that are at the beginning of a bucket of length 2 is also 1, but the cost of searching for a word at the end of a bucket of length 2 is 2; and so on. Adding up these numbers and averaging gives

$$\frac{1}{1319}(1 \times 359)$$

$$+ (1 + 2) \times 156$$
$$+ (1 + 2 + 3) \times 82$$
$$+ (1 + 2 + 3 + 4) \times 37$$
$$+ (1 + 2 + 3 + 4 + 5) \times 19$$
$$+ (1 + 2 + 3 + 4 + 5 + 6) \times 18$$
$$+ (1 + 2 + 3 + 4 + 5 + 6 + 7) \times 5$$
$$+ (1 + 2 + 3 + 4 + 5 + 6 + 7 + 8) \times 2$$
$$= 1.944$$

In other words, an average successful search in this hash table involves about two comparisons.

Mathematical analysis of hash tables shows that if n words are stored in a table of size m, and if the hash table is behaving properly, the average number of comparisons in a successful search would be

$$1 + \frac{n - 1}{2m}$$

This says that in our case, with $n = 10{,}000$ and $m = 20{,}000$, a "good" hash function would result in about 1.25 comparisons per search. By this standard, 2 comparisons per search is rather poor. The improved hash function gives rather different statistics for this input:

Number of nonempty buckets:	1281
Average length of nonempty buckets:	1.03
Maximum bucket length:	2
Buckets of length 1:	1243
Buckets of length 2:	38

The cost of the average successful search in this table is $(1243 + 38 + 2 \times 38)/1319$ $= 1.03$. The difference is reflected in the timings shown in the last two lines of Table 9.1. Though this sample is still too small to show a dramatic improvement, the sample input containing all distinct words shows the difference clearly.

The difference in the hash functions is perhaps brought out most clearly by plotting the size of each bucket. Figure 9.12 shows, for each of the 20,000 buckets, the bucket sizes used by the bogus hash function in color and the sizes of the 19,991 buckets used by the good hash function in black. (Note that although most buckets are empty—that is, of size zero—this does not show up clearly in the plot, because the lines are thicker than $1/20{,}000$ of the width of the plot.) What is most striking about this plot is that the bad hash function uses buckets only in the range 0 to 2000, less than one-tenth of the available buckets; the remaining 18,000 positions in the table may as well not exist. The good hash function, on the other hand, uses the entire table.

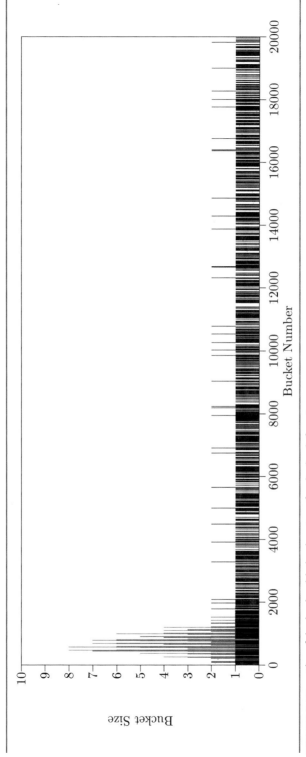

FIGURE 9.12 Plot of the hash table bucket sizes for the hash functions.

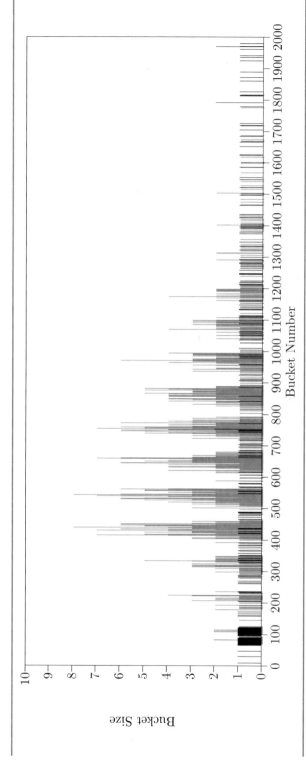

FIGURE 9.13 Plot of the hash table bucket sizes for buckets 0 to 2000 for the hash functions.

Figure 9.13 shows a magnified view of the first 2000 buckets. Here we see that not only does the bad hash function use a mere tenth of the hash table, but even within this range it distributes the words in a highly nonuniform way. Indeed, there is a simple explanation for the peaks around 430, 540, and so on: Most words consist mainly of lower-case letters, whose ASCII codes are in the range 97 to 122. Let us say, then, that the average ASCII code for a lower-case letter is 109.5. On average, then, we would expect a four-letter word to hash to 438, a five-letter word to hash to 547.5, and so on. Though the plots don't show exactly where the peaks are, we clearly see heavy concentrations of words in the general neighborhood of $n \times 109.5$ for n ranging from 2 to 11.

Exercises—Fifth Set

1. Samples of text taken from the real world tend to exhibit "locality" of reference, meaning that when a word occurs more than once, all its occurrences are likely to be close to one another. This suggests another way of representing a table, called a *self-organizing* table. In such a table, when a new word is added, it is placed in a highly accessible place, and when a new occurrence of a word already in the table is encountered, that word is moved to a more accessible place in the table. Program these three variants on the idea of a self-organizing table:
   (a) Starting from version 1 of the **table** class, modify **addOccurrence** in two ways: (1) The search for a word should start from the *end* of the array, so that words added more recently will be found more quickly. (2) When it finds a word already in the table, it moves that word one position closer to the end of the list (by swapping it with the word that follows it).
   (b) Starting from version 1 of the **table** class, modify **addOccurrence** in the same ways as in part 1(a), with this exception: When it finds a word already in the table, it moves that word all the way to the end of the table, shifting every other word down.
   (c) In version 3, the individual buckets may be self-organizing. To achieve this, modify **addOccurrence** so that when it finds a word already in the table, it moves that word to the front of its bucket.

2. When creating a concordance, one usually wants to gather more information than the number of occurrences of a word. For each word, store the number of the line on which it first occurs and the line on which it last occurs. Modify **readWord** to count line numbers (that is, newline characters) and keep the current line number in a global variable. Modify the **word** class to store the two line numbers, **table::addOccurrence** to update those numbers, and **table::listEntries** to print them.

3. Generalize your solution to Exercise 2 to store *all* line numbers on which a word occurs. Add an **intList*** data member to **word** and use it to store each line number on which the word occurs. Again, modify **table::addOccurrence** and **table::listEntries** to store and print these line numbers.

★ 4. Generalize your solution to Exercise 3 to keep the *context* of each occurrence of each word—the word that precedes it and the word that follows it. When printing the concordance, print four columns, giving the line number, the preceding word, the word, and the following word. For example, if the first word in the concordance is "a" and it occurs on lines 12, 31, 33, and 40, the start of the listing might be

```
31      in      a     list
12      in      a     sequence
33      on      a     computer
40      with    a     hundred
```

Here, we have printed the line number in a field of width 4 and each of the words in a field of width 10; the width of the last three fields should be calculated based on the longest word being printed. Furthermore, within the listing of a word—a, in this case—the occurrences are printed in alphabetical order of the preceding word; when the preceding word is the same, the ordering is based on the following word; if both the preceding and following words are the same (not shown here), the line number is used. In other words, the list should be sorted on the main word, then the preceding word, then the following word, then the line number. Do this by changing the comparison operation (**operator<**) on **word** objects.

5. Add statements to the hash table in version 3 of the **table** class to collect three numbers: average bucket length, maximum bucket length, and standard deviation of the bucket lengths. All three can have an effect on the performance of the class. The average bucket length has an obvious relation to efficiency; a single long bucket can degrade the performance considerably; and a high standard deviation, even with a low average, indicates that there may be many buckets of well above average length. Using a body of text of your own choosing, compute these values. Try to improve the performance of the class by adjusting two values: the size of the table (the larger the table the better, but even a very large table of nonprime size may do poorly; for example, try making **maxTableSize** 100,000) and the multiplier used in the hash function (for which we currently use **256**). Once you get the average bucket size down to 1.05, pick a new text of approximately the same size and try it again. Devise a hash function that gives good performance for both inputs.

6. The great improvement, shown in Table 9.1, of the ordered array over the unordered one seems rather surprising, especially as concerns the first input (10,000 distinct words). However, it may be explained by looking at the 10,000 words more closely.
   (a) What is the performance of the two versions for a sequence of words that is in strictly ascending order (that is, each word is different from, and lexicographically greater than, its predecessor)?
   (b) What is their performance if their input is in strictly *descending* order?
   (c) Test your answers to the above questions by experiment. Generate a sequence of 10,000 distinct words and run four experiments, inserting the words in ascending and descending order using the unordered and ordered array representations. (You may use more or fewer than 10,000 words if your computer is either much faster or much slower than the authors'.)
   To generate the sequence of words, just use a four-element character array and generate strings **aaa, aab,..., aaz, aba**, and so on, until you've generated the 10,000th word (**oup**). Just simulate the odometer of a car: Increment the rightmost character unless it is **z**; in that case, reset it to **a** and increment the middle character, unless it is **z**; in that case, reset it to **a** and increment the leftmost character.

★ 7. Recall the spreadsheet problem introduced in Exercise 4 on page 413. A cell can depend upon the values in other cells. We want to detect when there is a circularity in the dependencies among the cells.

In Exercise 4, we imposed the (severe) restriction that each cell could depend on at most one other cell. We can now lift this restriction, by using a more general representation of the dependencies among the cells. Represent the row of the spreadsheet (we'll still confine ourselves to a single row) by an array of n pointers to `intList`s. The ith `intList` contains the numbers of the cells on which the ith cell depends.

The input is in the form of n lines, each containing zero or more numbers in the range $0, \ldots, n-1$, terminated by -1. The numbers on the ith line are the cells on which cell i depends; if the only number is -1, the ith cell doesn't refer to any other cells.

For example, if the input is

```
-1
0 -1
1 3 -1
1 4 -1
-1
```

it indicates that cells 0 and 4 do not depend on any other cells, cell 1 depends on cell 0, cell 2 on cells 1 and 3, and cell 3 on cells 1 and 4. This would be stored internally in the form

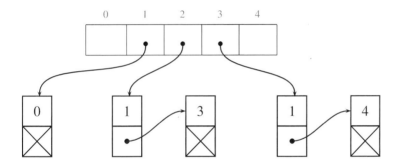

representing the abstract structure:

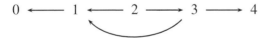

Determine whether there is a cycle in this spreadsheet. Again, use a boolean array `visited`, initialized to `false`. Define the recursive function `void visit (int vertex)`, which sets `visited[vertex]` to `true` and then recursively visits all the vertices on which `vertex` depends. If `visit` is ever called with a vertex that has already been visited, there is a cycle.

Two-Dimensional Arrays

Two-dimensional arrays, in which data are arranged in a rectangle, are common in everyday life. For example, Table 9.2 shows the annual consumption of energy in

	Coal	Natural gas	Petroleum products	Hydroelectric power	Nuclear power	Other	Total
1989	18.9	19.4	34.2	2.9	5.7	0.3	81.1
1990	19.1	19.3	33.6	3.0	6.2	0.2	81.2
1991	18.8	19.6	32.9	3.1	6.6	0.2	81.0
1992	18.9	20.3	33.5	2.8	6.7	0.2	82.2
1993	19.6	20.8	33.8	3.1	6.5	0.2	83.8
Total	95.3	99.4	160.0	14.9	31.7	1.1	409.3

TABLE 9.2   U.S. energy consumption, by source, 1989–1993, in quadrillions of Btu. (*Statistical Abstract of the United States,* 114th Ed., Bernan Press, Lanham, Maryland, 1994.)

the United States (in 10^{15} Btu) by source for the years 1989–1993. Such tables are often shown with "column totals" (in this case, these represent the total amount of energy in each source for the five years), "row totals" (total energy consumption for each year), and a "grand total" (total energy consumption for the entire five-year period).

In this section we present the fundamentals of working with two-dimensional arrays and then give two major examples: drawing shapes on a computer screen and solving systems of linear equations.

9.7.1   Two-Dimensional Array Basics

C++ provides a natural way of representing a table like Table 9.2: as a two-dimensional array. The declaration of an array **energyTable** with five rows and six columns,

```
const int numYears = 5;
const int numSources = 6;
float energyTable[numYears][numSources];
```

creates a two-dimensional array of variables, as shown in Figure 9.14. The individual variables in this array are referenced using two numbers: a row and a column number. So the top row contains variables **energyTable[0][0]**, **energyTable[0][1]**,..., **energyTable[0][5]**; the second row, variables **energyTable[1][0]**,..., **energyTable[1][5]**; and the last row, the variables **energyTable[4][0]**,..., **energyTable[4][5]**.

BUG ALERT 9.7   **Don't Use Commas for Indexing Two-Dimensional Arrays**

If you know another programming language or have seen matrices used in mathematics, you will probably be tempted to write **energyTable[0, 0]**. This is wrong, but, unfortunately, it is possible that C++ will let it pass without giving a compile-time error, so you need to be careful.

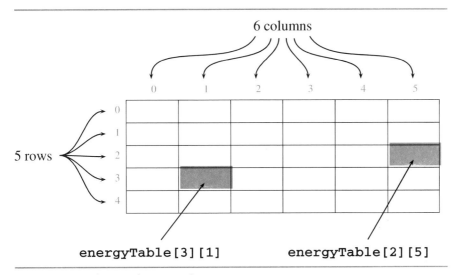

FIGURE 9.14 The two-dimensional array `energyTable`

To illustrate the use of two-dimensional arrays, we present the program to read the 30 numbers contained in the upper left part of the array shown in Table 9.2 and print the totals shown in that table. As with one-dimensional arrays, the most common method of processing two-dimensional arrays is to use a **for** loop. However, here you use *nested* **for** loops, in which the outer loop iterates over the rows (or columns) and the inner loop iterates over the columns (or rows). For example, here is a loop that reads the 30 numbers needed to fill **energyTable**, one row at a time:

```
for (int y=0; y<numYears; y++)
    for (int s=0; s<numSources; s++)
        cin >> energyTable[y][s];
```

Let's trace this. Assume that the inputs are the numbers 18.9, 19.4, . . . , 0.3, 19.1, 19.3, . . . , 0.2; that is, the input data are given in row-by-row order. The outer **for** loop sets **y** to 0 and executes the inner **for** loop; it executes the input statement six times, with **s** ranging from 0 to 5. The effect is to read the first six inputs and place them in **energyTable[0][0]**, . . . , **energyTable[0][5]**. The outer **for** loop then increments **y** to 1 and again executes the inner **for** loop. It again executes the input statement six times, reading the next six inputs into **energyTable[1][0]**, . . . , **energyTable[1][5]**. This continues until, at the fifth iteration of the outer loop, **y** is 4 and the inner loop is executed for the last time reading the last six inputs into **energyTable[4][0]**, . . . , **energyTable[4][5]**. After completion of this loop, the array is as shown in Figure 9.15.

The next step in the program is to compute the annual totals, combining all energy sources for each year. That is, for each year **y** we want to add up all the numbers **energyTable[y][s]** for all **s**. We'll store the annual totals in a one-dimensional array. We again use nested **for** loops to process **energyTable**:

	0	1	2	3	4	5
0	18.9	19.4	34.2	2.9	5.7	0.3
1	19.1	19.3	33.6	3.0	6.2	0.2
2	18.8	19.6	32.9	3.1	6.6	0.2
3	18.9	20.3	33.5	2.8	6.7	0.2
4	19.6	20.8	33.8	3.1	6.5	0.2

FIGURE 9.15 The array `energyTable`, after input loop.

	Coal	Gas	Oil	Hydro	Nuclear	Other	Total
1989	18.9	19.4	34.2	2.9	5.7	0.3	81.1
1990	19.1	19.3	33.6	3	6.2	0.2	81.2
1991	18.8	19.6	32.9	3.1	6.6	0.2	81
1992	18.9	20.3	33.5	2.8	6.7	0.2	82.2
1993	19.6	20.8	33.8	3.1	6.5	0.2	83.8
Total	95.3	99.4	168	14.9	31.7	1.1	409.3

FIGURE 9.16 Output from energy table program.

```
// Compute total energy use for each year
float yearTotals[numYears];

for (y=0; y<numYears; y++) {
  // Compute total for year y
  yearTotals[y] = 0;
  for (s=0; s<numYears; s++)
    yearTotals[y] = yearTotals[y] + energyTable[y][s];
}
```

The totals for each source are computed similarly, and the grand total is computed by summing all the yearly totals (or, equivalently, the source totals). The only trick to printing the table, aside from getting the column headings to line up nicely, is being careful to print newlines in the right places. The final program given here produces the output shown in Figure 9.16.

```
main () {
  const int numSources = 6;
  const int firstYear = 1989, numYears = 5;

  float energyTable[numYears][numSources];

  for (int y=0; y<numYears; y++)
    for (int s=0; s<numSources; s++)
      cin >> energyTable[y][s];

  // Compute total energy use for each year
  float yearTotals[numYears];
```

```
for (y=0; y<numYears; y++) {
  // Compute total for year y
  yearTotals[y] = 0;
  for (s=0; s<numYears; s++)
    yearTotals[y] = yearTotals[y] + energyTable[y][s];
}

// Compute total use of each source
float sourceTotals[numSources];

for (s=0; s<numSources; s++) {
  // Compute total for source s
  sourceTotals[s] = 0;
  for (y=0; y<numYears; y++)
    sourceTotals[s] = sourceTotals[s] + energyTable[y][s];
}

// Compute total energy use
float totalEnergy = 0;
for (y=0; y<numYears; y++)
  totalEnergy = totalEnergy + yearTotals[y];

cout << setw(7) << " "
     << setw(6) << "Coal"
     << setw(7) << "Gas"
     << setw(7) << "Oil"
     << setw(7) << "Hydro"
     << setw(9) << "Nuclear"
     << setw(6) << "Other"
     << setw(7) << "Total"
     << "\n";

for (y=0; y<numYears; y++) {
  cout << setw(6) << firstYear+y;
  for (s=0; s<numSources; s++)
    cout << setw(7) << energyTable[y][s];
  cout << setw(7) << yearTotals[y] << "\n";
}
cout << setw(6) << "Total";
for (s=0; s<numSources; s++)
  cout << setw(7) << sourceTotals[s];
cout << setw(7) << totalEnergy << "\n";
}
```

9.7.2   Passing Two-Dimensional Arrays to Functions

In the program above, we did not give a function to read the array's values, but instead placed the input loop in the main program itself. To give such a function, we need to explain how to pass two-dimensional arrays to functions; this task is slightly different from passing one-dimensional arrays.

As in the one-dimensional case, when a two-dimensional array is passed to a function, a pointer is passed. This way, assignments made to the array inside the function are seen by the caller after the function's return. However, it is *not* legal to declare the array as a simple pointer:

```
const int size = ...;

void read2DArray (float *A) {
  for (int i=0; i<size; i++)
    for (int j=0; j<size; j++)
      cin >> A[i][j];
}
```

Nor is it legal to declare it as a two-dimensional array while omitting the array bounds:

```
void read2DArray (float A[][]) {
  for (int i=0; i<size; i++)
    for (int j=0; j<size; j++)
      cin >> A[i][j];
}
```

The rule is that both array bounds can be given (as we will do in our examples), or the *first* bound may be omitted. So

```
void read2DArray (float A[size][size]) {
  for (int i=0; i<size; i++)
    for (int j=0; j<size; j++)
      cin >> A[i][j];
}
```

and

```
void read2DArray (float A[][size]) {
  for (int i=0; i<size; i++)
    for (int j=0; j<size; j++)
      cin >> A[i][j];
}
```

are both legal. The reason is that without knowing the length of a row (the second array bound), the calling function will not be able to determine how to place items in the array.

9.7.3   Initializing Two-Dimensional Arrays

Two-dimensional arrays may be initialized by nesting one-dimensional array initializers inside a set of braces. For example, `energyTable` could be declared and initialized like this (but again, this should be done only if `energyTable` is global, which is *not* the case in our program, as some C++ compilers do not permit initialization of local arrays):

```
float energyTable[numYears][numSources] =
  {
    {18.9, 19.4, 34.2, 2.9, 5.7, 0.3},
    {19.1, 19.3, 33.6, 3,   6.2, 0.2},
    {18.8, 19.6, 32.9, 3.1, 6.6, 0.2},
    {18.9, 20.3, 33.5, 2.8, 6.7, 0.2},
    {19.6, 20.8, 33.8, 3.1, 6.5, 0.2}
  };
```

You may omit the first bound (**numYears**, in this case) and C++ will determine it, but you may not omit the second.

A special case of this initialization allows for arrays of character strings. Recall from Section 9.4 that when you write a string, C++ creates a character array just large enough to hold the string (plus the terminating null character). You can use this feature to initialize an array of strings, making possible a neater version of the **printDigits** function defined on page 315.

```
char digitNames[][6] =
  {"zero", "one", "two", "three", "four",
   "five", "six", "seven", "eight", "nine"};

void printDigit (int n) { cout << digitNames[n]; }
```

Functions **printMillenary** (page 324) and **printDecade** (page 99) can also be programmed this way; see Exercise 5.

9.7.4 Drawing Shapes

An important use of two-dimensional arrays is to represent the image appearing on a computer screen. The picture is divided into a rectangular grid of *pixels* (*pic*ture *el*ements), as shown in Figure 9.17. The color to be displayed at each point is stored in an array, called a *frame buffer*, which is produced by the program and read by the video-display hardware. To change what appears on the screen,

pixel
frame buffer

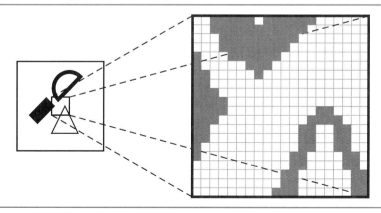

FIGURE 9.17 Picture made up of tiny pixels.

the program just has to write into the frame buffer; the new image appears instantly (to human eyes).

resolution   The number of pixels in the frame buffer—the *resolution* of the display device—varies; 1000×1000 is the approximate resolution of present-day workstation screens. By increasing the resolution while keeping the physical screen size constant, the amount of detail in displayed images can be increased; the disadvantage is the additional memory for the larger frame buffer and the greater time needed to write an image into it.

Another variable quantity is the number of available colors for each pixel. Some systems have only two—black and white—whereas some have 256 different colors, and yet others have millions. More colors are better, but again it requires additional memory if each pixel has a wide range of values.

Given a system based on a frame buffer, as we've been describing, we will draw two simple shapes: lines and circles. For our examples, we use a two-color image:

```
15    enum colors {black, white};
```

whose resolution is given by two global symbolic constants, **width** and **height**. We use a two-dimensional array to represent the frame buffer, but hide the representation in a class. We want to provide just four member functions— **clearScreen**, **displayScreen**, **drawLine**, and **drawCircle**—but we've included some others for illustrative purposes. The **drawHorizontalLine**, **drawVerticalLine**, and **drawLongLine** functions will be obsolete after **drawLine** is written; **drawLine1** is a preliminary version of **drawLine**; and **drawCircle1** is a preliminary version of **drawCircle**. We will drop these once we write **drawLine** and **drawCircle**. **setPixel** is a private member function used to set pixels in the frame buffer (after bounds checking).

```
class Screen {
private:
  colors frameBuffer[width][height];

  void setPixel (int col, int row, colors c) {
    if ((0 <= col && col < width) &&
        (0 <= row && row < height))
      frameBuffer[col][row] = c;
  }

public:
  Screen () ;

  void clearScreen () ;

  void displayScreen () ;

  void drawLine (int x1, int y1, int x2, int y2) ;

  void drawCircle (int x0, int y0, int r) ;
```

```
// Following functions are for illustrative purposes only

void drawHorizontalLine (int row) ;

void drawVerticalLine (int col) ;

void drawLongLine (float m, float b) ;

void drawLine1 (int x1, int y1, int x2, int y2) ;

void drawCircle1 (int x0, int y0, int r) ;
};

void Screen::clearScreen () {
  for (int col = 0; col < width; col++)
    for (int row = 0; row < height; row++)
      frameBuffer[col][row] = white;
}

Screen::Screen () { clearScreen(); }
```

The array is initially set to all white (a blank screen) by having the constructor call **clearScreen**. Position **fb[0][0]** represents the pixel in the upper left
corner of the screen, **fb[0][width-1]** the upper right, **fb[height-1][0]** the
lower left, and **fb[height-1][width-1]** the lower right.

Note that here the column number is the first array index, and the row number is the second; **fb[c][r]** represents the pixel at column **c**, row **r**. This follows
the convention in analytical geometry, where points are represented as pairs (x, y),
with x giving the position on the horizontal axis (the column), y the position on
the vertical axis (the row). However, the convention is not followed perfectly. In
graphics the origin (point $(0, 0)$) is taken to be the pixel in the upper left corner,
so that *higher* row numbers represent *lower* screen positions.

As our first, rather trivial, examples, these functions draw horizontal and
vertical lines, respectively, completely across the screen:

```
78   void Screen::drawHorizontalLine (int row) {
79     for (int col = 0; col < width; col++)
80       setPixel(col, row, black);
81   }
82
83   void Screen::drawVerticalLine (int col) {
84     for (int row = 0; row < height; row++)
85       setPixel(col, row, black);
86   }
```

We have no way to draw our frame buffer on a computer screen,[5] but in
general, **displayScreen** will have the form

---

[5]There *is* a way to do this, of course, but it goes beyond the scope of this book. More importantly,
there is no *portable* way to do it—that is, no way that will work on all computers.

```
void Screen::displayScreen () {
  for (int row = 0; row < height; row++) {
    for (int col = 0; col < width; col++)
      if (frameBuffer[col][row] == black)
        <draw black pixel at position (row, col)>
      else
        <draw white pixel at position (row, col)>
  }
}
```

In our examples (such as Figure 9.18), we assume a 60 × 90 screen,

```
17   const int width = 90,
18             height = 60;
```

This is high enough resolution for the shapes to look decent, but low enough for you to get a more detailed view of individual pixels.

Given these functions, these lines,

```
Screen scr;
for (int row = 10; row < height; row = row+10)
  scr.drawHorizontalLine(row);
for (int col = 10; col < width; col = col+10)
  scr.drawVerticalLine(col);
scr.displayScreen();
```

produce the picture shown in Figure 9.18.

Drawing slanted lines is more challenging than drawing vertical or horizontal lines. A straight line can be described as the set of points (x, y) satisfying an equation of the form

$$y = mx + b$$

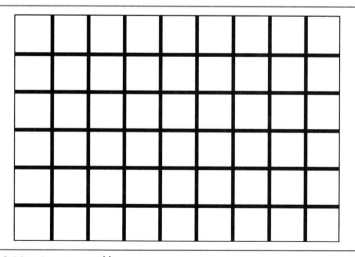

FIGURE 9.18   Drawing grid lines.

where *m* and *b* are real numbers. *m* is called the *slope*, and *b* is the *y-intercept*. The larger the value of *m*, the more vertical the line; if $m = 0$, the line is perfectly horizontal; if $m = 1$, the line is slanted at a 45° angle; if *m* is much greater than 1, the line is nearly vertical. (It is impossible, however, to describe a perfectly vertical line with this equation, because that would require an infinite slope.)

Using this equation directly, we can write a function to draw any nonvertical line across the screen.

```
88   void Screen::drawLongLine (float m, float b) {
89     for (int col = 0; col < width; col++) {
90       int row = round(m*col + b);
91       setPixel(col, row, black);
92     }
93   }
94
```

It is necessary that the slope **m** be a floating-point number, so we do our calculations in floating-point numbers. These are converted to integers to be used as screen positions. The function that does the conversion is

```
int round (float x) {
  return (x+0.5);
}
```

Recall that a floating-point number is converted to an integer by truncating the fractional part. Adding .5 and then truncating has the effect of rounding (for positive numbers), which is what we want to do here.

Given this definition of **drawLongLine**, the statements

```
scr.clearScreen();
scr.drawLongLine(.3, 2);
scr.drawLongLine(1, 5);
scr.drawLongLine(3, 10);
scr.displayScreen();
```

produce the picture shown in Figure 9.19.

There are three problems with this function. First, we don't normally want to draw a line across the screen; instead, we want to draw a line between two points. Second, this function is unable to draw vertical lines; there is no way to request it to do so, because we cannot make the first argument infinity.

The third and most subtle problem is that **drawLongLine** fails to draw all lines equally well. Notice the difference in the rendering of the top and middle lines as compared to the third line. The first two, which are more nearly horizontal than the third (with slopes of .3 and 1, respectively), look fine with one pixel drawn in each column. The third, more vertical line (slope = 3) is drawn very weakly, with only seventeen pixels to represent the entire line. (The second line has 55 pixels, though it is only about 50 percent longer than the third.) The reason for this is that **drawLongLine** draws at most one pixel per column, which makes sense only when $m \leq 1$. When $m > 1$, the line should be drawn with one pixel per *row*. To do this, we just reverse the roles of *x* and *y*, recasting

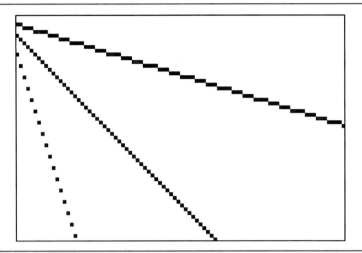

FIGURE 9.19   Drawing long lines.

the equation above as

$$x = (y - b)\big/ m$$

and iterate over the rows instead of the columns.

Including all of these improvements leads to our first version of **drawLine**.

```
95    void Screen::drawLine1 (int x1, int y1, int x2, int y2) {
96      int row, col;
97
98      if (x1 == x2) { // vertical line
99        if (y2 < y1)
100         swap(y1, y2); // force y1 <= y2
101       for (row = y1; row <= y2; row++)
102         setPixel(x1, row, black);
103     }
104     else {
105       float m = (y2-y1)/float(x2-x1),
106             b = y1-m*x1;
107       if (abs(m) < 1.0) {
108         if (x2 < x1) {   // force (x1,y1) to left of (x2,y2)
109           swap(x1, x2);
110           swap(y1, y2);
111         }
112         for (col = x1; col <= x2; col++) {
113           row = round(m*col + b);
114           setPixel(col, row, black);
115         }
116       }
117       else { // abs(m) >= 1.0
118         if (y2 < y1) {   // force (x1,y1) above (x2,y2)
119           swap(x1, x2);
120           swap(y1, y2);
121         }
```

```
122            for (int row = y1; row <= y2; row++) {
123              int col = round ((row-b)/m);
124              setPixel(col, row, black);
125            }
126          }
127        }
128    }
```

The calls

```
        scr.clearScreen();
        scr.drawLine1(45, 0, 45, 60);
        scr.drawLine1(0, 30, 90, 30);
        scr.drawLine1(10, 0, 70, 14);
        scr.drawLine1(50, 50, 55, 20);
        scr.displayScreen();
```

produce the picture in Figure 9.20. `drawLine1` can draw partial lines and vertical lines, and it draws lines with slope greater than 1 as strongly as those with slope less than 1.

`drawLine1` is not a line-drawing function that would be used in real graphics applications. It draws lines quite well, but it's slow. Drawing a single pixel requires several floating-point arithmetic operations, which are considerably slower than integer operations; when a line contains hundreds or thousands of pixels (and a larger shape may contain hundreds of lines), the cost of these operations adds up. An algorithm called *Bresenham's algorithm* draws a line using only integer arithmetic operations.

Suppose we are drawing a line between points (x_0, y_0) and (x_n, y_n), such that $x_0 < x_n$ and $y_0 \leq y_n$ and the line has a slope $\Delta y / \Delta x$ (where $\Delta y = y_n - y_0$ and $\Delta x = x_n - x_0$) that is positive and less than or equal to 1. In drawing such a line, we iterate over the columns drawing a pixel in each. Because the line is more nearly horizontal than vertical, we know that after we draw a pixel at position

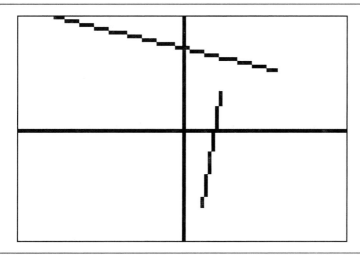

FIGURE 9.20   Drawing lines correctly.

(x_i, y_i), the next pixel will be drawn either at $(x_i + 1, y_i)$ or $(x_i + 1, y_i + 1)$. In other words, the question at each iteration is whether or not to increment the y value. J. E. Bresenham discovered that this question could be answered by doing calculations involving only integer operations.

The proper y value to use for $x_{i+1} = x_i + 1$ is simply a matter of which value, y_i or $x_i + 1$, is closer to the actual value, $y = mx_{i+1} + b$; that is, which of d_1 and d_2 is smaller, where

$$d_i = y - y_i$$
$$d'_i = y_{i+1} - y$$

(Note that d_i and d'_i are both nonnegative.) Defining

$$p_i = \Delta x(d_i - d'_i)$$

we can not only assert that $d_i > d'_i$ if and only if p_i is positive, but also prove the following:

$$p_{i+1} = \Delta x(d_{i+1} - d'_{i+1})$$
$$= p_i + 2\Delta y - 2\Delta x(y_{i+1} - y_i) \tag{9.1}$$

In other words, we can calculate every value of p_i from the previous value, and the calculation uses only integer operations. Now we only need a starting value, and it can be shown that

$$p_0 = 2\Delta y - \Delta x$$

This leads us to Bresenham's algorithm:

1. Draw (x_0, y_0) and calculate p_0.
2. Repeat for values of i from 1 to $\Delta x - 1$:
    (a) Calculate $x_{i+1} = x_i + 1$.
    (b) Calculate $y_{i+1} = y_i + 1$, if $p_i > 0$, and $y_{i+1} = y_i$, otherwise.
    (c) Draw a pixel at (x_{i+1}, y_{i+1}).
    (d) Use formula (9.1) to calculate p_{i+1}.

This code is given in Figure 9.21, but only for the case we've been discussing: $x_0 < x_n$, $y_0 \le y_n$, and a line with positive slope less than or equal to 1; we'll leave it to the exercises to finish it. The code follows the algorithm just given exactly, except that in calculating the new value of **p** it uses the fact that in formula (9.1) $y_{i+1} - y_i$ is either 0 or 1 (depending on whether $p_i > 0$) to simplify the computation.

Finally, we look at **drawCircle**. A circle is the set of points at a given distance r from a given point (x_0, y_0). Since the distance of a point (x, y) from the center (x_0, y_0) is

$$\sqrt{(x - x_0)^2 + (y - y_0)^2},$$

we can define the circle as all points (x, y) satisfying the equation

$$(x - x_0)^2 + (y - y_0)^2 = r^2$$

```
void Screen::drawLine (int x1, int y1, int x2, int y2) {
  // This version of drawLine works only if x1<x2, y1<y2,
  // and the slope of the line is positive and <= 1
  int dx = x2-x1;
  int dy = y2-y1;
  int p = 2*dy - dx;
  int x = x1,
      y = y1;
  setPixel(x, y, black);
  for (x=x1+1; x<=x2; x++) {
    if (p > 0) y++;
    setPixel(x, y, black);
    if (p < 0)
      p = p + 2*dy;
    else
      p = p + 2*(dy - dx);
  }
}
```

FIGURE 9.21   Bresenham's algorithm for drawing lines (incomplete).

Instead of using this equation directly, we can simplify the discussion by assuming that the center of the circle is at $(0, 0)$, which gives the equation

$$x^2 + y^2 \;=\; r^2$$

or

$$y \;=\; \sqrt{r^2 - x^2}$$

(where both the positive and negative roots correspond to points on the circle). When a pair (x, y) satisfying this equation is found, we just translate it to $(x_0 + x, y_0 + y)$ and draw a point there, as illustrated in Figure 9.22. This discussion leads directly to our first circle-drawing function:

```
149   void Screen::drawCircle1 (int x0, int y0, int r) {
150     int x, y;
151     int r2 = r*r;
152
153     for (x = -r; x <= r; x++) {
154       y = round(sqrt(r2 - x*x));
155       setPixel(x0+x, y0+y, black);
156       setPixel(x0+x, y0-y, black);
157     }
158   }
```

The statements

```
scr.clearScreen();
scr.drawCircle1(45, 30, 5);
scr.drawCircle1(45, 30, 15);
scr.drawCircle1(45, 30, 25);
scr.drawCircle1(45, 30, 35);
scr.displayScreen();
```

produce the output shown in Figure 9.23.

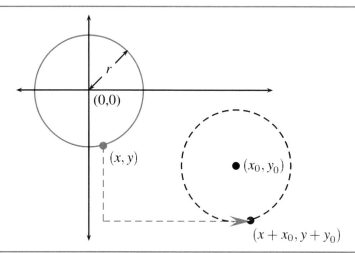

FIGURE 9.22   Compute circle relative to $(0, 0)$, then translate to (x_0, y_0).

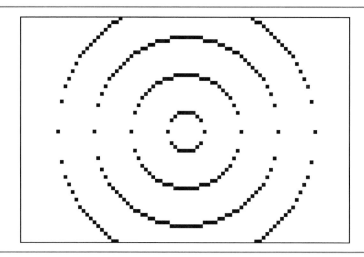

FIGURE 9.23   Drawing circles—first try.

Like **drawLongLine**, **drawCircle1** draws circles poorly, because it favors the more horizontal parts of the circle (the top and bottom), drawing them much more strongly than the sides. It is also quite inefficient because of all the calls to **sqrt**, a time-consuming function.

Both the picture quality and the efficiency of this function can be improved by observing that it is really necessary to compute only one-eighth of the points on the circle directly—those at angles between 0° and 45°, the first *octant* of the circle—and symmetry can be used to find the rest. Figure 9.24 shows how. Given a circle centered at (0, 0) and a point (*x, y*) in the first octant of the circle, we can immediately find seven other points in the other octants of the circle. The func-

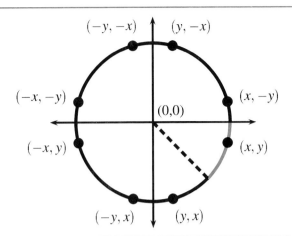

FIGURE 9.24   Computing one point on the circle gives seven others.

tion `drawCircle` makes use of this observation. It iterates over rows, selecting columns in which to draw a pixel, until the column number equals or exceeds the row number, indicating that it has exhausted the first octant. Each time it finds a point to draw in the first octant, it draws the corresponding points in the other seven octants as well.

```
160  void Screen::drawCircle (int x0, int y0, int r) {
161    int x, y;
162    int r2 = r*r;
163
164    y = 0;
165    x = r;
166    do {
167      setPixel(x0+x, y0+y, black);
168      setPixel(x0+y, y0+x, black);
169      setPixel(x0-y, y0+x, black);
170      setPixel(x0-x, y0+y, black);
171      setPixel(x0-x, y0-y, black);
172      setPixel(x0-y, y0-x, black);
173      setPixel(x0+y, y0-x, black);
174      setPixel(x0+x, y0-y, black);
175      y++;
176      x = round(sqrt(r2 - y*y));
177    }
178    while (y <= x);
179  }
```

Drawing the same circles we tried to draw in Figure 9.23 produces much more satisfactory results, shown in Figure 9.25.

Bresenham has provided a more efficient algorithm for drawing circles, following the same idea as his line-drawing algorithm; see Exercise 10.

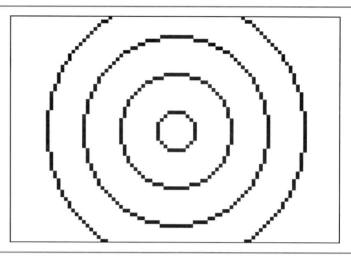

FIGURE 9.25   Drawing circles.

9.7.5 Solving Linear Systems

Our last example is one of the most basic of all mathematical computations on a computer: the solution of a system of simultaneous linear equations. This problem demonstrates the use of subarrays of two-dimensional arrays, exactly analogous to our uses of subarrays of one-dimensional arrays earlier in this chapter. It is also a lovely example of the use of recursion.

We are presented with a set of equations in the variables, or *unknowns*, x_0, ..., x_{n-1}:

$$\begin{array}{ccccccccc}
a_{00}x_0 & + & a_{01}x_1 & + & \cdots & + & a_{0,n-1}x_{n-1} & = & b_0 \\
a_{10}x_0 & + & a_{11}x_1 & + & \cdots & + & a_{1,n-1}x_{n-1} & = & b_1 \\
\vdots & & \vdots & & & & \vdots & & \vdots \\
a_{n-1,0}x_0 & + & a_{n-1,1}x_1 & + & \cdots & + & a_{n-1,n-1}x_{n-1} & = & b_{n-1}
\end{array}$$

and we need to find values for the unknowns that will satisfy all n equations simultaneously.

Gaussian elimination   The method known as *Gaussian elimination* is—with its numerous variants—the basic method used in solving such systems. It is a recursive method, which we can derive by asking our usual question: *Assuming* that we are able to solve smaller systems—say, those consisting of $n - 1$ equations in $n - 1$ unknowns—how can we use that capability to solve the n-equation system? There is a simple answer to this question: We can *eliminate* variable x_{n-1} by expressing it in terms of the remaining variables:

$$x_{n-1} = (b_{n-1} - a_{n-1,0}x_0 - \cdots - a_{n-1,n-2}x_{n-2})/a_{n-1,n-1} \qquad (9.2)$$

(if $a_{n-1,n-1}$ is not zero) and then substituting this into the other equations. For example, the first equation becomes

$$a_{00}x_0 + \cdots + a_{0,n-2}x_{n-2} + a_{0,n-1}(b_{n-1} - a_{n-1,0}x_0 - \cdots)/a_{n-1,n-1} = b_0,$$

which we can write as

$$\left(a_{00} - \frac{a_{0,n-1}a_{n-1,0}}{a_{n-1,n-1}}\right)x_0 + \cdots + \left(a_{0,n-2} - \frac{a_{0,n-1}a_{n-1,n-2}}{a_{n-1,n-1}}\right)x_{n-2}$$

$$= b_0 - \frac{a_{0,n-1}b_{n-1}}{a_{n-1,n-1}}$$

Eliminating x_{n-1} from each of the other equations in this way, we end up with $n-1$ equations in the variables $x_0, \ldots, x_{n-2}$. Solving this system—which we've assumed we can do—yields values for those variables, and we can use Equation (9.2) to find the value of x_{n-1}, solving the original system.

We need to show that the base case can be solved, but that is easy. The system of one equation in one unknown

$$ax = b$$

has the solution $x = b/a$, if $a \neq 0$.

So we might express this algorithm as

```
solve (system E of n equations in n unknowns) {
  if (n == 1)
    // system is ax = b
    return (b/a);
  else {
    eliminate last equation, yielding system E';
    solve(E'), yielding x(0), ..., x(n-2);
    x(n-1) = value obtained from equation (8.1);
    return (x(0), ..., x(n-2), x(n-1));
  }
}
```

The representation of the basic system of n equations is simple. We'll use a two-dimensional array containing the values a_{ij} and a one-dimensional array containing the values b_i:

```
float A[n][n];
float B[n];
```

As for returning the vector of values, we'll pass in an array **X** to be filled in by **solve**.

The key observation here is that we can place the coefficients of the smaller system of equations in the upper left portion of **A**. When **solve** is called, we need to tell it which subarray of **A** (and **B**) contains the system it has to solve. When **solve** is called from outside, the subarray is, of course, the entire array. In the first recursive call, it is the subarray whose lower right limit is **A[n-2][n-2]**, with right-hand sides of the equations given by **B[0]** ... **B[n-2]**. In the next recursive call, the lower right limit is **A[n-3][n-3]**, and the right-hand sides are **B[0]** ... **B[n-3]**. Thus, the recursive calls see smaller and smaller parts of the upper left portion of **A**. In the final recursive call, **solve** will be asked to solve a system whose upper and lower limits meet; that is, the only coefficient is **A[0][0]**.

Here, then, is **solve**, along with the auxiliary function **computeXi**, which performs the computation given in Equation (9.2); **eliminate** will be given subsequently.

```
void computeXi (float A[n][n], // Using A[0][0]..A[i-1][i-1]
                float B[n],    // and B[i],
                float X[n],    // and X[0]..X[i-1], compute
                int i) {       // X[i] using equation (8.1)
  float t = B[i];
  for (int j=0; j<i; j++)
    t = t - A[i][j]*X[j];
  X[i] = t/A[i][i];
}

void solve (float A[n][n], // Solve system whose coefficients
                           // are in A[0][0]..A[i][i],
            float B[n],    // with right-hand sides B[0]..B[i]
            float X[n],    // Place solutions
            int i          // in X[0]..X[i]
            ) {
  if (i == 0) // one-equation system - solve directly
    X[0] = B[0]/A[0][0];
  else {
    eliminate(A, B, i);    // eliminate Xi;  new system is in
                    // A[0][0]..A[i-1][i-1] and B[0]..B[i-1]
    solve(A, B, X, i-1);   // Fill in X[0]...X[i-1]
    computeXi(A, B, X, i); // calculate X[i] from A, B,
                           // and X[0]...X[i-1]
  }
}
```

eliminate alters the values in $A[0][0] \ldots A[i][i]$ and $B[0] \ldots B[i]$ to represent the smaller system. Since it needs to modify each of the values in each of the rows of the submatrix, a doubly nested loop structure is the clear choice.

```
void eliminate (float A[n][n], float B[n], int i) {
  // Eliminate variable xi from system whose
  // coefficients are in  A[0][0]..A[i][i],
  // with right-hand sides B[0]..B[i]
  float m;

  for (int j=0; j<i; j++) {
    m = A[j][i] / A[i][i];
    B[j] = B[j] - m*B[i];
    for (int k=0; k<i; k++)
      A[j][k] = A[j][k] - m*A[i][k];
  }
}
```

solve works fine for many examples. For example, if **n** = 3 and we provide the following values for **A** and **B** (we'll leave it to the reader to write the input loops),

$$
\text{A}: \quad
\begin{matrix}
1.0 & 1.0 & 1.0 \\
1.0 & 2.0 & 2.0 \\
1.0 & 1.0 & 2.0
\end{matrix}
\qquad
\text{B}: \quad
\begin{matrix}
1.0 \\
1.0 \\
2.0
\end{matrix}
$$

solve will find the solution **X** = 1 − 1 1.

However, **solve** can also fail. Given this input,

$$
\text{A}: \quad
\begin{matrix}
1.0 & 2.0 & 2.0 \\
2.0 & 4.0 & 4.0 \\
1.0 & 1.0 & 2.0
\end{matrix}
\qquad
\text{B}: \quad
\begin{matrix}
1.0 \\
2.0 \\
2.0
\end{matrix}
$$

the program produces this odd-looking output:

```
NaN NaN NaN
```

NaN means "not a number," indicating something's wrong. However, the *program* hasn't really failed here. This system has no solution—or rather, no unique solution—because the equations just don't contain enough information. Since the second equation is obtained from the first by multiplying both sides by 2, it adds no additional information, and what we really have is *two* equations in three unknowns. That is not enough to give a definite answer.

On the other hand, here we give the same equations as in the first example above, only in a different order:

$$
\text{A}: \quad
\begin{matrix}
1.0 & 1.0 & 2.0 \\
1.0 & 2.0 & 2.0 \\
1.0 & 1.0 & 1.0
\end{matrix}
\qquad
\text{B}: \quad
\begin{matrix}
2.0 \\
1.0 \\
1.0
\end{matrix}
$$

solve again produces the **NaN** output. This is distressing. Changing the order of the equations in a system doesn't change the solution. What has gone wrong?

We'll see the problem by printing out intermediate values, as usual. We add a call to **write2DArray** at the end of **eliminate** to print A and run it on the last example. Its output is

```
-1 -1 2
-1 0 2
1 1 1

-Inf -1 2
-1 0 2
1 1 1
```

The first array printed is **A** after one step of elimination. The important part of **A** at that point is the 2×2 array in the upper left, because this gives the coefficients in the smaller system of equations. Here we see exactly what caused the problem: **A[1][1]**, representing the coefficient of variable x_1, which we need to eliminate from this system, is zero. Remember that the elimination process works only if the coefficient $a_{n-1,n-1}$ of x_{n-1} is nonzero. Thus, even though we started with a system in which the coefficient of x_2 was nonzero, the elimination process produced a system in which the coefficient of x_1 was zero, and the attempt to solve the smaller system recursively failed.

This can be fixed easily. Although $a_{n-1,n-1}$ might be zero, at least one of the coefficients $a_{i,n-1}$ of x_{n-1} in one of the equations must be nonzero. Otherwise, there is no useful information about x_{n-1} in the entire system, and therefore no unique value for it. Furthermore, changing the order of the equations in the system won't change the order of the results. These considerations lead us to the following

partial pivoting

solution: If $a_{n-1,n-1}$ is zero, find an i such that $a_{i,n-1}$ is nonzero; then swap row i and row $n-1$, as well as the values b_i and b_{n-1}, and proceed as before. This method is known as *partial pivoting*. We've added a function `partialPivot` (with its auxiliary function `swapRows`) and then put a call to `partialPivot` in `solve`.

```
void swapRows (float A[n][n], int w, int j, int i) {
  // Swap first w+1 elements of rows j and i of A
  for (int k=0; k<=w; k++)
    swap(A[j][k], A[i][k]);
}

void partialPivot (float A[n][n], float B[n], int i) {
  // Swap rows so that A[i][i] is non-zero
  int j = i-1;
  while ((j >= 0) && (A[j][i] == 0))
    // Find row with non-zero first element
    j--;
  if (j == -1) {
    cout << "Pivoting failed:  system unsolvable\n";
    exit(1);
  }
  swapRows(A, i, j, i);
  swap(B[j], B[i]);
}

void solve (float A[n][n],  // Solve system whose coefficients
                            // are in A[0][0]..A[i][i],
            float B[n],     // with right-hand sides B[0]..B[i]
            float X[n],     // Place solutions in X[0]..X[i]
            int i) {
  if (i == 0) // one-equation system - solve directly
    X[0] = B[0]/A[0][0];
  else {
    if (A[i][i] == 0)
      partialPivot(A, B, i); // swap rows so A[i][i] != 0
    eliminate(A, B, i);      // eliminate Xi;  new system is in
                             // A[0][0]..A[i-1][i-1] and B[0]..B[i-1]
    solve(A, B, X, i-1);     // Fill in X[0]...X[i-1]
    computeXi(A, B, X, i);   // calculate X[i] from A, B,
                             // and X[0]...X[i-1]
  }
}
```

This version of **solve** produces the same answer for both arrangements of the system given above.

The time complexity of Gaussian elimination is not hard to calculate. On an $n \times n$ matrix, the first step is elimination of variable x_{n-1}; this requires that a simple $\Theta(1)$ calculation be performed for each element in the $(n-1) \times (n-1)$ submatrix, a total of $\Theta(n^2)$ time. The next step is to solve an $(n-1) \times (n-1)$ matrix recursively. On return from the recursive call, there is a linear amount of work to do to compute x_{n-1}, so we won't count that. Overall, then, the time to solve an $n \times n$ matrix is $\Theta(n^2 + (n-1)^2 + \cdots + 1)$, which is $\Theta(n^3)$. Pivoting involves only a linear amount of additional work in each call and so will not alter this result.

Exercises—Sixth Set

☞ 1. Write a program to construct and print the following *n*-by-*n* arrays, where *n* is a symbolic constant in the program.
  (a) The *identity matrix* `I`, a floating-point array that has values of 1 along the diagonal (that is, in positions `I[j][j]` for all `j` between 0 and $n - 1$) and zeros elsewhere.
  (b) The matrix `A` that has value `i+j` in location `A[i][j]`.
  (c) The matrix that has zeros around the outer border, ones just inside that, twos just inside that, and so on. For example, if $n = 5$, this matrix is

```
0 0 0 0 0
0 1 1 1 0
0 1 2 1 0
0 1 1 1 0
0 0 0 0 0
```

☞ 2. An *n*-by-*n* array is *symmetrical* if `A[i][j] = A[j][i]` for all `i` and `j`. Write a boolean-valued function of a floating-point array that returns **true** if the array is symmetrical and **false** if not.

3. The *transpose* of a square matrix `m` is the matrix `t` such that `t[i][j] = m[j][i]` for all `j` and `i`. Write a program to read in a square matrix and compute and print its transpose. Then calculate the transpose *in place*, that is, change `m` to its transpose by rearranging its elements, instead of placing the transpose into a separate array.

4. Operations analogous to those used with ordinary numbers can be defined on matrices. For example, matrices can be added "componentwise," meaning that `A+B` is the matrix `C` such that for all `i` and `j`, `C[i][j] = A[i][j]+B[i][j]`. The *zero matrix* (the matrix containing all zeros) acts as the identity for matrix addition, just as zero is the identity for addition of numbers. Define the addition operation:

```
void addMatrices (float A[n][n], float B[n][n], float C[n][n])
```

This function adds `A` and `B` and places the result in `C`.
  Matrix multiplication is more complicated. The product of `A` and `B` is the matrix `C` such that

$$C[i][j] = \sum_{k=0}^{n-1} A[i][k] \times B[k][j].$$

(The identity matrix defined above is the identity for multiplication.) Define **multMatrices** analogous to **addMatrices**.

☞ 5. Rewrite functions **printMillenary** (page 324) and **printDecade** (page 99) using arrays of character strings.

6. A maze can be represented by a two-dimensional boolean array in which true elements represent walls and false ones represent hallways, for example:

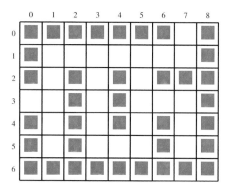

Write a program to move a mouse through a maze so represented using the algorithm in Chapter 1.

7. Complete the **drawLine** function shown in Figure 9.21.

★ 8. Add operations **drawBox** and **drawDisk** to the **Screen** class. These calls draw *filled* shapes. **drawBox** is given three corners of a rectangle and draws the rectangle with the interior filled in in black. **drawDisk** has the same arguments as **drawCircle**, but it draws the circle filled in in black.

9. Use the line-drawing operations of the **Screen** class and the **drawBox** function defined in the previous exercise to draw a checkerboard.

★ 10. Bresenham's circle-drawing algorithm has the same overall structure as his line-drawing algorithm. Suppose we are drawing the highlighted arc of the circle in Figure 9.24. Starting from the point $(r, 0)$, where r is the radius of the circle, the next point to draw is at either $(r, 1)$ or $(r - 1, 1)$. In general, in drawing this arc, if the last point drawn was (x_i, y_i), then the next point to draw is either $(x_i, y_i + 1)$ or $(x_i - 1, y_i - 1)$. We will compute quantities p_i that will indicate by their sign which of the two points to draw next. We will not explain the justification for the following formulas; you may look in any book on computer graphics for more details.

We begin at point $(x_0, y_0) = (r, 0)$ and proceed to draw pixels at points (x_i, y_i), computed as follows for $i \geq 0$:

$$(x_{i+1}, y_{i+1}) = \begin{cases} (x_i, y_i + 1) & \text{if } p_i < 0, \\ (x_i - 1, y_i + 1) & \text{otherwise,} \end{cases}$$

until we draw a point (x_i, y_i) such that $x_i = y_i$. The quantities p_i are computed as follows:

$$p_1 = 3 - 2r$$

$$p_{i+1} = \begin{cases} p_i + 4y_i + 6 & \text{if } p_i < 0, \\ p_i + 4(y_i - x_i) + 10 & \text{otherwise.} \end{cases}$$

Being able to draw this arc is the key to drawing the circle. The tasks of drawing the other seven arcs and centering the circle at a point other than $(0, 0)$ are easily accomplished in the same way we as we did them in **drawCircle**. Program Bresenham's circle-drawing algorithm and compare its performance to that of **drawCircle**.

★ 11. In Exercise 7 on page 472, you determined whether the dependencies in a spreadsheet were circular. An important part of that program was the representation of the dependency structure. We used an *n*-element array (*n* being the number of cells in the spreadsheet) containing pointers to `intLists`.

An alternative representation of that structure employs an *n*-by-*n* boolean matrix `adjacency`. If cell `i` depends on cell `j`, then `adjacency[i][j]` is set to `true`; otherwise it is set to `false`. Redo that exercise using this so-called *adjacency matrix* representation of the dependency structure.

Design a class `dependencies` that provides the operations necessary to do the spreadsheet computation but is abstract enough so that it can be implemented using either of the two representations without its clients being affected by the choice.

12. Develop a program that reads text and translates it into braille. The braille alphabet is a system of writing for the blind; it uses patterns of raised dots in a 3-by-2 array to represent letters and digits:

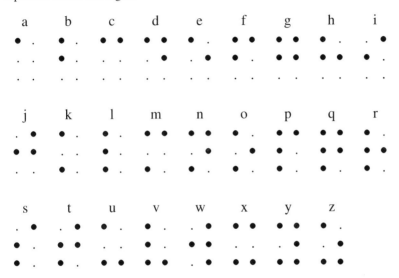

(The symbol "●" indicates a raised dot on the page; "." indicates that the paper is smooth.) The pattern

capital

. .

. .

. ●

means that the letter following is an upper-case letter. The pattern

digit

. ●

. ●

● ●

means that the letter following should be interpreted as a digit: "a" for 1, "b" for 2, . . . , "i" for 9, and "j" for 0. Your program should write three lines of output for each line of input, using an "x" to represent a "●" and a blank to represent a ".". Ignore characters other than letters and digits. Leave one space between adjacent letters and two spaces between adjacent words. Write a blank line between successive lines of braille. For instance, applied to the first sentence of this exercise, your program should produce output like this:

```
    XX X  X  X  X  X  XX  X    XX X  X  XX X  X  XX
       X  X X    XX X    X X       X  XX  X XX XX
    X          XX     X  X  X       X  X  X     X     X

    X  X  X    X  X  X  X  XX  X    X  X  XX  X  X  XX XX
    XX XX      XX XX  X     X  X  XX  X    XX      X  X
    X          X  X          X  X    XX X      X

    X  X  X  XX  X  X  X    X  X   X   X  X   X XX  X  X
    XX XX      X  X  X      XX  X  X   X  XX  X   X XX  X
    X  X      X  X  X      X      X       X      X  X  X

    X  X  X    X  X  X  X
    X  XX    X  X  X   X
       X          X  X
```

13. Write a program to translate a string of characters into Morse code. Letters (with case ignored), periods, and commas should be translated to the dot and dash sequences as shown in Table 9.3; other characters should be translated into a space, except the space, which should be translated into two spaces.

14. The American Bankers' Association font E–13B is used to print numbers on checks in magnetically readable ink. It is a simple font employing a 7 by 7 grid, as follows:

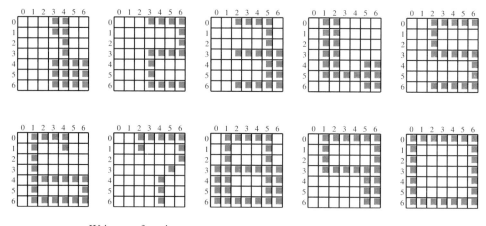

Write two functions:

(a) **void printE13B (int digit)** prints **digit** (an integer between 0 and 9), using **X**'s for the filled-in boxes and leaving the others blank.

(b) **int readE13B (boolean grid[7][7])** has as its argument an array of booleans purporting to contain a character in the E–13B font, in the obvious way. **readE13B** returns the corresponding digit, or −1 if **grid** does not contain any of the ten E–13B characters.

a	· —	h	· · · ·	o	— — —	v	· · · —
b	— · · ·	i	· ·	p	· — — ·	w	· — —
c	— · — ·	j	· — — —	q	— — · —	x	— · · —
d	— · ·	k	— · —	r	· — ·	y	— · — —
e	·	l	· — · ·	s	· · ·	z	— — · ·
f	· · — ·	m	— —	t	—	·	· — · · — · —
g	— — ·	n	— ·	u	· · —	,	— — · · — —

TABLE 9.3 The International Morse Code. (see Exercise 13)

To solve this problem, employ a *three-dimensional* array:

```
boolean E13B[10][7][7] = ...
```

Three-dimensional arrays work just as you would expect: `E13B[i][j][k]` gives the value of the `[j][k]` position in `E13B[i]`. The initialization list has braces nested three deep. With this array correctly initialized, both functions are quite simple to program. A function accepting a three-dimensional array as an argument must specify at least the second and third array bounds.

Summary

A *one-dimensional array* is a collection of variables. It is declared using the syntax

```
<type> <array name>[<size>]
```

Examples are

```
int answers[100];        // 100 integers
char firstName[20];      // 20 characters
intList *listHeads[10];  // 10 pointers to intLists
time sunrise[365];       // 365 time objects
```

Any of the variables in an array can be accessed by subscripting, as in `answers[15]` or `firstName[i]`. The valid subscripts of an array range from zero to the size of the array minus one. Furthermore, the amount of time required to obtain an element of an array is very small and *constant*; that is, it does not depend on *which* element is referenced.

When an array is passed as an argument to a function, C++ passes only the address of the first item in the array. In other words, it does not make a copy of the array. In a function, a one-dimensional array argument can be declared as an array or a pointer; it makes no difference in the programming of the function. If the argument is declared as an array, the size of the array can be omitted, allowing the function to operate on arrays of any size.

By convention, sequences of characters, or *strings*, are represented by character arrays containing the null character, `'\0'`, as a terminator. This gives strings a limited ability to grow and shrink within the bounds of the array. Include `string.h` to obtain access to some useful string functions, listed in Appendix C.

Three popular methods for sorting the contents of an array are *selection sort*, *insertion sort*, and *quicksort*. Selection sort and insertion sort have quadratic time complexity, although insertion sort runs much faster when the array is already partially sorted. Quicksort is quadratic in the worst case, but on average it has $n \log n$ time complexity; in practice, it has excellent efficiency.

Binary search is a very fast—$\log n$, where n is the size of the array—method of searching for an item in a *sorted* array. A *hash table* is a data structure in which the items that are stored are spread out evenly instead of being all bunched up. This is accomplished by computing the location of the item as a function of the item itself. For storing and retrieving large amounts of data, hash tables are extremely efficient.

A two-dimensional array is a rectangular grid of variables in which a single variable is accessed by providing *two* indices. A two-dimensional array declaration has the form

```
float USEnergy[5][6];
time monthlyAppointments[31][16];
```

Two indices must be provided to access an element: `USEnergy[year][type]`, `monthlyAppointments[14][3]`.

Two-dimensional arrays are used to represent images on a computer screen. Bresenham has provided efficient algorithms, using only integer operations, for drawing lines and circles. Another use of two-dimensional arrays is to represent matrices in mathematical calculations. An example is the solution of a system of linear equations, which can be done by the method of Gaussian elimination.

No new keywords were introduced in this chapter.

10

A Multi-File Application

Chapter Preview

Large C++ programs are broken into multiple files; in this chapter we explain how that is done. Many C++ programs obtain data from, and write results to, files; we explain how to do file input and output (I/O) in this chapter. As an illustration of these "real-life" C++ facilities, we develop a large C++ application—the largest in this book: a program that reads picture specifications in a special form and draws the specified pictures. In addition to being divided into multiple files and doing file I/O, this program involves a number of new programming concepts, including *lexing*, *parsing*, and *tree traversal*. These are the same concepts employed by C++ compilers to process C++ programs.

I n concentrating on developing algorithms, we have not covered everything you need to know to write a real, full-sized C++ program. In this chapter, we cover *multiple-file programs* (Section 10.1) and *file input and output* (Section 10.2). We then illustrate these features by developing a large application, called **psl**, for Picture Specification Language. **psl** reads files containing specifications of pictures made up of circles, squares, and rectangles and draws the specified pictures.

Programs are divided into multiple files to reduce the difficulty of editing and compiling them, to allow several programmers to work on different parts simultaneously, and to maintain a logical organization. However, breaking a program into pieces requires that certain principles be observed, the most important being that any variable, function, or class must be declared before it is used. We show how to break a program into multiple files in the first section of this chapter. This also gives us an opportunity to explain the mysterious **#include** lines that we have always placed at the beginning of our programs.

Data are stored in files on a computer, and programs often need to read their input from files or write their results into files. C++ employs similar methods for doing file input/output (*I/O*) as we have used for terminal I/O. Once we learn how to *open* files—that is, tell C++ that we want to read data from, or put data into, a particular file—we will be able to do I/O by the same methods we've been using for terminal I/O. This topic is explored in Section 10.2.

I/O

A final "real-world" topic is how to provide arguments to the program when it is first started. In Section 10.3, we cover how C++ programs read arguments from the "command line." (This discussion is applicable only to users operating in command-oriented environments such as DOS or UNIX, where program execution is initiated by typing a command, not to those using graphical environments like the Apple Macintosh or Microsoft Windows, where program execution is initiated by clicking on an icon.)

Section 10.4 introduces *context-free grammars*, a method for defining the syntax of languages like PSL and C++. Context-free grammars play an important role in defining the PSL language and writing the **psl** program.

In Section 10.5 we begin our discussion of the **psl** program. **psl** reads descriptions of simple pictures, given in a highly structured form, and draws the pictures on the screen. The **psl** program consists of about 650 lines of C++ code, broken up into twelve files. Aside from illustrating the topics discussed in Sections 10.1 and 10.2, **psl** illustrates a number of new programming concepts that are especially important in programs whose input is highly flexible although its structure conforms to strict rules. These include *lexing*, *parsing*, and *tree processing*.

Section 10.5 gives a "user's guide" for the PSL language, the language in which pictures are specified. To give a precise specification of the PSL language, we define its syntax formally, using a *context-free grammar*. This grammar will also guide us in implementing **psl**.

The bulk of the chapter is in Section 10.6, presenting the **psl** program. **psl** begins by *parsing* the picture specification, resulting in the construction of a *syntax tree*. Syntax trees are just one type of *tree structure*, an important concept in computer science. We discuss how to represent syntax trees in C++ and give several examples of tree-processing functions.

All of the C++ code for **ps1** is given in Section 10.7 at the end of the chapter.

We chose **ps1** as a final example in this text because its processing of picture specifications has a great deal in common with the processing of C++ programs by the C++ compiler. In particular, a compiler begins by parsing the program, based on a context-free grammar for C++. We point out analogies between PSL and C++ processing at various points in the chapter. The example is also a fitting conclusion to the book, as it makes use of virtually every major topic we have covered.

10.1

Separate Compilation

source file
object file

Until now, all the C++ programs we have written have been *single-file* programs. Each program was contained in a single *source file*—that is, a single file of C++ code. As shown in Figure 10.1, such a file is compiled into a single *object file*, which contains the translation of the source program into a form that the computer can directly execute, as explained in Chapter 1. The object file is sometimes called a *binary*.

When programs become very long, this simple organization has severe drawbacks. In general, the single file lacks the structure to make the program manageable; just as a program without functions is hard to understand, so is a program contained in a single file. As a result of this lack of structure, it becomes

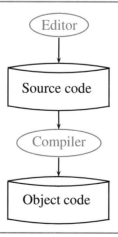

FIGURE 10.1   Compiling a single source file

difficult for a group of programmers to work on different parts of the program simultaneously, as is frequently required to complete a large program. Another drawback of a single source file is that the process of compiling takes a lot of time. In real life, many programs contain hundreds of thousands of lines of C++ code and take hours to compile. By splitting the program into multiple files, and compiling only the files that have changed, much of this time can be saved.

Therefore, programs are divided into several files, as shown in Figure 10.2. The compiler is executed separately on each source file, producing an object file for each. These object files are combined into one object file for execution by a program called the *linker*.[1] (Usually, the compiler will automatically run the linker, so you may not even be aware of its existence, but every computer has one.)

linker

The division of a program into multiple files must follow certain rules regarding the order of classes, functions, and global variables. One rule is that a function or class cannot be split into two files. That is, every opening brace ({) must have its corresponding closing brace (}) in the same file.

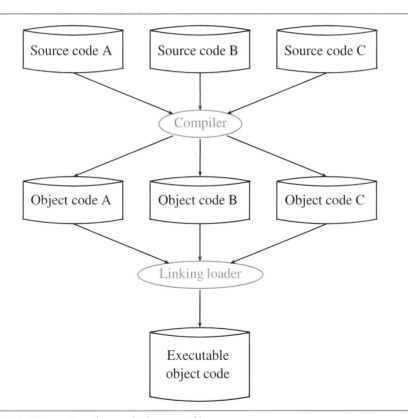

FIGURE 10.2   Compiling multiple source files

[1]The linker is also called the *linking loader* or *linkage editor*.

The most important rule about splitting programs into multiple files is that every class, function, or global variable must be *declared* before it is *used*. It does not have to be *defined*—though it can be—but it must be declared. Here is where the distinction between *declarations* and *definitions* becomes important. A declaration of a class or function gives the "basic outline" of the class or function, without completely defining it. In the case of a function, this "basic outline" is the function's *prototype* (see Section 6.3):

Function prototype	Function definition

void error (char *c) ;
or
void error (char *) ;
	void error (char *c) {
	    cout << c;
	    exit(1);
	}

In the case of a class, the basic outline includes all the data members and prototypes of all the member functions:

Class declaration

class time {
private:
    int minute, int hour;
public:
    time (int m) ;
    time addMinutes (int m) ;
    . . .
};

Usually, definitions of small functions—such as most constructors—are included in the class declaration. The definition is completed by giving the definitions of its remaining member functions. Normally, all of these member function definitions are given in one file; remember that definitions of functions given after the class must use the function's full name (for example, `time::addMinutes`).

The declaration of a global variable is the same as the *definition* of that variable, but with the word **extern** placed at the beginning:

Variable declaration	Variable definition
extern int tableSize;	int tableSize;

The keyword **extern** tells the C++ compiler that the variable is defined in a separate file. Again, every file that uses the variable must contain a *declaration* of that variable. Among all the files making up the program, exactly one must contain the variable's *definition*.

The point to remember is that clients of a function or class, or users of a variable, can be compiled as long as they have seen the *prototype* of the function or the *declaration* of the class or variable. As a simple example, the following two files can be compiled separately and then linked together to create a running program:

file1.C	file2.C
`#include <iostream.h>`	`#include <iostream.h>`
`// Declare printSquare`	`// Define printSquare`
`void printSquare (int n) ;`	`void printSquare (int n) {`
	`    cout << n << " squared = "`
`// Use printSquare`	`        << n*n << '\n';`
`main {`	`}`
`    int i;`	
`    cout << "Enter integer: ";`	
`    cin >> i;`	
`    printSquare(i);`	
`}`	

Although these two files *compile* separately, producing two object files, neither can *run* separately. After both are compiled, they must be *linked* together in order to execute. (The method of running the compiler and linker, and running the program itself, varies greatly among different systems.)

Here is another version of the program in the previous paragraph, using the global variable **n** to store the value that **printSquare** is to print:

file1.C	file2.C
`#include <iostream.h>`	`#include <iostream.h>`
`void printSquare () ;`	`int n; // definition of n`
`extern int n; // declaration of n`	
	`void printSquare () {`
`main {`	`    cout << n << " squared = "`
`    cout << "Enter integer: ";`	`        << n*n << '\n';`
`    cin >> n;`	`}`
`    printSquare();`	
`}`	

To summarize, the rule is that functions, classes, and global variables must be declared in any file in which they are used, prior to their first use. In a large, multi-file program, there may be hundreds of functions, classes, and global variables that are used in many different files. The programmer should not have to copy all those prototypes and declarations in each file, so C++ provides the `include` mechanism. If you place the line

```
#include "filename"
```

in a file and compile it, C++ looks for the file named *filename* in the current directory and inserts the contents of that file into the file being compiled. For example, we could divide the foregoing program (in the version in which **n** is a parameter) into three files with exactly equivalent results (here giving the third file the name **fundecl.h**):

file1.C	file2.C
`#include <iostream.h>`	`#include <iostream.h>`

`#include "fundecl.h"`	`void printSquare (int n) {`
	`    cout << n << " squared = "`
	`        << n*n << '\n';`
	`}`

`main {`
`    int i;`
`    cout << "Enter integer: ";`
`    cin >> i;`
`    printSquare(i);`
`}`	

fundecl.h
`void printSquare (int n) ;`

When **file1.C** is compiled, as soon as the line `#include "fundecl.h"` is read, the file **fundecl.h** is inserted in its place, so the result is indistinguishable from the previous example.

A universally respected convention in the C++ world is that function prototypes and class and global variable declarations are placed into files ending with **.h** for "header." There are usually several header files, included in varying combinations in different source files. You will often see source files with several **#include** lines at the beginning.

What about the **#include** lines you have been placing in your files from the start?

```
#include <iostream.h>
#include <iomanip.h>
```

They are similar to the one we just introduced, and do exactly what we've just explained—they insert the files **iostream.h** and **iomanip.h** into the source file. But you never created files by that name, so where do they come from? That is what the angle brackets mean: Because we include **<iostream.h>** rather than **"iostream.h"**, C++ looks for these files in a special place on your system, not in the current directory. That is the difference between **#include <***file***>** and **#include "***file***"**.

As you can tell from their names, `iostream.h` and `iomanip.h` are header files: They contain class and variable declarations and function prototypes. You can ask your system administrator where these files are and look at them. For example, `iostream.h` contains the declaration of classes `istream` and `ostream`. `istream` defines member functions such as

```
istream& istream::operator>> (char *);
istream& istream::operator>> (int&);
istream& get (char&);
```

which we have been using all along. `iomanip.h` contains declarations for `setw` and `setfill`.

The declarations in these files allow programs that use these functions to be compiled. There are also source files that define the functions declared there, but we don't see them. Instead, we get the object files containing the compiled object code implementing those functions. Object code files supplied with your compiler that contain implementations of functions declared in system header files are called *libraries*. A complete picture of the compilation process is shown in Figure 10.3.

Normally, many such libraries are included when you get a compiler. An example we have already used is the mathematical function library. To call functions such as `sqrt`, you must include `math.h`, which provides their prototypes. The object files in your program are linked with the math library to form a single object file. (Appendix B lists the prototypes of most of the functions in `math.h`.)

There is one more rule you should be aware of when attempting to divide your program into multiple files: You may not declare a class more than once. It is surprisingly difficult to avoid doing so, because you may need to include two header files, both of which need to include the same third header file. By including the first two, you are including the third twice. If that third header file contains a class declaration, you will get a compiler error. You can usually avoid this problem simply by being careful, but it can be very burdensome. A general solution is described in Section E.2 of Appendix E.

10.2

The Stream Library

The screen on your computer terminal and a file stored on your computer's disk seem totally different. Yet, they share the characteristic that characters can be written to them. Similarly, the keyboard and files share the property that characters can be read from them. To exploit this commonality, C++ employs the notion of a *stream*: a sequence of characters. There are two types of streams: those that a program can *write to* (a file or display device), and those a program can *read from* (a file or keyboard).

stream

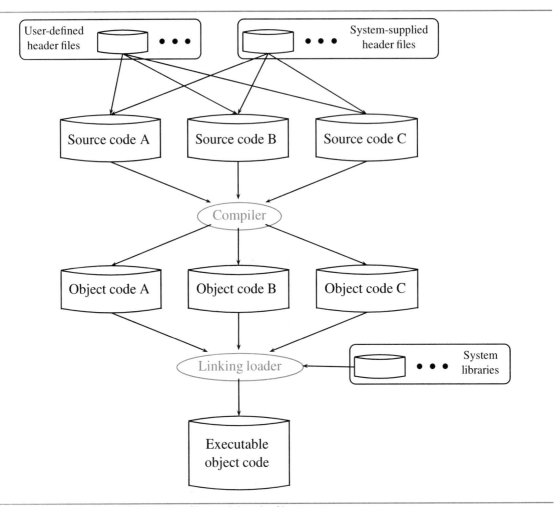

FIGURE 10.3   Compiling multiple source files, with header files

cout is an *output stream*—a variable of type **ostream**—initialized to your computer screen. As we have seen, the class **ostream** defines overloaded versions of **operator<<**, such as

```
ostream& ostream::operator<< (int)
ostream& ostream::operator<< (float)
ostream& ostream::operator<< (char)
ostream& ostream::operator<< (char *)
```

It defines many other member functions as well, but we have not used them in this book.

cin is an input stream—a variable of type **istream**—initialized to the keyboard. **istream** contains several overloaded definitions of **operator>>**, as well as two other functions we have found useful in the past:

```
istream& istream::operator>> (int&)
istream& istream::operator>> (float&)
istream& istream::operator>> (char&)
boolean istream::eof ()
char istream::get()
```

In other words, we have been using the classes `ostream` and `istream` implicitly. Their declarations are given in system header file `iostream.h`. That is why we included this header file in all our programs.

Streams associated with files are similar to `cout` and `cin` but are objects of different classes. `ifstream` is for files used only for input in a program, and `ofstream` is used for files used only for output. Both classes are declared in `fstream.h`.

We consider `ifstream` first. An `ifstream` object can be created by calling the zero-argument constructor `ifstream::ifstream ()`. The main difference between `ifstream` and `istream` is that `ifstream` is equipped with a two-argument member function,

```
void ifstream::open (char *file, int mode)
```

whose job is to "open" the file named in its first argument. *Opening a file* for input means searching the disk for a file with that name, making sure the program has permission to read the file, and remembering the file's location on the disk. Once the file has been opened, this `ifstream` object can be used to read characters from it, using the same operations as were provided in `istream`, including overloaded versions of `operator>>`, `ifstream::eof`, and `ifstream::get`. (The second argument to `open`, the "mode," is used to give options when opening a file; for our purposes, it is always `ios::in`.)

opening a file

A file can also be opened at the time the `ifstream` object is created, by using the two-argument constructor

```
ifstream::ifstream (char *file, int mode)
```

Its arguments are identical to those of the `open` function.

`ofstream` likewise has a zero-argument constructor and an `open` function,

```
void ofstream::open (char *file, int mode)
```

as well as a two-argument constructor:

```
ofstream::ofstream (char *file, int mode)
```

Opening a file for output is different from opening it for input. The disk is first searched for a file with the given name. However, if that search fails, a *new* file by that name is created. The opening of the file fails if you lack permission to create a new file. If the search succeeds, however, the program must decide what to do with the file with the same name as the output. The decision depends on the `mode` argument. If the `mode` argument is `ios::out`, the file's contents are deleted, and after executing the program the contents of the file will be just what was written to the file by the program. If the `mode` argument is `ios::app`, the file's contents are preserved, and data written by this program are appended to the end of the file. The opening of the file fails if the file exists but you lack permission to write to it. **ofstream** is otherwise similar to **ostream**, providing, in particular, all the same overloadings of **operator<<**.

closing a file   When you do not need a file any more, you can *close* it by sending it the **close** message. It is not usually *necessary* to do so, because when any program terminates, it automatically sends the **close** message to all **ifstream** and **ofstream** objects. However, sending the **close** message to the streams you have opened is good programming practice and *is* necessary if you want to *reopen* the same file during the same run of the program.

The member functions **boolean ifstream::fail ()** and **boolean ofstream::fail ()** can be used to determine whether opening a file was successful. The **fail** message should always be sent after you attempt to open a file. If it returns **true**, the file was not opened—perhaps because you misspelled its name or because you lack permission to read it or write it—and some error action should be taken.

As an example of the use of these classes, this program copies the contents of the file **inputfile** into **outputfile**.

```
#include <iostream.h>
#include <fstream.h>
#include <stdlib.h>

void copyFile (ifstream &is, ofstream &os) {
  char ch = is.get();
  while (!is.eof()) {
    os << ch;
    ch = is.get();
  }
}

main () {

  ifstream ifs("inputfile", ios::in);
  if (ifs.fail()) {
    cout << "inputfile cannot be opened:  either it does not\n"
         << "exist, or you lack permission to read it.\n";
    exit(1);
  }
  ofstream ofs("outputfile", ios::out);
  if (ofs.fail()) {
    cout << "outputfile cannot be opened; this probably means\n"
         << "you lack permission to write to it.\n";
    exit(1);
  }

  copyFile(ifs, ofs);
}
```

We've used **get** instead of **operator>>** for reading from **inputfile** to ensure all whitespace characters (spaces and newlines) are read, just as we did in Section 7.7 when reading from **cin**.

One other member function defined in **ifstream**, which we will use later in this chapter, is **putback (char c)**, which places a character that was just read from the input stream using **get** *back into the input stream*, so that the *next* call to **get** will return that character again. This is useful when scanning a file for a character that is at the beginning of a useful sequence of characters; by putting that first character back, the entire sequence of characters can be processed more easily. For example, here is a function that adds all the numbers that occur at the beginnings of lines in a file:

```
int addInitialNumbers (ifstream& numfile) {
  int sum = 0;
  boolean atStartOfLine = true;
  char inputchar;
  int inputint;

  inputchar = numfile.get();

  while (!numfile.eof()) {
    // sum = sum of all integers occurring at the
    //    beginning of lines
    // atStartOfLine is true if, and only if, the
    //    last character read was a newline
    if (atStartOfLine && isDigit(inputchar)) {
      numfile.putback(inputchar);
      numfile >> inputint;
      sum = sum + inputint;
    }

    if (inputchar == '\n')
      atStartOfLine = true;
    else
      atStartOfLine = false;

    inputchar = numfile.get();
  }

  return sum;
}
```

When this function sees a digit at the beginning of a line, it puts it back in the input stream so that the subsequent use of **operator>>** will read the entire number. Without the call to **putback**, **operator>>** would drop the first digit of every number it reads.

Note that you must include **fstream.h** to use classes **ifstream** and **ofstream**. Some other member functions defined in these classes are listed in Appendix D.

10.3

Command-Line Arguments

To run a program in a command-line environment like UNIX or DOS (as opposed to a graphical environment like the Apple Macintosh or Microsoft Windows), a user types the name of the program, along with any arguments the program needs. For example, one might run the PSL program, **psl**, by entering

```
psl pic1.psl
```

where **pic1.psl** is the name of a file containing the input to **psl**.

For some programs there may be several arguments. For example, this is one way to display the contents of **file1** and **file2** in UNIX systems:

```
cat file1 file2
```

cat is a program that has an arbitrary number of command-line arguments.

The arguments are passed into the program as follows: The system divides up the command line into sequences of nonblank characters (spaces are ignored), and each sequence is placed into a string. Then, an array is constructed containing pointers to these strings:

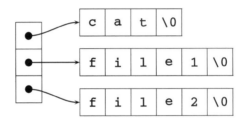

This array is passed as an argument to **main**. Until now, we have always assumed **main** to be a zero-argument function, but really it has two arguments. The second argument is the array of strings just shown; it is conventionally called **argv**. The first argument, called **argc**, is an **int** giving the length of **argv** (3, in our example). Thus, the full prototype of **main** is

```
int main (int argc, char *argv[])
```

When the program begins execution, **main** can check **argc** to make sure it has the correct number of command-line arguments, and then look at these arguments in **argv**.

Notice the **int** return value of **main**. It can be used to return a result from the entire execution of the program. This is usually used, if at all, simply to indicate that the program has failed to execute properly for some reason; a return value other than zero means a failure has occurred. When you don't want to return any such indication, you can declare the return type of **main** to be **void**.

As an example, the program in Section 10.2 that copies **inputfile** to **outputfile** could obtain the two filenames from the command line, as follows:

```
int main (int argc, char*argv[]) {

  if (argc != 3) {
    cout << "Correct usage: copy <file1> <file2>\n";
    exit (1);
  }
```

```
    ifstream ifs(argv[1], ios::in);
    if (ifs.fail()) {
      cout << argv[1] << " cannot be opened:  it does not\n"
           << "exist, or you lack permission to read it.\n";
      exit(1);
    }

    ofstream ofs(argv[2], ios::out);
    if (ofs.fail()) {
      cout << argv[2] << " cannot be opened; you probably\n"
           << "lack permission to write to it.\n";
      exit(1);
    }

    copyFile(ifs, ofs);
  }
```

The function **copyFile** is the same as on page 512. Such a program is obviously far more useful than the previous one, because it can be used to copy files with different names without recompiling the program.

Exercises—First Set

☞ 1. Take any program you have written that contains a class definition and divide it into three files: a header file containing the class declaration, a source file containing the definitions of the class's member functions, and a source file containing the remaining functions (including **main**).

2. Modify the file-copying program so that it prompts the user for both filenames. It should ask the user whether the contents of the input file should replace the output file (as we've done) or be appended to it. Furthermore, if the user enters either filename as a single dash (-), use the standard input (that is, read from **cin**) or standard output (**cout**), respectively.

3. Extend the program from Exercise 2 to allow the user to enter more than one filename on the input line, separated by spaces. All these files should be copied to the output file in order (either replacing the contents or being appended to them).

10.4

Context-Free Grammars

Context-free grammars are widely used to define the syntax of computer languages like C++, and can be found in many programming language books and manuals. We introduce the formalism in this section so that we can use it in the next section to define the syntax of PSL.

  A context-free grammar is a list of rules called *productions*. Each production has the form $A \rightarrow w$, where A is one of a finite set of *variables* and w is a sequence of variables and *literals*; w can be of any length, including zero.

context-free grammar

production

variable

literal

$$\text{expression} = \text{term} + \text{term} + \cdots + \text{term}$$
$$\text{term} = \text{factor} * \text{factor} * \cdots * \text{factor}$$
$$\text{factor} = \text{a number or a parenthesized expression}$$

FIGURE 10.4   *Rules defining expression syntax, copied from page 371.*

The variables in a context-free grammar represent sets of syntactically correct phrases; these sets are called *syntactic categories*. A production of the form $A \rightarrow w$ says that one way to construct a phrase in syntactic category A is to write w. If w contains a variable B, and there is a production $B \rightarrow u$ in the grammar, B can be replaced by u; if u has length zero, B can be deleted from w. Continuing this process, every variable in w can be either deleted or replaced by a string of literals. w is then a phrase in the syntactic category A.

A context-free grammar we have already used, implicitly, is the one defining arithmetic expressions for the calculator in Section 8.8. Rules defining the syntax of expressions were given in a box on page 371 and are reproduced here in Figure 10.4. These rules can be cast as a context-free grammar, where we have written variables in **bold** and literals in `computer display` type in color:

1	**Expression**	$\rightarrow$	**Term**
2	**Expression**	$\rightarrow$	**Term** `+` **Expression**
3	**Term**	$\rightarrow$	**Factor**
4	**Term**	$\rightarrow$	**Factor** `*` **Term**
5	**Factor**	$\rightarrow$	**Integer**
6	**Factor**	$\rightarrow$	`(` **Expression** `)`

Leaving the syntax of integers to your intuition, this gives the same set of expressions as the rules given in Figure 10.4. The difference is that we have used recursion here in place of the ellipses in Figure 10.4. For example, rules 1 and 2 can be read as saying: An **Expression**—that is, a phrase in the syntactic category **Expression**—is either a **Term**, or a **Term** followed by a plus sign followed by an **Expression**. Since an **Expression** can be a **Term** followed by a plus sign followed by an **Expression**, it can be a **Term** followed by a plus sign followed by a **Term** followed by a plus sign followed by an **Expression**. Carrying this logic through, we see that an **Expression** can be any number of **Term**s separated by plus signs. This is what the rules on page 371 say more directly.

Rules 3 and 4 say that a **Term** is either a **Factor** or a **Factor** followed by a multiplication sign followed by a **Term**. Rules 5 and 6 say that a **Factor** is either an **Integer** or an **Expression** enclosed in parentheses. For example, `1*2+(3*4+5)*6+7` is seen to be an **Expression** by the following reasoning, analogous to that used on page 371:

1. Since `2` is a **Factor**, it is a **Term**. Since `1` is a **Factor**, expression `1*2` is a **Factor** followed by a multiplication sign followed by a **Term**; therefore, it is a **Term**.

2. Similarly, `3*4` is a **Term**. Since `5` is a **Factor**, it is a **Term**, so it is an **Expression**. Thus, `3*4+5` is a **Term** followed by a plus sign followed by an **Expression**, so it is in turn an **Expression**, and (`3*4+5`) is a **Factor**. (`3*4+5`)`*6` is a **Factor** followed by a multiplication sign followed by a **Term**, so it is a **Term**.

3. `7` is a **Factor**, so it is a **Term**, so it is an **Expression**.

4. (`3*4+5`)`*6+7` is the **Term** (`3*4+5`)`*6` followed by a plus sign followed by the **Expression** `7`, so it is an **Expression**.

5. `1*2+`(`3*4+5`)`*6+7` is the **Term** `1*2` followed by a plus sign and then the **Expression** (`3*4+5`)`*6+7`, so it is (at last) an **Expression**.

Another example of a context-free grammar is this fragment of the context-free grammar for C++ statements:[2]

1	**Statement**	$\rightarrow$	**AssignmentStatement** ;
2	**Statement**	$\rightarrow$	**CompoundStatement**
3	**Statement**	$\rightarrow$	if (**Expression**) **Statement**
4	**Statement**	$\rightarrow$	if (**Expression**) **Statement** else **Statement**
5	**Statement**	$\rightarrow$	while (**Expression**) **Statement**
6	**CompoundStatement**	$\rightarrow$	{ **StatementList** }
7	**StatementList**	$\rightarrow$	**Statement**
8	**StatementList**	$\rightarrow$	**Statement StatementList**

For example, we see that

```
if (x == 0) {
  y = x+1;
  while (z < y)
    z = z+3;
}
```

is a **Statement**. Since `x == 0` is an **Expression**, this code forms a **Statement** by rule 3, as long as { `y = x+1; ...`} is a **Statement**. It is one by rule 1, because it is a **CompoundStatement** by rule 5. That is because it is a **StatementList** by rule 7, consisting of a **Statement** (`y = x+1;`) followed by a `StatementList`; the latter consists of the single statement `while (z < y) z = z+3;`, which is a **StatementList** because it is a **Statement** (rule 6).

10.5

A Picture Specification Language

PSL is a language for describing simple pictures consisting of squares, rectangles, and circles. In this section, we give some examples of PSL specifications and then

---

[2]The full context-free syntax for C++ appears in B. Stroustrup, *The C++ Programming Language*, 2nd ed., Addison-Wesley, Reading, MA, 1991.

give a precise definition of PSL. In the next section, we present the **psl** program, which reads these descriptions and draws the pictures they describe.

A PSL picture specification consists of the description of the size and shape of a simple figure and the specifications of other figures connected to it; those figures have the same form, including connecting figures. For example,

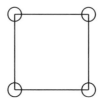

was produced by the specification

```
1    square(100)
2      connecting ne/c (circle (10))
3      connecting se/c (circle (10))
4      connecting sw/c (circle (10))
5      connecting nw/c (circle (10))
```

Line 1 says the main figure is a 100×100 square. In line 2, a circle of radius 10 is drawn with its center located at the northeast corner of the square. Lines 3, 4, and 5 specify that similar circles are drawn at the other corners of the square. The sizes are not given in any fixed units of length, as the actual sizes of the shapes is determined by the output device. What matters is the *relative* sizes of the shapes—for example, that the square has sides ten times the length of the circles' radius. We could just as well have said the square has size 10 and the circles size 1.

We can place circles just outside the square, or at its center, or offset from its center. The specification

```
1    square(100)
2      connecting ne/sw (circle (10))
3      connecting c/c (circle (30))
4      connecting c/w (circle (5))
5      connecting c/e (circle (10))
```

creates the figure

Line 1 specifies the square, as above, and line 2 the small circle at the upper right; the specification **ne/sw** says that the northeast corner of the square connects to the southwest point of the circle. Line 3 draws a large circle in the center of the square (c/c means the center of the square coincides with the center of the circle). Line 4 draws the small circle just to the right of the center of the square (c/w means the center of the square meets the west side of the circle), and line 5 draws the larger circle to its left.

Drawing a square with circles *inside* the corners is a little trickier. The specification

```
1    square (100) connecting ne/ne (circle(20))
```

produces the figure

which is not exactly what we want. The circles can be positioned inside the square by locating them relative to a smaller square, and not drawing the smaller square.

```
1    square(100)
2      connecting c/c (
3        invisible square (80)
4          connecting ne/c (circle (10))
5          connecting se/c (circle (10))
6          connecting sw/c (circle (10))
7          connecting nw/c (circle (10))
8      )
```

The large square contains a smaller square, which in turn has connected circles at each corner. However, the smaller square is **invisible**, meaning it is not drawn; its only purpose is to aid in positioning the four circles. The result is the picture

The square shown is of size 100×100. The circles are centered on the corners of an 80×80 square that is invisible.

The only other available shape is a rectangle. In this picture, a rectangle contains two groups of eight squares arranged in a circular pattern.

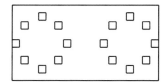

It is obtained by drawing a rectangle containing two invisible circles, which in turn contain eight squares each.

```
 1   rectangle (100, 50)
 2     connecting w/w (invisible circle (20)
 3          connecting e/e (square (5))
 4          connecting s/s (square (5))
 5          connecting w/w (square (5))
 6          connecting n/n (square (5))
 7          connecting ne/ne (square (5))
 8          connecting se/se (square (5))
 9          connecting sw/sw (square (5))
10          connecting nw/nw (square (5))
11     )
12     connecting e/e (invisible circle (20)
13          connecting e/e (square (5))
14          connecting s/s (square (5))
15          connecting w/w (square (5))
16          connecting n/n (square (5))
17          connecting ne/ne (square (5))
18          connecting se/se (square (5))
19          connecting sw/sw (square (5))
20          connecting nw/nw (square (5))
21     )
```

To reduce repetition in specifications, as in the last example, part of a specification can be placed in a separate file and read into the middle of a specification. For example, if the file **squares.psl** contains

```
 1   clear circle (20)
 2          connecting e/e (square (5))
 3          connecting s/s (square (5))
 4          connecting w/w (square (5))
 5          connecting n/n (square (5))
 6          connecting ne/ne (square (5))
 7          connecting se/se (square (5))
 8          connecting sw/sw (square (5))
 9          connecting nw/nw (square (5))
```

then the last picture can be specified by

```
 1   rectangle (100, 50)
 2     connecting w/w ("squares.psl")
 3     connecting e/e ("squares.psl")
```

The part of the specification that says **"squares.psl"** is replaced by the contents of **squares.psl**, exactly as if they had appeared there originally. This is comparable to the **#include** facility in C++ itself. We refer to this as the *include facility* of PSL, and to the files that are read in as *included files*.

PSL has one last feature: the ability to *scale* (expand or reduce) a picture. This is particularly useful in conjunction with the include facility, since it allows a picture to appear at a different size from the original. For example,

```
1    square (100)
2      connecting c/c (scale (2.0) "squares.psl")
3      connecting c/c ("squares.psl")
4      connecting c/c (scale (0.5) "squares.psl")
```

produces

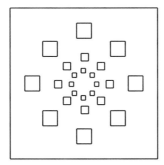

10.5.1   A Precise Definition of PSL

The C++ program we present in this chapter—the PSL program—reads a file containing a PSL specification and produces as its output an image, using the **Screen** class developed in Chapter 9. If a specification is contained in a file **spec.psl**, we can enter the command

```
psl spec.psl
```

The program reads the file **spec.psl**, processes it (reading any files it may include), and produces the specified image.

When developing any program, it is essential to have a precise specification of what the program is to do. With the smaller programs we have written in the rest of this book, a brief description in English sufficed. For a large program such as **psl**, whose input has a specific and highly structured form, much more care must be taken in describing what the valid inputs are and exactly what the program does for any input.

To help define PSL precisely, we give its context-free grammar in Figure 10.5. As explained in Section 10.4, the rules describe the structure of PSL specifications. They should be read like this:

- A **Picture** is either
    —The word **scale** followed by an opening parenthesis, a **Float** (described in rule 18), a closing parenthesis, and an **UnscaledPicture**; or
    —An **UnscaledPicture**.
- An **UnscaledPicture** consists of a **Shape** followed by a **SubpictureList**.
- A **SubpictureList** is either
    —Nothing; or
    —A **Subpicture** followed by a **SubpictureList**.

and so on. Rules 16 through 18 are special; we explain them below.

1	**Picture**	→	scale (**Float**) **UnscaledPicture**
2	**Picture**	→	**UnscaledPicture**
3	**UnscaledPicture**	→	**Shape SubpictureList**
4	**SubpictureList**	→	
5	**SubpictureList**	→	**Subpicture SubpictureList**
6	**Subpicture**	→	connecting **Direction** / **Direction** (**Picture**)
7	**Shape**	→	**Color Primitive Size**
8	**Color**	→	
9	**Color**	→	invisible
10	**Primitive**	→	square
11	**Primitive**	→	circle
12	**Primitive**	→	rectangle
13	**Size**	→	(**Integer Size2**
14	**Size2**	→	)
15	**Size2**	→	, **Integer**)
16	**Direction**	→	c, n, e, s, w, ne, se, sw, or nw
17	**Integer**	→	any sequence of digits
18	**Float**	→	any sequence of digits with a period, beginning with a digit

FIGURE 10.5   The PSL grammar

syntax tree   *Syntax trees* are a helpful way to think about context-free grammars. A syntax tree graphically shows the use of the rules to form a particular specification. For example, rule 2 tells us to form a **Picture** by writing an **UnscaledPicture**. This permits us to write this small syntax tree:

The "(2)" indicates that we've used rule 2. Rule 3 tells us that an **UnscaledPicture** can consist of a **Shape** followed by a **SubpictureList**, giving

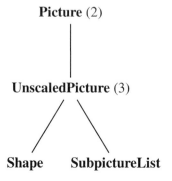

A **Shape** consists of a **Color** followed by a **Primitive** and a **Size:**

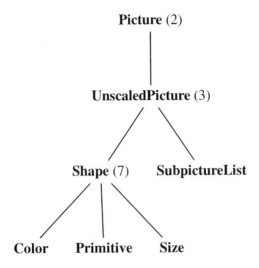

Continuing in this way—"expanding" variables by using productions of the grammar—we can produce a tree that is *complete* in the sense that there are no variables left to be expanded using a production in Figure 10.5. An example of a complete syntax tree is given in Figure 10.6; there are no variables left unexpanded. The literals are drawn in color in this syntax tree to emphasize that when placed in sequence, they form a picture specification, namely

```
square (100) connecting c/c (circle (50))
```

which produces this picture:

Thus, the valid PSL specifications are formed by constructing syntax trees, starting with the variable **Picture**, and then writing down all the literals in the order in which they appear in the tree. These literals comprise the *leaves* (or *frontier*) of the tree.

leaves
frontier

Note that not all the sequences of literals are valid specifications. For example,

```
square (100) connecting circle (50)
```

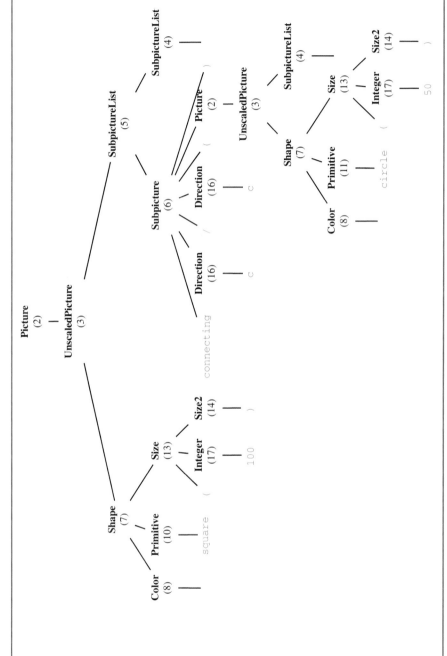

FIGURE 10.6 Syntax tree for `square (100) connecting c/c (circle (50))`.

is ungrammatical: there is no syntax tree whose frontier is that sequence. A **Picture** can begin with `square (100) connecting`, but this must be followed by a **Direction**, and `circle` is not a **Direction**. Thus, just as there can be syntax errors in C++ programs, there can be syntax errors in PSL specifications.

We need to explain rules 16, 17, and 18, which don't look like the others:

16	**Direction**	→	c, n, e, s, w, ne, se, sw, or nw
17	**Integer**	→	any sequence of digits
18	**Float**	→	any sequence of digits with a period, beginning with a digit

These are not really context-free productions at all—just informal descriptions of certain allowable strings. In the implementation, it is more efficient to treat these categories separately, appealing to the informal descriptions given here. In syntax trees we expand the variable **Direction** with any of the nine literals representing directions, the variable **Integer** with any positive integer, and the variable **Float** with any number having a decimal point (provided that there is at least one digit preceding the decimal point).

We will see that the first major processing step in the **psl** program, after reading a specification, is the construction of its syntax tree—that is, the syntax tree whose frontier matches the specification. This step is called *parsing*.   *parsing*

Now that we have a precise definition of the syntax of picture specifications, we can say exactly what picture is described by any specification; that is, we can say exactly what picture the **psl** program should draw. A specification contains a number of shapes, but how big is each shape, and where is it located? The size of a shape is given explicitly and is then multiplied by the scaling factor, if one has been given. Note that scaling factors build up multiplicatively, so in the specification

```
... scale (0.4) ... connecting c/c (scale (0.25) circle (10) ...)
```

the circle is scaled by $0.4 \times 0.25 = 0.1$, and its radius is thus 1 rather than 10.

Determining the locations of the shapes in a picture is more difficult. The first shape in a picture is located at the center of the screen. Now consider the problem of determining where $shape_2$ is drawn—that is, the location of its center—in the specification

$$shape_1 \text{ connecting } dir_1/dir_2 (\text{ } shape_2 \text{ ... })$$

The center of $shape_2$ is determined by the two directions dir_1 and dir_2 and by the type and size of $shape_1$ and $shape_2$. Assuming that we already know where the center of $shape_1$ is, dir_1 determines a point p; if dir_1 is c, then p is the same as the center of $shape_1$; if it is not c, p is a point on the perimeter of $shape_1$, as illustrated in Figure 10.7. Once p is determined, we work backwards to find the center of $shape_2$. If dir_2 is c, then the center of $shape_2$ is p. Otherwise, the center of $shape_2$ has to be computed so that dir_2 of $shape_2$ ends up at point p.

For example, suppose the specification is

```
circle (10) connecting e/w (square (8) ... )
```

and we have determined from the surrounding shapes that the center of the circle is at $(25, 20)$. Since the circle has a radius of 10, its east point is $(35, 20)$; this is

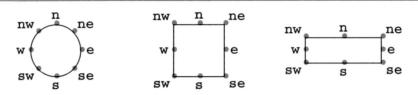

FIGURE 10.7   Perimeter points on circles, squares, and rectangles

the point called *p* in the previous paragraph. Thus, the west point of the square must be at (35, 20). Since this is a square whose side has a length of 8, the center is 4 units due east of its west point; specifically, it is (39, 20).

Exercises—Second Set

1. Write a PSL specification to produce this picture:

2. For the following PSL specification, calculate the center of each shape, assuming the square is centered at (50, 50).

```
square (20)
  connecting n/s (circle (5))
  connecting se/w
    (circle (10) connecting ne/sw (rectangle (30, 10)))
```

3. Draw the syntax tree for this PSL specification:

```
rectangle (20, 10)
  connecting e/w (scale (2.0) square (5))
```

10.6

The PSL Program

The program **psl** does its work in two major steps: First it reads and parses the input; that is, it creates a syntax tree for that input (or displays an error message if the input contains a syntax error) and stores this syntax tree internally. Second, it "traverses" the syntax tree to produce a list of "shapes" which can be displayed using the **Screen** class.

The program consists of eight source code files and three header files. The source files[3] are listed here in the order in which they are used to process picture specifications (which is also the order in which we cover them in this section).

  psl.C contains the function **main**, which reads the command-line argument and calls functions to process the file.

---

[3] Systems vary in the filename extensions used for C++ source programs; extensions in use include C, cc, and cpp.

preprocess.C defines the function **preprocess**, which reads the input file and all its included files and creates a temporary file containing the entire specification.

lexer.C performs *lexical analysis,* or *lexing:* a processing step preliminary to parsing.

parse.C contains the function **parse**, as well as a variety of auxiliary functions, which converts the input into a syntax tree.

shape.C defines the member functions of the **Shape** class.

shapelist.C defines member functions of the class **ShapeList** (analogous to our other list classes).

computeshapes.C defines function **computeShapes**, which takes a syntax tree as input and produces a list of shapes: objects of the **Shape** class.

screen.C defines member functions of the **Screen** class. This class has the same declaration as the **Screen** class defined in Chapter 9, but we use a different definition, for reasons we explain in Section 10.6.7.

The overall structure of the program is illustrated in Figure 10.8. It shows the processing of the specification given on page 521. That specification uses the include feature to include file **squares.psl**. The names of the files that contribute to each phase are given on the right-hand side of the figure.

The remaining subsections describe the functions and classes defined in each source file; the header files are covered as needed. Most of these subsections are divided into two parts, the first describing *what* the classes and functions defined in the source file do and the second explaining *how* those functions work. Read the first parts of all the sections first to see how the components of the program fit together. All of the C++ files for this program will be given at the end of the chapter (*following* the Summary), starting on page 563, beginning with the three header files (**psl.h**, **lexer.h**, and **shape.h**), followed by the source files listed above.

10.6.1 psl.C

This file contains the declarations of two global variables—**theInput** and **computedShapes**—and the function **main**. **main** performs these actions, which reflect the structure shown in Figure 10.8:

1. Check that there is exactly one command-line argument.
2. Open the specification file named on the command line.
3. Open the temporary file, called **psltempfile**, for output.
4. Call **preprocess** to copy the specification file, plus all included files, to the temporary file.
5. Close the temporary file and then open it for input. The global variable **theInput** contains the **ifstream** object connected to the temporary file.
6. Call **parse** to construct the syntax tree of the specification.
7. Call **computeShapes** to create the list of the **Shape** objects in the specified picture. The address of this list is placed into the global variable **computedShapes**.
8. Send the **draw** message to **computedShapes**.

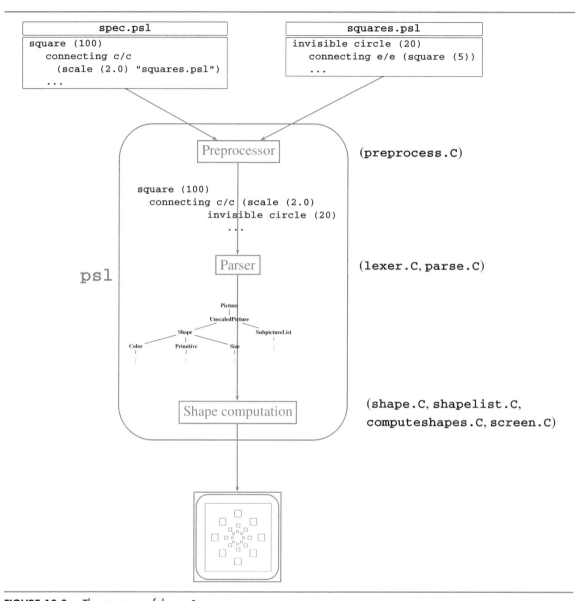

FIGURE 10.8   The structure of the **psl** program.

Here is the definition of **main**:

```
//
// psl.C - gives main program for PSL processor, as
//    well as definition of global variable theInput.
//
// Author:  R. Holly Kamin
// Last modified: 4/4/95
//
```

```
#include "psl.h"
#include "shape.h"

ifstream theInput; // temporary file containing
      // complete specification, after preprocessing

extern ShapeList *computedShapes; // list of shapes
      // produced by call to computeShapes

const char tempfilename[] = "psltempfile";

void main (int argc, char *argv[]) {
  if (argc != 2) {
    cout << "Usage: psl <filename>\n";
    exit(1);
  }

  // Open specification file
  ifstream inputfile(argv[1], ios::in);
  if (inputfile.fail()) {
    cout << "Unable to open file " << argv[1] << "\n";
    exit(1);
  }

  // Open temporary file for output
  ofstream tempfile(tempfilename, ios::out);
  if (tempfile.fail()) {
    cout << "Unable to open temporary file for output\n";
    exit(1);
  }

  // Copy specification, plus included files, to temporary file
  preprocess(inputfile, tempfile);
  tempfile.close();

  // Open temporary file for input
  theInput.open(tempfilename, ios::in);
  if (tempfile.fail()) {
    cout << "Unable to open temporary file for input\n";
    exit(1);
  }

  // Parse specification
  SyntaxTreeNode *tn = parse();
  // Traverse syntax tree; put list of shapes in computedShapes
  computeShapes(tn);
  // Draw computed shapes
  Screen screen;
  computedShapes->draw(screen);
}
```

10.6.2   preprocess.C

This file contains the function

```
void preprocess (ifstream& input, ofstream& temp)
```

It copies the file **input** into **temp**. If while reading **input** it encounters an included file—that is, it sees a file name in double quotes—it copies that file into **temp** before copying the rest of **input**. The result is that **temp** contains the complete specification, with no uses of the include facility.

Implementation

preprocess is a standard input loop, reading file **input** until it reaches end of file. However, when it sees a double quote, it must include the file named in quotes. It scans for the filename (stores all the characters up to the closing double quote), opens the file for input, then recursively calls itself to copy that file.

```
void preprocess (ifstream& input, ofstream& temp) {
  char c = input.get();
  while (!input.eof()) {
    if (c != '"')
      temp << c;
    else { // copy included file
      // Read name of included file
      char includedFile[100];
      int i = 0;
      c = input.get();
      while (c != '"') {
        includedFile[i] = c;
        i++;
        c = input.get();
      }
      includedFile[i] = '\0';

      // Open included file
      ifstream inputfile(includedFile, ios::in);
      if (inputfile.fail()) {
        cout << "Unable to open included file "
             << includedFile << "\n";
        exit(1);
      }

      // Copy included file to temporary file
      preprocess(inputfile, temp);
    }

    c = input.get();
  }
}
```

10.6.3 lexer.C

lexical analysis   *Lexical analysis* divides the input characters into chunks that can be easily processed by the parser. The lexical analyzer, or *lexer,* also has the job of discarding spaces and newline characters, because they have no significance in parsing and do not affect the meaning of a specification.

token   To understand the role of lexing, just consider ordinary English. Sentences are made up of words, which are in turn made up of letters. Here, the characters correspond to letters, the entire PSL specification is a "sentence," and the lexical chunks, or *tokens,* are the words.

In a PSL specification, there are 19 distinct tokens that may occur:

```
(           )          ,          /          scale   connecting
invisible   square   circle   rectangle   c       n              e
s           w        ne       se          sw      nw
```

Further, there are two *lexical categories*—integer and float. Each of these categories contains many tokens, but for the parser they can be treated as just two tokens, because the syntactic structure of a specification depends only on the presence of an integer or floating-point number, not on its value. The two lexical categories and the 19 distinct tokens constitute most of the enumerated type `TokenType` in `psl.h`:

```
23    enum TokenType {intnum, floatnum, oparen, cparen, comma, slash,
24                    scale, connecting,
25                    center, north, east, south, west,
26                    northeast, southeast, southwest, northwest,
27                    square, circle, rectangle, invisible,
28                    endoffile, badToken};
```

We treat the end-of-file condition as a token, and we include one catch-all token for invalid inputs. All together, there are 23 types of tokens.

The lexical analyzer delivers tokens to the parser. That is, it reads characters from the input file, skips over spaces and newlines, reads a single token, and returns that token to its caller.

The file `lexer.C` (page 570) provides the function `void getToken ()` and the global variable `theLexer` of type `FSM`. When a client function wants to read a token, it calls `getToken`. `getToken` does not return a value, but after it returns, `theLexer` can be interrogated to determine the token that was recognized. We will look at the class `FSM` in detail in the implementation section, but for now we need to know only that it provides the following member functions (among others):

> `TokenType FSM::type ()` returns the `TokenType` of the token last recognized by its receiver.

> `int FSM::intValue ()` and `float FSM::floatValue ()` return values associated with lexical categories `intnum` and `floatnum`. If the token returned by `type()` is `intnum` or `floatnum`, it means only that the token is one of the tokens in that category. The specific integer or float that was read is obtained by calling the appropriate one of these member functions.

> `void FSM::error (char *)`: Used by the lexer and the parser to print an error message and terminate the processing of a specification when an error is detected.

Thus, clients call `getToken`, which sends messages to `theLexer` directing it to read characters until it reaches the end of a token. The client then uses the aforementioned `FSM` member functions to discover what that token was. For example, if the input file contains the characters

```
square (50)
```

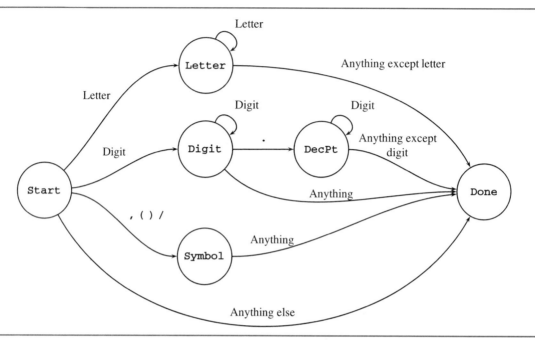

FIGURE 10.9   Finite-state machine implemented by `FSM::feedCharacter`

then `getToken` will be called five times. After the first call, `theLexer.type()` will return the token `square`. After the second call, the call `theLexer.type()` will return `oparen`. After the third call, `theLexer.type()` will return `intnum`, and the call `theLexer.intValue()` will return 50. After the fourth call, the token will be `cparen`, and after the fifth it will be `endoffile`. There should be no more calls to `getToken` after that.

Implementation

FSM stands for *finite-state machine,* the mathematical term for a system, such as the alarm watch discussed in Section 6.6, that can be described by a transition diagram like those of Sections 3.5 and 6.6. **FSM** objects represent states in the transition diagram shown in Figure 10.9. The declaration of **FSM** is given in `lexer.h`:

```
// States names all the states in the transition diagram
// for the lexical analyzer for PSL.

const int numStates = 6;
enum States {Start, Letter, Digit, DecPt, Symbol, Done};

// FSM implements the transition diagram for PSL.
// reset initializes the state to Start, and
// feedCharacter makes a transition.
// Various data are computed during transitions;
// operations are provided to access those data.
```

```
class FSM {
private:
  States state;      // current state of finite-state machine
  char buffer[maxTokenLength];  // char's in this token
  int charcount;     // length of this token
  int ivalue;        // value of this token, if an integer
  float fvalue;      // value of this token, if a float
  TokenType ttype;   // type of token

public:
  FSM () : state(Start), charcount(0)
           {}

  void error (char *msg) ;

  void feedCharacter () ;

  boolean tokenReady () { return (state == Done); }

  TokenType type () { return ttype; }

  int intValue () { return ivalue; }

  float floatValue () { return fvalue; }

  void reset () ;
};
```

feedCharacter is the member function that moves an **FSM** object from one state to another, making the state transition on the character it reads from the character stream. It is the most complex and most important operation in the **FSM** class, and we explain its operation in detail below. tokenReady indicates when the final state, called **Done**, has been reached. reset, defined in lexer.C, sets the state to **Start** to begin reading a new token:

```
void FSM::reset () {
  state = Start;
  charcount = 0;
  ivalue = 0;
  fvalue = 0.0;
}
```

When we discuss feedCharacter, it will become clear why data members charcount, ivalue, and fvalue are reinitialized as they are.

theLexer is a global variable containing an **FSM** object, to which the getToken function sends characters:

```
FSM theLexer;
extern ifstream theInput;

void getToken () {
  theLexer.reset();
  while (!theLexer.tokenReady())
    theLexer.feedCharacter();
}
```

The `getToken` function starts `theLexer` in the `Start` state and continually calls `feedCharacter` until `theLexer` is in the `Done` state (that is, until `theLexer.tokenReady()` returns `true`). When `getToken` is done, `theLexer` has scanned the next token that the parser needs to see.

Now we are ready to discuss `feedCharacter`. To make it easier to follow the transition diagram on which it is based, `feedCharacter` classifies characters into one of seven character classes, given in the type `CharacterClass` in `lexer.C`:

```
const int numCharacterClasses = 7;
enum CharacterClass {letter, digit, period, symbol,
                     whiteSpace, eof, nothingElse};
```

`letter` represents lower-case letters (there are no upper-case letters in PSL specifications except in filenames), `whiteSpace` the space and newline characters, `digit` any digit character, and `symbol` any one of

```
,  (  )  /
```

`period` represents a period. `nothingElse` represents all other characters. The function `classify`, called from `feedCharacter`, returns a character's class.

```
CharacterClass classify (char c) {
  if (c == ' ' || c == '\n')
    return whiteSpace;
  else if (c >= 'a' && c <= 'z')
    return letter;
  else if (c >= '0' && c <= '9')
    return digit;
  else if (c == '(' || c == ')' || c == '/' || c == ',')
    return symbol;
  else if (c == '.')
    return period;
  else
    return nothingElse;
}
```

`eof` does not represent a specific character but rather represents the condition of being at the end of the input file; it is treated separately, as we will see. The transitions in Figure 10.9 are based on character classifications, so this categorization allows the diagram to be followed easily.

`feedCharacter` begins by reading a character from `theInput` and determining its classification. When it reaches the end of file, it pretends it has read a character of class `eof`:

```
void FSM::feedCharacter () {

  char c = theInput.get();
  CharacterClass cc;

  if (theInput.eof())
    cc = eof;
  else
    cc = classify(c);
```

The transition diagram of Figure 10.9 is represented by a two-dimensional array:

```
States transitions[numStates][numCharacterClasses] = {
//
//                               white          nothing
//    letter  digit  period symbol Space  eof    Else
//    ======  =====  ====== ====== =====  ===   =======
// Start:
     {Letter, Digit, Done,  Symbol, Start, Done, Done},
// Letter:
     {Letter, Done,  Done,  Done,   Done,  Done, Done},
// Digit:
     {Done,   Digit, DecPt, Done,   Done,  Done, Done},
// DecPt:
     {Done,   DecPt, Done,  Done,   Done,  Done, Done},
// Symbol:
     {Done,   Done,  Done,  Done,   Done,  Done, Done},
// Done:
     {Done,   Done,  Done,  Done,   Done,  Done, Done}};
```

Note the order of the states in the declaration of type **States** and the order of the character classes in **CharacterClasses**. This array follows those orders, as indicated in the comments. For example, **transitions[DecPt][digit]**—that is, **transitions[3][1]**—represents the transition from state **DecPt** on character **digit**; its value is state **DecPt**, as it should be according to Figure 10.9.

Each time a transition is made in this diagram, an action is taken. That action may depend upon the state being moved to, or the state moved from, or the character that was read. Thus, the structure of **feedCharacter** is

```
void FSM::feedCharacter () {

  char c = theInput.get();
  CharacterClass cc;

  if (theInput.eof())
    cc = eof;
  else
    cc = classify(c);

  States priorState = state;
  state = transitions[state][cc];
  switch (state) {
    case Start:  <action when reaching state Start>
    case Letter: <action when reaching state Letter>
    case Digit:  <action when reaching state Digit>
    case DecPt:  <action when reaching state DecPt>
    case Symbol: <action when reaching state Symbol>
    case Done:   <action when reaching state Done>
  }
}
```

Here are the actions taken when moving to any of the states except **Done**, which is treated afterwards:

Start: The only way to enter the **Start** state is if the input value was a space or newline character; since these characters are ignored, no action is required.

```
case Start:
  break;
```

Letter: Most of the tokens in PSL are just strings of letters. As long as we continue to see letters, we will just gather them into a character string (**buffer**, a data member of **FSM**). We'll figure out which token we have after all the letters have been read.

```
case Letter:
  buffer[charcount] = c;
  charcount++;
  if (charcount == maxTokenLength)
    error("token too long");
  break;
```

Digit: When we first see a digit, we assume that it is part of an integer. We want to compute that integer and store it in the data member **ivalue**, which is initialized to zero. Here we've used the same idea we used in Section 8.8: Each time a digit is read, the value of the digits previously read is multiplied by 10 and the value of the new digit is added. For example, if the digits are **234**, when the **2** is read, **ivalue** gets the value 2; when the **3** is read, **ivalue** becomes 23 ($2 \times 10 + 3$); and when the **4** is read, **ivalue** becomes 234 ($23 \times 10 + 4$).

```
case Digit:
  // ivalue must have been initialized to zero
  // before this token was read.
  ivalue = 10*ivalue + (c-'0');
  break;
```

DecPt: This state is reached upon seeing a decimal point, after seeing at least one digit (so **ivalue** has been assigned a value). It is then reached repeatedly as long as more digits are seen. Just as **ivalue** is recomputed each time state **Digit** is entered, so **fvalue** should be computed when **DecPt** is entered. The first time this state is entered, the integer value in **ivalue** should be converted to a floating-point value; this is accomplished by assigning it to **fvalue**. **DecPt** is then repeatedly entered as digits are read. Each digit is divided by the next power of 10 and added to **fvalue**. We've used **ivalue** to keep track of the powers of 10. (**pow** is a function in the math library; **pow(m, n)** returns **m** raised to the power **n**.)

```
case DecPt:
  if (cc == period) { // first time entering this state
    fvalue = ivalue;
    ivalue = 1;  // use to count decimal position
  }
```

```
  else { // c must be a digit
    fvalue = fvalue + ((c-'0') / pow(10.0, ivalue));
    ivalue++;
  }
  break;
```

Symbol: This state is reached when the character is one of

, ( ) /

Store the character in `buffer`.

```
case Symbol:
  buffer[0] = c;
  charcount = 1;
  break;
```

The `Done` state can be entered from any of the other states, and its action depends upon the state from which it arrived (stored in `priorState`). Note, however, that when `Done` is reached, it is always *after reading one character past the last token*. Since this character should be fed into the finite-state machine at the start of the *next* token, the character is placed back into the input by calling `ifstream::putback`. However, this is not done if `cc` is `eof`, because it is not really a character. For each state from which `Done` may have been entered, there is a different action:

Start: As shown in Figure 10.9, it is possible to reach `Done` directly from `Start` only when the input character has category `eof`, `period`, or `nothingElse`. Of these, `eof` corresponds to the `endoffile` token, but the other two classes represent erroneous input.

Letter: The null character is placed in `buffer` and `typeOfWord` is called to determine the token corresponding to this string. `typeOfWord` does a simple lookup in an array of strings; it is listed in Section 10.7.6. If no token corresponds, `typeOfWord` returns `badToken`, and an error is reported.

Digit: `ivalue` holds the correct value; it only remains to set `ttype` to `intnum`.

DecPt: Similarly, set `ttype` to `floatnum`; `fvalue` holds the correct value.

Symbol: Look in `buffer[0]` to determine which symbol was seen, and set `ttype` accordingly.

This explains the code executed when `feedCharacter` puts the `FSM` in the `Done` state:

```
case Done:
  if (cc != eof)
    theInput.putback(c); // We've read one
              // character past end of token
  switch (priorState) {
    case Start:
      if (cc == eof)
        ttype = endoffile;
```

```
            else
              error("illegal character");
            break;
          case Letter:
            buffer[charcount] = '\0';
            ttype = typeOfWord(buffer);
            if (ttype == badToken)
              error("illegal token");
            break;
          case Digit:
            ttype = intnum;
            break;
          case DecPt:
            ttype = floatnum;
            break;
          case Symbol:
            switch (buffer[0]) {
              case '(': ttype = oparen;  break;
              case ')': ttype = cparen;  break;
              case ',': ttype = comma;   break;
              case '/': ttype = slash;   break;
            }
            break;
          case Done:
            ; // can't happen
        }
        break;
    }
```

The entire function is listed in Section 10.7.6.

10.6.4 parse.C

> A tree's a tree. How many more do you need to look at?
>
> —Ronald Reagan
> (quoted in the *Sacramento Bee,* Sept. 12, 1965)

parse.C defines the function **SyntaxTreeNode *parse ()**. It calls **getToken** repeatedly to read all the tokens in the input, determines their syntactic structure, builds a syntax tree, and returns that syntax tree to the caller (**main**).

The syntax tree is the central item of data in the PSL program. It is constructed here and then used to produce the picture in **computeshapes.C**. It is important to understand how syntax trees are represented. The details of the parsing process—*how* the correct syntax tree is constructed—will be left to the implementation section, but the representation of the syntax tree produced by the parse function will be explained now.

Some terminology concerning trees is helpful for this discussion. Look at the sample syntax tree on page 524. The variables and literals in the tree are called *nodes*. Whenever a variable node has other nodes below it, they are called the *children* of that node; the node is called the *parent*. Note that the number of children that a node has is the same as the number of symbols (both variables and literals) on the right-hand side of a production for that variable. Literal nodes never have children.

    Our method of representing syntax trees in **psl** is simple. Each node is represented by an object of type **SyntaxTreeNode**, and the lines connecting the nodes are represented by pointers (going from the higher node, or parent, to the lower nodes, or children). Because some nodes—specifically **Direction**, **Integer**, and **Float** nodes (rules 16 through 18)—have additional information beside the production number, **SyntaxTreeNode** objects can contain values of type **TokenType**, **integer**, or **float**. Thus, the **SyntaxTreeNode** class is declared in **psl.h** as

```
30    class SyntaxTreeNode {
31    private:
32      int productionNum;
33      SyntaxTreeNode *children[3];
34      TokenType direction;   // used when productionNum = 16
35      int ivalue;            // used when productionNum = 17
36      float fvalue;          // used when productionNum = 18
37
38    public:
39      SyntaxTreeNode (int p)
40        : productionNum(p) {}
41
42      SyntaxTreeNode (int p, int v)
43        : productionNum(p), ivalue(v) {}
44
45      SyntaxTreeNode (int p, float v)
46        : productionNum(p), fvalue(v) {}
47
48      SyntaxTreeNode (int p, TokenType dir)
49        : productionNum(p), direction(dir) {}
50
51      SyntaxTreeNode (int p, SyntaxTreeNode *c1)
52        : productionNum(p)
53      {
54        children[0] = c1;
55      }
56
57      SyntaxTreeNode (int p, SyntaxTreeNode *c1,
58                             SyntaxTreeNode *c2)
59        : productionNum(p)
60      {
61        children[0] = c1;
62        children[1] = c2;
63      }
64
65      SyntaxTreeNode (int p, SyntaxTreeNode *c1,
66                             SyntaxTreeNode *c2,
67                             SyntaxTreeNode *c3)
```

node
children

parent

```
68            : productionNum(p)
69        {
70          children[0] = c1;
71          children[1] = c2;
72          children[2] = c3;
73        }
74
75        int getProduction () { return productionNum; }
76
77        int getIntValue () { return ivalue; }
78
79        float getFloatValue () { return fvalue; }
80
81        TokenType getDirection () { return direction; }
82
83        SyntaxTreeNode *getChild (int n) { return children[n]; }
84      };
```

Each node contains a production number and an array of three pointers for the children of the node. There is no need to place the variable name in a node, because the production number determines the variable. As we will see shortly, in our representation of syntax trees, a node can have at most three children. Each node also contains data members of type **TokenType**, **int**, and **float**. These are used for productions 16, 17, and 18, respectively. Although every node has these three data members, a given object uses at most one of them.

SyntaxTreeNode is a simple class, consisting of several constructors and several operations to access the data members of a node. Its seven constructors include one to construct a node containing an integer (the production number will be 17), one for a node containing a float (production 18), one for a node containing a direction (production 16), and one each for constructing a node with zero, one, two, or three children. Member functions are provided to obtain the production number, the integer, float, or direction, or any of the children of a node. The parsing operation constructs the syntax tree in the heap, using **new** to allocate nodes.

A **SyntaxTreeNode** is used to represent a syntax tree almost exactly as on page 524. There are two exceptions:

1. Any node *not* containing a variable is omitted. For most tokens, like **square** or **(**, the token itself simply adds no useful information. For the three cases where the exact token is important—directions, integers, and floats—the token value is stored in the parent's node.
2. There will be no nodes with production number 2. If a picture has a scale factor, its production number is 1; otherwise it is 3.

Thus, the top part of the syntax tree on page 524 is represented by the following collection of **SyntaxTreeNode**s (in each node, we have shown only the relevant data members):

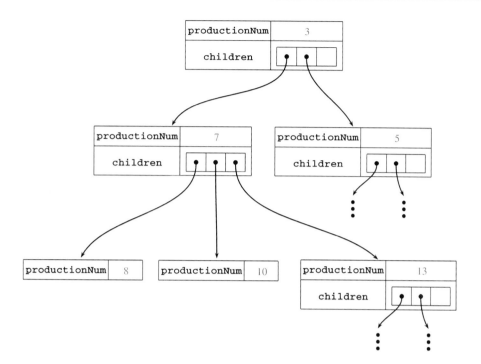

With this representation, no node has more than three children. Nodes for productions 6 and 7 have three.

The subsequent computation—computing the list of shapes to be displayed on the screen—looks at this syntax tree using the member functions just described. As long as you understand the structure of the syntax tree, you can understand that computation. In the following subsection, we explain *how* the syntax tree is constructed for a given specification.

Implementation

Parsing is the process of constructing a syntax tree whose frontier matches some input. There are many methods of parsing. The one we use is called *recursive descent*. It is the same method we used in programming the calculator in Chapter 8. *recursive descent*

We have said that PSL specifications are, by definition, the frontiers, or leaves, of syntax trees that have **Picture** as their topmost variable. But notice that for any variable there is a set of syntax trees having that variable as its topmost node, and each such tree has a frontier. In parsing terminology, the variable *derives* the frontier. For example, **Shape** can derive `square (50)`, `invisible circle (1)`, and `rectangle (5, 6)`, among many others. **Size** can derive `(50)`, `(1)`, `(5, 6)`, and many others. *derives*

The idea of recursive descent parsing is to define a separate function for each variable in the grammar. That function is responsible for constructing syntax trees for the strings that variable derives. These functions are mutually recursive—they call one another in complicated and possibly cyclic ways—so they are all declared at the beginning of `parse.C` (page 573).

For example, `parseShape` parses strings derivable from **Shape**. There is only one production for **Shape**, production 7,

$$7 \quad \textbf{Shape} \quad \rightarrow \quad \textbf{Color Primitive Size}$$

and it says that a string is derivable from **Shape** if it consists of a string derivable from **Color**, followed by a string derivable from **Primitive**, followed by a string derivable from **Size**. So `parseShape` calls `parseColor`, `parsePrimitive`, and `parseSize`, and then allocates a node (with production number 7) pointing to the syntax trees returned by those three calls:

```
SyntaxTreeNode *parseShape () {
  SyntaxTreeNode *tn1 = parseColor();
  SyntaxTreeNode *tn2 = parsePrimitive();
  SyntaxTreeNode *tn3 = parseSize();
  return new SyntaxTreeNode(7, tn1, tn2, tn3);
}
```

Note how closely `parseShape` follows the right-hand side of production 7.

Primitive has three productions:

$$10 \quad \textbf{Primitive} \quad \rightarrow \quad \text{square}$$
$$11 \quad \textbf{Primitive} \quad \rightarrow \quad \text{circle}$$
$$12 \quad \textbf{Primitive} \quad \rightarrow \quad \text{rectangle}$$

`parsePrimitive` looks at the input token and decides whether to return a node with production number 10, 11, or 12 (with no children in any case); if the input token is none of these three, a syntax error has occurred.

```
SyntaxTreeNode *parsePrimitive () {
  if (theLexer.type() == square) {
    getToken();
    return new SyntaxTreeNode(10);
  }
  else if (theLexer.type() == circle) {
    getToken();
    return new SyntaxTreeNode(11);
  }
  else if (theLexer.type() == rectangle) {
    getToken();
    return new SyntaxTreeNode(12);
  }
  else
    theLexer.error("expected primitive shape");
}
```

Aside from the calls to `getToken`, which we explain below, it does exactly what we described.

The `parse` functions all have a similar form. When there is more than one production for a variable, the function looks at the input token to determine which production to use, then calls the `parse` functions corresponding to any variables on the right-hand side of that production, and then checks and skips over any literals on the right-hand side. To take one more example, **Picture** has two productions:

1   **Picture** $\rightarrow$ scale (**Float**) **UnscaledPicture**
2   **Picture** $\rightarrow$ **UnscaledPicture**

`parsePicture` starts by looking at its first token. If the token is `scale`, that means production 1 is to be used; otherwise production 2 is to be used. To parse production 1, `parsePicture` calls `getToken` once, to skip over `scale`, and again, to skip over the opening parenthesis; it calls `parseInteger` to read the integer (`parseInteger` returns a node with production number 17), then skips over the closing parenthesis, and finally calls `parseUnscaledPicture`. The nodes returned by `parseInteger` and `parseUnscaledPicture` are placed into a new node, and that node's address is returned. In case the first token was not `scale`, `parsePicture` calls `parseUnscaledPicture` and returns whatever that call returns. (It never creates a node with production number 2.)

```
SyntaxTreeNode *parsePicture () {
  if (theLexer.type() == scale) {
    getToken();
    if (theLexer.type() != oparen)
      theLexer.error("expected opening parenthesis");
    getToken();
    SyntaxTreeNode *tn1 = parseFloat();
    if (theLexer.type() != cparen)
      theLexer.error("expected closing parenthesis");
    getToken();
    SyntaxTreeNode *tn2 = parseUnscaledPicture();
    return new SyntaxTreeNode(1, tn1, tn2);
  }
  else
    return parseUnscaledPicture();
}
```

We will not go through every **parse** function; they are all given in **parse.C** on page 573, and all follow the logic we have described. All of them, however, share one puzzling but important feature: the handling of **getToken**. It is tricky to call **getToken** at the correct times, because some **parse** functions can do their work by reading only the tokens derivable from the variable, whereas others must necessarily read *past* the derivable tokens. **Primitive** is an example of the former type of variable. **SubpictureList** is an example of the latter: It cannot know whether it is done parsing until it has looked one token past the last **Subpicture** (because it cannot otherwise tell that there are no more connecting shapes). However, when a **parse** function is called, it has to know whether the string it is attempting to derive begins with the token last read or with the next token. The resolution of this conflict is simply to enforce the following conventions:

1. Whenever a **parse** function is called, the first token derivable from that function should already have been read.
2. Every **parse** function should read one token past the end of the string it derives.

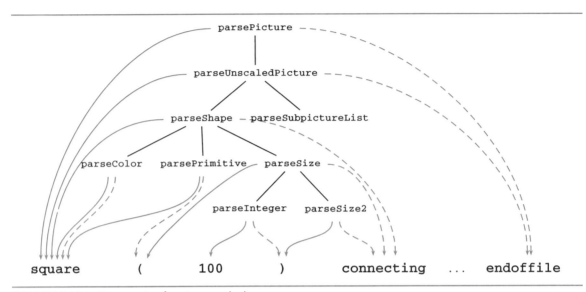

FIGURE 10.10   How parsing functions read tokens.

These conventions are illustrated in Figure 10.10. The tree shown in that figure is similar to the (first part of) the syntax tree in Figure 10.6 on page 524, but it shows how **parse** functions call other **parse** functions. For example, **parseColor**, **parsePrimitive**, and **parseSize** are children of **parseShape** because **parseShape** calls those three functions. For each **parse** function, the solid colored line shows the token that was read before calling that function, and the dashed colored line shows the token that was read before returning from that function.

For example, consider **parsePrimitive**. When it is called, **theLexer** has the first (and only) token of the primitive, which must be **square**, **circle**, or **rectangle**. That token constitutes the entire string that will be derived by **parsePrimitive**. However, to follow the convention, **parsePrimitive** must read the next token before returning. As another example, **parseInteger** is called after the integer it is to parse has been read. It must advance the input to the next token to follow the convention.

Consider **parsePicture** again. When it is called, the first token has already been read. Suppose it is **scale**. The next **getToken** should get an **oparen**, and the next a **floatnum**. Notice that after return from **parseFloat**, **theLexer** is tested for a **cparen** *without* a call to **getToken** first; that is because, according to the convention, **parseFloat** must already have read past the number it was parsing. After recognizing the **cparen**, **parsePicture** calls **getToken** once more, to ensure that the first token in the **UnscaledPicture** has been read as per the convention, before it calls **parseUnscaledPicture**.

As a final example, here is the function **parse** given at the end of **parse.C**; it is the function called from **main**:

```
SyntaxTreeNode *parse () {
  getToken();
  SyntaxTreeNode *tn = parsePicture();
  if (theLexer.type() != endoffile)
    theLexer.error("premature end of specification");
  else
    return tn;
}
```

All it does is to call **getToken** and then **parsePicture**; the call to **getToken** is to ensure that the first token of the picture has been read before **parsePicture** is called.

Each **parse** function produces the portion of the tree that derives its part of the input. Therefore, the overall effect of these calls is to construct the syntax tree for the entire specification.

10.6.5   shape.C **and** shapelist.C

With parsing done, the next stage of processing is to produce a list of "shapes," which are then drawn. The computation is done in **computeshapes.C**. Here, we will discuss the two classes **Shape** and **ShapeList**, which are used to represent the result of calling **computeshapes**.

The **Shape** and **ShapeList** classes are declared in **shape.h** and completed in **shape.C** and **shapelist.C**, respectively. **ShapeList** is analogous to our other list classes. Its value field is of type **Shape**. Its only other distinguishing feature is the member function **draw**, defined in **shapelist.C** (page 579), which simply sends the **draw** message to each **Shape** object in the list.

Shape objects are the specific shapes—circles, squares, and rectangles, with their locations and sizes—that make up the final picture. Before looking at the member functions of **Shape**, note the class **Point**, used to represent positions on the screen. It is defined (as well as declared) in **shape.h**:

```
// Points are simply pairs of floating-point numbers.
// Operations allow access to each item in the pair,
// and "component-wise" addition of pairs.
class Point {
private:
  float x, y;

public:
  Point (float a, float b) : x(a), y(b) {}

  float getX () { return x; }

  float getY () { return y; }

  Point operator+ (Point p) { return Point(x+p.x, y+p.y); }
```

Shape is declared in **shape.h**:

```
// Shape objects are primitive shapes, with enough detail
// (type of shape, size, and location) to be drawn
class Shape {
private:
  TokenType primShape;  // circle or rectangle
  float eastDist,       // distance from center to east edge
        northDist,      // to north edge
        northeastDist,  // to northeast corner
        neAngle;        // angle to northeast corner
  Point centerOfShape;
  boolean visible;      // false if invisible, true o.w.

  float angleTo (TokenType dir) ;
    // Compute angle to any direction;  angle to northeast
    // is given by data member neAngle

  float distanceTo (TokenType dir) ;
    // Compute distance to any direction;  distances to
    // east, north, and northeast are given by data members

public:
  Shape (TokenType prim, float radius, boolean vis) ;

  Shape (TokenType prim, float eastRadius,
         float northRadius, boolean vis) ;

  void draw (Screen&) ;

  Point computePerimeterPoint (TokenType dir) ;
    // Compute perimeter point in direction dir

  void computeCenter (Point p, TokenType dir) ;
    // Compute and fill in center, given that point p
    // is to fall at direction dir.
```

Its two constructors are used to create shapes with a single *length* (circles and squares) and shapes with both a *width* and a *height* (rectangles), respectively. In the first, **radius** is the distance from the center of the shape to the east point; this is just the radius of a circle or half the length of the side of a square. In the second, **eastRadius** is the distance from the center to the east point, **northRadius** the distance from the center to the north point. In each case, the argument **vis** indicates whether the shape is invisible (**vis** = **false**) or not.

There are three other public member functions:

void draw (Screen *s) sends the appropriate **drawLine** or **drawCircle** message to **s** to draw this shape.

Point computePerimeterPoint (TokenType dir) finds the point at which **dir** occurs on this shape. For example, if the shape is a circle having radius 5 and its center is (13, 30), then if **dir** is **east**, computePerimeterPoint returns the point $(18, 30)$. In computing north and south perimeter points, account must be taken of the "upside-down" nature of screen coordinates; the further south (lower on the screen) a point, the *higher* its y coordinate. So, if a square with side 10 has its center at $(15, 15)$, then its **south** perimeter point is $(15, 20)$. **dir** may also be **center**, in which case computePerimeterPoint returns the center of the shape.

void computeCenter (Point p, TokenType dir) finds the center of a shape, given its dimensions and the point to which it is connected. When a shape is first constructed, its dimensions are supplied; they are easily obtained just by looking at a small part of the syntax tree. We call this *position-independent* information. The only missing piece of information is the position itself (that is, the center of the shape), which can be determined only by knowing the point to which this shape is connected and how it is connected. **computeCenter** is given a point **p** and a compass point in this shape that is supposed to fall at point **p**. From there, the center of this shape is computed and filled in. For example, if the south point of a circle of radius 5 is to fall at location $(20, 30)$, then its center must fall at $(20, 25)$. If the northeast point of a square with sides of length 10 is to fall at $(100, 150)$, then the center must be at $(95, 155)$.

Implementation

The **Shape** class implements only two shapes: circle and rectangle. The first constructor provides an interface to a client that wishes to create a square, but internally **Shape** treats squares as rectangles.

The **Shape** constructors, defined in **shape.C** (page 576) set all the data members of the class.[4]

```
Shape::Shape (TokenType prim, float radius, boolean vis)
  : primShape(prim), centerOfShape(0, 0), eastDist(radius),
    northDist(radius), neAngle(Pi/4), visible(vis)
  // Use for circle or square;  for square, radius
  // is half of length of side
{
  if (prim == circle)
    northeastDist = radius;
  else {
    primShape = rectangle;
    northeastDist = radius * Sqrt2;
  }
}
```

[4]Constants **Pi** and **Sqrt2** are defined at the beginning of **shape.C**.

```
Shape::Shape (TokenType prim, float eastRadius,
              float northRadius, boolean vis)
  : primShape(prim), centerOfShape(0, 0), eastDist(eastRadius),
    northDist(northRadius), visible(vis)
  // Use for rectangle;  eastRadius is half of length,
  // northRadius is half of height
{
    northeastDist = sqrt(eastDist*eastDist + northDist*northDist);
    neAngle = atan(northDist/eastDist);
}
```

All of the data members but `centerOfShape`—that is, all the position-independent values—retain their values permanently; `centerOfShape` obtains its true value by subsequently receiving the `computeCenter` message. Most of the data members are illustrated in Figure 10.11.

> `TokenType primShape`: Either `circle` or `rectangle`. The one-argument constructor sets this to `rectangle` if its first argument is `square`.
>
> `float eastDist, northDist, northeastDist`: The distance from the center of the shape to the various points on the shape's perimeter. For circles, all three quantities are identical. For squares, the **radius** argument to the first constructor should be half the length of a side, and `northeastDist` is correctly set to this quantity multiplied by $\sqrt{2}$. For rectangles, `eastDist` and `northDist` are half the length and height, respectively, and `northeastDist` is calculated by the Pythagorean formula.
>
> `float neAngle`: The angle to the northeast point on the perimeter, expressed in radians. For squares and circles this is always $\pi/4$ radians (45 degrees). For rectangles it is calculated using the **atan** function in the mathematical library.
>
> `Point centerOfShape`: This is filled in as $(0, 0)$ by the constructors, only because C++ insists it be initialized, but the real center is calculated later by sending the `computeCenter` message.
>
> `boolean visible`: `true` if the shape was not specified as `invisible`.

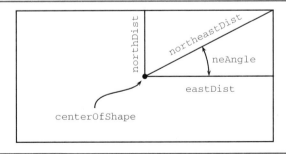

FIGURE 10.11   Data members of **Shape** class

The public member functions are **draw**, **computePerimeterPoint**, and **computeCenter**. **draw** is straightforward, using **drawCircle** and (four calls to) **drawLine** from the **Screen** class. **Shape** keeps values in floating-point form, so they must be rounded to integers to call those functions. For rectangles, first the northeast point is calculated; then a line is drawn to the southeast, then to the southwest, then to the northwest, and back to the northeast. Note that since we are drawing on a screen, where *higher* values on the vertical axis represent *lower* positions on the screen, the southeast point has a larger *y* value than the northeast point.

```
void Shape::draw (Screen& s) {
  Point p1(0, 0);
  int x, y;
  int length, height;
  if (visible) {
    switch (primShape) {
      case circle:
        s.drawCircle(round(centerOfShape.getX()),
                     round(centerOfShape.getY()),
                     round(eastDist));
        break;
      case rectangle:
        length = round(eastDist*2);
        height = round(northDist*2);
        p1 = computePerimeterPoint(northeast);
        x = round(p1.getX());
        y = round(p1.getY());
        s.drawLine(x, y, x, y+height);
        s.drawLine(x, y+height, x-length, y+height);
        s.drawLine(x-length, y+height, x-length, y);
        s.drawLine(x-length, y, x, y);
        break;
    }
  }
}
```

computePerimeterPoint is called when a shape is to be attached to a perimeter point of the receiver. (This assumes that the center of the receiver has already been filled in by a call to **computeCenter**.) It must find the point on the perimeter of the shape corresponding to the direction given by its argument. We have done this in a very general way. By finding the angle θ and distance r to the perimeter point (we will show how subsequently), we obtain a vector in polar coordinates. The function **Point vector (float angle, float magnitude)**, given at the beginning of **shape.C**,

```
Point vector (float angle, float magnitude) {
  // Convert polar to Cartesian coordinates
  // However, use "upside-down" Cartesian coordinates,
  // since we're talking about points on a screen
  return Point(magnitude*cos(angle), -magnitude*sin(angle));
}
```

converts this vector to Cartesian coordinates using the correspondence

$$(r, \theta) \text{ in polar coordinates } = (r\cos\theta, r\sin\theta) \text{ in Cartesian coordinates}$$

However, to account for the "upside-down" nature of screen coordinates, we need to negate the y value, giving $(r\cos\theta, -r\sin\theta)$. **computePerimeterPoint** find θ and r, calls **vector**, then adds the resulting vector to the center of the shape using the overloading of **operator+** given in the **Point** class (in **shape.h**):

```
Point Shape::computePerimeterPoint (TokenType dir) {
    // Compute perimeter point in direction dir
    return centerOfShape + vector(angleTo(dir), distanceTo(dir));
}
```

In turn, r and θ are computed by calls to private member functions **float distanceTo (TokenType dir)** and **float angleTo (TokenType dir)**, respectively. Note that for the case when the direction is **center**, r is 0, **vector** returns (0, 0), and the result is just the center of the shape.

distanceTo is easy to understand. **Shape** data members **eastDist** and **northDist** give the distances to the points on the horizontal and vertical axes, respectively; **northeastDist** is the distance to all intermediate compass points:

```
float Shape::distanceTo (TokenType dir) {
    // distance from center to direction dir
    switch (dir) {
      case center:
            return 0;
      case east:
      case west:
            return eastDist;
      case south:
      case north:
            return northDist;
      case northeast:
      case southeast:
      case southwest:
      case northwest:
            return northeastDist;
    }
}
```

For points on the axes, θ is always a multiple of $\pi/2$ radians (90 degrees). For the northeast perimeter point, θ is given by data member **neAngle**; the angles for other intermediate compass points are found by reflecting **neAngle** across one or both axes, which is accomplished by negating the angle, adding π, or both. See Figure 10.12.

```
float Shape::angleTo (TokenType dir) {
    switch (dir) {
      case center:      return 0;
      case east:        return 0;
      case south:       return -Pi/2;
      case west:        return Pi;
```

```
      case north:      return Pi/2;
      case northeast:  return neAngle;
      case southeast:  return -neAngle;
      case southwest:  return Pi+neAngle;
      case northwest:  return Pi-neAngle;
    }
  }
```

`computeCenter` is called after the position-independent quantities in a shape have been filled in. Its arguments are a point **p** and a direction **dir**. The center of the shape is to be calculated in such a way that the point on the perimeter given by **dir**—that is, `computePerimeterPoint(dir)`—will equal **p**. This is no more difficult than `computePerimeterPoint`. Just take the vector computed there, *reverse its direction* (by adding π to θ), and add it to **p**:

```
  void Shape::computeCenter (Point p, TokenType dir) {
    centerOfShape = p + vector(Pi+angleTo(dir), distanceTo(dir));
  }
```

10.6.6 computeshapes.C

This file defines function `void computeShapes (SyntaxTreeNode *)`. It is given the syntax tree produced by **parse**, and it places into the global variable `computedShapes` a list of all the shapes in the picture. Sending the **draw** message to `computedShapes` completes the computation.

Implementation

`computeShapes` and its various auxiliary operations in this file do their work by "traversing" the syntax tree, calculating sizes and positions of the shapes in the specification. Traversing a syntax tree is a process for which recursion is extremely useful. Before discussing `computeShapes` itself, let's look at some other, simpler, examples of tree traversals.

The first question in processing a syntax tree is, How can we visit all the nodes in the tree? Suppose we want to do something as simple as listing all the

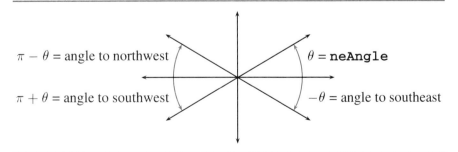

$\pi - \theta$ = angle to northwest

$\pi + \theta$ = angle to southwest

$\theta = $ **neAngle**

$-\theta$ = angle to southeast

FIGURE 10.12 Computing angles to intermediate compass points

production numbers in the tree. It's easy to do if we can get to every node, but how can we do that? The answer is *recursion*. Consider a node with two children, such as the top node in the tree on page 541. If we have managed to reach that node (and printed 3), we can visit its two children *recursively*. The structure of our function might be

```
void printProdNums (SyntaxTreeNode *tn) {
  cout << tn->getProduction() << '\n';
  printProdNums(tn->getChild(0));
  printProdNums(tn->getChild(1));
}
```

Of course, this function works only for nodes with two children, and it lacks a base case. A more general version is, in abstract form,

```
void printProdNums (SyntaxTreeNode *tn) {
  cout << tn->getProduction() << '\n';
  for (<every child ch of tn>)
    printProdNums(ch);
}
```

This not only handles nodes with any number of children; it also includes the base case: nodes with no children.

The only problem is that we don't know how many children **tn** has, and there is no member function in **SyntaxTreeNode** that tells us (for the functions in **computeshapes.C**, it is not needed). So we will write a function named **countChildren** and then complete **printProdNums**.

```
int numChildren[18] =
  // Number of children for production number n is
  // given in numChildren[n-1]
  {2, 1, 2, 0, 2, 3, 3, 0, 0, 0, 0, 0, 2, 0, 1, 0, 0, 0};

int countChildren (SyntaxTreeNode *tn) {
  return numChildren[tn->getProduction()-1];
}

void printProdNums (SyntaxTreeNode *tn) {
  cout << tn->getProduction() << "\n";
  for (int i=0; i<countChildren(tn); i++)
    printProdNums(tn->getChild(i));
}
```

For the syntax tree on page 541, the first part of the output from this function is

```
3
7
8
10
13
...
5
...
```

Note the order in which the production numbers are printed. Suppose the output statement were moved *after* the loop. Can you tell what the output would be? Try it.

As another example, suppose we want to print the production numbers with indentation based on the level of the node in the tree. The partial output in the preceding paragraph would become

```
3
  7
    8
    10
    13
      . . .
  5
    . . .
```

This function is similar to the previous one, but it needs an extra argument that gives the indentation for the subtree being printed:

```
void printProdNumsIndented (SyntaxTreeNode *tn, int indent) {
  cout << setw(indent) << "" << tn->getProduction() << "\n";
  for (int i=0; i<countChildren(tn); i++)
    printProdNumsIndented(tn->getChild(i), indent+2);
}

void printProdNumsIndented (SyntaxTreeNode *tn) {
  printProdNumsIndented(tn, 0);
}
```

Writing tree traversals is not hard if you use our usual approach to recursion: *Assume* that the function works on the children of a node, and then compute the function for this tree from its values on the children. As a last example, the following function counts the size of the syntax tree (that is, the total number of nodes in it):

```
int countSize (SyntaxTreeNode *tn) {
  int size = 1; // count this node
  for (int i=0; i<countChildren(tn); i++)
    size = size + countSize(tn->getChild(i));
  return size;
}
```

Exercise 1 gives a number of simple tree traversals you can use to improve your skills before proceeding.

When `computeShapes (SyntaxTreeNode *tn)` is called, its argument is a pointer to a syntax tree for an entire picture specification, whose production number is 1 or 3. It calls the overloaded definition of `computeShapes`:

```
void computeShapes (SyntaxTreeNode *tn, // picture to be drawn
                    Point dirPoint,     // with this point
                    TokenType dir,      // in this direction
                    float scale)        // scaled by this
```

This version of `computeShapes` and the function

```
void computeSubpictures
            (SyntaxTreeNode *tn,  // associated shapes
             Shape sh, // shape to which they are connected
             float scale)
```

are the functions that actually traverse the syntax tree. They will be the focus of our discussion here. This file also contains functions

```
Shape computeShape (SyntaxTreeNode *tn, // Must be production 7
                    Point dirPoint,      // This point is at
                    TokenType dir,       // this direction
                    float scale)         // Scale by this amount
```

and its auxiliary function

```
Shape computePosIndInfo (SyntaxTreeNode *tn, // Production 7
                         float scale)
```

which are called by `computeShapes` to compute a single shape. They will be explained after we've discussed the tree traversal.

The overall plan here is that `computeShapes` is called when a node for production 1 or 3 (**Picture** or **UnscaledPicture**) is visited, whereas `compute-Subpictures` is called when a node for production 4 or 5 (**SubpictureList**) is visited. These two functions are mutually recursive: **Picture** and **UnscaledPicture** syntax trees contain **SubpictureList** subtrees, and vice versa. Furthermore, `computeShapes` calls function `computeShape` to construct a `Shape` object from a production 7 (**Shape**) node.

The reason we use two mutually recursive functions to traverse the syntax tree is that the two types of nodes need different kinds of information. Referring to the syntax tree on page 524, consider the **UnscaledPicture** node on the bottom right. It needs to know where the shape it contains (a circle) will be placed. To calculate this, it needs to know the radius of the circle, which it can get from the **Shape** subtree itself. However, it also needs two pieces of information that it cannot get from that subtree: the point it is connected to (in this case, the center of the 100×100 square) and the perimeter point of the circle that connects to that point (in this case, the center of the circle). That is why `computeShapes`, which handles **UnscaledPicture** nodes, has among its arguments a `Point` and a `TokenType` parameter called `dir`.

Consider, on the other hand, the **SubpictureList** node near the top right of the tree. The program may have to place many connected shapes (although there is only one in this particular tree). Since the direction of each connection may vary and is given in the **Subpicture** subtrees, all it needs to know is the `Shape` object to which it is connecting other shapes. Thus, its arguments include a `Shape`.

In addition, any picture may be scaled, in which case all the shapes contained in that picture are scaled, so the `float` argument `scale` is passed to both functions.

Before looking at the internal details of these two functions, consider the one-argument version of `computeShapes`:

```
void computeShapes (SyntaxTreeNode *tn) {
  // tn is node for production 1 or 3, the top node in
  // the syntax tree of the entire specification.
  // The first shape in a specification is centered in
  // the middle of the screen, scaled by 1 by default.
  float scale = 1.0;
  if (tn->getProduction() == 1) { // scale factor given
    scale = tn->getChild(0)->getFloatValue();
    tn = tn->getChild(1);
  }
  computeShapes(tn, Point(width/2, height/2), center, scale);
}
```

The entire specification is centered in the middle of the screen and scaled by 1.
The size of the screen is given by the two integer constants **width** and **height**,
defined in **shape.h**. Its center is, therefore, at the point $(\text{width}/2, \text{height}/2)$.
We see that a production 3 (**UnscaledPicture**) node is calculated by calling the
four-argument version of **computeShapes** with arguments specifying that the
center of the picture is to be located at the center of the screen, and the scale
factor is 1. A production 1 (**Picture**) node is handled similarly, its production 3
child is passed to the four-argument version of **computeShapes** with the same
arguments, except for the **scale** argument.

Now consider the four-argument version of **computeShapes**:

```
void computeShapes (SyntaxTreeNode *tn, // picture to be drawn
                    Point dirPoint,     // with this point
                    TokenType dir,      // in this direction
                    float scale)        // scaled by this
{
  // tn is node for production 1 or 3
  if (tn->getProduction() == 1) { // scale factor given
    scale = scale * tn->getChild(0)->getFloatValue();
    tn = tn->getChild(1);
  }
  SyntaxTreeNode *tn1 = tn->getChild(0),  // shape
                 *tn2 = tn->getChild(1);  // associated pictures
  // Compute one primitive shape and add it to computedShapes
  Shape sh = computeShape(tn1, dirPoint, dir, scale);
  computedShapes = new ShapeList(sh, computedShapes);
  // Then compute all shapes connected to it
  computeSubpictures(tn2, sh, scale);
}
```

Consider first the case of a production 3 node. Such a node has two children, the
first a **Shape** and the second a **SubpictureList**. There is enough information in
the arguments to this function and in the first child itself to compute its shape
(including its position on the screen). This is done by a call to **computeChild**
(explained below), and the returned shape is placed on the list **computedShapes**.
It is this shape to which the shapes in the second child are connected, so it is
passed, along with the second child, to **computeSubpictures**.

For a production 1 node, **computeShapes** adjusts the scale factor and then
computes the shape of its production 3 child. (Although we have seen that this
routine is never called from the one-argument version of **computeShapes** with

a production 1 node, it may be called recursively, from `computeSubpictures`, with one.)

`computeSubpictures` handles a production 4 node by doing nothing. A production 5 node contains a **Subpicture** (which in turn contains two **Direction** nodes and a **Picture**) and a **SubpictureList** node. The first direction is used to compute a perimeter point on the containing shape, and this point is passed, along with the second **Direction** and the **Picture** subtree, to `computeShapes`. `computeSubpictures` then calls itself recursively to process the second child of the production 5 node.

```
void computeSubpictures
              (SyntaxTreeNode *tn,   // associated shapes
               Shape sh, // shape to which they are connected
               float scale)
{
  // tn is for production 4 or 5.  If 5, then it has
  // two children, and the first child has three children.
  if (tn->getProduction() == 4)
    return;
  SyntaxTreeNode *subpic = tn->getChild(0);
  TokenType dir1 = subpic->getChild(0)->getDirection(),
           dir2 = subpic->getChild(1)->getDirection();
  Point perimPoint = sh.computePerimeterPoint(dir1);
  computeShapes(subpic->getChild(2), perimPoint, dir2, scale);
  computeSubpictures(tn->getChild(1), sh, scale);
}
```

Thus, by mutual recursion, `computeShapes` and `computeSubpictures` visit every node with production number 1, 3, 4, or 5. In this way they can compute every shape in the picture.

The function `computeShape` is called by `computeShapes` to produce a shape given by a production 7 node. Note again that most of the information needed to draw a shape—all but its center—can be calculated from the production 7 subtree with no information about the connecting shapes; only the scale factor is needed. `computePosIndInfo` computes all of this position-independent information, returning a shape. Using the arguments that were passed to it from `computeShapes`, `computeShape` can calculate the center of the new shape.

```
Shape computePosIndInfo (SyntaxTreeNode *tn, // Production 7
                         float scale)
{
  // Create a shape and compute all information that is
  // independent of its position - everything but its center.
  // This is just a matter of finding the primitive shape and
  // its size (scaled by scale).
  int visProd = tn->getChild(0)->getProduction(),  // 8 or 9
      primProd = tn->getChild(1)->getProduction(); // 10, 11, 12
  boolean vis = (visProd == 8);    // true, if visible shape
  SyntaxTreeNode *sizenode = tn->getChild(2);  // Production 13
  int size1 = sizenode->getChild(0)->getIntValue();
  SyntaxTreeNode *size2node = sizenode->getChild(1);
  int size2;
```

```
        if (size2node->getProduction() == 15)
          size2 = size2node->getChild(0)->getIntValue();
        if (primProd == 10) // square
          return Shape(square, scale*size1/2, vis); // divide by 2
            // because length, not radius, is given in specification
        else if (primProd == 11) // circle
          return Shape(circle, scale*size1, vis);
        else // rectangle
          return Shape(rectangle, scale*size1/2, scale*size2/2, vis);
      }

      Shape computeShape (SyntaxTreeNode *tn, // Must be production 7
                          Point dirPoint,     // This point is at
                          TokenType dir,      // this direction
                          float scale)        // Scale by this amount
      {
        Shape sh = computePosIndInfo(tn, scale);
        sh.computeCenter(dirPoint, dir);
        return sh;
      }
```

10.6.7 screen.C

An implementation of the **Screen** class was given in Chapter 9. It provides the member functions **drawLine** and **drawCircle**, and those are the functions we used in **Shape::draw**.

However, it is worth mentioning that the **Screen** class can be modified to allow for output to be performed by other methods rather than going directly to the screen.

The version of **Screen** we used to produce the pictures in this chapter is shown on page 581. It produces commands for a drawing program. These commands have the form

```
\psline(x,y)(x',y')
\pscircle(x,y){r}
```

where **x**, **y**, **x'**, **y'**, and **r** are integers. These commands are given to the drawing program, which created the figures in this chapter.

Exercises—Third Set

1. Program the following tree-traversal functions:
   (a) **int countSquares (SyntaxTreeNode *)** counts the number of squares (that is, occurrences of production 10) in a picture.
   (b) **int height (SyntaxTreeNode *)** computes the *height* of a tree, that is, the longest distance from the top node to a leaf node.
   (c) **SyntaxTreeNode *mirror (SyntaxTreeNode *)** computes the mirror image of a picture. This is a picture with the same shapes and sizes, but with all directions reversed: north becomes south, east becomes west, northeast becomes southwest, and so on.
   (d) **void mirrorM (SyntaxTreeNode *)** is similar to **mirror** but is a mutating operation. It should change its argument to its own mirror image. In other words, after calling **mirrorM(t)**, t should be the same syntax tree as would have been returned from **mirror(t)**. You will need a new mutating member function

```
void SyntaxTreeNode::setDirection (TokenType t)
```

that allows the **direction** of a **SyntaxTreeNode** object to be changed to **t**.

2. Line numbers should be included in error messages printed by **psl**. You can keep track of line numbers by counting newline characters, but there is an added difficulty here. Errors are found only when looking at the temporary file produced by **preprocess**; if the include facility is used, the line numbers in the temporary file don't match those in the original files. Add information to the temporary file that allows the original filename and line number to be deduced. Modify **getToken** to check for this information and store it, and modify **FSM::error** to print the filename and line number of each error. (The filenames and line numbers in the temporary file can be surrounded with special characters that do not otherwise occur, and **getToken** can read this information without passing it on to **feedCharacter**. The information should be placed into the temporary file whenever the file being read changes.)

3. Every language should have a way of including comments in a program or specification. These comments should be recognized and eliminated by the lexer. There are a number of commenting styles in use. Implement each of the following commenting styles in PSL. This will require a change in the transition diagram and, consequently, the lexer (especially **feedCharacter**), but it should involve no other changes.

   (a) *C++ style, but with a one-character comment starter*: Comments start with a single character and run through the end of the line. To avoid confusion with the current use of /, use the semicolon (;) as the comment starter.

   (b) *C++ style*: Comments start with // and continue to the end of the line. Because comments start with *two* / characters, you can distinguish them from the existing use of /.

   (c) *"Parenthesized" style*: Comments begin with an open brace ({) and end with a closing brace (}). The advantage of this style is that a line can contain a comment at the beginning, with meaningful code after it, and an entire group of lines can be "commented out" with the insertion of only two characters. (C++ actually allows a similar comment style, which we haven't used; see Appendix E.)

   (d) *Parenthesized style, with nesting*: In the pure parenthesized style, a comment ends with the first closing brace, even if there was another opening brace preceding it. For example, suppose we have a line like this:

   ```
   { comment 1 } real code { comment 2 }
   ```

   and we attempt to comment out the entire line by placing braces before and after it:

   ```
   {
   { comment 1 } real code { comment 2 }
   }
   ```

   We have shown in color how the braces match up; the *real code* is not commented out. The problem is that comments don't nest. Implement a nested comment style. Maintain a comment-level counter, initialized to zero. Opening braces increment it, closing braces decrement it (but are legal only when the counter is nonzero), and every character encountered while the counter is nonzero is considered part of the comment.

4. Allow shapes in a picture to be labeled with text, by adding the production

   | 19 | **Primitive** | $\rightarrow$ | **String** |
   | 20 | **String** | $\rightarrow$ | any sequence of characters surrounded by single quotes |

That is, a string is a new kind of shape. (We've used single quotes to avoid conflict with the include facility.) For purposes of computing compass points, a string is considered to be a rectangle whose height is 6 and whose length is 3 times the number of characters. For example, the specification

```
rectangle (50, 20)
   connecting c/c ('Bingo!' connecting s/n (circle (3))
                            connecting e/w (square (6))))
```

produces the picture

Since **string** is already a type of token, there is no need to change the lexical analyzer. However, the parser needs to change (we have given the new production a high number so as to avoid changes in most of the parsing functions). Most of all, the **Shape** class needs to be changed.

5. Add the primitive shape **oval** to PSL. This requires changes in most parts of the program. Add **oval** as a new token and the production

19 **Primitive** → oval

to the grammar. You may assume that the **Screen** class has a **drawOval** function, but the **Shape** class still needs to know how to calculate the data members for ovals. The second constructor will be used for both ovals and rectangles, with the **eastRadius** and **northRadius** arguments having the same meaning as for rectangles. **neAngle** is also the same as for rectangles, but **northeastDist** is calculated by the formula

$$ne\ \sqrt{(1 + \tan^2 \theta)/(n^2 + e^2 \tan^2 \theta)}$$

where n is **northDist**, e is **eastDist**, and θ is **neAngle**. Just as the **Shape** class only represents rectangles and not squares, it will no longer need to represent circles, because they are simply a special case of ovals.

★ 6. In Chapter 8 we wrote a function to read and evaluate arithmetic expressions. There we found no need to build a syntax tree; the expression could just be evaluated as it was read. However, some types of processing of arithmetic expressions are easier if a syntax tree is constructed first. In this exercise, we explore some examples.

(a) Modify the calculator given in Chapter 8 to read, parse, and build a syntax tree for an input expression. Use the grammar given on page 516, extended with the productions

Expression	→	**Term - Expression**
Term	→	**Factor / Term**
Factor	→	**Variable**

where a variable is any single letter. Follow the model we have used in this chapter, defining a lexer, a type of "tokens," a syntax tree class, and so on.

(b) Define a member function **float eval ()** in the syntax tree class. It should evaluate an expression just as the calculator did. (Syntax tree nodes containing variables can be ignored; just have them evaluate to zero.)

(c) Write a member function **void print ()** that prints the expression represented by a syntax tree. You will need to insert parentheses (which are not explicitly included in the syntax tree), but you should try to minimize them.

(d) Write a member function `SyntaxTreeNode *differentiate ()` that constructs a new expression representing the partial derivative of the receiver with respect to the variable **x**. For example, if **expr** points to the syntax tree for the expression **x*x + 10*y**, then **expr->differentiate()** should return the syntax tree for **2*x** (or an equivalent expression).

(e) In writing **differentiate**, you will find that the resulting expressions contain many unnecessary operations, such as addition of 0 and multiplication by 1. Write a member function **void simplify ()** that "cleans up" an expression by doing various algebraic simplifications: eliminate multiplication by one; eliminate multiplication and addition of zero; change expressions of the form *e*/*e* to 1 and expressions of the form **1/(1/***e***)** to *e*; and so on. **simplify** is a mutating operation; it changes its receiver to the simpler form.

Summary

Programs in C++ can be divided into multiple files, called *source files,* so long as every name (of a function, class, or variable) is declared before it is used. This rule can be difficult to follow, because a function defined in one file may need to call a function or use a variable defined in another. The multiple files are tied together through the use of *header files,* which contain class and variable declarations and function prototypes used by more than one source file. Each source file that needs the declarations given in a header file includes it using the **#include** facility. This permits the file to be *compiled* separately. To run the program, all the object files produced by the compiler from various source files must be *linked* together; every name declared in the header files must be defined in one of the object files.

A source file may use **#include** to include both system-supplied header files (using **#include <file>**) and user-created header files (using **#include "file"**). When the program is to be run, the linker may combine user-generated object files and system-supplied object files (also called *libraries*).

Global variable declarations look exactly like ordinary variable declarations but are preceded by the keyword **extern**. The usual variable "declaration" syntax should properly be called a *definition*, because it allocates memory for the variable. Header files should not contain global variable definitions but can contain global variable *declarations*. A variable's definition should be given in exactly *one* source file.

In C++, input and output are done using *streams*. **cout** and **cin** are streams that are predefined in every C++ program that includes **iostream.h**. **cout** is an output stream (an object of class **ostream**); output streams have overloaded definitions of **operator<<**. **cin** is an input stream (an object of class **istream**); input streams have overloaded definitions of **operator>>** as well as member functions **eof** and **get**.

A stream may be connected to a file, in the sense that output goes into that file or input comes from that file. Streams that are connected to files are objects of class **ifstream** or **ofstream**, declared in **fstream.h**. To create an input stream called **ifs** attached to a file **inputfile**, construct an **ifstream** object and send it the **open** message,

```
ifstream ifs;
ifs.open("inputfile", ios::in);
```

or call the two-argument **ifstream** constructor:

```
ifstream ifs("inputfile", ios::in)
```

Then, for example, if **c** is a **char** variable, **ifs >> c** will read a character from **inputfile** into **c**.

To create an output stream called **ofs** attached to a file **outputfile**, construct **ofs** and send the **open** message to it,

```
ofstream ofs;
ofs.open("outputfile", ios::out);
```

or call the two-argument **ofstream** constructor:

```
ofstream ofs("outputfile", ios::out)
```

The second argument to **open** or to the constructor—the *mode*—for an **ofstream** may be either **ios::out** or **ios::app**. In either case, subsequent calls to **ofs <<** *<expression>* will place the value of *<expression>* in **outputfile**. With the first form (using **ios::out**), the previous contents of **outputfile** (if any) will be destroyed and its only contents will be the contents you write; with the second form (using **ios::app**) the output from this program will be appended to the contents of the file for an **ofstream**.

A file can be closed by sending the **close** message to the **ifstream** or **ofstream** object to which it is connected.

An attempt to open a file may fail, either because the file doesn't exist or because you don't have permission to use it. After calling **open** or the two-argument constructor, you should send the message **fail** to the stream (that is, call **ifs.fail()** or **ofs.fail()**); it will return the boolean value **true** if the file could *not* be opened, and **false** otherwise.

The **main** function in a C++ program can receive arguments from the command line. The system takes the program name and the arguments on the command line and places each one in a character array, then places a pointer to each array into another array, conventionally called **argv**. It passes two arguments to **main**: an integer (called **argc**), giving the number of entries in **argv**, and the address of **argv**. A common command-line argument is the name of a file, which the program can attempt to open for input or output.

Languages processed by computer—such as PSL and C++—are almost always defined by a *context-free grammar*. A context-free grammar is a set of *productions* of the form $A \rightarrow w$, where A is one of a finite set of *variables* and w is a string of zero or more variables and *literals*. Productions can be used to form *syntax trees*. When all the variables occurring in a syntax tree have children, so that the bottom, or *frontier*, of the syntax tree contains only literals, this string of literals is a sentence in the language defined by the grammar.

Parsing is the process of finding a syntax tree whose frontier matches a given input string. In practice, the input is divided into units, called *tokens*, by the *lexer*. Lexers are usually written using transition diagrams (also known as *finite-state machines*). Tokens are analogous to words in natural languages; the characters correspond to letters and entire inputs to sentences.

One simple method of parsing is *recursive descent*. Each variable in the grammar has an associated function responsible for parsing strings derivable from that variable. These functions follow very closely the productions of the grammar.

Once a syntax tree has been constructed, it is traversed to produce output. Tree traversal is a naturally recursive process.

The keyword introduced in this chapter is
```
extern
```

10.7

The `ps1` **Program**

This section gives the listings of every file in the **ps1** program, beginning with the three header files. To better help you understand the program structure, the diagram in Figure 10.13 shows which source (**.C**) files include which header (**.h**) files. All the system header files we need—**iostream.h, iomanip.h**, and so on—are included in **ps1.h**, which in turn is included in every source file. **preprocess.C** includes only **ps1.h**; **lexer.C** and **parse.C** include **ps1.h** and **lexer.h**; and the remaining source files include **ps1.h** and **shape.h**.

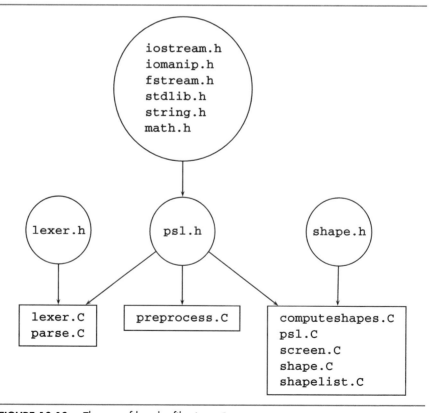

FIGURE 10.13   The use of header files in **ps1**.

10.7.1 psl.h

```
//
// psl.h - main header file for PSL processor.
//   Includes declarations of enum type TokenType
//   and class syntaxTreeNode.  These are the types
//   used to communicate between the two major phases
//   of the PSL processor, parsing and shape computation.
//
// Included in: all source files
//
// Author:  R. Holly Kamin
// Last modified: 4/4/95
//

#include <iostream.h>
#include <iomanip.h>
#include <fstream.h>
#include <stdlib.h>
#include <string.h>
#include <math.h>

enum boolean {false, true};

enum TokenType {intnum, floatnum, oparen, cparen, comma, slash,
                scale, connecting,
                center, north, east, south, west,
                northeast, southeast, southwest, northwest,
                square, circle, rectangle, invisible,
                endoffile, badToken};

class SyntaxTreeNode {
private:
  int productionNum;
  SyntaxTreeNode *children[3];
  TokenType direction;  // used when productionNum = 16
  int ivalue;           // used when productionNum = 17
  float fvalue;         // used when productionNum = 18

public:
  SyntaxTreeNode (int p)
    : productionNum(p) {}

  SyntaxTreeNode (int p, int v)
    : productionNum(p), ivalue(v) {}

  SyntaxTreeNode (int p, float v)
    : productionNum(p), fvalue(v) {}

  SyntaxTreeNode (int p, TokenType dir)
    : productionNum(p), direction(dir) {}
```

```
SyntaxTreeNode (int p, SyntaxTreeNode *c1)
  : productionNum(p)
{
  children[0] = c1;
}

SyntaxTreeNode (int p, SyntaxTreeNode *c1,
                       SyntaxTreeNode *c2)
  : productionNum(p)
{
  children[0] = c1;
  children[1] = c2;
}

SyntaxTreeNode (int p, SyntaxTreeNode *c1,
                       SyntaxTreeNode *c2,
                       SyntaxTreeNode *c3)
  : productionNum(p)
{
  children[0] = c1;
  children[1] = c2;
  children[2] = c3;
}

int getProduction () { return productionNum; }

int getIntValue () { return ivalue; }

float getFloatValue () { return fvalue; }

TokenType getDirection () { return direction; }

SyntaxTreeNode *getChild (int n) { return children[n]; }
};

// Function declarations:

void preprocess (ifstream&, ofstream&) ;

SyntaxTreeNode *parse() ;

void computeShapes (SyntaxTreeNode *) ;
```

10.7.2 `lexer.h`

```
//
// lexer.h - Declaration of FSM is the most important part
//    of this file.  Also includes declarations of function
//    getToken and FSM object theLexer.
//
// Included in: lexer.C, parse.C
//
// Author:  R. Holly Kamin
// Last modified: 4/4/95
//

const int maxTokenLength = 20;

// States names all the states in the transition diagram
// for the lexical analyzer for PSL.

const int numStates = 6;
enum States {Start, Letter, Digit, DecPt, Symbol, Done};

// FSM implements the transition diagram for PSL.
// reset initializes the state to Start, and
// feedCharacter makes a transition.
// Various data are computed during transitions;
// operations are provided to access those data.
class FSM {
private:
  States state;       // current state of finite-state machine
  char buffer[maxTokenLength];  // char's in this token
  int charcount;      // length of this token
  int ivalue;         // value of this token, if an integer
  float fvalue;       // value of this token, if a float
  TokenType ttype;    // type of token

public:
  FSM () : state(Start), charcount(0)
          {}

  void error (char *msg) ;

  void feedCharacter () ;

  boolean tokenReady () { return (state == Done); }

  TokenType type () { return ttype; }

  int intValue () { return ivalue; }

  float floatValue () { return fvalue; }

  void reset () ;
};

extern FSM theLexer;
void getToken ();
```

10.7.3 shape.h

```
//
// shape.h - declaration of Screen, Point, and Shape classes.
//
// Included in: computeshapes.C, ps1.C, screen.C, shape.C,
//              shapelist.C
//
// Author:  R. Holly Kamin
// Last modified: 4/4/95
//

enum colors {black, white};

const int width = 100;
const int height = 100;

class Screen {
private:
  colors frameBuffer[width][height];

  void setPixel (int col, int row, colors c) {
    if ((0 <= col && col < width) &&
        (0 <= row && row < height))
      frameBuffer[col][row] = c;
  }

  void setCirclePoints (int x0, int y0, int x, int y) ;

public:
  Screen () ;

  void displayScreen () ;

  void drawLine (int x1, int y1, int x2, int y2) ;

  void drawCircle (int x0, int y0, int r) ;
};

// Points are simply pairs of floating-point numbers.
// Operations allow access to each item in the pair,
// and "component-wise" addition of pairs.
class Point {
private:
  float x, y;

public:
  Point (float a, float b) : x(a), y(b) {}

  float getX () { return x; }

  float getY () { return y; }

  Point operator+ (Point p) { return Point(x+p.x, y+p.y); }
};
```

```
// Shape objects are primitive shapes, with enough detail
// (type of shape, size, and location) to be drawn
class Shape {
private:
  TokenType primShape; // circle or rectangle
  float eastDist,      // distance from center to east edge
        northDist,     // to north edge
        northeastDist, // to northeast corner
        neAngle;       // angle to northeast corner
  Point centerOfShape;
  boolean visible;     // false if invisible, true o.w.

  float angleTo (TokenType dir) ;
    // Compute angle to any direction;  angle to northeast
    // is given by data member neAngle

  float distanceTo (TokenType dir) ;
    // Compute distance to any direction;  distances to
    // east, north, and northeast are given by data members

public:
  Shape (TokenType prim, float radius, boolean vis) ;

  Shape (TokenType prim, float eastRadius,
         float northRadius, boolean vis) ;

  void draw (Screen&) ;

  Point computePerimeterPoint (TokenType dir) ;
    // Compute perimeter point in direction dir

  void computeCenter (Point p, TokenType dir) ;
    // Compute and fill in center, given that point p
    // is to fall at direction dir.
};

// ShapeList is a standard list class, plus draw function
class ShapeList {
private:
  Shape value;
  ShapeList *nextEntry;
public:
  ShapeList (Shape v, ShapeList *next)
    : value(v), nextEntry(next)
  {}

  Shape getValue () { return value; }

  ShapeList *getNextEntry () { return nextEntry; }

  void draw (Screen&) ;
};
```

10.7.4 ps1.C

```
//
// ps1.C - gives main program for PSL processor, as
//    well as definition of global variable theInput.
//
// Author:  R. Holly Kamin
// Last modified: 4/4/95
//

#include "psl.h"
#include "shape.h"

ifstream theInput; // temporary file containing
      // complete specification, after preprocessing

extern ShapeList *computedShapes; // list of shapes
      // produced by call to computeShapes

const char tempfilename[] = "psltempfile";

void main (int argc, char *argv[]) {
  if (argc != 2) {
    cout << "Usage: psl <filename>\n";
    exit(1);
  }

  // Open specification file
  ifstream inputfile(argv[1], ios::in);
  if (inputfile.fail()) {
    cout << "Unable to open file " << argv[1] << "\n";
    exit(1);
  }

  // Open temporary file for output
  ofstream tempfile(tempfilename, ios::out);
  if (tempfile.fail()) {
    cout << "Unable to open temporary file for output\n";
    exit(1);
  }

  // Copy specification, plus included files, to temporary file
  preprocess(inputfile, tempfile);
  tempfile.close();

  // Open temporary file for input
  theInput.open(tempfilename, ios::in);
  if (tempfile.fail()) {
    cout << "Unable to open temporary file for input\n";
    exit(1);
  }

  // Parse specification
  SyntaxTreeNode *tn = parse();
  // Traverse syntax tree; put list of shapes in computedShapes
```

```
      computeShapes(tn);
      // Draw computed shapes
      Screen screen;
      computedShapes->draw(screen);
    }
```

10.7.5 preprocess.C

```
//
// preprocess.C - function preprocess copies the input file
//    to the temporary file, recursively copying included files
//
// Author:  R. Holly Kamin
// Last modified: 7/14/95
//

#include "ps1.h"

void preprocess (ifstream& input, ofstream& temp) {
  char c = input.get();
  while (!input.eof()) {
    if (c != '"')
      temp << c;
    else { // copy included file
      // Read name of included file
      char includedFile[100];
      int i = 0;
      c = input.get();
      while (c != '"') {
        includedFile[i] = c;
        i++;
        c = input.get();
      }
      includedFile[i] = '\0';

      // Open included file
      ifstream inputfile(includedFile, ios::in);
      if (inputfile.fail()) {
        cout << "Unable to open included file "
             << includedFile << "\n";
        exit(1);
      }

      // Copy included file to temporary file
      preprocess(inputfile, temp);
    }

    c = input.get();
  }
}
```

10.7.6 `lexer.C`

```
//
// lexer.C - member functions of class FSM, declared in
//   lexer.h, plus the definition of global variable theLexer
//   of type FSM, and the client function getToken.
//
// Author:  R. Holly Kamin
// Last modified: 4/4/95
//

#include "psl.h"
#include "lexer.h"

FSM theLexer;
extern ifstream theInput;

void getToken () {
  theLexer.reset();
  while (!theLexer.tokenReady())
    theLexer.feedCharacter();
}

const int numCharacterClasses = 7;
enum CharacterClass {letter, digit, period, symbol,
                     whiteSpace, eof, nothingElse};

CharacterClass classify (char c) {
  if (c == ' ' || c == '\n')
    return whiteSpace;
  else if (c >= 'a' && c <= 'z')
    return letter;
  else if (c >= '0' && c <= '9')
    return digit;
  else if (c == '(' || c == ')' || c == '/' || c == ',')
    return symbol;
  else if (c == '.')
    return period;
  else
    return nothingElse;
}

const int numTokenWords = 15;

char words[numTokenWords][11] =
  {"scale", "connecting", "c", "n", "e", "s", "w",
   "ne", "se", "sw", "nw", "square", "circle",
   "rectangle", "invisible"};
TokenType correspondingToken[numTokenWords] =
  {scale, connecting, center, north, east, south, west,
   northeast, southeast, southwest, northwest,
   square, circle, rectangle, invisible};

TokenType typeOfWord (char *buf) {
  // Compute TokenType corresponding to given string.
```

```
    for (int i=0; i < numTokenWords; i++)
      if (strcmp(buf, words[i]) == 0)
        return correspondingToken[i];
    return badToken;
}

States transitions[numStates][numCharacterClasses] = {
//
//                                      white       nothing
//     letter  digit  period symbol  Space   eof   Else
//     ======  =====  ====== ======  =====   ===   =======
// Start:
     {Letter, Digit, Done,   Symbol, Start, Done, Done},
// Letter:
     {Letter, Done,  Done,   Done,   Done,  Done, Done},
// Digit:
     {Done,   Digit, DecPt,  Done,   Done,  Done, Done},
// DecPt:
     {Done,   DecPt, Done,   Done,   Done,  Done, Done},
// Symbol:
     {Done,   Done,  Done,   Done,   Done,  Done, Done},
// Done:
     {Done,   Done,  Done,   Done,   Done,  Done, Done}};

void FSM::error (char *msg) {
  cout << "Error: " << msg << endl;
  exit(1);
}

void FSM::feedCharacter () {

  char c = theInput.get();
  CharacterClass cc;

  if (theInput.eof())
    cc = eof;
  else
    cc = classify(c);

  States priorState = state;
  state = transitions[state][cc];
  switch (state) {
    case Start:
      break;
    case Letter:
      buffer[charcount] = c;
      charcount++;
      if (charcount == maxTokenLength)
        error("token too long");
      break;
    case Digit:
      // ivalue must have been initialized to zero
      // before this token was read.
      ivalue = 10*ivalue + (c-'0');
      break;
```

```
        case DecPt:
          if (cc == period) { // first time entering this state
            fvalue = ivalue;
            ivalue = 1;   // use to count decimal position
          }
          else { // c must be a digit
            fvalue = fvalue + ((c-'0') / pow(10.0, ivalue));
            ivalue++;
          }
          break;
      case Symbol:
        buffer[0] = c;
        charcount = 1;
        break;
      case Done:
        if (cc != eof)
          theInput.putback(c); // We've read one
                      // character past end of token
        switch (priorState) {
          case Start:
            if (cc == eof)
              ttype = endoffile;
            else
              error("illegal character");
            break;
          case Letter:
            buffer[charcount] = '\0';
            ttype = typeOfWord(buffer);
            if (ttype == badToken)
              error("illegal token");
            break;
          case Digit:
            ttype = intnum;
            break;
          case DecPt:
            ttype = floatnum;
            break;
          case Symbol:
            switch (buffer[0]) {
              case '(': ttype = oparen;  break;
              case ')': ttype = cparen;  break;
              case ',': ttype = comma;  break;
              case '/': ttype = slash;  break;
            }
            break;
          case Done:
            ; // can't happen
        }
        break;
    }
  }
```

```
void FSM::reset () {
  state = Start;
  charcount = 0;
  ivalue = 0;
  fvalue = 0.0;
}
```

10.7.7 parse.C

```
//
// parse.C - functions to parse a PSL specification and
//    produce a syntax tree (SyntaxTreeNode *).  Method is
//    recursive-descent, so there is one function for each
//    variable in the grammar.  Clients call parse.
//    Functions call getToken to get tokens.
//
// Author:  R. Holly Kamin
// Last modified: 4/4/95
//

#include "ps1.h"
#include "lexer.h"

// The grammar:
//
// 1.  Picture      ->  scale ( Float ) Unscaled-picture
// 2.                |  Unscaled-picture
// 3.  Unscaled-picture  -> Shape SubpictureList
// 4.  SubpictureList  ->
// 5.                |  Subpicture SubpictureList
// 6.  Subpicture   ->
//                 connecting  Direction / Direction ( Picture )
// 7.  Shape        ->  Color Primitive Size
// 8.  Color        ->
// 9.                |  invisible
// 10. Primitive    ->  square
// 11.               |  circle
// 12.               |  rectangle
// 13. Size         ->  ( Integer  Size2
// 14. Size2        ->  )
// 15.               |  , Integer )
// 16. Direction    ->  c, n, e, s, w, ne, se, sw, or nw
// 17. Integer      ->  any sequence of digits
// 18. Float        ->  any sequence of digits with a period

SyntaxTreeNode *parsePicture () ;
SyntaxTreeNode *parseUnscaledPicture () ;
SyntaxTreeNode *parseSubpictureList () ;
SyntaxTreeNode *parseSubpicture () ;
SyntaxTreeNode *parseShape () ;
SyntaxTreeNode *parseColor ();
SyntaxTreeNode *parsePrimitive ();
SyntaxTreeNode *parseSize ();
SyntaxTreeNode *parseSize2 ();
```

```
SyntaxTreeNode *parseDirection ();
SyntaxTreeNode *parseInteger () ;
SyntaxTreeNode *parseFloat () ;

SyntaxTreeNode *parseInteger () {
  if (theLexer.type() != intnum)
    theLexer.error("expected number");
  int v = theLexer.intValue();
  getToken();
  return new SyntaxTreeNode(17, v);
}

SyntaxTreeNode *parseFloat () {
  if (theLexer.type() != floatnum)
    theLexer.error("expected number");
  float v = theLexer.floatValue();
  getToken();
  return new SyntaxTreeNode(18, v);
}

SyntaxTreeNode *parsePicture () {
  if (theLexer.type() == scale) {
    getToken();
    if (theLexer.type() != oparen)
      theLexer.error("expected opening parenthesis");
    getToken();
    SyntaxTreeNode *tn1 = parseFloat();
    if (theLexer.type() != cparen)
      theLexer.error("expected closing parenthesis");
    getToken();
    SyntaxTreeNode *tn2 = parseUnscaledPicture();
    return new SyntaxTreeNode(1, tn1, tn2);
  }
  else
    return parseUnscaledPicture();
}

SyntaxTreeNode *parseUnscaledPicture () {
  SyntaxTreeNode *tn1 = parseShape();
  SyntaxTreeNode *tn2 = parseSubpictureList();
  return new SyntaxTreeNode(3, tn1, tn2);
}

SyntaxTreeNode *parseSubpictureList () {
  SyntaxTreeNode *tn1, *tn2;
  if (theLexer.type() == connecting) {
    tn1 = parseSubpicture();
    tn2 = parseSubpictureList();
    return new SyntaxTreeNode(5, tn1, tn2);
  }
  else
    return new SyntaxTreeNode(4);
}
```

```
SyntaxTreeNode *parseDirection () {
  TokenType dir = theLexer.type();
  getToken();
  if ((center <= dir) && (dir <= northwest))
    return new SyntaxTreeNode(16, dir);
  else
    theLexer.error("expected direction");
}

SyntaxTreeNode *parseSubpicture () {
  // Last token is "connecting"
  getToken();
  SyntaxTreeNode *tn1 = parseDirection();
  if (theLexer.type() != slash)
    theLexer.error("expected /");
  getToken();
  SyntaxTreeNode *tn2 = parseDirection();
  if (theLexer.type() != oparen)
    theLexer.error("expected opening parenthesis");
  getToken();
  SyntaxTreeNode *tn3 = parsePicture();
  if (theLexer.type() != cparen)
    theLexer.error("expected closing parenthesis");
  getToken();
  return new SyntaxTreeNode(6, tn1, tn2, tn3);
}

SyntaxTreeNode *parseShape () {
  SyntaxTreeNode *tn1 = parseColor();
  SyntaxTreeNode *tn2 = parsePrimitive();
  SyntaxTreeNode *tn3 = parseSize();
  return new SyntaxTreeNode(7, tn1, tn2, tn3);
}

SyntaxTreeNode *parseColor () {
  if (theLexer.type() == invisible) {
    getToken();
    return new SyntaxTreeNode(9);
  }
  else
    return new SyntaxTreeNode(8);
}

SyntaxTreeNode *parsePrimitive () {
  if (theLexer.type() == square) {
    getToken();
    return new SyntaxTreeNode(10);
  }
  else if (theLexer.type() == circle) {
    getToken();
    return new SyntaxTreeNode(11);
  }
  else if (theLexer.type() == rectangle) {
    getToken();
    return new SyntaxTreeNode(12);
  }
```

```
        else
          theLexer.error("expected primitive shape");
      }

      SyntaxTreeNode *parseSize () {
        if (theLexer.type() != oparen)
          theLexer.error("expected opening parenthesis");
        getToken();
        SyntaxTreeNode *tn1 = parseInteger();
        SyntaxTreeNode *tn2 = parseSize2();
        return new SyntaxTreeNode(13, tn1, tn2);
      }

      SyntaxTreeNode *parseSize2 () {
        if (theLexer.type() == cparen) {
          getToken();
          return new SyntaxTreeNode(14);
        }
        else if (theLexer.type() == comma) {
          getToken();
          SyntaxTreeNode *tn = parseInteger();
          if (theLexer.type() != cparen)
            theLexer.error("expected closing parenthesis");
          getToken();
          return new SyntaxTreeNode(15, tn);
        }
      }

      SyntaxTreeNode *parse () {
        getToken();
        SyntaxTreeNode *tn = parsePicture();
        if (theLexer.type() != endoffile)
          theLexer.error("premature end of specification");
        else
          return tn;
      }
```

10.7.8 shape.C

```
//
// shape.C - member functions of class Shape,
//    plus function vector
//
// Author:  R. Holly Kamin
// Last modified: 4/4/95
//

#include "psl.h"
#include "shape.h"

const float Pi = 3.1415926536,
            Sqrt2 = 1.41421356;
```

```
Point vector (float angle, float magnitude) {
  // Convert polar to Cartesian coordinates
  // However, use "upside-down" Cartesian coordinates,
  // since we're talking about points on a screen
  return Point(magnitude*cos(angle), -magnitude*sin(angle));
}

Shape::Shape (TokenType prim, float radius, boolean vis)
  : primShape(prim), centerOfShape(0, 0), eastDist(radius),
    northDist(radius), neAngle(Pi/4), visible(vis)
  // Use for circle or square;  for square, radius
  // is half of length of side
{
  if (prim == circle)
    northeastDist = radius;
  else {
    primShape = rectangle;
    northeastDist = radius * Sqrt2;
  }
}

Shape::Shape (TokenType prim, float eastRadius,
              float northRadius, boolean vis)
  : primShape(prim), centerOfShape(0, 0), eastDist(eastRadius),
    northDist(northRadius), visible(vis)
  // Use for rectangle;  eastRadius is half of length,
  // northRadius is half of height
{
  northeastDist = sqrt(eastDist*eastDist + northDist*northDist);
  neAngle = atan(northDist/eastDist);
}

int round (float x) {
  return (x+0.5);
}

void Shape::draw (Screen& s) {
  Point p1(0, 0);
  int x, y;
  int length, height;
  if (visible) {
    switch (primShape) {
      case circle:
        s.drawCircle(round(centerOfShape.getX()),
                     round(centerOfShape.getY()),
                     round(eastDist));
        break;
      case rectangle:
        length = round(eastDist*2);
        height = round(northDist*2);
        p1 = computePerimeterPoint(northeast);
        x = round(p1.getX());
        y = round(p1.getY());
        s.drawLine(x, y, x, y+height);
        s.drawLine(x, y+height, x-length, y+height);
```

```
            s.drawLine(x-length, y+height, x-length, y);
            s.drawLine(x-length, y, x, y);
            break;
        }
    }
}

float Shape::distanceTo (TokenType dir) {
  // distance from center to direction dir
  switch (dir) {
    case center:
            return 0;
    case east:
    case west:
            return eastDist;
    case south:
    case north:
            return northDist;
    case northeast:
    case southeast:
    case southwest:
    case northwest:
            return northeastDist;
  }
}

float Shape::angleTo (TokenType dir) {
  switch (dir) {
    case center:    return 0;
    case east:      return 0;
    case south:     return -Pi/2;
    case west:      return Pi;
    case north:     return Pi/2;
    case northeast: return neAngle;
    case southeast: return -neAngle;
    case southwest: return Pi+neAngle;
    case northwest: return Pi-neAngle;
  }
}

Point Shape::computePerimeterPoint (TokenType dir) {
  // Compute perimeter point in direction dir
  return centerOfShape + vector(angleTo(dir), distanceTo(dir));
}

void Shape::computeCenter (Point p, TokenType dir) {
  centerOfShape = p + vector(Pi+angleTo(dir), distanceTo(dir));
}
```

10.7.9 shapelist.C

```
//
// shapelist.C - member functions of class ShapeList.
//   The only function defined here is draw.
//
// Author:  R. Holly Kamin
// Last modified: 4/4/95
//

#include "ps1.h"
#include "shape.h"

void ShapeList::draw (Screen& s) {
  if (nextEntry != NULL)
    nextEntry->draw(s);
  value.draw(s);
}
```

10.7.10 computeshapes.C

```
//
// computeshapes.C - functions to assign to variable
//   computedShapes a list of Shape objects calculated
//   from a syntax tree, and the definition of computedShapes
//
//   void computeShapes(SyntaxTreeNode *) is called by
//     main.  Other functions are auxiliary.
//
// Author:  R. Holly Kamin
// Last modified: 4/20/95
//

#include "ps1.h"
#include "shape.h"

ShapeList *computedShapes = NULL;

void computeShapes (SyntaxTreeNode *, Point, TokenType, float) ;
Shape computeShape (SyntaxTreeNode *, Point, TokenType, float) ;

void computeShapes (SyntaxTreeNode *tn) {
  // tn is node for production 1 or 3, the top node in
  // the syntax tree of the entire specification.
  // The first shape in a specification is centered in
  // the middle of the screen, scaled by 1 by default.
  float scale = 1.0;
  if (tn->getProduction() == 1) { // scale factor given
    scale = tn->getChild(0)->getFloatValue();
    tn = tn->getChild(1);
  }
  computeShapes(tn, Point(width/2, height/2), center, scale);
}
```

```
void computeSubpictures (SyntaxTreeNode *, Shape, float);

void computeShapes (SyntaxTreeNode *tn, // picture to be drawn
                    Point dirPoint,      // with this point
                    TokenType dir,       // in this direction
                    float scale)         // scaled by this
{
  // tn is node for production 1 or 3
  if (tn->getProduction() == 1) { // scale factor given
    scale = scale * tn->getChild(0)->getFloatValue();
    tn = tn->getChild(1);
  }
  SyntaxTreeNode *tn1 = tn->getChild(0),  // shape
                 *tn2 = tn->getChild(1);  // associated pictures
  // Compute one primitive shape and add it to computedShapes
  Shape sh = computeShape(tn1, dirPoint, dir, scale);
  computedShapes = new ShapeList(sh, computedShapes);
  // Then compute all shapes connected to it
  computeSubpictures(tn2, sh, scale);
}


Point computePoint(Shape, TokenType, TokenType);

void computeSubpictures
            (SyntaxTreeNode *tn,  // associated shapes
             Shape sh, // shape to which they are connected
             float scale)
{
  // tn is for production 4 or 5. If 5, then it has
  // two children, and the first child has three children.
  if (tn->getProduction() == 4)
    return;
  SyntaxTreeNode *subpic = tn->getChild(0);
  TokenType dir1 = subpic->getChild(0)->getDirection(),
            dir2 = subpic->getChild(1)->getDirection();
  Point perimPoint = sh.computePerimeterPoint(dir1);
  computeShapes(subpic->getChild(2), perimPoint, dir2, scale);
  computeSubpictures(tn->getChild(1), sh, scale);
}


Shape computePosIndInfo (SyntaxTreeNode *tn, // Production 7
                         float scale)
{
  // Create a shape and compute all information that is
  // independent of its position - everything but its center.
  // This is just a matter of finding the primitive shape and
  // its size (scaled by scale).
  int visProd = tn->getChild(0)->getProduction(),  // 8 or 9
      primProd = tn->getChild(1)->getProduction(); // 10, 11, 12
  boolean vis = (visProd == 8);    // true, if visible shape
  SyntaxTreeNode *sizenode = tn->getChild(2);  // Production 13
  int size1 = sizenode->getChild(0)->getIntValue();
  SyntaxTreeNode *size2node = sizenode->getChild(1);
  int size2;
```

```
    if (size2node->getProduction() == 15)
      size2 = size2node->getChild(0)->getIntValue();
    if (primProd == 10) // square
      return Shape(square, scale*size1/2, vis); // divide by 2
        // because length, not radius, is given in specification
    else if (primProd == 11) // circle
      return Shape(circle, scale*size1, vis);
    else // rectangle
      return Shape(rectangle, scale*size1/2, scale*size2/2, vis);
}

Shape computeShape (SyntaxTreeNode *tn, // Must be production 7
                    Point dirPoint,     // This point is at
                    TokenType dir,      // this direction
                    float scale)        // Scale by this amount
{
  Shape sh = computePosIndInfo(tn, scale);
  sh.computeCenter(dirPoint, dir);
  return sh;
}
```

10.7.11   screen.C

```
//
// screen.C - member functions of class Screen.
//    A version of this class is developed in Chapter 8,
//    but here we use a simpler version, relying on an
//    external program to actually display shapes.
//
// Author:  R. Holly Kamin
// Last modified: 4/4/95
//

#include "ps1.h"
#include "shape.h"

Screen::Screen () {
}

void Screen::displayScreen () {
}

void Screen::drawLine (int x1, int y1, int x2, int y2) {
  cout << "\\psline(" << x1 << ","
       << -y1 << ")("
       << x2 << ", "
       << -y2 << ")\n";
}

void Screen::drawCircle (int x0, int y0, int r) {
  cout << "\\pscircle(" << x0 << ","
       << -y0 << "){"
       << r << "}\n";
}
```

Precedence Rules

The following table is adapted from B. Stroustrup's *The C++ Programming Language*, 2nd ed., Addison-Wesley Publishing Co., Reading, MA, 1994. Operators are given in *decreasing order* of "precedence," with operators of equal precedence grouped together. Unless otherwise indicated by parentheses, operators of higher precedence are applied before operators of lower precedence, so, for example, `a*b+c` is evaluated as `(a*b)+c`. With one exception, binary operators of equal precedence associate from left to right—for example, `a/b*c` is evaluated as `(a/b)*c`. The exception is the assignment operator `=`, which associates from right to left. All unary operators associate from right to left.

Operator	Name	Use	Page
.	Member selection	*<object>* . *<member>*	191, 198
->	Member selection	*<pointer>* -> *<member>*	243
[]	Subscripting	*<pointer>* [*<expr>*]	398
()	Function call	*<expr>* (*<expr-list>*)	610
++	Increment	*<variable>* ++	19
--	Decrement	*<variable>* --	27
sizeof	Size of type	sizeof (*<type>*)	602
!	Not	!*<expr>*	58
-	Unary minus	- *<expr>*	57
+	Unary plus	+ *<expr>*	
&	Address of	& *<variable>*	240
*	Dereference	* *<expr>*	241
new	Create	new *<type>*	250
delete	Create	delete *<pointer>*	307
*	Multiply	*<expr>* * *<expr>*	23
/	Division	*<expr>* / *<expr>*	23
%	Modulo (remainder)	*<expr>* % *<expr>*	23
+	Add	*<expr>* + *<expr>*	23
-	Subtract	*<expr>* - *<expr>*	23
<<	Left shift	*<expr>* << *<expr>*	30
>>	Right shift	*<expr>* >> *<expr>*	30
<	Less than	*<expr>* < *<expr>*	56
<=	Less than or equal	*<expr>* <= *<expr>*	56
>	Greater than	*<expr>* > *<expr>*	56
>=	Greater than or equal	*<expr>* >= *<expr>*	56
==	Equal	*<expr>* == *<expr>*	56
!=	Not equal	*<expr>* != *<expr>*	56
&	Bitwise *and*	*<expr>* & *<expr>*	606
^	Bitwise exclusive *or*	*<expr>* ^ *<expr>*	606
|	Bitwise inclusive *or*	*<expr>* | *<expr>*	606
&&	*and*	*<expr>* && *<expr>*	58
||	*or*	*<expr>* || *<expr>*	58
? :	Conditional expression	*<expr>* ? *<expr>* : *<expr>*	605
=	Assign	*<variable>* = *<expr>*	26
*=	Multiply and assign	*<variable>* *= *<expr>*	607
/=	Divide and assign	*<variable>* /= *<expr>*	607
%=	Modulo and assign	*<variable>* %= *<expr>*	607
+=	Add and assign	*<variable>* += *<expr>*	607
-=	Subtract and assign	*<variable>* -= *<expr>*	607
<<=	Shift left and assign	*<variable>* <<= *<expr>*	607
>>=	Shift right and assign	*<variable>* >>= *<expr>*	607
&=	Bitwise *and* and assign	*<variable>* &= *<expr>*	607
|=	Bitwise inclusive *or* and assign	*<variable>* |= *<expr>*	607
^=	Bitwise exclusive *or* and assign	*<variable>* ^= *<expr>*	607

B

Mathematical Functions in math.h

The following functions are available in **math.h**. For each function we give the prototype, together with a brief description. Other mathematical functions may be available too, depending on the C++ compiler. In reading the prototypes, consider the type **double** to be like **float**; it is explained in Appendix E—see page 602.

Name/Use	Meaning
`double acos(double x)`	Arc cosine (in radians) of x; x must be in the range $[-1, 1]$
`double asin(double x)`	Arc sine (in radians) of x; x must be in the range $[-1, 1]$
`double atan(double x)`	Arc tangent (in radians) of x
`double atan2(double y, double x)`	Arc tangent (in radians) of y/x
`double cos(double x)`	Cosine of x (in radians)
`double sin(double x)`	Sine of x (in radians)
`double tan(double x)`	Tangent of x (in radians)
`double cosh(double x)`	Hyperbolic cosine of x
`double sinh(double x)`	Hyperbolic sine of x
`double tanh(double x)`	Hyperbolic tangent of x
`double acosh(double x)`	Arc hyperbolic cosine of x
`double asinh(double x)`	Arc hyperbolic sine of x
`double atanh(double x)`	Arc hyperbolic tangent of x
`double exp(double x)`	Exponential of x; e^x
`double log(double x)`	Natural logarithm of x; $\ln x$
`double log10(double x)`	Decimal logarithm of x; $\log_{10} x$
`double modf(double x, double *y)`	Integer/fraction parts of x: returns the fractional part of x; the integer part is stored in y
`double pow(double x, double y)`	Power of x: returns x^y
`double sqrt(double x)`	Square root of x; $\sqrt{x}$
`double ceil(double x)`	Ceiling of x; returns the smallest integer greater than or equal to x
`double floor(double x)`	Floor of x; returns the greatest integer less than or equal to x
`double fabs(double x)`	Absolute value of x

APPENDIX

C

Useful Libraries

There is a wealth of libraries commonly available to the C++ programmer; for example, in Appendix B we gave a list of the most commonly used mathematical functions available in the library **math.h**. In this appendix, we discuss **ctype.h** and **string.h** (for handling characters and arrays of characters, respectively), and **stdlib.h** (an eclectic collection of useful functions). The **.h** files discussed here are just a tiny part of those available; others include functions for getting and manipulating the computer's clock time (**time.h**), dealing with complex numbers (**complex.h**), and so on.

In the following prototypes, the type **size_t** is (essentially) an unsigned integer; for details, see Appendix E, page 610. The type **const char *** can be considered the same as **char ***. The type **void *** means a pointer to anything.

C.1

ctype.h

The file **ctype.h** provides functions that determine what sort a character is—letter, digit, punctuation, and so on. There are also functions to convert upper-case letters to lower-case, and vice versa:

int isalnum(int c)	Return a nonzero value if **c** is a letter or a digit; return zero otherwise.
int isalpha(int c)	Return a nonzero value if **c** is a letter; return zero otherwise.

`int isdigit(int c)`	Return a nonzero value if c is a digit; return zero otherwise.
`int islower(int c)`	Return a nonzero value if c is a lower-case letter; return zero otherwise.
`int ispunct(int c)`	Return a nonzero value if c is a printable character that is *not* a letter, digit, or space.
`int isspace(int c)`	Return a nonzero value if c is a "white space" character (space, tab, newline, and so on).
`int isupper(int c)`	Return a nonzero value if c is an upper-case letter; return zero otherwise.
`int tolower(int c)`	Return the lower-case equivalent of an upper-case letter c. If c is not an upper-case letter, return c.
`int toupper(int c)`	Return the upper-case equivalent of a lower-case letter c. If c is not a lower-case letter, return c.

C.2

string.h

The following are some of the more useful functions for handling arrays of characters.

`char *strcat(char *s1,` `   const char *s2)`	Concatenate to the end of string s1 a copy of the string s2 so that the first character of s2 overwrites the \0 at the end of s1. Return s1.
`char *strchr(char *s, int c)`	Find the first occurrence in s of the character c. Return a pointer to the occurrence, if found, NULL if not found.
`int strcmp(const char *s1,` `   const char *s2)`	Compare strings s1 and s2. Return 0 if the strings are equal, a negative value if s1 is lexicographically less than s2, and a positive value if s1 is lexicographically greater than s2.
`size_t strcspn(const char *s1,` `   const char *s2)`	Return the length of the prefix of the string s1 *not* containing any character from the string s2.

`size_t strlen(const char *s)`	Return the length of the string **s**, *not* including the \0 at the end.
`char *strncat(char *s1,` `   const char *s2, size_t n)`	Just like `strcat` (above), but appends at most n characters.
`char *strpbrk(const char *s1,` `   const char *s2)`	Find the first occurrence in the string **s1** of any character in the string **s2**. Return a pointer to the occurrence, if found, **NULL** if not found.
`char *strrchr(const char *s,` `   int c)`	Find the last occurrence in the string **s** of the character **c**. Return a pointer to the occurrence, if found, **NULL** if not found.
`size_t strspn(const char *s1,` `   const char *s2)`	Return the length of the prefix of string **s1** containing *only* characters from the string **s2**.
`char *strstr(const char *s1,` `   const char *s2)`	Find the first occurrence in the string **s1** of the string **s2**. Return a pointer to the occurrence, if found, **NULL** if not found.

C.3

stdlib.h

`void abort()`	Terminate the program abnormally; streams may not be closed.
`int abs(int n)`	Return the absolute value of an integer **n**.
`double atof(const char *s)`	Convert a prefix of the string **s** to a `float` value, returning that value.
`int atoi(const char *s)`	Convert a prefix of the string **s** to an `int` value, returning that value.

`void bsearch(const void *k,`
`   void* a, size_t n, size_t s,`
`   int (*) (const void *x,`
`   const void *y))`
	Use binary search (see page 460) to search for **k** in the array **a** of **n** items of size **s**. The last argument is the comparison function, which is called with two pointers to array elements and must return an integer less than, equal to, or greater than zero when, respectively, **x < y**, **x == y**, **x > y** (see Appendix E, page 610).

`void exit(int n)`	Terminate the program normally with exit status n, closing all streams.
`void qsort(void* a, size_t n,` `size_t s, int (*)(const void` `*x, const void *y))`	Use quicksort (see page 443) to sort the array a of n items of size s. The last argument is the comparison function, which is called with two pointers to array elements and must return an integer less than, equal to, or greater than zero when, respectively, `x < y`, `x == y`, `x > y` (see Appendix E, page 610).
`int rand()`	Return a pseudo-random `int`.
`void srand(unsigned int n)`	Set the seed for the pseudo-random numbers produced by `rand()`. An `unsigned int` is, as the type name suggests, an unsigned integer; see Appendix E, page 602.

D

Input/Output with
`iostream.h` *and* `iomanip.h`

The first section of this appendix covers methods of formatting output and input; it can be read at any time after reading Chapter 2. The second section discusses various stream classes and their operations; much of it is a review of material in Section 10.2, and it can be read at any time after reading Chapter 6.

D.1

Formatting Output and Input

In various sections of this book we described the simplest forms of output. Sometimes, however, we need to make output conform to particular styles. We saw, for example, that by using `setw(w)` we could force a value to be printed in a
manipulator   field of width **w**. `setw` is called a *manipulator*. We have seen other manipulators too: `endl`, `flush`, and `setfill` are all manipulators. Manipulators appear as arguments to the `<<` or `>>` operator, but instead of being printed, they modify the output or input of subsequent values. Some modify the output or input only of the very next value; some modify all subsequent output or input until a different manipulator is given. The manipulators available in C++ are found in `iostream.h` and `iomanip.h`.

To format output the following manipulators are available in **iostream.h**:

iostream.h manipulators for output			
Manipulator	**Purpose**	**Duration**	**Page**
endl	Output newline and flush output	Not applicable	32
flush	Flush output	Not applicable	32
dec	Use decimal notation	Until changed	
hex	Use hexadecimal notation	Until changed	
oct	Use octal notation	Until changed	

The manipulators **dec**, **hex**, and **oct** allow us to specify the base (*radix*) used in printing or reading a number: decimal, hexadecimal (base 16), or octal (base 8), respectively. The indicated radix remains in effect for this stream until changed by another manipulator. Thus the statement

```
cout << hex << 100 << endl;
```

prints

```
64
```

because $100_{10} = 64_{16}$. Similarly,

```
cout << oct << 100 << endl;
```

prints

```
144
```

because $100_{10} = 144_8$. **dec** is the default, but you sometimes need the manipulator to force decimal output for values that would otherwise be printed in hexadecimal or octal notation (like pointers).

Other manipulators for formatting output are available in **iomanip.h**:

iomanip.h manipulators for output			
Manipulator	**Purpose**	**Duration**	**Page**
setw (int w)	Set field width to w	Next output	19
setfill (int c)	Set fill character to c	Next output	188
setbase (int b)	Set base format to b	Until changed	
setprecision (int p)	Set float/double precision to p	Until changed	
setiosflags (long f)	Set output format flag f	Until unset	
resetiosflags (long f)	Unset output format flag f	Until unset	

Two of these, **setw** and **setfill**, have already been discussed in the text: `setw(w)` sets the field width for the next output to `w`, and `setfill(c)` sets the fill character to `c` for the next output. `setprecision` specifies the number of significant digits to be used in the output with types **float** or **double**; the precision specified remains in effect until changed by another use of **setprecision**. Thus

```
for (int i=1; i<9; i++) {
  cout << "Precision = " << i << ": "
       << setprecision(i) << 3.1415926 << endl;
}
```

prints

```
Precision = 1: 3
Precision = 2: 3.1
Precision = 3: 3.14
Precision = 4: 3.142
Precision = 5: 3.1416
Precision = 6: 3.14159
Precision = 7: 3.141593
Precision = 8: 3.1415926
```

flags   Some of the output formats are controlled by switches, called *flags*, that are turned on with the manipulator **setiosflags** and off with the manipulator **resetiosflags**. The flags available[1] are

Flag	Effect
`ios::fixed`	Use a fixed number of digits to right of the decimal point for **float** and **double**
`ios::internal`	Pad numbers (with fill character) between the sign and the number
`ios::left`	Pad numbers (with the fill character) on left
`ios::right`	Pad numbers (with the fill character) on right
`ios::scientific`	Use scientific notation for **float** and **double**
`ios::showpos`	Use an explicit plus sign for positive numbers
`ios::uppercase`	Use upper-case **E** for scientific notation

---

[1]These flags are elements of an **enum** type local to the class `ios`; see Section E.7.5 of Appendix E for a discussion of local types.

Thus, for example, if we always want to show dollar amounts with two decimal digits, we would use

```
cout << setiosflags(ios::fixed)
     << setprecision(2)
     << 3.0 << endl;
```

and get the output

```
3.00
```

because the flag `ios::fixed`, when turned on, causes **float** and **double** to be printed with a fixed number of digits to the right of the decimal point; the number of digits is given by **setprecision**.

Note that these flags *stay turned on* (and therefore govern the way numbers are printed) until they are turned off by **resetiosflags**.

Manipulators can also be used to alter the way in which input values are read. **dec**, **hex**, and **oct** alter the way in which numeric inputs are interpreted; for example, after inserting the **hex** manipulator, the input **10** is interpreted as $16 = 10_{16}$.

`iostream.h` manipulators for input

Manipulator	Purpose	Duration
dec	Use decimal notation	Until changed
hex	Use hexadecimal notation	Until changed
oct	Use octal notation	Until changed

D.2

The Stream Library

In most of this book we have printed output on the output stream **cout**—normally, the computer screen—and read input from the input stream **cin**—normally, the keyboard. In Chapter 10 we saw how to write and read files with the operators `<<` and `>>`. In this section we review the various operations and classes we have covered, and we add some new operations.

We confine our discussion to the four most important classes for I/O: **istream**, **ostream**, **ifstream**, and **ofstream**. **cin** is an **istream** object; **cout** is an **ostream** object. To use **cin** and **cout**, you must include **iostream.h**. Files are read by associating them with **ifstream** objects and written by associating them with **ofstream** objects. To construct **ifstream** and **ofstream** objects, you must include **fstream.h**.

Although `cin` and `cout` are normally associated with the keyboard and screen, respectively, most systems provide a way to change that association when a program is run. Thus, input or output can be directed to a file without changing the program. Because such a facility is provided by the system and is external to the program, we have not covered it in this book.

In addition to `cin` and `cout`, two other output streams are predefined in every C++ program: `cerr` and `clog`. Both are normally associated with the computer screen. The difference between them is that `clog` is *buffered*, like `cout`, so that output is stored up and printed only when necessary, whereas `cerr` is *unbuffered*, so that output goes to the screen immediately. Thus, `cerr` behaves as if every output statement ends with `<< flush`. This makes it a useful alternative to using `cout` with `flush` or `endl` when debugging information or error messages need to be printed. Furthermore, if a program is run with `cout` directed to a file, `cerr` need not be redirected; thus, ordinary output goes to the file, but error messages go to the screen.

A complete understanding of C++ I/O requires a knowledge of inheritance and derived types, which we cover in Appendix E; however, for our current purposes, you need only know the following:

1. `ifstream` is derived from `istream`, so *operations applicable to* `istream` *objects are also applicable to* `ifstream` *objects* (but not vice versa).
2. `ofstream` is derived from `ostream`, so *operations applicable to* `ostream` *objects are also applicable to* `ofstream` *objects* (but not vice versa).

For example, the output formatting manipulators presented in the previous section can be used with both `ofstream` and `ostream` objects. Moreover, if you overload `operator<<` to output objects of user-defined type `mytype`, giving it the prototype

```
ostream& operator<< (ostream& os, mytype x)
```

it can be used with an `ostream` object or an `ofstream` object:

```
mytype myobject;
cout << myobject;
ofstream ofs(...);   // create ofstream object
ofs << myobject;     // use operator<< to write myobject to file
```

In the remainder of this section we present a sequence of tables showing many of the constructors and member functions of these four classes. Most have already been covered earlier in the book. Table D.1 shows the constructors of `ifstream` and `ofstream`. Table D.2 shows the operations that are available on `istream` (and therefore also on `ifstream`). Table D.3 shows the operations available on `ostream` (and therefore also on `ofstream`). Table D.4 shows the operations peculiar to `ifstream` and `ofstream`.

In the constructors for `ifstream` and `ofstream` (Table D.1), and in the **open** function (Table D.4), values `ios::in`, `ios::out`, and `ios::app` are used for the **mode** argument. These are elements of the **enum** type **open_mode**, local to the class **ios**; see Section E.7.5 of Appendix E for a discussion of local types.

Constructor	Comment	Page
ifstream ()	Use **open** to open file.	511
ifstream (char *fn, int mode)	**fn** is filename. **mode** should be ios::in.	511
ofstream ()	Use **open** to open file.	511
ofstream (char *fn, int mode)	**fn** is filename. **mode** can be ios::out or ios::app.	511

TABLE D.1   ifstream and ofstream constructors

The istream operators **peek**, **ignore**, and **getline** are the only new operations in these tables. **peek** is the same as **get** followed by **putback**. **ignore** just reads and discards the indicated number of characters. **getline** reads an entire line of input (that is, all the characters up to a newline character) into a character array. **putback**, **ignore**, and **getline** return their receiver; this allows the receiver to be tested using **fail** to determine whether it is in a good state.

Member Function	Comment	Page
istream& operator>> (type&)	Overloaded for primitive types *type*.	215
char get ()	Get next character; do *not* skip white space.	301
int eof ()	True if last character has been read.	
istream& putback (char c)	Place **c** back into input stream.	513
char peek ()	Look at next character, but do not advance input pointer; next call to **get** or **peek** will return same character.	
istream& ignore (int Limit, char Delim)	Discards **Limit** characters, stopping either if it reaches end of file before then or if it encounters character **Delim**.	
istream& ignore (int Limit)	Discards **Limit** characters, stopping if it reaches end-of-file before then.	
istream& getline (char *buffer, int Limit)	Place line of input into array **buffer**, up to **Limit** characters.	
boolean fail ()	True if receiver is in an error state that disallows I/O; mainly used with **ifstream** object to test whether an attempt to open a file has succeeded.	512

TABLE D.2   istream member functions

Member Function	Comment	Page
`ostream& operator<< (type)`	Overloaded for primitive types *type*.	210
`boolean fail ()`	True if receiver is in an error state that disallows I/O; mainly used with `ofstream` object to test whether an attempt to open a file has succeeded.	512

TABLE D.3   `ostream` member functions

Member Function	Comment	Page
`void open (char *fn, int mode)`	Opens file for output (`ofstream::open`) or input (`ifstream::open`); arguments are the same as for two-argument constructor.	511
`void close ()`	Disconnect file from stream. File can now be opened again.	512

TABLE D.4   `ifstream` and `ofstream` member functions

Other C++ Features

O ur goal has been to present *principles of programming* in C++, not *language features*. Indeed, we have been rather sparing in introducing language features, introducing only enough to express the principles and avoid awkward or nonidiomatic usages.

This appendix provides a reading knowledge of C++ as it is used in the real world, by briefly covering many of the omitted language features. With the material in this appendix and that in the text, we have covered all but its most esoteric features. The sections of this appendix can be read independently of one another; Table E.1 lists the sections of the book that contain prerequisites for reading each section of the appendix.

Most of the features in this appendix are mere details or syntactic shortcuts; for example, there are a number of operators we have not mentioned. One feature, however, is of great importance and some conceptual difficulty: *class inheritance*. We supply more explanation of that topic than of the conceptually simpler features.

C++ evolved from an earlier language, called simply C. The name of the new language is a pun on the incrementing operator; it is "incremented C." C had most of the features of C++ but lacked classes. Some of what we present here are features of C that are retained in C++ for compatibility—and still appear in many C++ programs—but have been superseded by newer and better ones. We present them not because we favor their use, but to allow you to read programs that use them.

Appendix section	Can be read after
E.1 Old-style comments	Chapter 2
E.2.1 `#define`	Chapter 4
E.2.2 `#ifdef`	Section 10.1
E.3.1 The `sizeof` operator	Section 7.1
E.3.2 Other built-in types	Chapter 9
E.3.3 Type conversions	Section 7.1
E.3.4 `const` declarations	Section 7.1
E.3.5 Integers as booleans	Chapter 5
E.3.6 Operators	Chapter 2
E.3.7 Pointer arithmetic	Chapter 9
E.3.8 `typedef`	Chapter 2
E.3.9 Functions as arguments	Chapter 9
E.4 Inline functions	Chapter 4
E.5 Control structures	Chapter 5
E.6 Templates	Chapter 7
E.7.1 Syntax of classes	Chapter 6
E.7.2 Structures	Chapter 6
E.7.3 Friend functions	Chapter 6
E.7.4 Mutually recursive classes	Section 7.1
E.7.5 Local definitions	Chapter 6
E.8 Class inheritance	Chapter 6

TABLE E.1   Prerequisites for the sections in Appendix E

E.1

Old-Style Comments

Text between the symbols `/*` and `*/` (not necessarily on the same line) is ignored. Thus, several lines of code can be "commented out" by inserting `/*` before the first line and `*/` after the last line. Depending upon the editor you use, it may be easier to insert these two lines than to place `//` at the start of every line. However, you must be careful with old-style comments. Any occurrence of `*/`, even if it is just ending a comment included in one of the lines you're commenting out, ends the comment. That is, if you attempt to comment out a line that contains a comment:

```
... /* comment */ ...
```

by placing comment brackets before and after it,

```
/*
... /* comment */ ...
*/
```

then the first `*/` ends the comment, and the `...` at the end of the line is not considered to be in the comment.

The Preprocessor

We stated on page 508 that lines of the form `#include <filename>` or `#include "filename"` are replaced by the contents of the file called `filename`. The C++ compiler starts by performing this replacement and only afterwards begins to parse and compile the program. This beginning phase of the compiler is called *preprocessing*.

The preprocessor is capable of performing some other modifications to the program as well. Instructions to the preprocessor are always signaled by lines that begin with the pound sign (`#`). The most important of these instructions, aside from `include`, are `#define` and `#ifdef`.

In describing the actions of the preprocessor we will call the program you present to the compiler the *source program* and the program that comes out of the preprocessor the *preprocessed program*.

E.2.1 `#define`

Though the use of symbolic constants is clearly preferable, an earlier method of defining constants was to write a line of the form

```
#define <name> <value>
```

such as

```
#define maxArraySize 1000
#define Pi 3.14159
#define greeting "Hello, stupid\n"
```

Every subsequent occurrence of *<name>* in the source program is replaced by *<value>* to produce the preprocessed program.

The preprocessor can also be used to define "lightweight" functions, also called *macros*. If you include a line of the form

macro

```
#define <name>(<parameter-list>) <expression>
```

then any occurrence of the *<name>* with the correct number of arguments is replaced by the *<expression>* (with the parameters replaced by the corresponding arguments). For example, if this line appears in your program:

```
#define error(str) cout << "Error: " << str << "\n"
```

and this line occurs in the program:

```
error("invalid input");
```

then the latter is replaced by

```
cout << "Error: " << "invalid input" << "\n"
```

Just as the definition of constants using **#define** is superseded by the symbolic constants of Chapter 2, the definition of macros is largely superseded by the "inline function" feature explained later in this appendix (page 613).

E.2.2   #ifdef

Programs that are intended to be compiled and run on a variety of computers teem with code fragments of the form

```
#ifdef <name>
   ...
#endif
```

This checks whether the **<name>** has previously been defined using **#define** (the value given to it is immaterial; it matters only whether or not it has been defined), and if so, the lines between the **ifdef** line and the **endif** line will be included in the preprocessed program. If not, those lines are omitted from the preprocessed program. The inverse is

```
#ifndef <name>
   ...
#endif
```

conditional compilation

which compiles the lines between the first and last only if **<name>** has *not* been defined. This feature is called *conditional compilation.*

What is it for? Slight differences among computers, operating systems, and compilers—too technical to explain here—require that certain operations be done differently on different systems. To take one example, different computers treat floating-point numbers differently, so some functions in the mathematical function library need different declarations for their argument and return types. The **include** file **math.h** for one compiler includes these lines (the type **double** is explained in Section E.3.2):

```
#ifdef  sparc
#define FLOATFUNCTIONTYPE       double
...
#endif

#ifdef  i386
#define FLOATFUNCTIONTYPE       float
...
#endif
```

sparc stands for the SPARC workstation (a computer built by Sun Microsystems, Inc.), whereas **i386** is a symbol for the Intel 80386 processor (the processor in many IBM-compatible PCs made in the early 1990s). When a compiler is producing object code files for one of these machines, it defines the corresponding symbol. Thus, when a program is being compiled for a SPARC workstation, if it includes **math.h**, then the symbol **FLOATFUNCTIONTYPE** will be equated to the symbol **double**; if the same program is compiled for a PC that uses the 80386 processor, **FLOATFUNCTIONTYPE** will be equated to **float**. Subsequent lines in **math.h** give function prototypes with return type **FLOATFUNCTIONTYPE**, making those prototypes correct for either system.

Another important use of conditional compilation is to avoid collisions among **include** files, a problem alluded to in Section 10.1. It is illegal to declare a class more than once, but it can be difficult to avoid doing so when there are many **include** files. For example, suppose you have a file **complex.h** that declares the class **complex**, and files **cmathone.h** and **cmathtwo.h** that declare various mathematical functions on complex numbers. The latter files both contain the line

```
#include "complex.h"
```

A problem arises if you need to use functions from both files. If you place these lines in your program,

```
#include "cmathone.h"
#include "cmathtwo.h"
```

you are, perhaps unknowingly, including **complex.h** twice. The compiler will complain that you have declared the class **complex** twice.

The conditional compilation facility can solve this problem. Let **complex.h** define a special symbol and then check whether that symbol is defined, as follows:

```
#ifndef __complex__
#define __complex__
class complex {
   ...
};
#endif
```

The first time **complex.h** is included in another file, __ **complex**__ has not been defined (it is customary to choose an odd name like this, to minimize the chances that someone has defined this symbol for totally unrelated reasons), so the definition of the class is compiled. At the same time, the symbol is defined, so that the next time **complex.h** is included, the class declaration will not be compiled. In short, this ensures that the class declaration will not be compiled more than once.

E.3

Data Types

We have introduced the major built-in data types **int**, **float**, **char**, and pointer. In this section we fill in some details about these and other types.

E.3.1 The `sizeof` Operator

bit   Every data value in a computer is represented as a binary number. The number
of binary digits, or *bits*, in a given type of value varies with the computer and
compiler but is the same for all values of a given type. Usually, *but not always*,
integers are 32 bits long, floating-point numbers 32 bits, characters 8 bits, and
pointers 32 bits. Notice that all these sizes are multiples of 8; a group of eight bits
byte   is called a *byte*.

You can determine the number of bits used in the representation of various
types of data by using the **sizeof** operator. It is a one-argument operator whose
argument is a type; it returns an integer that gives the number of bytes in values
of that type. For example, the program

```
enum boolean {true, false};

main () {
  cout << "ints are " << sizeof(int) << " bytes\n";
  cout << "floats are " << sizeof(float) << " bytes\n";
  cout << "pointers are " << sizeof(float*) << " bytes\n";
  cout << "booleans are " << sizeof(boolean) << " bytes\n";
}
```

outputs

```
ints are 4 bytes
floats are 4 bytes
pointers are 4 bytes
booleans are 4 bytes
```

on one computer. You can generally assume that all pointers are of the same
length, regardless of what they point to. Notice that booleans, which really need
only one bit, use 32 bits.

E.3.2 Other Built-In Types

A number of variants of the built-in types are provided, mainly to increase or
decrease the size. The most important are **short** (for small integers; usually 16
bits); **long** (for large integers; usually 32 bits; this type is mainly used on computers in which **int** is 16 bits); and **double** (for large floating-point numbers;
usually 64 bits). Of these, **double** is heavily used in scientific computations,
but **short** and **long** are used rarely. Note that **char**, which is almost always one
byte, can be used for really small integers.

The integer types—**char**, **short**, **int**, and **long**—can be modified by the
word **unsigned**. A variable of type **unsigned int** assumes values from zero to
the maximum capacity of an **int**. For example, with 32-bit integers, the range
of an **int** variable is $-2,147,483,648$ to $2,147,483,647$, and the range of an
unsigned int variable is 0 to $4,294,967,295$.

The **sizeof** operator can also be used to find the length of values of user-
defined types. Normally, the length of an object is just the sum of the lengths
of its data members. For example, on the computer that produced the foregoing

output, `sizeof(intList)` (page 256) returns 8 (four bytes for the integer, four for the pointer). There are exceptions, though. For example, on the same computer, `sizeof(charList)` (page 302) also returns 8, even though the two data members are a `char` (1 byte) and a pointer (4 bytes).

`sizeof` can be applied to a data value and will give the number of bytes in that value. (In this case, the parentheses may be omitted.) This is useful for finding the length of an array, which, again, is normally just the size of the values it contains multiplied by its length. Thus, if `A` is an array of 10 `int`s, `sizeof A` will return 40.

E.3.3   Type Conversions

It is occasionally necessary to transform a value from one type to another. This is called *type conversion*. For example, you may want to pass an integer into a function that takes a floating-point argument, or you may want to assign an integer to a floating-point variable.

type conversion

Some type conversions are performed automatically. For example, as a convenience to the user, `int`s are automatically converted to `float`s when necessary. This seems harmless, because no information is lost in the conversion. Similarly, `char` is automatically converted to `int`, `int` to `long`, and `float` to `double`. In each case, the conversion entails no loss of information.

Other conversions are not performed. If you pass a pointer into a function that expects an integer argument, or attempt to assign a `time` value to a `float` variable, the compiler issues an error message. In these cases there is no sensible conversion to do.

In yet other cases the compiler does the conversion but issues a warning message. For example, some compilers convert `float`s to `int`s by truncating the fractional part, but they issue a warning message. In these cases the conversion is sensible but may cause loss of information.

The compiler, likewise, declines to convert a pointer-to-`T1` to pointer-to-`T2` if `T1` and `T2` are different types. One important exception to this rule is that any pointer can be converted to type `void*` (but not vice versa). This is why we say `void*` represents a "pointer-to-anything." An example of this conversion is given below in Section E.3.9. (Another exception to the rule is discussed in Section E.8.)

In some cases the compiler can convert between types, but does so only if specifically requested to by the programmer. To request that an expression `e` be converted to type `T`, use a *cast*:

cast

```
(T) e
```

For example, assignments 1, 3, and 4 in the following listing, which would otherwise provoke error messages or warnings from the compiler, will be compiled with no complaints:

```
1    int i = (int) 4.95;        // assigns 4 to i
2    void *pv = new time(9, 0); // legal assignment to void*
3    time *tptr = (time*) pv;    // must cast void* to time*
4    float *fptr = (float *)&i;  // must cast int* to float*
```

In line 3 the same pointer that was assigned to **pv** is assigned to **tptr**; thus, **tptr** now points to a valid **time** object containing the time 9:00 A.M. The conversion in line 4 is a different matter: **i** is not converted to a **float**, but **fptr** points to it, and we have told the compiler that it points to a **float**. It is not at all clear what this means or what the outcome will be (for example, what will **cout << *fptr** print?), and it is probably a mistake; nonetheless, the compiler does not complain.

E.3.4   const **Declarations**

We have introduced only one use of the **const** keyword in the text: for defining simple constants, usually integers or floats. Several other uses are common in C++ code.

First, a pointer variable **p** can be declared to be constant. However, there are two possible meanings for this: Either **p** itself is constant and cannot be changed by assignment, or what is in the location pointed to by **p** is constant. In other words, either

```
p = ...
```

or

```
*p = ...
```

is illegal.

So which is it? That depends upon the exact form of the declaration of **p**. The declaration

```
float *const p = ...;
```

declares that **p** itself is constant, so that assignments of the first form are illegal. (Note that in this case the initialization of **p** is absolutely essential, because there will be no other way to give **p** a value.) The declaration

```
const float *p = ...;
```

declares that "**p** is a pointer to a constant **float**"; that is, the value **p** points to cannot be changed by assigning to ***p**.

An extremely common use of **const** in C++ programs occurs in function headers. When a function parameter is declared as **const**, it indicates that the function will not assign to that parameter. (If the parameter is a pointer, it says that the location pointed to will not be changed by the function.) For example, the function **strcpy** given on page 430, which copies one string into another, might be declared as

```
void strcpy (char target[], const char source[]) ;
```

or, equivalently,

```
void strcpy (char *target, const char *source) ;
```

meaning that the value referred to by the second argument is not changed by the function. Any assignment to ***source** in the body of the function is an error. Furthermore, it is an error to pass **source** as an argument to a function that does *not* declare its argument to be **const**. In other words, declaring an argument **const** says that this argument is not changed during the execution of this function, either by the function itself or by any function that it calls.

You sometimes see **const** added at the end of a member function header:

```
intList *intList::find (const int key) const { ... }
```

The second use of **const** says that the receiver of this message will not be changed by the function call. Any assignment to any of the receiver's data members in the body of this function is an error.

E.3.5   Integers as Booleans

We defined the enumerated type **boolean** early in the text and used it whenever we wanted a value to represent the outcome of a test—that is, a truth value. However, in reality, truth values in C++ are represented by integers. Zero represents **false**, and *any nonzero* value represents **true**. For example, if integer variable **i** is initialized to 10, then the loop

```
while (i) {
  cout << i << ' ';
  i--;
}
```

prints the numbers from 10 down to 1 and then stops.

E.3.6   Operators

We have covered all the arithmetic operators (**+, -, *, /, %**), comparison operators (**==, !=, <, >, <=, >=**), and logical operators (**!, &&, ||**), as well as the increment and decrement operators (**++, --**). This leaves the *bitwise operators*, the *conditional operator*, and the *assignment operators*, all of which will be introduced in this section. We also need to explain the use of (some of) these operators on pointers.

To understand the *bitwise operators*, remember that all numbers in a computer are represented in binary. These operations combine pairs of integers on a bit-by-bit basis. They are listed and explained in Table E.2.

bitwise operators

The *conditional operator* (**?:**) is a *ternary* (three-argument) operator—the only one in C++. An expression of the form

```
<expr1> ?  <expr2> : <expr3>
```

is evaluated by evaluating **<expr1>** and then returning the value of either **<expr2>** or **<expr3>**, depending on whether **<expr1>** is true or false. For

Operator	Explanation	Example (in decimal and binary)
&: bitwise *and*	Each bit in the result is obtained from the two corresponding bits in the arguments using the *and* operation: 1 if both bits are 1, 0 otherwise.	108 & 85 = 68 01101100 & 01010101 = 01000100
|: bitwise inclusive *or*	Each bit in the result is obtained from the two corresponding bits in the arguments using the OR operation: 0 if both bits are 0, 1 otherwise.	108|85 = 126 01101100 | 01010101 = 01111110
^: bitwise exclusive *or*	Each bit in the result is obtained from the two corresponding bits in the arguments using the *exclusive or* operation: 0 if both bits are the same, 1 otherwise.	108^85 = 57 01101100 ^ 01010101 = 00111001
~: bitwise *not*	Each bit in the result is obtained from the corresponding bit in the argument using the *not* operation: 0 if the bit is 1, 1 if it is zero.	~108 = 147 ~ 01101100 = 10010011
<<: left shift	Shift bits of the first argument left the number of places indicated by the second argument. (For sufficiently small numbers, m << n is equal to $m \times 2^n$.)	58 << 2 = 232 00111010 << 2 = 11101000
>>: right shift	Shift bits of the first argument right the number of places indicated by the second argument. (m << n is equal to $m/2^n$.)	58 >> 2 = 14 00111010 >> 2 = 00001110

TABLE E.2   Bitwise operations of C++.

example, $(x==0)$? y : y/x returns the value of y if x is zero and the value of y/x otherwise. As another example, the assignment

```
x = <expr1> ? <expr2> : <expr3>;
```

is equivalent to

```
if (<expr1>)
  x = <expr2>;
else
  x = <expr3>;
```

The *assignment operators* provide a simple shorthand for some common forms of assignment statement, such as

```
x = x + <expression>;
```

Specifically,

```
x += <expression>;
```

is equivalent to the previous statement. All the assignment operators work this way. If **x** is a variable (that is, an expression that can legally appear on the left-hand side of an assignment statement), and **e** is an expression, then the following equivalences hold:

This	is equivalent to
x += e	x = x+e
x -= e	x = x-e
x *= e	x = x*e
x /= e	x = x/e
x %= e	x = x%e
x &= e	x = x&e
x |= e	x = x|e
x ^= e	x = x^e
x <<= e	x = x<<e
x >>= e	x = x>>e

x++ and **x--** are equivalent to **x += 1** and **x -= 1**, respectively.

Contrary to our use of **=**, **++**, and **--** in this book, these operators actually form expressions and can be used inside larger expressions. For example, if **x** has the value 10, then

```
x++*(x+5)
```

evaluates to 160. **x++** is evaluated first; it *returns* 10 (the value of **x**) but also *increments* **x** to 11. **x+5** is evaluated next; since **x** is now 11, it evaluates to 16. The product of 10 and 16 is 160. Was that confusing? That's why we don't use it.

This raises the question, "What values do the other assignment operators return?" The answer is simple: They return the value that is assigned. In other words, **x = e** returns the value of **e**, **x += e** returns the value of **x+e**, and so on.

There is one surprise, though: **++** (and similarly **--**) can be used both in the *postfix* form we've used before (**x++**) and in a *prefix* form (**++x**). Both increment **x**, but the values they return, when used in expressions, differ: **x++** returns the value of **x** *prior to being incremented,* whereas **++x** returns the incremented value.[1] Again, these values matter only when the expression appears within a

---

[1]For this reason it has been said that C++ should really be called ++C.

larger expression; when these expressions are used as statements, their value doesn't matter. For example, a[i++] = 10 and a[++i] = 10 are different; the first assigns 10 to a[i], the second assigns 10 to a[i+1] (and both increment i). On the other hand, i++; A[i] = 10; is the same as ++i; A[i] = 10; (both are equivalent to a[++i] = 10). A typical example of the use of these operators within an expression is this loop that searches for the value **x** in an array **A**:

```
i = 0;
while (i<n && A[i++] != x) ; // Note: ++i would be wrong!
```

This idiom is very popular in C++.

The fact that = is an operator explains why a statement like

```
if (x = y) ...
```

is not a syntax error, even though it is almost certainly a mistake. As far as C++ is concerned, **x = y** is an *expression* that returns an integer (which, as explained above, is also a truth value). Thus, even though the programmer probably intended to write **x == y**, the C++ compiler cannot give an error message, because the code might be legitimate. In fact, this type of code is used heavily when processing strings, because the null character at the end of a string has integer value zero and can be used to terminate a loop. Thus, the function **strcpy** given on page 430 might be written more concisely as

```
void strcpy (char target[], char source[]) {
  int i = 0;
  while (target[i] = source[i++]) ;
}
```

This loop has no body. The condition accomplishes the copying of one character and the incrementing of the index variable, and the loop terminates when a zero is assigned.

E.3.7 Pointer Arithmetic

The connection between pointers and arrays is closer than we implied in Chapter 9. Anything that can be done using array subscripting can be done using pointers.

Pointer arithmetic refers to the ability to perform certain operations on pointers, most importantly, adding an integer to a pointer. If a pointer **p** is pointing to an item within an array,

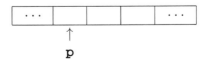

then `p+1` points to the next item in the array, `p+2` to the item after that, and so on:

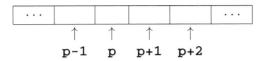

Thus, since an array `A` is really a pointer, we have the following equivalence:

$$A[i] \equiv *(A+i).$$

Furthermore, if `A` is of length `n`, then `A+n` is the address just past the end of `A`. Thus, a simple initialization loop,

```
for (int i=0; i<n; i++) A[i] = 0.0;
```

can be written entirely using pointer arithmetic:

```
for (float *p=A; p<A+n; p++) *p = 0.0;
```

Note that the comparison operator `<` can be used with pointers; it works correctly as long as the pointers being compared are within the same array (or just past the end of the array). An array-reversing loop,

```
int i = 0, j = n-1;
while (i < j) {
  float tmp = A[i];
  A[i++] = A[j];
  A[j--] = tmp;
}
```

becomes

```
float *pi = A, *pj = A+n-1;
while (pi < pj) {
  float tmp = *pi;
  *(pi++) = *pj;
  *(pj--) = tmp;
}
```

As a final example, the **strcpy** function defined in the previous subsection (page 608), written in the most concise form, is

```
void strcpy (char target[], char source[]) {
  while (*target++ = *source++) ;
}
```

So who cares about all this? Using pointers is *slightly* more efficient than array subscripting. We don't recommend this kind of thing—it produces unreadable code, which is almost always a more important consideration than the slight increase in speed—but you will see it quite a lot.

E.3.8 typedef

A synonym for a type can be introduced by using the **typedef** facility. A declaration of the form

```
typedef <type1> <name>;
```

makes **<name>** a synonym for **<type1>**. After this **typedef**, it makes no difference whether a variable is declared as having **<type1>** or **<name>**.

This feature might be used simply to abbreviate a long type name or to introduce a more descriptive name for a type, as in

```
typedef intList* intListPtr;
```

A declaration **intListPtr ilp;** is indistinguishable from **intList* ilp;**.

A more important use, however, is to promote portability among different computers. Suppose you have a variable **count** that will contain large integers—not large enough to need more than 32 bits, but too large to be accommodated in 16 bits. Declaring it to have type **int** would be a mistake, because on some systems the size of **int** is 2 bytes (16 bits). On the other hand, declaring it to have type **long** would result in its using 8 bytes on some systems—a waste of memory. The best solution is to use a type synonym, say **largeint**. **count** can be declared as having type **largeint**, and a **typedef** can be given in an **include** file. On systems that have 32-bit **int**s, the **typedef** would be

```
typedef int largeint;
```

and on those that have 16-bit **int**s, it would be

```
typedef long largeint;
```

An example of such a use is provided by the type **size_t**, used in some declarations in Appendix C. This is not actually a separate type but instead is a synonym of one of the built-in types you know about, such as **unsigned int** or **unsigned short**. Its **typedef** is in a system header file that is automatically included whenever you include a header file that uses it (such as **string.h**). It is used to represent the type of array indices, because the range of array indices varies among machines. It is usually an unsigned integer type, because indices cannot be negative.

E.3.9   Functions as Arguments

Pointers can point to functions as well as to ordinary data values. If **f** is a function, **&f** is its address; if a variable **fptr** contains that address, then **f** can be called by writing **(*fptr)(...)**.[2]

---

[2]Note that because function application has higher precedence than the dereferencing operator (see Appendix A), ***fptr(...)** would be wrong. This would mean that the value returned from the call **fptr(...)** is to be dereferenced.

This odd-seeming feature is actually very useful. For example, you might want to define a function **plot** that can plot functions. Rather than have it plot a single function, it would be preferable to have it plot any function that is passed to it as an argument.

How can we declare a variable that holds a pointer to a function? The answer lies in the basic idea of the C++ declaration syntax. A declaration of the form

```
int <expression containing variable>;
```

can be read as saying that whenever the expression appears, its value will have type **int**. For example, the declaration **int *p** says that "the expression ***p** has type **int**," which is just an indirect way of saying that **p** has type pointer-to-**int**.

Complex declarations can be understood the same way. For example,

```
float *A[10];
```

says that an expression of the form ***A[...]** has type **float**, which says, indirectly, that **A** is an array of pointers-to-**float**.

This principle applies when declaring a variable that is to hold a pointer to a function. As explained above, if **fptr** is such a function, then it can be used in a context like **(*fptr)(...)**. Its declaration then simply needs to give the type of the arguments and result of such an expression. For example,

```
int (*fptr)();
```

declares **fptr** to be a pointer to a function having no arguments and returning an integer.

```
float *(*gptr)(int);
```

declares **gptr** to be a pointer to a function that has one **int** argument and returns a pointer to a **float**.

An example is the **plot** function previously mentioned:

```
void plot (int (*f)(int)) {
  for (int i=0; i<20; i++)
    cout << setw(2) << i << ':'
         << setw((*f)(i)) << ' ' << "*\n";
}
```

plot has as its argument a pointer to a function that takes an **int** argument and has an **int** result. It plots its values in the range 0 to 19. For example, for this function and main program, the output, shown in Figure E.1, is a plot of the so-called "Witch of Agnesi" function:

```
const int a=20;

int WitchOfAgnesi (int i) {
  return a*a*a/(i*i + a*a);
}

void main () {
  plot(&WitchOfAgnesi);
}
```

```
 0:                                    *
 1:                                   *
 2:                                   *
 3:                                   *
 4:                                   *
 5:                                   *
 6:                                  *
 7:                                  *
 8:                                  *
 9:                                 *
10:                                 *
11:                                *
12:                               *
13:                               *
14:                              *
15:                              *
16:                             *
17:                            *
18:                            *
19:                            *
```

FIGURE E.1   Plot of the "Witch of Agnesi" function.

Another use of this feature is in the quicksort function declared in **stdlib** (see Appendix C, page 589):

```
void qsort(void*, size_t, size_t,
           int(*)(const void*, const void*));
```

Here, **qsort** is defined to have four arguments: a pointer (**void*** means "pointer-to-anything"), two array indices, and a pointer to a function. The latter is not named, but the declaration says it is a pointer to a function having two pointer arguments and returning an **int**. This last argument represents a comparison function that will be applied to elements of the array; when applied to two values, it must return a negative number if the first is less than the second, a positive number if the first is greater, and zero if they are equal. Thus, to sort an array **A** of five **int**s, define a function **intCompare** to compare integers in this way (subtracting the second from the first is a simple way to obtain appropriate values) and call

```
qsort(A, 5, sizeof(int), &intCompare);
```

It is worth looking at this call more closely as an illustration of **void***. Though the prototype of **qsort** says that its first argument is of type **void***, we can pass **A**, which is of type **int***, because there is an automatic conversion from **int*** to **void***. Let's look now at the definition of **intCompare**. The obvious solution is wrong:

```
int intCompare (int *i1, int *i2) {
    return (*i1-*i2);
}
```

because the types don't match the prototype of **qsort**. **qsort** expects its last argument to be (a pointer to) a function whose arguments are of type **void***, but we have passed it (a pointer to) a function whose arguments are of type **int***. This doesn't work, because the compiler will *not* automatically convert a **void*** to an **int***. So we must define **intCompare** to accept **void*** arguments and cast them to **int***s. We can use this definition:

```
int intCompare (void *i1, void *i2) {
  int *p1 = (int *)i1,
      *p2 = (int *)i2;
  return (*p1-*p2);
}
```

or this more concise, but equivalent, one:

```
int intCompare (void *i1, void *i2) {
  return (*(int*)i1-*(int*)i2);
}
```

E.4

Inline Functions

We strongly favor using many functions instead of writing a single "monolithic" program. Doing so makes the program easier to write, read, debug, and modify. Unfortunately, the act of calling a function is not free but can be rather costly.

For example, programs A and B do essentially the same computation:

Program A	Program B
	```float addPi (float x) {```
	``` return x+3.14159;```
```main () {```	```}```
``` float x = 1;```	
``` for (int i=0; i<1000000; i++)```	```main () {```
``` x = x+3.14159;```	``` float x = 1;```
```}```	``` for (int i=0; i<1000000; i++)```
	``` x = addPi(x);```
	```}```

Yet on one computer, program A runs in 0.7 seconds, but program B takes 1.4 seconds. Such is the cost of function calling.

This cost can in some cases be reduced by simply adding the word **inline** at the beginning of the function definition:

```
inline float addPi (float x) {
  return x+3.14159;
}
```

This tells the C++ compiler to copy the body of the function wherever the function is called, effectively making program B identical to program A. In our example, this reduces the running time to 0.7 seconds, exactly the same as for version A.

As a general rule, *functions defined inside a class declaration are automatically treated as if they were declared* `inline`. Since the use of classes tends to lead to many small functions, this has the important effect of reducing the cost of using those functions and, accordingly, of using classes.

However, to the C++ compiler the `inline` declaration (whether explicit or implicit) is only a recommendation, which it may ignore. Different C++ compilers have differing rules about when to follow and when to ignore `inline` declarations, but all refuse to inline a function that is recursive, and many refuse to inline a function that contains a `while` loop. (You may recall our statement on page 201 that member functions with loops cannot be defined inside a class declaration. We can now explain why: Functions defined inside a class are *implicitly* declared `inline`, so compilers that won't inline functions with loops issue an error message in this case.)

E.5

Control Structures

Two statements we have not covered allow for premature termination of a loop. The statement `continue` inside a loop causes termination of the *current* iteration of the loop, without terminating the loop itself. For example, this loop prints every index `i` of `a` such that `A[i] = A[i-1]`:

```
for (int i=1; i<n; i++) {
  if (A[i] != A[i-1])
    continue;
  cout << i << "\n";
}
```

`goto` is a more general construct that allows you to pass control to any other point in a function. Its most common use is to exit from two or more nested loops (`break` can be used to exit from one loop):

```
while (...)
  ...
  while (...) {
    ...
    if (irrecoverableError) goto emergency;
    ...
  }
  ...
}
emergency: ...
```

The label (`emergency`, in this case) can be any identifier. It must be defined (by giving its name followed by a colon) exactly once within the function. One warning, however: A label cannot be defined immediately before a closing brace; that is, the construct

```
label:
}
```

is always a syntactic error. To get around this problem, place a semicolon—actually, a *null statement*—just after the label, as in

```
label: ;
}
```

E.6

Templates

We have defined in this book a number of classes of the form

```
class type List {
private:
  type value;
  type List *nextEntry;
public:
  type List (type v, type List* l)
  : value(v), nextEntry(l) {}

  type getValue () { return value; }

  type List *getNextentry () { return nextEntry; }
};
```

that differed only in the actual type name substituted for **type:** int, char, and so on. C++ has a *template* feature, which permits us to replace all those definitions by a single "generic" definition:

```
template <class T>
class list {
private:
  T value;
  list *nextEntry;
public:
  list (T v, list *l) : value(v), nextEntry(l) {}

  T getValue () { return value; }

  list *getNextentry () {return nextEntry; }
};
```

In effect, this automatically defines an infinite set of classes, with names like list<int>, list<float>, list<char*>, even list<list<int>>. We can declare variables using these class names and invoke the constructors with those names:

```
list<int> *ilis = new list<int>(10, NULL);
list<char*> *strlist = new list<char*>("ren",
                            new list<char*>("stimpy", NULL));
cout << ilis->getValue() << strlist->getValue() << "\n";
```

This feature is very popular and has spawned the development of libraries of generic "container" classes, classes that represent such objects as lists, sets, tables, and trees.

E.7

Classes

Here we discuss some features of classes not covered in the text proper. A major feature of classes, *inheritance*, is discussed in the final section of this appendix.

E.7.1   Syntax of Classes

Contrary to our explanation in Chapter 6 and our usage throughout the text, the keywords **public** and **private** can be interspersed through a class declaration. Member declarations are public or private according to the most recent occurrence of one of these keywords. Thus, the class definition

```
class C {
private:
 <data member declarations>
public:
 <constructors and member functions>
};
```

is equivalent to this one:

```
class C {
public:
 <constructors and member functions>
private:
 <data member declarations>
};
```

There can even be several **public** and **private** keywords:

```
class C {
public:
 <some constructors and member functions>
```

```
private:
 <some data member declarations>
public:
 <the remaining constructors and member functions>
private:
 <the remaining data member declarations>
};
```

Another form often seen, equivalent to the above, is

```
class C {
 <data member declarations>
public:
 <constructors and member functions>
};
```

That is, the members of a class are private by default.

Unlike ordinary variables and functions, members may be used in other member functions *before* they are declared. In effect, the compiler scans the class declarations and gathers all the member declarations before looking at the member function definitions.

E.7.2 Structures

We have advised strongly against making data members public. Nonetheless, public data members do allow for some notational conciseness. For example, the program to compute Fibonacci numbers given on page 343, using public data members rather than accessor functions, is

```
class intPair {
public:
  int x, y;
  intPair (int u, int v) {x = u; y = v;}
};

intPair fibonacciPair (int n) {
  // Compute the nth and (n+1)st Fibonacci numbers,
  // returning the pair of values.
  if (n == 0)
    return intPair(0,1);
  else {
    intPair p = fibonacciPair(n/2);
    if ((n % 2) == 0)
      return intPair(2*p.x*p.y - p.x*p.x, p.x*p.x + p.y*p.y);
    else
      return intPair(p.x*p.x + p.y*p.y, 2*p.x*p.y + p.y*p.y);
  }
}

int fibonacci (int n) {
  // Compute the nth Fibonacci number.
  return fibonacciPair(n).x;
}
```

Since the data members are accessed directly, the parentheses needed to call the accessor functions are avoided.

structures   Indeed, historically, classes did not have private data members and were not even called classes—they were called *structures*. C++ retains a special keyword, `struct`, that can be used in place of `class` and is different from `class` in just one way: Members of a `struct` are *public* by default. This allows `intPair` to be written as

```
struct intPair {
  int x, y;
  intPair (int u, int v) {x = u; y = v;}
};
```

The `fibonacci` and `fibonacciPair` functions above are unchanged.

E.7.3   Friend Functions

We have stated that only a member function of a class `C` can access the private members of `C` objects. It can access the private members of its receiver by simply naming them, and it can access the private members of other `C` objects (such as parameters or global variables) by using dot notation.

friend   There is, however, a way for a class to grant a nonmember function access to the private members of its objects: by declaring it to be a *friend*. Friend functions are *not* members of the class. They are just ordinary functions (or members of other classes) that have been given the special right to access private members of objects of this class, using dot notation.

For example, the `intPair` class could keep its data members private while granting special access to `fibonacci` and `fibonacciPair`:

```
class intPair {
  friend intPair fibonacciPair (int) ;
  friend int fibonacci (int) ;
  int x, y;
public:
  intPair (int u, int v) {x = u; y = v;}
};
```

A common use of this feature is to allow the overloading of `operator<<` or `operator>>`. As we saw in Chapter 6, these functions cannot be overloaded as members of a class (because their left-hand argument is of type `ostream` or `istream`), so they are normally overloaded as clients that call a separate member function to do the real work:

```
class C {
private:
  int a, b;
public:
  void print (ostream &os) {
    os << a << b;
  }
  ...
};
```

```
ostream& operator<< (ostream &os, C c) {
  c.print(os);
  return os;
}
```

`operator<<` cannot print the private members of `c` directly, because it is a client, and clients cannot see private members. If the class `C` were to declare `operator<<` a friend, `print` could be eliminated:

```
class C {
private:
  ...
public:
  friend ostream& operator<< (ostream&, C);
  ...
};

ostream& operator<< (ostream &os, C c) {
  os << c.a << c.b;
  return os;
}
```

A member function `void f (C)` of another class, say `D`, can be declared a friend of `C` by using its full name, `D::f`. Furthermore, an entire class—that is, every member function of the class—can be declared a friend with one declaration. Thus, `C` can contain the friend declarations

```
friend void D::f (C) ;
friend class E ;
```

In the definition of `f` in `D`, the private members of its argument, or of any `C` objects, can be accessed using dot notation, and likewise for all member functions of the class `E`.

Since friend functions are not members, it makes no difference whether the `friend` declaration occurs in the public or private part of the class.

E.7.4 Mutually Recursive Classes

Just as it is illegal for a class `C` to contain a data member of type `C`, it is illegal for a class `C` to contain a data member of type `D` while the class `D` contains a data member of type `C`:

```
class C {
private:
  D d;
  ...
};

class D {
private:
  C c;
  ...
};
```

On the other hand, it is fine for the two classes to contain *pointers* to each other. However, the obvious way of writing this is wrong:

```
class C {
private:
  D *dptr;
  ...
};

class D {
private:
  C *cptr;
  ...
};
```

The C++ compiler will issue an error message for the declaration of `dptr`, because it does not yet know that `D` is a class. To tell it that you are going to define `D` later, you can give an abbreviated declaration of `D`, as follows:

```
class D;

class C {
private:
  D *dptr;
  ...
};

class D {
private:
  C *cptr;
  ...
};
```

E.7.5 Local Definitions

Classes may contain local definitions of variables and types. If declared in a class `C`, a locally defined name can be referred to outside the class—if it is public—using its full name (that is, with the `C::` prefix). Such a name is distinct from any name defined outside the class.

static data member

We begin with local definitions of variables. A locally defined variable, called a *static data member*, is like a global variable except that it must be referred to by its full name outside the class. Furthermore, if it is `private`, it can be used only in the class's functions (meaning its member functions, constructors, and friends). A local variable is declared like a data member, except that the keyword `static` is added at the beginning of its declaration, but it acts like a global variable: It comes into existence when the program starts executing and remains in existence until the end of the program. Unlike a data member, there is just a single instance of a local variable—*not* one instance per object. The only reasons to use a static data member instead of a global variable are that there is no danger of its name overlapping with other global variables, and that, if desired, it can be made private to the class.

An example is the variable `count` used to count the number of `time` objects that have been created:

```
class time {
private:
  int hour, minute;
  static int count;

public:
  time (int h, int m) { hour = h; minute = m; count++; }

  time addMinutes (int m) { ... }

  void printTime () { ... }

  void printCount () { cout << count; }
};
```

Each time the constructor is called, it increments `count`. Because `count` is private, no clients can mention it directly. A member function has to be added to print it; that is the purpose of `t.printCount()`.

The static data member `count` needs to be initialized. Its declaration in the class is *only* a declaration; a definition must be provided outside the class (see the discussion of declarations versus definitions in Chapter 10). In effect, `time::count` is a global variable, and, like any global variable, it must be defined somewhere outside of any function:

```
int time::count = 0;
```

Note that this definition of `time::count` is legal even though `count` is private. This is a special, one-time exception to the privacy of `count`; functions outside `time` still cannot refer to `count` (or `time::count`). If `count` were a public static data member of `time`, clients could refer to it using the name `time::count`.

Member functions can also be static, meaning that they act like ordinary functions (no implicit receiver argument) but are referred to by their full names and may be private to the class. If `printCount` were declared to be static (but still public),

```
class time {
private:
  int hour, minute;
  static int count;

public:
  ...

  static void printCount () { cout << count; }
};
```

then clients could call it in this way:

```
time::printCount()
```

The full name of **printCount** is used. Since there is no receiver, **printCount** cannot refer to ordinary data members, but it can refer to static data members.

A class may also have local data type declarations. For example, a class may have a local enumerated type:

```
class time {
private:
  int hour, minute;
  ampm dayHalf;

public:
  enum ampm {am, pm};
  ...
};
```

A client can use the type **time::ampm** and its members, **time::am** and **time::pm**, as long as it uses their full names. Unlike static data members and functions, locally defined types are never private. However, if **ampm** were declared in the private part of the class, its data values **am** and **pm** would be private.

Another example of a local data type declaration is the declaration of a class within another class. This is generally used when the enclosing class is the only client of the nested class.

E.8

Class Inheritance

One of the most important and highly touted features of C++—indeed, of all object-oriented languages—is *inheritance*. It allows a programmer to "customize" a class for a specific application without modifying that class at all. Instead, a new class is defined that uses ("inherits from") the first class and adds or redefines its member functions as necessary. By allowing for the reuse of existing classes, inheritance can be highly advantageous in its ability to provide varying functionality without code explosion.

derived class   A class **D** is said to be *derived from* a class **B** (or, equivalently, **B** is a *base*
base class   *class* of **D**) if the declaration of **D** has the form

```
class D : public B {  // D is derived from B
  ...
};
```

The body of **D** follows the usual syntax. The new part is the **: public B** in the first line. With **D** derived from **B**, the objects of **D** contain all the data members of objects of **B** as well as the data members declared in **D**, and they respond to all the member functions defined in **B** as well as those defined in **D**. Furthermore, the declaration of **D** can *redefine* member functions defined in **B**, thereby overriding the behavior of those member functions when they are applied to D objects.

As an example, recall the `time` class introduced in Chapter 6. Here is a version that includes only `advanceMinutes` (the mutating operation to advance the time by a certain number of minutes) and `printTime`:

```
class time {
private:
  int hour, minute;

public:
  time (int h, int m) { hour = h; minute = m; }

  void advanceMinutes (int m) {
    int totalMinutes = (60*hour + minute + m) % (24*60);
    if (totalMinutes < 0)
      totalMinutes = totalMinutes + 24*60;
    hour = totalMinutes/60;
    minute = totalMinutes%60;
  }

  void printTime () {
    if ((hour == 0) && (minute == 0))
      cout << "midnight";
    else if ((hour == 12) && (minute == 0))
      cout << "noon";
    else {
      if (hour == 0)
        cout << 12;
      else if (hour > 12)
        cout << hour-12;
      else
        cout << hour;
      cout << ':' << setfill('0') << setw(2) << minute;
      if (hour < 12)
        cout << "AM";
      else
        cout << "PM";
    }
  }
};
```

Suppose we wished to have a class representing more exact time, counting seconds as well as minutes and hours. We may want to retain our current definition—not every client wants to have such exact time—while adding a new class, `preciseTime`, which is mostly the same as `time` but has a new data member, `second`, and a new member function, `void advanceSeconds (int)`. This can be accomplished with inheritance:

```
class preciseTime : public time {
private:
  int second;
```

```
public:
  preciseTime (int h, int m, int s) : time(h, m), second(s)
  {}

  void advanceSeconds (int s) {
    int advMinutes = s / 60;
    second += s % 60;
    if (second < 0) {
      advMinutes--;
      second += 60;
    }
    else if (second >= 60) {
      advMinutes++;
      second -= 60;
    }
    advanceMinutes(advMinutes);
  }
};
```

Objects of this class have data members `hour`, `minute`, and `second` and member functions `advanceMinutes`, `printTime`, and `advanceSeconds`. The program

```
int main () {
  preciseTime lunchtime(6, 10, 0);
  lunchtime.advanceSeconds(60);
  lunchtime.printTime(); cout << "\n";
  lunchtime.advanceSeconds(-61);
  lunchtime.printTime(); cout << "\n";
}
```

prints

```
6:11AM
6:09AM
```

The constructor `preciseTime::preciseTime (int, int, int)` is explained in the following subsections. It is not important to understand the function `advanceSeconds` in detail; in general, it adjusts the data member `second`, determines by how many minutes (if any) the time is being advanced, and then calls `advanceMinutes`. Since `preciseTime` objects inherit the member functions of `time`, they can respond to `advanceMinutes`.

Note that `printTime` does for `preciseTime` objects exactly what it did for `time` objects: It prints the `hour` and `minute` data members. It does not automatically adjust itself to print the `second` member. We will see how to do that in the next section.

derivation
hierarchy

A class can have any number of derived classes, and those derived classes can in turn have further derived classes, creating a *derivation hierarchy*. A class in the hierarchy inherits the members of all the classes above it in the hierarchy.

E.8.1   Private, Public, and Protected Members

Private members of a class cannot be accessed either by clients (of course) or by the member functions of its derived classes. Public members can be accessed by both clients and derived classes. Often it is helpful to give derived classes access to members without allowing clients that access. For this reason, a new visibility classification—*protected*—is available.

The keyword `protected` can be used instead of `public` or `private`. Members declared after this keyword are visible to classes derived from this one but not to its clients. Thus, when there is the possibility that a class will have derived classes, it is best to use `protected` rather than `private`. Inherited protected members are considered to be protected members of the derived class (visible to derived classes, hidden from clients), and inherited public members are considered to be public members of the derived class (visible to everyone).

For example, we may want to define `printTime` differently in the class `preciseTime` than in `time`. This can be done by overriding `printTime` in the derived class. However, this definition does not work,

```
class preciseTime : public time {
...

  void printTime () {
    if ((hour == 0) && (minute == 0))
      cout << "midnight";
    else if ((hour == 12) && (minute == 0))
      cout << "noon";
    else {
      if (hour == 0)
        cout << 12;
      else if (hour > 12)
        cout << hour-12;
      else
        cout << hour;
      cout << ':' << setfill('0') << setw(2) << minute;
      cout << ":" << setfill('0') << setw(2) << second;
      if (hour < 12)
        cout << "AM";
      else
        cout << "PM";
    }
  }

};
```

because it accesses the private data members of `time`. The remedy for this is to change the definition of `time` to

```
class time {
protected:
  int hour, minute;

public:
  ... as above ...
};
```

Such a change—making the `private` data members `protected`—has no effect on existing clients of `time` and does not allow them access to `hour` and `minute`, but it does allow such access to `preciseTime` and to any other classes derived from `time`.

E.8.2   Constructors

When an object of a derived class is created, C++ naturally wants to call a constructor of that class. However, it also wants to call a constructor from the base class to initialize the data members declared in that class. The general rule is that the base class's constructor is executed first, followed by that of the derived class. In general, given a class hierarchy

```
              B
              |
              D
              |
              :
              |
              E
```

if a new **D** object is created, the constructors will be called in the order **B::B**, **D::D**, ..., **E::E**. This way, each class in the hierarchy is responsible for initializing data members declared at that level.

Only one question remains. If a base class doesn't have a zero-argument constructor, where will it get the arguments for its constructor? The answer is, "In the initialization list of the derived class's constructor." Specifically, in derived class **D** the constructor's initialization list should include a call to **B::B**:

```
class D : public B {
  ...
  D (...) : B(...), ...
  {
    ...
  }
  ...
};
```

It is important to understand that **D** *does not contain a data member of type* **B**. The initialization list is perhaps misleading in this regard. All other entries are used to initialize data members; the **B(...)** calls another constructor, which initializes data members.

The constructor given already for **preciseTime** is an example of this feature. A **preciseTime** object is initialized by providing three integers. The hour and minute should be set by the base-class constructor, **time::time (int, int)**, and the second by the derived-class constructor. The call **time(h, m)** in the initialization list of the **preciseTime** constructor allows the **time** constructor to do this initialization.

E.8.3 Virtual Functions and Dynamic Binding

Whenever a function is called or a message sent in a C++ program, it is possible to determine, without running the program, which function or member function will be invoked. Even when a function is overloaded or when a member function is overridden in a derived class, this principle continues to hold. It may be complicated and require a deep understanding of the C++ compiler, but, in principle, every time a function is called or a message is sent, the exact function that will be invoked can be determined *at compile time*. This principle is known as *static binding of functions.*

static binding

We now come to a place in C++ where this principle is violated. If a member function is declared **virtual** in a base class (by placing the keyword **virtual** at the beginning of its prototype or definition), then when that message is sent to an object of that class or any class derived from it, the call is *dynamically bound*. This means that the function actually invoked depends upon the class of its receiver. Since the member function may be redefined in derived classes, this can make a difference.

We begin with a very simple, but artificial, example to explain the concept:

```
class B {
public:
  void g () { cout << "I'm a B object\n"; }
  void f () { g(); }
};

class D : public B {
public:
  void g () { cout << "I'm a D object\n";}
};
```

Here we have *not* used the **virtual** keyword, so the actions of these classes can be understood from prior principles. Two cases are of interest, namely the calls on lines 4 and 6 below:

```
1    B aBobject;
2    D aDobject;
3    aBobject.g();   // Prints: I'm a B object
4    aBobject.f();   // Prints: I'm a B object
5    aDobject.g();   // Prints: I'm a D object
6    aDobject.f();   // Prints: I'm a B object
```

Lines 3 and 5—aBobject.g() and aDobject.g()—have an obvious effect, printing I'm a B object and I'm a D object, respectively. Line 4—aBobject.f()—does not involve inheritance (it would work exactly the same if class D didn't exist), so its effect is explained by the principles of Chapter 6: It sends f to aBobject, which in turn sends g to aBobject, which prints I'm a B object. Line 6—aDobject.f()—is more problematic. It sends f to aDobject, which in turn sends g to aDobject. What happens now? The principle of static binding tells us that the function invoked by B::f must be determined at compile time. We have already agreed that this function is `B::g`. So the answer is that line 6 prints `I'm a B object`.

An argument can be made that this violates the basic principle of object-oriented programming. If a message like `g` is sent to an object of class `D`, that object should respond to the message *as an object of class* `D`. `D` objects respond to `g` by printing `I'm a D object`. This requires that the call to `g` in the body of `f` invoke `B::g` for objects of type `B` and invoke `D::g` for objects of type `D`. Yet the principle of static binding bars this possibility.

Declaring `g` **virtual** in the base class tells C++ that calls to `g` should be *dynamically bound*, invoking whichever `g` is appropriate for the receiver—`B::g` for `B` objects, `D::g` for `D` objects:

```
class B {
public:
  virtual void g () { cout << "I'm a B object\n"; }
  void f () { g(); }
};

class D : public B {
public:
  void g () { cout << "I'm a D object\n";}
};
```

Looking again at the sequence of statements above, the call `aDobject.f()` in line 6 sends the `f` message to `aDobject`, which in turn sends the `g` message to `aDobject`. Because `g` is virtual, this last call is based on the receiver of `g`; its receiver in this case is of type `D`, so `D::g` is invoked, and the output is `I'm a D object`. The effect of the other calls is unchanged. (*Syntactic note:* In the derived class, the **virtual** keyword may be added to the definition of `g`, or it may be omitted. It makes no difference: The **virtual** declaration in the base class ensures that all calls to `g` are dynamically bound.)

The combination of class inheritance and virtual functions is extremely powerful and accounts for much of the popularity of C++. It permits a derived class to reuse the member functions inherited from its base class, while ensuring that those inherited functions behave correctly on objects of the derived class.

From a client's point of view, it generally doesn't matter that a class is derived from another. Variables of type `B` and `D` are declared in the same way, and constructors are used in the same way as always. However, there is one circumstance when it does matter: when the client doesn't know the exact type of an object. Suppose, for example, that the client is building a list of objects that may be either `B` or `D` objects. Here the following important rules about type conversions come into play:

- A `B` object *cannot* be converted to a `D` object. In particular, the assignment

  ```
  aDobject = aBobject;
  ```

  is illegal.

- A D object *can* be converted to a B object. In particular, the assignment

  ```
  aBobject = aDobject;
  ```

  is legal. However, this is rarely useful.
- A B pointer *cannot* be converted to a D pointer. If **aBpointer** is of type **B***
  and **aDpointer** is of type **D***, then the assignment

  ```
  aDpointer = aBpointer;
  ```

  is illegal.
- A D pointer *can* be converted to a B pointer. Furthermore, *the object pointed
  to by the* D *pointer retains its identity as a* D *object.* Thus, not only is

  ```
  aBpointer = aDpointer;
  ```

  a legal assignment, but the object referred to by **aBpointer** continues to
  be a D object. This means, most importantly, that, in terms of our example
  above, **aBpointer->g()** invokes D::g, not B::g.

  This crucially important rule allows our hypothetical client to build a
  list of B and D objects. So long as the list is declared to have entries of type
  B*, they can point to either B or D objects. When a message is sent to one of
  those entries, it responds as appropriate to its type.
- A D& object *can* be converted to a B&. In particular, if a function has an
  argument of type B&, and a D object is passed to the function, in the body
  of the function the argument behaves as a D object. For example, given
  function

  ```
  void sendf (B& x) { x.f(); }
  ```

  the call **sendf(aDobject)** prints **I'm a D object**.

E.8.4 Example

As a final example, we define a hierarchy inspired by the **Shape** class of Chapter 10 (but this discussion is independent of that chapter). The hierarchy consists of four classes:

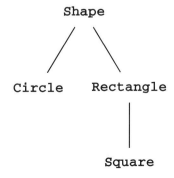

In addition to constructors, each of these classes has two public member functions:

```
void draw (Screen& s)
Point computePerimeterPoint (Direction d)
```

Direction is an enumerated type, giving the four major compass directions,

```
enum Direction {east, south, west, north};
```

and **Point** (see page 545) is a structure containing a pair of floating-point numbers:

```
struct Point {
  float x, y;
  Point (float a, float b) : x(a), y(b) {}
};
```

draw draws a shape on a screen (see Chapter 9), and **computePerimeterPoint** finds the point on the perimeter of a shape corresponding to a given direction.

Every shape has a *center* and provides a method **distanceTo** to compute the distance from the center to any of the four compass points. (**distanceTo** is used by **computePerimeterPoint**.) The definition of **Shape** is[3]

```
class Shape {
protected:
  Point center;
  virtual float distanceTo (Direction) = 0;

public:
  Shape (Point c) : center(c) {}
  virtual void draw (Screen &) = 0;
  virtual Point computePerimeterPoint (Direction) ;
};

Point Shape::computePerimeterPoint (Direction d) {
  float dist = distanceTo(d);
  switch (d) {
    case east:  return Point(center.x+dist, center.y);
    case south: return Point(center.x, center.y+dist);
    case west:  return Point(center.x-dist, center.y);
    case north: return Point(center.x, center.y-dist);
  }
}
```

We have used a feature here we didn't mention before. To give the prototypes of virtual functions without giving their definitions—since the **distanceTo** and **draw** functions have real definitions only in derived classes—we write **= 0;**.

---

[3] As mentioned in Chapters 9 and 10, graphics applications use an "upside-down" coordinate system in which points appearing higher on a screen have lower *y* coordinates. That is why **dist** is added to go south and subtracted to go north.

Clients never create **Shape** objects (**Shape** is an *abstract class*), but they   *abstract class*
create **Circle**, **Rectangle**, and **Square** objects. Each of these has its own constructor and its own definition of **draw** and **distanceTo**:

```
class Circle : public Shape {
protected:
  float radius;

public:
  Circle (float r, Point c) : radius(r), Shape(c) {}

  void draw (Screen &s) {
    s.drawCircle(center.x, center.y, radius);
  }

  float distanceTo (Direction d) {
    return radius;
  }
};

class Rectangle : public Shape {
protected:
  float halfwidth, halfheight;

public:
  Rectangle (float w, float h, Point c)
    : halfwidth(w/2), halfheight(h/2), Shape(c)
  {}

  float distanceTo (Direction d) ;

  void draw (Screen &s) ;
};

float Rectangle::distanceTo (Direction d) {
  switch (d) {
    case east:
    case west:
      return halfwidth;
    case north:
    case south:
      return halfheight;
  }
}

void Rectangle::draw (Screen &s) {
  Point ne(center.x+halfwidth, center.y-halfheight);
  Point se(center.x+halfwidth, center.y+halfheight);
  Point sw(center.x-halfwidth, center.y+halfheight);
  Point nw(center.x-halfwidth, center.y-halfheight);
  s.drawLine(ne.x, ne.y, se.x, se.y);
  s.drawLine(se.x, se.y, sw.x, sw.y);
  s.drawLine(sw.x, sw.y, nw.x, nw.y);
  s.drawLine(nw.x, nw.y, ne.x, ne.y);
}
```

```
class Square : public Rectangle {
public:
  Square (float r, Point c) : Rectangle(r, r, c) {}

  float distanceTo (Direction d) {
    return halfheight;
  }
};
```

In the absence of inheritance—as in the **Shape** class of Chapter 10—**Shape** would have a data member that indicated the type of shape represented by an object. Functions **draw** and **computePerimeterPoint** would have to test that data member and behave appropriately. The addition of a new shape would require a change in the definitions of those functions. The advantage of inheritance is that a new shape can be added without disturbing any existing code. For example, we can add the derived class **Triangle** by defining **distanceTo** and **draw**:

```
class Triangle : public Shape {
protected:
  // data members for representing triangles

public:
  Triangle (...) ;

  float distanceTo (Direction d) ;

  void draw (Screen &s) ;
};
```

This does not save any of the hard work of programming these operations, but the key point is that existing functions are not touched.

E.9

Remaining Features

Some features of C++ are not covered either in the main part of this book or in this appendix. Just so the reader will know that these features exist, we list them here and state their purpose, but give no examples or explanation.

- *Destructors.*   These are special member functions (of which a class **C** can have only one, called **C:~C**) that are called to "de-initialize" an object when that object ceases to exist (either because the function that created it exits, or due to a call to **delete**).
- *Exceptions.*   A fairly new feature of C++, exceptions make it possible to exit from many function calls at once.
- *Multiple inheritance.*   A class can be derived from more than one base class, inheriting all the members of each of its base classes. Multiple inheritance is far more complicated than the single inheritance we introduced

earlier in this appendix, because it raises issues such as the order in which constructors of the base classes are called, what to do when two base classes have members with the same name, and many others.

- *Standard libraries.*   There are a number of standard libraries that were not covered in Appendices B and C. Particularly important is the *standard template library*, which defines a number of data structures (such as lists and tables) along with efficient operations on them, such as searching and sorting.

Further Reading—
An Annotated Bibliography

Cave ab homine unius libri.
(Beware the man of one book.)

—Latin saying

The purpose of this bibliography is twofold. First and foremost, it is designed to help you find further details about the material presented in this book. Second, it is intended as a *vade mecum*—traveler's guide—to the breadth of computer science. These two purposes overlap to some extent, because the choice of examples presented in this book was motivated by a desire to give you a taste of a wide selection of important topics.

The mouse-in-the-maze example, used to motivate and describe (in a nontechnical way) the process of designing an algorithm and writing a program, was used in the early 1960s in classes given by IBM for systems engineer trainees. More recently, the idea was extended considerably in

> Pattis, R. E., *Karel the Robot* (2nd ed., revised by J. Roberts and M. Stehlik), John Wiley and Sons, New York, 1995,

to include not only the simple mouse instructions we used in Chapter 1 but also an entire programming language. Pattis's book is a pleasant, nontechnical introduction to programming.

You have by now learned a great deal about C++. Further technical details of the language can be found in

> Stroustrup, B., *The C++ Programming Language,* 2nd ed., Addison-Wesley Publishing Co., Reading, MA, 1994.

There are a number of good books on the craft of programming. This material transcends the C++ language itself—good style, careful program development, and efficient techniques apply to any language.

> Kernighan, B. W., and P. J. Plauger, *The Elements of Programming Style,* 2nd ed., McGraw-Hill, New York, 1978,

points out the stylistic shortcomings of many published programs, explaining how they should have been written. Efficiency considerations are the focus of

> Bentley, J. L., *Writing Efficient Programs,* Prentice-Hall, Englewood Cliffs, NJ, 1982,

which examines how to get programs to run faster.

There is no better way to acquire a good programming style than to read and study programs written by masters of the craft. A nice collection can be found in

Bentley, J. L., *Programming Pearls,* Addison-Wesley, Reading, MA, 1986
Bentley, J. L., *More Programming Pearls,* Addison-Wesley, Reading, MA, 1988,

which are compilations of Bentley's columns that appeared in the *Communications of the ACM.*

Reading the programs of others is not sufficient, however. You have to practice to acquire the skill. In

Wetherell, C., *Études for Programmers,* Prentice-Hall, Englewood Cliffs, NJ, 1978,

there are outlined a number of intriguing programming projects, called "études." Each étude includes a discussion of a problem and some hints on how to solve it, but the solution is left to the reader.

One of the most important programming techniques presented in this book is recursion. Our coverage in Chapter 8, and use thereafter, is much more extensive than in other introductory programming texts; still, there is a great deal of material that we did not cover. See

Rohl, J. S., *Recursion via Pascal,* Cambridge University Press, Cambridge, 1984
Roberts, E. S., *Thinking Recursively,* John Wiley and Sons, New York, 1986,

for further examples and techniques.

Our presentation of programming included a stress on the analysis of the algorithms implemented. This stress is deserved; many grotesque algorithms have been unthinkingly implemented when far better choices were available. Analysis of the underlying algorithms is the only precise way to understand a program's behavior. An excellent place to begin a study of the analysis of algorithms is

Cormen, T. H., C. E. Leiserson, and R. L. Rivest, *Introduction to Algorithms,* MIT Press, Cambridge, MA, 1990 (copublished by McGraw-Hill, New York).

Having learned C++, you might want to explore other programming languages. Programming languages are classified by the predominant "programming paradigm" they support. Traditional languages like C are based on the *imperative* paradigm; with the addition of classes, this becomes the *object-oriented* paradigm. Other paradigms include the *functional* and *logic-based* paradigms. An overview of other programming languages is given in

Kamin, S. N., *Programming Languages: An Interpreter-Based Approach,* Addison-Wesley, Reading, MA, 1990.

The functional paradigm, in which algorithmic processes are expressed by defining functions rather than by a sequence of operations, has had a strong influence on our presentation of C++, especially in Chapters 7, 8, and 10. The best known functional languages are LISP and Scheme. You can read more about them in

> Winston, P. H., and B. K. P. Horn, *LISP,* 2nd ed., Addison-Wesley, Reading, MA, 1984
>
> Wilensky, R., *Common LISPcraft,* W. W. Norton, New York, 1986
>
> Abelson, H., G. J. Sussman, and J. Sussman, *Structure and Interpretation of Computer Programs,* MIT Press, Cambridge, MA, 1985 (copublished by McGraw-Hill, New York)

Another functional language of interest is the language included in Mathematica®, a system for doing mathematics on computer. See

> Gaylord, R. J., S. N. Kamin and P. R. Wellin, *Introduction to Programming with Mathematica,* Telos/Springer-Verlag, New York, 1993,

for an introduction.

You should definitely learn about the internal structure of computers. C++ and many other programming languages disguise the computer's structure in many ways, insulating you from it. But what goes on beneath the surface is important to know, because it impinges on how and why languages do what they do. Some standard introductions to computer architecture are

> Patterson, D. A., and J. L. Hennessy, *Computer Organization and Design: The Hardware/Software Interface,* Morgan Kaufmann Publishers, Inc., San Mateo, CA, 1993
>
> Ward, S. A., and R. H. Halstead, *Computation Structures,* MIT Press, Cambridge, MA, 1990 (copublished by McGraw-Hill, New York).

In the early days, computers were used solely for mathematical calculations, such as linear-system solving by Gaussian elimination, which we covered in Chapter 9. For the mathematically inclined, there are many interesting questions about the efficiency and accuracy of such numerical algorithms. An up-to-date introduction is

> Skeel, R. D., and J. B. Keiper, *Elementary Numerical Computing with Mathematica,* McGraw-Hill, New York, 1993.

Graphics is an intensively studied subdiscipline of computer science; several of our major examples were drawn from this area. See

> Hearn, D. and M. P. Baker, *Computer Graphics,* 2nd ed., Prentice-Hall, Englewood Cliffs, NJ, 1994,

for a general introduction.

The example we gave in Chapter 10—the `psl` program—is similar in structure to a compiler for a high-level programming language like C++. The topics of lexing and parsing and the use of syntax trees are covered in books on compilers, such as

> Aho, A., R. Sethi, and J. Ullman, *Compilers: Principles, Techniques, and Tools,* Addison-Wesley, Reading, MA, 1986.

For a discussion of the simulation of human behavior by computer, see

Dean, T., J. Allen, and Y. Aloimonos, *Artificial Intelligence: Theory and Practice,* Addison-Wesley, Reading, MA, 1995.

Also in this regard, a fascinating history of computer chess playing can be found in

Levy, D., *Chess and Computers,* Computer Science Press, Woodland Hills, CA, 1976.

Finally, you might be interested in the genesis of modern computers. If so, look at

Goldstine, H. H., *The Computer from Pascal to von Neumann,* Princeton University Press, Princeton, N.J., 1972

Randell, B., editor, *The Origins of Digital Computers,* 3rd ed., Springer-Verlag, Berlin, 1982.

Solutions to ☞ Exercises

> I am not bound to please thee with my answer.
>
> —Shakespeare
> *The Merchant of Venice*

Chapter 1—First Set

1. The algorithm underlying the program on page 6 will find an exit if one exists. Since an entrance is indistinguishable from an exit, the mouse will eventually go out the entrance.

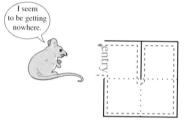

2. The new algorithm needs to keep a wall on the mouse's left. We use the same methods that we used with the original algorithm on page 6. To check if the mouse has a wall on its left, it must **turn left**, then ask whether it is facing a wall. If it is facing a wall, it must then **turn right** until it is not facing a wall. This is written as

```
turn left;
while (facing a wall?) {
  turn right;
}
```

The mouse can then **step forward**, assured that it will not crash into a wall. This process needs to be repeated until the mouse is out of the maze:

```
step forward;  //  This takes the mouse into the entrance.
while (not outside the maze?) {
  turn left;
  while (facing a wall?) {
    turn right;
  }
  step forward;  // How do we know that the
                 // mouse is not facing a wall?
}
```

Compare this to the original code on page 6. It is *symmetrical*; that is, **turn right** is replaced by **turn left**, **turn left** is replaced by **turn right**, and everything else remains the same.

6. Since the mouse always hugs a wall, we can ask how many walls can connect to a room. The definition of *maze* on page 2 gives a room four corners. A mouse can enter a room, turn, and leave the room once at each of those corners. It can therefore enter (and leave) a room four times. Here's an example where room A is visited four times:

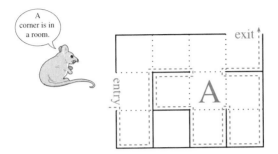

7. To see whether the mouse is facing north, we can follow the algorithm: If the mouse is not facing north, turn the mouse to the right. Then, if the mouse is still not facing north, turn to the right. If we keep going, we will eventually be facing north.

```
while (not facing north?) {
  turn right;
}
```

Chapter 2—First Set

2. The code that produces Figure 2.1 starts at $-10°C$ and goes to $+10°C$. There are 21 different integers from -10 to $+10$. In general, the number of integers between two integers i and j (where j is the larger) is $j - i + 1$. By substitution, we get $10 - (-10) + 1 = 21$. This is one example of the infamous *off-by-one error* (sometimes called the *fence post error*) that plagues computer science.

3. Using the same compiler as mentioned in Chapter 2, our results are as follows, but in some cases your results will be different.
   (a) We omitted the semicolon on line 20 and got the following:

   ```
   line 21: Error: Use ";" to terminate statements.
   ```

   (b) We added a semicolon on line 20, and the program executed the same as the original.
   (c) The result of the change was

   ```
   line 22: Error: mian() is expected to return a value.
   ```

   (d) We changed the { on line 4 and received the messages

   ```
   line 10: Error: Badly formed expression.
   line 14: Error: Type name expected instead of "<<".
   line 15: Error: Type name expected instead of "=".
   ```

```
line 16: Error: ")" expected instead of "<=".
line 18: Error: Type name expected instead of "<<".
line 20: Error: Type name expected instead of "++".
6 Error(s) detected.
```

(e) In integer arithmetic, $9/5$ is evaluated as 1. The result is

DEGREES C	DEGREES F
-10	22
-9	23
-8	24
⋮	⋮
8	40
9	41
10	42

(f) If the number is less than or equal to 10, the output will begin at the number. If the number is greater than 10, there is nothing written except the titles. Here's the result when -10.0 is changed to -5.0:

DEGREES C	DEGREES F
-5	23
-4	24.8
-3	26.6
⋮	⋮
8	46.4
9	48.2
10	50

(g) This change causes output that is incremented by 0.5°C:

DEGREES C	DEGREES F
-10	14
-9.5	14.9
-9	15.8
⋮	⋮
9	48.2
9.5	49.1
10	50

(h) This change causes output that is incremented by 2°C:

DEGREES C	DEGREES F
-10	14
-8	17.6
-6	21.2
⋮	⋮
6	42.8
8	46.4
10	50

(i) This change causes output that is incremented by $-1°C$. Since `Celsius` is getting smaller, it will never reach $+10°C$. This program executes forever.

```
DEGREES C  DEGREES F
   -10          14
   -11        12.2
   -12        10.4
    ⋮           ⋮
```

4. The modified program is

```cpp
#include <iostream.h>
#include <iomanip.h>

main () {
//  Create a table of corresponding Celsius and
//  Fahrenheit temperatures from -10 to +10 deg Fahrenheit.

   float  Celsius,     // The Celsius temperature.
          Fahrenheit;  // The Fahrenheit temperature.

   cout << "DEGREES F  DEGREES C\n";
   Fahrenheit = -10.0;
   while (Fahrenheit <= 10.0) {
     Celsius = (Fahrenheit - 32.0) * 5.0 / 9.0;
     cout << setw(7) << Fahrenheit << "     "
          << setw(7) << Celsius << "\n";
     Fahrenheit++;   // Increment the Celsius value.
   }
}
```

It produces the output

```
DEGREES F  DEGREES C
   -10      -23.3333
    -9      -22.7778
    -8      -22.2222
     ⋮          ⋮
     8      -13.3333
     9      -12.7778
    10      -12.2222
```

Chapter 2—Second Set

1.
`first_entry`	This is a valid C++ identifier.
`2nd`	This is invalid; it begins with a number.
`right-hand-side`	This is invalid; it contains a "-".
`dataType`	This is valid.
`FATHER`	This is valid.
`break`	This is invalid; it is a keyword.
`last one`	This is invalid; it contains a space.

2.   −6543210.0   -6.54321e6   or   -6543210e0
       .897654321   8.97654321e-1   or   0.897654321e0
       3×10^{45} 3e45
       0.000061   6.1e-5   or   0.000061e0
       45.8×10^{-3} 4.58e-2   or   45.8e-3

3. (a) Fahrenheit = (9.0 / 5.0) * (Kelvin + 273.16) + 32.0;
    (b) Kelvin = Celsius - 273.16;
    (c) Kelvin = (5.0 / 9.0) * (Fahrenheit - 32.0) + 273.16;

Chapter 3—First Set

1.  ```
    if (score >= 90)
       cout << "A";
    else if (score >= 80)
       cout << "B";
    else if (score >= 60)
       cout << "C";
    else if (score >= 50)
       cout << "D";
    else
       cout << "Fail";
    ```

5. Both **heatingDegDays** and **coolingDegDays** use the same formula, so we calculate it first and then decide where the result is placed. We subtract **degDays** from **coolingDegDays**, because subtracting a negative number is equivalent to adding a positive number.

    ```
    degDays = 65.0 - ((highTemp + lowTemp) / 2.0);
    if (degDays > 0)
       heatingDegDays = heatingDegDays + degDays;
    else
       coolingDegDays = coolingDegDays - degDays;
    ```

17. (a)   !((!!p) && (q || q))   =   !(p && (q || q))   !!p == p
                                 =   !(p && q)   q || q == q
                                 =   !p || !q   DeMorgan's law

    (b)   (p || (p && q)) && !(!q && !r)
                                 = (p || (p && q)) && (q || r)   DeMorgan's law
                                 = p && (q || r)   Absorption

19. *nand* is short for "not and," giving the expression **!(A && B)**, which by DeMorgan's law (from Table 3.5) is **!A || !B**.

Chapter 3—Second Set

1.  ```
    #include <iostream.h>
    #include <iomanip.h>

    main () {
    // Add the ordinal suffix to a positive integer.
      int x;
    ```

```
      cout << "Enter an integer >= 0: ";
      cin >> x;
      cout << "The ordinal form is " << x ;

      if ((x % 100 > 10) && (x % 100 < 14))
        cout << "th.";
      else {
        switch (x % 10) {
          case 1:  cout << "st."; break;
          case 2:  cout << "nd."; break;
          case 3:  cout << "rd."; break;
          default: cout << "th.";
        }
      }
      cout << "\n";
    }
```

2. `result = (x < 1.00005);`

3.
```
    switch(class) {
        case FirstClass:
          cost = .32;
          if (weight > 1)
            cost = .32 + (0.23 * floor(weight));
          break;

        case AirMail:
          cost = .50;
          if (weight > .5)
            cost = 0.50 + (0.50 * floor(weight*2.0));
          break;

        case PostCard:
          cost = .20;
          break;

        case Book:
          if (weight <= 1)
            cost = 1.24;
          else if ((weight * 16 > 1) && (weight * 16 <= 7))
            cost = 1.24 + (0.50 * floor(weight * 16));
          else
            cost = 1.25 + 3.00 + (0.31 * floor((weight*16)-6);
          break;
    }
```

4. The **break** statement at the end of **case 0** is missing. If **x** is zero, first **s** is assigned 0, then since **x** is not less than 0, **s** is assigned 1. See Bug Alert 3.7 (page 75).

Chapter 4—First Set

1.
```
    #include <iostream.h>
    #include <iomanip.h>

    //  Print the song "This Old Man"
```

```
void verse (int n,       // What the old man played
                char *what) // What he played it on
{
// Print the verse
  cout << "This old man, he played " << n << ",\n"
          << "He played nick nack " << what << ";\n"
          << "Nick nack paddy whack, give a dog a bone,\n"
          << "This old man came rolling home.\n\n";
}

main () {
  verse(1, "on my drum");
  verse(2, "on my shoe");
  verse(3, "on my tree");
  verse(4, "on my door");
  verse(5, "on my hive");
  verse(6, "on my sticks");
  verse(7, "all round heaven");
  verse(8, "on my gate");
  verse(9, "on my line");
  verse(10, "on my hen");
}
```

5.
```
boolean Xor (boolean A, boolean B) {
// return the "exclusive or" of two variables.
  return ((A && !B) || (!A && B))
}
```

Chapter 4—Second Set

1.
```
enum meridian {AM, PM};

void fracToTime
      (int &h, int &m, int &s, meridian &halfDay, float f) {
// Convert day fraction to a time

  s = floor(f*60*60*24);   // number of seconds
  halfDay = AM;
  h = s / 3600;            // number of hours
  s = s % 3600;            // number of seconds left
  if (h > 12) {            // fix AM and PM
    h = h - 12;
    halfDay = PM;
  }
  m = s / 60;              // number of minutes
  s = s % 60;              // number of seconds left
}
```

5.
```
void swap (int &firstVariable, int &secondVariable) {
// Swap two integers.
  int tempVariable = firstVariable;
  firstVariable = secondVariable;
  secondVariable = tempVariable;
}
```

6. This function requires the use of `lastDayOfMonth` on page 106 and `leapYear` on page 104.

```
void previousDay (int& m, int& d, int& y) {
// Decrement date m, d, y to previous day

  if (d != 1)                   // not the first day
    d --;
  else if (m != 1) {            // first day of month
    m --;
    d = lastDayOfMonth(m,y);
  }
  else {                        // first day of year
    d = 31;                     // reset day
    m = 12;                     // reset month
    y --;                       // prev year
  }
}
```

Chapter 4—Third Set

1. (a) This function requires `GregorianDayNumber` on page 122.

```
int GregorianDaysLeft (int month, int day, int year) {
// Return the number of days left in the year (gregorian).
   return GregorianDayNumber(12, 31, year) -
          GregorianDayNumber(month, day, year);
}
```

(b) This function requires `JulianDaysLeft` on page 122.

```
int JulianDaysLeft (int month, int day, int year) {
// Return the number of days left in the year (julian).
   return JulianDayNumber(12, 31, year)
          - JulianDayNumber(month, day, year);
}
```

5.
```
enum season {Fall, Winter, Spring, Summer};

season seasonFromDate (int month, int day) {
// Return the season associated with the date.

  if (day <= 20) // If we're before the 21st, jump back a month.
    month --;       // Now all the seasons have 3 different months
                    // except Winter, which has 0, 1, 2, and 12.
  switch (month/3) {
    case 1: return Spring;
    case 2: return Summer;
    case 3: return Fall;
    default: return Winter;
  }
}
```

13. (a) `date - x` is the number of days `x` is before `date`. `(date - x) % 7` is the number of days the most recent `x`-day of the week is before `date`.

```
int xdayOnOrBefore (int date, weekday x) {
  return date - ((date - x) % 7);
}
```

(b) To find the **x**-day prior to a given date, call **xdayOnOrBefore(date-1,x)** where **x** is the **x**-day we're looking for. To find the **x**-day following a given date, call **xdayOnOrBefore(date+7,x)**. To find the **x**-day nearest a given date, call **xdayOnOrBefore(date+3,x)**. To find the **x**-day on or after a given date, call **xdayOnOrBefore(date+6,x)**.

(c)
```
int nthxDay(int n, int x, int m, int y) {
    if (n < 0)
       // return the xday following n weeks before the end of
       // the month
       return xdayOnOrBefore(
         absoluteFromGregorian(m,
                               lastDayOfGregorianMonth(m, y),
                               y)
           + (7 * n) + 7, x);
    else
       // return the xday prior to n weeks after the first of
       // the month
       return xdayOnOrBefore(
         absoluteFromGregorian(m, 1, y)
           + (7 * n) + 7, x);
}
```

Chapter 5—First Set

1. (a)
```
void printMonth (int month) {
   // Print the name of the month.

   switch (month) {
     case 1:  cout << "January";   break;
     case 2:  cout << "February";  break;
     case 3:  cout << "March";     break;
     case 4:  cout << "April";     break;
     case 5:  cout << "May";       break;
     case 6:  cout << "June";      break;
     case 7:  cout << "July";      break;
     case 8:  cout << "August";    break;
     case 9:  cout << "September"; break;
     case 10: cout << "October";   break;
     case 11: cout << "November";  break;
     case 12: cout << "December";  break;
   }
}
```

(b)
```
void printGregorianCalendar (int month, int year) {

   // Print a calendar for the specified month, year, (Gregorian)

      const int width = 3;       // width of a column in the calendar
      const int separation = 2; // spaces between columns
```

```
      int firstOfMonth = absoluteFromGregorian(month,1,year) % 7;
                    // day of the week of the first of the month
                    // 0 means Sunday, 1 means Monday, etc.
      int firstSaturday = 7 - firstOfMonth;
                    // date of first Saturday in the month

      // Write the heading
      printMonth(month);
      cout << ", " << year << "\n"
           << setw(width)             << "Sun"
           << setw(width+separation) << "Mon"
           << setw(width+separation) << "Tue"
           << setw(width+separation) << "Wed"
           << setw(width+separation) << "Thu"
           << setw(width+separation) << "Fri"
           << setw(width+separation) << "Sat"
           << "\n";

      // Leave firstOfMonth blank days on the first line
      cout << setw(firstOfMonth*(width+separation)) << "";

      // Write the days of the month, going to a new line
      // after every Saturday except the last day of the month
      for (int i = 1;
           i <= lastDayOfGregorianMonth(month,year);
           i++) {
        cout << setw(width) << i;
        if ( (i % 7) == (firstSaturday % 7) &&
           (i != lastDayOfGregorianMonth(month,year)) )
           // begin new week after Saturday
           cout << "\n";
        else
           // otherwise just add column separation
           cout << setw(separation) << "";
      }
      cout << "\n";
    }

22. void printEuropeanCalendar (int month, int year) {

    // Print a calendar for the specified month, year, (European)

      const int width = 3; //width of a column in the calendar
      const int separation = 2; //spaces between columns

      int firstOfMonth = absoluteFromGregorian(month,1,year) % 7;
                    // day of the week of the first of the month
                    // 0 means Sunday, 1 means Monday, etc.
      int firstSunday =  8 - firstOfMonth;
      if (firstSunday > 7)
         firstSunday = firstSunday - 7;
                    // date of first Sunday in the month

      // Write the heading
      printMonth(month);
```

```
cout << ", " << year << "\n"
      << setw(width)            << "Mon"
      << setw(width+separation) << "Tue"
      << setw(width+separation) << "Wed"
      << setw(width+separation) << "Thu"
      << setw(width+separation) << "Fri"
      << setw(width+separation) << "Sat"
      << setw(width+separation) << "Sun"
      << "\n";

// Leave 7-firstSunday blank days on the first line
cout << setw((7-firstSunday)*(width+separation)) << "";

// Write the days of the month, going to a new line
// after every Sunday except the last day of the month
for (int i = 1;
     i <= lastDayOfGregorianMonth(month,year);
     i++) {
  cout << setw(width) << i;
  if ((i % 7) == (firstSunday % 7) &&
     (i != lastDayOfGregorianMonth(month,year)) )
    // begin new week after Sunday
    cout << "\n";
  else
    // otherwise just add column separation
    cout << setw(separation) << "";
}
cout << "\n";
}
```

Chapter 5—Second Set

1.
```
#include <iostream.h>

main () {
int count = 7;                  // must be at least 7 eggs.

while (count % 2 != 1 || count % 3 != 1 ||
       count % 4 != 1 || count % 5 != 1 ||
       count % 6 != 1 || count % 7 != 0)
  // we have not reached a solution
  count ++;

cout << "The solution is " << count << "\n";
}
```

Chapter 5—Third Set

1. To verify that the code segment is correct, we need to make the observation that a score can only be the maximum *and* the minimum if it is the first score read. If the score just encountered is less than the first score, it cannot be the maximum. Similarly, if it is larger than the first score, it cannot be the minimum. If the score read is equal to the first score, there is no need to change the minimum or maximum. Because of this, there is no need to check whether every score after the first is both a minimum and

a maximum, since it is one, the other, or neither. If it is a maximum, it cannot be a minimum and there is no need to check. This observation will speed up the execution time of our program by saving unnecessary comparisons.

2. In order to find the median, we need to "remember" all the scores. If we have seen n numbers so far, we can easily construct a situation where any one of those n numbers could be the median, so after reading n numbers, we must save n numbers—all the numbers we have seen. We do not yet know how to do this; we'll see how in Chapter 7.

Chapter 6—First Set

1. (a)
```
void printMilitaryTime () {
    // Print the receiver's time in military format.
    cout << setfill('0') << setw(2) << hour
      << setfill('0') << setw(2) << minute;
}
```

(b)
```
time addHours (int h) {
    // Return a time h hours after the receiver's time
    // or before it, if h is negative
    int totalMinutes = (60 * (hour + h) + minute) % (24*60);
    if (totalMinutes < 0)
      totalMinutes = totalMinutes + 24*60;
    return time(totalMinutes/60, totalMinutes%60);
}
```

(c)
```
boolean isPM () {
    // Return whether the receiver's time is in the PM
    return (hour >= 12);
}
```

2.
```
void printTime () {
    // Print the receiver's time.
    if ((hour == 0) && (minute == 0))
      cout << "midnight";
    else if ((hour == 12) && (minute == 0))
      cout << "    noon";
    else {
      if (hour == 0)
        cout  << setfill(' ') << setw(3) << 12;
      else if (hour > 12)
        cout  << setfill(' ') << setw(3) << hour-12;
      else
        cout  << setfill(' ') << setw(3) << hour;
      cout << ':' << setfill('0') << setw(2) << minute;

      if (hour < 12)
        cout << "AM";
      else
        cout << "PM";
    }
}
```

3.
```
#include <iostream.h>
#include <iomanip.h>

//
// time objects represent times during a single day.
//
class time {
private:
  int hour, minute, second;

public:
  time (int h, int m, int s) {
    hour = h; minute = m; second = s;}

  time addSeconds (int s) {
    // Return a time s seconds after the receiver's time
    // or before it, if a is negative.
    int totalSeconds =
      (3600*hour + 60*minute + second + s ) % (24*60*60);
    if (totalSeconds < 0)
      totalSeconds = totalSeconds + 24*60*60;
    return time(totalSeconds / 3600,
               (totalSeconds % 3600) / 60,
                totalSeconds % 60);
  }

  void printTime () {
    // Print the receiver's time.
    if ((hour == 0) && (minute == 0))
      cout << "midnight";
    else if ((hour == 12) && (minute == 0))
      cout << "    noon";
    else {
      if (hour == 0)
        cout  << setfill(' ') << setw(3) << 12;
      else if (hour > 12)
        cout  << setfill(' ') << setw(3) << hour-12;
      else
        cout  << setfill(' ') << setw(3) << hour;
      cout << ':' << setfill('0') << setw(2) << minute;
      cout << ':' << setfill('0') << setw(2) << second;

      if (hour < 12)
        cout << "AM";
      else
        cout << "PM";
    }
  }
};
```

4.
```
#include <iostream.h>
#include <iomanip.h>

int leapYear (int y) {
  return (((y % 4) == 0) && ((y % 100) != 0))
    || ((y % 400) == 0);
}
```

```
    int lastDayOfMonth (int m, int y) {
      switch (m) {
        case 2:
          if (leapYear(y))
            return 29;
          else
            return 28;
        case 4:
        case 6:
        case 9:
        case 11: return 30;
        default: return 31;
      }
    }


    //
    // date objects represent Gregorian dates.
    //
    class date {
    private:
      int month, day, year;

    public:
      date (int m, int d, int y) {month = m; day = d; year = y;}

      date incrementDay () {
        // Return the date following the receiver's date.
        int newMonth = month;
        int newDay = day;
        int newYear = year;
        if (newDay != lastDayOfMonth(newMonth,newYear))
          newDay++;
        else { // last day of month
          newDay = 1;                      // reset day
          newMonth = (newMonth % 12) + 1; // next month
          if (newMonth == 1)              // next year
            newYear++;
        }
        return date(newMonth, newDay, newYear);
      }

      void printDate () {
        // Print the receiver's date.
        cout << month << '/' << day << '/' << year;
      }
    };
```

Chapter 6—Second Set

```
1.    boolean equals (time t) {
        // Return whether the receiver's time is t
        return (t.hour == hour) && (t.minute == minute);
      }
```

```
boolean after (time t) {
  // Return whether the receiver's time after t
  return ((hour > t.hour) ||
          ((hour == t.hour) && (minute > t.minute)));
}


int subtractTimes (time t) {
  // Return the difference in minutes between the
  // receiver's time and t.
  int totalMinutes = hour * 60 + minutes
    - (t.hours * 60) - t.minutes;

  // remove negative numbers
  if (totalMinutes < 0)
    totalMinutes = -totalMinutes;
  return totalMinutes;
}
```

Chapter 6—Third Set

1. These functions need to be within the **Class time** definition:

```
int getHour ()   {
  if (AM)
    return hour;
  else
    return hour + 12;
}

int getMinute () { return minute; }
```

Chapter 6—Fourth Set

1. The following code,

```
#include <iostream.h>
#include <iomanip.h>

enum boolean {false,true};

void f (float x) {cout << "First Function f\n";}
void f (int i, float x) {cout << "Second Function f\n";}

void g (int i, int j) {cout << "First Function g\n";}
void g (float x, float y) {cout << "Second Function g\n";}

main () {
  cout << "(a) ";
  f(10);
  cout << "(b) ";
  g(10,10.1);
}
```

produces the output

  (a) `First Function f`
  (b) `First Function g`

From this we can see that (with this compiler) integers will be converted to floats, floats will be converted to integers, and booleans will be converted to integers. Integers will not be converted to the boolean type by this compiler. The first function to appear in the code will be chosen if there is no exact match.

    The code

```
void h1 (int i, boolean p) {cout << "First Function h1\n";}
void h1 (boolean p, int i) {cout << "Second Function h1\n";}

void h2 (boolean p, int i) {cout << "First Function h2\n";}
void h2 (int i, boolean p) {cout << "Second Function h2\n";}
```

gives the errors

```
Error: Overloading ambiguity between h1(int, boolean)
       and h1(boolean, int).
Error: Overloading ambiguity between h2(boolean, int)
       and h2(int, boolean).
```

Again, your computer may give different results.

2. Notice that `subtractMinutes` returns a `time`, whereas `subtractTimes` returns an `int`:

```
time operator- (int m) { return difference(m); }

int operator- (time t) { return difference(t); }

time difference(int m) { return addMinutes(-m); }

int difference(time t) {
    // Return the difference in minutes between the
    // receiver's time and t.
int totalMinutes = hour * 60 + minutes -
    (t.hours * 60) - t.minutes;
if (totalMinutes < 0)              // remove negative numbers
   totalMinutes = -totalMinutes;
return totalMinutes;
```

3. First we implement the operators as member functions:

```
boolean operator== (time t) {// == overloaded member
  return ((hour == t.hour) && (minute == t.minute));
}

boolean operator> (time t)  {// > overloaded member
  return (!operator<(t) && !operator==(t))
}

boolean operator>= (time t) {// >= overloaded member
  return !operator<(t)
}
```

```
boolean operator<= (time t) {// <= overloaded member
  return !operator>(t)
}

boolean operator!= (time t) {// != overloaded member
  return !operator==(t)
}
```

Next we implement them as client functions, which require only the member functions **operator==** and **operator<**.

```
boolean operator> (time t1, time t2) {// > overloaded client
  return (!(t1 < t2) && !(t1 == t2));
}

boolean operator>= (time t1, time t2) {// >= overloaded client
  return !(t1 < t2);
}

boolean operator<= (time t1, time t2) {// <= overloaded client
  return !(t1 > t2);
}

boolean operator!= (time t1, time t2) {// != overloaded client
  return !(t1 == t2);
}
```

Chapter 6—Fifth Set

1. The only function to change is **A**.

```
void A () {
  switch (s) {
    case displayTime:  cout << "turn light on\n"; break;
    case setTimeHour:  clockTime.advanceMinutes(60); break;
    case setTimeMin:   clockTime.advanceMinutes(1); break;
    case displayAlarmTime:
            cout << "momentarily sound buzzer\n"; break;
    case setAlarmHour: alarmTime.advanceMinutes(60); break;
    case setAlarmMin:  alarmTime.advanceMinutes(1); break;
  }
```

Chapter 7—First Set

1. The output for line 8 is

```
100 200
0xeffffb2c 0xeffffb28 0xeffffb28
```

The pictures look like

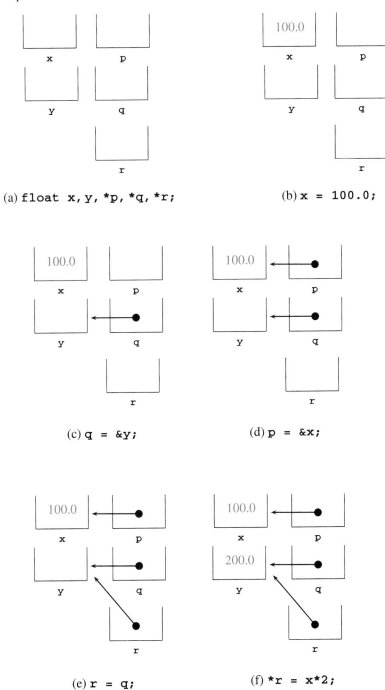

(a) `float x, y, *p, *q, *r;`

(b) `x = 100.0;`

(c) `q = &y;`

(d) `p = &x;`

(e) `r = q;`

(f) `*r = x*2;`

We can see that the output matches the picture. `p` has a different address from `q` and `r`, which have the same address.

2.
```
    void swap (int *p1, int *p2) {
    // Swap two integers
      int temp = *p1;
      *p1 = *p2;
      *p2 = temp;
    }

    main() {
      int i = 10, j = 20;
      int *ip, *jp;
      ip = &i;
      jp = &j;
      swap(ip, jp);
      cout << i << " " << j << "\n";
    }
```

Chapter 7—Second Set

1. (a)
```
    int sum (intList *list) {
      // Sum a list of integers.
      int sum = 0;
      intList* ptr = list;
      while (ptr != NULL) {
        // ptr points to an element of list
        sum = sum + ptr->getValue();
        ptr = ptr->getNextEntry();
      }
      return sum;
    }
```

   (b)
```
    int frequency (intList *list, int p) {
      // Count the frequency of p in a list of integers.
      int count = 0;
      intList* ptr = list;
      while (ptr != NULL) {
        // ptr points to an element of list
        if (ptr->getValue() == p)
          count ++;
        ptr = ptr->getNextEntry();
      }
      return count;
    }
```

   (c)
```
    void minmax (intList *list, int& min, int& max) {
      // find the minimum and maximum of a list of integers.

      if (list == NULL) {          // an empty list
        min = 0;
        max = 0;
      }
      else {                       // a non-empty list
        min = list->getValue();
        max = list->getValue();
        intList* ptr = list->getNextEntry();
```

```
          while (ptr != NULL) {
            // ptr points to an element of list

            if (ptr->getValue() < min)
              min = ptr->getValue();
            else if (ptr->getValue() > max)
              max = ptr->getValue();

            ptr = ptr->getNextEntry();
          }
        }
      }

2. (a) intList *copy (intList *list) {
        // make a copy of list.

        intList *newList = NULL;    // The start of the newList.
        intList *ptr = list;        // Where in the original list.

        while (ptr != NULL) {
          // ptr has not reached the end of the list
          newList = new intList(ptr->getValue(), newList);
          ptr = ptr->getNextEntry();
        }
        return reverse(newList);
      }

   (b) intList *extractPositive (intList *list) {
        // make a copy of list with only positive numbers

        intList *newList = NULL;    // The start of the newList.
        intList *ptr = list;        // Where in the original list.

        while (ptr != NULL) {
          // ptr has not reached the end of the list

          if (ptr->getValue() >= 0)
            newList = new intList(ptr->getValue(), newList);
          ptr = ptr->getNextEntry();
        }
        return reverse(newList);
      }

   (c) intList *remove (intList *list, int p) {
        // make a copy of list with all occurrences of p removed

        intList *newList = NULL;    // The start of the newList.
        intList *ptr = list;        // Where in the original list.

        while (ptr != NULL) {
          // ptr has not reached the end of the list

          if (ptr->getValue() != p)
            newList = new intList(ptr->getValue(), newList);
          ptr = ptr->getNextEntry();
        }
        return reverse(newList);
      }
```

Chapter 7—Third Set

```
1.  intList *readForwardList () {
      int inputval;
      intList *front = NULL;

      cout << "Enter number: "; cin >> inputval;

      while (!cin.eof()) {
        if (front != NULL)
          front->addToEndM(inputval);
        else
          front = new intList(inputval, NULL);
        cout << "Enter number: "; cin >> inputval;
      }
      cout << "\n";
      return front;
    }
```

```
2. (a)  int sum() {   // as a member function
          if (nextEntry == NULL)
            return value;
          else
            return value + nextEntry->sum();
        }
```

```
   (b)  int frequency(int n) {   // as a member function
          int count = 0;
          if (nextEntry != NULL)
            count = nextEntry->frequency(n);
          if (value == n)
            count ++;
          return count;
        }
```

Chapter 7—Fourth Set

```
1.  intList *readForwardList () {
      int inputval;
      intList *front = NULL;

      cout << "Enter number: "; cin >> inputval;

      while (!cin.eof()) {
        if (front != NULL)
          front->addToEnd(inputval);
        else
          front = new intList(inputval, NULL);
        cout << "Enter number: "; cin >> inputval;
      }
      cout << "\n";
      return front;
    }
```

```
2.   intList *addInOrder(int n) {
       intList* newList = NULL;
       if (nextEntry != NULL)
         if (n < value)                    // not yet
           newList = new intList(value, nextEntry->addInOrder(n));
         else if (n == value)              // We're done
           newList = new intList(value, nextEntry);
         else                              // add it here
           newList = new intList(n, new intList(value, nextEntry));
       return newList;
     }
```

Chapter 7—Fifth Set

```
1.   #include <iostream.h>
     #include <iomanip.h>

     enum boolean {false, true};

     // Read in a list and compare it with its reverse.

     class charList {
     private:
       char value;
       charList *nextEntry;

     public:
       charList (char v, charList *next)
         : value(v), nextEntry(next)
       {}

       boolean operator== (charList c) {
         if (value != c.value)
           return false;
         else if (nextEntry == NULL && c.nextEntry == NULL)
           return true;
         else
           return (*nextEntry == *(c.nextEntry));
       }

       boolean operator!= (charList c) {
         return !(operator==(c));
       }

       char getValue () { return value; }

       charList *getNextEntry () { return nextEntry; }

       charList *charList::reverseAcc () { return reverseAcc(NULL); }

       charList *charList::reverseAcc (charList *acc) {
       // reverse a list
         if (nextEntry == NULL)
           return new charList(value, acc);
```

```
        else
           return nextEntry->reverseAcc(new charList(value, acc));
    }
};

charList *readForwardcharList () {
// read in a charList

  charList *input = NULL;

  char ch = cin.get();
  while (ch != '\n') {
    input = new charList(ch, input);
    ch = cin.get();
  }
  return input->reverseAcc();
}

main () {
  charList* 11 = readForwardcharList();

  if (*11 == *(11->reverseAcc()))
    cout << "\n a palindrome \n";
  else
    cout << "\n not a palindrome \n";
}
```

Chapter 8—First Set

1.  ```
    void printDecimal (int n, int p) {
    // Write a number n * 10^p in decimal.

      if (n > 9) {
        printDecimal(n/10, p+1);
        cout << " + ";
      }
      cout << n%10 << "*1" << setw(p) << setfill('0') << "";
    }
    ```

2.  ```
    void printBinary (int n, int p) {
    // Write a number n * 2^p in binary.

      if (n > 1) {
        printBinary(n/2, p+1);
        cout << " + ";
      }
      cout << n%2 << "*2^" << p ;
    }

    void printBinary(int n) {
      printBinary(n, 0);
    }
    ```

5. We use **needComma** in much the same way we use **needBlank**. We set **needComma** to true only after we've printed a millenary.

```
     boolean needComma;   // a global variable used to keep track
                          // of whether a comma is needed before
                          // the next word

void printString (char *s) {
// Write a string, preceded by a blank if needed.
  if (needComma)
    cout << ",";
  if (needBlank)
    cout << " ";
  cout << s;
  needBlank = true;
  needComma = false;
}


void printMillenary (int n) {
// Write the name of the power of a 1000.
  switch (n) {
    case 1: printString("thousand"); break;
    case 2: printString("million");  break;
    case 3: printString("billion");  break;
    case 4: printString("trillion"); break;
  }
  needComma = true;
}
```

We must also make sure to initialize **needComma** to false:

```
void printNumber (int n) {
//   Write a number in English words according to the
//   American nomenclature. The number can be as large as
//   needed--it is only necessary to extend the switch
//   statement in printMillenary to include "quadrillion",
//   "quintillion", "sextillion", and so on.
  needBlank = false;
  needComma = false;
  if (n > 0)
    printBigNumber(n,0);
  else if (n < 0) {
    printString("minus");
    printBigNumber(-n,0);
  }
  else { // (n == 0)
    printString("zero");
  }
}
```

Chapter 8—Third Set

3. To evaluate the multiplication of a one-digit number and an n-digit number, we need to examine the size of x_{left}, x_{right}, y_{left} and y_{right}. Let's assume that x is the one-digit number. y_{left} and y_{right} have $n/2$ digits, x_{left} has one digit, and x_{right} has no digits. Therefore A is the product of an $n/2$-digit number and zero, B is the product of an $n/2$-digit number and a one-digit number, and C will be the product of an $n/2$-digit number and a

one-digit number. The recurrence equation for this is $T(n) = kn + 2T(n/2)$. Table 8.2 tells us this is $\Theta(n \log n)$.

5.
```
Integer mult (int digit, int carry) {
// Recursively multiply receiver by digit and add carry

   if (digits != NULL) {
     int i = digits->getDigit() * digit + carry;
     return shift(-1).mult(digit,i / radix).shift(1) + i%radix;
   }
   else
     return Integer(carry);
}

Integer mult (Integer L) {
// Multiply the least significant bit of L with the
// receiver.  Add this to the (recursive) product of
// most significant digits of the receiver first multiplied
// by L then shifted one position.

   if (L != 0)
     return mult(L.digits->getDigit(),0) +
             mult(Integer(L.sign,
                     L.digits->getNextDigit())).shift(1);
   else
     return Integer(0);
}
```

Chapter 8—Fourth Set

1. (a) When the evaluator sees the parenthesis, it will call **expression**, which calls **term**, which calls **factor**, which skips the opening parenthesis, reads an expression (in this case 1+1), then reads what should be a closing parenthesis. Since there is no closing parenthesis, we attempt to read past the end of the **charList** and get the message

Segmentation fault

The sequence of calls is

Enter expression
  Enter term
    Enter factor
    Skip '('
      Enter expression
        Enter term
          Enter factor
          Read 1
          Exit factor **with** 1
        Exit term **with** 1
      Skip '+'
        Enter term
          Enter factor

Read 1
Exit factor **with 1**
Exit term **with 1**
Exit expression **with 2**
Skip ')' **(Cause of error)**

(b) In this case, the evaluator finishes its evaluation before the close parenthesis (and anything following it) is read. The sequence of calls is

Enter expression
  Enter term
    Enter factor
    Read 1
    Exit factor **with 1**
  Exit term **with 1**
Skip '+'
  Enter term
    Enter factor
    Read 1
    Exit factor **with 1**
  Exit term **with 1**
Exit expression **with 2**
Done. We've never looked at the ')'.

2.  ```
    int expression (charList *&e) {
      // Recursively evaluate an expression as
      //   term + expression

      int value = term(e);
      if (e->getValue() == '+') {
        e = e->getNextEntry(); // skip + sign
        value = value + expression(e);
      }
      return value;
    }

    int term (charList *&e) {
      // Recursively evaluate a term as
      //   factor * term

      int value = factor(e);
      if (e->getValue() == '*') {
        e = e->getNextEntry(); // skip times sign
        value = value * term(e);
      }
      return value;
    }
    ```

3. The function **number** requires a second parameter to keep track of what has been encountered so far so that it can shift it the appropriate amount. The recursive definition of this number is
    ```

> number = digit number
> number = digit

```
int factor (charList *&e) {
  // Recursively evaluate a factor as a number or
  // an expression in parentheses.

  int value = 0;
  if (isDigit(e->getValue())) // number
    value = number(e, 0);
  else { // parenthesized expression
    e = e->getNextEntry();   // skip opening parenthesis
    value = expression(e);
    e = e->getNextEntry();   // skip closing parenthesis
  }
  return value;
}

int number (charList *&e, int partial) {
  // Recursively evaluate a number as a digit or
  // a digit followed by partial number

  int value = 0;
  int hold = 0;
  if (isDigit(e->getValue())) {
    value = charToInt(e->getValue()) + partial*10;
    e = e->getNextEntry();               // skip number
    if (isDigit(e->getValue()))
        value = number(e, value);
  }
  return value;
}
```

Don't forget to add **number** to the prototypes at the top of the program:

```
int term (charList *&e);
int factor (charList *&e);
int number (charList *&e, int partial);
```

Chapter 9—First Set

1.  ```
    #include <iostream.h>
    #include <iomanip.h>

    const int inputMax = 1000;

    main () {
      int A[inputMax],B[inputMax],C[inputMax];
      int D[inputMax],E[inputMax],F[inputMax];
      int size = 0;
      int n;
    ```
    ```

```
cout << "Enter first number: ";
cin >> n;
while (!cin.eof()) {
  // The first size inputs are stored in
  // A[0] .. A[size-1]
  A[size] = n;
  size++;
  cout << "Enter next number: ";
  cin >> n;
}

// Running Sums
B[0] = A[0];
C[size-1] = A[size-1];
for (int i=1; i<size; i++) {
  B[i] = B[i-1] + A[i];
  C[size-1-i] = C[size-i] + A[size-1-i];
}

// Pairwise Differences
for (i=0; i<size-1; i++)
  D[i] = A[i+1] - A[i];

// Three way averages
for (i=0; i<size-2; i++)
  E[i] = (A[i+2] + A[i+1] + A[i])/3;

// Increasing Values
F[0] = A[0];
int currentF = 0;    // Last used spot in F[]
for (i=1; i<size; i++)
  if (A[i] > F[currentF]) {      // it's larger
    currentF ++;                 // next free spot
    F[currentF] = A[i];          // store it
  }

// Printout all arrays
    cout << "\n\n" << setw(4) << "i"
         << setw(6) << "A[i]"
         << setw(6) << "B[i]"
         << setw(6) << "C[i]"
         << setw(6) << "D[i]"
         << setw(6) << "E[i]"
         << setw(6) << "F[i]" << "\n";
 for (i=0; i<size; i++)
    cout << setw(4) << i
         << setw(6) << A[i]
         << setw(6) << B[i]
         << setw(6) << C[i]
         << setw(6) << D[i]
         << setw(6) << E[i]
         << setw(6) << F[i] << "\n";

}
```

Here's a sample execution:

```
Enter first number: 12
Enter next number: 23
Enter next number: 56
Enter next number: 34
Enter next number: 90
Enter next number: 78
Enter next number: ^D
```

i	A[i]	B[i]	C[i]	D[i]	E[i]	F[i]
0	12	12	293	11	30	12
1	23	35	281	33	37	23
2	56	91	258	-22	60	56
3	34	125	202	56	67	90
4	90	215	168	-12	0	0
5	78	293	78	0	0	0

Chapter 9—Second Set

1. (a)
```
int sum (int A[], int size) {
    // sum from A[0] to A[size-1]
    int total = 0;

    for (int i=0; i < size; i++)
      total = total + A[i];
      // total contains sum of A[0] ... A[i]

    return total;
}
```

(b)
```
int frequency (int A[], int size, int p) {
    // count occurrences of p in A[0] to A[size-1]
    int count = 0;

    for (int i=0; i < size; i++)
      if (A[i] == p)
        count ++;
      // count contains number occurrences of
      // p in A[0] to A[i]

    return count;
}
```

(c)
```
int max (int A[], int size) {
  // find maximum of A[0] to A[size-1]
  int maximum = A[0];

  for (int i=1; i < size; i++)
    if (A[i] > maximum)
      maximum = A[i];
    // maximum contains maximum of A[0] to A[i]

  return maximum;
}
```

```
(d) void insert (int A[], int size, int p) {
    // insert p as the first element of A[0] to A[size]

      for (int i=size-1; i >= 0 ; i--)
        A[i+1] = A[i];
        // the array A[i+1] to A[size] has been shifted

      A[0] = p;
    }
(e) void insertInOrder (int A[], int size, int p) {
    // insert p in ascending order in A[0] to A[size]

      for (int i=size-1; i >= 0 ; i--) {
        if (A[i] > p)
          A[i+1] = A[i];
        else {
          A[i+1] = p;          // store the new item
          break;               // we're done
        }
        // the array A[i+1] to A[size] has been shifted
      }
    }
(f) void find (int A[], int size, int p) {
    // find p in A[0] to A[size-1]
      for (int i=0; i < size ; i++)
        if (A[i] == p)
          return i;
        // the array A[0] to A[i] has been searched

      return -1;
    }
```

Chapter 9—Third Set

```
1. (a) void upcase (char *source) {
         // replace all lower case with upper case
         int i = 0;
         while (source[i] != 0) {
           // there are chars left in source
           if ((source[i] >= 'a') && (source[i] <= 'z'))
             // source[i] is lower case
             source[i] = source[i] - 'a' + 'A';
           i++;
         }
       }
   (b) char *join(char *s1, char* s2) {
         // join two strings
         char *target = new char[strlen(s1) + strlen(s2)];
         int i = 0;
         int j = 0;
         while (s1[i] != 0) {
           // there are chars left in s1
           target[i] = s1[i];
           i++;
         }
```

```
        while (s2[j] != 0) {
          // there are chars left in s2
          target[i+j] = s2[j];
          j++;
        }
        target[i+j] = 0;
        return target;
      }
```

(c)
```
char *joinInOrder(char *s1, char* s2) {
  // join two strings in lexicographical order
  if (less(s1,s2))
    return join(s1,s2);
  else
    return join(s2,s1);
}
```

(d)
```
void squeezeSpaces (char *source) {
  // remove all spaces
  int i = 0;
  int j;
  while (source[i] != 0) {
    // there are chars left in source (by count i)
    if (source[i] == ' ') {
      j = i;                    // shift remainder of string
      while (source[j] != 0) {
        // there are chars left in source  (by count j)
        source[j] = source[j+1];
        j++;
      }
    }
    else
      i++;
  }
}
```

2.
```
main () {
  // Make sure sentences begin with a capital letter.

  boolean change = false;// Have we made a change for this '.'?
  char ch;
  cout << "Enter a string: ";
  while (!cin.eof()) {
    // There is more data.
    ch = cin.get();
    if (ch == '.')
      change = true;
    else if (change && (ch >= 'a') && (ch <= 'z')) {
      // ch is lower case and change is true
      ch = ch - 'a' + 'A';
      change = false;
    }
    else if (change && (ch != ' ') && (ch != '\n'))
      // ch is not a space or newline
      change = false;
    cout << ch;
  }
}
```

Chapter 9—Fourth Set

1. Notice that mostly the parameter types have changed—very little else. We overloaded the < and <= operators for both `appointment` and `appointment*` to facilitate this.

```
class appointment {
private:
  time appointmentTime;
  char description[100];
public:
  boolean operator<(appointment a) {
    return (appointmentTime < a.appointmentTime);
  }
  boolean operator<=(appointment a) {
    return (appointmentTime <= a.appointmentTime);
  }
};

enum boolean {false, true};

boolean operator<(appointment* a1,appointment* a2) {
  // this calls the appointment member function
  // boolean operator<(appointment)
  return (*a1 < *a2);
}

boolean operator<=(appointment* a1,appointment* a2) {
  // this calls the appointment member function
  // boolean operator<=(appointment)
  return (*a1 <= *a2);
}

void swap (appointment* &a, appointment* &b) {
  appointment* temp = a;
  a = b;
  b = temp;
}

int findMinimum (appointment* A[], int lo, int hi) {
  if (lo == hi)
    return lo;
  else {
    int locationOfMin = findMinimum(A, lo+1, hi);
    if (A[lo] < A[locationOfMin])
      return lo;
    else
      return locationOfMin;
  }
}

void selectionSort (appointment* A[], int lo, int hi) {
  // A[0]..A[lo-1] contain the smallest values in A,
  // in ascending order.
  if (lo < hi) {
    swap(A[lo], A[findMinimum(A, lo, hi)]);
    selectionSort(A, lo+1, hi);
  }
}
```

```
void insertInOrder (appointment* A[], int hi, appointment* x) {
  // Insert x into A[0] ... A[hi-1], filling in
  // A[hi] in the process.  A[0] ... A[hi-1] are sorted.
  if (hi == 0 || A[hi-1] <= x)
    A[hi] = x;
  else {
    A[hi] = A[hi-1];
    insertInOrder(A, hi-1, x);
  }
}

void insertionSort (appointment* A[], int hi) {
  // Sort  A[0] ... A[hi]
  if (hi > 0) {
    insertionSort(A, hi-1);
    insertInOrder(A, hi, A[hi]);
  }
}

int medianLocation (appointment* A[], int i, int j, int k) {
  if (A[i] <= A[j])
    if (A[j] <= A[k])
      return j;
    else if (A[i] <= A[k])
      return k;
    else
      return i;
  else // A[j] < A[i]
    if (A[i] <= A[k])
      return i;
    else if (A[j] <= A[k])
      return k;
    else
      return j;
}

int partition (appointment* A[],
               int lo, int hi, appointment* pivot) {
  if (hi == lo)
    if (A[lo] < pivot)
      return lo;
    else
      return lo-1;
  else if (A[lo] <= pivot) // A[lo] in correct half
    return partition(A, lo+1, hi, pivot);
  else {                   // A[lo] in wrong half
    swap(A[lo], A[hi]);
    return partition(A, lo, hi-1, pivot);
  }
}

int partition (appointment* A[], int lo, int hi) {
  swap(A[lo], A[medianLocation(A, lo+1, hi, (lo+hi)/2)]);
  int m = partition(A, lo+1, hi, A[lo]);
  swap(A[lo], A[m]);
  return m;
}
```

```
void quickSort (appointment* A[], int lo, int hi) {
  int m;

  if (hi > lo+1) { // there are at least 3 elements,
                   // so sort recursively
    m = partition(A, lo, hi);
    quickSort(A, lo, m-1);
    quickSort(A, m+1, hi);
  }
  else // 0, 1, or 2 elements, so sort directly
    if (hi == lo+1 && A[hi] < A[lo])
      swap(A[lo], A[hi]);
}
```

3. Here are the iterative versions:

```
enum boolean {false, true};

void swap (float &a, float &b) {
  float temp = a;
  a = b;
  b = temp;
}

int findMinimum (float A[], int lo, int hi) {
  int locationOfMin = lo;
  for (int i = lo+1; i <= hi; i++)
    // A[locationOfMin] is smallest value among A[lo]..A[i-1]
    if (A[i] < A[locationOfMin]) locationOfMin = i;
  return locationOfMin;
}

void selectionSort (float A[], int lo, int hi) {
  for (int i = lo; i < hi-1; i++)
    // A contains the same values as it did originally, but
    // in a different order;  the elements A[0]..A[i-1]
    // contain the i smallest values in A in ascending order.
    swap(A[i], A[findMinimum(A, i, hi-1)]);
  }
}

void insertInOrder (float A[], int hi, float element) {
  // A[0] ... A[hi-1] are sorted;  A[hi] is unoccupied
  int i = hi-1;
  while (i >= 0 && A[i] >= x) {
    // Original elements in A[0]..A[hi-1] are now in two
    // parts:  A[0]..A[i] and A[i+2]..A[hi].  All the values
    // in the latter part are greater than element, as is A[i].
    A[i+1] = A[i]; // shift A[i] right
    i--;
  }
  A[i+1] = x;
}

void insertionSort (float A[], int hi) {
  // Sort  A[0] ... A[hi]
```

```
  for (int i=1; i<hi; i++)
    insertInOrder(A, i, A[i]);
}

int medianLocation (appointment* A[], int i, int j, int k) {
  if (A[i] <= A[j])
    if (A[j] <= A[k])
      return j;
    else if (A[i] <= A[k])
      return k;
    else
      return i;
  else // A[j] < A[i]
    if (A[i] <= A[k])
      return i;
    else if (A[j] <= A[k])
      return k;
    else
      return j;
}

int partition (float A[], int lo, int hi, float pivot) {
  while (lo < hi) {
    if (A[lo] > pivot) { // A[lo] in wrong half
      swap(A[lo], A[hi]);
      hi = hi-1;
    }
    else
      lo = lo+1;
  }
  if (A[lo] < pivot)
    return lo;
  else
    return lo-1;
}

int partition (appointment* A[], int lo, int hi) {
  swap(A[lo], A[medianLocation(A, lo+1, hi, (lo+hi)/2)]);
  int m = partition(A, lo+1, hi, A[lo]);
  swap(A[lo], A[m]);
  return m;
}

void quickSort (float A[], int lo, int hi) {
  int m;

  if (hi > lo+1) { // there are at least 3 elements,
                   // so sort recursively
    m = partition(A, lo, hi);
    quickSort(A, lo, m-1);
    quickSort(A, m+1, hi);
  }
  else // 0, 1, or 2 elements, so sort directly
    if (hi == lo+1 && A[hi] < A[lo])
      swap(A[lo], A[hi]);
}
```

Chapter 9—Fifth Set

1. (a)
```
class table {
  private:
    word words[maxTableSize];
    int size;

  public:
    table () : size(0) {}

    void addOccurrence (char *str) {
      word w(str);
      if (size == 0) {
        words[size] = w;
        size++;
      }
      else {
        int i = size;
        if (size > 0)
          while (i >= 0 && words[i] != w) i--;
        if (i < 0) { // add w as new entry
          words[size] = w;
          size++;
        }
        else { // word already in table; increment count
          words[i].incrFrequency();
          if (i < size-1)
            swap(words[i], words[i+1]);
        }
      }
    }

    void listEntries () ;
};
```

(b)
```
class table {
  private:
    word words[maxTableSize];
    int size;

  public:
    table () : size(0) {}

    void addOccurrence (char *str) {
      word w(str);
      if (size == 0) {
        words[size] = w;
        size++;
      }
      else {
        int i = size;
        if (size > 0)
          while (i >= 0 && words[i] != w) i--;
        if (i < 0) { // add w as new entry
          words[size] = w;
          size++;
        }
```

```
              else { // word already in table; increment count
                words[i].incrFrequency();
                word temp = words[i];
                for (int j=i; j < size; j++)
                  words[j] = words[j+1];
                words[size] = temp;
              }
            }
          }

        void listEntries () ;
      };

(c) class table {
      private:
        wordList *words[maxTableSize];

      public:
        table () ;  // initialize words to all NULL

        void addOccurrence (char *str) {
          word *w = new word(str);
          // Calculate preferred location of w
          int h = hash(str);
          if (words[h] == NULL)
            words[h] = new wordList(w, NULL);
          else {
            wordList *findw = words[h]->find(w);
            if (findw == NULL)
              words[h] = new wordList(w, words[h]);
            else {
              findw->getValue()->incrFrequency();
              swapContents(findw->getValue(), words[h]->getValue());
            }
          }
        }

        void listEntries () ;
      };
```

Chapter 9—Sixth Set

```
1.  void print (int A[inputMax][inputMax], int size) {
    // Print a size-1 by size-1 matrix.

      for (int i=0; i < size; i++) {
        for (int j=0; j < size; j++)
          cout << setw(4) << A[i][j];
        cout << "\n";
      }
      cout << "\n";
    }


    int min(int a, int b) {
    // Find the minimum of two integers
```

```
      if (a < b)
        return a;
      else
        return b;
    }

  main () {
    int A[inputMax][inputMax];
    int n, i, j;

    cout << "Enter number";
    cin >> n;

    // Identity maxtrix
    for (i=0; i < n; i++)
      for (j=0; j < n; j++)
        A[i][j] = (i == j);
    print(A,n);

    // A[i][j] = i+j
    for (i=0; i < n; i++)
      for (j=0; j < n; j++)
        A[i][j] = i + j;
    print(A,n);

    // Borders with 0, etc
    for (i=0; i < n; i++)
      for (j=0; j < n; j++)
        A[i][j] = min(min(i,j),min(n-j-1,n-i-1));
    print(A,n);
  }
```

2. Notice that the j loop does not go all the way to **size**, keeping j < i. This prevents double comparisons (both j with i and i with j) and identical comparisons (i with i).

```
    #include <iostream.h>
    #include <iomanip.h>

    const int inputMax = 1000;

    enum boolean {false,true};

    boolean symmetrical (int A[inputMax][inputMax],int size) {
      for (int i=0; i < size; i++)
        for (int j=0; j < i; j++)
          if (A[i][j] != A[j][i])
            return false;
      return true;
    }
```

5.
```
    char *millenary[] = {"", "thousand", "million",
                         "billion", "trillion"};

    char *decade[] = {"twenty", "thirty", "forty",
                      "fifty", "sixty", "seventy",
                      "eighty", "ninety"};
```

```
void printMillenary (int n) {
// Write the name of the power of a 1000.
  printString(millenary[n]);
}

void printDecade (int n) {
// Write the name of a multiple of 10.
  printString(decade[n-2]);
}
```

Chapter 10—First Set

1. We are using the appointment book code on page 261. In the file **main.C** we have

```
#include <iostream.h>
#include <iomanip.h>
#include "time.h"

// Print a schedule for the period starting at time start,
// with numberOfAppts entries, apptLength minutes apart.
void printSchedule (time start,
                    int apptLength,
                    int numberOfAppts) {
  for (int i=0; i<numberOfAppts; i++) {
    start.printTime();
    cout << " _____ \n";
    start = start.addMinutes(apptLength);
  }
}

int main () {
  printSchedule(time(8, 30), 30, 6);
}
```

In the file **time.h** we have

```
class time {
private:
  int hour, minute;

public:
  time (int h, int m) { hour = h; minute = m; }

  time addMinutes (int m);
  void printTime ();
};
```

In the file **time.C** we have

```
#include <iostream.h>
#include <iomanip.h>
#include "time.h"

time time::addMinutes (int m) {
```

```
    // Return a time m minutes after the receiver's time
    // (or before it, if m is negative).
    int totalMinutes = (60*hour + minute + m) % (24*60);
    if (totalMinutes < 0)
      totalMinutes = totalMinutes + 24*60;
    return time(totalMinutes/60, totalMinutes%60);
  }

  void time::printTime () {
    // Print the receiver's time.
    if ((hour == 0) && (minute == 0))
      cout << "midnight";
    else if ((hour == 12) && (minute == 0))
      cout << "noon";
    else {
      if (hour == 0)
        cout << 12;
      else if (hour > 12)
        cout << hour-12;
      else
        cout << hour;
      cout << ':' << setfill('0') << setw(2) << minute;
      if (hour < 12)
        cout << "AM";
      else
        cout << "PM";
    }
  }
```

Chapter 10—Second Set

1.  ```
    rectangle (50, 15)
        connecting c/e
            (clear rectangle (23,10)
                connecting w/w (circle (4))
                connecting c/c (circle (3))
                connecting e/e (circle (2)))
    ```

2. Since we know the center of the square is $(50, 50)$, its north point is at $(50, 40)$. If this is the south point of a circle with a radius of 5, the circle's center is at $(50, 35)$. The square's southeast point is $(60, 60)$. This gives the circle with a radius of 10 a center of $(70, 60)$ and a northeast point of $(77, 53)$. The rectangle therefore has a center of $(92, 48)$.

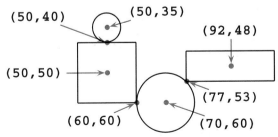

3. See Figure S.1 (next page).
    ```

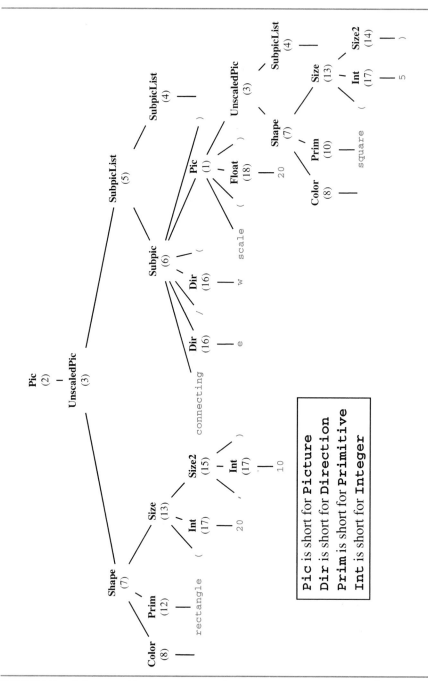

FIGURE S.1   Solution to Chapter 10, Second Set, Exercise 3: a syntax tree for `rectangle(20,10) connecting e/w (scale (20) square(5))`

Chapter 10—Third Set

1. (a)
```cpp
int countSquares (SyntaxTreeNode *tn) {
    // count the number of squares in a tree.

    int sum = 0;
    if (tn->getProduction() == 10)  // a square
        sum = 1;
    for (int i=0; i<countChildren(tn); i++)
        sum = sum + countSquares(tn->getChild(i));
    return sum;
}
```

(b)
```cpp
int height (SyntaxTreeNode *tn) {
    // calculate the (maximum) height of a tree.
    int max = 0;
    for (int i=0; i<countChildren(tn); i++)
        if (max < height(tn->getChild(i)))
            max = height(tn->getChild(i));
    return max + 1;
}
```

(c)
```cpp
TokenType reverseDirection (TokenType t) {
    // reverse the direction of a TokenType
    switch (t) {
        case north:     return south;
        case northeast: return southwest;
        case east:      return west;
        case southeast: return northwest;
        case south:     return north;
        case southwest: return northeast;
        case west:      return east;
        case northwest: return southeast;
    }
}

SyntaxTreeNode *mirror (SyntaxTreeNode *tn) {
    switch (countChildren(tn)) {
    case 0:
        if (tn->getProduction() == 16)      // A direction
            return new SyntaxTreeNode(16,
                        reverseDirection(tn->getDirection()));
        else
            return new SyntaxTreeNode(tn->getProduction());
    case 1:
        return new SyntaxTreeNode(tn->getProduction(),
                            mirror(tn->getChild(0)));
    case 2:
        return new SyntaxTreeNode(tn->getProduction(),
                            mirror(tn->getChild(0)),
                            mirror(tn->getChild(1)));
    case 3:
        return new SyntaxTreeNode(tn->getProduction(),
                            mirror(tn->getChild(0)),
                            mirror(tn->getChild(1)),
                            mirror(tn->getChild(2)));
    }
}
```

(d)
```
void mirrorM (SyntaxTreeNode *tn) {
  if (tn->getProduction() == 16)        // A direction
    tn->setDirection(reverseDirection(tn->getDirection()));
  for (int i=0; i<countChildren(tn); i++)
    mirror(tn->getChild(i));
}
```

This uses the member function **setDirection**:

```
class SyntaxTreeNode {
private:
        .
        .
        .
public:
        .
        .
        .

  void setDirection (TokenType t) {direction = t;}
};
```

Index